Historical Dictionary
of the
1 9 6 0s

Historical Dictionary
of the
1 9 6 0s

EDITED BY JAMES S. OLSON

ASSOCIATE EDITOR: SAMUEL FREEMAN

Greenwood Press
Westport, Connecticut • London

Library of Congress Cataloging-in-Publication Data

Historical dictionary of the 1960s / edited by James S. Olson ;
associate editor, Samuel Freeman.
     p. cm.
    Includes bibliographical references and index.
    ISBN 0–313–29271–X (alk. paper)
    1. United States—History—1961–1969—Dictionaries. I. Olson,
James Stuart, 1946–
   E841 H58 1999 *C, 2*
   973.923—dc21   97–2231

British Library Cataloguing in Publication Data is available.

Library of Congress Catalog Card Number: 97–2231
ISBN: 0–313–29271–X

First published in 1999

Greenwood Press, 88 Post Road West, Westport, CT 06881
An imprint of Greenwood Publishing Group, Inc.
www.greenwood.com

Printed in the United States of America

The paper used in this book complies with the
Permanent Paper Standard issued by the National
Information Standards Organization (Z39.48–1984).

10 9 8 7 6 5 4 3 2 1

Contents

Preface

There is a schizophrenic quality to American life in the 1960s. Perhaps the term "manic" decade would be appropriate. Few other eras in U.S. history have begun with more optimistic promise and ended in more pessimistic despair. When John F. Kennedy entered the White House in January 1961, the United States was the hope of the world, the repository of morality and power, and the president pretended to have the will to exercise that virtue and might in support of freedom, democracy, capitalism, and progress. Ten years later, American power abroad seemed wasted, even dissipated, in the jungles of Indochina, and critics at home cast doubt on whether the United States really was the "land of the free and the home of the brave." The assassination of President John F. Kennedy marked the beginning of the change, but it was followed by other assassinations, the civil rights movement, the antiwar movement, the youth rebellion, campus protest, and repeated riots in American cities, all of which blamed the country's problems on its existing institutions.

Americans had long held the view that the United States was a democratic, egalitarian nation, but protests from African Americans, Hispanic Americans, Native Americans, and women brought that conviction into doubt. The idea that the Constitution protected the average citizen from abuses of government power came into question over Vietnam and the activities of the Central Intelligence Agency (CIA) and the Federal Bureau of Investigation (FBI). Finally, Americans had long prided themselves on being the world's only hope for downtrodden, oppressed people, but as the Vietnam War escalated in the 1960s, the image of the United States as a global bully became much more common.

In *Historical Dictionary of the 1960s*, I have tried to take an encyclopedic look at the decade. Readers should know that I wrote all of the unsigned entries. An asterisk following a term indicates that it is a main entry. In addition to biographies of prominent individuals, I have included a variety of political, military, social, cultural, religious, economic, and diplomatic topics that made the 1960s a very unique decade in U.S. history. I wish to express my gratitude to the other contributors and to my editors at the Greenwood Publishing Group, who have been most patient and understanding. The staff of the Newton Gresham Library at Sam Houston State University has been particularly helpful.

A

ABEL, IORWITH WILBER. I. W. Abel was born August 11, 1908, in Magnolia, Ohio. After graduating from high school and attending a local business college, Abel got a job as a molder. In 1936, he enthusiastically supported the formation of the Congress of Industrial Organizations and the "Little Steel" strike of 1937. He rose steadily through the ranks of the United Steelworkers of America, becoming its national secretary-treasurer in 1952. In 1965, Abel successfully unseated David J. McDonald as president of the United Steelworkers. He earned a reputation as an enlightened labor leader who worked for racial equality, industrial stability, and union democracy. A lifelong Democrat, Abel was a consistent voice in support of liberal social and economic policies. He stepped down as head of the United Steelworkers in 1977. I. W. Abel died August 10, 1987.
REFERENCES: John Herling, *Right to Challenge: People and Power in the Steelworkers*, 1977; *New York Times*, August 11, 1987.

ABERNATHY, RALPH DAVID. Ralph David Abernathy was born March 11, 1926, in Linden, Alabama. He graduated from Alabama State College in 1950 and earned a master's degree at Atlanta University in 1951. Abernathy then entered the ministry. During the great struggles of the civil rights movement* of the late 1950s and 1960s, he was a trusted friend, confidant, and assistant to Rev. Martin Luther King, Jr.,* in the Southern Christian Leadership Conference* (SCLC). Abernathy was also a national civil rights leader in his own right. When King was assassinated in April 1968, the mantle of the SCLC fell on Abernathy. At the time of his death, King was working in support of the garbage collectors of Memphis, Tennessee, who had gone on strike for better wages and working conditions. Abernathy brought the strike to a successful conclusion for the workers and then went on to complete the Poor People's

Campaign,* which brought thousands of poor people to Washington, D.C., in 1968 for several weeks of protests, demonstrations, and political lobbying.

Unfortunately, Abernathy proved unable to match Martin Luther King's influence. He had all of King's passion but none of his charisma, and the Southern Christian Leadership Conference declined in influence under his direction. He resigned the directorship in 1977 to run for Congress. Andrew Young's seat had become available when he accepted appointment as ambassador to the United Nations. But Abernathy ran a weak campaign, securing only 5 percent of the vote in the Democratic primary. He died April 17, 1990.

REFERENCES: Ralph Abernathy, *And the Walls Came Tumbling Down: An Autobiography*, 1989; *New York Times*, April 18, 1990.

ABRAMS, CREIGHTON. Creighton Abrams was born in Springfield, Massachusetts, September 16, 1914. Described as ''tough,'' ''crusty,'' and ''gruff,'' Abrams graduated from West Point in 1936. Considered one of the great combat officers of World War II, Abrams served in General George Patton's Third Army and took part in the relief of Bastogne. Upon assuming command of Military Assistance Command, Vietnam (MACV) in July 1968, when General William Westmoreland* left, Abrams shifted American tactics in the direction of small-unit operations in an attempt to keep pressure on Vietcong* and North Vietnamese army* (NVA) forces while avoiding the heavy American casualties that often resulted from Westmoreland's large-scale ''search and destroy''* sweeps. Also, in the latter half of 1968, Abrams launched the Accelerated Pacification Campaign, in which the United States and South Vietnam committed a major share of their military resources to controlling the Vietnamese countryside. The campaign enjoyed only short-term success.

As MACV commander, Abrams was responsible for implementing the Vietnamization* program, which had originated in the Lyndon B. Johnson* administration and which was announced with much public fanfare in 1969 by President Richard M. Nixon.* Abrams viewed the Cambodian incursion of 1970 as a means of keeping Vietcong and NVA pressure off the gradual American withdrawal mandated by Vietnamization. Although Abrams privately doubted the ability of the South Vietnamese army to replace U.S. troops effectively, he was successful in carrying out the American troop withdrawal. During his tenure as MACV commander, Abrams saw American strength reach its peak (543,482) in April 1969, and he also witnessed the departure of the last U.S. Army combat unit from Vietnam in August 1972. Abrams was promoted to chief of staff of the U.S. Army in 1972, a post he held until his death September 4, 1974.

REFERENCES: R. E. Dupuy, *The Compact History of the U.S. Army*, 1973; David Halberstam, *The Best and the Brightest*, 1972; George C. Herring, *America's Longest War: The United States in Vietnam, 1950–1975*, 1986; *New York Times*, September 5, 1974; Lewis Sorley, *Thunderbolt: General Creighton Abrams and the Army of His Times*, 1992.

Sean A. Kelleher

ACCURACY IN MEDIA. The consumer interest group Accuracy in Media was organized in 1969 by a group of people convinced that mass media reporting of the Vietnam War* was hopelessly biased by antiwar liberals. Accuracy in Media's political philosophy has been quite conservative. It is convinced that the media are antiwar, antibusiness, and pro-environmentalism and that such newspapers as the *New York Times* and the *Washington Post* and NBC, ABC, and CBS News have too much influence on American policymakers. Leaders of Accuracy in Media work to balance American journalism through personal contact with media leaders and by exerting influence on conservative political leaders.
REFERENCE: Loree Bykerk and Ardith Maney, *U.S. Consumer Interest Groups: Institutional Profiles*, 1995.

ACHESON, DEAN GOODERHAM. Dean Acheson was born on April 11, 1893, in Middletown, Connecticut. He graduated from Yale in 1915 and went on to Harvard, where he earned a law degree in 1918. Acheson served as private secretary to Supreme Court Justice Louis Brandeis until 1921, and, except for a brief stint in 1933 as undersecretary of state, practiced law privately in Washington, D.C., until 1941, when he was appointed assistant secretary of state. He became undersecretary of state in August 1946 and secretary of state under Harry Truman in July 1946. Acheson left the State Department in 1953 when Dwight D. Eisenhower* became president.

During the 1960s, Presidents John F. Kennedy* and Lyndon B. Johnson* frequently sought out Acheson's advice on foreign policy matters, especially Vietnam War* issues. As one of the "Wise Old Men,"* a group of senior foreign policy experts, Acheson promoted escalation of the war in 1965, viewing it as just another example of Cold War* Communist aggression; however, he soon soured on the conflict. By 1966 he was expressing grave reservations, and in 1967 he urged President Johnson to de-escalate the war. In March 1968, at a meeting of the Wise Old Men, Acheson told Johnson that the war was a lost cause. Johnson felt betrayed, and Acheson's days as a foreign policy advisor were over. Dean Acheson died on October 12, 1971.
REFERENCES: Dean Acheson, *Present at the Creation*, 1969; *New York Times*, October 13, 1971; Walter Isaacson and Evan Thomas, *The Wise Old Men: Six Friends and the World They Made*, 1986.

ACID. During the 1960s, the term "acid" was used as a synonym for LSD. People who readily used the drug were known as "acidheads."
REFERENCE: Todd Gitlin, *The Sixties: Years of Hope, Days of Rage*, 1987.

ACTION FOR CHILDREN'S TELEVISION. Action for Children's Television is a children's advocacy group founded in 1968 by Peggy Charren in Boston. Charren was concerned about the overcommercialization of children's television,* deceptive advertising targeting juvenile viewers, the lack of variety in children's television programming, and the general dearth of high-quality productions. Action for Children's Television lobbyists began working the corridors of the Federal Communication Commission (FCC), trying to get new guidelines and regulations passed for children's television programming. Their crusade experienced its first real success in 1974, when the FCC adopted a Children's Television Report and Policy Statement, which required broadcasters to limit the amount of advertising during children's programming to 9.5 minutes per hour on weekends and 12 minutes on weekdays. In response, the National Association of Broadcasters voluntarily designated one hour of prime time each evening for "family viewing" and launched a series of scientific, cultural, and historic specials and news shows.

REFERENCE: Loree Bykerk and Ardith Maney, *U.S. Consumer Interest Groups: Institutional Profiles*, 1955.

ACTION ON SMOKING AND HEALTH. Action on Smoking and Health was a consumer interest group organized in 1967 by John F. Banzhaf III to eliminate cigarette smoking in the United States. The Surgeon General* Report in 1964 had clearly outlined the health risks of smoking, and Banzhaf wanted to get that message circulated more widely in the United States. Action on Smoking and Health still operates today, but its early successes in the 1960s included the Federal Communications Commission's decision in 1969 to allow antismoking messages to be broadcast on television and its 1971 decision to ban cigarette commercials from television.

REFERENCE: Loree Bykerk and Ardith Maney, *U.S. Consumer Interest Groups: Institutional Profiles*, 1995.

AD HOC TASK FORCE ON VIETNAM. The Tet Offensive* of 1968 dealt a death blow to the American war effort in Vietnam by undermining the political atmosphere at home. Doubtful congressmen began evaluating their positions while the military was requesting greater investment of resources in the conflict. Late in February 1968, General William C. Westmoreland* asked President Lyndon B. Johnson* for the deployment of 200,000 more troops to Southeast Asia, and the president convened the Ad Hoc Task Force on Vietnam to evaluate Westmoreland's request. The debate was also taking place in the midst of the presidential primary campaign of 1968, in which Lyndon Johnson was facing considerable pressure from Senators Eugene McCarthy* of Minnesota and Robert F. Kennedy* of New York.

Clark Clifford,* the new secretary of defense, chaired the group. The debate was wide-ranging, dealing with the Vietnam War* in particular and American commitments abroad in general. General Maxwell Taylor* and Walt W. Rostow,* both presidential advisers, supported the commitment, as did General Earle Wheeler,* chairman of the Joint Chiefs of Staff, but the escalation was opposed by other prominent people, including Paul Nitze,* deputy undersecretary of defense, and Paul Warnke,* assistant secretary of defense. Although

Clifford took no formal position in the debate, his own doubts about the nature of the war were confirmed. The military could provide no realistic prediction of when the war could be wound down and brought to a successful conclusion. Those opposing the escalation prevailed, and Westmoreland received only 25,000 of the 200,000 troops he requested. Later in March, President Lyndon Johnson announced his decision not to run for reelection and to de-escalate the war effort.

REFERENCES: Harry F. Summers, Jr., *Vietnam War Alamanac*, 1985; Clark M. Clifford, "A Viet Nam Reappraisal," *Foreign Affairs* (July 1969), 601–22; Clark Dugan and Steven Weiss, *The Vietnam Experience: Nineteen Sixty-Eight*, 1983.

ADAMS, HANK. An American Indian of Sioux and Assiniboin descent, Hank Adams was born on the Fort Peck Indian Reservation in Montana in 1947. A gifted athlete and student leader during high school, Adams moved to California after graduation and became involved in politics. He actively supported the John F. Kennedy* administration, and in 1964 he refused induction into the U.S. Army until the federal government made good on all treaties with American Indians. That same year he worked diligently to stage Marlon Brando's protest march to the Washington state capitol in Olympia to demand Indian fishing rights. In April 1964, Adams went into the army. When he left the military, he became director of the Survival of American Indians Association,* a group dedicated to Native American fishing rights. He focused his attention in 1968 on the Nisqually River near Franks Landing, Washington, where he protested state attempts to limit Indian net fishing. In January 1971, Adams was shot on the shore of the Puyallup River near Tacoma, where he had intentionally set an illegal fishing trap. Since that time, he has continued his struggle to exempt Indians from state fish and game regulations.

REFERENCE: Duane Champagne, ed., *The Native North American Almanac*, 1994.

ADAMS-WESTMORELAND CONTROVERSY. Because the war in Vietnam was a war of attrition,* in which U.S. strategy rested on killing more enemy troops than North Vietnam and the Vietcong* could put in the field, accurate statistics became critically important in evaluating the successes and failures of American military policy. During the war, a fierce battle raged between the Central Intelligence Agency* (CIA) and the Military Assistance Command, Vietnam (MACV), over the number of enemy troops in South Vietnam, the rate at which North Vietnam infiltrated its soldiers into South Vietnam, and the volume of enemy supplies reaching those troops.

Sam Adams, a young CIA intelligence officer, believed that General William Westmoreland* and the MACV seriously underestimated enemy strength in South Vietnam. The calculus was important. If Adams were correct, the United States would need a far higher commitment of combat troops in Vietnam in order to win the war. He became the center of a growing controversy because MACV and higher echelons in the CIA rejected his numbers. As it turned out,

Adams's estimates of enemy truth strength had been accurate. In order for Westmoreland's strategy of attrition to have succeeded, he would have needed far more than the 548,000 troops he had in Vietnam in 1968.

In 1975, still frustrated, Adams publicized his charges in *Harper's* magazine. CBS News produced a documentary on the controversy in January 1982, charging Westmoreland with conspiring to report low figures for the enemy. Westmoreland sued for libel, but the resulting court trial in 1985 found support for Adams's original contention and vindication for his lonely vigil. Westmoreland and CBS settled their suit out of court.

REFERENCE: Bob Brewin and Sydney Shaw, *Vietnam on Trial: Westmoreland v. CBS*, 1986.

THE ADVENTURES OF OZZIE AND HARRIET. *The Adventures of Ozzie and Harriet* was one of the most popular situation comedies in American television* history. First telecast by ABC in 1952, the show detailed the ''real life'' of the Nelson family—Ozzie, Harriet, David, and Ricky—who played themselves on the series. America watched the Nelsons raise their children on the air and turn from young adults to middle-aged adults. The boys grew from adolescents to married young adults, with all of the interests and disinterests of American young people. *Ozzie and Harriet* presented an idealized portrait of the American family that played well in the 1950s but became increasingly irrelevant in turbulent 1966. The last episode of *The Adventures of Ozzie and Harriet* was broadcast on September 3, 1966.

REFERENCE: Tim Brooks and Earle Marsh, *The Complete Directory to Prime Time Network and Cable TV Shows*, 1995.

AEROBICS. In the mid-1960s, Dr. Kenneth Cooper, an air force physician, coined the term ''aerobics'' to describe any form of exercise that elevated an individual's heart rate above 130 beats per minute for a sustained period of time. Jogging, running, racquetball, squash, cycling, swimming, and vigorous walking were the best exercises. Cooper developed what he called the ''twelve-minute test'' to evaluate fitness. An individual who, walking or running, covered only a mile in twelve minutes was in poor shape. Anybody who could cover 1.75 miles in that time was in excellent shape. In 1968, Cooper published his book— *Aerobics*—explaining his philosophy of physical fitness. The book became a best-seller, selling more than 3 million copies and launching the jogging-running craze in the United States.

REFERENCE: Randy Roberts and James S. Olson, *Winning Is the Only Thing: Sports in America since 1945*, 1989.

AFFIRMATIVE ACTION. The term ''affirmative action'' refers to a series of rules and regulations that evolved throughout the 1960s, 1970s, and 1980s in an attempt to counteract the effects of historical discrimination against certain designated minority groups. With the Civil Rights Act* of 1964, most types of formal, legal discrimination had been eliminated, but civil rights advocates soon realized there were many other practices and traditions, such as seniority rights and aptitude tests, that continued to militate against the hiring and promotion of minority workers. On September 24, 1965, President Lyndon B. Johnson* responded to that problem by issuing an executive order requiring all federal contractors to use "affirmative action" in making sure that minority workers were hired in numbers consistent with their ratio in the population. In *Griggs v. Duke Power Company* in 1971, the Supreme Court invalidated the use of intelligence tests that had the effect of limiting minority hiring and promotion. Companies began to use a variety of criteria, not just intelligence tests, in making their hiring decisions. The Equal Employment Act of 1972 then extended "affirmative action" requirements to educational institutions.

Critics charged, however, that in many instances affirmative action requirements rigidified into hiring and promotion quotas and then constituted reverse discrimination against white males, violating their Fourteenth Amendment right to equal protection under the law. Those claims became politically significant in the mid-1970s, when the American economy stagnated. A number of cases wound their way through the federal courts protesting affirmative action. In 1978, the Supreme Court heard the *Regents of the University of California v. Bakke* case. Allan Bakke had been denied admission to the University of California at Davis medical school. But because of the school's quota system for admission, several minority students with lower grade point averages and lower test scores had been admitted. Bakke claimed that the practice constituted reverse discrimination. The Court ruled that rigid, special preference admission programs were unconstitutional. After the Bakke decision, quotas were dead, although affirmative action programs that actively sought to hire or admit minority workers were still legal.

During the Reagan years of the 1980s, affirmative action continued to be a divisive political issue; minority groups charged President Ronald Reagan with gutting civil rights programs, and conservative whites praised him for ending reverse discrimination. The real meaning of affirmative action continued to be muddled. In *Fullilove v. Klutznick* in 1980, the Supreme Court upheld federal legislation requiring that 10 percent of all federal public works projects be reserved for minority contractors, regardless of whether or not they were low bidders on a project. By the early 1990s, with the American economy in a recession, criticisms of affirmative action programs surfaced again, generally with Democrats defending them and Republicans opposing them. When Republicans prevailed during the elections of 1994 and took control of the U.S. Senate and the House of Representatives, opponents of affirmative action gained the upper hand in the policy debate. In the election of 1996, California voters passed Referendum 209, which outlawed the use of race and gender in determining college admission and state employment and in the awarding of state contracts.

REFERENCES: Katharine Greene, *Affirmative Action and Principles of Justice*, 1990; Stephen L. Pevar, *The Rights of Indians and Tribes: The Basic ACLU Guide to Indian and Tribal Rights*, 1992.

AFRICAN AMERICANS. See **CIVIL RIGHTS MOVEMENT** and **BLACK POWER**.

•

THE AFRO. Long hair was the style of the 1960s among young men, and for African Americans the fad took the form of the so-called Afro haircut. In 1967 James Brown released his record "Say It Loud—I'm Black and I'm Proud," and the "black pride" movement was under way. One of its symbols was the Afro haircut. Abandoning the practice of straightening their hair with harsh chemicals or even cropping it close to their heads in the name of black pride, young African-American men let their hair grow long. The tight curls, teased up with a wide-tined comb and spray cans of Afro Sheen, gave the hairdo a symmetrical, rounded look that identified the wearer as someone who was black and proud of it. Prominent figures like Angela Davis, Jimi Hendrix, and Huey Newton also sported Afros by the late 1960s. In Chicago, the Blackstone Rangers, an African-American gang, said they liked the Afro because it cushioned the blows of police clubs.
REFERENCE: Jane Stern and Michael Stern, *Encyclopedia of Pop Culture*, 1992.

AGENCY FOR INTERNATIONAL DEVELOPMENT. Congress established the Agency for International Development (AID) in 1961. Its purpose was to administer the economic development programs that were included in U.S. foreign aid. At the time, American policymakers were deeply worried about the spread of communism, especially in the Third World, and they believed that economic development was one way of preventing communists from getting a foothold. President John F. Kennedy* named Fowler Hamilton to head AID. The key AID program in the early 1960s was the Alliance for Progress.* In addition to long-term development programs, AID became involved in counterinsurgency* programs during the Kennedy administration, especially in Latin America and Indochina. By the time of the Lyndon B. Johnson* administration (1963–1969), AID was spending $2 billion a year on its programs and had missions in seventy countries.

Because of the Vietnam War,* AID became increasingly unpopular in the late 1960s and 1970s, with Congress steadily limiting its authority and cutting its budget. AID programs became less political and more humanitarian in focus, emphasizing refugee assistance, food production, population control, and public health. AID personnel dropped from 20,000 people in 1968 to only 6,000 in 1978. At that point its size and mission stabilized.
REFERENCE: Paul G. Clark, *American Aid for Development*, 1972.

AGENT ORANGE. Agent Orange was the name for the primary chemical herbicide used by U.S. military forces between 1962 and 1970 to defoliate forested areas near the Demilitarized Zone* in South Vietnam and near the borders between Cambodia, Laos, and South Vietnam. Because of the guerrilla nature of enemy forces, American soldiers frequently had a difficult time finding them and were often surprised in ambushes. By spraying the toxin from fixed-wing aircraft and helicopters into the forest, American pilots tried to destroy the foliage that was being used by the Vietcong* as cover. Military planners dubbed the project "Operation Ranch Hand."

During Operation Ranch Hand, 11.22 million gallons of Agent Orange were dumped on South Vietnam. Agent Orange contained equal amounts of 2,4-dichlorophenoxyacetic acid (2,4-D) and 2,4,5-trichlorophenoxyacetic acid as well as small amounts of 2,3,7,8-tetrachlorodibenzo-p-dioxin (TCDD). Although Agent Orange was rarely sprayed directly on American troops, soldiers frequently came into contact with the chemical when on patrol in defoliated areas. The military reduced the use of Agent Orange after receiving reports of its toxicity.

After the war, many Americans and South Vietnamese exposed to the dioxin developed health problems ranging from cancer to chronic skin rashes. Critics of the defoliation campaign also complained about an unusually high number of children born with birth defects. For years the Department of Defense and Dow Chemical, the principal manufacturer of the defoliant, insisted that no correlation existed between the reported health problems and exposure to Agent Orange. Nevertheless, thousands of Vietnam veterans began seeking financial compensation for themselves and their families. They brought a class-action suit against Dow Chemical and other manufacturers. Without ever agreeing to culpability, the chemical companies voluntarily established a $180 million fund to compensate alleged victims. The issue remains in litigation today.

REFERENCES: Clifford Linedecker, *Kerry, Agent Orange and an American Family*, 1982; Carol Van Strum, *A Bitter Fog: Herbicides and Human Rights*, 1983.

Carol Nguyen

AGNEW, SPIRO THEODORE. Spiro Agnew was born November 9, 1918, in Baltimore. Before World War II he attended Johns Hopkins University and the Baltimore Law School, and after serving in an army unit during the war, he graduated from the Baltimore Law School in 1947. Agnew began practicing law and working in local Republican politics, and in 1957 he was appointed to the Baltimore County Zoning Board of Appeals. He won election to the position of county executive in 1962, and in 1966 he won the governorship of Maryland, defeating a segregationist Democrat and earning liberal credentials. During his two terms as governor, however, Agnew became increasingly conservative and strident in his rhetoric. In 1968, he supported Richard Nixon's* candidacy for president, and Nixon rewarded him with the spot of running mate. They won the election over Democrat Hubert H. Humphrey,* and Agnew became the vice president of the United States in 1969.

As vice president, Agnew carried the battle to the opponents and critics of the Nixon administration. Critics of the Vietnam War,* whether in Congress or on campus, were the special targets of Agnew's alliterative verbal assaults. The baiting and buzzwords of the 1950s were dusted off for reuse, together with many new ones of Agnew's invention. But while Agnew carried the cudgels for the Nixon administration, serving as an unofficial verbal hit man, his excesses often inflamed an already overheated national debate, and the vice president himself was severely criticized for exacerbating the situation.

Thus, when Agnew's past caught up with him, those who had been the victims of his denunciation could hardly conceal their delight. During his years as county executive and governor in Maryland, Agnew had accepted kickbacks on government contracts. Investigators brought those crimes to light during his term as vice president. Faced with the threat of prosecution and impeachment for violation of bribery, conspiracy, and tax laws, on October 10, 1973, Agnew entered into a plea bargaining agreement, pleading no contest (nolo contendere) to one count of income tax evasion. He also resigned from the vice presidency. For the remainder of his life, Spiro Agnew kept a very low profile. He died September 17, 1996.

REFERENCES: Spiro T. Agnew, *Go Quietly... Or Else*, 1980; *New York Times*, September 18–19, 1996.

Joseph M. Rowe, Jr.

AIKEN, GEORGE DAVID. George David Aiken was born on August 20, 1892, in Dummerston, Vermont. He graduated from high school in 1909 and went to work in his family's agriculture and nursery business, but farming did not really suit him. In 1920 he won election as head of the local school board and enjoyed the political give-and-take. He then turned to full-time politics. Like most Vermonters, Aiken declared himself a Republican. In 1930, he won a seat in the state legislature and soon made a name for himself, earning the respect of his constituents and his political peers. He won the lieutenant governorship in 1935, and in 1937 Vermont voters picked him as their new governor. Aiken served two terms and proved to be more progressive politically than most Vermonters expected. However, they loved his honesty and his iconoclasm. In 1940, he won a seat in the U.S. Senate.

Aiken spent thirty-five years in the U.S. Senate, becoming one of its most senior and highly respected members. From his long-term position on the Senate Foreign Relations Committee, he could be trusted to reflect the popular will on diplomatic issues, and in 1966, when he publicly advised President Lyndon B. Johnson* to withdraw U.S. troops from Vietnam, the Washington establishment shuddered. Aiken became the country's highest profile opponent of the war. He came to consider Vietnam a national tragedy. In 1975 Aiken retired from the

Senate and returned to his beloved farm in Vermont. He died on November 19, 1984.

REFERENCES: George G. Aiken, *The Aiken Senate Diary*, 1976; *New York Times*, November 20, 1984; Joseph M. Rowe, Jr., ''George David Aiken,'' in James S. Olson, ed., *Historical Dictionary of the Vietnam War*, 1988.

AIR AMERICA. During the course of U.S. involvement in Indochina during the 1950s and 1960s, the Central Intelligence Agency* (CIA) carried out a variety of clandestine and intelligence-gathering activities. In doing so, the agency often established subdivisions known as ''proprietaries''—organizations that masked themselves as legitimate private business enterprises. One of these proprietaries was Air America. To maintain its cover as a legitimate enterprise, Air America operated a cargo transportation business, hauling freight throughout Indochina, Southeast Asia, and East Asia. It was a highly profitable venture because of the unprecedented volume of air traffic the Vietnam War* brought to the region. During the course of the war, more than two-thirds of Air America flights actually consisted of legitimate freight operations. It was enough to keep even many Air America employees from realizing that the company was actually a front for the Central Intelligence Agency.

Air America's primary mission, however, was to assist the CIA in carrying out its Vietnam War*-related activities. More often than not, Air America recruited its pilots and crew members from Vietnam veterans, who had experience in the region and who took the jobs because salaries far exceeded those in private industry. Although Air America occasionally used fighter pilots and combat aircraft in combat situations, most of its activities involved the delivery of money, personnel, and supplies to remote regions of Vietnam, Cambodia, Laos, and Thailand. Nevertheless, the missions could be extremely dangerous, since Air America flights frequently landed in and took off from enemy-controlled territory. To maintain secrecy, flights often took place at night or under bad weather conditions.

REFERENCES: Christopher Robbins, *Air America*, 1979; Stafford T. Thomas, ''Air America,'' in James S. Olson, ed., *Dictionary of the Vietnam War*, 1988.

THE ALAMO. Making a film about the Alamo—the great battle in the fight for Texas independence in 1836—had been a lifelong dream of John Wayne,* and in 1959 he finally had the financing and the time to do it. Filmed in Brackettsville, Texas, in 1959, *The Alamo* was released in October 1960, just before the presidential race between John F. Kennedy* and Richard M. Nixon.* Its interpretive point of view was pure John Wayne. The Texans were heroes, and the Mexicans were interlopers out to crush freedom. The film was loaded with not-so-subtle Cold War* rhetoric, with the Texans synonymous with liberty and the Mexicans with despotism. Critics panned the movie, but it did well at the box office and has remained an enduring film for television and video rentals.

REFERENCE: Randy Roberts and James S. Olson, *John Wayne, American*, 1995.

ALCATRAZ ISLAND. On November 9, 1969, a group of American Indian college students and urban Indian people from the San Francisco Bay Area set out in a chartered boat to circle Alcatraz Island and symbolically claim the island for Indian people. On November 20, 1969, this symbolic occupation of Alcatraz Island turned into a full-scale occupation when Indian students from San Francisco State University, the University of California, Berkeley, the University of California, Santa Cruz, and the University of California, Los Angeles, joined with urban Indian people from the greater San Francisco Bay Area and reoccupied the island, claiming title by "right of discovery."

The newly formed Alcatraz organization, Indians of All Tribes,* Inc., demanded clear title to Alcatraz Island, the establishment of an American Indian University, an American Indian Cultural Center, and an American Indian Museum. The Indian occupiers on Alcatraz Island kept Americans aware of the occupation and their demands by publishing a newsletter, *Rock Talk*, and by starting their own radio program—"Radio Free Alcatraz." As a result, letters and telegrams began to pour in to government officials, including President Richard M. Nixon.* The mood of the public could be summed up in a telegram sent to Nixon on November 26, 1969, that read: "For once in this country's history let the Indians have something. Let them have Alcatraz."

The Indian occupiers successfully held the island until June 11, 1971, and Alcatraz soon became a rallying cry for the new American Indian activism that would continue into the mid-1970s under the names of red power* and the American Indian Movement.* This activism included the 1972 occupation of the Bureau of Indian Affairs headquarters in Washington, D.C., which lasted for seven days, and the occupation of Wounded Knee in 1973, which lasted for seventy-one days. The occupation of Alcatraz Island represents the longest continuous occupation of a federal facility by a minority group in the history of the United States, and on Alcatraz modern activism finds its roots. Alcatraz set in motion a wave of overtly nationalist Indian militancy that ultimately resulted in abandonment of the termination* program and the adoption of a policy of Indian self-determination.*

The nineteen-month occupation of Alcatraz Island is a watershed event in the American Indian protest and activist movement. The Alcatraz occupation brought together hundreds of Indian people who came to live on the island and thousands more who identified with the call for self-determination, autonomy, and respect for Indian culture. The Indian people who organized the occupation and those who participated either by living on the island or by working to solicit donations of money, water, food, clothing, or electrical generators came from all walks of life. As the occupation gained international attention, Indian people came from Canada and South America and from Indian reservations across the United States to show support for those who had taken a stand against the federal government. Thousands came, some stayed, and others carried the message home to their reservations that Alcatraz was a clarion call for the rise of Indian activism.

Today Alcatraz Island remains a strong symbol of Indian activism and self-determination and a rallying point for unified Indian political activities. On February 11, 1978, Indian participants began the "Longest Walk" to Washington, D.C., to protest the government's ill treatment of Indian people. That walk began on Alcatraz Island. On February 11, 1994, American Indian Movement leaders Dennis Banks,* Clyde Bellecourt,* and Mary Wilson met with Indian people to begin the nationwide "Walk for Justice." That walk began on Alcatraz Island. On Thanksgiving Day of each year since 1969, Indian people have gathered on Alcatraz Island to honor those who participated in the occupation and those who share in the continuing struggle for Indian self-determination. The 1969 occupation of Alcatraz Island stands out as the most symbolic, the most significant, the most successful Indian protest action of the modern era.

REFERENCES: Peter Blue Cloud, *Alcatraz Is Not an Island*, 1972; Troy R. Johnson, *The Occupation of Alcatraz Island: Indian Self-Determination and the Rise of Indian Activism*, 1996.

Troy Johnson

ALI, MUHAMMAD. Muhammad Ali was born Cassius Clay on January 18, 1942, in Louisville, Kentucky. He grew up in the poor, black neighborhoods of Louisville and found an identity for himself in the gymnasium, where he began boxing when he was twelve years old. A gifted athlete with unusual speed and quickness, given his big size, Clay won two Golden Gloves championships. When he was just eighteen, he won a gold medal for boxing at the 1960 Olympic Games in Rome. He returned to Louisville a national hero, and a consortium of local businessmen decided to finance his run for the heavyweight championship of the world.

Brash, outspoken, and a marketing genius, Clay fancied himself another Gorgeous George, the outlandish professional wrestler who preened before the press in elaborate outfits and bragged incessantly about his abilities. Clay bragged as well. The difference, of course, was that professional boxing was a real sport and Clay was among the best, and perhaps the very best, boxer ever to step into a ring. He rose through the ranks and finally got a shot at the heavyweight title in 1964. The reigning champion was Sonny Liston,* a man of few words, whose reputation for ferocity was unmatched. Clay bragged about humiliating Liston in the ring, and the world waited for the young challenger to get what was coming to him. He did. Clay delivered an unmerciful beating to Liston and won the heavyweight championship.

The next day, Clay stunned the sports world by announcing his conversion to the Nation of Islam and the change of his name from Cassius Clay to Muhammad Ali. At the time, the so-called Black Muslims, led by Elijah Muhammad,* were considered a radical, subversive force in the United States. Ali defended his title against all comers, rarely even being challenged by his opponents. Outside the ring, he constantly had to defend his religious beliefs, which were genuine, against the criticisms of non-Muslims.

He soon found himself, however, elevated from sports icon in the United States to draft-dodger and a political prisoner of sorts. The escalation of the Vietnam War* in 1965 had created enormous personnel demands for the United States military, and draft* calls increased dramatically in volume. Ali failed an army intelligence test and was at first classified as unfit for duty, but he was reclassified late in 1966. He then appealed for deferment as a religious conscientious objector, but the selective service rejected the request. Early in 1967, Ali announced that he would not go to war against the Vietnamese. "I ain't got no quarrel with those Vietcong, anyway," he said. "They never called me nigger." On April 18, 1967, he refused to take the oath and enter the U.S. Army. The World Boxing Association almost immediately stripped him of his title, and in June 1967 a federal jury convicted him of draft evasion. Ali was sentenced to five years in prison and fined $10,000.

To African Americans and antiwar* activists, Ali became an overnight sensation and a hero. He was twenty-five years-old and at the peak of his athletic skills, but state boxing commissions refused to issue him a license, and the State Department would not allow him to travel abroad. Unable to fight, Ali travelled widely throughout the country, denouncing the Vietnam War and promoting the Nation of Islam. He appealed his case, and in June 1970 the U.S. Supreme Court overturned the conviction. Ali returned to the ring, regained the heavyweight championship in October 1974, and went on to lose and regain the championship two more times. He retired from boxing in 1980.

Since then, Ali has become a beloved figure throughout the world. A gentle man who has remained faithful to his religion, Ali has come to epitomize the best combination of pride and humility. Suffering from Parkinson's Syndrome, a neurological disorder caused, in this case, by too many blows to the head over the years, Ali thrilled global television audiences in July 1996 when he was selected to light the torch at the summer Olympic games in Atlanta.

REFERENCES: Muhammad Ali, *The Greatest*, 1975; Thomas Hauser, *Muhammad Ali*, 1991; John Ricks, "Muhammad Ali," in James S. Olson, ed., *Dictionary of the Vietnam War*, 1988.

ALLIANCE FOR PROGRESS. In 1958, President Juscelino Kubischek of Brazil proposed the creation of a development fund to boost the South American economies and eliminate a breeding ground for communism. Fidel Castro's* triumph in Cuba gave the proposal more urgency. On August 17, 1961, at the Inter-American Conference in Punta del Este, Uruguay, President John F. Kennedy* proposed an "Alliance for Progress" through which the Organization of American States would establish, over the course of ten years, a $100 billion development fund, of which the United States would supply $20 billion. Kennedy hoped to achieve a 2.5 percent annual growth in gross national product throughout Latin America, to bring about a more equitable distribution of income, to improve public health, and to provide low-cost housing for the poor.

Although the Alliance for Progress was temporarily very popular in Latin

America, it soon degenerated into a politically controversial program. The United States insisted on keeping control of it, while Latin American countries wanted a more multilateral approach. The United States established an Inter-American Committee for the alliance in January 1964, but this did not improve the program. During the Lyndon B. Johnson* administration, U.S. appropriations for the alliance declined, while bilateral aid programs were increased. The alliance gradually disappeared into the general foreign aid program of the United States. Some economists and historians have argued that the alliance's objectives of anticommunism and social and economic reform were inherently contradictory and that most of the money found its way into the hands of Latin American elites that already controlled the social, political, and economic institutions of the continent.

REFERENCES: Jerome Levinson and Juan de Oñis, *The Alliance That Lost Its Way*, 1970.

ALIANZA FEDERAL DE PUEBLOS LIBRES. See **FEDERAL ALLIANCE OF FREE TOWNS**.

ALTAMONT. On December 6, 1969, the Rolling Stones* put on a concert at the Altamont Raceway in California. More than 200,000 people attended the concert, and it has gone down in the history of the 1960s as the end of an era. The Stones asked the Hell's Angels, a motorcycle gang, to provide security for the concert. It turned out to be a disaster. At the time, the Rolling Stones were cultivating their image as the bad boys of rock and roll—five young men who were into rock, drugs, and rebellion. The Altamont concert did them justice. Large numbers of the audience were doing a variety of drugs, and the Hell's Angels, in an act of so-called security enforcement, beat a young concertgoer to death. The killing was captured on film and became the center of a documentary film entitled *Gimme Shelter*. For some historians of rock and roll and the 1960s, the Altamont concert marked the end of the era of the peace-and-love cult of the 1960s.

REFERENCE: *New York Times*, December 7–8, 1969.

ALTIZER, THOMAS JONATHAN JACKSON. Thomas J. J. Altizer was born September 28, 1927, in Cambridge, Massachusetts. He attended St. John's College in Annapolis, Maryland, during 1944–1945. After a short period in the U.S. Army, he received a B.A. (1948), M.A. (1951), and Ph.D. (1955) from the University of Chicago. His career has included positions at Wabash College (1954–1956) in Crawfordsville, Indiana, Emory University (1956–1968) in Atlanta, Georgia, and the State University of New York (1968–) at Stony Brook, where he is currently professor of English and religious studies. Altizer is noted as the main leader of the "death of God" movement of the 1960s.

He and William Hamilton* wrote a series of essays that were published under the title *Radical Theology and the Death of God* in 1966. During the years from

1965 to 1968, his radical views were debated throughout the nation. While many assailed him for his unorthodoxy, most attacked him without reading more than the sensational headlines. What he seems to have meant in his writings was that the transcendent God became immanent in Jesus Christ, and with the death of Jesus, "God is dead." He proposed "Christian" atheism to replace traditional Christianity because transcendence was no longer meaningful for modern, secular human beings. Meaning and significance in the universe had passed with the "death of God." At Emory University, affiliated with the Methodist Church, his views received substantial criticism. Since he taught liberal arts outside the school of theology, he was able to withstand the pressure by agreeing to teach "death of God" theology only to his graduate students.

REFERENCES: Thomas J. J. Altizer, *Radical Theology and the Death of God*, 1968; *Library Journal*, May 15, 1966; *Contemporary Authors*, New Revised Series, vol. 3, 24; *Current Biography*, 1967, 9–11; *The Encyclopedia of Religion*, vol. 1, 478.

Bobby J. James

ALVAREZ, EVERETT, JR. Everett Alvarez, Jr., was born in Salinas, California, in 1937. He graduated from Santa Clara University in 1960 with a degree in electrical engineering. During the Vietnam War,* he was a naval pilot. Stationed on the USS *Constellation* in the South China Sea, he was piloting an A-4 Skyhawk when it was shot down over North Vietnam on August 5, 1964, in the midst of the Gulf of Tonkin* incident. Alvarez was transferred to the "Hanoi Hilton"* prison and spent the next eight years as a prisoner of war. He was the first American pilot taken prisoner. Upon his release in February 1973, he took a master's degree in systems analysis at the Naval Post-Graduate School. Between 1976 and his retirement from the navy in 1980, Alvarez headed the navy's Air System Command in Washington, D.C. After his retirement from the military, he served for a year as deputy director of the Peace Corps* and then spent more than a decade as deputy administrator of the Veterans Administration.

REFERENCES: Ignacio García, "America Says 'Welcome Home,' " *Nuestro* 6 (November 1982); San Antonio *Sunday Express News*, October 2, 1983.

AMERICAN CONSERVATIVE UNION. The American Conservative Union (ACU), a right-wing, anticommunist political action group, was founded in Washington, D.C., in 1964. Committed to the promotion of capitalism, the destruction of communism, military preparedness, tax reductions, and cuts in federal spending, the ACU endorsed Arizona senator Barry Goldwater* for president in the election of 1964* and Richard Nixon* in the election of 1968.

REFERENCE: Alan Crawford, *Thunder on the Right*, 1980.

AMERICAN FRIENDS OF VIETNAM. The American Friends of Vietnam, or Vietnam Lobby, began in 1950 with a meeting between Professor Wesley Fishel of Michigan State University and Ngo Dinh Diem,* a Vietnamese nationalist and anti-communist then living in self-imposed exile. Fishel brought

Diem to the United States and put him in touch with Cardinal Spellman,* Senators Mike Mansfield* and John Kennedy,* and Supreme Court Justice William Douglas,* all of whom became Lobby supporters. They were soon joined by an odd assortment of former leftist intellectuals, conservative generals, and liberal politicians. The Cold War* was underway in 1950, and the Friends of Vietnam was concerned about the popularity of Ho Chi Minh,* a communist, and his successful rebellion in French Indochina. They wanted to find an "independent nationalist alternative" to "communist totalitarianism," and they hoped to build such a movement around Ngo Dinh Diem. In April 1954, Senator John Kennedy delivered a speech and denounced any negotiated settlement in Vietnam that awarded political power to Ho Chi Minh.

After the fall of the French fortress of Dien Bien Phu to Ho Chi Minh's Vietminh Army, the American Friends of Vietnam lobbied successfully and convinced the Eisenhower* administration that Diem, an anti-communist untainted by French or Japanese association, was right for premier of South Vietnam, a new political entity created by the Geneva Accords of 1954. Ho Chi Minh became head of North Vietnam. The Accords provided that elections would be held within two years to reunite the country under either Ho Chi Minh or Ngo Dinh Diem.

Eisenhower, however, never really warmed to Diem. His suspicions proved correct when Diem systematically alienated much of the South Vietnamese population, thereby dramatically strengthening the Vietcong* rebels. But the American Friends of Vietnam manuevered Eisenhower into escalating support for "Free Vietnam" against Communist aggression. This required depicting Diem as an Asian democrat, no easy job given Diem's often antidemocratic remarks. The Vietnam Lobby eventually created a number of myths to bolster American support for Diem: (1) the "miracle myth" of political stability, economic development, and land reform; (2) the "democratic myth" justifying refusal to hold reunification elections because Communists would win by subverting the election process; (3) the myth that refugees moving south were portrayed as peasants "voting with their feet" against "Communist oppression"; and (4) the myth that North Vietnamese aggression necessitated Diem's totalitarian measures and substantial increases in American military assistance.

Although the myths contained grains of truth, they rested on a precarious foundation of exaggeration and falsehood. Land reform was a failure, and Diem's favoritism toward northern refugees created animosity among native southerners. Ho Chi Minh was a hero even in the south and would have defeated Diem in both northern and southern Vietnam in a fair election. Rather than common peasants, northern refugees were almost exclusively Catholics who had served either in the French colonial government or the French Union Forces and were urged to migrate by U.S. General Edward Lansdale's propaganda campaign. The Vietcong organized resistance to Diem despite North Vietnam's initial opposition. Diem's assassination in 1963 by South Vietnamese generals all but destroyed the American Friends of Vietnam as a lobbying group.

REFERENCES: Samuel Freeman, "American Friends of Vietnam," in James S. Olson, ed., *Dictionary of the Vietnam War*, 1988; Robert Sheer and Warren Hinckle, "The Vietnam Lobby," *Ramparts*, January 25, 1969, 31–36; Denis Warner, *The Last Confucian*, 1963.

AMERICAN INDEPENDENT PARTY. In 1968, Governor George Wallace* of Alabama established the American Independent Party (AIP) to serve as the political vehicle for his 1968 third-party campaign for the presidency. Headquartered in Montgomery, Alabama, the AIP promoted Wallace's candidacy and a platform emphasizing states' rights, law and order, escalation of the Vietnam War,* middle- and working-class tax reductions, strong national defense, and local control of schools. Wallace selected former air force general Curtis LeMay* as his running mate. They managed to get the AIP ticket on the ballots of all fifty states, and Wallace won 9,901,151 popular votes (13.54 percent of the total) and forty-seven electoral votes.

REFERENCE: Theodore White, *The Making of a President, 1968*, 1969.

AMERICAN INDIAN CHICAGO CONFERENCE. The American Indian Chicago Conference of 1961 proved to be a milestone in the history of Native American activism. During the 1950s, the National Congress of American Indians (NCAI) became internally divided between a younger generation of primarily urban Indians and an older generation of more traditionally oriented reservation leaders. The younger activists resented the fact that the older traditionalists dominated the National Congress of American Indians and began to express their discontent. Urban-born, university-educated, and imbued with a Pan-Indian spirit, the younger Indians felt the NCAI had capitulated to white control through the Bureau of Indian Affairs. The depth of their discontent became abundantly clear at the American Indian Chicago Conference.

Sol Tax, a professor of anthropology at the University of Chicago, assisted the NCAI in organizing the conference. Its purpose was to present the new John F. Kennedy* administration with a comprehensive Indian policy package. More than 500 Indians from sixty-seven tribes attended. Although the NCAI adopted resolutions demanding the preservation of Indian land rights and cultural traditions, the younger delegates—led by Clyde Warrior, a Ponca; Melvin Thom, a Paiute; and Herbert Blatchford, a Navajo—criticized the conference as too accommodationist, too cautious, and too patient. They called for a formal condemnation of American racism, ethnocentrism, and paternalism. When their demands went unfulfilled, they formed the National Indian Youth Council, a far more strident group of American Indian activists.

REFERENCE: James S. Olson and Raymond Wilson, *Native Americans in the Twentieth Century*, 1984.

AMERICAN INDIAN LAW CENTER. The American Indian Law Center was established in 1967 by the law school of the University of New Mexico. Under the direction of Philip S. Deloria, the center became independent of the university in 1977, although it is still housed in the law school, and staff members work closely with law school students and faculty. During its twenty-nine-year history, the American Indian Law Center has focused its activities on the analysis of federal, state, and local policies affecting Indian people, assisting tribal governments with legal issues, improving relationships between tribal and state governments, and helping to prepare Indian undergraduate students for law school.

REFERENCE: Nell Jessup Newton, "American Indian Law Center," in Mary B. Davis, ed., *Native America in the Twentieth Century: An Encyclopedia*, 1994.

AMERICAN INDIAN MOVEMENT. The American Indian Movement (AIM) was established in Minneapolis in 1968 by a group of Anishinabes (Chippewas) protesting police brutality. Among its founders were Dennis Banks,* Mary Jane Williams, and George Mitchell. They used the Black Panthers* as a model for their organization. In urban areas of the United States, where the police forces were composed overwhelmingly of whites who lived in the suburbs, relationships between policemen and minority communities were usually tense and hostile. Indian people, AIM leaders claimed, were often harassed and beaten by police. AIM also wanted to lobby for improved city services for urban Indians. In one of their first acts, they established an "Indian patrol" to monitor police activities.

Using insurgent political tactics, AIM soon established chapters in major American cities and participated in the 1969 occupation of Alcatraz Island* by Indians of All Tribes.* Federal law said that abandoned U.S. government property should revert to its previous owners, and they claimed that Alcatraz, an abandoned federal penitentiary, belonged to Indians. Russell Means,* an Oglala Sioux raised in Oakland, California, became active in AIM in the early 1970s. On July 4, 1971, he led a protest at Mount Rushmore, and later in the year, on Thanksgiving Day, an AIM group occupied Plymouth Rock in Massachusetts and painted it red in symbolic protest. In February 1972, Means led a "caravan" of more than 1,000 Indians into Gordon, Nebraska, to protest the murder of Raymond Yellowthunder, an Oglala, and the community's refusal to indict the killers. The protest succeeded in securing the indictments and eventual convictions of the white men involved in the crime.

AIM leaders actively participated in "fish-ins" in the Pacific Northwest to protest state fish and game laws, and in 1972 they organized the "Trail of Broken Treaties" caravan to Washington, D.C., and the occupation of the Bureau of Indian Affairs (BIA) building. In 1973, AIM orchestrated the seventy-one-day occupation of Wounded Knee, South Dakota. The occupation began as a symbolic protest of Oglala Sioux politics, but once the Federal Bureau of Investigation (FBI) sent in 250 agents to surround the protesters, it became a broad-based protest of the plight of American Indians. When it was over, the occupation had become the symbol of the red power* movement.

Soon after the occupation of the BIA building, several hundred AIM members traveled to Rapid City, South Dakota, to protest the murder of Wesley Bad Heart Bull, an Oglala. Darold Schmitz, a white man, was charged with manslaughter in the case, but AIM protesters demanded an indictment of first-degree murder. On February 6, 1973, more than 200 AIM protesters fought with police in Custer, South Dakota, over the incident.

By that time, trouble had erupted as well at the Pine Ridge reservation. Oglala traditionalists resented the leadership of Richard Wilson, who headed the federally backed tribal government. When they protested his leadership, the government dispatched sixty federal marshals to Pine Ridge. The traditionalists asked AIM for support. AIM protesters arrived at Pine Ridge, and on February 28, 1973, an armed confrontation began in the village of Wounded Knee. The standoff lasted for seventy-one days, with AIM committed to the notion of tribal sovereignty and the federal government committed to the destruction of the American Indian Movement. The federal government then brought hundreds of charges against AIM leaders for their participation in the standoff, but of the 562 indictments, only fifteen convictions resulted, and these were for minor offenses. In the election for the tribal presidency of the Pine Ridge Reservation in 1974, AIM nominated Russell Means for the office. In the election, Wilson won by a narrow margin, and although the Civil Rights Commission recommended decertification of the election because of irregularities, the Bureau of Indian Affairs let it stand.

In 1975, AIM established a protest encampment at Jumping Bull near the Oglala village. Federal agents joined forces with the GOONS (Richard Wilson's Guardians of the Oglala Nation) and attacked the encampment. During the confrontation, a firefight took place. One AIM member and two federal agents were killed. Three AIM members—Bob Robideau, Darrell Butler, and Leonard Peltier—were brought to trial. Robideau and Butler were acquitted by an all-white jury, but Peltier was convicted of murder and given two life sentences.

After Wounded Knee, AIM membership gradually declined. AIM tended to be overrepresented by Sioux and Chippewas and failed to significantly broaden its tribal representation. The end of the Vietnam War* took a great deal of steam out of protest movements in general, and the civil rights movement* entered a long period of decline in the 1970s. With the passage of the Indian Self-Determination Act of 1974, many Indian peoples felt they had succeeded, at least temporarily, in reversing the direction of government Indian policy. In 1974, Russell Means emerged as national chairperson of AIM. He promoted the International Indian Treaty Council* movement in the late 1970s. In 1978, Dennis Banks organized the "Longest Walk"* demonstration, which memorialized the Caravan of Broken Treaties protest of 1972. Since then, AIM has functioned more at the local than the national level, promoting Indian civil rights.

REFERENCES: Ward Churchill and Jim Vander Wall, *Agents of Repression: The FBI's Secret War against the Black Panther Party and the American Indian Movement*, 1988;

Rex Weyler, *Blood of the Land: The Government and Corporate War against the American Indian Movement*, 1982.

AMERICAN INDIAN MOVEMENT FOR EQUAL RIGHTS. The American Indian Movement for Equal Rights (AIMFER) was founded in 1969 by the National Indian Youth Council.* It was a civil rights advocacy group. One of its first targets was the Bureau of Indian Affairs (BIA), which had relatively few Indian people in management positions. Eventually, they wanted to create an all-Indian Bureau of Indian Affairs completely separate from the federal government. During their most vocal period in the 1970s and early 1980s, AIMFER members worked as watchdog groups in BIA offices trying to promote the hiring and advancement of American Indians.
REFERENCE: Armand S. La Potin, *Native American Voluntary Organizations*, 1986.

AMERICAN INDIANS. See **RED POWER**.

AMERICAN NAZI PARTY. In November 1958, George Lincoln Rockwell* founded the American Nazi Party in Arlington, Virginia. Anti-Semitic, antigay, antiblack, and anti-Catholic, the American Nazis protested the civil rights movement* and engaged in joint protest demonstrations with the Ku Klux Klan. After Rockwell was assassinated in 1967, Matthew Koehl took over leadership of the party, but by that time the American Nazi Party was in an advanced state of decline.
REFERENCE: Michael Newton and Judy Ann Newton, *The Ku Klux Klan: An Encyclopedia*, 1990.

AMERICAN UNIVERSITY SPEECH (1963). In U.S. diplomatic history, President John F. Kennedy's* American University speech is considered a critical event in the Cold War.* Delivered on June 9, 1963, at American University in Washington, D.C., the speech offered an olive branch to the Soviet Union. Rather than wallowing in Cold War rhetoric, Kennedy called for a reduction in mutual suspicions because both superpowers had an interest in peace and an end to the arms race. He also proposed negotiations to end the atmospheric testing of nuclear weapons. ''We all inhabit this small planet,'' Kennedy proclaimed. ''We all breathe the same air. We all cherish our children's future. And we are all mortal.'' Some historians of U.S. foreign policy see the American University speech as the first episode in the era of detente.
REFERENCE: Alonzo L. Hamby, *The Imperial Years: The U.S. since 1939*, 1976.

AMERICANS FOR DEMOCRATIC ACTION. Americans for Democratic Action (ADA) was a liberal political action group founded in Washington, D.C., in 1947. Most of its supporters were pro-New Deal liberals worried about the post–World War II threat to dismantle the government safety net established during the 1930s. They endorsed Harry Truman for president in 1948, Adlai Stevenson in 1952 and 1956, John F. Kennedy* in 1960, Lyndon B. Johnson* in 1964, and Hubert H. Humphrey* in 1968. During the 1960s, under the leadership of people like John Kenneth Galbraith,* Bella Abzug, Allard K. Lowenstein,* and Michael Harrington,* the ADA became even more liberal, calling for expansion of the welfare state, increased government regulation of business abuses, an end to the Vietnam War,* and civil rights and civil liberties for all Americans. During the 1960s, the Americans for Democratic Action became widely recognized as one of the most liberal political action groups in the United States.

REFERENCES: Clifton Brock, *Americans for Democratic Action*, 1963; Hal Libros, *Hard Core Liberals*, 1975.

AMERIND. In 1969, the leaders of the National Indian Youth Council* established AMERIND, Inc. to fight employment discrimination against Native Americans. A number of Bureau of Indian Affairs (BIA) employees had filed employment discrimination suits against the federal government, especially in the BIA's Gallup and Albuquerque, New Mexico, offices. AMERIND's stated objective has been to fight employment discrimination against Indian workers in the Bureau of Indian Affairs, the U.S. Public Health Service, and other federal agencies serving Native Americans.

REFERENCE: Duane Champagne, ed., *Chronology of Native North American History*, 1994.

ANDREWS, JULIE. Born Julia Elizabeth Wells October 1, 1935, in Walton-on-Thames, England, Julie Andrews exhibited extraordinary vocal talent even as a child. At the age of twelve she performed in the *Starlight Roof* and several years later at the London Palladium. She won the role as Polly Browne in *The Boy Friend* in 1954. Two years later, Julie Andrews became a certifiable Broadway star, creating the role of Eliza Doolittle in *My Fair Lady*. She returned to London in 1958 to continue the role, and in 1960 she was cast as Queen Guinevere in *Camelot*. From there, Andrews made the jump into film, starring in *Mary Poppins* (1964), for which she won an Academy Award as Best Actress, *The Americanization of Emily* (1964), *The Sound of Music* (1965), *Torn Curtain* (1966), *Hawaii* (1966), *Thoroughly Modern Millie* (1967), *Star!* (1968), *10* (1979), *S.O.B.* (1981), and *Victor/Victoria* (1982), for which she won an Oscar nomination for best actress. Since then, she has continued her recording and acting career.

REFERENCES: John Cottrell, *Julie Andrews: The Story of a Star*, 1968; Robert Windeler, *Julie Andrews*, 1970.

THE ANDY GRIFFITH SHOW. *The Andy Griffith Show* was a popular, low-key television* domestic comedy. This sitcom was in the 1950s tradition in which family problems and troubling situations were solved during a single episode. The series was part of the popular rural comedy genre of CBS during the 1960s and first aired October 3, 1960. It starred Andy Griffith as Sheriff Andy Taylor, Ronny Howard as his son Opie Taylor, Frances Bauvier as Aunt Bee Taylor, Don Knotts as deputy Barney Fife, and Jim Nabors as gas station attendant Gomer Pyle.

The Andy Griffith Show appealed to a wide audience. Its characters had relatable human qualities. Critics agreed it was the best-written rural sitcom of the 1960s. The series spawned the spin-off *Gomer Pyle, U.S.M.C.*, in 1964. The popularity of the series allowed it to continue as *Mayberry R.F.D.* in 1968 after Andy Griffith decided to leave the show. *Mayberry R.F.D.* retained many of the familiar characters.

During the times of uncertainty in the 1960s, *The Andy Griffith Show* focused on hope. As the network news examined student and police riots and civil rights demonstrations, the series tried to reassure Americans of the stability of family and community. Although Andy Taylor was symbolic of authority and government, the sheriff practiced understanding and promoted his open-minded philosophic ideology.

The Andy Griffith Show did not die through cancellation, as most rural comedies did in the early 1970s. It was transformed into a new series in 1968 following the decision of the main character to leave. In its final season *The Andy Griffith Show* ranked number one in home viewing. Its successor, *Mayberry R.F.D.*, was as popular as the original series. The last telecast of *The Andy Griffith Show* aired September 16, 1968. Today the series is still popular in rerun syndication throughout the United States.

REFERENCES: Tim Brook and Earle Marsh, *The Complete Directory to Prime Time Network Shows: 1964–Present*, 1992; David Marc, *Demographic Vistas: Television in American Culture*, 1984.

Christopher Gore

THE ANIMALS. The Animals were one of the more popular rock-and-roll bands of the 1960s. Formed in Newcastle upon Tyne, England, in 1962, the group originally included Alan Price, Eric Burdon, Bryan Chandler, John Steel, and Hilton Valentine. Heavily influenced by African-American blues music, the Animals were part of the 1964 "British invasion"* of the United States. Their 1964 single "House of the Rising Sun" was a number one hit on both sides of the Atlantic. They followed "Rising Sun" with a number of other hits, including "Don't Let Me Be Misunderstood" (1965), "We Gotta Get Out of This Place" (1965), and "It's My Life" (1965). Personal and drug problems fractured the group late in 1965. Price left the group, and then so did John Steel. The Animals formally broke up at the end of 1966, just after their song "Don't Bring Me Down" reached the top ten.

REFERENCE: Patricia Romanowski and Holly George-Warren, eds., *The New Rolling Stone Encyclopedia of Rock and Roll*, 1996.

ANTIESTABLISHMENT. The term "antiestablishment" emerged as an adjective in the 1960s to describe a variety of groups opposed to the prevailing values and institutions of American society. Antiwar activists were "antiestablishment" in their opposition to the Vietnam War,* the draft,* and ROTC programs on campus. Countercultural groups like the hippies* were antiestablishment in their opposition to prevailing social and religious values. Various left-wing groups like the Students for a Democratic Society* (SDS) were antiestablishment in their opposition to the prevailing corporate, capitalist system in the United States.

REFERENCES: Ronald Fraser, *1968: A Student Generation in Revolt*, 1988; Todd Gitlin, *The Sixties: Years of Hope, Days of Rage*, 1987.

ANTIWAR MOVEMENT. During the 1950s, a few voices expressed concern about what was happening in Southeast Asia. One of them was Graham Greene, whose 1955 novel *The Quiet American* took exception to American policy there. The central figure was Alden Pyle, an American committed to coldly passionate abstractions—democracy, patriotism, falling dominoes, and the love of God. Greene's objective was to expose the fallacies of U.S. military policy in Vietnam.

Stationed in Saigon as a war correspondent in the early 1950s, Greene watched France leave and the United States arrive. The Americans had young, fresh faces and crew-cuts; they were Alden Pyles intent on doing good, "not to any individual person but to a country, a continent, a world." That was the problem. Americans defined good and evil in universal abstractions. Not many Americans were ready for Greene's prophetic message, offered by one of the novel's characters—Thomas Fowler—who tells Pyle: "In five hundred years there may be no New York or London, but they'll be growing paddy in these fields. . . . Do you think the peasant sits and thinks of God and Democracy when he gets inside his mud hut at night? . . . Isms and ocracies. Give me facts." Alden Pyle is murdered in the end. Michael Herr, in his book *Dispatches* (1977), said: "Maybe it was already over for us in Indochina when Alden Pyle's body washed up under the bridge at Dakao, his lungs full of mud."

Throughout the 1950s and early 1960s, Old Leftists—traditionally socialists and pacifists—were also beginning to marshall forces against the growing American involvement in Southeast Asia. In 1954, as the Eisenhower* administration considered military intervention to rescue the French garrison at Dien Bien Phu, the Friends Committee on National Legislation, a Quaker pacifist group, cautioned the United States against getting involved in a war in Vietnam, characterizing the conflict there as an internal revolution against a despotic regime. Instead, they called on American policymakers to implement a general settlement in Asia that "would shift the emphasis of the conflict from a military basis to a political and economic basis." The American Friends Service Committee, another Quaker group, called on the United States to resist military intervention in Vietnam in favor of a political settlement.

A. J. Muste,* a veteran American pacifist, headed the Fellowship of Reconciliation* (FOR). First established in 1914 during World War I, the FOR had long been the most influential pacifist group in Great Britain and the United States. In October 1964, Muste and the FOR officially endorsed draft resistance to denounce the increasing number of American military advisors being sent to Vietnam. They labeled their protest document "The Declaration of Conscience Against the War in Vietnam." Another anti-Vietnam pacifist group was the War Resistors League* (WRL). Founded in 1923 as a secular pacifist organization, the WRL had opposed U.S. intervention in World War II and in the Korean War. In 1963, under the direction of David Dellinger,* the WRL focused its protests on the expanding U.S. military advisement effort in Vietnam. The WRL sponsored a demonstration in New York City on May 16, 1964. During the protest, twelve men burned their draft* cards. In December 1964, the WRL organized the first nationwide demonstration in opposition to the Vietnam War.*

Except for Greene and the pacifists, however, the antiwar movement was a tiny fringe force in American politics. It also lacked any official voice in Washington, D.C. There were some exceptions; a few Cold Warriors had serious concerns about the war on pragmatic grounds. As early as 1961 Undersecretary of State George Ball* voiced opposition to a proposal by General Maxwell Taylor* and national security advisor Walt W. Rostow* to place an 8,000-man logistical task force in South Vietnam to serve as soldiers and/or economic and political workers. Ball told President John F. Kennedy* that any serious American military effort there "would have the most tragic consequences." Ball then issued a prophetic warning: "If we go down that road we might have, within five years, 300,000 men in the rice paddies of the jungles of Viet-Nam and never be able to find them. . . . You [Kennedy] better be damned careful."

Kennedy heard similar opinions from several other advisors. John Kenneth Galbraith,* the Harvard economist, told the president in April 1962 that Vietnam "could expand step by step into a major, long-drawn-out indecisive military involvement." Former ambassador to the Soviet Union W. Averell Harriman* then warned the president that President Ngo Dinh Diem* of South Vietnam "is a losing horse in the long run." George Kennan,* creator of the "containment"* idea and a former ambassador to the Soviet Union, urged Kennedy to be careful, to realize that nationalism, not communism, was the real issue in Vietnam.

A few early critical voices also sounded in Congress. On March 10, 1964, Senator Ernest Gruening* of Alaska deplored the waste of American lives. "All Vietnam," he wrote, "is not worth the life of a single American boy. . . . The loss of any American lives in Vietnam will someday be denounced as a crime." Five months later, when President Lyndon B. Johnson* turned the Gulf of Tonkin* incident into a *cause célèbre* and asked Congress for unlimited authority to wage war against North Vietnam, the vote in the Senate was 98 to 2 in favor, with only Senator Wayne Morse* of Oregon and Gruening dissenting.

There were also some vocal critics in the Saigon* press corps. From the very

beginning of the conflict, officials of the Kennedy, Johnson, and Nixon administrations criticized the press for impeding the war effort. They wanted reporters
to deliver positive news to the public, or at least news which reflected official
opinion. Most journalists did just that, uncritically passing on the official version
of events. But there were some renegades who kept reporting a steady erosion
of Diem's political base and equally steady gains for the Vietcong.* David
Halberstam* of the *New York Times*, Neil Sheehan of UPI, Nick Turner of
Reuters, Peter Arnett of the Associated Press, Bernard Kalb and Peter Kalisher
of CBS, James Robinson of NBC, Charles Mohr of *Time*, Francois Sully of
Newsweek, Pepper Martin of *U.S. News & World Report*, and Stanley Karnow
of *Time* argued that the regime of Ngo Dinh Diem was isolated and paranoid,
and that a stable democracy would never develop as long as the Ngo family
held power. In short, the United States and South Vietnam were losing.

But the opposition of Old Left pacifist groups, some Cold Warriors, a few
reporters, and a few congressmen was just not enough, and early in 1965 Johnson escalated the war by sending regular American ground troops to South
Vietnam. When Dwight Eisenhower left the White House in 1961, there were
only about 700 American troops in South Vietnam. That number jumped to
17,000 by at the end of 1963. At the end of 1965, more than 180,000 American
soldiers were already there and preparations were underway to send another
160,000 troops. Draft calls escalated just as quickly, as did U.S. casualties.*

Theological and social liberals in many mainstream Protestant churches were
uncomfortable with the escalation. They formed Clergy and Laymen Concerned
About Vietnam* (CALCAV) to mobilize the religious community against the
war. CALCAV was one of the first important channels for Jewish and Catholic
peace activism. CALCAV combined moral and pragmatic arguments in condemning the war, expressing its opposition in ways that kept it on good terms
with its white, middle-class, religiously motivated constituency.

Escalation inspired the antiwar movement, broadening its narrow base to include new elements in American society. Student groups, New Leftists,* and
civil rights activists took a critical look at the war. More than thirty other new
antiwar groups appeared in 1965, represented by an umbrella group—the National Coordinating Committee to End the War in Vietnam.*

The heart of the antiwar movement existed on university campuses. At the
University of Michigan in Ann Arbor, several faculty members organized a
"teach-in"*—modeled after the famous 1960 civil rights "sit-ins"—on March
24, 1965. More than 3,500 students attended the teach-in, where faculty members lectured about the war. Similar teach-ins occurred at many other colleges
and universities that spring. The teach-ins culminated on May 15, 1965, in the
"National Teach-In," which took place at 122 colleges and universities.

By the summer of 1965, New Left groups actively opposed the war. The
Students for a Democratic Society* (SDS) was the most visible. After the Gulf
of Tonkin incident* in 1964, SDS organized campus demonstrations and teach-
ins against the war and distributed "We Won't Go" petitions among young

men of draft age. On April 17, 1965, SDS staged a protest that brought more than 20,000 demonstrators to Washington, D.C. SDS membership quickly jumped from 2,000 to nearly 30,000 members. Other New Left groups—including the Catholic Peace Fellowship, the Emergency Citizens' Group Concerned About Vietnam, the "Another Mother for Peace" organization, and the National Emergency Committee of Clergy Concerned About Vietnam—also actively protested the war.

In mid-1965, several civil rights leaders also became concerned about the escalating war. Rev. James Bevel, a close associate of Rev. Martin Luther King,* Jr., proposed an alliance between the civil rights movement* and the antiwar movement. As deaths and casualties rose in 1966, the antiwar movement gained strength and the civil rights movement became more intimately involved with it. Civil rights leaders, especially Martin Luther King, Jr., took note of a troubling statistic. In 1965–1966, blacks constituted more than 20 percent of the war casualties, a number far higher than their percentage of the American population. Early in 1967, King argued that the war was destroying the civil rights movement at home and creating a black bloodbath in Vietnam.

Late in 1966, when U.S. troops in South Vietnam reached 385,000, the antiwar movement gained new liberal converts. Several Kennedy administration officials, including historian Arthur M. Schlesinger,* Jr., and economist John Kenneth Galbraith,* denounced the war. General David Shoup,* former commandant of the Marine Corps, testified in May 1966 that "I don't think the whole of Southeast Asia, as related to the present and future safety and freedom of this country, is worth the life or limb of a single American." General James Gavin* made a similar statement before the Senate Foreign Relations Committee in 1966. In Congress, Senators Wayne Morse* and Ernest Gruening* were no longer alone in their opposition. Senator George Aiken,* a Republican from Vermont, broke ranks with the administration in 1966. Senator Clifford Case, a New Jersey Republican, called for withdrawal as well. Republican Mark Hatfield* won a Senate seat from Oregon in 1966 because of his antiwar position. In New York, Republican Senator Jacob Javits* came out against the war. Such Republicans as Governor Nelson Rockefeller* of New York, Governor William Scranton of Pennsylvania, Mayor John Lindsay* of New York City, and Senator Hugh Scott of Pennsylvania denounced the war as well.

Democratic opposition intensified. In 1966 Johnson lost some of the most powerful Democrats in the United States Senate. Mike Mansfield,* the majority leader, had long urged the president to avoid escalation, and in 1966 he went public with his criticism. Senator Frank Church* of Idaho called for an end to the bombing of North Vietnam and a negotiated settlement. Senator J. William Fulbright* of Arkansas urged withdrawal from Indochina. He also staged a series of critical hearings by the Senate Foreign Relations Committee in 1966. Senator Vance Hartke* of Indiana wrote a public letter to the president in 1966 calling for an end to the war. Senators George McGovern* of South Dakota, Robert F.

Kennedy* of New York, Edward Kennedy* of Massachusetts, and Eugene Mc-
Carthy* of Minnesota voiced their doubts about the war late in 1966.

Throughout 1966 and early 1967, the antiwar movement gained momentum.
In January 1967 the Spring Mobilization to End the War in Vietnam* was
organized. A coalition of academics, students, and Old and New Leftists, they
sponsored mass demonstrations in the spring. On April 15, 1967, more than
130,000 demonstrators marched in New York City, as did another 70,000 in
San Francisco. Six months later, more than 100,000 people came to Washington,
D.C., for the "March on the Pentagon" demonstration. Photojournalists recorded the event for a worldwide media. People around the world realized how
unpopular the war had become in the United States.

Late in 1967, mainstream liberals invested their antiwar energies into Democratic Party politics. On November 30, 1967, Senator Eugene McCarthy* of
Minnesota announced his intention to run for the 1968 Democratic presidential
nomination. Two months later, the Vietcong launched the Tet Offensive.* Their
ability to stage such a broad-based attack stunned the American public. Eugene
McCarthy did surprisingly well in the New Hampshire primary on March 12,
after which Senator Robert Kennedy* of New York announced his own candidacy for the Democratic nomination. President Johnson, broken politically and
emotionally, decided not to run for reelection. Vice-President Hubert Humphrey* then announced his candidacy for the presidency.

At the August 1968 Democratic National Convention* in Chicago, while
Democrats jockeyed for political position and Hubert Humphrey came away
with the nomination, antiwar activists took to the streets outside the convention
hall. When Mayor Richard Daley* ordered the Chicago police to suppress the
demonstrations, officers violently waded into the demonstrators with dogs,
horses, and billy clubs. The televised images of the demonstrations and the
police attacks were proof that it was time for a political change in America.
Republican candidate Richard M. Nixon* won the election in November 1968.

By that time the antiwar movement was acquiring new allies on the right. To
be sure, there were many Americans who believed the war was immoral, and
millions more who thought the United States simply had no business there. But
there were millions of others—represented by former MACV General William
Westmoreland*; Admiral Ulysses S. Grant Sharp; and Senators Barry Goldwater* of Arizona, Richard Russell* of Georgia, Strom Thurmond* of South
Carolina, and Russell Long* of Louisiana—who proclaimed that if the United
States was not going to "win the war," the only reasonable, and moral, option
was withdrawal.

After the inauguration, Richard Nixon's delay in initiating policy changes
galvanized the antiwar movement. On March 26, Women Strike for Peace pick-
ets carried out the first large-scale antiwar demonstration since the inauguration.
Nixon responded with "Vietnamization,"* turning the war gradually over to
South Vietnam. In June 1969, he informed the country that he would pull 25,000
of 543,000 soldiers from Vietnam. Until he did, two antiwar groups—the Viet-

nam Moratorium Committee and the New Mobilization Committee to End the War in Vietnam—sponsored a series of nationwide protests on a monthly basis beginning in October 1969. Millions participated in the October 15 demonstrations. Thousands of soldiers in South Vietnam wore black armbands to support the demonstrations. Another nationwide demonstration took place in November.

By that time, the antiwar movement was beginning to run out of steam. As Nixon incrementally but steadily reduced the number of U.S. combat troops in Vietnam, the number of American casualties declined, as did the expense of the war. His invasion of Cambodia in 1970 brought the movement temporarily back to life, but the new policy of Vietnamization seemed a reasonable approach to most Americans.

REFERENCES: Charles DeBenedetti and Charles Chatfield, *An American Ordeal: The Antiwar Movement of the Vietnam Era*, 1990; David W. Levy, *The Debate Over Vietnam*, 1991; Melvin Small, *Johnson, Nixon, and the Doves*, 1988; Kathleen J. Turner, *Lyndon Johnson's Dual War: Vietnam and the Press*, 1985; Sandy Vogelgesang, *The Long Dark Night of the Soul: The American Intellectual Left and the Vietnam War*, 1974; Nancy Zaroulis and Gerald Sullivan, *Who Spoke Up? American Protest Against the War in Vietnam, 1963–1975*, 1984.

AP BAC, BATTLE OF (1963). The Battle of Ap Bac, which took place outside of Ap Bac village, forty miles southwest of Saigon* in the Mekong Delta, proved to be a watershed in the early history of the Vietnam War.* Several hundred Vietcong* troops dug into defensive positions along a one-mile canal connecting Ap Vac with a neighboring village. The position gave the Vietcong a clear view of surrounding rice fields. Soldiers from the Army of the Republic of Vietnam's (ARVN) Seventh Division, with a ten to one numerical superiority and helicopter support, assaulted the Vietcong positions. The results startled U.S. policymakers. The Vietcong destroyed five helicopters and killed sixty ARVN soldiers, sustaining only three casualties themselves. The Battle of Ap Bac exposed fatal weaknesses in ARVN and played a key role in convincing many U.S. policymakers that U.S. soldiers might eventually have to play a larger role in the war. ARVN had been no match for the Vietcong, and that reality would continue throughout the war.

REFERENCES: Stanley Karnow, *Vietnam: A History*, 1983; Joseph Buttinger, *Vietnam: A Dragon Embattled*, vol. 2, *Vietnam at War*, 1967.

APPALACHIAN REGIONAL DEVELOPMENT ACT OF 1965. Congress passed the Appalachian Regional Development Act in 1965 as part of Lyndon B. Johnson's* Great Society* "war on poverty."* The legislation was designed to provide approximately $250 million, along with subsequent appropriations of another $1 billion, to develop roads, highways, and water projects throughout the twelve states in the Appalachian mountain chain. The money was also to be used for conservation projects, public recreational facilities, health care facilities, wildlife refuges, and erosion prevention. Although the program as outlined under

the provisions of the 1965 act ended in 1975, many of its programs were continued in subsequent legislation.
REFERENCE: Niles M. Hansen, *Rural Poverty and the Urban Crisis: A Strategy for Regional Development*, 1970.

APOLLO PROGRAM. See **NATIONAL AERONAUTICS AND SPACE ADMINISTRATION.**

APTHEKER V. SECRETARY OF STATE. The Supreme Court under Chief Justice Earl Warren* earned a reputation for limiting the powers of the states and enhancing the rights and freedoms of individuals. That was especially true in how the Court interpreted First Amendment issues during the 1960s, including the freedom of association clause. The Court decided *Aptheker v. Secretary of State* on June 22, 1964. The vote was 7 to 2, and Justice Arthur Goldberg* wrote the majority opinion. The Subversive Activities Act of 1950 had permitted the U.S. government to deny passports to individuals who were members of subversive organizations. The Court declared portions of the act unconstitutional. The government could deny the right to travel to individuals who had joined such groups with the full knowledge of their subversive mission, but not to individuals who were not fully informed. The burden of proof rested on the government. Otherwise, the law was a violation of the freedom of association clause of the First Amendment.
REFERENCE: 378 U.S. 500 (1964).

AQUARIUS, AGE OF. During the late 1960s, the term ''age of Aquarius'' became synonymous with the decade itself. The counterculture,* hippies,* youth rebellion, and antiwar movement* collectively, at least among their own adherents, came to represent a new America where peace, individual liberty, ethnic, gender, and cultural diversity, and sexual freedom had become social norms rather than social exceptions. Proponents of the ''age of Aquarius'' also argued that a new generation of Americans who distrusted unbridled economic growth and technological change was coming to maturity in the United States, and they would eventually alter the face of America. In 1969, the rock group Fifth Dimension put these concepts to song and verse. Their hit record ''Aquarius/ Let the Sunshine In'' spent much of 1969 at the top of the pop music charts.
REFERENCES: William Braden, *The Age of Aquarius: Technology and the Cultural Revolution*, 1970; Ronald Fraser, *1968: A Student Generation in Revolt*, 1988; Todd Gitlin, *The Sixties: Years of Hope, Days of Rage*, 1987.

ARC LIGHT OPERATIONS. Arc Light was the U.S. Air Force code name for the use of B-52 bombers on enemy positions throughout Southeast Asia. The first Arc Light raid occurred on June 18, 1965, and the last ones in December 1973. The B-52s were used for strategic bombing, tactical air support, and

air interdiction. Some critics claimed that using B-52s in South Vietnam was like "swatting flies with sledgehammers."
REFERENCE: James S. Olson, ed., *Dictionary of the Vietnam War*, 1988.

THE ASSOCIATION. The Association was one of the most successful rock-and-roll bands of the 1960s, selling more than 15 million records during the decade. Formed in Los Angeles in 1965, the band included Jules Alexander, Terry Kirkman, Brian Cole, Ted Bluechel, Jim Yester, and Russ Giguere. They emphasized soft rock and ballad music. Their first hit appeared in 1966—"Along Comes Mary." In 1966, with "Cherish," they had their first number one hit. "Windy" was a number one hit in 1967, and "Never My Love" reached number two on the pop charts later in the year. The band then disappeared and failed at a revival in 1981.
REFERENCE: Patricia Romanowski and Holly George-Warren, eds., *The New Rolling Stone Encyclopedia of Rock and Roll*, 1996.

ATROCITIES. Guerrilla conflict is nothing new to American military history. During the American Revolution, the Civil War, the nineteenth-century Indian wars out west, and the Philippine insurrection just after the turn of the twentieth century, U.S. troops had been forced to fight as guerrillas or conduct operations against entrenched guerrilla enemies. The Vietnam War* was another example, but it followed in the wake of World War I, World War II, and the Korean War, all of which had been conventional conflicts employing infantry, artillery, air support, and enormous amounts of firepower.

Guerrilla wars often result in heavy civilian casualties, since an external army must do battle against an enemy in its own homeland. Unlike earlier wars in U.S. history, Vietnam brought home to most Americans the fact that their country, as well as the enemy, was capable of committing atrocities. The My Lai* massacre was the most notorious example, but throughout the war the media crackled with stories of civilian casualties, the torture and execution of Vietcong* prisoners, the throwing of Vietcong prisoners of war* out of helicopters, and the cutting off the ears of the Vietcong and North Vietnamese dead. Vietnam was ripe for atrocities; it was fought in a distant land against a different ethnic group.

Tired, frustrated, angry soldiers commit atrocities, and U.S. soldiers were all three. Unable to separate the Vietcong from civilians, they came to look upon all Vietnamese as combatants. The fact that booby traps* caused so many American casualties only made matters worse, since GIs were convinced that local civilians knew of the booby traps but refused to warn the soldiers about them. Most U.S. soldiers also resented the attitudes of South Vietnamese civilians, who often expressed the wish that the Americans would just go home. Many soldiers thought that they were fighting and dying for ingrates. Between 1965 and 1973, 278 army and marine soldiers were convicted of serious offenses—

murder, rape, and negligent homicide—against Vietnamese civilians. Civilian casualties in the field, both from accidents and atrocities, were far higher.

Furthermore, indiscriminate U.S. bombing and artillery assaults caused widespread civilian casualties. The war was being fought inside South Vietnam, against an elusive enemy that often mixed in with the civilian population. When U.S. forces went after enemy troops with conventional bombing and artillery, civilian casualties were inevitable. Even conservative estimates of civilian deaths in the Vietnam War total more than 250,000 people. Other estimates put the total at one million. Such widespread suffering was counterproductive, since it only made the South Vietnamese more anti-American and more willing to support Communist forces.

REFERENCES: Guenter Lewy, *America in Vietnam*, 1978; Philip Caputo, *A Rumor of War*, 1977; Peter D. Trooboff, ed., *Law and Responsibility in Warfare: The Vietnam Experience*, 1975.

ATTRITION. Throughout the years of the Vietnam War,* there was no shortage of suggestions on how to win the conflict. Presidents John F. Kennedy* and Lyndon B. Johnson* wanted to contain the war, to maintain it as a limited conflict. When it became apparent that limited measures were not effective, the United States gradually relied more and more on its massive military firepower to stop the spread of communism in South Vietnam. The U.S. military began massive bombings in communist-controlled territory in South Vietnam and eventually carried the bombing into Laos and North Vietnam. The American military attempted to approach the conflict on the same terms that the nation fought under in World War I, World War II, and the Korean War—crush the enemy with massive military firepower.

Although Kennedy and Johnson resisted the most extreme demands for escalation, they also refused to withdraw from the conflict, and over the course of eight years they made dozens of "compromise" decisions to modestly increase the American commitment and the level of firepower. Eventually, those series of modest decisions led to an extraordinary escalation. Between 1964 and 1973, the United States detonated more than 7 million tons of explosives on North Vietnam and South Vietnam, a greater volume of firepower than was employed during all of World War II. The tactical initiative remained with the enemy forces, and the United States developed into what became known as the "strategy of attrition." The only way to win the war was to kill so many enemy troops that they could no longer field combat-ready military units.

The strategy of attrition ultimately became a numbers game in which the United States was obsessed with body counts. In order to find the enemy, American military officials imposed relocation programs on millions of South Vietnamese peasants, removing them from ancestral villages and placing them in secured relocation camps. The removal of "friendly" civilians supposedly then left the jungles inhabited only by the "bad guys," so the United States declared those areas to be "free-fire zones"* and unloaded huge volumes of explosives.

To expose the enemy, the United States even launched Operation Ranch Hand,* an aerial defoliation campaign in which American aircraft sprayed the jungles with antiplant chemicals. The United States essentially laid waste to much of South Vietnam. The more desperate the United States became, the more frequent and violent the bombings became.

But the arithmetic of attrition was flawed from the very beginning. By any estimates, the United States would have had to kill as many as 250,000 enemy troops a year to even begin to seriously limit North Vietnam's ability to field decent combat units. The United States, of course, did not believe North Vietnam would be willing to absorb such heavy losses. But the United States badly underestimated their sense of commitment. They were willing to sacrifice up to a quarter of a million troops a year, but in order to inflict those kinds of losses, the United States would have had to have more than 1 million combat troops in Vietnam and have been willing to accept as many as 35,000 dead troops of its own a year. While North Vietnam was prepared politically to make that kind of commitment, the United States was not, and North Vietnam knew it. Under those circumstances, the strategy of attrition was doomed from the very beginning.

REFERENCES: Larry Berman, *Planning a Tragedy: The Americanization of the War in Vietnam*, 1982, and *Lyndon Johnson's War: The Road to Stalemate in Vietnam*, 1989; Robert L. Gallucci, *Neither Peace nor Honor: The Politics of American Military Policy in Vietnam*, 1989; Walter Isaacson and Evan Thomas, *The Wise Men. Six Friends and the World They Made*, 1986.

AUTOMOBILE INDUSTRY. The American love affair with the automobile began when Henry Ford and his Model T made the car affordable to millions of people. During the next half century, American society and the American economy came to revolve around the automobile. The 1960s, however, marked a great watershed in the history of the industry, primarily because of foreign competition. In 1949, foreign manufacturers sold only 12,000 units in the United States, while American companies sold more than 5 million units. During the 1950s, however, the Germans began to successfully sell the Volkswagen in the low-price segment of the market, and by the end of the decade, imports had gained a market share of 10 percent, selling more than 600,000 units in the United States.

Japanese manufacturers began to enter the market in the 1960s, providing lower-cost, more fuel-efficient trucks and automobiles to cost-conscious American buyers. By 1970 imports accounted for 1,230,000 unit sales in the United States, or 15.3 percent of the market. With the jump in oil prices in the 1970s, fuel-efficient foreign cars became even more popular, and in 1975 imports captured 18 percent of the market. By the late 1980s, that percentage had increased to more than 25 percent.

REFERENCES: James J. Fink, *The Car Culture*, 1975; James J. Fink, *The Automobile Age*, 1988; David Halberstam, *The Reckoning*, 1986.

AX HANDLE SATURDAY. On August 27, 1960, after ten days of sit-in*
protests by African-American demonstrators, hundreds of Ku Klux Klansmen
from Florida, Georgia, and Alabama arrived in Jacksonville, Florida. They purchased baseball bats and ax handles at local hardware and department stores and
went on a rampage, randomly beating black pedestrians on the streets of Jacksonville. Police watched the riot but did not intervene to protect black citizens.
Black and white students fought back, and by the afternoon more than 3,000
people were involved in the battle. One man was killed. Locals in Jacksonville
remember the day as ''Ax Handle Saturday.''
REFERENCE: Michael Newton and Judy Ann Newton, *The Ku Klux Klan: An Encyclopedia*, 1990.

B

BA GIA, BATTLE OF (1965). Between 1954 and 1965, the purpose of U.S. military advisors in Vietnam had been to train the Army of the Republic of Vietnam (ARVN) and prepare it for battle against Vietcong* and North Vietnamese forces. The Battle of Ba Gia in 1965 demonstrated how futile that effort had been. On May 29, 1965, near the hamlet of Ba Gia in Quang Ngai, more than 1,000 Vietcong troops attacked three ARVN battalions. The ARVN troops panicked and fled the battlefield, leaving behind their weapons. It took U.S. forces to dislodge the Vietcong from Ba Gia. The Vietcong then retook the hamlet a month later. Even though ARVN General Nguyen Chanh Thi had his own troops ready to reattack, he had them stand by and asked the U.S. Marines to do the job. Ba Gia was one of several critical battles in the spring of 1965 that convinced officials in the Lyndon Johnson* administration that ARVN would not be able to hold its own against Communist forces. The United States would have to take over the war.

REFERENCE: Shelby M. Stanton, *The Rise and Fall of an American Army: U.S. Ground Forces in Vietnam, 1965–1973*, 1985.

BAEZ, JOAN. Joan Baez was born January 9, 1941, in Staten Island, New York. Her father took a position as a professor of physics at Harvard University in 1957, and the family moved to Boston. Joan Baez was a child musical prodigy, and after settling in Boston, she became fascinated with folk music. She had a beautiful soprano voice and began singing folk music in Boston coffeehouses. After several brilliant performances at the Newport Music Festival in 1959 and 1960, she signed a recording contract and made several best-selling albums between 1960 and 1964.

As the civil rights movement* and the antiwar movement* gained momentum in the 1960s, Baez also acquired a national political reputation. She was a political liberal who was committed to peace, disarmament, and racial equality, all of which made her a natural leader to young Americans active in those movements. In 1966, to protest the Vietnam War,* Baez refused to pay her income taxes. She was subsequently arrested in Oakland, California, in 1967 for protesting outside the Northern California Draft Induction Center. Along with her husband, David Harris, Baez was also in César Chávez's* crusade to secure union recognition and better contracts for agricultural workers in California. In 1973, she visited Hanoi in North Vietnam and reported that American bombing campaigns over the years had caused widespread suffering among civilians.

Since the end of the Vietnam War, Baez has continued her singing career, performing in folk music festivals and on the college and university circuit. She has also been active in Amnesty International, an advocacy group committed to assisting political prisoners around the world.

REFERENCES: Joan Baez, *Daybreak*, 1968, and *And a Voice to Sing With: A Memoir*, 1986; Nancy Zaroulis and Gerald Sullivan, *Who Spoke Up? American Protest against the War in Vietnam, 1963–1975*, 1984.

BAG. The term ''bag'' emerged as a slang expression in the 1960s to refer to an individual's primary interest in life.

REFERENCE: Ruth Bronsteen, *The Hippy's Handbook—How to Live on Love*, 1967.

BAKER V. CARR. Throughout the 1960s, the Supreme Court continued the trends launched when Earl Warren* became chief justice in 1953. Very consistently, the Court struck down all forms of de jure segregation, expanded the rights of individuals, narrowed the powers of government, and labored to make sure that the Fifteenth Amendment's protection of voting rights was expanded. One of the most important of the voting rights decisions of the Warren Court was *Baker v. Carr*, decided on March 26, 1962, by a 6 to 2 vote. Justice William Brennan* wrote the majority opinion, which overturned *Colgrove v. Green* (1946) and implemented the ''one-man, one-vote'' doctrine for state legislatures. Until the 1960s, it was common in many state legislatures for rural districts with less population to have the same number of votes as urban districts with large populations. The Court ordered that such maldistribution of power was undemocratic and unconstitutional and a subject fit for federal court redistribution. The Court ordered the redrawing of legislative districts to make sure that all of them possessed equal populations, guaranteeing each individual citizen equal voting power.

REFERENCE: 369 U.S. 186 (1962).

BAKER, BOBBY. See THE BOBBY BAKER SCANDAL.

BALDWIN, JAMES. James Baldwin was born in New York City in 1924. He worked as a boy preacher in several storefront Harlem churches in the 1930s, and he displayed an early gift for writing. In 1945, armed with a Eugene Saxton Scholarship, Baldwin left the United States and took up permanent residence in

France, where his writing career flourished. His first novel—*Go Tell It on the Mountain*—was published in 1953. He followed that with an anthology of his own essays, *Notes of a Native Son*, in 1955. Baldwin's second novel, *Giovanni's Room*, appeared in 1956. Another collection of his essays, entitled *Nobody Knows My Name*, brought him critical acclaim in the United States.

During the civil rights movement* in the 1960s, James Baldwin was the preeminent literary voice of African Americans. His third novel—*Another Country*—was a critical and commercial success in 1962, and *The Fire Next Time* was a best-seller in 1964. It is considered by many to be the most telling, brilliant essay on the history of African-American protest. After his 1968 novel *Tell Me How Long the Train's Been Gone*, Baldwin entered a long period of literary dormancy. In the mid-1970s, however, he returned to print with *If Beal Street Could Talk* (1974), *The Devil Finds Work* (1976), *Little Man, Little Man: A Story of Childhood* (1977), and *Just above My Head* (1979). He was just as prolific in the 1980s, writing *Remember This House* (1980), *The Evidence of Things Not Seen* (1985), and *The Price of the Ticket* (1985). James Baldwin died November 30, 1987.

REFERENCE: James Campbell, *Talking at the Gates: The Life of James Baldwin*, 1991.

BALL, GEORGE WILDMAN. George Ball was born December 21, 1909, in Des Moines, Iowa. He graduated from Northwestern University in 1930 and took a law degree there in 1933. He worked two years for the Department of the Treasury before returning to practice law in Chicago. During World War II, Ball worked for the Lend Lease Administration until President Franklin D. Roosevelt appointed him director of the U.S. Strategic Bombing Survey to measure the effectiveness of U.S. bombing campaigns over Germany and Japan. Ball concluded that the bombing had only stiffened enemy resistance. Between 1945 and 1961, he practiced law in Washington, D.C., and in 1961 he became undersecretary of state.

In the John F. Kennedy* and Lyndon B. Johnson* administrations, Ball was an early and consistent opponent of U.S. Vietnam policy. He argued that South Vietnamese leaders like Ngo Dinh Diem* were corrupt, democracy would be impossible to build, and a land war in South Vietnam was unwinnable. Ball repeatedly advised Johnson to stop the bombing campaigns over North Vietnam because they would only make the North Vietnamese more determined. When Johnson continued to escalate the war, Ball grew frustrated and in 1966, resigned from the state department. When the Tet Offensive* of 1968 proved Ball's warnings correct, Johnson appointed him to the Senior Advisory Group to reevaluate U.S. military and political policies in Indochina. There Ball sounded the same warnings: Vietnam was not central to U.S. strategic interests and not worth the investment of so many lives and so much money. In 1969, when President Johnson vacated the White House for Richard Nixon,* Ball signed on as a senior partner with Lehman Brothers, an investment banking firm. Before his death in 1995, Ball had become the author of four books: *The Discipline of*

Power (1968), *Diplomacy in a Crowded World* (1976), and *The Past Has Another Pattern* (1982). Historians of the Vietnam War* today consider Ball to have been the most astute observer of modern U.S. foreign policy.
REFERENCE: David L. Di Leo, *George Ball, Vietnam, and the Rethinking of Containment*, 1991.

THE BAMBOO BED. In 1969, William Eastlake's novel *The Bamboo Bed* appeared. Set in Indochina during the Vietnam War,* *The Bamboo Bed* was an early literary attempt to expose the absurdities of U.S. military and political policies. Eastlake uses highly fantasized images to make his point, such as peace-loving, tambourine-beating hippies wandering through the Vietnamese jungles sprinkling flowers while U.S. bombers and artillery pulverize the countryside, and U.S. pilots, while airborne, having sex with U.S. Medevac nurses. Most critics had harsh things to say about *The Bamboo Bed*, but they did praise Eastlake for his effort in revealing just how contradictory U.S. policy in Vietnam had become.
REFERENCES: William Eastlake, *The Bamboo Bed*, 1969; Philip D. Beidler, *American Literature and the Vietnam War*, 1982.

BAN THE BOMB. The "Ban the Bomb" crusade was a political movement of the late 1950s and early 1960s designed to reduce the threat of nuclear warfare in the world. Norman Cousins, editor of the *Saturday Review*, was the leading force behind the movement. Cousins was joined by such luminaries as television performer Steve Allen, musician Pablo Casals, composer Leonard Bernstein,* pediatrician Benjamin Spock,* and black writer James Baldwin.* In 1957, they founded the National Committee for a Sane Nuclear Policy.* The group at first campaigned for reductions in the number of nuclear weapons and an end to the atmospheric testing of nuclear weapons, and it eventually endorsed universal disarmament. It also sponsored "Ban the Bomb" rallies, demonstrations, and petition-signing drives around the country. When President John F. Kennedy* negotiated the Nuclear Test Ban Treaty* with the Soviet Union in 1963, the committee worked tirelessly to see that the Senate ratified it. In 1969, the National Committee for a Sane Nuclear policy changed its name to SANE: A Citizens' Organization for a Sane World. By that time, however, the Ban the Bomb movement had been largely subsumed by the anti–Vietnam War* movement in the United States.
REFERENCE: Milton Katz, *Ban the Bomb*, 1987.

BANKS, DENNIS. Dennis Banks, an Anishinabe Native American, was born in 1930 on the Leech Lake Indian Reservation in northern Minnesota. In 1968, with Clyde Bellecourt* and other Indian community members, Banks organized the American Indian Movement* (AIM) to protect the traditional ways of Indian people, improve government-funded social services, and prevent the harassment of local Native Americans by police. On Thanksgiving Day 1970, while attempting to extend its activism to a national audience, Banks and other members of AIM seized the *Mayflower II*, the replica of the original ship that carried the Pilgrims to the North American continent. AIM members proclaimed Thanksgiving Day a national day of mourning in protest against the seizure of Indian lands by the early white colonists.

In February 1973, Banks and other AIM members led a protest in Custer, South Dakota, after the mother of murder victim Wesley Bad Heart Bull was pushed down a flight of stairs following a meeting with officials. Banks was arrested as a result of his involvement in the seventy-one-day occupation of Wounded Knee, South Dakota, in 1973. Acquitted of charges related to the occupation at Wounded Knee, Banks was convicted of assault with a deadly weapon without intent to kill and rioting while armed, charges stemming from the Custer incident. Jumping bail, Banks fled to California. Governor Jerry Brown refused to honor extradition requests from South Dakota, citing the strong hostility there against AIM members in general and Banks in particular. In March 1983, the Onondaga Nation, located south of Syracuse, New York, granted Banks asylum. Later in the year, after nine years as a fugitive, Banks surrendered to state authorities in Rapid City, South Dakota. He served approximately one year of a three-year sentence.

In the late 1980s, Banks actively protested the disturbance of Native American ancestral burial grounds by collectors and archaeologists. Due in part to Banks' efforts, the Smithsonian Museum agreed to return 25,000 Indian bones and other artifacts for reburial. Banks organized ceremonies for over 1,200 of these reinterment efforts. In 1988, Banks published his autobiography, *Sacred Soul*, in Japanese rather than English, citing English as the language of the conquerors. Banks played important roles in the movies *The Last of the Mohicans* (1992) and *Thunderheart* (1992).

REFERENCES: Arlene Ehrlich, "The Right to Rest in Peace," *Baltimore Sun*, October 22, 1989; David Holmstrom, "Oglala Sioux: Up from Wounded Knee, Parts 1–3," *Christian Science Monitor*, October 16–18, 1989; Stanley David Lyman, *Wounded Knee, 1973: A Personal Account*, 1991; Kenneth Stern, *Loud Hawk. The United States versus the American Indian Movement*, 1994; Rex Weyler, *Blood of the Land: The Government and Corporate War against the American Indian Movement*, 1984; Theodore W. Taylor, *American Indian Policy*, 1983.

David Ritchey

BARBIE. See **HANDLER, RUTH**.

BARNARD, CHRISTIAAN NEETHLING. Christiaan Neethling Barnard was born in 1923 and grew up in the village of Beauford West, South Africa. Barnard's father earned a living as a Dutch Reformed minister, making fifty-nine dollars a month; Barnard and his three brothers were raised in conditions bordering on poverty. He attended schools in Beauford West and in 1953 received his M.D. from University of Cape Town Medical School. Barnard, who was disappointed with the poor research facilities in Cape Town, journeyed to the United States at the end of 1955 and entered the University of Minnesota. He received a grant from the Danzain Foundation for Medical Research and began extensive research on heart surgery. In 1957 he performed his first heart operation. Barnard returned to Cape Town Medical School in 1958 and became director of surgical research. He continued his research and by the fall of 1967 had ten years' experience in major heart surgery.

Barnard began recruiting candidates for the most challenging surgical procedure ever attempted. He believed that he could successfully transplant a human heart. In 1967 he found his patient, Louis Washkansky, a wholesale grocer who was dying of heart disease at Groote Shuur Hospital. Washkansky was fifty-four years old, had extensive coronary artery disease with only 20 percent of the muscle in the left ventricle normal, and suffered from diabetes. Washkansky agreed to the operation. On the night of December 2, 1967, twenty-five-year-old Denise Duvall, hit by a car while crossing a Cape Town street, was rushed to Groote Shuur Hospital, where she died hours later. Duvall's heart was removed from her chest, examined, and put into a dish containing solution at 10 degrees centigrade to cool it. Washkansky was attached to a heart-lung machine, his empty pericardial cavity awaiting Duvall's healthy heart. The heart was placed in Washkansky's pericardial sac, where it was then rewarmed. To suppress the white blood cells that immediately invade any foreign organism placed in the body, Washkansky received massive doses of the drugs azathigorine and cortisone, supplemented with gamma rays from a cobalt-60 unit. These drugs prevented rejection by suppressing the immune system, but they left Washkansky defenseless against infection. On December 21, 1967, he contracted double pneumonia and died.

After successfully completing the heart transplant, Barnard received massive media attention. The Columbia Broadcasting System flew him to the United States to appear on the network television show *Face the Nation*. During his visit, Barnard was a guest of President Lyndon B. Johnson* and was feted wherever he went. On January 2, 1968, after returning to Cape Town, Barnard performed his second heart transplant operation. The recipient of the heart was Dr. Philip Blaiberg. The second operation was far more successful than the first. With the acquired knowledge of his first experience Barnard was able to stabilize Blaiberg, who was released seventy-four hours after his operation. Dr. Blaiberg is still alive and enjoys a moderate amount of activity.

Dr. Christiaan Barnard had been acclaimed for his many successes. He not only opened the science of cardiology but opened up the operating room for other organ transplants. Barnard has received fellowships in the American College of Cardiology and the American College of Surgery. He now resides in South Africa's Karoo region with his wife, Karin Setzkorn.

REFERENCE: Christiaan Barnard, *A Second Life: Memoirs*, 1993.

Amber Durden

BARNETT, ROSS ROBERT. Ross Barnett was born in Standing Pine, Mississippi, January 22, 1898. He served in the U.S. Army during World War I and graduated from Mississippi College in 1922. After teaching and coaching in the public schools for two years, Barnett went to Oxford and earned a law degree at the University of Mississippi in 1926. He then practiced law in Jackson, Mississippi, and became active in Democratic Party politics. After failing to win the governorship of Mississippi in 1951 and 1955, Barnett finally succeeded in the election of 1959, running on a strong segregationist plank.

But Ross Barnett's political career then collided with the civil rights movement.* He bitterly opposed school desegregation and tried to block James Meredith's* enrollment at the University of Mississippi in 1962. Barnett continued his obstructionist stance even after President John F. Kennedy* called in federal troops to guarantee Meredith's admission. The governor earned a contempt citation for refusing to cooperate. In 1963, he led the fight in Mississippi to reject the constitutional amendment outlawing the poll tax. The Mississippi constitution prohibited the reelection of a governor, and Barnett returned to private life in 1964. In 1967, he failed in a bid for the Democratic gubernatorial nomination. Ross Barnett died November 6, 1987.

REFERENCES: Russell H. Barnett, *Integration at Ole Miss*, 1965; Roy Glashan, *American Governors and Gubernatorial Elections, 1775–1975*, 1975; *New York Times*, November 7, 1987.

BAY OF PIGS INVASION (1961). Late in November 1959, the Dwight D. Eisenhower* administration made a decision to oppose the new Fidel Castro* regime in Cuba, although at the time the methods to be used were primarily economic coercion and propaganda campaigns. Inside the Central Intelligence Agency* (CIA), however, there was a strong movement to take positive steps to destabilize the Castro regime. Fidel Castro represented a communist beachhead in the Western Hemisphere, and his presence there was intolerable to many Americans. Allen Dulles, head of the Central Intelligence Agency, organized a special Cuban task force within the CIA, and the task force recruited thirty Cuban exiles to return to Cuba as local guerrilla leaders. They also formulated plans to commit acts of sabotage against Cuban military and economic installations. Early in 1960, Eisenhower approved Dulles' proposal to overthrow Castro through covert action.

In August 1960, the Eisenhower administration formally funded what the CIA was calling Operaton Pluto and authorized the Department of Defense to assist the CIA in building a paramilitary force composed of Cuban exiles living in south Florida. The CIA was confident, based on extensive interviews of the Cuban exiles, that the Castro regime was politically marginal and that it would not be too difficult to inspire a mass uprising against him. The fact that they were gathering their intelligence from upper- and middle-class exiles and that a natural anti-Castro bias was built into their opinions did not affect CIA planning.

They had already concluded that Fidel Castro's regime in Cuba was illegitimate and unpopular with the masses. The radio broadcasts were to prepare the Cuban population for an uprising, and an invasion of the island by the paramilitary expeditionary force would bring it about spontaneously.

After carefully surveying the political landscape, the CIA established the Cuban Democratic Revolutionary Front in May 1960 and headquartered it in Miami. Howard Hunt, who would later mastermind the 1972 break-in at the Democratic Party headquarters in the Watergate building, was placed in charge of planning for the operation. The CIA also began training guerrilla radio operators near Fort Myers, Florida, and recruited exiles to begin guerrilla military training at Fort Gulick in the Panama Canal Zone. Just in case the CIA would need to train a larger army, the agency established a training facility, named Camp Trax, in Guatemala.

The first exile recruits arrived there at the end of August 1960. The CIA also purchased Southern Air Transport Company to transfer men, weapons, and supplies to Camp Trax. To provide combat air support, the CIA assembled a contingent of B-26 bombers and C-46 transports and recruited American pilots from the Alabama Air National Guard. Finally, for naval transport and support, the CIA purchased ships from a bankrupt company known as Mineral Carriers in Key West, Florida. In November, news of the training group began to leak to the press. Operation Pluto would not be a secret. Its scale was way too large for a covert action. By that time the CIA had also decided to change the nature of Operation Pluto from guerrilla infiltration to a conventional amphibious landing. The timing for the invasion was set for March 1961.

By early February 1961 there were about 1,400 exiles in training in Guatemala. They called themselves Brigade 2506. Brigade 2506 was divided into six small "battalions" and a heavy weapons group. There was also a commando group of 168 troops scheduled to make a diversionary attack on the island. The CIA had also arranged for another 500 troops to be staged in the Miami area and prepared to reinforce the main units if such reinforcement proved necessary. By early February, as the training reached completion, the numbers of stories in American and Havana newspapers about the groups had completely blown whatever covert intentions the CIA had. Although the new president, John F. Kennedy,* would not permit any overt U.S. naval or air support for the invasion, he enthusiastically approved the planned invasion.

The invasion took place in mid-April at the Bay of Pigs, but it proved to be an unmitigated disaster. The diversionary invasion failed to take place because of heavy seas, and the CIA's promise that Castro's air forces would not be able to respond to the invasion for at least two days was woefully wrong. Because of all the publicity about the training of the exile army, Castro had placed his own armed forces in a state of readiness. Within hours the Cuban air force had sunk two supply ships. Also, the CIA promise that more than 5,000 anti-Castro Cuban guerrillas would join Brigade 2506 went unfulfilled. Only fifty Cubans joined the brigade once it had hit the beaches. The CIA had also scattered the

1,400 troops along more than thirty-six miles of beach. Three days into the operation, Brigade 2506 had used up all of its ammunition, broken up, and dispersed into the swamps, and Castro's troops then arrested them one by one.

The Bay of Pigs invasion was an unbelievable propaganda coup for Fidel Castro, who could not have been more pleased at the CIA folly in planning the invasion and its bungling of the entire affair. He now had proof for all the world to see that the United States was a counterrevolutionary entity bent on his destruction. Although the CIA expected the Cuban people to rise up en masse against the Castro regime once the exile brigade had landed, exactly the opposite took place. Castro enjoyed widespread support among the Cuban lower classes. Once it was clear that the invasion was American-backed, Brigade 2506 was doomed to failure. In that sense the Bay of Pigs helped even more to legitimize the revolution throughout Cuba. In December 1962, 1,179 prisoners of the Bay of Pigs mission were ransomed for $53 million worth of pharmaceutical supplies and heavy construction equipment.

REFERENCE: James S. Olson and Judith E. Olson, *The Cuban-Americans: From Tragedy to Triumph*, 1995.

THE BEACH BOYS. The Beach Boys were an extraordinarily popular rock-and-roll band during the 1960s. Formed in Hawthorne, California, in 1961, the Beach Boys included Brian Wilson, Dennis Wilson, Carl Wilson, Al Jardine, and Mike Love. They became symbols of so-called California rock and California teenager life—driving, surfing, and dating. In 1962, under contract with Capitol Records, they put together a string of megahits, including "Surfin' Safari" (1962), "Surfin' USA" (1963), "Surfer Girl" (1963), "In My Room" (1963), "Don't Worry Baby" (1964), "I Get Around" (1964), "Fun, Fun, Fun" (1964), "Help Me Rhonda" (1965), "California Girls" (1965), and "Good Vibrations" (1966). By that time, however, Brian Wilson had had a nervous breakdown and stopped serving as the band's producer. The group declined into obscurity except as nostalgia performers, but in 1988 it had another number one hit—"Kokomo."

REFERENCE: David Leaf, *The Beach Boys*, 1985; David Leaf, *The Beach Boys and the California Myth*, 1978.

BEAT. The word "beat" was actually a combination of three words, coming from "jazz beat," a musical form Beatniks* especially enjoyed; feeling "beat" or crushed by the vapid, dry square world; and "beatitude," a spiritual quest in which they tried to find meaning in an existential universe.

REFERENCE: Bruce Cook, *The Beat Generation*, 1971.

BEATLEMANIA. The term "Beatlemania" was coined in 1964, when the Beatles rock group came on tour in the United States. It referred to the mass hysteria exhibited by mobs of Beatles fans. See THE BEATLES.

THE BEATLES. The British rock group the Beatles comprised four working-class musicians from Liverpool. They are considered to have been the most important influence on popular music and the most successful performing group in history. The Beatles were also the first of the rock groups whose domination of American popular music in the 1960s became known as the British invasion.

They began performing in the late 1950s as skiffle players, first in Liverpool and later in Hamburg, Germany. They took their name from a play on the name of Buddy Holly's band, the Crickets, and called themselves first the Silver Beatles, shortening the name later to the Beatles. From the beginning, the group's primary writers were John Lennon and Paul McCartney. They were joined on guitar and vocals by George Harrison and later, on drums, by Ringo Starr. In 1961, they acquired a manager, Brian Epstein, who has often been given credit for their later success.

The Beatles recorded their first number one hit in the United Kingdom in 1963 with "Please Please Me." The record generated no chart action in the United States, nor did their first album, *Introducing the Beatles*. One year later, however, their single, "I Want to Hold Your Hand," reached number one, and, four months later, the group held the top five positions on America's charts. The wave of popularity, dubbed "Beatlemania," that followed the Beatles' career was unprecedented in music history and will arguably never be repeated.

From their 1963 first release to their dissolution in 1971, the Beatles permanently raised global standards for popular music. They exhibited an uncanny ability to successfully incorporate musical ideas from widely divergent sources; and their lyrics, concepts, and production techniques were considered to be on the cutting edge of the industry.

The Beatles introduced an unprecedented lyrical sophistication, offering social commentary and addressing philosophical concerns that stretched the intellectual boundaries of rock music. They invented the concept album and introduced the idea of record covers as art form. The first fully realized concept album, *Sergeant Pepper's Lonely Hearts' Club Band*, may be the best-known rock album of all time. They were also innovators in the use of unusual instruments and electronic production techniques. They experimented with movies, garnering two solid successes in *Hard Day's Night* and *Help!*, which became cult favorites, plus the animated film *Yellow Submarine*, which was a critical and financial success in Europe and America. Their single foray into television, 1967's *Magical Mystery Tour*, was unsuccessful, but the accompanying sound track album sold in the millions.

The Beatles stopped touring in 1966, citing safety concerns. Although they continued to record as a group, they began to pursue individual projects, and, by 1969, rumors of their dissolution had become rampant. Not until 1971, however, did the group announce the official breakup.

Throughout the 1970s, rumors persisted of a "Fab Four" reunion. Then, in 1980, John Lennon was murdered by an obsessed fan, and the group became history. During the eight years they performed as a group, the Beatles produced music that, to date, has resulted in sales of more than 100 million singles and more than 100 million albums.

REFERENCES: Ray Coleman, *McCartney: Yesterday and Today*, 1996; Maxwell MacKenzie, *The Beatles: Every Little Thing*, 1998.

Sammie Miller

BEATNIKS. Late in the 1950s, the beatniks emerged as the most characteristic element of American pop culture. Herbert Caen, a columnist for the *San Francisco Examiner*, coined the term after "Sputnik," the name of the successful Soviet orbital vehicle in 1957. He took the suffix "nik" and added it to the word "beat." Beatniks inaugurated the 1960s as a time of nonconformity and rebellion. They wore black, turtleneck sweaters, baggy sweatshirts, cheap dungarees, sunglasses, sandals, and dark berets and first appeared in San Francisco and Venice, California, the Left Bank of Paris, and Greenwich Village in New York City. Beatnik women were adorned in leotards, gaudy jewelry, and ballet slippers and wore their hair long and straight. With a feigned moroseness, they disdained the material world and enjoyed their own alienation. Real beats like Jack Kerouac or Ken Kesey and Allen Ginsberg hated the "beatnik" phenomenon as a vulgarization of their own true movement. Ginsberg once asked reporters never to refer to him as a "beatnik," since he considered the word an insulting epithet. In 1958, *San Francisco Examiner* reporter June Miller wrote a series of articles on the beatniks, which made their way on to the wire services and into newspaper pages throughout the country. Their image as rebels was eclipsed in the mid-1960s by the emergence of hippies.*

REFERENCES: Bruce Cook, *The Beat Generation*, 1971; John Arthur Maynard, *Venice West: The Beat Generation in Southern California*, 1991; Steven Watson, *The Birth of the Beat Generation, 1944–1960*, 1995.

BEATS. During the late 1950s and early 1960s, the "beat generation" emerged as an early precursor to the anti-institutional, antibureaucracy, and antiwar counterculture* of the 1960s. It was primarily a literary rebellion, a cultural, rather than a political, phenomenon. Most beatniks opposed racism, militarism, and economic exploitation, but they were far more interested in personal liberation and the celebration of heterosexuality and homosexuality, hallucinatory drug use, and mystical religion. The leading lights of the "beat" movement were writers Jack Kerouac, who wrote *On the Road* (1957) and *The Dharma Bums* (1958); Gary Snyder, who wrote *The Old Ways* (1972); poet Allen Ginsberg, who wrote *Howl* (1956); Ken Kesey, who wrote *One Flew over the Cuckoo's Nest* (1962); and William Burroughs, who wrote *Naked Lunch* (1959).

The beats first appeared in major cities, especially San Francisco and New York, where young people gathered for jazz concerts, poetry readings, and drug and alcohol use. Outsiders considered them rebellious, self-indulgent, and undisciplined, but the major focus of the beats was to broaden the range of human experience by stepping outside existing social conventions. It did not matter whether those conventions were economic, cultural, religious, or sexual. Critics accused the beats of being rootless. In a sense they were; they were known for their travels, primarily because they resisted the limitations that private property and social station imposed on people. Beats also distrusted the complexities of modern technology and preferred simple crafts and simple machines. They rejected the narrow conventions of sectarian Western religions in favor of the mysticisms inherent in Buddhism and Hinduism. Bureaucracies of all sorts were also alien to the beats, primarily because large organizations developed stifling conventions of their own and valued the impersonal over the personal.

By the mid-1960s, however, the beats lost their lock on the fringe of American culture. They were eclipsed by the new counterculture that emerged on college campuses after 1963. Beats were far less overtly political than the counterculture, but they were far more concerned about introspection, moods, energy, and words. Some historians look to Ken Kesey as the link between the beats and the counterculture. He is sometimes viewed as the last of the beats and the first of the counterculture rebels.

REFERENCES: Bruce Cook, *The Beat Generation*, 1971; John Arthur Maynard, *Venice West: The Beat Generation in Southern California*, 1991; Steven Watson, *The Birth of the Beat Generation, 1944–1960*, 1995.

BEAUTIFUL. In the 1960s, the term ''beautiful'' emerged in the hippie* counterculture* as a slang expression indicating enthusiastic approval for something.
REFERENCE: Ruth Bronsteen, *The Hippy's Handbook—How to Live on Love*, 1967.

BECK, DAVID. David Beck was born in Stockton, California, June 16, 1894. After dropping out of high school, Beck took extension courses at the University of Washington and then got a job as a laundry worker. He became active in local union politics. He became a laundry driver and joined the local of the International Brotherhood of Teamsters, Chauffeurs, Warehousemen, and Helpers (IBT) in 1917. During the 1920s, he served several terms as local union president and went to work full-time for the IBT as an organizer in 1927. In 1937, Beck organized and became president of the Western Conference of Teamsters, and in 1952, he was elected international president of the IBT. He did not run for reelection in 1957 because he was under investigation by the McClellan Committee of the U.S. Senate. Convicted of income tax fraud, Beck spent 1962 to 1965 in a federal penitentiary. After his release, he built a successful real estate business in Seattle. In 1983, at the age of eighty-nine, Beck participated in a speaking tour for the teamsters. He died in 1989.
REFERENCE: Donald Garnel, *The Origins of Teamster Power in the West*, 1972.

BELIEVER. The slang expression ''believer'' emerged during the 1960s to refer to a dead soldier, usually an enemy soldier, in Vietnam. Later in the decade it became a more generic term to describe the victims of crimes and accidents.
REFERENCE: James S. Olson, ed., *Dictionary of the Vietnam War*, 1988.

BELLECOURT, CLYDE. Clyde Bellecourt, an Ojibway Native American, was born in 1939 on the White Earth Reservation in Minnesota. Bellecourt, with Dennis Banks* and other Native American community leaders, cofounded the American Indian Movement* in Minneapolis in July 1968. The American Indian Movement (AIM) was originally formed to improve government-funded social services to urban neighborhoods and to prevent the harassment of local Native Americans by police. Increasingly confrontational, Bellecourt and other AIM leaders implemented an armed occupation of the tiny South Dakota hamlet of Wounded Knee on February 27, 1973. Bellecourt was elected to the council of the AIM-declared "Nation of Wounded Knee" and eventually cosigned the peace agreement ending the confrontation. Not long after Wounded Knee, Bellecourt was shot in the stomach by Carter Camp, another occupation leader.

During the 1972 occupation of the Bureau of Indian Affairs building in Washington, D.C., Bellecourt helped draft the twenty-point document presented to the government. Although AIM demands were ignored, the government did establish a task force that met with movement leaders and promised to make no arrests in connection with the occupation. Bellecourt also worked extensively to raise funds for AIM-sponsored projects and was briefly associated with militant black activist Stokely Carmichael.*

In the 1990s, Bellecourt lobbied energetically on behalf of the Mille Lac Chippewa during their struggle to maintain traditional walleyed pike harvests along the shores of Flathead Lake in Minnesota. Earlier successes in Wisconsin allowed Native Americans to continue their treaty-guaranteed right to maintain their traditional subsistence fishing economy. Powerful opposition in Minnesota, led by former Minnesota Viking football coach Bud Grant, persuaded the state legislature to reject an agreement that would have allowed the tribe to harvest about half of the walleyed pike in Flathead Lake.

REFERENCES: Margaret L. Knox, "The New Indian Wars: A Growing Movement Is Gunning," *Los Angeles Times*, November 7, 1993; Edward Lazarus, *Black Hills, White Justice: The Sioux Nation versus the United States, 1775 to the Present*, 1991; Stanley David Lyman, *Wounded Knee, 1973: A Personal Account*, 1991; Kenneth Stern, *The United States versus the American Indian Movement*, 1994; Rex Weyler, *Blood of the Land: The Government and Corporate War against the American Indian Movement*, 1984.

David Ritchey

BELLOW, SAUL. Saul Bellow was born July 10, 1915, in Lachine, Quebec, Canada, to Russian Jewish immigrant parents. He was raised in Montreal, and after earning a bachelor's degree at Northwestern University he settled permanently in an ethnically mixed neighborhood in Chicago. A gifted writer, Bellow wrote his first book in 1944—*Dangling Man*. Although the book was not a commercial success, it did secure him an enthusiastic following among American literati. His 1953 novel *The Adventures of Augie March*, however, won Bellow commercial success as well as critical acclaim. The novel was a commentary on American life from the perspective of Augie March, a sort of Jewish Huck Finn stuck in a modern, urban world. *Henderson the Rain King*, a novel set in a mythical Africa and published in 1959, further cemented his reputation as a major American novelist. In 1964, Bellow wrote his greatest novel, *Herzog*, which revolves around Moses Herzog, a middle-class Jewish intellectual living in the United States. One of the great literary figures of the twentieth century, Bellow was awarded the Nobel Prize in literature in 1976 after publishing *Humboldt's Gift*.

REFERENCES: Daniel Fuchs, *Saul Bellow: Vision and Revision*, 1984; Gilbert M. Porter, *Whence the Power? The Artistry and Humanity of Saul Bellow*, 1974.

BEN CASEY. *Ben Casey* was one of the most popular television series of the 1960s. A medical drama, it first aired on October 7, 1961, for ABC. Vince Edwards starred as Dr. Ben Casey, with Sam Jaffe as Dr. David Zorba. The setting is a major metropolitan hospital, and the series' realism—it dealt honestly with death, crime, and emotional problems—was consistent with the growing skepticism of the decade. The last episode of *Ben Casey* was broadcast on March 21, 1966.

REFERENCE: Tim Brooks and Earle Marsh, *The Complete Directory to Prime Time Network and Cable TV Shows*, 1995.

BEN SUC. During the Vietnam War,* the village of Ben Suc became a symbol of the futility of U.S. military policy. Located approximately thirty miles northwest of Saigon in Binh Duong Province, Ben Suc had a population of just over 5,500 people in 1965. The village was on the fringe of the so-called Iron Triangle,* also known as War Zone D. The Iron Triangle was a hotbed of Vietcong* activity, and American soldiers repeatedly found themselves engaging in search and destroy* operations there. The political environment in Ben Suc frustrated U.S. troops. In 1964 Vietcong soldiers had driven troops of the Army of the Republic of Vietnam* (ARVN) from Ben Suc, and villagers there openly cooperated with the Vietcong, protecting them, hiding them, and allowing them to place booby traps* throughout the area. Despite repeated assaults and U.S. air strikes between 1965 and 1967, ARVN troops had been unable to dislodge the Vietcong from the village and its immediate environs.

Late in 1966, U.S. military officials decided to launch Operation Cedar Falls* in order to wipe out Vietcong activity in the Iron Triangle. Although Ben Suc was located just beyond the northwestern tip of the Iron Triangle, it became a key objective of Operation Cedar Falls.* On January 8, 1967, 420 U.S. soldiers invaded Ben Suc. They expected heavy resistance but encountered only sporadic small-arms fire. The soldiers relocated the entire Ben Suc population to a refugee camp. Then, a U.S. engineering battalion leveled the village, destroying homes, buildings, fruit trees, and grapefruit fields. Miles of underground tunnels used for hiding Vietcong soldiers crisscrossed Ben Suc, and the engineers blew up the tunnels. When the troops and the engineering battalion left Ben Suc, nothing was left.

Two days later, Vietcong troops returned to Ben Suc. Journalists in the Saigon* press corps learned of the reoccupation and used the story to illustrate the implausibilites inherent in U.S. military policy. Less than thirty miles from Saigon, U.S. and ARVN troops, in order to root out enemy soldiers, had destroyed a village and turned 5,500 people into refugees. In the end, they had not achieved their objective of eliminating Vietcong activity in the area. In 1967, journalist Jonathan Schell wrote a bestselling indictment of U.S. policy, entitling the book *The Village of Ben Suc*. As a result, U.S. policymakers and the general public began to have serious doubts about the merits of fighting a war of attrition* in Vietnam.

REFERENCES: Jonathan Schell, *The Village of Ben Suc*, 1967; Bernard William Rogers, *Cedar Falls-Junction City: A Turning Point*, 1974.

BEN TRE. Like Ben Suc*, Ben Tre was a South Vietnamese city that symbolically exposed the bankruptcy of U.S. policy in Indochina. Ben Tre was the capital of Kien Hoa Province, located south of Saigon* along the coast of the South China Sea. During the Tet Offensive* of 1968, Vietcong* troops captured the city, and U.S. forces had to retake it. Thousands of U.S. and Army of the Republic of Vietnam* (ARVN) troops participated in the invasion, which included massive air strikes. When the dust settled and Ben Tre had been recaptured, 550 Ben Tre residents—civilians and Vietcong—were dead and another 1,200 had been wounded. Similar assaults occurred all over South Vietnam during the war, but Ben Tre became famous when an American journalist asked a U.S. Army major to justify such indiscriminate use of air power and artillery. The major remarked, ''It became necessary to destroy the town in order to save it.'' Antiwar* activists circulated the quote widely to underscore their opposiiton to the war.

REFERENCE: Peter Baestrup, *Big Story: How the American Press and Television Reported and Interpreted the Crisis of Tet 1968 in Vietnam and Washington*, 1983.

BENNETT, ROBERT. Robert Bennett, an Oneida Indian, was born in 1912 in Oneida, Wisconsin. He attended the Haskell Institute in Kansas and then earned a law degree at Southeastern University in Washington, D.C. With his law degree in hand, Bennett accepted a position with the Bureau of Indian Affairs (BIA), where he worked as an administrative assistant on the Navajo Reservation in New Mexico. With the outbreak of World War II, Bennett took a leave of absence from the BIA and served honorably in the Marine Corps. After the war, he returned to the Bureau of Indian Affairs, and in 1966 he was named commissioner of Indian affairs, only the second Native American to hold the position. He headed the BIA until his resignation in 1969, when the Richard M. Nixon* administration came into office. During his tenure with the BIA,

Bennett was an indefatigable proponent of self-determination.* Since his retirement, he has remained active in promoting Indian rights.

REFERENCE: Duane Champagne, ed., *Chronology of Native North American History*, 1994.

BERGER, SAMUEL DAVID. Samuel David Berger, a career diplomat who played an important role in formulating U.S. military policy in Vietnam, was born in New York City on December 6, 1911. In 1934 he received a Ph.D. in economics from the University of Wisconsin, spent several years working as a statistician and labor economist, and then, in 1945, joined the state department. After diplomatic assignments in Great Britain, Japan, New Zealand, and Greece, Berger became ambassador to South Korea in 1961. In 1968, President Lyndon B. Johnson* named him deputy ambassador to South Vietnam, a post Berger remained in until 1972. Berger served as a liaison between the United States, the Army of the Republic of Vietnam (ARVN), and President Nguyen Van Thieu.* In an attempt to keep ARVN in a secondary political role, he staunchly supported the government of Nguyen Van Thieu. Berger believed that it was possible to build a permanent, non-communist government in Saigon.* He supported both the invasion of Cambodia in 1970 and the disastrous invasion of Laos in 1971. After leaving Saigon in 1972, Berger signed on with the Foreign Service Institute. He died February 16, 1980.

REFERENCES: Department of State, *Biographic Register*, 1974; Clark Dougan and Steven Weiss, *The Vietnam Experience: Nineteen Sixty-Eight*, 1983; *New York Times*, February 17, 1980.

BERLIN CRISIS. At the end of World War II, the defeated Germany was occupied by troops from the United States, France, Great Britain, and the Soviet Union. Diplomats from all four nations eventually divided the country into four zones, one for each of the occupying powers. Eventually, the four zones were consolidated into two. One became West Germany, and the other became Soviet-dominated East Germany. The city of Berlin was also divided into two zones. East Berlin fell within the Soviet bloc and West Berlin was in the American orbit.

The city of West Berlin soon became a bone of contention in the Cold War.* Because of its political liberties and consumer economy, West Berlin attracted tens of thousands of refugees from East Berlin, which was fast becoming a dreary, oppressive symbol of communism's inherent contradictions. In June 1948, the Soviet Union precipitated a Cold War crisis by cutting off all rail and highway traffic into West Berlin. Such a move was easy for the Soviets because both West Berlin and East Berlin were located well within the boundaries of East Germany. President Harry S Truman responded with the Berlin airlift, flying supplies into West Berlin for nearly a year in order to keep the city from surrendering. The crisis ended in May 1949, when the Soviets reopened the highways and rail lines.

Berlin remained a source of international tension for the next decade. The flow of refugees from East Berlin to West Berlin continued unabated, and the prosperity of West Berlin became a distinct embarrassment for the Russians. To that embarrassment was added fear in 1958, when a rearmed West Germany acquired nuclear weapons. In November 1958, Soviet premier Nikita Khrushchev* reacted by calling for a nuclear-free Germany and the end of the four-power occupation of the country. If the United States would not agree to his demands, he threatened to conclude a separate peace with East Germany and close off all access to West Berlin. Khrushchev kept postponing his deadline on an agreement, and the crisis continued to fester throughout 1959 and 1960.

Berlin provided President John F. Kennedy* with the first superpower confrontation of his administration. At the Vienna summit conference of 1961, Kennedy and Khrushchev spent a good deal of time discussing Berlin, but they could reach no accommodation. In August 1961, to stem the tide of refugee migration, the Soviets constructed the Berlin Wall, dividing the city in two. Border guards were given instructions to shoot-to-kill individuals trying to escape East Berlin for West Berlin. Kennedy did not respond to construction of the wall, but it did end the crisis because Khrushchev soon declared that the Soviet Union had achieved its objectives and no longer needed to worry about the four-power occupation of West Germany or the presence of nuclear weapons there.

REFERENCES: Roger Morgan, *The United States and West Germany*, 1974; Jack Schick, *The Berlin Crisis, 1958–1962*, 1974.

BERLIN WALL. See **BERLIN CRISIS**.

BERNSTEIN, LEONARD. Leonard Bernstein was born in Lawrence, Massachusetts, August 25, 1918, to Russian-Jewish parents. He attended the Boston Latin School and received an undergraduate degree from Harvard in 1939. A child musical prodigy, Bernstein had decided to be a composer and a conductor. He then studied conducting at the Curtis Institute in Philadelphia. Bernstein's many talents soon became apparent to the musical world. He wrote Symphony No. 1 ("Jeremiah") in 1942 at the age of twenty-three. At the time, he was struggling to make a living as a musician. In 1943, he was named assistant conductor of the New York Philharmonic, and when Bruno Walter became sick on November 14, 1943, Bernstein took over and conducted the orchestra to rave reviews. In the symphonic world, Leonard Bernstein at the age of twenty-five had become famous.

Bernstein eventually became what the *New York Times* called the "Renaissance man of American music." In addition to Symphony No. 2 ("The Age of Anxiety") in 1949 and Symphony No. 3 ("Kaddish") in 1963, Bernstein wrote the scores to the Broadway musicals *On the Town* (1949), *Peter Pan* (1950), *Wonderful Town* (1953), *Candide* (1956), and *West Side Story* (1957). His operatic compositions included *Trouble in Tahiti* and *Candide*, and among his works for ballet were *Fancy Free* and *Facsimile*. In 1958, Bernstein was named conductor of the New York Philharmonic, and the next year he wrote the very well received book *The Joy of Music*. He remained at the helm of the New York Philharmonic until retiring in 1969.

After leaving the New York Philharmonic, Bernstein continued to conduct and compose. He was also active politically. A liberal Democrat, Bernstein lent his support to the civil rights movement* and the antiwar movement* in the 1960s and 1970s, and during the 1980s he worked to raise money for AIDS research and to end discrimination against those infected with the HIV virus. Leonard Bernstein died October 14, 1990.

REFERENCES: *New York Times*, October 15, 1990; Joan Peyser, *Bernstein: A Biography*, 1987.

BERRIGAN, DANIEL. Daniel Berrigan was born in Virginia, Minnesota, May 9, 1921. In 1939, he began studying to become a Jesuit, and he was ordained in 1952. Berrigan wrote poetry and joined the faculty of Le Moyne College in 1957. He taught there until 1963. By that time, he was a committed social activist, against war and poverty and in favor of civil rights. He helped found the Catholic Peace Fellowship in 1964 and Clergy and Laity Concerned about Vietnam* in 1965. Opposition to the Vietnam War* soon became his reason for being. He attended antiwar rallies around the country and visited Hanoi* in 1967 to negotiate the release of several American prisoners of war.

Berrigan turned to civil disobedience on May 17, 1968, when, along with his brother Philip and several others, he destroyed selective service records in Catonsville, Maryland. The "Catonsville Nine" were charged with conspiracy and destruction of government property, found guilty, and sentenced to three years in federal prison. Berrigan jumped bail in April 1970 and spent eight months underground until the Federal Bureau of Investigation (FBI) caught up with him. He then began serving his prison sentence. During the rest of the decade, after being paroled in January 1972, Berrigan continued to protest the war. In 1975 he was arrested for digging a hole on the White House lawn to protest nuclear weapons, and in 1980, as one of the "Plowshares Eight," he broke into a General Electric plant and sprinkled fake blood on nuclear warhead cones. Since then, Berrigan has become an opponent of war and abortion, which he likens to mass murder.

REFERENCES: Daniel Berrigan, *No Bars to Manhood*, 1970; John Kinkaid, "Daniel Berrigan," in James S. Olson, *Dictionary of the Vietnam War*, 1988; Charles Meconis, *With Clumsy Grace: The American Catholic Left, 1961–1975*, 1979.

BERRIGAN, PHILIP (FRANCIS). Philip Berrigan was born in Two Harbors, Minnesota, October 5, 1923. He began attending St. Michael's College in Toronto in 1941 but was drafted into the U.S. Army in 1943. He served with valor during combat in the European theater and after World War II received a bachelor's degree from the College of the Holy Cross in Worcester, Massachusetts.

In 1955, Berrigan was ordained a Jesuit priest. He was assigned as a high school teacher in New Orleans, where he earned a degree in secondary education at Loyola and then a master's degree at Xavier University. Berrigan was so active in local civil rights efforts that church superiors transferred him in 1964 to a seminary in New York, where he promptly founded the Emergency Citizens Group Concerned about Vietnam and helped establish the Catholic Peace Fellowship.

Increasingly radicalized about the Vietnam War,* he joined his brother Daniel in acts of civil disobedience. On October 27, 1967, Philip Berrigan broke into the Baltimore Customs House and poured blood on selective service files there. The act earned him a felony conviction, but while he was waiting for trial, he joined Daniel and several others in breaking into another selective service facility—this one in Catonsville, Maryland—and destroying more files. Federal authorities sentenced him to six years in prison, but he jumped bail on April 9, 1970, and began conspiring to blow up heating systems in government buildings in Washington, D.C., and federal authorities accused him of conspiring to kidnap national security adviser Henry Kissinger.* He was arrested late in April 1970 and began serving his prison sentence. Berrigan was paroled in December 1972. In 1975 he was arrested for digging a hole on the White House lawn to protest nuclear weapons, and in 1980, as one of the "Plowshares Eight," he broke into a General Electric plant and sprinkled fake blood on nuclear warhead cones.

REFERENCES: Daniel Berrigan, *No Bars to Manhood*, 1970; John Kinkaid, "Daniel Berrigan," in James S. Olson, *Dictionary of the Vietnam War*, 1988; Charles Meconis, *With Clumsy Grace: The American Catholic Left, 1961–1975*, 1979.

THE BEVERLY HILLBILLIES. *The Beverly Hillbillies* was one of the most successful rural comedies of the 1960s. It was created by Paul Henning for CBS and first aired September 26, 1962. Within a few weeks the comedy ranked in the Nielsen's top ten. The series starred Buddy Ebsen as multimillionaire Jed Clampett, Irene Ryan as "Granny" Moses, Donna Douglas as Elly May Clampett, Max Baer, Jr., as cousin Jethro Bodine, Raymond Bailey as banker Milburne Crysdale, and Nancy Culp as bank secretary Jane Hathaway.

Demographic studies showed *The Beverly Hillbillies* had a mass appeal to an audience of all ages and differing economic backgrounds. It was popular with everyone except the television* critics. The series ranked as the number one television program for its first two seasons, maintained its popularity throughout most of the 1960s, and even had a spin-off, *Petticoat Junction,** in 1963.

The characters supplied outlandish entertainment during the insecurity and uncertainty of the 1960s by creating situations beyond the acceptance of an intelligent modern society. The appeal of the rural comedy allowed feelings of superiority, which provided feelings of security. Each comical episode promoted underlying traditional American values and customs of conduct for which the audience may have had a nostalgic longing.

The decline and death of *The Beverly Hillbillies* and other rural comedies came after a revolution in television comedy and a decision by CBS to take a gamble on changing demographics. Comedy had begun a transition in the later 1960s. Political humor was increasing in urban popularity with the creation of the *Smothers Brothers Show* and *Laugh-In*. Number one-ranked CBS was overwhelmed with successful rural comedies but saw the transition taking place. The popularity of *The Beverly Hillbillies* had recently declined, and the highly concentrated rural audience did not attract the advertisers of the urban areas.

On September 7, 1971, CBS decided to make a clean cut and severed its four remaining rural comedies from the network. *The Beverly Hillbillies* had been successful because of its popularity with the people in the 1960s. Its episodes are still popular today in rerun syndication throughout the South. Eight of its episodes are ranked in Nielsen's "Top-Ranked Programs of All Times." This total is more than that for any other comedy. The lone enemy, the television critics, had to kick the dead series one last time. In 1972 *Time Magazine* voted CBS the award for "Most Encouraging Sign of Improved Network Taste" after it canceled *The Beverly Hillbillies*.

REFERENCE: Stephen Cox, *The Beverly Hillbillies*, 1993.

Christopher Gore

BEWITCHED. *Bewitched* was one of the most popular situation comedies of the 1960s on American television.* Produced by ABC and first telecast on September 17, 1964, *Bewitched* was escapist fare during a decade of antiwar and civil rights protests. Elizabeth Montgomery starred as Samantha Stephens, a witch trying to live in the mortal world of her husband, Darrin (Dick York and then Dick Sargent), who worked as an advertising executive. Samantha's mother, Endora (Agnes Moorehead), disdained the mortal world and constantly tried to bring Samantha back to the occult. The last episode of *Bewitched* was broadcast on July 1, 1972.

REFERENCE: Tim Brooks and Earle Marsh, *The Complete Directory to Prime Time Network and Cable TV Shows*, 1995.

BIAFRA. The catastrophic civil war in Nigeria, which led to mass deaths in the Biafra region, became the international humanitarian cause of the 1960s. In May 1967, the eastern region of Nigeria, which consisted primarily of Igbo tribal members, seceded from Nigeria and proclaimed itself the Republic of Biafra. For decades, Igbo tribesmen began moving west into regions of Nigeria traditionally occupied by Hausa and Yoruba peoples. In 1966, an Igbo-led coup d'état succeeded in Nigeria, but a Hausa coup the next year toppled the Igbos. During the Hausa uprising, more than 30,000 Igbos were slaughtered, and another million fled back to the western regions of the country. Odemegwu Ojukwu, the Igbo governor of the eastern region, feared that Igbo people were no longer safe in Nigeria, so he led the May 1967 secession.

Nigerian forces reacted to the secession immediately. Determined to bring Biafra back into the country, Nigerian military forces imposed an airtight blockade around Biafra, making sure no supplies went in and no refugees came out. Biafrans were soon starving by the millions. The international community worried that Biafra's example might inspire similar tribal secessions throughout Africa but did little to save Biafra. International relief organizations could not break the siege, even though they distributed photos of television footage of starving Biafran children. When Biafran forces finally surrendered in 1970, more than one million people had starved to death. It was the worst demographic disaster of the 1960s.

REFERENCE: John Okpoko, *The Biafran Nightmare*, 1986.

BIEN HOA, BATTLE OF (1964). The Battle of Bien Hoa on November 1, 1964, was an important turning point in the Vietnam War.* Indirectly, the incident inspired an escalation of the conflict that proved to be irresistible. Bien Hoa was the capital city of Bien Hoa Province and was located twenty miles north of Saigon.* After the Gulf of Tonkin* incident in August 1964, President Lyndon B. Johnson* decided to launch air strikes against North Vietnam. In order to do so, the United States constructed an air base at Bien Hoa. Once U.S. military personnel and expensive military aircraft were stationed at Bien Hoa, it became a target for Vietcong* attacks. Vietcong sappers assaulted the base on November 1, 1964, killing four American soldiers and destroying five U.S. aircraft. The attack played an important role in the Johnson administration's decision to station regular U.S. ground troops in South Vietnam, since the aircraft and personnel stationed at Bien Hoa needed to be protected. The first U.S. ground troops were deployed to South Vietnam in the spring of 1965.

REFERENCES: *New York Times*, November 2–4, 1964; George W. Ball, ''Top Secret: The Prophecy the President Rejected,'' *The Atlantic* 230 (July 1972), 35–49.

THE BIG BANG. The ''big bang'' concept in astrophysics evolved from the primeval atom model, envisioned by Belgian cosmologist and theologian Georges Lemaitre. It asserted that a dense nucleus exploded outward and disintegrated to form the present universe. Conversely, American physicist George Gamow proposed a universe born in nuclear fission. With graduate student Ralph Alpher, Gamow expounded the idea and published it in the 1948 April edition of *Physical Review*. It was not popularly accepted because it failed to explain heavy element formation. The same year, Alpher and Robert Herman, an associate of Gamow, questioned the fate of radiation released when the universe became transparent—theoretically, the most ancient observable radiation. The heavy element dilemma and the radiation question prevented immediate acceptance of Alpher and Gamow's theory, coined the ''big bang.'' Margaret and Geoffrey Burbidge, William Fowler, and Fred Hoyle resolved the heavy element mystery in 1957 with their concept of stellar nucleosynthesis. Discovery of the cosmic background radiation in 1965 ushered forth a new cosmological era.

Princeton physicist Robert H. Dicke perceived that radio telescopes might be used to detect the theorized background radiation. With P. J. E. Peebles, a Princeton researcher, P. G. Roll and D. T. Wilkinson, Princeton staffers, construction of a small dish antenna to detect the radiation was begun in 1964 atop the Princeton biology building. Their efforts ended when, in 1965, the radiation background was discovered by Arno Penzias and Robert Wilson of the Bell Research Laboratories. At the time, emerging technology was the visible stimulus that prompted the discovery, as was evident in the team's contemporary twenty-foot horn antenna employed in communication satellites experiments. In retrospect, historians wonder why the discovery was not made earlier. The radiation background could have been identified as early as 1941, when Canadian astronomer Andrew McKellar concluded that relevant spectral absorption lines were caused by interstellar cyanide molecules excited by a radiation with temperature 2.3 K. Several subsequent observers narrowly failed to identify the cosmic background radiation.

Regardless, the discovery of the isotropic background radiation with a temperature of approximately 3 K and a spectrum analogous to that of a black body had a profound effect on the 1960s and astronomy in general. Specifically, the big bang concept, first to be substantially endorsed by empirical science, replaced the dominant steady-state theory, a philosophically pleasing creation idea. In 1967, Robert Wagoner at Stanford University, with Fowler and Hoyle at Caltech, formulated the modern standard model of the big bang. It further strengthened the big bang theory by asserting the creation, by mass, of approximately three times as much hydrogen as helium—nearly the ratio observed in stars. The theory has permitted calculation of events during the first minutes of creation, though billions of years ago. It has helped shape the current concepts of particle physics.

REFERENCES: A. D. Berger, ed., *The Big Bang and George Lemaitre*, 1983; David N. Schramm, *The Big Bang and Other Explosions in Nuclear Particle Astrophysics*, 1995.

Andrew Koehl

THE BIG VALLEY. *The Big Valley* was a popular western broadcast by ABC in the late 1960s. Set in the San Joaquin Valley of California in the 1870s, *The Big Valley* starred Barbara Stanwyck as Victoria Barkley, Richard Long as Jarrod Barkley, Peter Breck as Nick Barkley, Lee Majors as Heath Barkley, and Linda Evans as Audra Barkley. The Barkleys are ranchers trying to build a life for themselves in the lawless West. First broadcast on September 15, 1965, *The Big Valley* played to large audiences until 1969, when its ratings began to plummet. Some television* historians argue that westerns lost their relevance during the 1960s. The last episode of *The Big Valley* was broadcast on May 19, 1969.

REFERENCE: Tim Brooks and Earle Marsh, *The Complete Directory to Prime Time Network and Cable TV Shows*, 1995.

THE BILLY SOL ESTES SCANDAL. Billy Sol Estes was a west Texas businessman in the 1960s. In 1953, the National Chamber of Commerce had named Estes one of America's ten outstanding young men. A devout elder in the Church of Christ and a lay preacher, Estes had settled in Pecos, Texas, in 1951 and went into the cotton business. Soon he was raising cotton and selling anhydrous ammonia, a cotton-growth-enhancing chemical fertilizer. He also began heavily leveraging himself to launch a grain storage business, a proposition that allowed him to take advantage of generous federal crop subsidies. While he was on the rise, Estes bragged widely of his connections, dropping the names of people like Senate majority leader Lyndon B. Johnson.*

By 1959, however, Estes had overextended himself. He could not generate the cash flow necessary to service the debt he had accumulated, so he began to sell, and then lease back, fictitious chemical fertilizer tanks. Using the mortgages on the nonexistent tanks, he borrowed nearly $30 million from banks and finance companies. He also fraudulently acquired cotton land allotments well beyond the limits of the law. In 1962, a Pecos, Texas, newspaperman exposed the scheme. Senator John L. McClellan had his Permanent Investigations Subcommittee of the Government Operations Committee look into the scandal. The Department of Agriculture fined Estes $500 million for his participation in illegal subsidy schemes. The fertilizer scheme, however, earned him a felony conviction and nearly seven years in a federal penitentiary. Estes was not rehabilitated. In 1979, eight years after his parole, he was convicted of income tax evasion, mail fraud, and interstate transportation of stolen property. He was sentenced to ten years in prison and was released in 1983.

REFERENCE: Pam Estes, *Billie Sol: King of the Texas Wheeler-Dealers*, 1983.

THE BIRMINGHAM BOMBING. The civil rights movement* came to Birmingham, Alabama, in 1963. Rev. Fred Shuttlesworth was leading a local campaign to integrate downtown department stores and to bring about the hiring of black clerks in those establishments. When white business leaders balked at Shuttlesworth's proposals, Rev. Martin Luther King, Jr.,* and the Southern Christian Leadership Conference* (SCLC) decided to make a national example of Birmingham.

When the SCLC demonstrators marched in Birmingham, police chief Bull Connor pulled out all the stops. He unleashed police dogs on demonstrating children and opened up on the adults with fire hoses capable of taking the bark off trees at ninety feet. Amid all the violence, King and his supporters turned the other cheek, maintaining their loyalty to nonviolence. Network news teams recorded the events and broadcast them nationwide to a disbelieving nation. King himself was arrested for defying a court order to stop demonstrating, and his subsequent "Letter from the Birmingham Jail" proved to be a popular, ennobling plea for equality in America.

The final straw in the Birmingham saga occurred on September 15, 1963. White racists planted a bomb in the black Sixteenth Street Baptist Church, and it detonated on Sunday morning, killing four black girls who were in Sunday school. Rioting erupted in Birmingham. Outrage over the bombing spread throughout the country, and public officials of every persuasion condemned the carnage. Civil rights historians today look back upon the bombing as the seminal event in the movement. It gave the entire country a single image of the destructiveness of white supremacy notions. The four little girls became martyrs in the freedom struggle of millions of African Americans.

REFERENCE: David Burner, *Making Peace with the Sixties*, 1996.

BIRTH CONTROL PILL. The birth control pill was certainly one of the most revolutionary pharmaceutical developments in United States history. Led by Margaret Sanger, the birth control movement had long urged limiting family size as a means of preserving the health and economic vitality of women and children, but the lack of reliable, convenient birth control technologies consistently compromised the movement's success. During the 1950s, however, with funding from Planned Parenthood, endocrinologist Gregory Pincus developed the first safe, reliable method of interrupting female ovulation. In 1960 the U.S. Food and Drug Administration approved use of the "pill," and Searle pharmaceutical company was soon manufacturing and distributing it.

Some social commentators have linked the sexual revolution of the 1960s to the development of the birth control pill. They argued that because the pill eliminated the threat of unwanted pregnancy, women were free to become more sexually active. The pill also allowed women to time and space their children to fit family and career needs. With the advent of the pill, birth rates plummeted in the United States and Western Europe. By the 1980s, 90 percent of married couples in the United States used contraceptives, and the pill was the most popular choice.

REFERENCES: Angus McLaren, *A History of Contraception: From Antiquity to the Present Day*, 1990; James Reed, *From Private Vice to Public Virtue: The Birth Control Movement and American Society since 1830*, 1978.

BLACK, HUGO LAFAYETTE. Hugo LaFayette Black was born February 27, 1886. His family lived in the heart of Alabama cotton country. When Hugo was three, the family moved to Ashland, a town of about 350, where his father bought and operated a general store. The younger Black attended Ashland College, and from there he went to the University of Alabama to pursue a medical career. But after one year he switched to law and graduated with an LL.B. in 1906.

He practiced law in Ashland and then Birmingham. In addition to his clients, he served as legal counsel to the miners' union and the carpenters' union. In 1910, he was appointed police court judge, a part-time position that he retained for about eighteen months. Then, in 1915, he was elected county solicitor (prosecutor) for Jefferson County. When the United States entered World War I, Black resigned his position to join the army. He rose to the rank of captain in the Eighty-First Field Artillery and also served as adjutant of the nineteenth Artillery Brigade. After the war he returned to Birmingham.

When Senator Oscar Underwood announced his intention to retire in 1926, Black decided to run for the Senate. He simply took off on his own, covering the back country alone in his Model-T, speaking anywhere he could find listeners and staying with anyone who would put him up. His vigorous campaign won him the nomination over three opponents, and at that time in Alabama the Democratic nomination was tantamount to election. In his first term, Black did what was expected of junior members. He remained discreetly in the background while he studied the legislative process to learn how the system worked. At the same time he began a lifelong habit of reading extensively to make up for the deficiencies of his early education, concentrating on history, economics, and philosophy. He consumed the writings of Thomas Jefferson and studied the accounts of the Federal Convention of 1787 as well as the records of the state ratifying conventions. It gave him a deep reverence of the Constitution.

When he felt prepared, he plunged into the work of the Senate by joining Senator George W. Norris of Nebraska in the fight for public operation of Muscle Schoals in his home state of Alabama. Elected to a second term in the Democratic sweep of 1932, Black soon emerged as a conspicuous figure in the Senate. He was an enthusiastic backer of the New Deal, voting for all the major measures proposed in Congress during Franklin D. Roosevelt's first term, except one—he strongly opposed the National Industrial Recovery Act, which he felt from the first was doomed to failure. During the New Deal, he was also a staunch friend of labor. In 1933 Black launched a series of investigations into the policies, costs, and salaries of the U.S. Shipping Board, a matter that had interested him since the late 1920s. He was extremely critical of subsidies. In 1935, Black was given credit for passing the Public Utility Holding Company Act. He created an uproar when, as chairman of the Senate Lobby Investigating Committee, he tried to subpoena some 5 million telegrams as evidence of the high-pressure tactics of lobbyists. He was rebuffed by the courts and roundly criticized in the press.

His relatively brief career in the Senate was cut short when President Roosevelt nominated him for the Supreme Court on August 12, 1937, to replace conservative justice Willis Van Devanter. The Senate voted confirmation, and on the same day Justice Black took the oath of office. He then sailed for Europe on vacation. While he was still abroad, a new controversy swirled around Black. A series of articles in the *Pittsburgh Post-Gazette* revealed that he had joined the Ku Klux Klan on September 11, 1923, and resigned on July 9, 1925, as he began his campaign for the Senate. These revelations set off a new round of denunciation and defense. Black himself said nothing from Europe, but after his return to the United States, he explained in a radio address that he had joined the Klan but resigned and never rejoined. In an interview not published until after his death, Black explained that because many lawyers in Birmingham and many jurors belonged to the Klan, he too had to join to have an equal advantage with juries.

He took his seat on the Court and quickly emerged as a consistent dissenter.

His minority opinions prompted continued attack by conservatives and support by liberals. If there was any lingering doubt about his Klanism, he soon dispelled it with his strong defense of individual and minority rights. In 1940, he wrote the majority opinion in the case of *Chambers v. Florida*, vacating the conviction of four blacks whose confessions had been obtained under duress, a violation of the Fourteenth Amendment. Also in 1940, in *Smith v. Texas*, Justice Black wrote the majority opinion that a black defendant had not received a fair trial because blacks were excluded from the jury.

Justice Black found himself in frequent conflict with Justice Felix Frankfurter* over the Bill of Rights. Black insisted that the guarantees contained in the First and Fifth Amendments were absolute, that there was nothing equivocal about the language in the Bill of Rights. When the First Amendment said, "Congress shall make no law . . . ," it meant precisely that—no law. For Black, the Bill of Rights extended absolute protection of individual liberties to every American against federal government action, and the Fourteenth Amendment provided the same protection against the actions of state governments. Justice Frankfurter rejected such a concept. He believed that the guarantees of the Bill of Rights had to be balanced against other considerations. Thus, the two men were often in conflict over the issue of individual rights. After Frankfurter retired in 1962, however, the tide turned in favor of Black's point of view.

Occasionally, Justice Black aroused the wrath of liberals for his opinions. In *Karematsu v. United States* (1944), he upheld the authority of the federal government to remove the Japanese from along the Pacific coast. Especially in his later years, liberals accused him of turning conservative because he declined to defend civil rights demonstrations under First Amendment rights, upheld the constitutionality of the Virginia poll tax, and refused to overturn an anti–birth control law in Connecticut. But Justice Black insisted that these opinions were consistent with his views on constitutional guarantees. In poor health, Black retired from the Supreme Court late in August 1971. On Sunday, September 24, 1971, he died at age eighty-five from inflammation of the arteries and a stroke that he had suffered the previous Sunday. Eight days before his death, he had resigned from the Supreme Court after thirty-four years of service as one of the foremost champions of individual rights in the Court's history.

REFERENCES: John P. Frank, *Mr. Justice Black*, 1949; James J. Magee, *Mr. Justice Black: Absolutist on the Court*, 1980; *New York Times*, September 26, 1971.

Joseph M. Rowe, Jr.

BLACK BERETS. The Black Berets were a Chicano activist group formed in 1969. Modeled after the Black Panthers,* they engaged in a number of protest movements and community service projects in California and New Mexico. They had a limited appeal in the Mexican-American community, however, because of their radical, anticapitalist ideology.

REFERENCE: Matt S. Meier and Feliciano Rivera, *Dictionary of Mexican American History*, 1981.

BLACK PANTHERS. The Black Panthers were a militant African-American civil rights organization of the 1960s and 1970s. The group was founded in Oakland, California, in 1966 by Huey Newton* and Bobbie Seale.* Rejecting the middle-class values of white society and the nonviolent, civil disobedience tactics of mainstream civil rights organizations, the Black Panthers appealed to unemployed black young men living in urban ghettos. They asserted the right to defend themselves against racist attacks by the white power structure, especially the police, imposed a militaristic discipline on members, advocated arming the black community, and espoused a militant machismo philosophy.

Not surprisingly, armed conflict frequently occurred between Black Panther militants and urban police. In Chicago, police killed Panther leaders Fred Hampton and Mark Clark during a raid. Bobby Seale and Huey Newton were indicted for shooting several policemen. Charges were dropped against Seale, but Newton was convicted and spent nearly two years in jail before the conviction was reversed on appeal. In 1968, Eldridge Cleaver,* Black Panther minister of information, ran for president of the United States on the Peace and Freedom Party* ticket. In 1969, their newspaper—*Black Panther*—had a circulation of 140,000. The Panthers espoused a philosophy of black nationalism and tried to maintain breakfast programs for poor children in the ghettos.

But there was also an extremely negative side to the Black Panthers. Drug abuse was all too common, and Panther violence was too often gratuitous, directed at one another as well as at police. In most cities, the children's breakfast program was frequently based on extortion and racketeering, threatening to firebomb those business establishments that did not contribute. There were powerful antifeminist, antiwomen rhetoric and values among Black Panther leaders. Early in the 1970s, the Panthers rejected their emphasis on violence and tried to focus on political organization. By then, however, the group was in an advanced state of decline. Today, the Black Panthers continue to exist only in Oakland, California, where they are only a shadow of their former selves.

REFERENCES: David Burner, *Making Peace with the Sixties*, 1996; Gene Marine, *The Black Panthers*, 1969.

BLACK POWER. In 1964, when Congress passed the Civil Rights Act, the fledgling civil rights movement* achieved a major victory. Along with a series of Supreme Court decisions in the late 1940s and 1950s, Jim Crow* segregation was dead, on the law books at least. But in spite of the legislative victories, the African-American community still faced poverty, de facto segregation, and institutional racism. A younger generation of impatient black leaders reacted with the black power movement.

The shift to "black power" appeared in two guises, one spontaneous and emotional, the other deliberate and ideological. In August 1965 the Watts ghetto of Los Angeles exploded when thousands of African Americans rioted after a young black was arrested for reckless driving. White businesses were looted, snipers fired at police, and before it was over, thirty-four people were dead, more than a thousand wounded, and over $40 million worth of property destroyed. There was another racial rebellion in Newark, New Jersey, in 1967, and in the summer of 1967, Detroit was engulfed in a major conflagration, with angry African Americans turning on police and white-owned businesses. The assassination of Martin Luther King, Jr.,* in April 1968 caused racial uprisings in many cities; and nine years later, when an electrical failure darkened New York City for a night, thousands of unemployed African Americans and Puerto Ricans engaged in an orgy of looting. In every instance the eruptions were unpremeditated rebellions, illegal to be sure, against the frustrations of ghetto life. White America was outraged and frightened by the insurgency; but as they condemned the violence, whites also scrutinized the racial crisis as never before.

The ideological rise of black power came to the surface in 1966, even though signs of the philosophy had appeared earlier. After a lifetime of scholarly writing and support of black political activism, W.E.B. Du Bois finally despaired of changing America and joined the Communist Party. The Black Muslims, founded by Elijah Muhammad* in 1930, rose to national prominence in the 1960s. Preaching the ultimate doom of "devil" whites and the triumph of blacks, the Muslims took up where Marcus Garvey had left off, calling for black pride, black enterprise, and a separate black state. They also called on African Americans to think less about being nonviolent and more about returning violence for violence. In 1959 Robert Williams, a National Association for the Advancement of Colored People (NAACP) leader in North Carolina, was dismissed from the NAACP for advocating violence in self-defense; escaping to Cuba after allegedly kidnapping an elderly white couple, he became leader of the Revolutionary Action Movement (RAM).

But all these groups were relatively obscure until James Meredith,* an African American, decided to prove in 1966 that he could march to Jackson, Mississippi, during voter registration week without harassment. One day into the march, he was wounded by a shotgun blast, and civil rights leaders from all over the country descended on Mississippi to complete the "freedom march." But while Martin Luther King, Jr., still spoke of nonviolent civil disobedience, Stokely Carmichael,* the young leader of the Student Nonviolent Coordinating Committee (SNCC), startled the nation by ridiculing nonviolence and crying out for black power. On the other side of the country, Huey Newton* and Bobby Seale* established the Black Panthers* in Oakland, California, and called for African-American control of the urban ghettos.

Despite the rhetoric of black power and the fear it sent through white America, it meant different things to different people. To whites, the slogan was incendiary, somehow implying that the social order was about to undergo revolutionary change. To the Congress of Racial Equality* (CORE), black power meant direct political action through the Democratic Party and the mobilization of African-American votes in the South. The Black Panthers and SNCC viewed it as community control; they demanded African-American police and African-American firemen in African-American neighborhoods, African-American teachers and principals in African-American schools, and African-American–owned businesses to serve the African-American market. To some radical groups—including the Black Panthers, RAM, the Republic of New Africa, and SNCC—black power implied the use of retaliatory violence to end poverty and discrimination.

REFERENCES: William L. Van Deburg, *New Day in Babylon: The Black Power Movement and American Culture, 1965–1975,* 1992; Herbert Haines, *Black Radicals and the Civil Rights Mainstream, 1954–1970,* 1988.

BLACK SOLDIERS. Because the Vietnam War* coincided with the militant stage of the civil rights movement,* the role played by blacks in the Indochinese conflict became a major controversy. Existing draft* regulations in 1965 provided exemptions to young men attending college or working in certain critical occupations, both of which discriminated in favor of middle-class whites. Black leaders like Martin Luther King, Jr.,* argued that young blacks were more likely to be drafted than whites and, once drafted, more likely to get dangerous infantry assignments. They were correct. Although blacks constituted about 13.4 percent of the American population in 1966, they had sustained more than 20 percent of the combat deaths in Vietnam up to that time. Concerned about those percentages and about the diversion of assets away from domestic problems, King condemned Vietnam as a racist war in 1967. Even before that, heavyweight champion Muhammad Ali* had startled the nation by saying, "I ain't got nothing against them Vietcong*" and later refusing to be drafted.

The criticisms did not fall on deaf ears. After 1967 both the U.S. Army and the Marine Corps made conscious efforts to reduce black battlefield casualties, and by the end of the American combat effort in 1972, blacks had sustained approximately 5,700 of the 47,200 battlefield deaths of U.S. personnel—about 12 percent of the total.

REFERENCES: Martin Binkin et al., *Blacks in the Military,* 1982; Lawrence M. Baskir and William A. Strauss, *Chance and Circumstance: The Draft, the War, and the Vietnam Generation,* 1978; Wallace Terry, *Bloods: An Oral History of the Vietnam War by Black Veterans,* 1984; Stanley Goff and Robert Sandfors, *Brothers: Black Soldiers in the Nam,* 1982.

BLOW-UP. *Blow-Up* was a controversial film of the 1960s. Because of its sexual content, the Production Code denied it a seal, essentially blackballing the film and giving it huge, free publicity. The movie was written and directed by Michelangelo Antonioni and starred David Hemmings as photographer Thomas, Vanessa Redgrave as Jane, and Sarah Miles as Patricia. The film follows Thomas on his frenetic search for work and conquests, and it has a dark twist when he accidentally photographs a crime. Thomas is a talented, gadabout, celebrity, freelance photographer perfect for the 1960s—self-indulgent, restless, starstruck, morally confused, and horny.

REFERENCE: *New York Times,* December 19, 1966.

BLOW YOUR MIND. In the 1960s, the term "blow your mind" emerged in the hippie counterculture* as a slang expression for a sense of being absolutely overwhelmed by a new idea or a new perception.

REFERENCE: Ruth Bronsteen, *The Hippy's Handbook—How to Live on Love*, 1967.

BLUE LAKE. Blue Lake in northwest New Mexico is an ancient holy place to the Taos Indians. They view it as a religious shrine, the source of life, and a manifestation of the great spirit of the universe. Blue Lake, economically and spiritually, was the center of their lives. But in 1906, the federal government incorporated Blue Lake and the surrounding 48,000 acres into the Kit Carson National Forest. Later, the U.S. Forest Service opened the area to non-Indian hunters, fishermen, and campers. Taos Indian leaders began demanding return of the lake, and in 1965 the Indians Claims Commission offered the tribe $10 million and 3,000 acres near the lake. Paul Bernal, a Taos leader, rejected the offer, telling the Indian Claims Commission: "My people will not sell our Blue Lake that is our church, for $10 million, and accept three thousand acres, when we know that fifty thousand acres is ours. We cannot sell what is sacred. It is not ours to sell." Blue Lake became a symbol of Indian land claims and a rejection of the notion that cash settlements could make up for assaults on Indian culture. In 1970, President Richard M. Nixon* came to support the Taos claim, and Congress passed the Taos Blue Lake Act, returning the lake and 48,000 acres to the tribe.

In 1996, however, Blue Lake and the Taos Indians were once again in the headlines. Although they had won the return of much of their land in 1970, the Taos people soon became concerned about the number of non-Indian vacation homes that began to sprout near the reservation. In order to generate the revenue needed to purchase neighboring land and get the non-Indians out, the tribe secured approval from the Department of the Interior in 1995 to open a gambling casino. They purchased $10 million of nearby ranch land, made a down payment of $1 million, and took out a mortgage on the rest. But early in 1996, U.S. attorney general John Kelly ordered the Taos Indians to shut down the casino, since they did not enjoy approval from the state of New Mexico to keep it open. Nine other New Mexico tribes were similarly ordered to close their casinos. The Taos Indians were concerned that if they lost gambling revenue, they would have had to default on the mortgage and lose the land. The other tribes had similar concerns about land purchases and tribal services.

Closing ranks, the Indians refused to obey the order and filed suit in the district court. They also approached the state legislature, asking for specific legislative authorization to continue operating, but non-Indian business owners in Santa Fe and Albuquerque opposed the casinos because they drain off tourists' discretionary spending. By the spring of 1996, the tribes affected by the decision were threatening to block Interstate highways 10, 20, and 25, disrupting transportation and commerce, if the casinos were shut down. To this day the issue remains unresolved.

REFERENCES: Vine Deloria, Jr., *American Indians, American Justice*, 1983; *Houston Chronicle*, January 13, 1996; *New York Times*, February 11, 1996; James S. Olson and Raymond Wilson, *Native Americans in the Twentieth Century*, 1984.

THE BOBBY BAKER SCANDAL. In 1955, Senate Majority Leader Lyndon B. Johnson* hired Robert Gene ''Bobby'' Baker as his secretary. Baker had developed some expertise in congressional politics by serving as a Senate page and then as a legislative strategist. His salary was $9,000 a year, and his net worth was $11,000. Eight years later, Baker was worth more than $2.5 million. But on September 12, 1963, the *Washington Post* revealed that Baker had been improperly using political power and office to secure special defense contracts for Serv-U Corporation, a vending machine company he had established. The Senate Rules Committee launched an investigation of Baker's business affairs, even though Vice President Lyndon B. Johnson tried to block it. Republicans accused Baker of making sure that Johnson had received kickbacks on several government contracts to defense industry corporations.

Baker was also accused of accepting illegal contributions to various Democratic campaign funds. In the election of 1964,* Republican candidate Barry Goldwater* argued that the Bobby Baker scandal reached all the way into the White House, but the charges never stuck. In January 1967, Baker was convicted of income tax evasion, theft, and conspiracy to defraud the government. Sentenced to a one-to-three-year stretch in federal prison, he served seventeen months before his release in 1972.

REFERENCES: Vaughn Bornet, *The Presidency of Lyndon B. Johnson*, 1983; Paul Conkin, *Big Daddy from the Pedernales*, 1986.

BODY BAG. The term ''body bag'' emerged in the 1960s to describe the plastic used to retrieve from the field of battle the bodies of dead U.S. Soldiers in Vietnam. Eventually, more than 58,000 American soldiers were brought back to base camps in body bags before mortician crews prepared them for shipment to the United States.

REFERENCE: James S. Olson, ed., *Dictionary of the Vietnam War*, 1988.

BODY COUNT. Once a week during the course of the Vietnam War,* the Pentagon released what came to be known as the ''body count''—the number of Vietcong* and North Vietnamese enemy soldiers killed and wounded during the previous seven days. Comparisons were often made with the numbers of U.S. and South Vietnamese casualties as well. Vietnam was a guerrilla war in which territorial acquisition was irrelevant. Americans fought a war of attrition,* not geography, hoping to kill so many enemy soldiers that North Vietnam and the Vietcong would not be able to continue the fight. Secretary of Defense Robert McNamara* and General William Westmoreland* came to rely on the body count to evaluate the progress of the war.

For several reasons, body count figures were unreliable. Because of combat conditions, estimates of enemy dead were often made from aerial surveillance or memory. Distinguishing military from civilian casualties was often difficult in Vietnam. Sometimes counts were duplicated, and at other times even rough estimates could not be made. It was also common for U.S. military officers—anxious to receive high-quality, career-boosting efficiency reports—to exaggerate body counts. Body counts became a joke among American journalists in Vietnam, who considered Pentagon estimates completely unreliable. The fact that the enemy lost only one-sixth as many weapons as it lost people lent credibility to those who accused the Pentagon of gross exaggeration. Such a discrepancy meant either that large numbers of civilians were killed along with the Vietcong, that the body count figures were seriously inflated, or both. At the end of the war, American officials estimated that 666,000 Vietcong and North Vietnamese had died during combat in South Vietnam between 1965 and 1974, and that American air strikes had killed 65,000 people in North Vietnam.

REFERENCES: Guenter Lewy, *American in Vietnam*, 1978; John E. Mueller, ''The Search for the 'Breaking Point' in Vietnam: The Statistics of a Deadly Quarrel,'' *International Studies Quarterly* 24 (December 1980), 497–519.

BOMBING OF SOUTHEAST ASIA. During the Vietnam War,* as U.S. forces became more heavily involved in the conduct of the war, reliance on conventional tactics and firepower steadily increased. Fighting a guerrilla war in South Vietnam would take many years and require a heavy investment in economic and political infrastructure, and U.S. policymakers did not feel they could afford such a long-term effort. Instead, they decided to get the war over with as quickly as possible by fighting a war of attrition*—killing so many enemy troops that North Vietnam and the Vietcong* could no longer replace their casualties. Air power became a key component in that decision, and during the 1960s and 1970s, U.S. forces conducted an unprecedented air campaign throughout Indochina.

Although U.S. air operations began in 1961 with Operation Farmgate, in which U.S. pilots trained Vietnamese pilots and often accompanied them into combat, U.S. bombing campaigns formally began after the Gulf of Tonkin* incident. On August 7, 1964, Congress passed the Gulf of Tonkin Resolution,* giving President Lyndon Johnson* power to do whatever was necessary to protect U.S. forces and to assist South Vietnam in preserving its national security. Johnson then unleashed a bombing campaign against North Vietnam. Most of the attacks were confined below the twentieth parallel and targeted bridges and radar installations. The Pentagon dubbed the bombing campaign ''Operation Rolling Thunder,''* and that code name continued to be used until November 1968.

Johnson initially hoped that after a taste of U.S. military might North Vietnamese leaders would back away from the war and negotiate a settlement. But the bombing only stiffened North Vietnamese resolve. Concluding that he had not used enough force, Johnson expanded the bombing to several metropolitan areas of Vietnam. On May 22, 1965, U.S. aircraft bombed a North Vietnamese army barracks at Quang Soui. Still, North Vietnam did not show any inclination to negotiate, and the president ordered B-52 strikes on North Vietnam. To do so, the U.S. Air Force constructed six bases in Thailand. By early 1968 it took more than 55,000 military personnel to operate those bases, which included 600 aircraft. By November 1, 1968, when Operation Rolling Thunder came to an end, United States and South Vietnamese aircraft had conducted 304,000 tactical air strikes against enemy targets, while B-52s had completed 2,380 sorties. The targets of choice included railroad tracks, rolling stock, bridges, air strips, military bases, radar sites, warehouses, supply depots, factories, highways, and anti-aircraft installations. During the course of Operation Rolling Thunder, more than 643,000 tons of U.S. bombs fell on enemy targets.

The bombing resumed in 1969 when President Richard M. Nixon* entered the White House. For years U.S. military officials had been frustrated about the ability of enemy troops to escape destruction by crossing into the jungles of Cambodia and from there staging attacks on U.S. troops. Hoping to weaken the enemy by eliminating these sanctuaries, President Nixon launched secret B-52 bombing raids over Cambodia. The sorties began on March 18, 1969, and continued until May 26, 1970. Although the bombing temporarily disrupted enemy troop movements, it also expanded the war deep into a country that was already in the midst of a civil war. Nixon's decision in the spring of 1970 to invade Cambodia, which inspired vast strategic bombing runs over Cambodia, turned much of the country into a war zone and eventually strengthened the Communist political position there.

The bombing campaign posed special challenges to U.S. military planners. Because of the limited nature of the war and a commitment on the part of the Johnson administration to keep the conflict from expanding throughout Southeast Asia or from triggering any direct military intervention by the Soviet Union and the People's Republic of China, political constraints were constantly imposed on the bombing campaign. The last thing the administration wanted was for a bombing campaign to go awry and lead to a broader war. Coordination of bombing operations was not simply a matter of tactical and strategic planning by military officials. It also included constant input from the State Department, the National Security Agency, cabinet officials, and the White House. In many cases, bombing targets were chosen—or not chosen, for that matter—because of political constraints. As a result, bombing operations never achieved their full military potential.

Even if they had, there were no guarantees that bombing would have achieved its political and strategic objectives. U.S. military planners hoped to employ strategic bombing campaigns to achieve three objectives: to convince North Vietnamese leaders that the price of war was too high and that a negotiated settlement was their only alternative to national destruction; to disrupt the North Vietnamese economy to make the production and shipment of war goods more difficult; and to stop the flow of supplies and troops along the Ho Chi Minh Trail* to North Vietnamese and Vietcong forces in South Vietnam.

The bombing campaigns failed to achieve any of those objectives. Instead of bringing North Vietnamese leaders to the negotiating table, it only stiffened their resolve. North Vietnamese civilians steadily became more anti-American as casualties mounted. To limit the effects of the bombing on the economy, North Vietnamese leaders all but depopulated the city of Hanoi, reducing its population from more than one million in 1964 to only 250,000 by 1970 and dispersing manufacturing facilities into rural areas. U.S. military planners also learned that bombing had relatively little effect on pre-industrial economies. Nor was air interdiction very effective. Although the United States staged continuous bombing campaigns over the Ho Chi Minh Trail during the war, the North Vietnamese steadily increased the shipment of goods and soldiers into South Vietnam. By the time the war ended, the Ho Chi Minh Trail included more than 12,000 miles of roads through heavily jungled, mountainous terrain. When the war finally ended in 1973, U.S. tactical aircraft had flown more than 400,000 bombing sorties and B-52s nearly 127,000. They had dropped more than 6,162,000 tons of explosives.

The bombing also had a deleterious effect on South Vietnam. In order for the government of South Vietnam to stand alone and resist Communist aggression, it needed the political support of its own people. But the U.S. bombing campaigns worked against that process. Because it was so difficult to distinguish enemy troops from civilians, U.S. bombing was often quite indiscriminate, causing large numbers of civilian casualties among the South Vietnamese population. These casualties created extraordinary resentment among millions of South Vietnamese and made it more difficult, even impossible, for the United States to generate any widespread political support there. In that sense, the bombing was counterproductive.

REFERENCES: David A. Anderton, *The History of the U.S. Air Force*, 1981; Carl Berger, ed., *The United States Air Force in Southeast Asia, 1961–1973: An Illustrated Account*, 1977; Walter Boyne, *Boeing B-52: A Documentary History*, 1981, and *The Development of the Strategic Air Command: A Chronological History*, 1982; James N. Eastman, Jr., et al., eds., *Aces and Aerial Victories: The United States Air Force in Southeast Asia, 1965–1973*, 1976; Stanley Karnow, *Vietnam: A History*, 1983; Roger D. Launius, "Bombing of Southeast Asia," in James S. Olson, ed., *Dictionary of the Vietnam War*, 1988; James Clay Thompson, *Rolling Thunder: Understanding Policy and Program Failure*, 1980.

BONANZA. *Bonanza* was one of the most successful programs in American television* history. It was a western melodrama set in the "Ponderosa Valley" near Virginia City, Nevada, in the 1860s. Produced by NBC, *Bonanza*'s first episode was broadcast on September 12, 1959. It starred Lorne Greene as Ben Cartwright, Michael Landon as "Little Joe" Cartwright, Dan Blocker as "Hoss" Cartwright, and Pernell Roberts as Adam Cartwright. The Cartwrights were a prosperous ranching family who had to deal with all of the social, economic, ethnic, and cultural challenges facing settlers in the far West. *Bonanza* was the highest-rated television show in America from 1964 to 1967, and its theme song—"Bonanza"—sold a gold record. The last episode of *Bonanza* was broadcast on January 16, 1973.

REFERENCE: Stephen Calder, *The Ponderosa Empire*, 1995.

BOND, JAMES. James Bond was a character in Ian Fleming's series of highly profitable espionage novels of the 1950s and 1960s. A special agent for the British secret service, Bond romanced beautiful women and foiled the evildoers of the world. During the 1960s, a series of enormously popular James Bond films starred actor Sean Connery. They included *Dr. No* (1963), *From Russia with Love* (1964), *Goldfinger* (1965), *Thunderball* (1965), *You Only Live Twice* (1967), and *Diamonds Are Forever* (1971). President John F. Kennedy* was a particular fan of the books and films.

REFERENCE: Andrew Lycett, *Ian Fleming: The Man behind James Bond*, 1995.

BOND, JULIAN. Julian Bond was born in Nashville, Tennessee, January 14, 1940. His parents were both college professors, and he attended Morehouse College. A class there taught by Rev. Martin Luther King, Jr.,* permanently raised Bond's consciousness about civil rights issues. During his junior year at Morehouse, Bond organized sit-ins* at lunch counters to promote desegregation. In 1960, with one semester left before graduation, he quit school for a position with the *Atlanta Inquirer*, a weekly black newspaper. He went on to become managing editor of the paper. Bond was also active in the Student Nonviolent Coordinating Committee (SNCC), becoming its communications director in 1962. In 1965, Bond won election to the Georgia legislature from Atlanta's 111th district.

His election precipitated a constitutional crisis. Bond was an outspoken opponent of the Vietnam War,* and legislators in the Georgia house refused to seat him. Bond appealed through the federal courts, arguing that his First Amendment rights were being violated. The U.S. Supreme Court agreed with him and forced his seating in 1966. To protest the racist structure of the Democratic Party in Georgia, Bond formed the insurgent Georgia Loyal National Democratic Party to contest the regular Georgia Democratic Party's credentials at the 1968 national convention in Chicago. They succeeded in winning half of the Georgia delegate allotment at the convention. In 1974, Bond was elected to the state senate, a post he still holds.

REFERENCES: John Neary, *Julian Bond: Black Rebel*, 1971; Thomas Rose, *Black Leaders: Then and Now*, 1984.

BONNIE AND CLYDE. *Bonnie and Clyde* was one of the 1960's most popular and important films. It was directed by Arthur Penn and released in 1967. Set in depression-era Texas, Oklahoma, and Missouri, the film starred Warren

Beatty as Clyde Barrow and Faye Dunaway as Bonnie Parker, real-life bank robbers who became popular icons in the 1930s. Michael J. Pollard played sidekick C. W. Moss, while Gene Hackman had a supporting role as Buck Barrow, Clyde's brother. Estelle Parsons played Buck's wife, Blanche. Because resentment against banks was so great during the depression, bank robbers often became folk heroes among lower-class, blue-collar Americans. Arthur Penn's film was graphically violent, more so than any other mainstream film of its time, and Bonnie and Clyde were at best antiheroes responsible for stealing from greedy bankers but also for killing innocent people accidentally. Critics either loved or hated the film, but it was a box office success that cemented Beatty's and Dunaway's reputations as Hollywood superstars. Nihilistic, violent, and morally ambiguous, *Bonnie and Clyde* was a perfect symbol of 1960s angst in the United States.

REFERENCE: Lorrine Glennon, ed., *Our Times: An Illustrated History of the 20th Century*, 1995.

BOOBY TRAPS. The term "booby trap" exists in U.S. military lexicon to describe a hidden, makeshift device left behind to kill and wound troops after enemy soldiers have left a combat zone. During the Vietnam War,* the Vietcong* and North Vietnamese employed booby traps to great success. The most dangerous booby traps included hollowed-out coconut logs packed with gunpowder and triggered with a trip wire; walk bridges with ropes almost cut away; concealed punji sticks (sharpened bamboo sticks); buried bullets pointing straight up with firing pins located on bamboo stubs; and the "Malay whip log," a tree trunk attached to two trees by a rope. During the course of the war, most U.S. casualties* were caused by booby traps. American troops often held South Vietnamese civilians responsible for not informing them of the location of booby traps. The South Vietnamese did so because they were either conspiring with the Vietcong and North Vietnamese or because they felt intimidated by the enemy.

REFERENCES: Christian Appy, *Working Man's War*, 1993; Edgar C. Doleman, Jr., *The Vietnam Experience: Tools of War*, 1984; Peter Goldman and Tony Fuller, *Charlie Company: What Vietnam Did to Us*, 1983.

THE BOSTON STRANGLER. The term "Boston Strangler" was press jargon in the early 1960s for a vicious rapist and killer in Boston. Between 1962 and his arrest in 1964, Albert Henry DeSalvo raped and murdered thirteen women in their own homes. The victims were strangers to him, which made their deaths even more frightening to the general public. DeSalvo confessed to police but then refused to testify at his trial. He was convicted nevertheless and sentenced to life in prison. DeSalvo would be among the first murderers to be described as "serial killers." He died in prison November 28, 1973.

REFERENCE: *New York Times*, January 12, 1967.

BOUVIER, JACQUELINE. Jacqueline Bouvier was born July 28, 1929, in East Hampton, Long Island, to Jack and Janet Bouvier, members of the social elite in America. On July 22, Jackie's parents were divorced by a Reno, Nevada, court, which left her father paying for all of Jackie's expenses and receiving liberal visitation rights. The result of this settlement was a battle over the affection of Jackie and her sister. Her father won at first until her mother's marriage to Hugh Auchincloss, one of America's leading socialites, which gave her mother the upper hand.

In 1944, Jackie entered Miss Porter's School in Farmington, Connecticut, one of the leading boarding schools for girls in the United States. In the autumn of 1947, Jackie entered Vassar College in Poughkeepsie, New York, and stayed there through her sophomore year, when she went to France. She finished her college career at George Washington University in Washington, D.C. After graduation she accepted a job at the *Washington Times-Herald*, which led to her first introduction to John F. Kennedy.* He asked Jackie to marry him when she was in London on business, and they were married on September 12, 1953.

Seven years after they were married, Jackie became the First Lady when Kennedy was elected president of the United States. Jackie Kennedy soon became one of the most popular, recognizable women in the world. After J.F.K.'s assassination on November 22, 1963, she became involved with Aristotle Socrates Onassis, the Greek shipbuilding tycoon. They were married October 20, 1968. Their marriage, based more on convenience and status than real romance, ended on March 15, 1975, when Aristotle Onassis died in a French hospital from complications after surgery.

After Onassis' death, Jackie Kennedy Onassis became a successful businesswoman, an editor at Doubleday, and an important leader of the Kennedy clan. She will undoubtedly go down as one of the world's greatest women as well as the most popular First Lady. She died of a lymphoma May 19, 1994.

REFERENCES: Christina Anderson, *Jack and Jackie*, 1996; Ellen Ladowksy, *Jacqueline Kennedy Onassis*, 1997; Richard Taylor, *Jackie*, 1990.

Jerry Jay Inmon

BOYLE, WILLIAM ANTHONY. William "Tony" Boyle was born in Bald Butte, Montana, December 1, 1904. He went to work as a coal miner and became active in the local activities of the United Mine Workers of America (UMW). Boyle rose through the union ranks and served as a personal assistant to John L. Lewis between 1948 and 1960. He was elected international president of the UMW in 1963. Rank-and-file members came to resent Boyle's leadership of the union. They suspected him of the corrupt use of union funds and a lack of responsiveness to their needs. In 1969, Joseph A. Yablonski challenged Boyle for the UMW presidency. Boyle defeated Yablonski in the election, but Yablonski and his family were murdered in their homes shortly thereafter. In 1972, the Department of Labor invalidated the 1969 election as hopelessly fraudulent, and Arnold Miller defeated Boyle in the presidential election. Boyle was sub-

sequently convicted of illegally using union funds for political purposes and of conspiring to murder Yablonski. He received an extended prison sentence. Tony Boyle died May 31, 1985.
REFERENCE: *New York Times*, June 1, 1985.

BREAKFAST AT TIFFANY'S. *Breakfast at Tiffany's* was one of the most popular films of the early 1960s. Based on a short story by Truman Capote and directed by Blake Edwards, the film was released in 1961 and starred Audrey Hepburn as Holly Golightly. Holly Golightly was an early version of the anti-hero that the 1960s popularized. An antiestablishment* rebel, Golightly shoplifts at Woolworth's for the thrill of it, feigns sophisticated intelligence at fancy cocktail parties, and manages to have breakfast one morning at Tiffany's, the upscale New York jeweler. Golightly is a transitional figure between the ideal domestic woman of the 1950s and the outspoken feminist of the 1970s. She is girlish in her charms but not sexually aware, and she is emotionally independent yet financially dependent on wealthy men.
REFERENCE: *New York Times*, October 6, 1961.

BRENNAN, WILLIAM JOSEPH, JR. William Joseph Brennan, Jr., was born in Newark, New Jersey, April 25, 1906. He received his undergraduate degree from the University of Pennsylvania and his law degree from Harvard. He prac- ticed law in Newark after leaving Harvard, specializing in labor law, which was evolving quickly in the wake of the Wagner Act of 1935. During World War II, he joined the army and served in a staff position to Undersecretary of War Robert Patterson. For a few years after the war, Brennan practiced law privately, but in 1949 he accepted an appointment as a judge in the New Jersey Superior Court system. He became a judge in the appellate division in 1950 and a justice on the New Jersey Supreme Court in 1952. Brennan was still serving in that position when President Dwight Eisenhower* named him to the U.S. Supreme Court in 1956. There he became part of the liberal majority of the Earl Warren* Court that revolutionized American jurisprudence. Many judicial historians con- sider Brennan to have been the "heart" of the Warren Court, a gentle moderate who nevertheless pushed the envelope of individual rights. During the 1970s and 1980s, Brennan often found himself in dissent, disagreeing with many of the conservative decisions of the Supreme Court under Warren Burger* and William Rehnquist. Brennan retired in 1990.
REFERENCES: Hunter Clark, *Justice Brennan:The Great Conciliator*, 1995; Roger L. Goldman, *Justice William J. Brennan, Jr.: Freedom First*, 1994.

BRIGHT, WILLIAM ROHL. William Rohl (Bill) Bright was born in Coweta, Oklahoma, November 19, 1921. He was raised in a devout Methodist household, and as a young man he became involved in the Hollywood Presbyterian Church in Hollywood, California. At Hollywood Presbyterian, genuine evangelicalism mixed easily with individual prosperity and social advancement. In 1946, Bright entered the Princeton Seminary, but he transferred to the Fuller Seminary in Pasadena, California, the next year.

Toward the end of his seminary years, Bright founded the Campus Crusade movement, rented an apartment near the campus of the University of California at Los Angeles, and began recruiting students to his college evangelical group. By the early 1960s, the Campus Crusade had established chapter groups on campuses throughout the United States. The Campus Crusade message to college students was that God loved them and had a plan for their lives and that Jesus redeems men and women from sin if individuals will receive him as their savior. In the mid-1960s, Bright founded Athletes in Action, an organization of gifted athletes who traveled around the country witnessing for Jesus Christ. By the early 1990s, Campus Crusade had an annual budget of $140 million.

REFERENCE: Richard Quebedeaux, *I Found It! The Story of Bill Bright and Campus Crusade*, 1979.

BRINKS HOTEL (SAIGON). The Brinks Hotel was located in downtown Saigon* and was often used during the early stages of the Vietnam War* buildup to house U.S. army officers. As such, it became a target for Vietcong* terrorists. On the morning of December 24, 1964, several Vietcong operatives planted a car bomb in the basement parking lot of the hotel. The bomb detonated at 5:45 P.M., during the dinner hour. In the ensuing explosion, two Americans died and fifty-eight were wounded.

The explosion came as a surprise to President Lyndon B. Johnson* and his advisors in the White house and the Pentagon, who had thought that Saigon was under U.S. and South Vietnamese control. Questions raced through official Washington, D.C., from the White House to the Pentagon to Capitol Hill. How could the Vietcong plant such a device and remain completely undetected? Had the Vietcong infiltrated the city to an even greater extent? Were they also present in other cities and towns of South Vietnam? And finally, how should the United States respond to such a blatant assault on U.S. soldiers?

The president mulled over the question. Some of his advisors urged him to launch a bombing* campaign over North Vietnam, but the president decided that such a course would be unwise. A massive bombing campaign would be an inappropriate response given that only two American lives had been lost, and bombing during the Christmas season might garner him international political criticism. He decided to bide his time and hope that the U.S. policy objective of training the Army of the Republic of Vietnam (ARVN) to defend the country would be realized. The bombing of the Brinks Hotel, however, made it abundantly clear that no area of South Vietnam, even U.S. military installations and barracks, was secure from Vietcong attack. It also convinced many of Johnson's closest advisors that only the commitment of regular U.S. combat troops could defeat the Vietcong.

REFERENCES: Stanley Karnow, *Vietnam: A History*, 1983; *New York Times,* December

25–28, 1964; Stafford T. Thomas, "Brinks Hotel," in James S. Olson, *Dictionary of the Vietnam War*, 1988.

BRITISH INVASION. The term "British invasion" was used in the 1960s and in subsequent rock-and-roll history to describe the arrival between 1964 and 1966 of several British rock bands, including the Beatles,* the Rolling Stones,* the Yardbirds, the Animals,* the Dave Clark Five,* Herman's Hermits,* and the Kinks. These groups dominated the pop charts on both sides of the Atlantic for several years, serving as a transition between the doo-wop rhythm-and-blues music of the late 1950s and early 1960s and the psychedelic rock of the later 1960s.
REFERENCE: Patricia Romanowski and Holly George-Warren, eds., *The New Rolling Stone Encyclopedia of Rock and Roll*, 1996.

BROOKE, EDWARD. Edward William Brooke was born into a middle-class Washington, D.C., family in 1919. During World War II, he served in an all-black army regiment and then returned to Washington, D.C., to attend Howard University. He graduated at the top of his class at the Boston University Law School, editing the *Law Review* and earning a reputation as a young man of wit, intelligence, and political savvy. He then practiced law and became active in Republican Party politics. In 1962, Brooke defeated Elliot Richardson in the GOP ("Grand Old Party") primary and went on to win election as the attorney general of Massachusetts. Brooke was elected to the U.S. Senate in 1966, the first African American to win that honor since Reconstruction.

Brook was convinced that the welfare state had gone too far, that it had robbed many poor men and women of their dignity. "You don't help a man," he often said, "by constantly giving him more handouts." As a Republican during the Richard M. Nixon* administration, Brooke found himself increasingly estranged from his own party because of the president's mixed record on civil rights and his commitment to appointing southern conservatives to the Supreme Court. After winning reelection in 1972, Brooke emerged as one of the leading figures in the liberal wing of the Republican Party. He was defeated for reelection in 1978 and returned to the practice of law.
REFERENCE: *Black Americans in Government*, 1969.

BROWN, H. RAP. H. Rap Brown was born in Baton Rouge, Louisiana, October 4, 1943. He first came to national attention in 1966, when he was an outspoken advocate of black power.* Brown was charged with inciting a riot in Cambridge, Maryland, in 1968, and his actions led to a clause in the Civil Rights Act* of 1968 that was known as the "H. Rap Brown Statute," making conspiracy to commit riot a federal offense. That same year he was convicted of carrying a firearm across state lines. He disappeared in 1970 to avoid prosecution for other crimes, resurfacing in 1972 after being wounded in a shoot-out with police. He was convicted of robbing a New York City saloon and sentenced to prison in 1974. In the penitentiary, he converted to Islam and opened a grocery store in Atlanta after his release.

REFERENCES: H. Rap Brown, *Die, Nigger, Die!* 1969; William L. Van Deburg, *New Day in Babylon: The Black Power Movement and American Culture, 1965–1975*, 1992; Herbert Haines, *Black Radicals and the Civil Rights Mainstream, 1954–1970*, 1988.

BROWN, JAMES. James Brown was born in Barnwell, South Carolina, May 3, 1933. Raised in poverty, Brown shined shoes and picked cotton as a child to make money. He was convicted of armed robbery in 1949 and spent three years in juvenile detention. After prison, Brown tried his hand at semipro boxing and minor league baseball. He also began singing gospel music with a group known as the Flames. In 1956, they had their first hit—"Please, Please, Please." Brown's music was influenced by gospel sounds, but it gradually acquired a sharper, rougher edge. In 1958, his song "Try Me" went to number one on the rhythm and blues charts. Later that year, he formed the James Brown Band.

The band received bigger and bigger bookings. Bedecked in his characteristic cape, Brown put on a stage show as well as a concert, with his trademark pumping hits, twisting foot, and floor splits. Raw and powerful, Brown's music became the most important in black rhythm and blues and included such hits as "Bewildered" (1961), "I Don't Mind" (1961), "Lost Someone" (1961), "Live at the Apollo" (1962), and "Out of Sight" (1963). In the mid-1960s, a number of Brown's rhythm and blues hits made their way into the top twenty of the pop charts. By that time, he had become recognized as the godfather of soul music—"Soul Brother Number One."

He was also an icon in the black community, a man who had overcome poverty and established an unparalleled reputation for independence and pride. His songs in the late 1960s reflected that point of view. He made the transition to funk music in the early 1970s, but his career began to decline in the mid-1970s. Financial problems beset him, and late in the 1980s he did time for assault. Paroled in 1991, Brown resumed his concert career.

REFERENCE: Patricia Romanowski and Holly George-Warren, eds., *The New Rolling Stone Encyclopedia of Rock and Roll*, 1996.

BROWN, SAMUEL WINFRED. Samuel Brown was born in Council Bluffs, Iowa, on July 27, 1943. He graduated from the University of Redlands in 1965, where he had come to oppose the Vietnam War,* and earned a master's degree in political science at Rutger's in 1966. In 1967, Brown took classes at Harvard Divinity School and became involved in Senator Eugene McCarthy's* campaign for the 1968 Democratic presidential nomination. When Hubert Humphrey* won the nomination and Richard Nixon* the general election, Brown decided to take his antiwar* feelings to the street. He founded the Vietnam Moratorium Committee, which staged massive antiwar rallies in 1969 and 1970. The committee disbanded in 1970, but Brown continued to speak out in favor of political candidates who favored a withdrawal of U.S. troops from Vietnam.

REFERENCE: Nancy Zaroulis and Gerald Sullivan, *Who Spoke Up? American Protest Against the War in Vietnam, 1963–1975*, 1984.

BROWN BERETS. The Brown Berets were founded in 1967 by David Sánchez in Los Angeles. Carlos Montez and Ralph Ramírez were also among the founders. At first organized to protest political brutality against the Hispanic community, the Brown Berets engaged in group patrols to monitor police activities. They soon became more militant, wearing the distinctive brown berets, army fatigues, and boots to emphasize the self-defense nature of their ideology. The Brown Berets intended to defend the Hispanic community against Anglo violence. Although chapters of the Brown Berets were established throughout the urban Southwest, the group was strongest in California and Texas.

In 1968, the Brown Berets organized a series of protests at high schools in California to demand improvements in public education for Hispanic children. Many of them were arrested and charged with a variety of narcotics, public order, and ideological crimes. They also engaged in several community service activities, the most important of which was the East Los Angeles Free Clinic, a medical facility funded by the Ford Foundation. In 1972, Sánchez led a Brown Beret ''invasion'' and ''occupation'' of Catalina Island off the southern coast of California, claiming that it was illegally taken from Mexican peoples. Later in the year, Sánchez disbanded the Brown Berets. The Brown Berets never had more than 5,000 members.

REFERENCE: Matt S. Meier and Feliciano Rivera, *Dictionary of Mexican American History*, 1981.

BRUCE, LENNY (LEONARD ALFRED SCHNEIDER). Lenny Alfred Schneider was born in Mineola, New York, in 1926. His mother was a popular local comic, and Lenny quit school after the eighth grade to pursue a career in show business. He served in the navy during the last year of World War II, and in 1946, with GI Bill checks coming in every month, he studied acting in Hollywood and began to get a few bookings as a stand-up comedian. He took the stage name of Lenny Bruce. In the staid conformity of the 1950s, he gained a certain notoriety because of his vulgar irreverence. He elevated street language into an art form. Nothing was sacred to Lenny Bruce—no word too obscene to repeat again and again, no personality too proper to subject to the most vile innuendos. His nightclub act was the harbinger of a new culture that would become endemic in the United States in the 1960s.

Bruce was also into the drug culture. In 1963, he was arrested for heroin possession, convicted, and committed to a rehabilitation center. When he was released, Bruce found it difficult to find work, primarily because most nightclub owners did not want to risk a backlash by booking him. In 1964, New York City police arrested him for obscenity after watching his act at the Cafe Au Go Go in Greenwich Village. The case became a cause célèbre in the artistic, literary, and entertainment communities, with supporters like Norman Mailer,*

Lionell Trilling, and John Updike defending his First Amendment right to freedom of speech. Bruce eventually lost the case and was sentenced to four months in prison. He never served a day, however. He appealed the conviction and stayed out of jail, but on August 3, 1966, he died of a morphine overdose. Police found him with the needle sticking out from his arm.

REFERENCES: Lenny Bruce, *How to Talk Dirty and Influence People*, 1965; *New York Times*, August 4, 1966.

BUCKLEY, WILLIAM FRANK, JR. William F. Buckley, Jr., was born November 24, 1925, in New York City to a well-to-do family. After a stint in the U.S. Army during World War II, Buckley attended Yale University, where he served as editor of the *Yale Daily News*. He graduated in 1950. In 1951, Buckley came to national attention when his book *God and Man at Yale* was published. The book was a powerful attack on the liberal biases in the curriculum at Yale. Buckley did not endear himself to the Yale faculty when he arranged to have the book distributed at the university's commencement ceremonies.

Buckley worked for the Central Intelligence Agency* from 1951 to 1952, and in 1954 he wrote his second book—*McCarthy and His Enemies*—a defense of the anticommunist movement. Buckley saw nothing wrong with a society's defending itself from alien ideas. In 1955, he cemented his reputation as one of America's leading conservatives when he launched the *National Review*, a weekly conservative political journal. In 1959, he wrote *Up from Liberalism*, a book that demanded an uncompromising, tough foreign policy toward the Soviet Union, which he considered the twentieth century's most evil force. In 1962, Buckley began writing ''On the Right,'' a syndicated weekly newspaper column. First broadcast over the Public Broadcasting System (PBS), his weekly television interview program *Firing Line* eventually became the longest continuing series in PBS history. By that time, Buckley had become an influential public figure in his own right and the widely recognized intellectual godfather of the modern conservative political movement. Today Buckley writes fiction and continues his political commentary.

REFERENCES: John B. Judis, *William F. Buckley, Jr.: Patron Saint of the Conservatives*, 1988; Mark Royden Winchell, *William F. Buckley, Jr.*, 1984.

BUMMER. The term ''bummer'' emerged as a slang expression in the 1960s to refer to a bad experience of any kind. Upon receiving bad news, a ''hip'' individual would simply utter ''Bummer,'' and everyone around him or her realized the nature of the news.

REFERENCE: Ruth Bronsteen, *The Hippy's Handbook—How to Live on Love*, 1967.

BUNDY, McGEORGE. McGeorge Bundy, an architect of U.S. policy during the Vietnam War,* was born in Boston, Massachusetts, on March 30, 1919. A brilliant student, he graduated from Yale in 1940 and served in the army during World War II, earning a reputation as a skilled planner and logician. He left the army in 1946 and signed on as a research assistant to former Secretary of State Henry L. Stimson, with whom he coauthored *On Active Service in Peace and War* (1948). By that time Bundy's star had risen in the Washington, D.C., political establishment. In 1948 he served as an advisor to Republican Thomas Dewey's presidential campaign, as a consultant to the Marshall Plan, and as a member of the Council on Foreign Relations. In 1953 he became dean of arts and sciences at Harvard, and in January 1961 President John F. Kennedy* named Bundy special assistant to the president for national security affairs.

After the assassination of President John Kennedy in 1963, Bundy emerged as one of President Lyndon B. Johnson's* most influential advisers, and because he believed that Vietnam was purely a Cold War* event in which Vietnamese communists were bent on overthrowing another country, he was in a position to exert tremendous personal influence on U.S. policymaking there. He was also a strong advocate of strategic bombing* campaigns over North Vietnam. In 1966, Bundy left the Johnson administration to become head of the Ford Foundation. He also continued, as one of the "Wise Old Men,* to advise the president on military and foreign policy. After the disastrous Tet Offensive* of 1968, Bundy told Johnson that gradual disengagement from Vietnam was the only viable option. In later years, Bundy wrote prodigiously, and his published works included *Presidential Power and Performance* (1980), *Danger and Survival: Choices About Nuclear Weapons in the First Fifty Years* (1990), and *Reducing Nuclear Danger* (1993). McGeorge Bundy died September 17, 1996.

REFERENCES: Kai Bird, *The Color of Truth: McGeorge Bundy and William Bundy, Brothers in Arms*, 1998; David Halberstam, *The Best and the Brightest*, 1972; Leslie Gelb and Richard Betts, *The Irony of Vietnam: The System Worked*, 1979; *New York Times*, September 17, 1996.

BUNDY, WILLIAM. William Bundy was born in Washington, D.C., on September 24, 1917. He graduated from Yale in 1939 and joined the U.S. Army. After mustering out of the military, Bundy entered Harvard Law School and received his degree there in 1947. Soon after leaving Cambridge, Bundy went to work for the Central Intelligence Agency* (CIA), rising quickly to the agency's upper echelons and impressing those around him with his brilliance. In 1961 he became deputy assistant secretary of defense for international security affairs. Because his brother McGeorge was a close advisor to President John F. Kennedy,* William quickly secured influence in Washington beyond the significance of his post at the Pentagon. In terms of Vietnam War* policy, he supported the government of Ngo Dinh Diem,* drafted what became the Gulf of Tonkin Resolution* in 1964, and called for escalation of U.S. commitment there. Like his brother McGeorge, he was a "Cold Warrior" and a leading "hawk"* in both the Kennedy and Johnson administrations. In 1964 he also became assistant secretary of state for Far Eastern affairs. Together with McGeorge, William Bundy devised the strategic bombing campaign over North Vietnam, which often included selecting specific targets. By 1967 he had moderated somewhat his position on the war, urging a negotiated settlement. Bundy left the State Department in 1969 to become editor of *Foreign Affairs*.

REFERENCES: Kai Bird, *The Color of Truth: McGeorge Bundy and William Bundy, Brothers in Arms*, 1998; David Halberstam, *The Best and the Brightest*, 1972; Leslie Gelb and Richard Betts, *The Irony of Vietnam: The System Worked*, 1979; *New York Times*, September 17, 1996; *Who's Who In America, 1967–1968*, 1968.

BUNKER, ELLSWORTH. Ellsworth Bunker was born in Yonkers, New York, on May 11, 1894. After graduating from Yale in 1916, he went to work for the National Sugar Company, rising through the corporate ranks to become president of the company in 1948. Because of the company's sugar interests in the Caribbean and Central America, Bunker developed an expertise in Latin American affairs. Between 1948 and 1951, he served as chairman of the board, then retired to launch a diplomatic career. In 1951 President Harry Truman named Bunker U.S. ambassador to Argentina. Similar posts followed, including ambassadorships to Italy, India, and Nepal. In 1962, as a U.S. troubleshooter, he helped settle the bloody West Irian dispute between the Netherlands and Indonesia. Between 1964 and 1966, Bunker served as the U.S. representative to the Organization of American States. President Lyndon B. Johnson* appointed him ambassador to South Vietnam in 1967, hoping Bunker could work some diplomatic magic there, but it was not to be. Bunker remained in South Vietnam until 1973, working with the regime of Nguyen Van Thieu* and trying to make a success of President Richard Nixon's* ''Vietnamization''* policy, but nothing succeeded. After the end of the war in 1973, Bunker became an ambassador at large and during the Jimmy Carter administration played a key role in developing the Panama Canal Treaties. Ellsworth Bunker died September 17, 1984.

REFERENCES: Lee H. Burke, *Ambassador at Large: Diplomat Extraordinary*, 1972; *New York Times*, September 18, 1984; *The Wall Street Journal*, September 18–19, 1984.

BURGER, WARREN EARL. Warren Earl Burger was born September 17, 1907, in St. Paul, Minnesota. He attended the University of Minnesota for two years and then earned his law degree at the St. Paul College of Law in 1931. He then practiced for a Minneapolis firm for the next twenty-two years. While practicing law, Burger became active in state Republican politics. He became well acquainted with Herbert Brownell, Thomas E. Dewey's presidential campaign adviser, and in 1953, when Brownell became Dwight D. Eisenhower's* attorney general, Burger was appointed assistant attorney general, where he headed the Department of Justice's civil division. His reputation as a conservative grew quickly there, especially in civil liberties and loyalty issues. In 1956, President Dwight D. Eisenhower appointed him to the U.S. Court of Appeals for the District of Columbia. There, his conservative reputation grew, particularly in his handling of criminal justice cases.

President Richard M. Nixon* agreed with Burger's view that the Constitution should be interpreted narrowly, and in 1969 he appointed Burger to replace Earl

Warren* as chief justice of the Supreme Court. Burger served until his retirement in 1986. He surprised conservatives by not stepping back from the decisions of the Warren years. The Warren decisions on school desegregation, one-person, one-vote, the right to privacy, and the *Miranda* description of defendants' rights survived. His Court also upheld the constitutionality of busing to achieve racial desegregation of public schools and affirmative action,* as well as the right of a woman to have an abortion. During the Watergate crisis, the Burger Court ordered the White House to hand over taped recordings to Congress, which eventually forced Richard M. Nixon's resignation. Warren Burger died June 24, 1995.

REFERENCES: Nancy Maveety, *Representation Rights: The Burger Years*, 1991; *New York Times*, June 25, 1995; Bernard Schwartz, *The Ascent of Pragmatism: The Burger Court in Action*, 1992.

BURNS, ARTHUR FRANK. Arthur Frank Burns was born in Stanislau, Austria, April 27, 1904. The family immigrated to the United States when Burns was still a child, and he earned a number of degrees, including a Ph.D. in economics in 1934. Burns' economic ideas were decidedly conservative, as were his Republican politics, but he was no ideologue. He served as chairman of the Council of Economic Advisers during the Dwight D. Eisenhower* administration and was later president of the National Bureau of Economic Research. In 1969, he came back into government service as an economic adviser to President Richard M. Nixon,* who appointed him head of the Federal Reserve Board in 1970. An expert on the business cycle, Burns argued that the violent swings in the American economy were things of the past, and he opposed business monopolies, wage-price controls, and social spending to stimulate an ailing economy. At the Federal Reserve Board, he argued that the board should concentrate more on managing the total supply of money in the economy rather than worrying about how monetary policy would affect credit market conditions. Burns left government service during the Jimmy Carter administration and retired to private life. He died June 26, 1987.

REFERENCES: *New York Times*, June 27, 1987; "Spotlight on Arthur Frank Burns," *Banking* 62 (1970), 47, 110.

BURROUGHS, WILLIAM S. William S. Burroughs was born February 5, 1914, in St. Louis, Missouri, to a patrician family. He rejected the trappings of upper-class success and spent many years on the streets, washing windows, collecting garbage, working as an exterminator, and passing out handbills to make a living. Addicted for years to hard drugs, Burroughs accidentally killed his own wife during a game of William Tell. When Burroughs tried his hand at writing, his book *Naked Lunch* became a cause célèbre among civil libertarians. Aristocratic and anarchistic, *Naked Lunch* features a drug addict as antihero and such characters as Clem Snide the Private Asshole and the Paregoric Kid. Excerpts of the novel first appeared in 1959 and caused controversy everywhere.

Boston officials ruled the book obscene and banned its sale in the city. *Naked Lunch* was published in its entirety in Europe in 1963, and in 1965, a Massachusetts state court overturned the Boston ban as a First Amendment violation. Burroughs died August 2, 1997.

REFERENCES: David Burner, *Making Peace with the Sixties*, 1996; Ted Morgan, *Literary Outlaw: The Life and Times of William S. Burroughs*, 1988; Jennie Skerl, *William S. Burroughs*, 1985.

BUSINESS-INDUSTRY POLITICAL ACTION COMMITTEE. The Business-Industry Political Action Committee was founded in 1963 by the National Association of Manufacturers to counter the growing influence of the American Federation of Labor–Congress of Industrial Organizations (AFL–CIO) Political Action Committee. Robert L. Humphrey served as its first president, and its board of directors was composed of major American business leaders. The mission of the Business-Industry Political Action Committee has been to promote free enterprise in the United States; the committee believes that the best way of achieving that goal is to reduce federal spending and balance the federal budget, reduce government controls on business, and control the growth of the federal bureaucracy. Its Candidate Review Committee reviews political candidates for national office in terms of their conservative credentials and endorses their campaigns.

REFERENCE: James S. Olson, ed., *Dictionary of United States Economic History*, 1991.

BUTCH CASSIDY AND THE SUNDANCE KID. *Butch Cassidy and the Sundance Kid* was one of the decade's most popular films. Released in 1969, it starred Paul Newman as Butch Cassidy, Robert Redford as the Kid, and Katherine Ross as the Kid's lover and Cassidy's sidekick. Cassidy and the Kid were train and bank robbers in an old West that was not so old anymore. As the nineteenth century gave way to the twentieth, the two men became an anachronism, gunslingers in an age when gunslingers were disappearing. Pursued relentlessly by train detectives, they decided to ply their trade in Latin America, where they were ultimately killed in a shoot-out with Bolivian police. Because Cassidy and the Kid were young, funny, handsome, and carefree antiheroes, they appealed to mainstream as well as counterculture* audiences. Burt Bachrach's original song for the film—''Raindrops Keep Falling on My Head''—rocketed to the top of the pop charts in 1969.

REFERENCE: Lawrence J. Quirk, *The Films of Paul Newman*, 1981.

BYE BYE BIRDIE. *Bye Bye Birdie* was one of the 1960s premier Broadway musicals. Written by Michael Stewart, with lyrics by Lee Adams and music by Charles Strouse, *Bye Bye Birdie* opened in New York at the Michael Beck Theater on April 14, 1960. It was the first Broadway musical to revolve around the new popular music, which had surfaced in the United States in the late 1950s. Conrad Birdie (played by Dick Gautier) is a new rock-and-roll sensation, but his manager, Albert Peterson (played by Dick Van Dyke), cannot seem to make enough money from the situation. Albert's secretary, Rosie (Chita Rivera), will not marry him until his financial affairs are in order. Like the real-life Elvis Presley, Conrad is about to get drafted, and like the real-life Jerry Lee Lewis, he gets in trouble for being with an underaged girl. A musical comedy, *Bye Bye Birdie* ends with Albert's quitting the business, marrying Rosie, and becoming a teacher. *Bye Bye Birdie* had 607 performances on Broadway before hitting the road.

REFERENCE: Kurt Ganzl, *The Encyclopedia of the Musical Theater*, 1994.

C

CABARET. *Cabaret* was a highly successful Broadway play of the 1960s. Premiering at the Broadhurst Theater in New York on November 20, 1966, *Cabaret* was adapted from Christopher Isherwood's *Berlin Stories* and the play *I Am a Camera* by Joe Masteroff. The music was by John Kander, and the lyrics by Fred Ebb. *Cabaret* starred Joel Grey as the master of ceremonies. A musical set in a cabaret in late Weimar Germany just before the Nazi takeover, *Cabaret* exposed the decadent racism and anti-Semitism of German society. It was sophisticated, dark, and frightening, a complete departure from the Rogers and Hammerstein musicals that had dominated Broadway for so long. *Cabaret* eventually had a run of 1,165 performances.
REFERENCE: Kurt Ganzl, *The Encyclopedia of the Musical Theater*, 1994.

CALLEY, WILLIAM LAWS, JR. William L. Calley, Jr., was born June 8, 1943, and grew up in Miami, Florida. After graduating from high school he worked a number of odd jobs before joining the U.S. Army in 1966. He completed officer's candidate school and was assigned to Company C of the 1st Battalion of the 20th Infantry. At the time the unit was stationed in Hawaii. Company commander Captain Ernest Medina* put Calley in charge of the 1st Platoon. They arrived in South Vietnam in December 1967 and deployed to Quang Ngai Province, where they were assigned to the 11th Infantry Brigade.

On March 16, 1968, during an operation in the village of My Lai,* Company C slaughtered nearly 500 Vietnamese civilians without encountering any Vietcong* resistance. A helicopter pilot observing the operation reported large-scale civilian casualties, but officers of the 11th Infantry Brigade—Colonel Oran K. Henderson and Major General Samuel W. Foster—conducted only a cursory investigation and concluded that nothing out of the ordinary had taken place at My Lai.

Over the course of the next year, rumors about the massacre circulated within the 11th Brigade, but the story did not make it into the media until April 1969, when Ronald L. Ridenhour, a Vietnam veteran who had heard about the incident, wrote a letter to President Richard M. Nixon* and thirty U.S. congressmen and requested an investigation. In November 1969, Lieutenant General William Peers launched a special investigation of the massacre. Calley was soon charged with war crimes. In his defense, Calley claimed that he was acting under orders received from Captain Medina, who allegedly instructed him to destroy every living thing in the hamlet. On March 29, 1971, William Calley was convicted of the first-degree murder of at least twenty-two Vietnamese noncombatants. The military judge sentenced him to life imprisonment at hard labor.

The conviction provoked a firestorm of political controversy. Many Americans felt Calley was taking the entire blame for the incident, that his military superiors were making him the scapegoat. President Richard M. Nixon, in tune with public opinion, ordered Calley released from the military stockade and placed under confinement in Calley's own base apartment. The president then implemented a formal review of the conviction and sentence. In August 1971, he reduced Calley's sentence to twenty years and then, in April 1974, to only ten years. William Calley was released on parole in November 1975.

REFERENCES: Joseph Goldstein, Burke Marshall, and Jack Schwartz, *The My Lai Massacre and Its Cover-Up: Beyond the Reach of the Law?*, 1976; Richard Hammer, *The Court-Martial of Lieutenant Calley*, 1971; James S. Olson and Randy Roberts, *My Lai: A Documentary History*, 1998; W. R. Peers, *The My Lai Inquiry*, 1979; John Sack, *Lieutenant Calley: His Own Story*, 1971.

CAMELOT. *Camelot*, one of the major musicals of the 1960s, opened at the Majestic Theater on Broadway on December 3, 1960. It was written by Alan Jay Lerner and based on T. H. White's *The Once and Future King*. The music was written by Frederick Lowe. The play starred Richard Burton as Arthur and Julie Andrews as Guenevere in a retelling of the King Arthur legend. Robert Goulet played Lancelot. In the popular culture of the 1960s, *Camelot* earned a larger-than-life place because President John F. Kennedy* heartily endorsed the play. Critics say that he fancied himself a modern version of King Arthur. After his death, journalist Theodore White perpetuated such a mythology, describing the Kennedy years before the assassination as a Camelot-like idyllic time in American history. The Kennedy years, he claimed, were like the first half of *Camelot*, when all is well in the Arthurian kingdom. In subsequent years, of course, when historians revealed a darker, sleazy side of the Kennedy administration, "Camelot" became a sarcastic way of referring to the assassinated president. *Camelot* eventually enjoyed 873 performances on Broadway.

REFERENCES: Kurt Ganzl, *The Encyclopedia of the Musical Theater*, 1994.

CARMICHAEL, STOKELY. Stokely Carmichael was born in Trinidad in the West Indies in 1941. His father was a carpenter. The family immigrated to the United States in 1952. Ghetto life in New York City was a shock to Carmichael, and after being admitted to the prestigious Bronx High School of Science, he developed equal contempt for white racists and white liberals. At the Bronx High School, Carmichael considered himself nothing more than a token or, in his words, the school's "black mascot."

Between 1961 and 1964, he was active in the Congress of Racial Equality* and participated in the freedom rides.* He entered Howard University in 1964 and soon emerged as the leader of the new Student Nonviolent Coordinating Committee* (SNCC), a civil rights organization that concentrated its efforts on voter registration drives in the South. The violence SNCC workers received in the South in 1963 and 1964 radicalized Carmichael. In 1966, he coined the term "black power"*—by which he meant black economic and political unity and self-defense against white violence. He became the antithesis of Martin Luther King, Jr.,* who continued to advocate nonviolent civil disobedience. Because of the rash of racial rebellions that swept through many cities between 1965 and 1968, Carmichael became the symbol of white America's fears.

By the late 1960s, Carmichael had abandoned any lingering support for working with white liberals in promoting black civil rights. He increasingly turned to Pan-African ideas, believing that only by uniting with black people all over the world could African Americans truly liberate themselves. In 1969, Carmichael moved to Guinea in West Africa, where he lived until his death on November 15, 1998.

REFERENCES: Stokely Carmichael, *Black Power*, 1972, and *Stokely Speaks: From Black Power Back to Pan-Africanism*, 1971; Robert Cwiklik, *Stokely Carmichael and Black Power*, 1993.

CARSON, RACHEL LOUISE. Rachel Louise Carson was a scientist, writer, and one of the leading conservationists of modern times. A marine biologist by training, she also possessed literary gifts that caused her nonfiction books and articles to be compared to those of Joseph Conrad and Herman Melville. Since the publication of her greatest work, *Silent Spring* (1962), Carson has become known as the seminal figure in the environmental movement.*

Rachel Carson was born in Springdale, Pennsylvania, in 1907. While growing up she spent much of her time outdoors. During this period she learned of her love of the outdoors and the animal world. She credited her interest in science to her mother, who taught her about the local flora and fauna. At an early age, her talent as a writer revealed itself. By the age of thirteen, she was publishing short stories in *St. Nicholas*, a children's magazine. She entered the Pennsylvania College for Women with the intention of majoring in English; however, a biology class renewed her interest in science, and, in 1929, she earned her B.A. in biology. She then entered Johns Hopkins University.

In 1930, she was appointed to the teaching staff of the university for summers, and she earned her M.A. at Johns Hopkins in 1932. One year earlier, Carson had joined the University of Maryland zoology staff, where she stayed until 1936. In 1936, Carson accepted a job with the U.S. Fish and Wildlife Service

(USFWS), a post she kept until 1952. In 1947 she was appointed the USFWS editor in chief and, as such, was responsible for writing most of the articles and pamphlets issued by the service. She also published articles in *Collier's, Yale Review*, and *The Science Digest*. In 1951 her book *The Sea around Us* was published. It was well received and won the National Book Award, as well as reaching the top of the nonfiction best-seller list. She left the USFWS in 1952 to devote herself to full-time writing. Her second book, *The Edge of the Sea*, was published in 1955. However, with her third book, *Silent Spring*, Carson reached international acclaim and founded the modern environmental movement.*

In the early 1960s, concerns over the way people had been treating the world were rising. More and more people were becoming interested, and *Silent Spring* lit the fire of the environmental movement. Like her other books, *Silent Spring* emphasized the interdependence and sanctity of all forms of life. It was an attack on the use of chemical fertilizers and pesticides by farmers and pointed out the potentially harmful effects of these on animals and humans. *The Saturday Review* called the book "a devastating, heavily documented, relentless attack upon human carelessness, greed, and irresponsibility." Because of the debate created by this book, President John F. Kennedy* ordered an investigation into the problem. In May 1963, the President's Science Advisory Committee agreed with the findings in *Silent Spring*, and this led to the banning of several dangerous chemicals, including DDT. Rachel Carson died in 1964. In May 1980, President Carter awarded her the Presidential Medal of Freedom.

REFERENCES: Liza Burby, *Rachel Carson*, 1996; Barbara Ravage, *Rachel Carson: The Gentle Crusader*, 1997.

Steven D. Smith

CASTRO, FIDEL. Fidel Castro was born August 13, 1927, in Mayari, Cuba. In 1950 he received a law degree from the University of Havana. An opponent of the Fulgencio Batista regime in Cuba, he led an attack on the Moncada military barracks in Santiago, Cuba, on July 26, 1953. Arrested, convicted, and sentenced to a fifteen-year prison term, Castro was released in 1955 under a general amnesty. He then went into exile in Mexico, not returning to Cuba until 1957, when he launched the rebellion against Batista. On December 31, 1959, the Batista government collapsed, and Castro came to power in Cuba.

An anti-imperialist nationalist, Castro had resented the long shadow cast over Cuba by the United States, and soon after his political triumph, he began nationalizing American-owned property on the island. He formally declared Cuba a socialist society in 1961. By that time, the United States had severed diplomatic relations with Cuba and had imposed an economic embargo on all Cuban-produced products.

Cuba's relations with the United States since 1959 have gone from bad to worse. The misguided U.S. attack on Cuba at the Bay of Pigs* in April 1961 failed miserably, succeeding only in strengthening Castro's grip on the Cuban

people. During the 1960s, more than 1 million Cubans fled the island for the United States, and the exodus continued in the 1970s and 1980s as the Cuban economy collapsed under the weight of its Marxist baggage. Despite predictions of his imminent demise, Fidel Castro was still firmly in control of Cuba in 1999.
REFERENCE: Lee Lockwood, *Castro's Cuba, Cuba's Fidel*, 1969.

CASUALTIES. Once U.S. military strategists decided to fight a war of attrition*—achieving victory by killing so many Vietcong* and North Vietnamese troops that the enemy could no longer field an army to fight—the number of killed and wounded soldiers became a number of overwhelming importance. Because it was so difficult in South Vietnam to distinguish enemy troops from civilian noncombatants, casualties among civilians ran quite high. Estimates of South Vietnamese civilian casualties between 1965 and 1974 range from 1,005,000 wounded and 430,000 killed to 800,000 wounded and 250,000 killed. Among American troops, 47,244 were killed in military action, while an additional 10,446 died from accidents or illness. The number of wounded in action totaled 304,000. Vietcong and North Vietnamese military deaths exceeded 660,000, while U.S. bombing over North Vietnam killed approximately 65,000 people. Among South Vietnamese military forces, nearly 224,000 were killed in action and 571,000 wounded.
REFERENCES: Edward S. Herman, *Atrocities in Vietnam: Myths and Realities*, 1970; Telford Taylor, *Nuremberg and Vietnam: An American Tragedy*, 1971; Guenter Lewy, *America in Vietnam*, 1978; Harry G. Summers, Jr., *Vietnam War Almanac*, 1985.

CATCH-22. *Catch-22* is the title of Joseph Heller's 1961 novel. A brilliant satire set on the imaginary island of Pianosa during World War II, the novel centers around bomber pilot Captain John Yossarian's efforts to survive. Flying bombers in World War II was deadly business, and Yossarian's commanding officer kept raising the number of missions a pilot had to complete before earning a leave. When Yossarian tries to get out of the service by feigning insanity, he collides head-on with Catch-22, a military regulation claiming that since a man must be insane to agree in the first place to go on bombing missions, his request for a mustering out of the military is proof positive that he is sane. Yossarian cannot get out of the service. The novel became a cultural icon of the 1960s because it spoofed large bureaucracies and their naive convictions about their ability to bring order to a chaotic world. By the mid-1960s, the term ''catch-22'' had entered the American vocabulary as a synonym for bureaucratic rules that possess no logic or sense and whose consequences are counterproductive. Many Americans came to view the U.S. military effort in Indochina as one enormous example of catch-22.
REFERENCE: Joseph Heller, *Catch-22*, 1961.

CENTER FOR STUDY OF RESPONSIVE LAW. The Center for Study of Responsive Law was established by Ralph Nader* in 1968. Financed by foun-

dation grants, the group became known as "Nader's Raiders"—zealous young lawyers out to use the legal system to protect consumers against business fraud. When Nader won his lawsuit against General Motors, he channeled the settlement money into his Center for Study of Responsive Law. The center's primary tactic is to conduct independent research into consumers' issues and then to disseminate its findings as widely as possible. The center still exists today.
REFERENCE: David Bollier, *Citizen Action and Other Big Ideas: A History of Ralph Nader and the Modern Consumer Movement*, 1989.

CENTRAL INTELLIGENCE AGENCY. The Central Intelligence Agency (CIA) had its origins in the Office of Strategic Services, an intelligence-gathering agency created by Congress during World War II. In 1947, Congress formally converted the Office of Strategic Services into the CIA. Since then, the CIA has been the premier branch of the United States intelligence establishment. By virtue of its original charter, the CIA was prohibited from operating within the United States. Its mission was to serve as a clearinghouse for all foreign intelligence operations of the United States. Subsequent legislation in 1949 allowed the CIA to employ secret administrative procedures and even insulated it from the congressional budget process.

During the 1960s, the Central Intelligence Agency operated all over the world, and it was deeply involved in the major foreign policy events of the decade, including the U-2* incident over the Soviet Union in 1960, the botched Bay of Pigs* invasion of Cuba in 1961, the Cuban missile crisis* of 1962, the invasion of the Dominican Republic* in 1964, and the conflict in Southeast Asia. CIA involvement in Vietnam began late in World War II when a special team from the Office of Strategic Services there allied itself with Ho Chi Minh* and his small Vietminh army in opposing Japanese occupation forces. After the war, the CIA supported first the French, and later, until the 1963 coup d'etat, the regime of Ngo Dinh Diem.* Until the Geneva Accords of 1954, a CIA team led by Colonel Edward Lansdale, working out of Saigon, had conducted psychological operations and paramilitary raids against the Vietminh and North Vietnamese. In 1961, the CIA launched its clandestine campaign in Laos,* recruiting nearly 10,000 Hmong tribesmen to attack the Ho Chi Minh Trail* and sever the infiltration route. Throughout the 1960s, the CIA worked to destroy the Vietcong* infrastructure, particularly through the Phoenix Program,* which included military operations against the National Liberation Front as well as targeted assassinations of Vietcong leaders.
REFERENCES: William E. Colby and Peter Forbath, *Honorable Men: My Life in the CIA*, 1978; Morton Halperin et al., *The Lawless State: The Crimes of the U.S. Intelligence Agencies*, 1976; Harry Howe Ransom, *The Intelligence Establishment*, 1970; John Prados, *Presidents' Secret Wars: CIA and Pentagon Covert Operations Since World War I*, 1986; Peer da Silva, *Sub Rosa: The CIA and the Uses of Intelligence*, 1978.

CENTRAL OFFICE FOR SOUTH VIETNAM. In 1964, North Vietnam established the Central Office for South Vietnam (COSVN), headquarters for their command and control liaison with the Vietcong.* Although nominally located in Tay Ninh Province, COSVN was actually a highly mobile command head-quarters, capable of relocating itself on a moment's notice, particularly when U.S. military forces operated nearby. COSVN was a small office of senior of-ficers and staff assistants, not a large bureaucratic complex. Throughout the war, U.S. military officials believed that if they could capture COSVN, they could deliver a logistical death blow to the enemy military effort. In 1970, General Creighton Abrams* speculated that the "successful destruction of COSVN head-quarters in a single blow would, I believe, have a very siginificant impact on enemy operations throughout South Vietnam."

In 1969, the desire to destroy the Central Office for South Vietnam became the driving force behind President Richard M. Nixon's* military policies in Cambodia. U.S. intelligence officials claimed to have located COSVN in the jungles of eastern Cambodia, and Nixon launched Operation Menu,* large-scale B-52 strikes, to destroy it. In 1970, much of the rationale for the combined U.S.-South Vietnam invasion of Cambodia was the desire to capture COSVN. Of course, they never located COSVN because they were searching for a huge, underground office complex that did not exist and never had existed. U.S. ob-session with capturing COSVN amused the North Vietnamese, confirming their belief that the Nixon administration simply did not understand the nature of the war.

REFERENCES: William Shawcross, *Sideshow: Kissinger, Nixon, and the Destruction of Cambodia*, 1979; Malcolm Caldwell and Tan Lek, *Cambodia in the Southeast Asia War*, 1973; Samuel Freeman, "Central Office for South Vietnam," in James S. Olson, ed., *Dictionary of the Vietnam War*, 1988; Jonathan Grant et al., *The Widening War in In-dochina*, 1971.

CHAPPAQUIDDICK. The accident on the Chappaquiddick bridge was one of the most controversial political events of the 1960s, wrecking Senator Edward Kennedy's* aspirations for the presidency. The incident occurred on the island resort of Martha's Vineyard in Massachusetts on July 18 or 19, 1969, around midnight. Senator Kennedy lost control of his 1967 Oldsmobile 88 and plunged off Dikes Bridge into Puocha Pond. He managed to escape the submerged ve-hicle, but his passenger, Mary Jo Kopechne, drowned.

Kennedy did not report the accident to the police but instead returned to the party the two had been attending and secured the assistance of a former U.S. attorney for the state of Massachusetts, Paul Mackham, and Mackham's cousin, Joseph Gargan. They allegedly returned to the scene of the accident, but belated attempts to rescue Kopechne failed. Kennedy reportedly swam the channel to the mainland, while his two companions returned to the party, leaving Kopechne in the water. Neither Kennedy nor the two men reported the accident to the police.

The wrecked car was spotted the following morning by two young boys searching for a place to fish and was thus reported to Edgartown police chief

Diminich Arena, who with the help of the fire department retrieved the vehicle. The vehicle was later identified as belonging to Senator Kennedy. Edgartown police launched a search for Kennedy, but around 8:30 A.M. Kennedy and his two assistants reported to Edgartown police headquarters. On July 25, 1969, Senator Edward Kennedy pleaded guilty to leaving the scene of an accident and was given a two-month suspended sentence and a one-year probation. The apparent miscarriage of justice gave rise to a widespread belief that a massive cover-up was taking place in Massachusetts.

The incident forever tarnished Edward Kennedy's political reputation. He had been partying with a single woman, and when his own driving caused the accident, he had apparently been more worried about his own political career than her life. Although Kennedy survived the incident in the state of Massachusetts and is now serving his sixth term in the U.S. Senate, his chances for national office were forever doomed. In 1972 and again in 1980 he made a run for the Democratic presidential nomination, but in each instance the legacy of Chappaquiddick undermined his campaign.

REFERENCE: Leo Dunmore, *Senatorial Privilege: The Chappaquiddick Cover-Up*, 1972.

Jerry Jay Inmon

CHÁVEZ, CÉSAR ESTRADA. César Estrada Chávez was born near Yuma, Arizona, March 31, 1927. He began working as a migrant farm laborer as a child and then spent the last years of World War II in the navy. In 1946, Chávez joined the National Agricultural Workers Union, and between 1952 and 1962, he worked for the Community Service Organization, the last two years as its general director. He resigned from the Community Service Organization because of its refusal to organize farmworkers. An ideological follower of the principles of nonviolence, Chávez relocated to Delano, California, in 1962 and established the National Farm Workers Association* (NFW). He gained national attention when the NFW joined with Filipino workers in their strike against Cochella Valley grape growers. He secured the support of a number of liberal politicians, including Senator Robert Kennedy* of New York. Although he encountered opposition from the International Brotherhood of Teamsters, which was also trying to organize farmworkers, Chávez was successful.

In 1966, the NFW merged with the Agricultural Workers Organizing Committee to form the United Farm Workers Organizing Committee (UFWOC), with Chávez as president. The UFWOC affiliated with the American Federation of Labor–Congress of Industrial Organizations in 1967 and launched a national boycott of all table grapes grown in California with nonunion labor. In 1969–1970, the boycott resulted in the signing of three-year labor contracts between the major growers and the union. During the 1970s, Chávez and the United Farm Workers tried, usually unsuccessfully, to organize farmworkers in Texas and engaged in severe jurisdictional disputes with the Teamsters. Chávez's critics, inside and outside the union, have charged him with being a terrible administrator and with advocating controversial psychological encounter groups and holistic medicine for his union members.

During the 1980s and early 1990s, Chávez became widely recognized as one of the twentieth century's most important civil rights advocates, doing for Mexican Americans* what Martin Luther King, Jr.,* had done for African Americans. He encouraged all Hispanics to take pride in their ancestral heritage and demand equality of economic opportunity in the United States. César Chávez died April 23, 1993.

REFERENCES: David Goodwin, *César Chávez*, 1991; Richard Griswold del Castillo, *César Chávez*, 1995; Joan London and Henry Anderson, *So Shall Ye Reap: The Story of César Chávez and the Farm Workers Movement*, 1970; *New York Times*, April 24, 1993.

CHESSMAN, CARYL. Caryl Chessman, nicknamed the "Red Light Bandit" by the press, was one of the most notorious criminals in United States history. In 1948 he was convicted in California of multiple acts of robbery, rape, and kidnapping. His method of criminal operation involved using a flashing red light on his automobile, pretending to be a law enforcement officer, to approach women in cars at night. He was sentenced to death for his crimes but soon became a cause célèbre among opponents of capital punishment around the world. While on death row at the San Quentin penitentiary, he also wrote a best-selling autobiography—*Cell 2455 Death Row*—whose royalties supplied him with the funds to mount an extended legal appeal. Chessman managed to avoid California's gas chamber for a record twelve years. He was finally executed on May 2, 1960.

REFERENCE: *New York Times*, May 3, 1960.

THE CHICAGO EIGHT. The term "Chicago Eight" refers to the trial of the decade in the 1960s. The youth rebellion, counterculture,* antiwar movement,* and black power* movement had all been powerful elements of the 1960s, and they all came together in a great conjunction in Chicago at the Democratic National Convention* in August 1968. Old-line pacifist groups like the Fellowship of Reconciliation* and the War Resisters League* came to Chicago to protest the Vietnam War* and the escalation of the conflict that had taken place during the Lyndon B. Johnson* administration. They were joined by such black power groups as the Black Panthers,* counterculture rebels in the Youth International Party,* or "yippies," radical organizations like the Students for a Democratic Society,* and a variety of other anti-Vietnam protest entities.

They gathered in Chicago and began protesting in the streets. Mayor Richard Daley* called out the Chicago police force to crush the demonstrations, and they did so with a vengeance. In front of a national television audience, what was later called a "police riot" took place as police waded into the demonstrators with tear gas and billy clubs. Police arrested the following leaders of the demonstrations and charged them with conspiracy to cross state lines in order to commit riot, obstruct justice, and give instructions in the construction and use of incendiary bombs: David Dellinger,* Rennard Davis, Thomas E. Hayden,* Abbott Hoffman,* Jerry Rubin,* Lee Weiner, John Froines, and Bobby Seale.*

The trial opened late in September 1969, and it soon turned into a media circus. While Judge Julius Hoffman presided in a most biased way against the defendants, defense attorneys tried to convert the trial into a hearing on the morality of the Vietnam War and the reality of racism in America. The defendants would not keep silent, hurling epithets at Judge Hoffman, unfurling Vietcong* flags, and shouting obscenities. Hoffman eventually slapped 175 charges of contempt on the defendants and their attorneys. Seale had to be gagged and chained to his seat before Hoffman declared a mistrial for him. The other seven defendants were acquitted on charges of conspiracy. The jury did, however, find Dellinger, Davis, Rubin, Hoffman, and Hayden guilty of inciting to riot. Over the next ten years, all of the convictions and contempt citations were overturned on appeal.

REFERENCE: Jason Epstein, *The Great Conspiracy Trial*, 1970.

CHICANO. During the late nineteenth century, the term "Chicano" was a pejorative reference employed by upper-class Mexicans to describe lower-class peasants and laborers. In the 1960s, however, Mexican-American* activists adopted the term as a reference of pride, a way of referring to Mexican Americans who enjoy a powerful sense of identity and who demand to be treated with equity and fairness by Anglo society.

REFERENCE: Matt S. Meier and Feliciano Rivera, *Dictionary of Mexican American History*, 1981.

CHILD, JULIA McWILLIAMS. Julia Child was born in 1912 and graduated from Smith College in 1938. She worked for the Office of Strategic Services during World War II and was assigned to Ceylon, where she became fascinated with the country's cuisine. When her husband was posted to Paris with the Foreign Service in 1948, Child accompanied him and attended the Cordon Bleu cooking school. In 1951, she founded her own cooking school—L'École des Trois Gourmandes. After ten successful years in Paris, Child wrote *Mastering the Art of French Cooking* and aimed it at the American market. She returned home in 1961 to live in Cambridge, Massachusetts. While promoting the book on Boston television, Child became a local hit and came to the attention of a producer of public television. In 1963, she began performing in *The French Chef* for public television. The show won an Emmy Award in 1966. By then, Julia Child was a television personality in her own right and the best-known chef in the United States. Since then she has only added to that reputation.

REFERENCE: Bill Stumpf, *Julia's Kitchen*, 1977.

CHIMEL V. CALIFORNIA. During the 1960s, the Supreme Court under the leadership of Chief Justice Earl Warren* continued its program of broadening

individual rights while narrowing those of federal, state, and government officials. In *Chimel v. California*, the court decided by a 6 to 2 vote to overturn its *United States v. Rabinowitz* decision of 1950, narrowing the constitutional boundaries of reasonable searches and seizures. In particular, the Court declared that law enforcement officials could conduct searches if acting during the process of arresting a suspect, but it limited the search to an area immediately surrounding the suspect—that is, an area in which the suspect could obtain a weapon or engage in the destruction of evidence. Just because a person was being arrested in his or her own home, the police could not search the entire house. Justice Potter Stewart wrote the majority opinion.
REFERENCE: 395 U.S. 752 (1969).

CHOMSKY, AVRAM NOAM. Avram Noam Chomsky, born December 7, 1928, in Philadelphia, is a famous American linguist and political activist. Chomsky graduated from the University of Pennsylvania in 1949 and then proceeded to earn his Ph.D. there in 1955. He then joined the faculty of the Massachusetts Institute of Technology (MIT). The father of what is known today as "transformational grammar," Chomsky's highly influential books—including *Syntactic Structures* (1957), *Aspects of the Theory of Syntax* (1965), and *Language and Mind* (1968)—pioneered the idea that language and universal grammar are innate, biologically determined human abilities.

Although Chomsky's contribution to modern linguistic theory is enormous, he is best remembered during the 1960s for his opposition to the Vietnam War.* He openly opposed the war as early as 1965, speaking widely on the northeastern campus circuit in 1966 and 1967, but he really made his mark on the antiwar movement* with the publication of his *American Power and the New Mandarins* in 1969. There he argued that the United States had become intoxicated with its own military and economic power, had assumed an ideology of superiority in world politics, and was destroying a society in the name of freedom. Although the causes of the war could be understood, he argued, they could not be justified. He accused American intellectuals of having become stooges of the business and government establishment. Finally, he criticized the media for generating propaganda and keeping the general population oblivious to the damages American military policies were doing to South Vietnam. Chomsky continues to teach at MIT. Most recently, he opposed U.S. policies in the Middle East and the Gulf War.
REFERENCES: *Who's Who in America, 1984–1985*, 1985; Noam Chomsky, *American Power and the New Mandarins*, 1969; Nancy Zaroulis and Gerald Sullivan, *Who Spoke Up? American Protest against the War in Vietnam, 1963–1974*, 1984.

Tracy Thompson

CHURCH, FRANK FORRESTER. Frank Church was born in Boise, Idaho, July 25, 1924. During World War II, he served as a military intelligence officer in China, India, and Burma, and in 1947 he graduated from Stanford University.

Church attended Harvard Law School for a year, but a bout with cancer brought him back west again, and in 1950 he graduated from the Stanford University Law School. Between 1950 and 1956, Church practiced law in Idaho and was active in Democratic politics, serving as chairman of the statewide Young Democrats organization. He won the party's nomination for the U.S. Senate in 1956 and went on to upset the Republican incumbent, Herman Welker. At thirty-two, Church was the youngest member of the Senate. He quickly earned a reputation as an outspoken liberal, and by supporting majority leader Lyndon B. Johnson* on civil rights* legislation, Church gained favor and was appointed to the prestigious Senate Foreign Relations Committee* in 1959. In 1960, he supported John F. Kennedy* for the presidential nomination, and in 1962 he won reelection.

After 1965, Senator Church became increasingly apprehensive about U.S. involvement in Southeast Asia. He warned against American support for repressive regimes such as that in Vietnam unless substantial progress was made toward reform. In 1965, he repeated this warning, contending that the rift in the communist world between the People's Republic of China and the Soviet Union had diminished the threat of "monolithic communism." In 1966, Church broke with the Johnson administration over Vietnam policy by calling for an end to the bombing. In 1970, he cosponsored the Cooper–Church Amendment* to prohibit American deployment of ground forces in Cambodia, setting off a six-month debate in the Senate. In 1972, in reaction to the Nixon administration's bombing of Hanoi and Haiphong and the mining of Haiphong Harbor, Church joined Senator Clifford Case of New Jersey in sponsoring a resolution seeking an end to all U.S. military activity in Southeast Asia. The proposal was considered the first step in the eventual adoption of the War Powers Resolution of 1973.

On the domestic front, Church chaired the Senate Select Committee on Intelligence, which investigated excesses and violations of law by the Central Intelligence Agency,* Federal Bureau of Investigation, and National Security Agency under the Nixon administration. In 1976, Church made a bid for the Democratic presidential nomination, but he lost to Governor Jimmy Carter of Georgia. In 1980, Church was defeated for reelection to the Senate. He continued to live in Washington, D.C., practicing international law until his death from cancer April 7, 1984.

REFERENCES: Mark Bill, *Frank Church, D.C., and Me*, 1995; *New York Times*, April 8, 1984.

Joseph M. Rowe, Jr.

THE CICERO MARCH (1966). In 1966, Martin Luther King, Jr.,* brought his civil rights movement* to the North, where the problem of de facto, rather than de jure, segregation kept white and black people separate in terms of housing, schools, and neighborhoods. He targeted Chicago, where 90 percent of black schoolchildren attended all-black schools, even though no formal laws or regulations mandated it. African-American children lived in neighborhoods where white people were never seen. Black public schools were overcrowded while white public schools had plenty of room. Nevertheless, the city of Chicago refused to bus children to achieve racial integration.

In 1966, King led a series of open housing marches as a way of protesting segregated neighborhoods. The reaction of whites to the marches was extraordinarily negative. Thousands of whites rallied to denounce King and demand that he leave their neighborhoods alone. The overt hostility surprised King. Even in Selma and Birmingham, Alabama, he had never encountered such vitriolic hatred. At a protest meeting in the Marquette Park neighborhoods of Chicago, King told white hecklers, "I think the people from Mississippi ought to come to Chicago to learn how to hate." In the Cicero area, several thousand National Guard troops had to be called out to protect a few hundred black protesters from 10,000 angry whites.

To end the trouble, Mayor Richard Daley* promised King that his administration would work to bring about integrated schools and open housing. King left Chicago, and Daley promptly forgot the promise. When he was reelected the next year by a 73 percent margin that included more than 80 percent of the black vote, Daley abandoned his pledge completely. But the Cicero march proved clearly that white racism was a national, not just a southern, problem.
REFERENCES: Alan B. Anderson and George W. Pickering, *Confronting the Color Line: The Broken Promise of the Civil Rights Movement in Chicago*, 1986; David Burner, *Making Peace with the Sixties*, 1996; David J. Garrow, *Bearing the Cross: Martin Luther King, Jr. and the Southern Christian Leadership Conference*, 1986; James R. Ralph, *Northern Protest: Martin Luther King, Jr., Chicago, and the Civil Rights Movement*, 1993.

CIVIL RIGHTS ACT OF 1960. During the 1950s, the Supreme Court's decision in *Brown v. Board of Education* (1954), desegregating the nation's public schools, and Martin Luther King, Jr.'s* bus boycott in Montgomery, Alabama, jump-started the civil rights movement* in the United States. In 1957, Congress passed a civil rights act that created the Civil Rights Commission to investigate reports of discrimination on the basis of race, religion, color, or national origin. It prohibited discrimination in voting rights as well as led to the establishment of the Civil Rights Division in the Department of Justice. A major shortcoming of the bill, however, was its lack of enforcement powers, so in 1960, at the request of President Dwight D. Eisenhower,* Congress passed another civil rights act. The Civil Rights Act of 1960 gave teeth to the Civil Rights Commission, made it a federal offense to obstruct federal court civil rights orders, and provided for federal marshals to monitor voting in areas with a history of discrimination.
REFERENCE: Hugh Davis Graham, *The Civil Rights Era: Origins and Development of a National Policy, 1960–1965*, 1990.

CIVIL RIGHTS ACT OF 1964. See **CIVIL RIGHTS MOVEMENT**.

CIVIL RIGHTS ACT OF 1965. See **VOTING RIGHTS ACT OF 1965**.

CIVIL RIGHTS ACT OF 1968. With passage of the Civil Rights Act of 1964 and the Voting Rights Act of 1965,* most vestiges of de jure discrimination, on the pages of the law books at least, were prohibited in the United States. But all of the legislation still had not done much to bring about integration, especially in areas of the North and West where segregated neighborhoods translated into completely segregated schools.

The problem was practice rather than legislation. Because banks, savings and loan institutions, and mortgage companies regularly practiced redlining—refusing to make loans to blacks to purchase homes in all-white neighborhoods—segregated housing was the rule in America. Many neighborhoods also had what they called "residential covenants"—pseudolegal agreements between neighborhood residents not to sell homes to blacks. Some city councils passed special zoning ordinances or complicated housing codes that made it cumbersome and difficult for black people to purchase homes in white neighborhoods. Renters had an equally difficult time because apartment owners in all-white complexes regularly refused to sign leases with minority families.

As part of its Great Society* program, the Johnson* administration wanted to bring about integrated housing in America by outlawing all of the practices working against desegregation. In order to get the measure through Congress, however, President Johnson had to agree to add to the bill an Anti-Riot Statute, nicknamed the "H. Rap Brown"* amendment, which increased the federal government's power to prosecute individuals for conspiracy to incite rioting and public disorder. With the support of Senator Everett Dirksen* of Illinois, who was the Republican minority leader in the Senate, Johnson pushed the Housing Act of 1968* and the Civil Rights Act of 1968 to address the problem. The Housing Act was designed to see to the construction of millions of new housing units in minority areas, while the Civil Rights Act struck down racially based residential covenants, attacked redlining, and prohibited property owners with more than four rental units from discriminating against prospective renters on the basis of race.

REFERENCES: David Burner, *Making Peace with the Sixties*, 1996; David J. Garrow, *Bearing the Cross: Martin Luther King, Jr. and the Southern Christian Leadership Conference*, 1986.

CIVIL RIGHTS MOVEMENT. The decade of the 1960s in the United States was the heyday of the civil rights movement. During the late 1940s and early 1950s, the Supreme Court had struck down several Jim Crow* institutions, especially segregated public school systems, and in 1960 Congress passed the Civil Rights Act* to strengthen the Civil Rights Commission and make attempts to enforce federal civil rights statutes a criminal offense.

The modern civil rights movement began on a commuter bus in Montgomery, Alabama. One day in 1955 Rosa Parks, tired after a long day of work, sat down on a city bus and refused to move to a back seat at the request of the driver. He forced her off the bus. The decision set off a chain reaction in which African Americans boycotted Montgomery city buses and pushed the system toward bankruptcy, demanding integration and more black bus drivers. The leader of the boycott, a young minister named Martin Luther King, Jr.,* rocketed to national prominence as the boycotts spread to other southern cities. Facing bankruptcy, the Montgomery transit system decided to integrate.

On February 1, 1960, African-American students from the Negro Agricultural and Technical College at Greensboro, North Carolina, entered several department stores and demanded service at lunch counters. When denied service because they were black, they refused to leave, and the "sit-in"* movement began. It quickly spread across the country; white and black students "sat in" in "white sections" of restaurants, theaters, bars, libraries, parks, beaches, and rest rooms, all in defiance of segregation statutes. Martin Luther King, Jr., became the unofficial leader of the movement, using nonviolent civil disobedience to startle whites into accepting social change.

Jailed in Atlanta for a department store sit-in in 1960, King was released after John F. Kennedy,* then the Democratic nominee for president, intervened with local authorities. The significance of the event was not lost on black people; they turned out in record numbers and helped to elect Kennedy.

In May 1961 the Congress of Racial Equality* (CORE) organized African-American and white "freedom riders"* to go into the South to see if interstate transportation facilities had been integrated; white mobs attacked the demonstrators, and federal troops had to be called in. The Southern Christian Leadership Conference* (SCLC) and the Student Nonviolent Coordinating Committee* (SNCC) sent thousands of freedom riders into the South until the Interstate Commerce Commission ruled that all terminals serving interstate carriers had to be integrated.

The pressure mounted in 1962 and 1963, especially after Martin Luther King, Jr., took his crusade to Birmingham, Alabama. Celebrating the centennial of the Emancipation Proclamation, his SCLC marched in favor of equal employment opportunities, integration of public facilities, and enforcement of court-ordered desegregation formulas. Birmingham police used tear gas and guard dogs against the demonstrators while millions of Americans watched on television.* When Medgar Evers,* director of the Mississippi National Association for the Advancement of Colored People (NAACP), was assassinated in June 1963, civil rights demonstrations erupted all over the South. Most Americans were convinced that African Americans had rarely been afforded the freedom and equality guaranteed by the Constitution. Sensitive to that problem and looking to the election of 1964,* when he would again need the African-American vote, President John Kennedy submitted a civil rights bill to Congress in 1963 calling for integration of all public facilities, even those privately owned, and the withholding of federal money from segregated institutions.

Southern opposition was fierce, but a string of events, tragic and ennobling, brought history and black demands together. In August 1963 nearly 250,000 people—led by the NAACP, SNCC, SCLC, American Jewish Congress, National Council of Churches, American Friends Service Committee, and the American Federation of Labor–Congress of Industrial Organizations (AFL–CIO)—gathered at the Lincoln Memorial to support the bill, and Martin Luther King, Jr., gave his famous "I Have a Dream" speech. One month later, when an African-American church in Birmingham was bombed on Sunday morning, and four children died, white sympathies were touched, and support for the civil rights bill grew stronger. Finally, in November 1963 John Kennedy was murdered in Dallas, Texas, and his successor, Lyndon Johnson,* pushed the civil rights bill as a legacy to the fallen leader, a sign of his own liberalism and a redemption of his home state. After a Senate cloture ended the filibuster in June 1964, the Civil Rights Act became law. It outlawed discrimination in voting, education, and public accommodations; established the Equal Employment Opportunity Commission; permitted the federal government to freeze funds to state and local agencies not complying with the law; and provided funds to the Department of Health, Education, and Welfare to speed desegregation of the schools.

The rhetoric over the Civil Rights Act of 1964, the pain and struggle to see it through Congress, and the rejoicing over its passage raised people's expectations. Some African Americans expected the act to make a difference right away, and when life did not change, they became frustrated. Some decided, as others had done when "massive resistance" began in the South, that more vigorous steps would have to be taken to reshape America.

The Civil Rights Act of 1964 did not put an end to segregation, but even had it done so, it had little to offer the black ghettos. As whites fled to the suburbs, businesses were relocating outside the city, making it more difficult for African Americans to find work. At the same time the whole American economy was shifting from a manufacturing to a service base; blue-collar jobs were steadily decreasing as white-collar ones became more plentiful. But white-collar jobs required educational and technical skills, and large numbers of underprivileged African Americans were unable to qualify. While earlier immigrants had used unskilled urban jobs as the bootstrap out of the ghettos, blacks no longer had those choices. They were trapped in a changing economy and a deteriorating physical environment, and their poverty became endemic and permanent, passing from one generation to the next. In 1970 more than one in three African-American families functioned below the poverty line, and the median black income was only about 60 percent that of whites. Unemployment was twice as high as for white workers, and joblessness for African-American teenagers reached more than 40 percent in some cities during the 1970s. A terribly poor African-American "underclass" emerged, made up of people who had never had jobs or lived in decent homes.

In the face of such debilitating economic problems, the end of formal segregation no longer took first place. For people worrying about how to pay their rent, utility, and food bills, whether or not their community was integrated was less important than how to support themselves. By the 1970s, African-American leaders turned their attention to poverty, de facto segregation, and institutional racism as the focus of their civil rights efforts.

Led by the NAACP, the African-American community set its sights on the end of de facto discrimination. The Civil Rights Act of 1968 had eliminated many forms of housing discrimination, but African-American leaders concluded that if school integration were to wait for integrated neighborhoods, it would probably never happen. They believed that busing children was the only way to overcome segregation in schools and second-class education for African-American children. To deal with black economic problems, CORE, National Urban League, SCLC, SNCC, and other African-American organizations demanded economic assistance and job training for educationally disadvantaged and low-income blacks and "affirmative action"* admissions, hirings, and promotions of African Americans by business, government, and universities. Congress passed the antipoverty program in 1965 to assist lower-class blacks and other poor people, and in the 1970s the Equal Employment Opportunity Commission* ordered government agencies, corporations, and universities to establish hiring, promotion, and admission policies favoring African Americans until the racial mix in American institutions, from the lowest service positions through the administrative hierarchy, reflected the racial composition of the whole society.

The African-American civil rights movement inspired similar efforts in the Hispanic and Native American communities. Before, the Hispanic civil rights movement had revolved around groups like the American GI Forum, the Unity Leagues, the Community Service Organization, and the League of United Latin American Citizens, and they had targeted de jure discrimination. Late in the 1950s, however, Mexican-American political activity became more intense. In 1958 the Mexican-American Political Association* (MAPA) was organized in California, as were the Political Association of Spanish-Speaking Organizations* (PASO) in Texas and the American Coordinating Council on Political Education (ACCPE) in Arizona. MAPA worked for only Mexican support, and the others for a coalition with white liberals, black activists, and labor unions, but all three tried to mobilize Mexican-American political power.

John Kennedy's campaign in 1960 worked through MAPA, PASO, and ACCPE to form Viva Kennedy* clubs, and in 1962 MAPA and PASO ran successful candidates in the Crystal City, Texas, elections. José Gutierrez* rose out of those elections and in 1970 formed La Raza Unida, a political party dedicated to community control of Mexican-American counties in south Texas. Corky Gonzalez* founded the Crusade for Justice* in 1965. Schooled in local politics and Denver antipoverty programs, Gonzalez demanded reform of the criminal justice system, an end to police brutality, and good housing, schools, and jobs for Mexican Americans. Culturally nationalistic, Gonzalez also sponsored Chicanismo, a pride in being Mexican American and in mestizo roots,

and a consciousness of ethnic origins that reflected an earlier Pachuco culture.
A host of Chicano writers and artists—including novelists Raymond Barrio and
Richard Vásquez, short story writer Daniel Garza, playwright Luis Valdez, and
painter Raul Espinoza—evoked the Chicano spirit, and Chicano studies programs swept through the schools of the Southwest in the 1970s and 1980s.

Reies Tijerina* was another Mexican-American activist of the 1960s and
1970s. After traveling widely in Spain and the United States, he formed the
Alianza Federal de Mercedes (Federal Alliance of Land Grants*) in 1963 and
demanded the return of land taken from *tejanos, californios,* and *nuevos mexicanos.* Militant and articulate, Tijerina was a charismatic leader who denounced
racism and called for ethnic solidarity. In 1966, claiming millions of acres in
New Mexico and urging secession, he "occupied" Kit Carson National Forest
and assaulted several forest rangers. On June 5, 1967, Tijerina and some of his
supporters raided the courthouse at Tierra Amarillo, New Mexico, shot two
deputies, released eleven Alianza members, and fled the town with several hostages. Sentenced to prison, Tijerina was paroled in 1971 on the condition that
he dissociate himself from the Alianza, and without his leadership the movement
died.

No Mexican-American leader rivaled César Chávez in influence. A counterpart in time and philosophy to Martin Luther King, Jr., he too believed in
nonviolence, but he was more committed to economic action than civil rights.
Born in 1927 in Yuma, Arizona, Chávez worked as a migrant laborer after his
parents lost their farm in a tax auction, but early in the 1950s, as a worker in
the Community Service Organization, he saw the potential of mass action. He
moved to Delano,* California, in 1962 and shortly thereafter organized the National Farm Workers (later the United Farm Workers). For two years he built
the union; then he struck the Delano grape growers, demanding better pay. The
growers refused, and Chávez turned the strike into a moral crusade, an appeal
to the conscience of America. The growers used violence, strikebreakers, and
anticommunist rhetoric; and Chávez appealed to white liberals like Robert Kennedy* and Hubert Humphrey,* labor unions like the AFL–CIO, black leaders
like Martin Luther King, Jr., and white students on college campuses. For five
years, Chávez led a national boycott of California grapes, fought the growers
as well as the Teamsters' Union, which tried to organize a rival union, and
finally, in 1970, succeeded in winning a long-term contract with the growers.
Chávez had been the most successful Chicano of all.

The Native American civil rights movement was unique in that the object of
the legislation was tribal governments. In 1968, Congress passed the Indian Civil
Rights Act* (ICRA), which authorized federal courts to intervene in intratribal
disputes and limited the power of tribes to regulate internal affairs. Many Native
Americans perceive it to be a threat to their self-determination* and have characterized it as an attempt by the federal government to preempt overall sovereignty.

Beginning in the early 1960s, Congress responded to numerous complaints by individual tribal members who contended that tribal officials were abusive and tyrannical. They appealed to Congress to pass legislation that would protect them from such mistreatment. Congressional hearings convened in 1962 to investigate their complaints of misconduct, and several congressmen concluded that individual Indians needed "some guaranteed form of civil rights against the actions of their own governments."

According to congressional records, the ICRA was passed to "ensure that the American Indian is afforded the broad Constitutional rights secured to other Americans . . . [in order to] protect individual Indians from arbitrary and unjust actions of tribal governments." Legislatively, it confers certain rights on all persons who are subject to the jurisdiction of a tribal government, and the act authorizes federal courts to enforce these rights. The purpose and scope of the Indian Civil Rights Act are similar to those of the U.S. Constitution; however, Congress did deny certain individual rights, which they felt were inherently dangerous to the survival of tribal self-government. Consequently, the ICRA guarantees almost all the fundamental rights enumerated in the U.S. Constitution, with several exceptions. Tribal governments are not subject to the Establishment Clause of the First Amendment, do not have to provide legal counsel (free of charge) to indigent defendants, and do not have to provide a trial by jury in civil cases or provide grand jury indictments in criminal cases.

REFERENCES: David Burner, *Making Peace with the Sixties*, 1996; Donald L. Burnett, "An Historical Analysis of the 1968 'Indian Civil Rights Act,' " *Harvard Journal of Legislation* 9 (1972); David J. Garrow, *Bearing the Cross: Martin Luther King, Jr. and the Southern Christian Leadership Conference*, 1986; Hugh Davis Graham, *The Civil Rights Era: Origins and Development of a National Policy, 1960–1965*, 1990; Hurst Hannum, *Autonomy, Self-Determination and Sovereignty: The Accommodation of Conflicting Rights*, 1990; Roxanne Dunbar Ortiz, *Indians of the Americas: Human Rights and Self-Determination*, 1984.

CLARK, TOM CAMPBELL. Tom Campbell Clark was born in Dallas, Texas, September 23, 1899. He graduated from the University of Texas in 1921, earned a law degree there in 1922, and then joined his father's Dallas law firm, which was well connected to the Democratic Party in Texas. From 1927 to 1932, he served as civil district attorney in Dallas. He then returned to private practice until 1937, when he was named special assistant in the Justice Department. Clark specialized in antitrust cases. During World War II, he focused on prosecuting fraudulent war claims against the federal government, which gained him the attention of Senator Harry Truman of Missouri, who was also actively investigating business fraud during the war. In 1943, Clark became assistant attorney general of the United States, and after the death of Franklin D. Roosevelt, President Harry Truman named Clark to his cabinet as attorney general. As attorney general, Clark was a zealous anticommunist. In 1949, Truman appointed him to the Supreme Court.

Clark began his career as a judicial conservative who gradually became more moderate during the evolution of the Supreme Court under Chief Justice Earl Warren.* Clark's most memorable written opinions involved banning school prayer in 1963 and upholding the constitutionality of the Civil Rights Act of 1964. To avoid any appearance of conflict of interest when President Lyndon B. Johnson* appointed his son, William Ramsey Clark, as attorney general, Clark resigned from the Court in 1967. He died June 13, 1977.

REFERENCES: Don Larrimer, *Bio-bibliography of Justice Tom Clark*, 1985; *New York Times*, June 14, 1977.

CLEAN AIR ACT OF 1970. During the late 1960s, the ecology movement gained momentum in the United States as consumers became increasingly concerned about the health risks associated with the quality of the air and water. In 1963, Congress had passed clean air legislation that provided $95 million in grants to assist local governments in developing programs to reduce air pollution. Air pollution was one of the leading environmental problems, and the primary culprit was auto emissions. Subsequent legislation (the Clean Air Act Amendments of 1965) authorized the federal government to set auto emission standards and launch research programs to reduce sulfur dioxide emissions. The Air Quality Act of 1967 greatly expanded federal control and research programs by appropriating more than $550 million. In March 1970, Senator Edmund Muskie, a Democrat from Maine, challenged the automobile industry to engage in what he called a "forced technology" and reduce harmful emissions by 90 percent. Under Muskie's sponsorship, Congress passed the Clean Air Act of 1970. It constituted a $1.1 billion program that required 1975 automobiles to reduce carbon monoxide and hydrocarbon emissions by 90 percent. Also, 1976 automobiles had to emit 90 percent less of the nitrogen oxides. The Environmental Protection Agency (EPA) was eventually assigned the responsibility of enforcing the legislation.

REFERENCE: James S. Olson, ed., *Dictionary of United States Economic History*, 1992.

CLEAVER, ELDRIDGE. Eldridge Cleaver was born in 1935 in Wabeseka, Arkansas. His family moved to Oakland, California, when Cleaver was still a child, and before he finished high school, he had been convicted of possessing marijuana. A series of convictions for drug offenses landed him prison terms at Soledad, Folsom, and San Quentin. During his confinement, Cleaver earned a high school diploma and converted to the Black Muslim* faith, becoming a dedicated follower of Malcolm X.* A gifted writer, Cleaver came out of prison in 1966 and began writing for publication. He was soon given a staff writer's position with *Ramparts*⃰ magazine.

Settling in Oakland, California, Cleaver became active in the Black Panther* Party and wrote his most famous book—*Soul on Ice* (1969)—part autobiography, part political philosophy. Raw in its expression of rage over American racism, *Soul on Ice* made Cleaver a household name in radical and student circles at the end of the 1960s. He fled the United States soon after the book's publication, escaping imprisonment for parole violations and trial on charges of assaulting Oakland police officers. Over the next decade, he lived in Cuba, the Soviet Union, and Algeria, evolving philosophically from a Marxist to a born-again Christian. He returned to the United States in 1977 and pleaded guilty to the assault charge. He was placed on probation and ordered to complete 2,000 hours of community service. In 1978, he wrote *Soul on Fire*.

In recent years, Cleaver's philosophical odyssey has continued. He became an ardent American patriot during the 1980s, regularly describing the United States as the ''freest and most democratic country in the world.'' He also appeared regularly at gatherings of fundamentalist religious groups. Cleaver died May 1, 1998.

REFERENCES: Eldridge Cleaver, *Soul on Ice*, 1969; Kathleen Rout, *Eldridge Cleaver*, 1991.

CLEOPATRA. The film *Cleopatra*, starring Elizabeth Taylor and Richard Burton, was released to extraordinary media hype in 1963. Taylor received an unprecedented salary of $1 million for the film, and the movie's entire cost—more than $30 million—was the most expensive, up to its time, in Hollywood history. The film also became a moral issue in early 1960s America. Debbie Reynolds, a young actress whose film *Tammy and the Bachelor* (1957) had made her America's sweetheart, married Eddie Fisher. Elizabeth Taylor had been married to producer Mike Todd until his death in a plane crash. While comforting her in her grief, Fisher fell in love with Taylor, and she with him. He divorced Debbie Reynolds and married Taylor. Then, on the set of *Cleopatra*, Taylor fell in love with costar Richard Burton and divorced Fisher. For many Americans, the whole episode was a tawdry example of Hollywood excess. The film bombed at the box office, earning its reputation as one of Hollywood's greatest disasters.

REFERENCES: Donald Spoto, *A Passion for Life*, 1995; Jerry Vermilye, *The Films of Elizabeth Taylor*, 1989.

CLERGY AND LAITY CONCERNED ABOUT VIETNAM. Clergy and Laity Concerned about Vietnam (CLCV) was founded in 1965 by an interdenominational group of religious leaders including Rev. John C. Bennett and Father Daniel Berrigan.* Early cochairs included Father Berrigan, Rabbi Abraham Heschel,* and Dr. Martin Luther King, Jr.* CLCV followed a moderate antiwar* course, advocating a negotiated settlement and holding teach-ins, fasts, vigils, and orderly antiwar activities. It sponsored a 2,000-member demonstration at the White House in January 1967 and a February Fast for Peace with over 1 million reportedly participating. Although CLCV participated in events with more radical antiwar groups, it consistently resisted radical activities such as draft* card burning and violent protest.

Late in 1966 CLCV commissioned a study entitled *In the Name of America*, indicting American involvement in Vietnam. It was published just before the 1968 Tet Offensive.* Drawing heavily on press reports and government documents, it argued that American involvement in Vietnam violated international law and that the United States and its allies were committing crimes against humanity. It focused on issues including uses and effects of napalm,* gas, and defoliants*; search and destroy* operations; treatment of prisoners; forced relocation and pacification programs; and the impact of artillery, aerial, and naval bombing.*

CLCV participated in the umbrella National Mobilization Committee protesting at the 1968 Democratic National Convention* in Chicago. Like other antiwar and peace organizations, CLCV was under surveillance and subject to infiltration by government intelligence and police agencies, including the Central Intelligence Agency's* Operation CHAOS* in 1969, which violated the CIA charter prohibiting domestic operations. Reflecting its expanding focus from Vietnam to U.S. military policies in general, CLCV changed its name in 1974 to Clergy and Laity Concerned. In the 1980s, the organization protested high schools' allowing armed forces recruiters and Reserve Officers' Training Corps (ROTC) programs on campus without giving equal time to peace organizations; opposed the Nestle Corporation's marketing of infant formula in Third World countries; and called for corporate divestment in South Africa.

REFERENCES: Nancy Zaroulis and Gerald Sullivan, *Who Spoke Up? American Protest against the War in Vietnam, 1963–1975*, 1984; Danile L. Migliore, "The Crisis of Faith in the Aftermath of Vietnam," *The Christian Century* 90 (June 13, 1973), 672–77; January 23, 1980; March 24, 1982.

Samuel Freeman

CLIFFORD, CLARK McADAMS. Clark Clifford was born at Fort Scott, Kansas, December 25, 1906. He attended Washington University in St. Louis and received his law degree there in 1928. Clifford practiced law in St. Louis until World War II, when he became an assistant to Harry S Truman's naval aide. In 1946 Clifford was named naval aide to the president. He resigned from the navy in June 1946 and joined Truman's staff as special counsel. During the next four years he became one of Truman's most trusted aides, playing key roles in the development of the Central Intelligence Agency* (CIA), the Department of Defense, the Truman Doctrine, and U.S. policy toward Israel. Clifford resigned and returned to private law practice in 1950, although he remained in Washington, D.C., as a prominent consultant. In 1960 he helped plan John F. Kennedy's* campaign strategy, and when Kennedy was elected president, Clifford headed the transition team. After the election, Kennedy named Clifford to the Foreign Intelligence Advisory Board to oversee CIA operations, and in 1963 Clifford broke into Lyndon B. Johnson's* inner circle. He planned Johnson's 1964 election campaign, and after the election Clifford advised the president on Vietnam, making frequent fact-finding trips to Southeast Asia and numbering himself among the "hawks."*

When Secretary of Defense Robert S. McNamara* resigned in 1968, Johnson persuaded Clifford to accept the cabinet post. He became the president's chief spokesman and defender on Vietnam policy. But after sounding out the generals on the future prospects in Vietnam, Clifford was dismayed that they had no timetable for completing the struggle. They just wanted more money, more men, and more weapons. With that sad prognosis, Clifford persuaded Johnson to put a lid on manpower allocations, limit bombing raids, and start peace negotiations.

In other foreign policy problems, such as the USS *Pueblo** incident, Clifford urged a cautious and restrained response. He assumed that China, not Russia, posed the major threat to U.S. interests in the future. He believed that U.S.– Soviet relations would be normalized, given time, through detente. In January 1969, the Nixon administration took office, and Clifford was replaced as secretary of defense by Melvin Laird* of Wisconsin. Back in private life, Clifford became increasingly critical of the Nixon administration's policy in Vietnam. In 1970, he branded the invasion of Cambodia as "reckless and foolhardy" and said that Nixon's policy of Vietnamization* was "a formula for perpetual war." He advocated an accelerated withdrawal from Vietnam in order to end the American role in ground fighting no later than December 31, 1970.

During the 1970s and 1980s, Clifford advised President Jimmy Carter and other Democratic politicians and practiced law at Clifford & Warnke in Washington, D.C. His reputation became somewhat tarnished in the early 1990s when he was accused of being involved in the scandals associated with the Bank of Credit and Commerce International. Clifford steadfastly maintained his innocence. He died on October 10, 1998.

REFERENCE: Clark M. Clifford, *Counsel to the President*, 1992.

Joseph M. Rowe, Jr.

CLINE, PATSY. Patsy Cline was the most popular female country and western vocalist of the 1960s. She was born Virginia Petterson Hensley. Her first big hit, "I Fall to Pieces," was released in 1961, and she followed it with another huge hit, "Crazy," which had been written by Willie Nelson. Patsy Cline died in an airplane crash in 1963.

REFERENCE: Margaret Jones, *Patsy*, 1994.

CLUB OF ROME. In April 1968, a group of thirty scientists, educators, economists, humanists, industrialists, and national and international civil servants gathered in the Italian capital to consider the future of the world economy. Out of their meeting emerged the Club of Rome, a group committed to keeping the world informed about the state of the global economy and environment. Between 1969 and 1972, the Club of Rome conducted what it called the Project on the Predicament of Mankind. Using computer models and assuming no change in population growth rates, the members of the Club of Rome predicted an ecological and economic disaster in the early decades of the twenty-first century. They warned that exponential population growth combined with continued industrialization would eventually send the world economy into a tailspin and lead to mass starvation and global suffering. The only answer, they argued, was the

establishment of limits to world growth. During the late 1960s and early 1970s, when the environmental movement* in the United States was especially strong, the apocalyptic predictions of the Club of Rome found a sympathetic audience.
REFERENCE: James S. Olson, ed., *Dictionary of United States Economic History*, 1992.

COFFIN, WILLIAM SLOAN, JR. William Sloan Coffin was born in New York City on June 1, 1924. After serving in the army during World War II, he worked for the Central Intelligence Agency* and then studied at Yale and Union Theological Seminary. He was ordained a Presbyterian minister in 1956 and in 1958 became chaplain at Yale. A political activist committed to civil rights* and antipoverty causes, Coffin was an early opponent of the Vietnam War.* He traveled widely around the country calling for draft* resistance and serving as an officer of the National Emergency Committee of Clergy Concerned About Vietnam. In 1968 Coffin was indicted and convicted for conspiring to assist draft resisters, but the convictions were eventually overturned. He left Yale in 1975 to pursue new interests in lecturing and writing. His books include *One to Every Man: A Memoir* (1977), *The Courage to Love* (1982), *Living the Truth in a World of Illusion* (1985), and *A Passion for the Possible: A Message to U.S. Churches* (1993).
REFERENCES: William Sloan Coffin, *One to Every Man: A Memoir*, 1977; Thomas Powers, *Vietnam, The War at Home*, 1984; Nancy Zaroulis and Gerald Sullivan, *Who Spoke Up? American Protest Against the War in Vietnam, 1963–1975*, 1984.

COLBY, WILLIAM EGAN. William Colby was born in St. Paul, Minnesota, on January 4, 1920. A brilliant young man, he entered Princeton University when he was sixteen and graduated in 1940. During World War II, he completed the U.S. Army's officer candidate school and was assigned to the fledgling Office of Strategic Services (OSS), an intelligence-gathering agency and fore-runner of the Central Intelligence Agency* (CIA). Covertly inserted into Nazi-occupied France, he fought with the French resistance. After the war, Colby received a law degree from Columbia University and went to work for the CIA. Nine years later, he was CIA station chief in South Vietnam. He returned to CIA headquarters in Washington, D.C., in 1962 to head up its Far East division and direct the operations of Air America,* a CIA subsidiary ferrying supplies and personnel to anti-Communist groups in Laos and Cambodia.

In 1968, Colby was reassigned to South Vietnam as deputy to General William Westmoreland.* His primary responsibility was direction of the Phoenix* program, a U.S.-sponsored initiative to destroy the Vietcong* infrastructure. Because the Phoenix program frequently involved assassinations of Vietcong leaders and sympathizers, it engulfed Colby in considerable controversy after the end of the war. In 1973, President Richard Nixon* named Colby head of the Central Intelligence Agency. Colby retired in 1976 and died in a canoeing accident in 1996.

REFERENCE: William Colby and Peter Forbath, *Honorable Men: My Life in the CIA*, 1978.

COLD WAR. The term "Cold War" has been used for a half century to describe the global struggle for influence between the United States and the Soviet Union and the People's Republic of China after World War II. They represented an ideological battleground between capitalism and communism, and by 1946 each side had concluded that the other was bent on its annihilation. During the 1940s, the Cold War included the Truman Doctrine of 1946, the Marshall Plan of 1947, the containment* policy, the Berlin Airlift of 1948, and the fall of China in 1949. During the 1950s, the Cold War continued with the Korean War, the Vietnamese intervention of 1954, the Suez crisis of 1956, the Lebanon intervention of 1958, and the beginnings of the Berlin crisis* in 1958.

The Cold War reached its peak in the early 1960s. President John F. Kennedy* preached a rhetoric of toughness, competition, and resolve, and when the Soviet Union decided to introduce interregional ballistic missiles into Cuba in 1962, the world came to the brink of nuclear disaster. The Cold War could have become the global meltdown. Both sides stepped back from the brink and resolved the crisis, but the event scared some sense into world leaders. To enhance communications between the United States and the Soviet Union, Kennedy and Soviet premier Nikita Khrushchev* installed the "hot line" in 1963, linking the White House and the Kremlin with a direct telephone line. Later in the year, the two countries signed the Nuclear Test Ban Treaty,* outlawing the atmospheric testing of nuclear weapons. Many historians of the Cold War, therefore, look to 1963 as the year in which detente between the two international rivals began.

REFERENCE: John Newhouse, *War and Peace in the Nuclear Age*, 1989.

COLTRANE, JOHN. John Coltrane was born September 23, 1926, in Hamlet, North Carolina. A gifted jazz saxophonist—tenor as well as soprano—he managed to bring jazz to a mass audience with his 1964 album *A Love Supreme*. Schooled by the likes of Dizzie Gillespie, Miles Davis, and Thelonius Monk, Coltrane introduced himself to larger audiences in 1959 with the album *Giant Steps*. In 1960, he brought out *My Favorite Thing*, a brilliant melodic departure from traditional jazz chord and harmonic rhythms. *A Love Supreme* in 1964 was his most brilliant work—melodic, hymnic, and mystical. Coltrane died July 17, 1967, at the age of forty-one.

REFERENCE: *New York Times*, July 18, 1967.

COLUMBIA UNIVERSITY DEMONSTRATIONS. During the last week of April 1968, a demonstration erupted at Columbia University that brought together many elements of the major protest and reform movements of the 1960s—the civil rights* movement, the black power* movement, the antiwar* movement, and the youth rebellion—and symbolized all that was good and bad about the era. The demonstration attracted worldwide media attention, exactly what the student protestors had hoped to achieve. Between 700 and 1,000 members of the Students for a Democratic Society* (SDS) and the Students Afro-American Society (SAS) seized and occupied five buildings on campus, including Low Library, which housed the offices of university president Grayson Kirk. The students demanded, among other things, that Columbia University stop construction of a gymnasium at Morningside Park, located near the campus and bordered by the African-American community in Harlem, and cut all ties with the Institute for Defense Analysis (IDA), a Department of Defense-sponsored consortium of major universities that helped the Pentagon analyze national security issues. By being so closely associated with the IDA, the university was guilty, at least in the minds of the student demonstrators, of complicity in the Vietnam War* and in other misguided U.S. foreign policy initiatives around the world, including Central Intelligence Agency* covert operations and the widespread deployment and threatened use of strategic nuclear weapons.

The confrontation began on April 23, 1968, at the sundial, a gathering place at Columbia for students. Mark Rudd,* head of the university's SDS chapter, staged the rally. Highly critical of the Vietnam War* and other U.S. foreign policies, SDS had already called for the severing of university ties with the Institute for Defense Analysis. After failing to gain entrance to the president's office in Low Library, the demonstrators moved on to Morningside Park, which had become a point of bitterly intense contention between the university and the African-American community in surrounding Harlem. The university's decison to construct a gymnasium there, which would be off-limits to community members, enraged black activists. After a confrontation with police in Morningside Park, Rudd led a group of students back to Hamilton Hall, where they staged a sit-in,* took Henry Coleman, acting dean of Columbia College, hostage, and issued their demands, which included amnesty from criminal prosecution and university disciplinary action. Coleman was not harmed and was later released.

The next day, SAS leaders asked Rudd to leave Hamilton Hall so that black students could issue demands of their own and attract media attention for their black power concerns. Rudd and the SDS agreed and then occupied Low Library. Several other halls—Fayerweather, Avery, and Mathematics—were soon occupied as well. When negotiations failed to end the crisis, New York City riot police were ordered in. At 1:30 a.m. on April 30, more than 1,000 police cleared Fayerweather, Avery, and Mathematics halls and Low Library. SAS students had already peacefully left Hamilton Hall. When students resisted arrest, the police used force, which led to charges of police brutality. The police successfully removed the students from the buildings.

But the event was not over. Mark Rudd and SDS planned and implemented a university-wide strike early in May, and on May 21 Rudd and 350 students reoccupied Hamilton Hall, this time to protest university disciplinary actions taken against the original demonstrators. Rudd demanded amnesty for himself and all other students. Again the policed moved in, but this time, in the process of removing the demonstrating students, they also attacked dozens of innocent bystanders. A subsequent investigating commission led by Harvard law professor Archibald Cox charged that they employed "brutality for which a layman can see no justification unless it be that the way to restore order in a riot is to terrorize civilians."

REFERENCES: Jerry L. Avorn, *Up Against the Ivy Wall: A History of the Columbia Crisis*, 1968; Mike Dennis, "Columbia University Demonstrations," in James S. Olson, ed., *Dictionary of the Vietnam War*, 1988; *New York Times*, April 24–30 and May 1–31, 1968.

COMBAT! Combat! was a popular television war drama of the 1960s. Starring Vic Morrow as Sergeant Chip Saunders and Rick Jason as Lieutenant Gil Hanley, *Combat!* was first broadcast by ABC on October 2, 1962. The program was set in Europe in 1944 and 1945, with a U.S. Army platoon fighting its way across the continent after D-Day. During 1964–1965 *Combat!* was in the top ten of the Nielsen ratings. It soon, however, fell victim to the increasing antiwar* climate in the United States. Although its ratings slipped some in 1966 and 1967, the viewing public was still tuning into the show in substantial numbers. ABC, however, abruptly canceled the show. The last episode of *Combat!* was broadcast on August 29, 1967. Several of the series' stars, including Vic Morrow, would later attribute its cancellation to the growing criticism of the war in Vietnam.

REFERENCE: Tim Brooks and Earle Marsh, *The Complete Directory to Prime Time Network and Cable TV Shows*, 1995.

COMMISSION ON CIVIL DISORDER. See KERNER REPORT.

COMMISSION ON THE RIGHTS, LIBERTIES, AND RESPONSIBILITIES OF THE AMERICAN INDIAN.

In the 1950s, federal Indian policy, which was committed to termination* and relocation, inspired bitter opposition from American Indian tribes. The termination and relocation policies were simply the most recent attempt by assimilationists to integrate Indians into the larger society. Fearing the loss of their culture and identity, most Indians protested the two policies and demanded self-determination.* In March 1957, when the controversy over termination was at its peak, the Fund for the Republic, a progressive philanthropic organization, decided to establish the Commission on the Rights, Liberties, and Responsibilities of the American Indian to examine the controversy and make recommendations.

Composed of Indian and non-Indian historians, anthropologists, and government officials, the commission spent nine years studying the plight of American Indians before issuing its final report in 1966. Instead of shedding new light on the challenges facing American Indians, the commission's report proved once again the cultural and political impasse that had developed in the United States over Indian rights. The report paid lip service to the idea of self-determination by insisting that Indian cultural pride should be preserved and that programs should be not imposed on them by outside authorities without their consent. But at the same time, the report employed typical assimilationist rhetoric, calling on Indian people to become "self-respecting and useful American citizen[s]" and to "participate in modern civilization," a practice certain to bring about the loss of their cultural heritage.

REFERENCE: William A Brophy and Sophie D. Aberle, *The Indian: America's Unfinished Business: Report on the Rights, Liberties, and Responsibilities of the American Indian*, 1966.

COMMONER, BARRY. Barry Commoner was born in Brooklyn, New York, in 1917. He received his bachelor's degree from Columbia University in 1937 and an M.A. and Ph.D. from Harvard, where he majored in biology. Commoner began a distinguished career in ecology, which eventually brought him a professorship at Washington University in St. Louis. During the 1960s, he founded the St. Louis Committee for Environmental Information and became a national scientific figure because of his books *Science and Survival* and *The Closing Circle*. The 1960s saw the beginnings of the modern environmental movement,* and Commoner became one of its leading gurus. He warned America about the unknown, long-range consequences of technology and the gradual destruction of the ecosphere through environmental pollution. Although the environmental movement declined in significance in the 1970s and 1980s, at least as a prominent political issue, Commoner maintained his crusade for a cleaner, simpler earth. In 1980 Commoner conducted a small-scale, independent run for the presidency, arguing that the future economic and social well-being of America depended on protecting the environment today.

Throughout the 1980s and early 1990s, Barry Commoner maintained his profile as one of the country's most visible and vocal environmentalists. Included in his recent publications is *Making Peace with the Planet* (1992).

REFERENCE: Barry Commoner, *Making Peace with the Planet*, 1992.

CON THIEN, BATTLE OF (1967–68). During the peak years of the Vietnam War,* in 1967–1968, Americans repeatedly heard the term "Hill of Angels," or Con Thien. Known also as the "Hill of Angels," Con Thien actually consisted of three hills, roughly 475 feet in height, just south of the Demilitarized Zone* (DMZ) in the eastern reaches of Quang Ngai Province. The hills sat astride a primary infiltration route by which the North Vietnamese* Army ferried troops, weapons, and supplies into South Vietnam. U.S. military planners made it a priority to interdict those troops and supply movements. To do so, General William Westmoreland* deployed the Third Marine Division to Con Thien. The marines soon found themselves in an unenviable position. Trained as assault troops, they were now under siege, defending fixed positions and frequently having to dig in against North Vietnamese artillery, which regularly shelled them from mountains in the DMZ.

In preparation for the Tet Offensive* of 1968, North Vietnamese General Vo Nguyen Giap* decided to use Con Thien to trick Westmoreland into thinking that North Vietnam was planning a huge conventional offensive south of the DMZ. Giap instigated a series of border battles in 1967 to distract American and Army of the Republic of Vietnam (ARVN) attention away from the most populated areas. These border clashes occurred at Con Thien, in the Central Highlands of the Cambodian-Laotian-South Vietnamese border, and in the rubber plantations near the Cambodian border in III Corps.

The artillery barrage against Con Thien intensified early in September 1967. The American media portrayed Con Thien as another Dien Bien Phu, but Westmoreland initiated Operation Neutralize to relieve the marines there. B-52s, naval bombardment, and army artillery pulverized the North Vietnamese positions around Con Thien, and by early October the North Vietnamese army abandoned the fight. Westmoreland claimed victory, citing more than 2,000 enemy dead, but Giap had succeeded in distracting U.S. miliary planners from his real objective: infiltrating tens of thousands of Vietcong* troops into South Vietnamese cities to carry out the Tet Offensive.

REFERENCES: Shelby L. Stanton, *The Rise and Fall of an American Army: U.S. Ground Troops in Vietnam, 1965–1973*, 1985; Wiliam M. Momyer, *Airpower in Three Wars*, 1978.

CONGLOMERATE. The term ''conglomerate'' has been used to describe highly diversified corporations that do business in several completely unrelated markets. The wave of conglomerate mergers began in the 1950s and accelerated in the 1960s; only 10 percent of the Fortune 500 companies are conglomerates, however. Management has usually decided to diversify for several reasons. One of the most important is simply a defensive move. Companies in rapidly changing industries have diversified in order to guarantee their futures. When new abortion laws and lifestyle changes dramatically reduced the number of births in the United States, for example, the Gerber Company went into the life insurance business in addition to its baby food products. A second strategy has been finding more profitable outlets for corporate funds. Borden Company, worried about the future of milk products sales, has diversified into chemicals, cosmetics, and fertilizers. In other situations, companies have acquired unrelated operations simply because some companies have been undervalued; by combining the book value of the two companies, net increases in profits and assets can be spectacular. Generally, the federal government has not taken antitrust action against conglomerates.

REFERENCES: Mansfield G. Blackford and K. Austin Kerr, *Business Enterprise in American History*, 1986; James S. Olson, ed., *Dictionary of United States Economic History*, 1992.

CONGRESS OF RACIAL EQUALITY. James Farmer* established the Congress of Racial Equality (CORE) in Chicago in 1942 and described its mission as a campaign to end the segregation of public facilities in America. CORE first used the tactic of sit-ins* to bring about the desegregation of restaurants in Chicago, and CORE chapters soon appeared in other major cities of the Midwest and Northeast. By the late 1950s, CORE was advocating, as were Martin Luther King, Jr.,* and his Southern Christian Leadership Conference,* the use of mass protest and passive resistance to achieve its goals.

CORE came to national attention in 1960, when it sponsored the famous sit-ins at Woolworth's lunch counters in Greensboro, North Carolina. Black students from North Carolina A&T College occupied restaurant seats and booths and refused to leave until they were served. From Greensboro, CORE went on to stage similar sit-ins throughout the South. Success in desegregating many southern restaurants gave the Congress of Racial Equality a national profile. Then, in 1961, CORE's status among civil rights activists increased even more when it sponsored the famous ''freedom rides''* to desegregate public transportation facilities in the South. Jesse Jackson* once said of CORE: ''It was the very soul of the civil rights movement.''

In 1966, however, the Congress of Racial Equality began to change. James Farmer stepped down and turned the reins of leadership over to Floyd McKissick.* At the time, the black power* movement was rising to ascendance in the civil rights movement,* and McKissick transformed CORE. He deemphasized CORE's history of interracial membership and worked to change it into an all-black organization. He also abandoned the rhetoric of nonviolent civil disobedience. In 1968, McKissick stepped down, and Roy Innis* assumed the presidency of CORE. At the time, CORE had chapters in thirty-three cities and a membership of more than 70,000 people. From that point on, however, its membership steadily declined, and chapter offices began closing. By the 1980s, CORE was barely functional.

REFERENCE: August Meier and Elliott Rudwick, *CORE: A Study in the Civil Rights Movement, 1942–1968*, 1975.

CONSERVATIVE PARTY. During the late 1950s and early 1960s, conservative Republicans in New York became increasingly concerned about the liberal political philosophy of the state's Republican leaders. Governor Nelson Rockefeller,* Senator Jacob Javits,* and Mayor John Lindsay* of New York were as liberal in their political philosophies as any liberal Democrat. To counter their influence, people like J. Daniel Mahoney, William Rickenbacker, and Frank Meyer formed the Conservative Party in New York City in 1962. They promoted local control of public schools, balanced federal and state budgets, cuts in foreign aid, a strong national defense, enactment of right-to-work laws, and strict anticommunism. The Conservative Party's constituency in New York consisted primarily of middle-class urban Democrats, usually Roman Catholics, and upstate Protestants. Their greatest success came in 1970, when James Buckley won a seat in the U.S. Senate.

REFERENCE: J. Daniel Mahoney, *Action Speaks Louder—The Story of the New York Conservative Party*, 1967.

CONSUMER FEDERATION OF AMERICA. The Consumer Federation of America is an omnibus group of more than 200 consumer organizations. It was founded in 1967 with the mission of lobbying Congress and state legislatures for consumer protection legislation. It also has research and public affairs divisions to distribute information about consumer issues. In addition, the Consumer Federation of America campaigns for the establishment of a cabinet-level federal consumer protection agency.

REFERENCE: James S. Olson, ed., *Dictionary of United States Economic History,* 1992.

CONTAINMENT POLICY. First pronounced by George Kennan in a 1947 article in *Foreign Affairs*, "containment" was the most important postwar American foreign policy. At first it was designed to keep Soviet expansionism under control, preferably behind its 1945 military boundaries. In the beginning, containment was nonmilitary, focusing on economic and technical assistance, and it was embodied in such programs as the Marshall Plan in 1947 and 1948 to rebuild the European economies and the Truman Doctrine to provide the funds Greece and Turkey needed to fight communist guerrillas. As the Cold War* escalated in the late 1940s, however, containment took on new global, military dimensions. After the fall of China in 1949, it came to imply the encirclement of the People's Republic of China and the Soviet Union with a network of military alliances: the North Atlantic Treaty Organization, the Baghdad Pact, the Southeast Asia Treaty Organization, and the enormous military buildup of the 1950s and 1960s. When the North Koreans invaded South Korea in 1950, the United States intervened in the conflict in the name of containment. Containment reached its peak during the Eisenhower* years and the tenure of Secretary of State John Foster Dulles (1953 to 1959).

When the French were expelled from Indochina after the Battle of Dien Bien Phu in 1954, the United States began increasing its commitment to prevent a communist takeover. American policymakers were applying the containment doctrine to Vietnam, assuming that Soviet and Chinese aggression was behind the North Vietnamese crusade to reunite the country. The domino theory* and the containment policy fitted nicely together in the 1950s and early 1960s. Not until the mid-1960s, however, when American policymakers began to see that communism was not a single, monolithic movement orchestrated from Moscow, did the application of containment to Vietnam begin to seem counterproductive. By the late 1960s and early 1970s, American policymakers accepted the importance of colonialism and nationalism in the history of the anti-French and anti-American movements in Vietnam. By that time as well, American policymakers realized that communism was a polycentric movement requiring creative, individual responses.

REFERENCES: John L. Gaddis, ''Containment: A Reassessment,'' *Foreign Affairs* 55 (July 1977), 873–87; Alexander L. George and Richard Smoke, *Deterrence in American Foreign Policy*, 1974; Douglas S. Blaufarb, *The Counterinsurgency Era: U.S. Doctrine and Performance, 1950 to the Present*, 1977.

COOPER, CHESTER. Chester Cooper was born January 13, 1917, in Boston. He received his education at MIT, New York University, and Columbia, and he took his Ph.D. at American University. Between 1945 and 1952, Cooper worked for the Central Intelligence Agency,* specializing in Asian affairs. In 1952, he was appointed to the National Security Council, eventually becoming deputy director of intelligence. In 1963, McGeorge Bundy* added Cooper to his White House national security staff, and Cooper found himself on the ground floor of Vietnam policymaking. He quickly became suspicious of the South Vietnamese regime and the feasibility of saving it from Vietcong* and North Vietnamese attack. He urged Bundy to seek a political and diplomatic solution and to make sure that the United States was not perceived as a new colonial power in Indochina. When Richard M. Nixon and the Republicans won the White House in the election of 1968,* Cooper returned to private life.

He spent a year writing *The Lost Crusade* (1970), a critique of U.S. Vietnam policy. He opposed the Cambodian invasion of 1970 because it widened the war and made it impossible to negotiate a genuine peace settlement in Paris. One of the first to recognize the plight of Amerasian children, Cooper asked the United States in 1973 to offer vigorous support for UNICEF's program to care for them. He also continued to write. His book *Growth in America* was published in 1976, and *Science for Public Policy* appeared in 1987.

REFERENCES: *Contemporary Authors*, vols. 29–32, 1978; Chester L. Cooper, *The Lost Crusade: America in Vietnam*, 1970; Samuel Freeman, ''Chester Cooper,'' in James S. Olson, ed., *Dictionary of the Vietnam War*, 1988.

COOPER, KENNETH. See AEROBICS.

CORNELL UNIVERSITY (1969). In 1969, Cornell University was the scene of a unique episode in the history of the black power* movement. Racial tensions had been growing on the campus, especially after a black female student was expelled for refusing to lower the volume of the soul music* she played in her dormitory room, and a Jesuit professor was accused of being a racist. A group of black students occupied the professor's office and then held his department chair and two secretaries hostage. When the incident ended, Cornell University president James Perkins refused to prosecute them, arguing that they were just ''trying to come to grips with the agonies of our society.''

Perkins' lack of will encouraged the militants, who then demanded immediate implementation of a black studies program at Cornell. When the university agreed to launch the program the next year, but not immediately, militant black students invaded Perkins' office, destroyed books in the library, and demanded the establishment of an autonomous, degree-granting college at Cornell. They physically attacked Perkins during a seminar on South African apartheid.

On April 18, 1969, some white students placed a burning cross on the lawn of a black female sorority. In response, black militants invaded and seized control of the Cornell student union. A number of white fraternity students tried to recapture the building from the blacks. Automatic weapons were smuggled to the black students, and the Cornell administration capitulated, agreeing to establish the black studies program and place it under the control of the militant students. When the black students exited the student union after the agreement, they smiled and raised their weapons in triumph, with a legion of news photographers taking their pictures for broadcast and publication.

REFERENCES: David Burner, *Making Peace with the Sixties*, 1996; David Grossvogel and Cushing Strout, *Divided We Stand: Reflections on the Crisis at Cornell*, 1971.

COUNTERCULTURE. The term ''counterculture'' was widely used in the 1960s and early 1970s to refer to a segment of American society that rejected middle-class values, racism, war, capitalism, sexual monogamy, and consumer culture. The ''counterculture'' inherited many of the traditions of the ''beat''* movement, but while the Beats had been literary and introspective, the counterculture was more overtly political. It opposed the Vietnam War,* private property, and the profit obsession of big business. The counterculture proclaimed the virtues of environmentalism, hallucinatory drugs, and sexual experimentation. For Theodore Roszak, who wrote *The Making of a Counterculture* (1969), Western civilization had created an ethos which separated, in the words of historian David Burner, ''the cerebral and observational faculties from the physical and sensual.'' Counterculture political radicalism, was dedicated to healing that fissure. The counterculture found expression in such groups as the Hippies,* Students for a Democratic Society,* and the Diggers, a communal movement that stole food from stores and repackaged it for distribution to the poor. The new world envisioned by the counterculture did not survive the 1970s.

REFERENCES: Ruth Bronsteen, *The Hippy's Handbook—How to Live on Love*, 1967; David Horowitz, Michael Lerner, and Craig Pye, eds., *Counterculture and Revolution*, 1972; Seymour Leventman, *Counterculture and Social Transformation*, 1982; Theodore Roszak, *The Making of a Counterculture*, 1969; Lewis Yablonsky, *The Hippie Trip*, 1968.

COUNTERINSURGENCY. In the jungles of Vietnam, U.S. soldiers found themselves fighting regular North Vietnamese Army* troop s as well as guerrilla troops native to South Vietnam, who mixed with the local civilian population. These Vietcong* troops were able to live off the land because they often enjoyed the active support of the local South Vietnamese population. Military strategists use the term "counterinsurgency" to describe the tactics needed to fight such an elusive enemy. "Pacification" was a common synonym for counterinsurgency. Central to effective counterinsurgency strategy was building the political loyalty of local civilians. If civilians were made to see the correctness of the American cause in South Vietnam, they would no longer harbor enemy guerrilla forces, making it easier for U.S. troops to find and destroy them. The way to win the "hearts and minds" of the local population was through effective economic development, decent housing, good schools for children, and adequate health care. If local South Vietnamese felt that siding with the United States would improve their everyday lives, winning the war would be a much easier task.

Unfortunately, the Lyndon Johnson* administration decided to deemphasize counterinsurgency in favor of a military solution to the war. Effective counterinsurgency, or political nation-building, is a time-consuming process that requires patience, determination, respect for local culture and tradition, and extreme caution in dealing with local civilian populations. Above all, for civilians to be won over politically, they must feel safe and secure. Reorienting the political attitudes of millions of people is no small task, and certainly not one accomplished overnight. Most strategists believed that a really effective United States counterinsurgency program in South Vietnam would have taken ten to fifteen years, at least, to implement.

From the very beginning of the American escalation of the war in 1965, antiwar* opposition at home was intense. Policymakers in the Johnson administration decided that counterinsurgency would take too long, and that the best way of bringing the war to an early conclusion was to fight a strategy of attrition* and annihilate so many North Vietnamese and Vietcong soldiers through conventional artillery attacks, strategic bombing, tactical bombing, and infantry search and destroy missions—that the enemy would no longer be able to field an army. In other words, the U.S. would kill enemy soldiers faster than Vietnamese population growth could replace them.

The strategy failed. First, the U.S. military machine was unable to kill Vietcong and North Vietnamese soldiers at a fast enough clip. The enemy proved able to field an increasingly large and an increasingly well-supplied army, in spite of massive U.S. firepower. Second, since most of the war was fought on South Vietnamese soil, indiscriminate U.S. firepower inadvertently inflicted millions of civilian casualties* and destroyed huge swaths of countryside. In the process, local South Vietnamese civilians came to resent the U.S. presence and became even more loyal to Communist forces. The strategy of attrition backfired, actually increasing anti-American sentiment in South Vietnam.

REFERENCES: Larry E. Cable, *Conflict of Myths: The Development of American Counter-Insurgency Doctrine and the Vietnam War*, 1986; Andrew F. Krepinevich, *The Army and Vietnam*, 1986; Robert Sellen, "Counterinsurgency," in James S. Olson, ed., *Dictionary of the Vietnam War*, 1988.

COWARD. *Coward*, written by Tom Tiede and published in 1968, was one of the first anti-Vietnam War* novels. Its main character is Private Nathan Long, a soldier who becomes an outspoken critic of the war. Eventually, he is court-martialed and sentenced to a combat tour of duty, where he eventually dies at the hands of the Vietcong.* Readers came away from *Coward* convinced that Vietnam was a futile military effort for the United States.
REFERENCES: Tom Tiede, *Coward*, 1968; Philip D. Beidler, *American Literature and the Experience of Vietnam*, 1982.

COX, HARVEY GALLAGHER. Harvey Cox was born in Phoenixville, Pennsylvania, May 19, 1929. Shortly after the end of World War II, when he was just seventeen, Cox left home and traveled to Europe, where he saw firsthand the ravages of war. He returned home and graduated from the University of Pennsylvania in 1951 with a degree in history. He took a divinity degree from Yale in 1955 and a Ph.D. from Harvard in 1963. Two years later, his first book, *The Secular City: Secularization and Urbanization in Theological Perspective*, became an international best-seller and made Cox the best-known theologian in the United States. The central theme of *The Secular City* was Cox's conviction that the secularization of human society was a necessary prerequisite to political and economic liberation. Traditional rituals and ceremonies were dead, and God made himself manifest in secular affairs through positive social change. In 1965 he wrote *God's Revolution and Man's Responsibility*.

It was a perfect theology for the 1960s. The antiwar movement,* civil rights movement,* environmental movement,* and antipoverty crusade were all manifestations of God's spirit on earth. Cox became a peace and civil rights activist during the decade, working for the Southern Christian Leadership Conference.* After the assassinations of Martin Luther King, Jr.,* and Senator Robert F. Kennedy* in 1968, Cox lived for a time in Cuernavaca, Mexico, and taught at the Center for Intercultural Documentation.

As the 1960s gave way to the 1970s, Cox's theological orientation shifted. His 1969 book, *The Feast of Fools: A Theological Essay on Festivity and Fantasy*, emphasized the inner spiritual life rather than social activism. In *The Seduction of the Spirit: The Use and Misuse of People's Religion* (1973), Cox took on the media and their ability to manipulate the masses and bemoaned the loss of commitment in American society. In 1977, he wrote *Turning East: The Promise and Peril of New Orientalism*, in which he worried about the tendency of Americans to use Eastern religions for self-fulfillment rather than for social change. Cox's other books have included *The Church amid Revolution* (1968), *Just As I Am* (1983), and *Religion in the Secular City: Toward a Postmodern Theology* (1984). Cox has taught at Harvard since 1982.
REFERENCES: Lonnie D. Kliever and John H. Hayes, *Radical Christianity: The New Theologies in Perspective*, 1968; Phyllis Clarke, ''Harvey Cox on the Secular City,'' in *Christianity and Marxism in Dialogue*, 1966.

CREDIBILITY GAP. The term ''credibility gap'' emerged during the 1960s to describe discrepancies between the public spin of official Washington and the reality of the Vietnam War.* During the John Kennedy* administration, members of the Saigon* press corps consistently printed highly pessimistic stories about Vietnam that contrasted sharply with official U.S. announcements. Journalists became suspicious of official Pentagon reports about the progress of the war. Events surrounding the Gulf of Tonkin* incident in August 1964 greatly escalated press skepticism about the trustworthiness of the Lyndon Johnson* administration. The term ''credibility gap'' first appeared on May 23, 1965, in an article by reporter David Wise in the *New York Herald Tribune*. A December 5, 1965, article written by Murray Marder for the *Washington Post* popularized the term. The Tet Offensive* of 1968 added fuel to the flames of the credibility gap. Just when General William Westmoreland* was predicting an end to the war because the enemy could no longer continue the fight, the Vietcong* launched a devastating offensive. During the 1970s, the Pentagon Papers and Watergate scandals only made the ''credibility gap'' seem even more obvious. REFERENCES: David Culbert, ''Johnson and the Media,'' in Robert Divine, ed., *Exploring the Johnson Years*, 1981; Peter Braestrup, *Big Story: How the American Press and Television Reported and Interpreted the Crisis of Tet 1968 in Vietnam and Washington*, 1983; Frances Frenzel, ''Credibility Gap,'' in James S. Olson, ed., *Dictionary of the Vietnam War*, 1988.

CREDIT CARDS. In 1949 Alfred Bloomingdale, Frank McNamara, and Ralph Snyder launched the era of the universal, third-party credit card when they founded Diners Club. The retail and gas credit cards were restricted to use in those industries, while the Diners Club card could be used to purchase goods and services at a variety of places around the country. Diners Club became the third party to the transaction, extending credit to the customer, providing customers to the seller, and charging them both for the service. The Diners Club saw credit as the product they were selling, not any particular commodity, service, or brand name. It was an uphill struggle. The airline, retail, and oil companies fought the idea because it competed with them, while many merchants resented the fee they were charged. But Diners Club stayed the course and pioneered a new industry.

After World War II, with the boom in consumer purchases, the market was ripe for a revolution in the consumer credit industry. In 1958 American Express, which had confined itself to issuing travelers checks, issued its own third-party, universal credit card, and the Hilton Hotel Corporation did the same with its Carte Blanche label. The Bank of America and Chase Manhattan Bank also issued their own universal credit cards in 1958. Chase Manhattan withdrew from the industry in 1962, but in 1966 Bank of America licensed its BankAmericard nationwide. To give themselves a more international image, they renamed the card VISA in 1976. Also, in 1966, a group of large banks decided to form the

Interbank Card Association. Eventually, their card became known as Master Charge, a name that changed in 1980 to MasterCard.
REFERENCE: Lewis Mandell, *The Credit Card Industry: A History*, 1990.

CRISPIE CRITTER. During the 1960s, the term "crispie critter" emerged in Vietnam to describe enemy soldiers who had been killed through burning to death. Eventually, the term was used as a slang expression in the United States to describe anybody who had died in a fire.
REFERENCE: James S. Olson, ed., *Dictionary of the Vietnam War*, 1988.

CRONKITE, WALTER LELAND. Walter Cronkite was born in St. Louis, Missouri, in 1916. During World War II, he served as a United Press war correspondent, and in 1950 he joined CBS television, rising to the top of the network. Between 1962 and 1981, Cronkite served as anchor and managing editor of the *CBS Evening News*. During those years, he earned a unique place of trust in the hearts of tens of millions of Americans, who came to respect his accuracy, wisdom, and temperance.

During the 1960s, Cronkite marked out the space program and the Vietnam War* as areas of expertise. The National Aeronautics and Space Administration (NASA) always gave him the royal treatment, and he reported everything from the first Mercury flights in the early 1960s to the moon landing in July 1969. He was an enthusiastic advocate of the space program. As for Vietnam, Cronkite tried to maintain an objective stance about the conflict, wanting to trust the judgment of U.S. military and political officials about the success of U.S. policies. Privately, his own sketicism about the war deepened between 1965 and late 1967, although he tried to maintain an on-the-air objectivity, accurately reporting both sides of the argument. The Tet Offensive* of 1968 was the last straw, as far as Walter Cronkite was concerned. He took a plane to Saigon* to assess the military and political situation and then broadcast on the evening news the following words, "The bloody experience of Vietnam is to end in stalemate." When President Lyndon Johnson* heard the comment, he despondently remarked, "If I have lost Walter Cronkite, I have lost Mr. Average Citizen." The president decided not to run for reelection.

Cronkite continued to anchor the *CBS Evening News* through the 1970s, retiring in 1981 when he turned 65. His departure from CBS was tinged with bitterness. Cronkite felt he had played a key role in building the program into a major force in American political and cultural life, but management had handled him cavalierly toward the end of his career. In 1996, he published his memoirs—*A Reporter's Life*—and in 1998 he signed on with CNN to anchor its coverage of John Glenn's* return to space flight as an astronaut aboard the space shuttle.
REFERENCES: Walter Cronkite, *A Reporter's Life*, 1996; David Halberstam, *The Powers That Be*, 1979; Hoyt Purvis, "Walter Cronkite," in James S. Olson, ed., *Dictionary*

of the Vietnam War, 1988; Kathleen J. Turner, *Lyndon Johnson's Dual War: Vietnam and the Press*, 1985.

CROW DOG, MARY. Mary Brave Bird was born on the Rosebud Sioux Reservation in 1953. During the late 1960s, discouraged about the social and economic problems on the reservation,* she became active in the American Indian Movement* and married Leonard Crow Dog, a Sioux medicine man. He was influential in working to revive the Ghost Dance among the Sioux. Mary Crow Dog published *Lakota Woman*, her autobiography, in 1990. The book detailed the problems of alcoholism and poverty in American Indian life. She also discussed the tension between modern feminism and traditional Indian values.
REFERENCE: Duane Champagne, ed., *The Native North American Almanac*, 1994.

CRUSADE FOR JUSTICE. In 1966, Rodolfo "Corky" Gonzales* founded Crusade for Justice in Denver. At its most fundamental level, Crusade for Justice was a civil rights organization demanding better education for Mexican-American* children, better jobs for Mexican-American parents, better housing for Mexican-American families, complete civil equality for all Mexican Americans, and the return of all Mexican-American land stolen after the Treaty of Guadalupe Hidalgo in 1848. Crusade members led protest marches and demonstrations for the hiring of more Chicano teachers and administrators. The most violent of those protests took place at West Side High School in Denver in 1969. Police riot squads were called in, and Gonzales was arrested. By that time, Crusade for Justice was among the most recognizable Mexican-American protest groups in the country.

In 1969, the crusade sponsored the first of several Chicano Youth Liberation Conferences in Denver, where workshops were held on political organization, Chicano culture, police brutality, and health and education issues. At the conference, crusade leaders issued *El Plan Espiritual de Aztlán*, which promoted self-determination* and Hispanic cultural nationalism. After the tumultuous days of the late 1960s and early 1970s, Crusade for Justice continued its crusade but with a significantly lower profile.
REFERENCE: Christine Marin, *A Spokesman of the Mexican American Movement: Rodolfo "Corky" Gonzales and the Fight for Chicano Liberation, 1966–1972*, 1977.

CUBAN AMERICANS. After Fidel Castro's* triumph in Cuba in 1959, an exodus of Cubans began from the island to the United States. The decisions of the Castro government during its first six months in power set in motion what became known as the "Golden Exile" from Cuba. Between January 1 and June 30, 1959, a total of 26,527 Cubans immigrated to the United States, the vast majority of them settling in Miami. Almost all of them were members of the Cuban elite who had been closely associated with the Batista government or with American-owned businesses on the island. They left the island when they lost all of their property, because they feared being arrested for supporting Fulgencio Batista, or because they were certain that the revolution would develop its own excesses, label them as counterrevolutionaries and enemies of the state, and punish them and their families.

They came to the United States full of bitterness about what they had lost in Cuba and full of commitment about overthrowing the Castro regime and regaining their assets. Relying on their sense of history, they thought the rebel government would be short-lived, that the United States would manage, as it had so often done in the past, to restore the upper class to power and protect its own investments on the island. Some of them even began to revive the old filibustering activities of the nineteenth century, in which American-based Cuban exiles planned the overthrow of the Cuban government.

The exodus of thousands of upper-class Cubans, the threats of the United States, and the strident counterrevolutionary rhetoric of the Cuban elite had a domino effect on the course of the revolution, inspiring more radicalization, more anti-Americanism, and more pro-Soviet policies on the part of the Castro regime. As the exodus from Cuba took place, the opposition forces inside Cuba became weaker and weaker. In the last six months of 1959 another 30,000 people left for the United States, and their exodus constituted the exporting of whatever hopes there were for counterrevolution. As the anti-Castro forces relocated to the United States, and as the United States continued to condemn the revolution, the ideologies of revolution and nationalism became even more closely entwined. As historian Louis H. Pérez, Jr., has written, "The defense of the revolution became synonymous with the defense of national sovereignty." Castro condemned the Catholic Church as a foreign, American-dominated body, just as he condemned the large corporations and landowners in Cuba. He also charged that the United States had supported the efforts of organized crime to penetrate Cuba and bring with it the evils of gambling, prostitution, pornography, and drugs. As the legitimate opposition dwindled in size, the revolution became more revolutionary, and with the threat of economic, political, and military action from the United States, Castro turned more and more to the Soviet Union for support.

In 1960 there were an estimated 124,416 people of Cuban descent living in the United States, but the political and economic events of the 1960s, on an international level and inside Cuba, had combined to send another 456,000 Cuban immigrants to the United States. In many ways they were a privileged group, at least compared to historical standards. Most of them were white, well educated, and blessed with important professional, technical, administrative, and entrepreneurial skills. Many of them already possessed substantial capital resources and investment portfolios. They also arrived as political refugees, victims of a dictatorial communist regime. When the Cubans naturalized as U.S. citizens, the vast majority of them became anticommunist, conservative Republicans, which provided the Republican Party with new political opportunities in what had once been part of the so-called solid South. The United States in the early to mid-1960s, before the Vietnam War* changed the ideological landscape, was an intensely, even jingoistically patriotic society. The "Golden Exiles" came into that anticommunist political culture as symbols not only of the malignant folly of Fidel Castro's revolution but of the magnificence of American society.

REFERENCE: James S. Olson and Judith E. Olson, *The Cuban-Americans: From Triumph to Tragedy*, 1995.

CUBAN MISSILE CRISIS (1962). Fidel Castro's* political triumph in Cuba in 1959 provided the Soviet Union with an unprecedented opportunity to establish a communist beachhead in the Western Hemisphere. Not only was Cuba engaged in a genuine revolution, but the Communist Party was playing a role in it. At the same time, the United States was threatening the Castro government with destruction. In the spring of 1960 the Russians resumed diplomatic relations with Cuba, which they had suspended in 1952, when Batista came into power; promised to purchase 425,000 tons of sugar now and 1 million tons annually thereafter; extended $100 million in economic assistance to Cuba; and agreed to sell petroleum to Cuba at below-market prices.

U.S. reaction was swift in coming. The Eisenhower* administration prohibited Texaco, Shell, and Standard Oil from refining the Soviet oil. At the end of June, Castro nationalized all foreign refineries. Early in July, Eisenhower announced that the United States would no longer purchase Cuban sugar. One month later, Castro nationalized all American-owned public utilities, sugar mills, and petroleum facilities. He followed that with the takeover of all North American-owned banks in Cuba. In October, the United States imposed a complete economic embargo on Cuba, and Castro then nationalized all American-owned publishing facilities, insurance companies, import-export businesses, port facilities, hotels, casinos, textile firms, chemical companies, mines, railroad and bus facilities, food-processing plants, and pharmaceutical concerns. Early in January 1961, the United States severed diplomatic relations with Cuba. By that time Cuba had already become part of the Soviet bloc.

Also by that time the United States had already made the decision to overthrow the Castro regime, and in the Cuban-American exile community of south Florida, the Eisenhower regime started to sow the seeds of counterrevolution, beginning its search for the recruits who would go home at the Central Intelligence Agency's* (CIA) bidding and overthrow the Castro regime. In August 1960 President Eisenhower formally funded what the CIA was calling Operation Pluto* and authorized the Department of Defense to assist the CIA in building a paramilitary force composed of Cuban exiles living in south Florida. The subsequent Bay of Pigs* invasion of April 1961 proved to be an unmitigated disaster for the United States and an extraordinary propaganda victory for Castro. He now had proof for all the world to see that the United States was a counterrevolutionary entity bent on his destruction.

The events of 1960 and 1961 led directly to the Cuban missile crisis* of October 1962. The combination of the economic embargo of Cuba and the

CIA's campaign against Fidel Castro had only served to drive the Cubans more deeply into the Soviet camp. Soviet premier Nikita Khrushchev* wanted to cement that relationship, and the Bay of Pigs had inspired him. Raised in the world of realpolitik, Khrushchev had been confused by the temerity of President John F. Kennedy's* effort to overthrow Castro. Why had not the Americans simply invaded Cuba outright using regular military forces, just as the Soviets had done in Hungary in 1956? Khrushchev concluded that Kennedy was a weak leader who would back down when bluffed. But at the very moment Khrushchev was reaching that conclusion, Kennedy had decided that his political future depended on demonstrating toughness and strength. He would never back down again. The stage was set for the missile crisis.

During August and September 1962, high-altitude American U-2 reconnaissance flights over Cuba revealed the presence of interregional ballistic missile silos, indicating that the Soviet Union intended to bring Cuba under its nuclear umbrella. The missiles could deliver warheads up to a distance of 1,500 miles, bringing most major American cities within Soviet range. President Kennedy weighed his options and decided on a forthright military policy designed to eliminate the Soviet nuclear threat from Cuba without being unnecessarily provocative. On October 22, 1962, the president announced the imposition of a naval quarantine around the island of Cuba. Somewhat like a blockade, the quarantine would not allow Soviet ships carrying missiles or nuclear warheads to enter Cuban ports. American naval vessels would search Soviet vessels for missile and warhead components and then destroy those implements. Kennedy also expressed his willingness to go to war—even nuclear war—over the issue, bluntly demanding that the Soviet Union dismantle and remove the missiles already in Cuba.

International tension ran high for the next six days, with world leaders wondering whether the Cold War* was finally about to become white-hot in a nuclear exchange between the superpowers. Fidel Castro pleaded with Nikita Khrushchev to launch a nuclear first strike against the United States, a request that the Soviet leader rejected as insane. In the end, Khrushchev was not willing to go to war over Cuba. It was too peripheral to Soviet national security. All the while, American and Soviet diplomats worked to find a face-saving way for both sides to end the crisis. On October 28, 1962, Soviet premier Nikita Khrushchev agreed to stop work on the missile sites and remove the missiles already in place. In return the United States pledged not to invade Cuba and, in a later, secret arrangement, to remove obsolete missiles from Turkey. The crisis was over.

REFERENCE: James S. Olson and Judith E. Olson, *The Cuban-Americans: From Triumph to Tragedy*, 1995.

CUSHING, RICHARD JAMES. Richard James Cushing was born in Boston August 24, 1895. He attended Boston College, graduated from St. John's Seminary in 1921, and took his vows as a Roman Catholic priest. For the next two years he labored as a parish priest in Roxbury and Somerville, Massachusetts, and in 1922 he was appointed assistant director of the Society for the Propagation of the Faith in Boston. Within a few years, he became director of the society. A fund-raiser without peer, Cushing was known for his accessibility, common sense, and pragmatism. In 1939 he was appointed auxiliary bishop of Boston, and in 1944 he became the archbishop of Boston. He remained at the head of that archdiocese for the rest of his life, receiving the red cap of a cardinal in 1958. Cushing was a vigorous supporter of Vatican II,* a friend of the Kennedy family, and an inveterate opponent of communism. Richard Cardinal Cushing was the most influential Roman Catholic prelate of his time. He died November 2, 1970.

REFERENCES: John H. Cutler, *Cardinal Cushing of Boston*, 1970; *New York Times*, November 3, 1970.

CUYAHOGA RIVER. The Cuyahoga River, which runs through Cleveland, Ohio, and into Lake Erie, became a symbol for the fledgling environmental movement in 1969. Heavy industrial, oil, and petrochemical discharges into the river, along with raw sewage and assorted debris, had badly polluted the Cuyahoga. For years a popular joke had circulated through Cleveland that ''anyone who falls in the Cuyahoga does not drown. He decays.'' But the jokes ended on June 22, 1969, when a match ignited the river. For twenty minutes, flames off the river climbed more than 200 feet in the air, consuming two bridges and darkening the downtown area with putrid, choking smoke. The burning of the Cuyahoga River was one of the top news stories of the year, and it provided environmentalists with the perfect symbol to promote the idea of clean water and sustainable development.

REFERENCES: *New York Times*, June 23–24, 1969.

D

DAK TO, BATTLE OF (1967). Dak To is a small, isolated village located in Kontum Province of the Socialist Republic of Vietnam, sparsely populated by Vietnamese civilians. During the years of the Vietnam War,* when Vietnam was divided at the seventeenth parallel into two countries, Dak To was in the region of South Vietnam designated II Corps by U.S. military authorities. The village possessed strategic significance because it was located on a primary infiltration route, in which Vietcong* and North Vietnamese Army* (NVA) forces moved supplies and troops into the central highlands of South Vietnam from Cambodia. A key goal of U.S. military planners during the war was to impede the enemy's ability to fight by stopping, or at least severely curtailing, the infiltration of troops and supplies into South Vietnam. Within months of President Lyndon Johnson's* decision in the spring of 1965 to escalate the war by introducing U.S. combat forces to South Vietnam, Dak To became the site of repeated skirmishes and military confrontations. U.S. Special Forces constructed a base camp at Dak To and trained local Montagnard tribesmen to patrol the infiltration route and alert U.S. artillery when major shipments of supplies and enemy troops were taking place.

By May 1967, the NVA began to establish a major presence in Dak To, moving in large numbers of troops from its 24th Regiment and building an elaborate system of bunkers, trenches, and tunnels along elevated ridgelines. In response, General William Westmoreland* deployed elements of the 173rd Airborne Brigade to Dak To. It was exactly what North Vietnamese strategists hoped he would do. They were planning the Tet Offensive* for early 1968, which involved Vietcong assaults on South Vietnamese cities and provincial capitals, and North Vietnam, in a series of border battles like Dak To, hoped to pull U.S. forces out of those cities and into the distant countryside.

Early in November 1967, U.S. forces assaulted the NVA positions. Within a matter of days, the battle centered on Hill 875. Westmoreland ordered more than

300 B-52* strikes and 2,000 fighter-bomber sorties on NVA positions, with the fighting intensifying into hand-to-hand combat between November 19 and 22. Late at night on November 22, the NVA 173rd Regiment simply withdrew, and an eerie silence settled in. Westmoreland hailed Dak To as a great U.S. military victory, but North Vietnam knew better. Although U.S. forces had inflicted heavy casualties on NVA and Vietcong troops, North Vietnam had fulfilled its strategic goal of pulling U.S. troops out of the cities in preparation for Tet.

REFERENCES: Samuel Freeman, "Battle of Dak To," in James S. Olson, ed., *Dictionary of the Vietnam War*, 1988; James S. Olson and Randy Roberts, *Where the Domino Fell: America and Vietnam, 1945–1995*, 1995; Shelby L. Stanton, *The Rise and Fall of an American Army: U.S. Ground Troops in Vietnam, 1965–1973*, 1985.

DALEY, RICHARD JOSEPH. Richard Joseph Daley was born May 15, 1902, in Chicago to an Irish-American working-class family. He grew up on the Southside, and after graduating from high school he went to work as a clerk in the Cook County controller's office. Daley attended law school at night at DePaul. A shrewd politician who understood the centrality of loyalty and personal rewards in an urban political machine, Daley rose quickly through the city's Democratic Party, succeeding at the precinct and ward level. He won election as a state representative in 1936, and two years later Daley took a seat in the state senate, which he occupied until 1946. That year, he suffered the only election defeat of his career when he failed in his bid to be sheriff of Cook County.

In 1947, Governor Adlai Stevenson of Illinois appointed Daley state revenue director, but he soon returned to Chicago when he was elected clerk of the Cook County Board of Commissioners. In 1953, Daley was chosen chairman of the Cook County Democratic Central Committee, which made him one of the most powerful politicians in Illinois. Using the chairmanship as a springboard, Daley was elected mayor of Chicago in 1955 and won reelection five more times. He was early into his sixth term when he died December 20, 1976.

His tenure in the mayor's office was successful. In fact, many public administrators considered Chicago one of the best-run cities in the country. He vastly improved the infrastructure, public transportation, and police and fire services, and he did it while keeping the city financially sound. During the 1960s, Richard Daley was considered one of the most powerful political figures in the United States. He had an iron grip on the Democratic Party in Chicago, and because of that he could deliver Illinois to Democratic presidential candidates. Some historians believe that Daley fraudulently manipulated the city's election returns in 1960 to make sure that John F. Kennedy* had enough votes to win Illinois and the presidency. In 1968, he bitterly opposed the antiwar movement* and encouraged Chicago police to brutalize the protesters who had gathered in the city for the Democratic presidential nominating convention.

REFERENCES: Eugene Kennedy, *Himself: The Life and Times of Mayor Richard J. Daley*, 1978; Mike Royko, *Boss: Richard J. Daley of Chicago*, 1971.

DANIEL BOONE. *Daniel Boone* was a popular television* western during the 1960s. Produced by NBC, the show was first broadcast on September 24, 1964, starring Fess Parker as the legendary American frontiersman Daniel Boone, who is trying to build a life for his family in late eighteenth-century Tennessee and Kentucky. It retained its popularity during the decade because of its relevance to larger events occurring in the United States at the time. Barry Rosenzweig supervised its writers, and he instructed them to portray Revolutionary America as England's Vietnam, with the Americans playing the role of Vietcong* guerrillas and the English as conventional soldiers. The last episode was broadcast on August 27, 1970.

REFERENCE: Tim Brooks and Earle Marsh, *The Complete Directory to Prime Time Network and Cable TV Shows*, 1995.

THE DAVE CLARK FIVE. The Dave Clark Five, formed in Tottenham, England, in 1961, were part of the so-called British invasion* of 1964–1965. The group included Dave Clark, Mike Smith, Rick Huxley, Lenny Davidson, and Denis Payton. Beginning with "Glad All Over" (1964), the Dave Clark Five had a string of seventeen singles that reached the top forty on the pop charts. Included in these hits were "Bits and Pieces," "I Like It Like That," "Because," "Over and Over," and "Catch Us If You Can." Beginning in 1968, however, their American popularity declined, although they still remained a popular group in England.

REFERENCE: Patricia Romanowski and Holly George-Warren, eds., *The New Rolling Stone Encyclopedia of Rock and Roll*, 1996.

DAVIS, ANGELA. Angela Yvonne Davis was born in Birmingham, Alabama, January 26, 1944. She attended Brandeis University as an undergraduate, where she came under the influence of Herbert Marcuse,* a Marxist philosopher. In Europe, she studied for a year under Marxist Theodore Adorno. After graduating from Brandeis, Davis began graduate school at the University of California at San Diego. She earned a master's degree in philosophy there in 1968 and had completed all of the requirements for the Ph.D., except for the dissertation, by 1969.

An African American concerned about the plight of her people, Davis became increasingly radical in the late 1960s. She became active in the Student Nonviolent Coordinating Committee* and took a teaching position at the University of California at Los Angeles (UCLA). In July 1968, Davis joined the Communist Party. The next year she traveled to Cuba, where she decided that African Americans had something in common with all Third World peoples. Later that year, she became a national figure when Governor Ronald Reagan* of California fired her from the teaching post at UCLA on the grounds that she was a communist.

By that time Davis was involved with defense of the Soledad brothers, one of whom was George Jackson, for murdering a prison guard. Jackson was killed trying to escape from San Quentin. On August 7, 1970, Jackson's younger brother Jonathan, using weapons registered in Davis's name, seized several hostages during a trial in Marin County. In a shoot-out that followed, Jackson was killed by police, but he murdered Judge Harold Haley before dying. Because Davis owned the weapons, she was charged with conspiracy to commit murder. Eventually, she was acquitted of the charges. Today, Davis teaches at San Francisco State University.

REFERENCES: Angela Davis, *Angela Davis: An Autobiography*, 1971, and *Women, Race, and Class*, 1981.

DAYS OF RAGE. The term "Days of Rage" describes a two-day melee in Chicago in October 1967. It was staged by the radical Weathermen,* a splinter group from Students for a Democratic Society.* Hundreds of Weathermen gathered in Chicago for a weekend of rioting. They marched through the downtown business district smashing cars, breaking windows, and harassing police. More than 300 of them were arrested for rioting. Ostensibly, their reason for gathering in Chicago was to "lead white kids into armed revolution." The Weathermen grew more and more violent during the rest of the 1960s, finally going underground in 1970.

REFERENCES: Ronald Fraser, *1968: A Student Generation in Revolt*, 1988; Todd Gitlin, *The Sixties: Years of Hope, Days of Rage*, 1987.

DEADHEAD. The term "Deadhead" emerged in the late 1960s and 1970s to describe an individual hooked on the music and the concerts of the Grateful Dead* band.

DEATH OF GOD. See ALTIZER, THOMAS JONATHAN JACKSON.

DEATH VALLEY DAYS. *Death Valley Days* was one of the longest-running programs in television* history. Always produced in syndication, *Death Valley Days* premiered in 1952 and remained on the air until 1975. Its setting was the harsh desert of California in the nineteenth century, where hard-bitten settlers tried to eke out an existence. It was narrated by Stanley Andrews from 1952 to 1965, Ronald Reagan* from 1965 to 1966, Robert Taylor from 1966 to 1968, and Dale Robertson from 1968 to 1972. Ronald Reagan, whose film career had gone into decline, became a household name again because of the series, catapulting him into a successful run for the California governorship in 1966.

REFERENCE: Tim Brooks and Earle Marsh, *The Complete Directory to Prime Time Network and Cable TV Shows*, 1995.

DECONSTRUCTIONISM. In 1967, with the publication of his book *De la Grammatologie* (Of Grammatology), French philosopher Jacques Derrida gave birth to the theory of deconstructionism, which had an enormous impact on the next generation of French and American philosophers and literary scholars. Derrida abandoned the long-held notion that the authority of the writer is absolute in the interpretation of a text. Instead, Derrida rejected traditional metaphysics and called for the "deconstructing" of literary texts. Language is imprecise, and meaning is infinitely variable, according to Derrida, and all statements of absolute value are meaningless. In determining the meaning of a text, the assumptions of the reader are as important as the intentions of the writer. Deconstructionism precipitated an intellectual civil war among French and American scholars that continues today.

REFERENCE: Christopher Norris, *Deconstructionism: Theory and Practice*, 1991.

DEER, ADA. Ada Deer, a Menominee, was born August 7, 1935, in Keshena, Wisconsin. In 1957, she graduated from the University of Wisconsin at Madison and then earned a master's degree in social work at Columbia. The battle to reverse the federal government's termination* of the Menominee Indians became Deer's passion in the late 1960s. By the early 1970s, she was vice president and chief Washington lobbyist of the National Committee to Save the Menominee People and Forest, and from 1973 to 1976 she served as chair of the Menominee Restoration Committee. Deer taught at the University of Wisconsin at Madison. She became assistant secretary for Indian affairs early in 1993, and a few months later President Bill Clinton named her head of the Bureau of Indian Affairs.

REFERENCE: Duane Champagne, ed., *The Native North American Almanac*, 1994.

DEFOLIATION. See OPERATION RANCH HAND.

DELANO GRAPE STRIKE. In 1965, Filipino grape pickers, who were members of the American Federation of Labor–Congress of Industrial Organization's (AFL-CIO) Agricultural Workers Organizing Committee (AWOC), implemented a strike against the grape growers of Delano, California. They wanted higher wages and recognition for the union. The growers responded by bringing in Mexican-American strikebreakers, and AWOC leaders turned to César Chávez* and his National Farm Workers Association (NFWA) for assistance. Chávez agreed, and the NFWA joined the strike.

Chávez then turned the strike into a liberal crusade. Civil rights and religious groups joined the movement, as did college students, antiwar* protesters, and prominent left-wing politicians. He secured the support of the Roman Catholic hierarchy and made the Virgin of Guadalupe the symbol of the strike. When growers brought in strikebreakers from around the country, Chávez launched a nationwide boycott of California grapes, urging his followers and labor union sympathizers everywhere not to eat another grape or drink a cup of wine until the California growers signed a contract with the union.

The growers tried to resist, sometimes violently, but Chávez told his people to respond with nonviolence and the people of the world to stop eating California grapes. By 1968, the boycott had spread to Western Europe. A year later, the first group of growers capitulated, and all of the other California growers had followed suit by 1970, giving workers a $1.75 per hour wage and signing three-year contracts with the union, now known as the United Farm Workers Organizing Committee.

REFERENCES: Dick Meister and Anne Loftis, *A Long Time Coming: The Struggle to Unionize America's Farm Workers*, 1977; Paul Fusco and George D. Horowitz, *La Causa, the California Grape Strike*, 1970; Jacques E. Levy, *César Chávez: Autobiography of La Causa*, 1975.

DELLINGER, DAVID. David Dellinger, America's premier living pacifist, was born in Boston, Massachusetts, on August 22, 1915, to a conservative Republican family. Dellinger attended Yale University, majoring in economics and graduating in 1936. By that time, he had decided on a career as a Protestant minister. A year of postgraduate study at Oxford and stints at two divinity schools turned him into a pacifist. War, he was convinced, was never an appropriate political response.

Dellinger's pacifism was no youthful flirtation. He was willing to suffer its consequences. When World War II erupted, he refused to register with the Selective Service, an act of defiance that earned him a one-year prison sentence. He was subsequently drafted into the U.S. Army, but he refused to report for duty. Dellinger was arrested and sentenced to two years in prison. He was paroled when the war ended. Once paroled, Dellinger lived in New Jersey and founded the Liberation Press, which promoted a variety of civil rights and antiwar causes. In 1956, he became editor of *Liberation*, a magazine devoted to radical pacifism. He was also active in the War Resisters League* (WRL).

In 1963, Dellinger and the War Resisters League targeted the Vietnam War* as a major concern and in doing so launched the antiwar movement.* On May 16, 1964, Dellinger and the WRL cosponsored in New York City an antidraft demonstration at which twelve men burned their Selective Service cards. The demonstration attracted widespread media attention. In December 1964, Dellinger used the WRL to organize the first nationwide protest demonstration against the Vietnam War. He was also the moving force behind the Committee for a Fifth Avenue Peace Parade, which demonstrated in New York City in October 1965.

Throughout the 1960s, Dellinger was the leading light in the antiwar movement. He earned the contempt of most Americans in 1968 and 1969 when he visited Hanoi, but as head of the Committee of Liaison with the Families of Servicement Detained in North Vietnam, he did negotiate the release of six prisoners-of-war.* He also played a key role in the demonstrations that took place in Chicago in 1968 during the Democratic National Convention.* As such, he was one of the defendants in the famous Chicago Eight* trial in February 1970. Although he was found guilty of contempt of court and inciting to riot, a federal appeals court overturned both convictions. He continued to oppose the Vietnam War until the final withdrawal of U.S. personnel from Saigon in 1975.

After Vietnam, Dellinger continued his pacifist career. In 1975, he founded

Seven Days, a pacifist magazine, and he actively opposed the Gulf War of 1991. In 1996, at the Democratic National Convention in Chicago, Dellinger appeared on national television frequently on news programs recalling the events of the Democratic National Convention of 1968.

REFERENCES: David Dellinger, *From Yale to Jail*, 1993, and *More Power Than We Know: The People's Movement Toward Democracy*, 1975; John Ricks, "David Dellinger," in James S. Olson, ed., *Dictionary of the Vietnam War*, 1988.

DELORIA, VINE, JR. Vine Deloria, Jr., author, attorney, educator, and grandson of a Yankton Sioux chief, was born in 1933 in Martin, South Dakota. Deloria graduated from Iowa State University in 1958 and received a law degree from the University of Colorado in 1970. Through his best-selling books *Custer Died for Your Sins* (1969) and *God Is Red* (1973), Deloria presented the details of the red power* activism agenda to a global audience. *Custer* remains one of the most incisive polemics written concerning the relationship of the U.S. government to the Native American. He is also the author of *American Indian Policy in the Twentieth Century* (1985); *American Indians, American Justice* (1983); *Behind the Trail of Broken Treaties: An Indian Declaration of Independence* (1985); *The Nations Within: The Past and Future of American Indian Sovereignty* (1984); and *Red Earth, White Lies: Native Americans and the Myth of the Scientific Fact* (1995).

Deloria served as the executive director of the National Congress of American Indians from 1965 to 1967 and provided leadersip in other organizations, such as the Citizens Crusade against Poverty and the Indian Rights Association. In 1971, he and two other Indian attorneys, Franklin D. Ducheneaux and Kirke Kickingbird, founded the Institute for the Development of Indian Law. The purpose of this nonprofit legal research organization was to strengthen the rights of Indian governmental and societal institutions in order to guarantee their ability to govern themselves in an efficient and sovereign manner. Since 1991, Deloria has taught political science at the University of Colorado at Boulder and remains a forceful and active spokesman for the Indian community.

REFERENCE: Robert Allen Warrior, "The Progressive Interview, Vine Deloria, Jr., 'It's About Time to Be Interested in Indians Again,' " *The Progressive* 54 (April 1990), 24–27.

David Ritchey

DEMILITARIZED ZONE. The Demilitarized Zone, a 10-mile-wide buffer, divided North Vietnam from South Vietnam. At the Geneva Conference of 1954, diplomats cut Vietnam into two countries and drew a boundary along the seventeenth parallel from the South China Sea to Laos. The DMZ was five miles of land north of the boundary and five miles of territory south of the boundary. At Geneva, the DMZ was proclaimed off limits to the military forces of both countries.

REFERENCE: Robert F. Randle, *Geneva, 1954*, 1969.

DEMOCRATIC NATIONAL CONVENTION OF 1968. In 1968, the Democratic Party held its presidential nominating convention in the city of Chicago, and the meeting proved to be the most raucus in U.S. political history. The convention, and demonstrations in the streets outside, served as a microcosm of the social and political tensions in American life, particularly those caused by the Vietnam War.* After the Tet Offensive* and Senator Eugene McCarthy's* strong showing in the New Hampshire primary, President Lyndon Johnson* had decided not to seek another term. Senator Robert Kennedy* of New York had announced his candidacy and done well in the primaries, but he was assassinated in June. Going into the convention, Senator McCarthy and Vice-President Hubert Humphrey* were the only viable candidates. Humphrey, of course, had the edge at the convention because he enjoyed the backing of most Democratic party politicians.

The convention was a disaster for the Democratic Party. Bitter debates over the Vietnam War* divided convention delegates, and outside, on the streets of Chicago, such leading antiwar protestors as Tom Hayden,* Abbie Hoffman,* Jerry Rubin,* David Dellinger,* and Rennard Davis led massive demonstrations. They denounced the war and what they called ''establishment'' domination of the Democratic Party. Chicago police—on the orders of Mayor Richard Daley,* who viewed the protesters as traitors to their country—viciously attacked the demonstrators. A subsequent investigation concluded that the incident had turned into a ''police riot.'' A national television audience watched the spectacle, which convinced millions of Americans that it was time for a political change. The Democratic National Convention finally nominated Hubert Humphrey for president and Senator Edmund Muskie of Maine for vice-president, but both men entered the campaign badly wounded. The catastrophe in Chicago gave Richard Nixon,* the Republican nominee, the upper hand.

REFERENCES: David Dellinger, *From Yale to Jail*, 1993; Norman Mailer, *Miami and the Siege of Chicago*, 1969; Theodore White, *The Making of the President, 1968*, 1969.

DENTON, JEREMIAH. During the Vietnam War,* Jeremiah Denton had the distinction of becoming one of the best known U.S. prisoners of war.* A naval pilot, he was shot down in June 1965, approximately 75 miles south of Hanoi. For the next seven years, he languished in North Vietnamese prisons, enduring beatings and torture for steadfastly refusing to answer his captors' questions. He came to national attention on one occasion while being interviewed for television. Although he answered the North Vietnamese questions, he was blinking his eyes in Morse code, transmitting the word ''torture'' to viewers. With the signing of the Paris Peace Accords* in 1973, Denton was one of the first U.S. prisoners of war* to be released. When he deplaned at Clark Field in the Philippines, he saluted smartly and said, ''Reporting for duty.'' The comment endeared him to millions of Americans. Denton won a seat in the U.S. Senate from Alabama in 1980, but he lost his reelection bid.

REFERENCES: Jeremiah A. Denton, *When Hell Was In Session*, 1976; John S. Bowman, *The Vietnam War: An Almanac*, 1985.

THE DICK VAN DYKE SHOW. *The Dick Van Dyke Show*, first broadcast on October 3, 1961, has become a classic of 1960s television* and could still be seen in reruns in the 1990s. It was a CBS production. Dick Van Dyke played Rob Petrie, a comedy writer for *The Alan Brady Show*. Mary Tyler Moore played his wife, Laura, and Rose Marie and Morey Amsterdam played Rob's writing colleagues—Sally Rogers and Buddy Sorrell. The program was a major hit in 1966, when Van Dyke and Moore decided to move on to other projects. The last episode of *The Dick Van Dyke Show* was telecast on September 7, 1966.

REFERENCE: Ginny Weissman, *The Dick Van Dyke Show*, 1993.

DICKERSON, NANCY CONNERS HANDSCHMAN. Nancy Dickerson was born in Milwaukee, Wisconsin, in 1927. She graduated from the University of Wisconsin in 1948, taught school for three years, and then spent some time as a clerk at George Washington University in Washington, D.C. She did not stay there for long, however, landing a position with the Senate Foreign Relations Committee. In 1954, she joined CBS television as a news producer, working with the *Face the Nation* series. Dickerson was not happy as a producer, however; she wanted to be a reporter, but there were no women in front of the cameras in the 1950s. In 1959, on assignment in Europe to produce a program on the women's army corps, she went off on her own and interviewed a number of prominent European leaders about the upcoming visit of Soviet premier Nikita Khrushchev* to the United States. Her work was so good that CBS put it on the air. Late in 1959, she managed to get an interview with Speaker of the House Sam Rayburn, a politician noted for his distance from the media.

In 1960, Nancy Dickerson became the first woman television correspondent for CBS News. The network also gave her her own weekly radio program— *One Woman's Washington*. In 1962, Dickerson signed a contract with NBC, with the assignment of covering Vice President Lyndon B. Johnson.* The Kennedy assassination catapulted Dickerson to prominence, because she now had the ear of the president of the United States. She soon became one of the most recognizable faces in television journalism. In 1970, Dickerson left NBC to work as a political commentator for syndication and to form her own independent production company. Her autobiography—*Among Those Present*—was published in 1976. Nancy Dickerson died on October 18, 1997.

REFERENCE: Nancy Dickerson, *Among Those Present*, 1976.

DIGGS, CHARLES. Charles Diggs was born in Detroit in 1922. He attended the University of Michigan and Fisk University before joining the army during World War II. After the war, Diggs attended Wayne State University's mortuary science program and started a funeral business. Active in local Democratic politics, he won a state senate seat in 1951. Three years later, Diggs was elected to the U.S. House of Representatives. In Congress, he specialized in the issue of de facto discrimination against African Americans in the U.S. military and in the federal government, and on many occasions he succeeded in getting the Pentagon to make policy changes designed to end discrimination against black servicemen and servicewomen.

Throughout the late 1960s and 1970s, Diggs was one of the most powerful black congressmen in the United States. He chaired the District of Columbia Committee and the Foreign Affairs African Subcommittee. In 1979, however, Diggs came under investigation for misappropriation of government funds, using money from his congressional staff budget to pay personal bills. He resigned his congressional seat in 1980 and was later convicted and sentenced to three years in prison. He served seven months in the federal prison at Maxwell Air Force Base in Montgomery, Alabama. After his release, he worked for a while as a special aide to the Congressional Black Caucus and then went into private business. Charles Diggs died on August 24, 1998.

REFERENCE: *New York Times*, November 28, 1981, and August 25, 1998.

DILLON, DOUGLAS. Douglas Dillon was born in Geneva, Switzerland, August 21, 1909. He graduated from Harvard in 1931 and went to work for the family investment business—Dillon, Read and Company. Later in the 1930s, he also became associated with the U.S. and Foreign Securities Corporation and the U.S. International Securities Corporation. A loyal Republican, Dillon supported Thomas E. Dewey's presidential campaigns in 1944 and 1948 and Dwight D. Eisenhower's* in 1952 and 1956. Eisenhower appointed Dillon ambassador to France in 1953. In 1958, Dillon returned home to serve as under-secretary of state for economic affairs. He became widely known in government circles for his efforts to coordinate economic policy and foreign affairs. He was also instrumental in the creation of the Inter-American Development Bank. In 1961 President John F. Kennedy* appointed Dillon to the cabinet post of secretary of the treasury, a position that he held until 1965, when he returned to Dillon, Read and Company.

REFERENCE: *Who's Who in America, 1991–1992*, 1992.

DINK. During the years of the Vietnam War,* the term ''dink'' was used by American soldiers as a racist reference to individuals of Vietnamese ethnic ancestry, whether they were enemy troops or Vietnamese civilians.

REFERENCE: James S. Olson, ed., *Dictionary of the Vietnam War*, 1988.

DIRKSEN, EVERETT McKINLEY. Everett McKinley Dirksen was born in Pekin, Illinois, January 4, 1896. He served in the U.S. Army during World War I and returned home to a variety of jobs until he was elected commissioner of finance in Pekin in 1927. He remained at that post until 1931, when he returned to school. In 1936, Dirksen earned a law degree from the University of Minnesota. He defied the odds in the election of 1932 by winning a seat in Congress as a Republican, and he remained there until 1948. In 1950 he won a seat from Illinois in the U.S. Senate. Dirksen was reelected in 1956, 1962, and 1968, serving his last ten years in the Senate as minority leader. A pragmatic politician whose natural conservatism could sometimes yield to more liberal persuasions, Dirksen was a major figure in the Senate during the 1960s. He died September 7, 1969.

REFERENCE: *New York Times*, September 8, 1969.

DISNEY, WALT. See *THE WONDERFUL WORLD OF WALT DISNEY*.

DIVINE, FATHER. George Baker, who became famous as Father Divine, was born around 1877 on Hutchinson Island, Georgia. Like many other southern African Americans, he headed north during World War II, and he settled in Sayville, Long Island, New York. He took over a local black congregation and soon earned a reputation for his unparalleled skill in providing food and lodging to those of his followers who were destitute. In 1933, he moved his operation to Harlem, where it became known as the Father Divine Peace Mission Movement. During the next decade, Divine established branch missions in most northern cities and came to be regarded as God himself by his followers.

Divine urged his followers to eschew racism, lust, tobacco, cosmetics, movies, and television. He forbade them to use the words "white" or "Negro" to refer to other people, and he preached the brotherhood of all people. Beyond that, there was no formal theology or ceremony. By the 1960s, Father Divine missions constituted a refuge for many black people facing unemployment and despair in the cities. He died September 10, 1965.

REFERENCES: Arthur H. Fauset, *Black Gods of the Metropolis*, 1971; *New York Times*, September 11, 1965.

DMZ. See **DEMILITARIZED ZONE**.

"DO YOUR OWN THING." The phrase "Do your own thing" emerged during the 1960s as a slogan of the counterculture.* Rebellious students, advocates of drug use, and hippies* used the term to reject any fidelity to conventional, middle-class values and morals and to try to legitimate any individual behavior that did not directly harm other people.

REFERENCE: David Lee Stein, *Living the Revolution: The Yippies in Chicago*, 1969.

DR. KILDARE. Like *Ben Casey, Dr. Kildare* was a popular television* medical drama of the 1960s. It was based on the successful series of *Dr. Kildare* movies of the 1940s. First broadcast by NBC on September 28, 1961, the series starred Richard Chamberlain as the young, sophisticated Dr. James Kildare and Raymond Massey as the wizened, irascible Dr. Leonard Gillespie. The scene was Blair General Hospital, a metropolitan teaching hospital, and Kildare was a

resident in internal medicine. The last episode was broadcast on August 30, 1966.
REFERENCE: Barbara Siegel, *Richard Chamberlain: An Actor's Life*, 1989.

DR. STRANGELOVE. The film *Dr. Strangelove: or How I Learned to Stop Worrying and Love the Bomb* was a dark comedy. The film starred Peter Sellers in a triple role as Group Captain Lionel Mandrake, President Merkley Muffley, and Dr. Strangelove; Sterling Hayden as the lunatic general Jack D. Ripper; George C. Scott as General Buck Turgidson; Slim Pickens as Major T. J. King Kong; and Keenan Wynn as Colonel Bat Guana. Released in 1964 at the peak of the post-Cuban missile crisis* paranoia about nuclear warfare, *Dr. Strangelove* sarcastically and satirically panned the prevailing notion that global nuclear warfare was a realistic military option, ridiculed the ongoing nuclear arms race between the United States and Soviet Union, and postulated the idea of the ultimate weapon—a doomsday device that would destroy the entire world in the event of any aboveground detonation of a nuclear device, even a test weapon or a nuclear accident.
REFERENCE: Charles Maland, '' 'Dr. Strangelove' (1964): Nightmare Comedy and the Cult of the Liberal Consensus,'' *American Quarterly* 31 (Winter 1979).

DR. ZHIVAGO. Based on Boris Pasternak's Russian novel *Dr. Zhivago*, the film *Dr. Zhivago* was released in 1965. Directed by David Lean, the film starred Omar Sharif, Julie Christie, Alec Guinness, Rod Steiger, and Geraldine Page. The film is set in Russia on the eve of the Bolshevik Revolution of 1917, during the subsequent civil war in Russia, and into the Soviet Union of the 1920s. The film follows Dr. Zhivago from his last year of medical school at the University of Moscow, out to the front as a military physician during World War I, back to Moscow during the starving time of 1918 and 1919, then out to a family farm west of the Ural Mountains, where he is captured by partisans and forcibly inducted into their guerrilla military unit. After serving a long stretch with the partisans, Zhivago escapes, and makes his way back to the family farm. The film ends in Moscow, where Zhivago dies of a heart attack. *Dr. Zhivago* was an elegant masterpiece of filmmaking, one of David Lean's greatest artistic achievements. It was also an extraordinarily popular film in the 1960s.
REFERENCES: Michael Anderegg, *David Lean*, 1984; Kevin Brownlow, *David Lean*, 1996.

DODA, CAROL. The cult of the breast produced its first caricature in July 1965. Carol Doda, a platinum blond dancer and waitress at the Condor Club in San Francisco's Tenderloin, discovered an infallible technique for increasing her tips. On a slack evening in July, she peeled off her bikini top and burlesqued for the patrons, establishing a new industry and introducing the word ''topless'' into the American vocabulary. Within days, she headlined the Condor Club's entertainment marquee, dancing topless on a raised platform, rocking back and forth on a swing roped to the ceiling, and selling an ocean of booze to a legion of mostly white, middle-class men. After a few months, Condor regulars noticed a bizarre, otherworldly quality to her breasts. When she danced, they did not jiggle. As she glided back and forth on the swing, they did not sag or flatten. Carol Doda's remarkable breasts possessed a life, indeed a superstructure, of their own.

Curious reporters inquired about their scientific properties. After months of disclaimers, the topless queen fessed up. She was the proud owner of silicone-enhanced breasts. Still in its infancy, the technology was crude. Doda regularly visited a physician who novocained her breasts and then repeatedly spot-injected 20 cc of liquid silicone until they were ready to burst. In subsequent years, her silicone would break up into freakish, wandering clumps of gel, but in 1965, she possessed the firmest breasts on the planet.

Topless clubs proliferated in the 1960s and 1970s, invading small towns as well as large cities and sometimes discreetly renaming themselves "gentlemen's clubs" in the 1980s and 1990s. Every few years religious organizations and women's groups unleashed political crusades to ban nude dancing, but most of the time the federal courts ruled "topless" enterprises as legitimate, if tasteless, forms of free expression protected by the First Amendment. In 1972, when California restricted topless dancing by prohibiting nudity in any business possessing a state liquor license, bar owners successfully appealed to the federal courts. With the litigation still in progress, a reporter asked Carol Doda if she worried about losing her job. She jiggled her breasts and giggled, "We could serve fruits and nuts and these guys would still show up. They don't come for the booze. They want a peek at my knockers."

REFERENCES: *San Francisco Examiner*, November 16, 1965; *New York Times*, December 10, 1972.

DODGE V. NAKAI (1969). The *Dodge v. Nakai* case of 1969 represented one of the first real tests of the Indian Civil Rights Act* of 1968. Before passage of the law, Indian tribes had been immune under federal common law from lawsuits. It was accepted at the time that the law would not permit individual Indians to launch civil rights lawsuits against tribal governments. But the *Dodge v. Nakai* case did just that. A non-Indian attorney brought suit against Raymond Nakai, chairman of the Navajo Tribal Council, seeking monetary damages in a dispute with the tribal council. The tribal council felt the suit was frivolous and out of order, since tribal sovereignty offered them immunity. The federal district court disagreed, upholding the suit against the tribal council, arguing that since Congress had established Indian civil rights in the 1968 legislation, the federal courts automatically received a jurisdiction more compelling than that of the tribes, essentially overriding the notion of tribal sovereign immunity.

REFERENCES: H. Barry Holt and Gary Forrester, *Digest of American Indian Law: Cases and Chronology*, 1990; Stephen L. Pevar, *The Rights of Indians and Tribes: The Basic ACLU Guide to Indian and Tribal Rights*, 1992; John R. Wunder, *"Retained by the People'': A History of American Indians and the Bill of Rights*, 1994; Wilcomb E. Washburn, *Red Man's Land, White Man's Law*, 1971; Charles F. Wilkinson, *American Indians, Time and the Law*, 1987.

THE DOMINICAN REPUBLIC CRISIS (1965). Ever since President James Monroe issued the Monroe Doctrine in 1823, U.S. foreign policy has been committed to American hegemony over the Western Hemisphere. During the nineteenth century, the United States insisted that the European powers establish no more colonial regimes in the Western Hemisphere. After World War II the United States became especially concerned about the establishment of communist regimes in Latin America and the Caribbean. Fidel Castro's* triumph in Cuba had been a nightmare for the United States, and Presidents John F. Kennedy* and Lyndon B. Johnson* were determined to see that it did not happen again.

In 1965, it almost did in the Dominican Republic. On April 24, 1965, an insurgent rebellion against the government of Donald Reid Cabral erupted in the Dominican Republic. The Johnson administration feared that the rebellion was a front for former Dominican president Juan Bosch, who was capable of establishing a communist regime. On April 28, U.S. ambassador W. Tapley Bennett asked for U.S. military intervention, and President Lyndon B. Johnson complied. The last thing he wanted was for a Caribbean nation to go communist during his administration. Johnson did manage to get a supportive resolution from the Organization of American States, although critics throughout Latin America condemned the invasion as an example of the continuing U.S. lack of respect for the political sovereignty of its neighbors. The multinational peacekeeping force remained in the Dominican Republic until September 1966. By that time a stable government had been established under the direction of President Joaquin Balaguer. The success in preventing a communist takeover in the Dominican Republic by injecting U.S. military forces into the crisis encouraged the Johnson administration to stay the course in Vietnam, even though the war there was a completely different situation.

REFERENCES: Piero Gleijeses, *The Dominican Crisis*, 1978; Abraham Lowenthal, *The Dominican Intervention*, 1972; Ted Szalc, *Dominican Diary*, 1965.

DOMINO THEORY. From the late 1940s to the early 1960s, the ''Domino Theory'' was a maxim of U.S. foreign policy in Southeast Asia and East Asia. President Harry Truman first gave rise to the idea in 1946 when he was promoting his Truman Doctrine to stop Communist guerrillas in Greece and Turkey. He claimed that if Greece and Turkey fell to communism, so would the rest of the Middle East, country by country, like a row of dominoes. In April 1954, during the Vietminh siege of the French fortress at Dien Bien Phu in Vietnam, President Dwight D. Eisenhower* resurrected the notion, arguing that if Vietnam fell to communism, the rest of Southeast Asia—Cambodia, Laos, Thailand, and Burma—would soon follow suit. If they fell, all of East Asia and the Pacific would be threatened. In the 1960s, John F. Kennedy* and Lyndon B. Johnson* both employed domino theory rhetoric to justify escalation of the war in Vietnam.

The domino theory got its real test in 1975, when North Vietnam overran Saigon* and reunited the country as the Socialist Republic of Vietnam. Cambodia and Laos soon went Communist as well. But Laos turned out to be the last domino to fall. The status quo prevailed in the rest of Southeast Asia and East Asia. Critics of the domino theory argue today that the only reason Cambodia and Laos went Communist was the misguided U.S. war in Indochina.

REFERENCES: Richard J. Barnet, *Roots of War: The Men and Institutions Behind U.S. Foreign Policy*, 1972; James S. Olson and Randy Roberts, *Where the Domino Fell: America and Vietnam, 1945–1995*, 1995.

THE DONNA REED SHOW. *The Donna Reed Show* was one of television's* most popular situation comedies in the late 1950s and 1960s. Produced by ABC, its first episode was broadcast on September 24, 1958. It starred Donna Reed as housewife Donna Stone, Carl Betz as her pediatrician husband, Shelley Fabares as her daughter Mary, and Paul Petersen as her son Jeff. The family lived in suburban Hilldale. The last episode of *The Donna Reed Show* was broadcast on September 3, 1966. *The Donna Reed Show* was a perfect symbol of the ideal, squeaky-clean traditional American family of the 1950s and early 1960s.

REFERENCE: Brenda Royce, *Donna Reed: A Bio-Bibliography*, 1990.

DONOVAN. Donovan Leitch was born in Glasgow, Scotland, May 10, 1946. When he was ten years old, the Leitch family moved to London. In 1965, several British television talent scouts heard some of Donovan's music, and they signed him to perform on the rock program *Ready Steady Go*. His first single record—"Catch the Wind"—did well, as did the next two, which were released in 1965: "Colours" and "Universal Soldier." Later that year, Donovan performed at the Newport Folk Festival in the United States. Donovan then rocketed to fame in America. His single "Sunshine Superman" became the number one hit single in 1966, and "Mellow Yellow" made it to number two in 1967. Some have described Donovan's music as "folk-rock hippie* mysticism." Other hit singles from 1967 to 1969 included "Epistle to Dippy," "There Is a Mountain," "Wear Your Love like Heaven," "Jennifer Jupiter," "Hurdy Gurdy Man," "Atlantis," and "Goo Goo Barabajagal (Love Is Hot)." By 1969, Donovan was deep into mystical studies under the Maharishi Mahesh Yogi,* and his recording career took a nosedive.

He tried to make a comeback in 1996, releasing his new album *Sutra*, but the recording was a commercial disappointment.

REFERENCE: Patricia Romanowski and Holly George-Warren, eds., *The New Rolling Stone Encyclopedia of Rock and Roll*, 1996.

"DON'T TRUST ANYONE OVER THIRTY." The phrase "Don't trust anyone over thirty" first emerged in the mid-1960s among members of the counterculture* to express their conviction that people over thirty years of age were part of an older, pre–World War II generation that did not understand the new world of drugs, peace, rock and roll, and open sexuality. Counterculture leaders like Jerry Rubin* and Abbie Hoffman* frequently repeated the phrase in front of student audiences in the 1960s.

REFERENCE: Christopher Bone, *The Disinherited Children: A Study of the New Left and the Generation Gap*, 1977.

THE DOORS. Jim Morrison, born James Douglas Morrison December 8, 1943, moved to California, where he became involved in the mass drug culture of the 1960s while attending the University of California at Los Angeles (UCLA). In 1965, he showed former classmate Ray Manzarek a few of his poems. The poetry impressed Manzarek, and he and Morrison mutually liked the idea of starting a rock band. Morrison would be the vocalist and write most of the songs, and Manzarek would be the organist. Jon Densmore joined as drummer, and Robby Krieger as guitarist. Morrison suggested "the Doors" as the band's title, inspired by *The Doors of Perception* by Aldous Huxley. The Doors began playing in Los Angeles clubs and had their breakthrough at the legendary club Whiskey a Go-Go, introducing the Doors as a dark, mysterious rock band compared to the "flower power" Haight-Ashbury scene springing up from San Francisco. Morrison also met his girlfriend Pamela Courson. Though both were unfaithful, they remained together until Morrison's death.

In 1966, Elektra Records signed the Doors. Their first self-titled album, *The Doors*, became a national success in 1967, containing the number one hit "Light My Fire," written by Robby Krieger. The same year the Doors released their second album, *Strange Days*, in which the song "Love Me Two Times" reached the charts. Jim Morrison remained estranged from his parents, brother, and sister, eventually cutting off all contact and withdrawing further into drugs and alcohol. Meanwhile, the Doors continued playing but often had problems due to Morrison's extreme actions, including his arrest on obscenity charges at a concert in New Haven, Connecticut, and their ban from *The Ed Sullivan Show*.

In 1968, the Doors were extremely popular in America and equally controversial. *Waiting for the Sun* became the third album released and was a number one hit, as well as the song "Hello, I Love You." The band enacted the song "Unknown Soldier" from the album, creating a musical film. The Doors also went on a brief European tour. At a concert later that year in Miami, Morrison was arrested and charged with "lewd and lascivious" behavior and released on bail.

The group released *The Soft Parade* in 1969, in which "Touch Me" was a hit. *Morrison Hotel*, released in 1970, made the Doors the first American rock group to achieve five gold albums in a row. The same year Elektra Records produced the group's first live album, *Absolutely Live*. Morrison also recorded *An American Prayer*, an album of his poetry reading. Meanwhile, the relations among the four group members worsened as Morrison fell into destructive alcoholism.

L.A. Woman would be the last album recorded by the original Doors. The record, which was released in 1971, contained the successful songs "Riders on the Storm" and "Lover Her Madly." The group was beginning to disintegrate, and in March 1971 Jim Morrison left with Pamela Courson for Paris. Exhausted from alcohol, drugs, and stardom, Morrison died July 3, 1971. The official cause of death was listed as heart failure. The remaining Doors, Manzarek, Krieger, and Densmore, went on to release two albums, *Other Voices* and *Full Circle*, which did very poorly. The trio broke up in 1972.

As a classic rock band, the Doors continue to have a tremendous influence. Their albums continue to sell, and the 1991 movie *The Doors* created additional resurgence in the Doors' music and essence. Jim Morrison has become an international legend as crowds still gather at his grave in Paris. Jim Morrison, like Elvis Presley and John Lennon, is one of the top-earning, deceased entertainers.
REFERENCES: James Riordan, *Break on Through: The Life and Death of Jim Morrison*, 1991; Bob Seymour, *The Death of James Morrison*, 1991.

Anne G. Woodward

DOO-WOP. The term "doo-wop" emerged in the late 1950s and continued throughout the 1960s as a reference to a form of rhythm and blues harmonic vocalizing. It involved the repetition of phonetic and nonsense syllables, such as "doo-wop," in intricate harmonic arrangements. The most representative rock-and-roll doo-wop singles included "Sh-Boom" by the Chords, "Earth Angel" by the Penguins, "Book of Love" by the Monotones, and "Little Darlin' " by Maurice Williams. Doo-wop had its origins in urban black vocal groups before it spread to white bands in the late 1950s.
REFERENCE: Patricia Romanowski and Holly George-Warren, eds., *The New Rolling Stone Encyclopedia of Rock and Roll*, 1996.

DOUGLAS, WILLIAM ORVILLE. William Orville Douglas, one of the most liberal Supreme Court justices in American history, was born October 16, 1898, in Maine, Minnesota. Raised in a desperately poor farm family, Douglas retained for his entire life a sensitivity to the plight of low-income people and a suspicion of corporate power. A polio attack in his childhood only intensified his compassion for the weak and suffering. He grew up in Yakima, Washington, and graduated from Whitman College in 1920 and then at the top of his class from Columbia University Law School. He tried for two years to work at a Wall Street law firm, but his own suspicions of his corporate clientele left him frustrated and unhappy. Douglas returned for a year to Yakima and then joined the law faculty at Columbia. In 1929, he moved to New Haven, Connecticut, to teach at Yale.

He soon earned a national reputation as an expert in finance law. In 1936, President Franklin D. Roosevelt brought Douglas to Washington as a member of the Securities and Exchange Commission (SEC), and in 1937 Douglas became chairman of the SEC. Douglas was a clear symbol of the "Second New Deal's" emphasis on corporate regulation, antitrust action, and progressive taxation. In 1939, Roosevelt named Douglas an associate justice of the Supreme Court to replace the retiring Louis Brandeis.

On the Roosevelt Court, Douglas maintained his reputation as an unabashed liberal. Throughout the 1930s and 1940s, he was a strong advocate of state taxation and regulation laws, clearly recognizing the principle of legislative supremacy and the "right to govern." He also was a general supporter of civil liberties and an opponent of government interference in them, except for wartime freedoms, where he believed that national emergencies sometimes justified extraordinary exercises of national power. Douglas was also a longtime protector of the rights of accused criminals to legal counsel and jury trials. Finally, he was a vigorous supporter of federal antitrust and pro-labor legislation.

During the 1940s and 1950s, Douglas's lifestyle and liberal views caused him severe political problems. Divorced three times between 1954 and 1966, he remarried quickly after each divorce and raised eyebrows in conservative Washington. Also, outspoken support of civil and criminal rights on the Warren Court raised the ire of conservatives, and in 1953 and 1970 Douglas faced impeachment charges. Special House judiciary subcommittees investigated him each time but found no grounds for impeachment. In January 1975 Douglas suffered a severe stroke. He tried to continue working, but his physical ailments weakened him, and he resigned in November 1975 after serving nearly thirty-seven years, longer than any other justice. William O. Douglas died January 19, 1980. REFERENCES: James C. Duram, *Justice William O. Douglas*, 1981; *New York Times*, January 20, 1980.

DOVE. During the 1960s and early 1970s, the term "dove" was used to refer to individuals in the United States who opposed the escalation of the Vietnam War.*
REFERENCE: James S. Olson, ed., *Dictionary of the Vietnam War*, 1988.

DOW CHEMICAL. See NAPALM.

DRAFT. Over 2 million men were inducted into military service during the Vietnam War* period in accordance with the Selective Service Act of 1948 and its ensuing extensions. The draft law provided for the registration of all males upon their eighteenth birthday. The president delegated authority in draft matters to the director of the selective service system. The director, his staff, and about 4,000 local draft boards throughout the country administered the system. Local draft boards were under the supervision of state directors, but quotas for inductees were set at the national level, which made its decision relative to the number of men from each state already in the military. The Department of Defense initiated draft calls for a given number of men, based on projected enlistments and needs. Draft deferments in terms of essential activities and critical occupations were defined by the Departments of Commerce and Labor. The secretary of defense defined the standards for physical, mental, and moral acceptability for military service.

Although the system operated under the regulations and standards drawn up at a national level, where the president could adjust induction numbers to meet changing political and military needs, local draft boards had considerable latitude in selecting men for service. Major inequities in the selective service system and its deferment procedures were recognized by both supporters and critics of the draft, but the majority of recommendations made by President Lyndon B. Johnson's* National Advisory Commission on Selective Service in 1967 to eliminate most deferments were not incorporated in the 1967 draft extension act. Both the inequities, where poor, rural, and minority young men were disproportionately drafted and sent to combat, and the increasing number of young men called to the draft made the selective service a natural target of the antiwar movement.* Antidraft activity ranged from Stop-the-Draft Week in October 1967 to break-ins of draft boards with the symbolic pouring of blood over the draft files.

As part of his policy of creating an all-volunteer U.S. military, President Richard M. Nixon* ended all draft calls in December 1972, and President Gerald Ford issued a proclamation terminating the remaining draft registration requirements in 1975. President Jimmy Carter, on January 21, 1977, pardoned all who had been convicted of violating the Selective Service Act during the Vietnam period. In 1979, President Carter reintroduced draft registration.

REFERENCES: Lawrence M. Baskir and William A. Strauss, *Chance and Circumstance: The Draft, the War, and the Vietnam Generation*, 1978; Stephen M. Kohn, *Jailed for Peace: The History of American Draft Law Violators*, 1986.

Linda Alkana

DYLAN, BOB. Robert Zimmerman was born on May 24, 1941, in Duluth, Minnesota. He grew up in Duluth and in Hibbing, Minnesota, an iron-mining town. An admirer of poet Dylan Thomas, Zimmerman changed his name to Bob Dylan and hit the road in his late teens, listening to folk music and beat poetry in cities around the country. In terms of his music, he looked to Woodie Guthrie almost as his alter ego, consciously imitating the legendary folk artist's style. By the early 1960s, Dylan had built a local reputation singing Guthrie ballads in the coffeehouses of Greenwich Village in New York City. He was discovered there by record producers.

Dylan released albums in 1962, 1963, and 1964, and two of his songs—"Blowin' in the Wind" and "The Times They Are A-Changin' "—quickly emerged as musical ensigns for the civil rights movement.* Dylan's music relied on simple melodies protesting social injustices. He never made any overtly anti-Vietnam songs, but he was nevertheless an icon in the antiwar movement.* In 1965, Dylan made a major artistic departure by adopting blues-based, rock-and-roll rhythms and going to electrically amplified instruments. In the process, with such albums as *Highway 61 Revisited* and *Blonde on Blonde*, he became the most influential figure in folk rock. Late in the 1960s, Dylan again reinvented himself artistically, meshing country-western rhythms with his own folk sounds. The album *Nashville Skyline* in 1969 was the best example of this style.

In the 1970s and 1980s, Dylan kept recording and performing, although his stature in the world of rock and roll had been largely eclipsed by new artists. His most prominent later works are *Blood on the Tracks* and *Desire* in 1975 and *Infidels* in 1983. Early in the 1990s, Dylan joined Roy Orbison,* George Harrison, and Tom Petty as one of the Travelling Wilburys.

REFERENCES: Clinton Heylin, *Bob Dylan*, 1995; Theodore Roszak, *The Making of a Counter Culture*, 1969; Richard Flacks, *Youth and Social Change*, 1971.

E

EASY RIDER. *Easy Rider* was a 1969 countercultural film that attracted a cult following. It starred Peter Fonda as Wyatt, Dennis Hopper as Billy, and Jack Nicholson as George Hanson. Wyatt and Billy leave on a cross-country motorcycle trip from California to New Orleans trying to "find the real America." Along the way they visit the "real" people—commune-based hippies,* poor farm families, and small towners. They pick up George Hanson, an alcoholic lawyer, in the cell of some small southern jail, and he joins them in their quest. The film celebrates "doing your own thing,"* drugs, rock and roll, and self-expression. Hanson is thrilled at the freedom he enjoys on the back seat of a motorcycle, but his is only a temporary stay, more a vacation than a lifestyle. Wyatt and Billy continue their journey. In the end, of course, they find the "real" America at the end of a double-barreled shotgun, where they are killed on a lonely stretch of highway by pickup truck-driving middle Americans who find them threatening.
REFERENCE: *New York Times*, July 15, 1969.

ECONOMIC OPPORTUNITY ACT OF 1964. In 1962, Michael Harrington* wrote a best-selling book entitled *Poverty in America*, which first exposed the millions of Americans who lived below what came to be called the "poverty line." Although the John F. Kennedy* administration had begun to talk about establishing some type of antipoverty program, President Lyndon B. Johnson* took the initiative in 1964 and made the "war on poverty"* the central part of his "Great Society"* programs. In his State of the Union address of January 8, 1964, Johnson called for a "war on poverty," and Congress responded by enacting the Economic Opportunity Act in August 1964. The legislation appropriated nearly $1 billion for a variety of work training, hiring incentives, education, Job Corps, and small business incentive programs. It also established an Office of Economic Opportunity to administer the program.
REFERENCE: James S. Olson, ed., *Dictionary of United States Economic History,* 1992.

THE ED SULLIVAN SHOW. *The Ed Sullivan Show* was the most popular and influential variety program in American television* history. First telecast on June 20, 1948, by CBS, the program was originally known as *Toast of the Town*. It was hosted by Ed Sullivan, a prominent New York entertainment journalist. Every Sunday evening for the next twenty-three years, Sullivan hosted the world's most popular performers. An invitation to *The Ed Sullivan Show* brought national exposure and certified the performer as part of the American mainstream. Elvis Presley* and the Beatles* were just two of the many acts that received influential national exposure on the program. By the late 1960s, however, viewers of the program had an older demographic profile, and CBS wanted to appeal to younger audiences. The last episode of *The Ed Sullivan Show* was broadcast on June 6, 1971.

REFERENCE: Jerry G. Bowles, *A Thousand Sundays: The Story of the Ed Sullivan Show*, 1980.

EDWARDS V. SOUTH CAROLINA. The so-called Warren Court of the 1950s and 1960s justifiably earned its reputation as the most liberal Supreme Court in U.S. history. Its liberal point of view was particularly evident in civil liberties decisions, especially in First Amendment freedom of speech and freedom of the press controversies. One example is *Edwards v. South Carolina*, decided by an 8 to 1 vote on February 25, 1963. Justice Potter Stewart* wrote the majority opinion. South Carolina authorities had arrested, tried, and convicted student demonstrators under ''breach-of-the-peace ordinances'' for conducting a peaceful protest march against racial discrimination. The Court overturned the convictions, arguing that they were violations of the First Amendment freedoms of speech, assembly, and petition.

REFERENCE: 372 U.S. 229 (1963).

EISENHOWER, DWIGHT DAVID. Dwight David Eisenhower was born October 14, 1890, in Denison, Texas. He was raised in Abilene, Kansas. Although his mother was a pacifist, Eisenhower attended the U.S. Military Academy at West Point, graduating in 1915. He spent the duration of World War I training troops at Camp Colt in Gettysburg, Pennsylvania. Although he begged for a transfer to a combat unit, Eisenhower was too good training other soldiers. During the 1920s, he filled a number of army assignments, earning a reputation as a skilled planner and logistics expert. He graduated at the top of his class in 1926 from the Command and General Staff School at Fort Leavenworth. He did similarly well at the National War College, graduating in 1928.

During his early career, Eisenhower had the opportunity of working under the leading lights of the U.S. Army. In 1926 he served on General John J. Pershing's staff, and from 1933 to 1935 he was assistant to Chief of Staff General Douglas MacArthur.* In 1935, he went to the Philippines with MacArthur and served as military adviser to the Filipino government. Eisenhower came back from the Philippines in 1939 with the rank of lieutenant colonel and assumed command of the fifteenth Infantry Regiment at Fort Ord, California. After a year at Fort Ord, he took over the ninth Army Corps at Fort Lewis, Washington.

After Pearl Harbor, Eisenhower was promoted to brigadier general and went to work as assistant chief of staff for war plans. He worked directly with Chief of Staff General George C. Marshall. Marshall was immediately impressed with Eisenhower's administrative abilities and organizational genius. In 1942, Marshall overlooked a number of senior general officers and appointed Eisenhower commanding general of U.S. forces training for European deployment. In August 1942, Marshall gave Eisenhower command of the Allied invasion of North Africa.

Eisenhower piled success upon success. In July 1943, he directed the invasion of Sicily, and in September he commanded the invasion of Italy. Marshall had no doubts about which of his officers should command the huge Allied invasion of France in June 1944. Eisenhower performed brilliantly, and in December 1944 he was promoted to general of the army. He accepted the German surrender in May 1945, and late in the year President Harry Truman appointed him chief of staff of the U.S. Army. He stepped down as chief of staff in 1948, spent two years as president of Columbia University, and then served as commanding general of North Atlantic Treaty Organization (NATO) forces from 1950 to 1952.

In 1952, the Republican Party brought Eisenhower home from Paris to run for the presidency. He defeated Democratic candidate Adlai Stevenson* and took the oath of office on January 20, 1953. He won a second term in 1956, again defeating Adlai Stevenson. Between Franklin D. Roosevelt in the 1930s and 1940s and Ronald Reagan* in the 1980s, Eisenhower was the only American president to serve two full terms. During his administration, he established a reputation for toughness, pragmatism, and good judgment. When he left the White House in 1961, he was viewed by most Americans as a wise, grandfatherly figure who had served his country with heroic distinction.

Eisenhower's health began to fail him in the 1960s, although he continued to be active in Republican Party politics and served as an elder statesman to Presidents Kennedy, Johnson, and Nixon,* offering gentle advice when it was solicited. Dwight D. Eisenhower died March 28, 1969.

REFERENCES: Stephen E. Ambrose, *Eisenhower: Soldier, General of the Army, President-Elect, 1890–1952*, 1983, and *Eisenhower: The President*, 1984.

THE ELECTION OF 1960. As the presidential election of 1960 approached, both parties geared up for victory. President Dwight D. Eisenhower* had completed two terms in the White House, and both Democrats and Republicans would be nominating new contenders. The GOP (Grand Old Party) nomination was close to an open-and-shut case. Vice President Richard M. Nixon* had been all but anointed by Eisenhower, and although Governor Nelson Rockefeller* of New York and Senator Henry Cabot Lodge* of Massachusetts expressed interest in running, neither could sustain a credible campaign. Nixon had the nomination in hand by the time of the Republican convention in Chicago at the end of July 1960. He selected Henry Cabot Lodge as his running mate.

The Democratic fight for the nomination, however, was wide open. Adlai Stevenson* had lost two elections in a row, and he did not stand a chance of securing the nomination for a third time. The mantle of the liberal wing of the party shifted to Senator Hubert Humphrey* of Minnesota, whose record on civil rights and support of a New Deal philosophy had few rivals. On the conservative side, Senator Lyndon B. Johnson* of Texas, the Senate majority leader and a legislative genius, announced his candidacy. So did Senator John F. Kennedy* of Massachusetts. Kennedy had the advantage of being young, charismatic, and moderate. He was identified with neither the liberals nor the conservatives in the Democratic Party, and his own legislative record had been decidedly non-ideological. Kennedy's greatest liability in 1960 was his religion. He was a Roman Catholic at a time in American history when that still mattered. No Catholic had ever been elected president, and millions of Bible-belt Protestants wanted to keep it that way.

The Democratic presidential primaries were dogfights, with Humphrey, Johnson, and Kennedy all staging strong campaigns. In the end, Kennedy's youthful charisma won out. He deftly handled the religion issue, promising to be his own man and not a tool of the pope, but he also appealed to the country's best instincts, asking Americans not to hold his religion against him, to demonstrate their commitment to freedom of religion by voting for him. It was a brilliant strategy, and he prevailed over Johnson and Humphrey. Kennedy won the Democratic nomination on the first ballot at the party's July convention in Los Angeles. He turned to Lyndon Johnson for his running mate.

Nixon's strategy was to campaign in all fifty states, to prove that he was a national, not a regional, candidate. Kennedy decided to focus all of his energies in the most populous states, where big electoral totals could be accumulated. His was a more efficient use of time. Nixon got tired because of all the traveling, and a bout with phlebitis also hurt him. Both men took a stand as the coldest of cold warriors, blasting one another for not being fervent enough in their opposition to the Soviet Union and world communism. The Democrats also manufactured the nonexistent issue of a missile gap between the United States and the Soviet Union, accusing the Eisenhower administration of allowing the United States to fall behind in the number of missiles and nuclear warheads and putting the nation at risk. The Republicans vehemently denied the charge. For their part, they charged Kennedy with being inexperienced and naive on the stage of world politics, contrasting him to Nixon.

The most innovative element of the campaign was the televised debates. On September 26 and October 7, 13, and 21, Nixon and Kennedy faced off before a national television* audience. Journalists asked each of them questions, and each candidate was allowed time to rebut the answers of his opponent. Nixon had been a first-class debater in high school and college, and he expected to be able to handle Kennedy easily. In fact, Nixon hoped to be able to expose Kennedy's lack of experience in matters of global significance.

But the Kennedy campaign was savvy about television. They knew that image and appearance, not answers and rebuttals, would matter in the debate. Kennedy was not going to try to win points from debate coaches; he wanted to strike a responsive chord with the voting public. A huge audience tuned in to the first debate. For several days before the debate, Kennedy had vacationed at the beach and gotten a good tan. Campaign media advisers knew that his face would require only a minimum of makeup before the camera lights. He also wore a dark blue suit, one that would contrast sharply with the gray background of the television studio. Nixon, on the other hand, campaigned up to the last minute and was tired and still ill on the day of the debate. He was pale and wore a gray suit, which tended to blend in with the set background. To television audiences, Kennedy appeared strong and healthy while Nixon seemed fatigued. Radio audiences and debate judges gave Nixon the nod in terms of the debate itself, but among television audiences, Kennedy was clearly the winner. There was no longer any doubt that he could hold his own against Nixon.

The election went down to the wire, too close for pollsters and political pros to call. The lead seesawed back and forth all evening long on November 8 and right through the morning of November 9. In the end, it all boiled down to Texas and Illinois. Lyndon Johnson had a death grip on the Democratic Party in Texas, and returns from corrupt counties in south Texas were slow in coming in, as if Johnson were waiting to see how many votes it would take to counter Republican strength in the Houston, Dallas, and San Antonio suburbs. The same thing happened in Illinois, where Mayor Richard Daley* of Chicago held up the city's vote count until Republican returns from southern Illinois were in. Out of 68.8 million votes cast, Kennedy won 34,226,731 to Nixon's 34,108,157, little more than a 118,000-vote difference.

Even then, however, the outcome was uncertain. Republicans all over the country, but especially in Texas and Illinois, screamed fraud and demanded recounts. The results in Hawaii were so close that a recount there had to be held. Although Nixon had won Mississippi, its electoral delegation was not bound by law to vote for the ticket. Nixon had a decision to make. He could demand a recount and throw the presidential succession into disarray, or he could bite his tongue and let Kennedy win. He decided on the latter course. If a recount were held, and he still lost, it would look like sour grapes. If he won a recount, it might precipitate a constitutional crisis. Nixon licked his wounds and kept his mouth shut. When the electoral votes were finally cast, Kennedy received 303 to Nixon's 229. John F. Kennedy was the next president of the United States.

REFERENCE: Theodore M. White, *The Making of the President, 1960*, 1961.

THE ELECTION OF 1962. During the congressional elections of 1962, the Republicans expected to make important gains, as the party that had lost the

previous presidential election had so often done in American history. They also thought the Kennedy administration was vulnerable. On the foreign policy front, the Bay of Pigs* fiasco, the erection of the Berlin* Wall, and the ongoing problems with communist guerrillas in Laos and Vietnam had been setbacks for the administration. But late in October, at the symbolic last minute of the campaign, the Cuban missile crisis* developed, and the world teetered on the brink of nuclear warfare. To most Americans, President Kennedy* handled the crisis with maturity, toughness, and skill, and the resolution of the crisis before the election boosted Democrats at the polls. When the election votes were counted, the Democrats lost only a handful of seats in the House of Representatives and actually gained five seats in the U.S. Senate, retaining their control of Congress. Republicans did win several important gubernatorial contests. Nelson Rockefeller* was reelected in New York, and George Romney* won the governorship in Michigan. But Richard Nixon,* in an ill-fated campaign against incumbent Pat Brown for the governorship of California, lost by a substantial margin.
REFERENCE: *New York Times*, November 7–8, 1962.

THE ELECTION OF 1964. Richard M. Nixon's* defeat at the hands of John F. Kennedy* in the election of 1960* had given conservatives the upper hand in the Republican Party. Although Nixon's anticommunist credentials were above reproach, he was a moderate on domestic policy and had been unable to prevail over Kennedy's so-called liberalism. Conservatives were convinced that Americans needed and wanted a real political choice and that if the Republican Party would really put forward a true conservative candidate, voters would respond positively.

The darling of Republican conservatives was Senator Barry Goldwater* of Arizona. Blunt, outspoken, and beholden to nobody, Goldwater was his own man. He minced few words in warning of the evils of world communism and the need for foreign policy vigilance, and he told Americans, again and again, that they must look to the private sector, not the federal government, for the solution to their social and economic challenges. At the Republican national convention in San Francisco in July, Goldwater got the nomination and picked New York congressman William Miller as his running mate.

Kennedy had relished the chance of running for reelection against Barry Goldwater, since he was certain that the Arizonan was way too conservative for most Americans. But Kennedy did not get the chance to run. When an assassin's bullet cut him down in November 1963, the presidency went to Lyndon B. Johnson.* During his first year in the White House, Johnson launched the Great Society* program of civil rights and antipoverty legislation, using the federal government in exactly the ways Goldwater opposed. Johnson won the Democratic nomination by acclamation and selected Senator Hubert H. Humphrey* of Minnesota as his vice presidential running mate. The election of 1964 provided voters with one of the clearest choices in American electoral history—a certifiable liberal, incumbent president running against a genuine conservative.

Goldwater ran an in-your-face campaign, never apologizing or trying to underplay his conservatism, telling the voters that Johnson and the Democrats were soft on communism, that the Great Society programs would eventually bankrupt America without solving any of the problems they were trying to address, and that the welfare state of entitlements and social security should be dismantled. Individuals should be liberated from government control to make money and stimulate economic growth; in the process, everyone would benefit.

Johnson had a field day with Goldwater's statements. He warned that if Goldwater won, the elderly would lose their monthly social security checks, farmers would lose their crop subsidies, the unemployed would lose their benefits, and the poor would be without the support of welfare, food stamps, and housing subsidies. The Democrats ran a series of highly misleading television commercials implying that a Goldwater victory might mean nuclear holocaust because the Arizona senator was too extreme. Americans listened intently to what the president was saying.

But the Democrats were still vulnerable on the foreign policy front in 1964. The Vietnam War* was going badly, actually slipping out of control, and military officials seemed unable to do much to stem the tide. Republican criticisms that the Democrats were losing Vietnam to the communists were beginning to resonate among voters, as was Goldwater's argument that Johnson just was not tough enough to be president. The president needed a dramatic illustration of his willingness to get tough with the communists, and at the end of July the North Vietnamese handed him one on a silver platter.

For years American naval vessels had conducted clandestine raids on North Vietnamese coastal communications facilities, and on July 31, 1964, North Vietnamese patrol boats attacked a U.S. destroyer in the Gulf of Tonkin. The attack was of no military significance, but Johnson saw his political opportunity and seized it. Several days later, when American sailors temporarily misread radar signals in the Gulf of Tonkin and mistakenly reported another enemy attack, Johnson sent to Congress what later became known as the Gulf of Tonkin Resolution,* asking for the power to implement whatever military measures were necessary to protect American lives. Congress gave him what he wanted, and Johnson used the resolution to begin a bombing campaign over North Vietnam. Middle America cheered the use of force, and Goldwater lost the only issue he really owned.

The election was over before it ever really began. Goldwater's strident rhetoric scared most Americans, and Johnson liberally took advantage of their fears. Liberal Republicans like Governor Nelson Rockefeller* of New York sat out the election, refusing to endorse Goldwater's candidacy. Goldwater did not have a chance. On the evening of November 3, 1964, the outcome was certain before the polls had even closed. The Republicans were in for a political catastrophe.

Johnson took 43,100,000 votes to Goldwater's 27,100,000 and 486 electoral votes to Goldwater's 49. It was the greatest landslide of the twentieth century, and Democrats increased their hold on both houses of Congress.
REFERENCE: Theodore M. White, *The Making of the President, 1964*, 1965.

THE ELECTION OF 1966. After their landslide victory in the presidential election of 1964, the Democratic Party was in its most enviable political position since the elections of 1932 and 1934 during the Great Depression. They controlled the House of Representatives and the U.S. Senate by huge majorities. President Lyndon B. Johnson* had then used that majority to promote his campaign for civil rights* and the war against poverty. By 1966, however, the Democrats were considerably more vulnerable. The rise of the black power* movement and African-American rebellions in several major cities in 1965 and 1966 had created the beginnings of a white backlash, and the war in Vietnam seemed out of control, with more and more American troops being deployed without any tangible progress in the war. Casualty rates climbed enormously, and the antiwar movement* was gaining strength. The elections proved just how vulnerable the Democrats were. Although the party retained control of Congress, they lost forty-seven seats in the House of Representatives and five seats in the U.S. Senate. Republicans also gained a net of eight governorships. The GOP (Grand Old Party) was well poised for the elections of 1968.
REFERENCES: *New York Times*, November 9–10, 1966.

THE ELECTION OF 1968. By 1968, the Republicans could smell victory in the air. Vietnam had become the Democrats' war, a quagmire of death, destruction, and dollars that seemed to have no end and was incapable of bringing Vietnamese communists to their knees. All through 1967, the administration had promised the country that the war was coming to its expected conclusion, but on the last day of January 1968, the communists unleashed the Tet Offensive,* a huge, coordinated, countrywide attack on American and South Vietnamese forces. Although American soldiers repulsed the attack and then all but wiped out the Vietcong* as a fighting force, the Tet Offensive proved to be a strategic triumph for North Vietnam. Americans were sick of the war and wanted out. They were tired of seeing their boys die for nothing.

The domestic front was no better for the Democrats. Although the president had put through Congress the greatest legislative package since the New Deal, the civil rights movement* had turned sour, with black power* rhetoric and burning, riot-torn cities giving tens of millions of middle- and working-class whites reason to wonder if Goldwater's prediction that big government could not solve anything might be true after all. Conservatives called the president "soft on crime" and demanded a new emphasis on law and order. Lyndon B. Johnson* wanted a second term in office, since it would give him the most presidential longevity, save for that of his idol Franklin D. Roosevelt, in U.S. history.

Republicans were dead set on denying him that record. After the debacle of 1964, conservative Republicans did not really have a chance of putting Goldwater or any of his ideological allies on a presidential ticket. But they were not about to give a liberal the ticket either. Nelson Rockefeller,* George Romney,* Charles Percy,* and John Lindsay* had all sat out the election of 1964,* refusing to back Goldwater and actually giving informal endorsements to Lyndon Johnson. Conservatives considered them spineless traitors. The Republicans needed a moderate, a middle-of-the-roader who had supported Goldwater in 1964 but carried none of the Arizona senator's ideological baggage. Only one man really filled the bill: Richard M. Nixon.*

But Nixon had a huge problem of his own. He lost, narrowly to be sure, the presidential election of 1960 to John F. Kennedy,* and then he had gone on to lose, not so narrowly, the California gubernatorial election in 1962 to Pat Brown. A two-time loser who had not had a winning election of his own since 1950, when he had entered the U.S. Senate, Nixon would have to prove in the Republican presidential primaries that he could win votes. He did, handily eliminating all of the other competition before the Republicans ever got to their August 1968 convention in Miami.

Goldwater had managed to deny Lyndon Johnson five states in the Deep South in 1964, and Nixon wanted to match and even improve on that record. To do so, he developed what later became known as the "southern strategy."* He wanted to appeal to discontented southern whites without coming out point-blank against the Civil Rights Act of 1964, which Nixon personally supported. Instead, he condemned antiwar protesters and urban rioters, called for law and order, and denounced the busing of schoolchildren to achieve desegregation. He also privately promised southern politicians—Republicans as well as Democrats—that if he won the election, he would see to it that conservatives and southerners were appointed to the federal bench.

Part of the southern strategy was also selecting the right vice presidential running mate. Conservatives had an especially close eye on this one, since many of them suspected that Nixon was actually quite liberal himself on domestic issues—a sort of conservative lamb in liberal wolf's clothing. Nixon wanted a law-and-order Republican, an ideological hit man who could push all of the right buttons among white southerners, taking the low campaign road while Nixon remained on the high road. He decided on Governor Spiro Agnew* of Maryland. Agnew had all of the law-and-order credentials and headed one of the border states, where Nixon needed to do well.

But the southern strategy was soon complicated by the entry of Governor George Wallace* of Alabama into the race. A states' rights conservative who hated the Civil Rights Act of 1964 and the Voting Rights Act of 1965* and wanted to turn back the clock on the civil rights movement,* Wallace would appeal to white voters in the Deep South and rob Nixon of that electoral base. Wallace picked former air force general Curtis LeMay* as his running mate. But Nixon still hoped that the southern strategy, along with having Spiro Agnew on the ticket, would give him strength in the Upper South and border states. What he did not realize was that Wallace's entry into the race would actually draw some blue-collar support in the North away from Democrats.

The Democrats had an even bigger challenge on their hands. Opposition to the Vietnam War* had spread from liberals to many conservatives, and President Johnson still seemed to have no way of getting out of the quagmire. The spectacular, surprise nature of the Tet Offensive at the end of January 1968 only deepened American cynicism about the war. The domestic front was no better for the Democratic Party. Urban riots and the rhetoric of black power had fractured the civil rights coalition and driven large numbers of whites, particularly blue-collar workers, into the conservative camp.

The depth of the division in the Democratic Party became clear in February 1968, when Senator Eugene McCarthy* of Minnesota, a vociferous opponent of the Vietnam War, challenged President Johnson in the New Hampshire presidential primary. Although McCarthy did not win the primary, he was only narrowly defeated by a sitting president. Within a matter of days, Senator Robert F. Kennedy* of New York, another antiwar Democrat, announced his candidacy for the presidential nomination. Convinced that his chances of renomination were threatened and his chances of reelection doomed, Johnson announced at the end of March his decision not to seek a second full term in the White House. That created a vacuum that Vice President Hubert Humphrey* decided to fill with his own run for the Democratic presidential nomination. When Senator Kennedy was assassinated in June 1968, the only two viable candidates remaining were Eugene McCarthy and Hubert Humphrey.

Humphrey went to the Democratic presidential convention* in Chicago in August 1968 with a lock on the nomination. But what happened there proved to be a catastrophe for the Democrats. Antiwar demonstrators took to the streets, blaming Democrats for the war, and Chicago police went after them and precipitated a riot. In front of a national television audience, the Democrats exposed their weaknesses. Humphrey selected Senator Edmund Muskie* of Maine as his vice presidential running mate, but he left Chicago with his candidacy badly damaged.

During the campaign, Humphrey finally charted an independent course on Vietnam, advocating a bombing halt and de-escalation, and preached what he called the "politics of joy," meaning a continuation of the Great Society.* Nixon campaigned on themes of law and order, making the federal government more efficient, and opposition to antiwar protesters. He also promised that he was more capable than the Democrats of negotiating a settlement to the Vietnam War. George Wallace continued his antifederal government, anti–civil rights, pro–states' rights crusade.

The nastiest issue of the fall campaign involved the Supreme Court. Chief Justice Earl Warren* had presided over the most liberal period in the Court's history. Uncertain about the outcome of the election of 1968, Warren decided to resign from the Court earlier than he had once planned in order to give

President Johnson the chance to replace him with a young liberal who would preserve his judicial legacy. Johnson jumped at the opportunity and submitted the name of Supreme Court justice Abe Fortas,* his old friend and confidant, to replace Warren. Nixon and the Republicans shouted their opposition immediately, arguing that selection of Warren's replacement ought to be the prerogative of the next president, whoever he might be, not the current one. They vowed to fight confirmation in the Senate.

Fortas proved to be his own worst enemy. During the controversy over his appointment in October 1968, the press revealed that during his tenure on the Supreme Court, Fortas had continued to advise the president politically and had accepted lecture fees, two practices that most jurists found unethical. The press had a field day with the news, and Republicans launched an ironclad filibuster in the Senate, which the Democrats could not stop. The Senate voted 45 to 43 to end the filibuster, but Senate rules required fifty-nine votes. Johnson withdrew the nomination.

At the end of October, to boost Humphrey's chances at the polls, President Johnson dramatically announced an end to the bombing campaigns over North Vietnam and the opening of peace negotiations in Paris. Soon, the presidential race was neck-and-neck between Humphrey and Nixon, and on election eve it had become a toss-up. Nixon worried that the election would slip out of his hands just as the election of 1960 had done. But it was not to be. When the votes were counted, Nixon had his lease on the White House. His victory margin had been razor-thin—31,785,480 votes to Humphrey's 31,275,166 and Wallace's 9,906,473. In the electoral college, Nixon had 301 to Humphrey's 191 and Wallace's 46. But Nixon failed to sweep other Republicans into Congress. The Democrats remained firmly in control of the House and the Senate.
REFERENCE: Theodore M. White, *The Making of the President, 1968*, 1969.

ELEMENTARY AND SECONDARY EDUCATION ACT OF 1965. A central element of President Lyndon B. Johnson's* "Great Society"* was the improvement of American education, and the Elementary and Secondary Education Act of 1965 became a keystone of federal education policy. There was a widespread belief that poor school systems perpetuated poverty in many areas of America. Because school funding was tied to the property tax base in most areas, a vicious cycle dominated the schools. The law therefore provided federal funds to improve school libraries, language laboratories, learning centers, and support services in poor school districts. As a result of the legislation, the funding of Indian schools—federal as well as state and local—increased dramatically.
REFERENCE: Lyndon B. Johnson, *The Vantage Point*, 1970.

ELKINS V. UNITED STATES. During the 1960s, the Supreme Court under the leadership of Chief Justice Earl Warren* continued its program of broadening individual rights while narrowing those of federal, state, and local gov-

ernment officials. *Elkins v. United States*, decided on June 27, 1960, involved Fourth Amendment protections against illegal searches and seizures. By a narrow 5 to 4 margin, with Justice Potter Stewart* writing the majority opinion, the Court prohibited the introduction in a federal court of any evidence illegally obtained by state authorities.
REFERENCE: 364 U.S. 206 (1960).

EMERGENCY FEED GRAIN ACT OF 1961. The chronic problem in American agriculture—overproduction—has inspired a number of proposed solutions. In 1961, Congress passed the Emergency Feed Grain Act in an attempt to stem the tide of massive surpluses and falling prices for grain sorghum and corn. Participating farmers who retired at least 20 percent of their land from production were paid a stipend estimated at 50 percent of their costs of production. They received certificates allowing them to take payment in cash or in Commodity Credit Corporation grain supplies. The bill succeeded in withdrawing more than 20 million acres from production and cut production by more than 420 million bushels.
REFERENCE: James S. Olson, ed., *Dictionary of United States Economic History,* 1992.

ENCLAVE STRATEGY. As the political situation deteriorated in South Vietnam in the early 1960s, a major debate ensued in the John F. Kennedy* and Lyndon B. Johnson* admnistrations about how best to deal with the crisis. In the Pentagon, traditionalists like Admiral Ulysses Sharp and General William Westmoreland* advocated a rapid buildup of conventional U.S. forces and a military defeat of the enemy through a massive, comprehensive offensive. Edward Lansdale, an employee of the Central Intelligence Agency* (CIA), urged the U.S. to emphasize counterinsurgency* and pacification tactics. Undersecretary of State George Ball* had serious reservations about introduction of American combat forces.

Eventually, General Westmoreland hit on a compromise. The so-called enclave strategy embraced the notion that the United States should secure the major cities and establish defensive enclaves throughout South Vietnam. From these secure cities, towns, and bases, U.S. troops would engage in aggressive search-and-destroy* patrols to locate and destroy enemy forces. At first, the U.S. military operated only in support of Army of the Republic of Vietnam (ARVN) troops. By the end of 1965, however, as doubts about ARVN's fighting abilities deepened, U.S. troops were already taking the initiative away from ARVN and engaging in direct search-and-destroy missions themselves. That remained the pattern of the war until 1969 and 1970, when the United States once again adopted a defensive posture and tried to hold on to enclaves.
REFERENCES: Samuel Freeman, "Enclave Strategy," in James S. Olson, ed., *Dictionary of the Vietnam War,* 1988; Harold K. Johnson, "The Enclave Concept: A 'License to Hunt'," *Army,* (April 1968); Andrew F. Krepinevich, Jr., *The Army and*

Vietnam, 1986; Bruce Palmer Jr., *The 25-Year War*, 1984; Peter Poole, *Eight Presidents and Indochina*, 1878; William R. Corson, *The Betrayal*, 1968.

ENGLE V. VITALE. The Supreme Court under Chief Justice Earl Warren* earned a reputation for limiting the powers of the state and enhancing the rights and freedoms of individuals. That was especially true in how the Court interpreted First Amendment issues during the 1960s. *Engle v. Vitale* was a good example. The case was decided on June 25, 1962, with Justice Hugo Black* writing the majority opinion. It was a 6 to 1 vote. The case revolved around the issue of prayer in school, in particular whether or not a public school could require students to recite a state-composed prayer. The Court decided that such a policy violated the establishment clause of the First Amendment. Even if the prayer was nondenominational, and objecting students were excused from participation, such a daily prayer was an obvious attempt by a governmental entity to promote religion. The decision raised, and continues to raise, bitter protests from fundamentalist groups in the United States.
REFERENCE: 370 U.S. 421 (1962).

ENTHOVEN, ALAIN. Alain Enthoven was born September 10, 1930, in Seattle Washington. In 1952, he received a degree in economics from Stanford, where he developed a fascination for public policy. After completing a Rhodes Scholarship at Oxford, he went for a Ph.D. in economics at the Massachusetts Institute for Technology, finishing there in 1956. At the time, the best place for a Democrat interested in public policy was the Rand Corporation; Enthoven worked from 1956 to 1960. With John Kennedy's* election in 1960, Enthoven became deputy assistant secretary at the Pentagon.

By 1966, he was senior assistant to Secretary of Defense Robert McNamara.* From that position, he continually expressed misgivings about U.S. policy in Vietnam. Enthoven believed that the key issue was nationalism, not communism, and that the key to long-term victory was political, not military. The decisions of the Kennedy and Johnson administrations to escalate the war only made matters worse. Few people listened, however, and Enthoven kept his point of view confined to policy discussion councils.

When Richard Nixon* and Republicans triumphed in the election of 1968,* Enthoven left public life for Litton Industries, where he became a vice president and then president of Litton Medical Services. He left Litton in 1973 to become a management professor at Stanford. He focused his expertise on health care issues, and in 1980 wrote *New Directions in Health Care* and *Health Plan*. In 1988, Enthoven wrote the influential *Theory and Practice of Managed Competition in Health Care Finance*.
REFERENCES: *Who's Who in America, 1984–1985*; Alain Enthoven and Wayne Smith, *How Much is Enough? Shaping the Defense Program, 1965–1969*, 1971.

ENVIRONMENTAL DEFENSE FUND. The Environmental Defense Fund was established in 1967 by Victor Yannacone. It was based in Long Island, New

York. Its first crusade was to expose the negative health effects of DDT, and from there the Environmental Defense Fund worked to analyze the economic and scientific claims of American industries and to assess the effects of toxic chemicals on soil, water, plants, and animal life. During the late 1960s and 1970s, the Environmental Defense Fund relied primarily on litigation to promote its interests, but in recent years it has broadened its tactics to include public health education as well.

REFERENCE: Loree Bykerk and Ardith Maney, *U.S. Consumer Interest Groups: Institutional Profiles*, 1995.

ENVIRONMENTAL MOVEMENT. Although the environmental movement really gained political momentum in the 1970s, particularly after the Earth Day demonstrations in April 1970, it had its origins in the political activism of the 1960s. The godmother of the movement was Rachel Carson, a biologist whose best-selling book *Silent Spring* (1962) captured the imagination of President John F. Kennedy* and millions of other Americans. It was an attack on the use of chemical fertilizers and pesticides by farmers and pointed out the potentially harmful effects of these on animals and humans. *The Saturday Review* called the book "a devastating, heavily documented, relentless attack upon human carelessness, greed, and irresponsibility." Because of the debate created by this book, Kennedy ordered an investigation into the problem. In May 1963, the President's Science Advisory Committee agreed with the findings in *Silent Spring*, and this led to the banning of several dangerous chemicals, including DDT.

From that point on, the environmental movement steadily gained momentum. Special interest groups like the Environmental Defense Fund appeared to lobby for a cleaner environment through federal government industrial standards. In 1963, Congress had passed clean air legislation that provided $95 million in grants to assist local governments in developing programs to reduce air pollution. Air pollution was one of the leading environmental problems, and the primary culprit was auto emissions. Subsequent legislation (the Clean Air Act Amendments of 1965) authorized the federal government to set auto emission standards and launch research programs to reduce sulfur dioxide emissions. The Air Quality Act of 1967 greatly expanded federal control and research programs by appropriating more than $550 million. In March 1970, Senator Edmund Muskie, a Democrat from Maine, challenged the automobile industry to engage in what he called a "forced technology" and reduce harmful emissions by 90 percent. Under Muskie's sponsorship, Congress passed the Clean Air Act of 1970. It constituted a $1.1 billion program that required 1975 automobiles to reduce carbon monoxide and hydrocarbon emissions by 90 percent. Also, 1976 automobiles had to emit 90 percent less of the nitrogen oxides.

Some environmentalists also began preaching dire macroenvironmental consequences for the world. In April 1968, a group of thirty scientists, educators, economists, humanists, industrialists, and national and international civil servants gathered in the Italian capital to consider the future of the world economy. Out of their meeting emerged the Club of Rome,* a group committed to keeping the world informed about the state of the global economy and environment. Between 1969 and 1972, the Club of Rome conducted what it called the Project on the Predicament of Mankind. Using computer models and assuming no change in population growth rates, the members of the Club of Rome predicted an ecological and economic disaster in the early decades of the twenty-first century. They warned that exponential population growth combined with continued industrialization would eventually send the world economy into a tailspin and lead to mass starvation and global suffering. The only answer, they argued, was the establishment of limits to world growth. During the late 1960s and early 1970s, when the environmental movement in the United States was especially strong, the apocalyptic predictions of the Club of Rome found a sympathetic audience.

At the height of the environmental movement in 1969, President Richard M. Nixon* proposed a series of laws that culminated in the Environmental Policy Act of 1969. The law required the federal government to direct each of its agencies to develop an environmental protection policy and also demanded that environmental impact studies be conducted before the implementation of any new government program. The law created a Council on Environmental Quality to serve as an advisory body on environmental concerns. Nixon staffed the Council on Environmental Quality in 1970, but since then its recommendations have had little impact on federal policy.

REFERENCE: James S. Olson, ed., *Dictionary of United States Economic History,* 1992.

ENVIRONMENTAL POLICY ACT OF 1969. See **ENVIRONMENTAL MOVEMENT.**

EQUAL EMPLOYMENT OPPORTUNITY COMMISSION. The Equal Employment Opportunity Commission (EEOC) was created on July 2, 1965, as directed by Title VII of the Civil Rights Act of 1964. Its charge was to prohibit employment discrimination on the base of race, color, religion, sex, or national origin. As a result of the Equal Employment Opportunity Act of 1972, its provisions also apply to state and local governments as well as federal agencies and private employers. At first its authority was limited to persuasion and conciliation, but amendments in 1972 empowered the EEOC to bring suit when necessary, and amendments in 1974 gave the EEOC power to file pattern and practice lawsuits as well.

The EEOC is a bipartisan commission of five members appointed for five-year terms. The most effective tactic employed by the EEOC has been to issue its employment guidelines, which most large employers gradually adopted in order to avoid lawsuits. The guidelines do not have the force of law, but the federal courts often rely on them in making decisions about individual discrimination cases. As a result of EEOC activities, overt employment discrimination

has been largely eliminated in the United States, and the principle of affirmative action* now plays a much more prominent role in the hiring and promotion procedures of most large employers.
REFERENCE: James S. Olson, ed., *Dictionary of United States Economic History,* 1992.

ESCOBEDO V. ILLINOIS. During the tenure of Chief Justice Earl Warren* (1953–1960), the Supreme Court assumed the most liberal constitutional profile in U.S. history, narrowing the powers of government officials and broadening the rights of individuals. A series of decisions revolving around the right-to-counsel clause of the Sixth Amendment substantially increased the rights of criminal defendants. One such case was *Escobedo v. Illinois,* decided on June 22, 1964, by a 5 to 4 vote. Justice Arthur Goldberg* wrote the majority opinion. The question revolved around the admissibility into trial of evidence acquired by police who had failed to inform a suspect of his or her right to counsel or who had ignored a request for counsel by a suspect. The Court decided that such evidence was not admissible.
REFERENCE: 378 U.S. 478 (1964).

ESTABLISHMENT. The term "establishment" emerged as a modifier in the 1960s to describe mainstream American society. Universities, corporations, the military, labor unions, and the middle and upper classes were all considered part of the "establishment."
REFERENCES: Ronald Fraser, *1968: A Student Generation in Revolt,* 1988; Todd Gitlin, *The Sixties: Years of Hope, Days of Rage,* 1987.

EVERS, MEDGAR. Medgar Evers was born in Decatur, Mississippi, July 2, 1925. He joined the U.S. Army in 1943, and when World War II was over, Evers enrolled at Alcorn A&M College. He graduated with a bachelor's degree in 1947 and sold insurance for several years. But his heart was in civil rights work, not business. When Evers was fourteen years old, he had witnessed the lynching of one of his father's friends. The man had allegedly insulted a white woman. Evers never forgot the incident. He joined the National Association for the Advancement of Colored People (NAACP) in 1952 and became a professional staff member in 1954, the same year he tried to enroll at the University of Mississippi. Evers rose quickly to become head of the NAACP in Mississippi.

He was diametrically opposed to segregation and more than once suffered a beating because of his refusal to go to the back of a bus or drink out of a racially designated fountain. He worked diligently at registering African-American voters and trying to end racial discrimination in the criminal justice system. Death threats became commonplace for the Evers family in the early 1960s. A target of Ku Klux Klan terrorists, Evers had his home firebombed in May 1963. On June 12, 1963, he was assassinated in the driveway of his home.
REFERENCES: *New York Times,* June 13, 1963; Adam Nossiter, *Of Long Memory: Mississippi and the Murder of Medgar Evers,* 1994.

F

FAIL SAFE. *Fail Safe* was a chilling film of the early 1960s that captured the prevailing fear of nuclear conflict in the United States during the post–Cuban missile crisis* heyday of the Cold War.* Released in 1964, *Fail Safe* was directed by Sidney Lumet and based on the book by Eugene Burdick and Harvey Wheeler. It starred Henry Fonda, Walter Matthau, Dan O'Herlihy, and Frank Overton. A taught, frightening drama, *Fail Safe* deals with the possibility of the system's failing. A nuclear bomb–armed American B-52 mistakenly crosses its "fail-safe" line—the point at which it either returns home or penetrates Soviet air space and initiates its bombing run—and heads for Moscow. The United States is unable to recall the plane, and the aircraft drops its bombload on Moscow. The only way to prove that the bombing is an unintentional mistake and prevent a thermonuclear holocaust is for the president of the United States (Henry Fonda) to have U.S. bombers incinerate New York City with a nuclear weapon.

REFERENCE: *New York Times*, September 16, 1964.

FALL, BERNARD. Author of the *Viet Minh Regime* (1956), *Le Viet Minh, 1945–1960* (1960), *Street without Joy* (1961), *The Two Viet Nams* (1963), *Viet Nam Witness* (1966), *Hell in a Very Small Place* (1966), and *Last Reflections on a War* (1967) and editor with Marcus Raskin of *The Viet Nam Reader* (1967), Bernard Fall was a recognized authority on Vietnam and the wars fought there. Born in 1926, Fall served in World War II with the French underground until the liberation and then with the French army until 1946. He was a research analyst at the Nuremberg War Crimes Tribunal and worked for the United Nations in the International Tracing Service. He came to the United States in 1951 on a Fulbright Scholarship, earning an M.A. and Ph.D. in political science at Syracuse University. He first went to Vietnam in 1953 to do research for his doctorate and returned for the sixth time on a Guggenheim Fellowship. When not in Vietnam, he was a professor of international relations at Howard University.

Fall was a complex man with a passion for Vietnam. He saw both wars there as tragedies. Although deep concern about communism in Indochina softened his criticism of both France and the United States, he held to the justice of an Indochina free of foreign domination, whether it be French, American, Chinese, or Russian. A critic of both French colonialism and American intervention, he distinguished clearly between the policies of governments and the human beings caught in between. Fall combined meticulous scholarship with a humane writing style. He wanted to see the war as it was experienced by those who were condemned to fighting it, and he wrote sensitively about their travails. He loved the Vietnamese people and had great respect and admiration for the forces of the Vietminh and National Liberation Front (NLF). On February 21, 1967, Bernard Fall was killed in the field with a U.S. Marine Corps unit when a Vietcong booby trap exploded.

REFERENCES: *New York Times*, February 22, 1967; Bernard Fall, *Hell in a Very Small Place*, 1966; *Last Reflections on a War*, 1967.

                                                                    Samuel Freeman

FALLOUT SHELTERS. Late in the 1950s, because of the Cold War* and the Soviet success in rocket technology, American fears about nuclear war reached a fever pitch. Films of the era symbolized the fear. In 1960, *On the Beach** told the story of nuclear holocaust, in which a nuclear war between the United States and the Soviet Union ended up killing all human beings on earth. In the early 1960s, such films as *Fail Safe*,* *The Bedford Incident*, and *Dr. Strangelove** escalated the paranoia. One manifestation of the nuclear fear was the fallout shelter craze. In July 1961, President John F. Kennedy* delivered a speech in which he told the country, ''In the event of attack, the lives of those families which are not hit in a nuclear blast and fire can still be saved if they can be warned to take shelter and if that shelter is available.''

The speech precipitated the fallout shelter craze of the late summer and fall of 1961. *Life* magazine featured a how-to article, and over the course of the next year, more than 200,000 American families invested in fallout shelters. New suburban housing developments enthusiastically advertised backyard fallout shelters. Critics, however, wondered if home fallout shelters really would protect people, especially after the Soviet Union detonated a huge, 60-megaton hydrogen weapon in October 1961. Fallout shelters continued to be built after 1961, but it was no longer a fad affecting millions of people.

REFERENCE: Howard Ball, *Justice Downwind: America's Atomic Testing Program in the 1950s*, 1985.

FAR OUT. The phrase ''far out'' emerged in the 1960s as a countercultural reference to any experience or idea that was highly pleasurable.

REFERENCE: David Lee Stein, *Living the Revolution: The Yippies in Chicago*, 1969.

FARMER, JAMES. James Farmer was born in Marshall, Texas, January 12, 1920. He received a bachelor's degree in chemistry from Wiley College and then decided to enter the Methodist ministry. In 1941 he received a bachelor of divinity degree from Howard University, but he refused ordination because he could not accept working in a segregated ministry. Instead, Farmer became race relations specialist for the Fellowship of Reconciliation,* a pacifist, antiwar group. He left the Fellowship of Reconciliation in 1942 to found the Congress of Racial Equality* (CORE) in Chicago.

Farmer was the first African-American civil rights leader to adopt the nonviolent civil disobedience tactics of India's great nationalist Mohandas Gandhi. In June 1943, he staged sit-in* demonstrations at segregated Chicago restaurants, and he succeeded in desegregating most of them. He also initiated what he called the ''standing line''—having large numbers of blacks wait in line outside establishments that would not give them access. During the 1950s, Farmer was one of the country's most prominent civil rights leaders, and in 1961 he had CORE launch the famous ''freedom rides.''* In 1960, the U.S. Supreme Court had outlawed segregation in public transportation facilities, and to test compliance with the law, Farmer sent blacks on buses and trains from northern terminals across state lines into the South. The demonstrations resulted in initial violence in Alabama and Mississippi and the eventual desegregation of public transportation facilities all over the South.

During the early 1960s, Farmer became increasingly concerned about the rise of black separatist sentiments among CORE members, and he stepped down as director in 1966. Floyd McKissick* succeeded him. In 1976, when Roy Innis* tried to use CORE to recruit black Vietnam veterans to fight as mercenaries in the civil war in Angola, Farmer resigned his membership in protest. In 1977, Farmer was appointed executive director of the Coalition of American Public Employees, a position he kept until 1982. Since then, Farmer has continued to teach, write, and lecture.

REFERENCES: James Farmer, *Lay Bare the Heart*, 1985; Jeff Sklansks, *James Farmer*, 1992.

FATHER KNOWS BEST. *Father Knows Best* was the quintessential situation comedy of the 1950s and early 1960s, portraying the Andersons as a stable, suburban, middle-class American family. CBS first broadcast *Father Knows Best* on October 3, 1954, and NBC picked up the series in 1955. *Father Knows Best* was back at CBS in 1958 and remained there until 1962, when ABC took over the series. Robert Young played Jim Anderson, the wise patriarch, with Jane Wyatt as his wife, Margaret. The children were Betty (Elinor Donahue), Bud (Billy Gray), and Kitten (Lauren Chapin). The family went through the typical problems of sibling and intergenerational rivalries, but all was fixed by the gentle wisdom of their father. The last episode of *Father Knows Best* was broadcast on April 5, 1963.

REFERENCE: Tim Brooks and Earle Marsh, *The Complete Directory to Prime Time Network and Cable TV Shows*, 1995.

THE F.B.I. *The F.B.I.* was one of the most popular police dramas in American television* history. It first aired on ABC on September 19, 1965, with Efrem Zimbalist, Jr., starring as Inspector Lewis Erskine and Philip Abbott as Special Agent Arthur Ward. To guarantee authenticity and avoid the wrath of the Federal Bureau of Investigation (FBI), ABC worked closely with the FBI, giving J. Edgar Hoover* complete control over the show's scripts. During its run, *The F.B.I.* scripts dealt with white-collar crime, radical bombings, communist espionage and subversion, and organized crime, all favorite targets of Hoover. The last episode of *The F.B.I.* was broadcast on September 8, 1974.
REFERENCE: Tim Brooks and Earle Marsh, *The Complete Directory to Prime Time Network and Cable TV Shows*, 1995.

FEDERAL ALLIANCE OF LAND GRANTS. The Federal Alliance of Land Grants (FALG) was a Mexican-American activist group founded by Reies Tijerina* in 1963. Tijerina's goal was to recover Mexican-American title to Spanish and Mexican land grants in New Mexico. FALG headquarters were in Albuquerque. The idea of regaining land appealed to young Chicano* activists as well as to the poor Mexican-American farmers of northwestern New Mexico. FALG grew slowly until 1964, when new federal regulations reduced the grazing rights on federal land of many small Mexican-American ranchers. FALG also staged several public protests. In July 1966, the group engaged in a protest march from Albuquerque to Santa Fe, New Mexico, and in October 1966 occupied the Echo Amphitheater at the Kit Carson National Forest.

The decline of the Federal Alliance of Land Grants began in 1967. Police charged several FALG members with vandalism and arson, and Tijerina dissolved the organization. He then replaced FALG with the new Alianza de Pueblos Libres. On June 3, 1967, Tijerina led a raid on the Tierra Amarilla courthouse in New Mexico to protest arrests of Alianza members. He was arrested, convicted, and sentenced to state prison for his actions in the raid. Tijerina was released from prison in 1971, and one of the terms of his parole was that he stay out of Alianza politics for five years. In 1976, he once again assumed the presidency of the Alianza.
REFERENCES: Patricia B. Blawis, *Tijerina and the Land Grants*, 1971; Richard Gardner, *Grito! Reies Tijerina and the New Mexico Land Grant War of 1967*, 1970; Peter Nabakov, *Tijerina and the Courthouse Raid*, 1969.

FELLOWSHIP OF RECONCILIATION. The Fellowship of Reconciliation (FOR) was an influential civil rights and antiwar organization of the 1950s and 1960s. Worldwide in scope, FOR had been founded in Great Britain in 1914. During the major wars of the twentieth century, FOR opposed the selective service system, assisted conscientious objectors, and opposed violent confron-

tations on the battlefield. A. J. Muste* was its most prominent leader, and in 1964 he formally spoke out against the conflict in Vietnam. After Muste's death in 1967, the Fellowship of Reconciliation continued its campaign against the draft and the war.
REFERENCE: Nancy Zaroulis and Gerald Sullivan, *Who Spoke Up? American Protest and the War in Vietnam, 1963–1975,* 1984.

FIDDLER ON THE ROOF. *Fiddler on the Roof* was one of the most popular musicals in Broadway history. Based on the stories of Sholom Aleichem, it premiered at the Imperial Theater in New York on September 22, 1964. The music was composed by Jerry Bock, Sheldon Harnick, and Joseph Stein. Produced by Harold Prince, the play was directed and choreographed by Jerome Robbins. *Fiddler on the Roof* is the story of Tevye the Milkman and his family, who live in a small village in prerevolutionary Russia, where they are forced to deal with the challenges posed to their Jewish faith by heavy-handed oppression and the more benign forces of assimilation. Amid all of the challenges, Tevye relies on tradition to anchor his life and interpret his world. *Fiddler on the Roof* continued on Broadway for more than eight years and 3,242 individual performances. Part of its stage success can also be attributed to the talents of Zero Mostel, who played Tevye throughout much of the run on Broadway.
REFERENCE: Kurt Ganzl, *The Encyclopedia of the Musical Theater,* 1994.

THE FIFTH DIMENSION. The Fifth Dimension was a very popular vocal group of the late 1960s and early 1970s. First organized in Los Angeles in 1966, the Fifth Dimension included LaMonte McLemore, Marilyn McCoo, Ron Towson, Florence LaRue, and Billy Davis, Jr. They had their first hit—"Go Where You Wanna Go"—in 1967 and followed that with "Up, Up and Away" in 1967, which reached number seven on the pop charts. The Fifth Dimension had two hits in 1968—"Stoned Soul Picnic" and "Sweet Blindness." The biggest hit of their career came in 1969, when their recording of "Aquarius/Let the Sunshine In" from the musical *Hair** rose to number one on the pop charts, selling nearly 2 million copies. "Aquarius" became an anthem of the 1960s counterculture.*
REFERENCE: Patricia Romanowski and Holly George-Warren, eds., *The New Rolling Stone Encyclopedia of Rock and Roll,* 1996.

FIFTY-MILE HIKE. During the John F. Kennedy* administration in the early 1960s, America became fascinated with the idea of physical fitness. Back in 1908, President Theodore Roosevelt had a company of U.S. Marines complete a fifty-mile hike in less than twenty hours. President Kennedy challenged General David M. Shoup,* commandant of the Marine Corps, to see if one of his companies could do the same. Shoup accepted the challenge, and his marines finished in twelve hours. Attorney General Robert F. Kennedy* then decided to walk fifty miles along the path of the C & O canal. So did his secretaries. The

Kennedys ignited the fad of the fifty-mile hike in 1963. That spring, hundreds of thousands of Americans also completed fifty-mile hikes.

REFERENCE: Randy Roberts and James S. Olson, *Winning Is the Only Thing: Sports in America since 1945*, 1989.

FINKBINE, SHERRIE. See **THALIDOMIDE**.

THE FIRE NEXT TIME. See **BALDWIN, JAMES**.

FITZGERALD, ALBERT. Albert Fitzgerald was born in Lynn, Massachusetts, in 1906. He went to work for General Electric after high school and joined the United Electrical Radio and Machine Workers of America (UERMWA). Fitzgerald rose quickly through the union ranks and was elected UERMWA president in 1941. Although he denied membership in the Communist Party, his politics were decidedly left of center. He became a Congress of Industrial Organizations (CIO) vice president in 1943, and after the war, he vigorously supported the political career of Henry A. Wallace and the Progressive Party. In 1949, the CIO expelled Fitzgerald and the UERMWA for being infiltrated by the Communist Party. Despite that experience, Fitzgerald remained at the helm of the UERMWA and in 1970 led the union in a successful strike against General Electric. Fitzgerald died April 3, 1982.

REFERENCE: *New York Times*, April 4, 1982.

FITZSIMMONS, FRANK EDWARD. Frank Fitzsimmons was born in Jeanette, Pennsylvania, April 7, 1908. He became a truck driver after leaving school, and in Detroit he joined the International Brotherhood of Teamsters, Chauffeurs, Warehousemen and Helpers of America. Jimmy Hoffa was head of the Detroit local, and Fitzsimmons rose through the Teamsters ranks along with him. Fitzsimmons became vice president of the Teamsters in 1961. In 1967, when Hoffa was imprisoned for jury tampering and fraud, Fitzsimmons became the new president of the union. Fitzsimmons' own politics were rather conservative, and he tended to be a loyal Republican. He died May 6, 1981.

REFERENCE: *New York Times*, May 7, 1981.

"FIVE O'CLOCK FOLLIES." "Five O'Clock Follies" was a term coined by the Saigon press corps to describe official press briefings conducted daily by the Joint United States Public Affairs Office (JUSPAO), the information arm of the Military Assistance Command Vietnam. Everyday at 5:00 p.m. at "Pentagon East"—the Tan Son Nhut airbase's Vietnam Office of Information in Saigon*— JUSPAO spokesmen met with reporters and briefed them on the military activities that had taken place the day before in Vietnam. The term reflected the prevailing mood among journalists that U.S. military effort had gone awry in Vietnam, despite government efforts to hide this. The briefings became legendary for confusion, double-talk, spin, and even highly inaccurate information, if not outright lying on the part of U.S. military officials. U.S. victories were always exaggerated and U.S. military defeats always minimized. Also, JUSPAO officials consistently overestimated enemy casualties.*

The daily "Five O'Clock Follies" clearly demonstrated how different the Vietnam War* was from World War I, World War II, and Korea. In those conflicts, American war correspondents had become accustomed to briefings in which information was released about troop advancements and the location of front lines, since progress in the conflict could be measured by territorial acquisition, the occupation of towns and cities, and the retreat of enemy forces. But in Vietnam, none of those traditional measures of progress was relevant. Vietnam had no fronts. The war was being fought throughout the country all of the time, with no fixed positions and no "front line." It was also a guerrilla war, in which enemy troops suddenly appeared, fought intensely, and then disappeared into the jungles. Journalists were unable to paint a comprehensive portrait of the war on any given day. Nor could U.S. military officials. Finally, JUSPAO officials rarely left the safe confines of Saigon to go into the field, where they might have been able to gather first-hand information. Instead, everything they passed on to reporters was second- or third-hand and often highly unreliable.

As a result, the "Five O'Clock Follies" exacerbated an already strained relationship between journalists and U.S. military officials. Their relationship became adversarial, and back home, helped fuel the so-called "credibility gap" between the American public and members of the Johnson and Nixon administrations.

REFERENCES: Peter Braestrup, *Big Story*, 1983; Frances FitzGerald, *Fire in the Lake: The Vietnamese and the Americans in Vietnam*, 1972; Samuel Freeman, "Five O'Clock Follies," in James S. Olson, ed., *Dictionary of the Vietnam War*, 1988; Daniel Hallin, *The Uncensored War: The Media and Vietnam*, 1986.

FLEXIBLE RESPONSE. The leading figure in the reorientation of American defense policy from massive retaliation to flexible response was General Maxwell Taylor.* Taylor had served as chief of staff of the army during the late 1950s, and he retired in 1959. But he had been a frustrated chief of staff. The "New Look" defense strategy was good for the air force and navy, which could deliver nuclear warheads, but bad for the army, which became a military stepchild. The "New Look," for Taylor at least, was pure folly, forcing the United States to resort to nuclear terror every time a political or military crisis developed somewhere in the world. Instead, Taylor pushed his "flexible response" military policy. Nuclear weapons should be available for reacting to a nuclear attack, but a strong, well-equipped army and Marine Corps should be available for conventional threats. Finally, the president should have a counterinsurgency* option to respond to guerrilla wars and political uprisings where conventional forces were inappropriate. Taylor's flexible response theory became a best-seller in his 1959 book, *The Uncertain Trumpet*.

President John F. Kennedy* and Attorney General Robert F. Kennedy* were impressed with Taylor's ideas, and he became a national security adviser to the administration. In 1962 they named him chairman of the Joint Chiefs of Staff. A dramatic shift then occurred in American defense policy toward limited or flexible response. Kennedy no longer wanted a policy of just nuclear sufficiency or balance with the Soviet Union; he wanted nuclear superiority. Kennedy also did not accept the concept of massive retaliation in the event of war and instead wanted a flexible response with conventional forces or possibly even the use of strategic nuclear weapons in a limited military theater. This reorientation in national policy provided the Kennedy administration with the means and rationale for intervention in Southeast Asia.

The Kennedy administration eventually expected to use counterinsurgency forces like the Green Berets* to train the South Vietnamese army to fight its own battles, employing only limited American conventional military power when absolutely necessary. Secretary of Defense Robert McNamara* designed and implemented the Kennedy defense program. It moved the United States away from a massive retaliation policy to one of a limited military strategy. It also included military assistance for the underdeveloped world to stop communist aggression and proposed a limited war policy. It became Kennedy's policy justification for U.S. involvement in Vietnam.

REFERENCES: William J. Rust, *Kennedy in Vietnam: American Foreign Policy, 1960–1963*, 1987; R. B. Smith, *An International History of the Vietnam War: The Kennedy Strategy*, 1987.

FLOWER CHILDREN. See HIPPIES.

FLOWER POWER. The term "flower power" emerged in the 1960s to refer to the counterculture* and hippie* movements. Advocates of peace, love, and reconciliation, the hippies hoped to restore tranquillity to America, not through the barrel of a gun but by broadening people's attitudes.

REFERENCE: James S. Olson, ed., *Dictionary of the Vietnam War*, 1988.

FONDA, JANE. Jane Fonda was born December 21, 1937, in New York City. As the daughter of actor Henry Fonda, who happened to be a somewhat distant parent, she was forced to develop her own identity. But after attending Vassar, she too went into acting. In 1954, she appeared opposite her father in *The Country Girl* in Omaha, Nebraska. Her acting talents were considerable, and she moved to New York to study under Lee Strasberg at the Actors' Studio.

In 1964, Fonda moved to Paris and married film director Roger Vadim, whose previous wife, Brigitte Bardot, had become an international sex symbol. He tried to do the same for Fonda, casting her in such films as *Circle of Love* (1964) and *Barbarella* (1968). In Paris when the Vietnam War* escalated, Fonda soon developed a strong aversion to the war. Her marriage was already breaking up, and she returned to the United States. Back home, Fonda became active in the Free Theater Association, which staged antiwar skits and programs at coffeehouses near U.S. military bases. She also participated in a variety of antiwar demonstrations. Revelations in December 1969 of the My Lai* massacre raised Fonda's antiwar consciousness even more. She sponsored the Winter Soldier investigations in Detroit in February 1971, in which dozens of Vietnam veterans testified that My Lai was not an isolated incident. That year, Fonda also won a Best Actress Oscar for her riveting performance in *Klute*.

In 1972, to make an even bolder statement against the Vietnam War, Fonda traveled to Hanoi in North Vietnam, where she visited with several U.S. prisoners of war* and spoke on the radio to American GIs all over Southeast Asia, urging them to join her in opposing an immoral war. She even posed next to antiaircraft guns. Comparing her to "Tokyo Rose," the Japanese-American woman who had made similar anti-American broadcasts during World War II, journalists dubbed Fonda "Hanoi Jane." Her activities in North Vietnam in 1972 earned her the enmity of millions of U.S. veterans.

After the war, Fonda resumed her acting career, winning another Academy Award for her performance in *Coming Home*. By then she was married to liberal activist Tom Hayden,* founder of Students for a Democratic Society* (SDS), and together they worked, in their words, for "civil rights, enviromental safety, and economic justice." She later divorced Hayden and became less politically active, marrying media mogul Ted Turner. She remains today a very popular American, except among veterans' groups, where she is loathed.
REFERENCES: Fred Lawrence Guiles, *Jane Fonda*, 1981; John Ricks, "Jane Fonda," in James S. Olson, ed., *Dictionary of the Vietnam War*, 1988.

FOOD AND AGRICULTURE ACT OF 1962. The chronic problem of overproduction in American agriculture plagued the John F. Kennedy* administration no less than it had his predecessors. In an attempt to reduce commodity surpluses, Congress passed the Food and Agriculture Act of 1962. The law established a price floor for feed grains at no less than 65 percent of parity as long as the production of corn, barley, and sorghum was cut by 20 to 50 percent. After 1963, the law allowed the secretary of agriculture to set a flexible price floor between 50 and 90 percent of parity. To further induce farmers to cut production, the law appropriated $70 million for converting farmland to conservation and recreational use; provided long-term government financing for rural redevelopment; and allowed the Farmers Home Administration to offer long-term loans for converting farmland to other purposes.
REFERENCE: James S. Olson, ed., *Dictionary of United States Economic History*, 1992.

FOOD AND AGRICULTURE ACT OF 1965. In a continuation of federal policies to reduce the amount of farmland in production, Congress passed the Food and Agriculture Act of 1965, which allowed the secretary of agriculture to pay farmers up to 40 percent of the value of the crops that could have been raised on land taken out of production for wildlife refuges, forest reserves, and public recreation.
REFERENCE: James S. Olson, ed., *Dictionary of United States Economic History*, 1992.

FOOD FOR PEACE ACT OF 1965. The Food for Peace Act of 1965 was an integral part of the foreign and domestic policies of Lyndon B. Johnson's* Great Society* plan for the United States and the world. The legislation authorized the president to distribute surplus farm commodities to fight famine abroad or to trade stored surpluses for strategic materials in a national emergency. Beyond that, the legislation was designed to provide U.S. assistance to Third World countries in improving their agricultural output by constructing adequate storage facilities, launching scientific research and extension programs, initiating agricultural industries, creating a climate favorable to outside investors, and improving infrastructures so that crops could be marketed. The Food for Peace program is still in effect as an important element of American foreign policy.
REFERENCE: James S. Olson, ed., *Dictionary of United States Economic History*, 1992.

FOOD STAMP ACT OF 1964. In 1939, Congress created the Food Stamp Program within the Department of Agriculture to allow poor people to purchase surplus commodities at retail stores through the use of government-issued stamps. The program was discontinued in 1943 because World War II virtually eliminated unemployment. Congress reauthorized the food stamp program in 1964 at the urging of Congresswoman Leonor Sullivan,* and it became part of President Lyndon B. Johnson's* antipoverty program.
REFERENCE: James S. Olson, ed., *Dictionary of United States Economic History*, 1992.

FORD, ARTHUR AUGUSTUS. Arthur Augustus Ford was born January 8, 1897, in Titusville, Florida. Ford was born as an Episcopalian, converted to the Baptist Church as a child, and then was excommunicated from the Baptists when he was seventeen because of his conversion to Unitarianism. He attended Transylvania College in Lexington, Kentucky, to prepare for the ministry, and in 1919 he became a pastor for the Christian Church in Barbourville, Kentucky.

Within a few years, Ford had begun the process by which he became a spiritualist. Convinced that the dead could be contacted through seances and that reincarnation was a reality, he became deeply involved in spiritualism. In 1926 Ford founded the First Spiritualist Church in New York. A decade later, he formed the International General Association of Spiritualists. By 1960, he was the most prominent spiritualist in the United States. In 1965 Ford conducted seances for Sun Myung Moon, head of the Unification Church, and in 1967 he conducted a nationally televised seance for Episcopal bishop James Pike.* Arthur Ford died January 2, 1971.
REFERENCE: Allen Spraggett and William V. Rauscher, *Arthur Ford: The Man Who Talked with the Dead*, 1973.

FORD, HENRY, II. Henry Ford II was born in Dearborn, Michigan, September 4, 1917. He spent four years studying sociology at Yale but did not graduate. After several years in the U.S. Navy during World War II, Ford was discharged in order to return to the Ford Motor Company and manage its wartime production. He became president of the company in 1945. In 1960, Ford resigned the presidency and became chairman of the board, a position he held until 1980. He literally saved the company from bankruptcy. He fired incompetent managers, implemented an effective audit system, retooled the company toward more effective automation systems, and revolutionized the design system, which produced the successful Falcon, Fairlane, Mustang, and Maverick models in the 1950s and 1960s. The great failure of Henry Ford II's era was the ill-fated Edsel. By the early 1970s, the Ford Motor Company was the third largest corporation in the United States. Ford died September 29, 1987.

REFERENCE: Victor Lasky, *Never Complain, Never Complain: The Story of Henry Ford II*, 1981.

FORRESTAL, MICHAEL VINCENT. Michael V. Forrestal was born November 26, 1927, in New York City. The son of James Forrestal, the first U.S. secretary of defense, he became an aide to W. Averell Harriman,* working on the Marshall Plan affairs, and in 1953 he received a law degree from Harvard. Forrestal practiced law in New York until 1962, when he joined the White House National Security staff. In late 1962 President John F. Kennedy* sent Roger Hilsman* and Forrestal on a fact-finding mission to South Vietnam. Their "balanced" report, delivered in early 1963, struck a middle ground between the optimism of U.S. embassy officials in Saigon and the pessimism of journalists. Forrestal and Hilsman had serious reservations about the Army of the Republic of Vietnam's (ARVN) effectiveness, saw flaws in the Strategic Hamlet Program, felt Ngo Dinh Diem* was increasingly isolated, and concluded that the United States and South Vietnam were "probably winning" but that the war would probably "last longer than we would like" and "cost more in terms of lives and money than we had anticipated." Their report reinforced the doubt about the accuracy of official estimates of progress.

In August 1963, the first Buddhist crisis paralyzed Diem's government as ARVN's generals plotted coups. Ambassador Henry Cabot Lodge* requested instructions from Washington, but it was a weekend, and most of Kennedy's key advisers were out of town. Forrestal drafted a response with Harriman and Hilsman, stating that the United States would no longer tolerate Ngo Dinh Nhu's* influence over Diem and calling for the removal of Nhu from power. Otherwise, U.S. support for Diem would end. Kennedy approved the cable but was later enraged when he found out that Secretary of Defense Robert McNamara* and Central Intelligence Agency* director John McCone had not seen it before it was sent. During the Lyndon B. Johnson* administration, Forrestal was a member of the White House national security staff. Believing that military reporting was grossly optimistic and supporting a negotiated settlement, Forrestal fell into disfavor with Johnson, was excluded from policy discussions, and resigned in 1965. He then returned to private law practice.

In subsequent years, Forrestal returned to Harvard as executive secretary of the Kennedy Institute for Politics, and from 1978 to 1980 he served as president of the U.S.–U.S.S.R. Trade and Economic Council. Michael Forrestal died January 11, 1989.

REFERENCES: Nelson Lichtenstein, ed., *Political Profiles. The Kennedy Years*, 1976; Loren Baritz, *Backfire*, 1985; Michael Maclear, *The Ten Thousand Day War*, 1981; *New York Times*, January 12, 1989.

Samuel Freeman

FORTAS, ABRAHAM. Abe Fortas was born in Memphis, Tennessee, in 1910 and worked his way through school playing the violin. He secured scholarships to Southwestern College in Memphis, graduated from there in 1930, and then went on to the Yale Law School, where he became the prize student of Professor William O. Douglas.* After graduating from Yale in 1933, Fortas remained on the Yale law faculty for four years while commuting to Washington, where he served as an assistant chief in the Agricultural Adjustment Administration's legal division. At Douglas' request, Fortas went to work for the Securities and Exchange Commission in 1934, and in 1939 he transferred to the Department of Interior. There Fortas served as undersecretary between 1942 and 1946. He cofounded the law firm of Arnold, Fortas, and Porter in Washington, D.C. In the process of building his business, Fortas became close friends with Lyndon B. Johnson.* Fortas brilliantly maneuvered Johnson through the fraud charges of his disputed 1948 senatorial election. Johnson returned the favor in 1965, appointing Fortas to the U.S. Supreme Court.

Fortas was a perfect fit for the Warren Court. He was a proponent of civil rights and civil liberties, and he reinforced the liberal philosophy of the Court. In 1968, Johnson tried to nominate Fortas to replace Chief Justice Earl Warren,* who was stepping down. Republicans bitterly objected, claiming that the next president should have the opportunity to fill the vacancy. Senate Republicans filibustered, and Johnson had to withdraw the nomination. In 1969, *Life* magazine published an exposé on Fortas, charging him with accepting a $20,000 payment, while sitting on the bench, from convicted stock manipulator Louis Wolfson. Although Fortas argued that he had already paid the money back, the furor would not die down. Fortas resigned his seat ten days after the article appeared. He then returned to private law practice. He died April 6, 1982.

REFERENCES: Laura Kalman, *Abe Fortas: A Biography*, 1990; *New York Times*, April 7, 1982.

THE FOUR SEASONS. The Four Seasons were one of the most popular rock-and-roll vocal groups of the late 1950s and early 1960s. Originally formed in Newark, New Jersey, in 1956, the group included Frankie Valli, Tommy DeVito, Nick DeVito, and Hank Majewski. They played the club circuit for six years, changing their name from the Four Seasons to the Four Lovers and back to the Four Seasons again. Their first big hit—"Sherry"—went all the way to number one on the pop charts in 1962, and they followed it with a second number-one hit in 1962—"Big Girls Don't Cry." During the next four years, the Four

Seasons had fifty recordings reach the top forty on the pop charts, including "Walk like a Man," "Ain't That a Shame," "I've Got You under My Skin," and "C'mon Marianne." But in 1966, their popularity declined rapidly. They revived for a time in the 1970s with such hits as "My Eyes Adored You" and "December 1963 (Oh What a Night)." After that, the group broke up.

REFERENCE: Patricia Romanowski and Holly George-Warren, eds., *The New Rolling Stone Encyclopedia of Rock and Roll*, 1996.

THE FOX. *The Fox* was one of the more sexually daring films of the 1960s. Directed by Mark Rydell and based on the novella of the same name by D. H. Lawrence and a screenplay by Howard Koch and Lewis Carlino, *The Fox* starred Sandy Dennis as Jill, Keir Dullea as Paul, and Anne Heywood as Ellen. The two women are intellectuals managing a farm in the rural Northeast until a man appears and upsets their lives. Jill is a lesbian who falls in love with Ellen, who accommodates that affection until the arrival of Paul. At the time, the sex scenes in *The Fox* were explicit for a mainstream movie, and its depiction of lesbianism was a first.

REFERENCE: *New York Times*, February 8, 1968.

FRAGGING. Except for the Mexican War, which generated intense opposition among northerners convinced that the conflict was a pretext for expanding slavery, no war in American history generated so much opposition as Vietnam. Opposition to the war affected every level of society and every American institution, including the military. "Fragging" is a clear illustration of just how endemic antiwar* sentiment had become in the U.S. Army.

The term "fragging" is taken from a fragmentation grenade, a deadly device used to kill overzealous officers or noncommissioned officers (NCOs). Such murders are nothing new in the history of warfare. In his memoirs *A Soldier Reports*, General William Westmoreland* concluded that fragging "increases when a sense of unit purpose breaks down and espirit de corps fails and when explosives and weapons are loosely controlled." History is replete with stories of military mutinies by soldiers upset with the decisions of superior officers or politicians. In Vietnam, disgruntled soldiers would throw a fragmentation grenade into the tent of an officer or NCO. The grenade was a perfect murder weapon, since it left behind little evidence. When it detonated, the grenade exploded into tens of thousands of pieces, more than enough to kill its victim but leaving criminal investigators nothing upon which to build a murder case. Fragging occurred in other ways as well. During firefights with enemy troops, U.S. soldiers might place the crosshairs of their own M-16s on an unpopular officer, kill him, and then blame the enemy for his death. They might not warn an officer or NCO of a booby trap* that everyone else had seen. Occasionally, they might even call in an artillery attack on an officer's position.

During Vietnam, there were relatively few fragging incidents until 1969, when the numbers began to increase. As part of his so-called Vietnamization* program, President Richard M. Nixon* had announced a plan to gradually withdraw U.S. soldiers from the theater of operations and replace them with South Vietnamese troops. Most U.S. military personnel quickly realized that it was only a matter of time before their own units were sent home. Since it was obvious that the United States was abandoning the war, many U.S. troops saw no purpose in risking their lives. Many had concluded that all of the dying to date had been for nothing. Zealous officers and NCOs who continued to put their men at risk became extremely unpopular. Army and Marine Corps criminal investigators concluded that there were 96 documented fraggings in 1969, and that the number escalated to 209 in 1970 and as many as 491 in 1971. The vast majority of fragging cases occurred in the army.

REFERENCES: Mike Dennis, "Fragging," in James S. Olson, ed., *Dictionary of the Vietnam War*, 1988; Eugene Linden, "Fragging and Other Withdrawal Symptoms," *Saturday Review* (January 1972), 12–17; Richard Holmes, *Acts of War: The Behavior of Men in Battle*, 1985.

FRANK, BILLY, JR. Billy Frank, Jr., a Nisqually Indian, was born in 1931 and raised in eastern Washington. Since the early 1960s, Frank has campaigned actively for Indian fishing rights, eventually emerging as a leader in the movement to exempt Native American peoples from state fish and game regulations in the Pacific Northwest. In the 1850s, Frank argued, the United States negotiated treaties with the tribes and provided those rights, and state governments cannot abrogate them. During the 1960s, Frank intentionally fished before and after state fishing seasons, which he considered acts of civil disobedience. He was arrested and jailed many times for his actions. Frank may have lost those battles, but he won the war in 1974, when the Supreme Court's Boldt decision upheld treaty fishing rights. Today, Frank is chairman of the Northwest Indian Fisheries Commission.

REFERENCES: Duane Champagne, ed., *The Native North American Almanac*, 1994; *New York Times*, November 26, 1992.

FRANKFURTER, FELIX. Felix Frankfurter was born to a Jewish family in Vienna, Austria, November 15, 1882. The family moved to New York City in 1894. Ambitious and brilliant, Frankfurter graduated from the City College of New York in 1901. He went on to become the top student in his class at Harvard Law School. After leaving Harvard, he returned to New York and accepted a position with Hornblower, Byrne, Miller, and Potter. In less than two years, Frankfurter went to work for Henry L. Stimson, the U.S. attorney for the southern district of New York. Frankfurter followed Stimson to the War Department in 1909 and remained there for five years.

In 1914, Frankfurter began his brilliant career at Harvard. Committed to the belief that the law was rooted in a social context, he insisted that his students study history, political science, sociology, and economics, as well as the law, and he secured a reputation for directing many of his most brilliant students into government service. During World War I, Frankfurter worked for the President's Mediation Commission and for the War Labor Policies Board.

During the 1920s, he reacted in horror when the Supreme Court assumed an activist, centralized role in overturning social legislation at the state level. It was, he believed, an unjust judicial assumption of legislative power and a violation of the principle of federalism. Frankfurter also earned a liberal reputation for his defense of Sacco and Vanzetti and such groups as the National Association for the Advancement of Colored People and the American Civil Liberties Union. During the New Deal years of the 1930s, Frankfurter acted as a legal adviser to the Roosevelt administration and sent dozens of his best students to work in New Deal agencies. In 1933, he also spent a year at Oxford University, where he met macroeconomist John Maynard Keynes and became a convert to his economic views. Upon returning to the United States in 1934, Frankfurter strongly encouraged Roosevelt to use government spending and tax policies as a means of stimulating the economy. In 1939, Roosevelt appointed him to the Supreme Court.

As a liberal, Frankfurter wanted the Court to be less likely than its predecessor to overturn legislative decisions at the federal and local level, where he considered democracy to be working in its purest form. Gradually, Frankfurter became a proponent of strict judicial self-restraint. By the time of the 1950s, when the Warren Court had become highly activist in overturning state laws limiting civil rights and civil liberties, Frankfurter's commitment to judicial self-restraint had transformed him, in the eyes of many, from a liberal to a conservative. He generally believed that the first eight amendments to the Constitution applied to Congress, and he was inclined to protect individual rights when the offending party was the federal government. But Frankfurter was not convinced that the Fourteenth Amendment to the Constitution required application of those same eight amendments to the activities of state government, so he was inclined not to have the Court intervene when offending activities took place at the state and local level. Frankfurter retired from the Court in 1962 and died February 22, 1965.

REFERENCES: H. N. Hirsch, *The Enigma of Felix Frankfurter*, 1981; Michael E. Parrish, *Felix Frankfurter and His Times*, 1982; Max Freedman, *Roosevelt and Frankfurter*, 1967.

FRANKLIN, ARETHA. Aretha Franklin was born in Detroit in 1942. Her father was a local Baptist minister, and she began performing in the church choir. By the early 1960s, for African-American performers to succeed commercially with white audiences, they had to abandon or at least de-emphasize black musical traditions. They had to "sound white." Aretha Franklin, however, was the first African-American artist to break that tradition. She had a supple, sassy voice, with a four-octave range, and the ability to improvise brilliantly. Franklin had all the gifts, and then some, of such great gospel singers as Mahalia Jackson and Clara Ward. She was unwilling to compromise her gifts and styles,

and because of the civil rights movement* and youth rebellion of the 1960s, white audiences were ready to appreciate her. Her 1967 album *I Never Loved a Man the Way I Loved You*, released by Atlantic Records, sold more than 1 million copies. All together, Franklin had five top-ten hits in 1967, including the single "Respect," which became an anthem of sorts for the civil rights and women's movements. In 1967, *Billboard* magazine named Franklin the "Queen of Soul" and the number one female recording artist in the United States.
REFERENCE: Lorrine Glennon, ed., *Our Times: An Illustrated History of the 20th Century*, 1995.

FREE-FIRE ZONES. The most frustrating dimension of the Vietnam War,* for troops in the field as well as for policymakers, was its guerrilla nature. Vietcong* troops lived among the civilian population of South Vietnam, and it often became impossible for U.S. soldiers to distinguish between enemy soldiers and noncombatants. The fact that the local civilian population was often hostile about the U.S. military presence in South Vietnam complicated matters.

This problem became especially acute when the United States decided to pursue a military resolution of the conflict. It had become obvious that a political solution through pacification, economic development, and education would take decades to achieve, but opposition to the conflict at home did not permit such an investment of time and resources. To end the war quickly, the Lyndon B. Johnson* administration opted for a war of attrition*—the massive expenditure of military firepower to pulverize the enemy into submission. Since the enemy lived among the civilian population, such a strategy was guaranteed to result in enormous casualties* among noncombatants. To deal with that problem, the U.S. Army came up with "free-fire zones," also known as "specified strike zones." Such areas had ostensibly been cleared of all civilian noncombatants, leaving only enemy troops behind, which then became targets for air and artillery strikes.

But the logic of free-fire zones had serious flaws. First, to clear an area of noncombatants meant relocating thousands of civilians from ancestral villages and herding them into internment camps. After they were gone, massive bombing would occur. Sometimes, civilians were not actually removed but only told to leave by the aerial dropping of leaflets or loudspeaker announcements. After a certain date, everybody still in the zone was considered the enemy and targeted for destruction. The results were obvious. Relocated villagers hated the troops who had taken them from their homes, and tens of thousands of noncombatants left behind in the free-fire zones were killed anyway. In the end, free-fire zones made the South Vietnamese even more resentful of U.S. policies and exacerbated an already impossible political situation.
REFERENCES: Frances FitzGerald, *Fire in the Lake: The Vietnamese and the Americans in Vietnam*, 1972; Sean Kelleher, "Free-Fire Zones," in James S. Olson, ed., *Dictionary of the Vietnam War*, 1988; Raphael Littauer and Norman Uphoff, eds., *The Air War in Indochina*, 1972.

FREE SPEECH MOVEMENT. The so-called free speech movement developed at the University of California (UC) at Berkeley in the fall of 1964. It proved to be the first college student uprising in post–World War II America. The civil rights movement* had acquired a strong base on the campus, and in order to rein it in, UC administrators imposed a regulation prohibiting student organizations from raising money on campus for off-campus causes. An alliance of outraged groups appeared immediately. Groups as different as the Student Nonviolent Coordinating Committee* (SNCC), the Congress for Racial Equality* (CORE), and the Young Republicans came together to protest the restriction.

On September 19, 1964, UC campus police arrested Jack Weinberg, who was trying to raise money for CORE. But when they tried to put him in a patrol car, hundreds of students spontaneously surrounded the automobile and prevented it from leaving the campus. The sit-down demonstration lasted for thirty-six hours, and in the end the police released Weinberg. The free speech movement was born.

Led by people like Mario Savio and Hal Draper, the free speech movement determined to give students a powerful voice in shaping university policy, something faculty members and administrators were not ready to accept. Throughout the 1964–1965 academic year, free speech activists at Berkeley disrupted classes, raised money for off-campus causes, and demanded a greater policy voice in university affairs. By 1965, with the Vietnam War* escalating, the free speech movement increasingly invested its energies in opposing the war as well as the university's ties to the Department of Defense. Many historians consider the free speech movement an important link between the civil rights movement* of the early 1960s and the antiwar movement* of the late 1960s.

REFERENCES: Hal Draper, *Berkeley: The New Student Revolt*, 1965; Max Heinrich, *The Spiral of Conflict: Berkeley, 1964*, 1971; Sheldon Wolin and John H. Schaar, *The Berkeley Rebellion and Beyond*, 1970.

FREEDOM AND PEACE PARTY. The Freedom and Peace Party was founded in 1968 by comedian and social activist Dick Gregory. Gregory's mission was to focus national attention on the need for empowering the civil rights movement* and de-escalating the war in Vietnam. More a college-speaking tour than presidential campaign, Gregory managed to receive only 47,133 votes in the 1968 election. The party then disintegrated.

REFERENCE: Richard C. Gregory, *Dick Gregory's Political Primer*, 1970.

FREEDOM BIRDS. During the Vietnam War,* GIs returning home after their tours of duty nicknamed the passenger aircraft leaving Saigon "Freedom Birds." Most of those passenger jets had been chartered from private companies, such as World Airways and Pan American. These companies ferried soldiers back and forth from the United States to Indochina under contract from the U.S. government. Among the troops arriving in Saigon, the mood was somber and depressing, for they knew what awaited them in the jungles. However, as soon as the jet containing those returning home lifted off the tarmac, the passengers erupted into spontanoeus cheers, and a party atmosphere prevailed across the Pacific Ocean. The private carriers employed stewardesses, who were often the first American women the GIs had seen in over a year. The "Freedom Birds" became a little bit of home—safe, secure, and populated by recognizable people. The flights home took less than twenty-four hours, which did not give the veterans much time to decompress. Some psychologists suggest that the "Freedom Birds," therefore, actually contributed to post-traumatic stress syndrome. Between 1965 and 1972 hundreds of thousands of U.S. soldiers had literally been in jungle firefights one day and then sitting in front of a television set drinking beer with family members the next. For many, the transition was too abrupt.

REFERENCES: Gloria Emerson, *Winners and Losers*, 1976; Rick Eilert, *For Self and Country*, 1983; Samuel Freeman, "Freedom Birds," in James S. Olson, *Dictionary of the Vietnam War*, 1988; John Wheeler, *Touched with Fire*, 1984.

FREEDOM DEMOCRATIC PARTY. The greatest challenge facing the civil rights movement* in the 1960s involved the deep ideological fissure in the Democratic Party. Its two primary bases of support—the liberal, working-class ethnic cities of the North and the conservative white voters of the "Solid South"—had diametrically opposed views of civil rights. Liberals were always afraid of offending southerners, especially the elderly white men who controlled so many congressional committees.

The Freedom Democratic Party dramatically exposed the tension between northern Democratic liberals and southern Democratic conservatives. After the bloody events of "Freedom Summer,"* leaders of the Student Nonviolent Coordinating Committee* (SNCC) decided to protest the lily-white composition of the Democratic Party in the South. SNCC activists organized separate Democratic Party caucuses in Mississippi to select the state's delegation to the 1964 Democratic presidential nominating convention. They called themselves the Freedom Democratic Party, denying the legitimacy of the regular Mississippi Democratic Party delegation because it had been selected in caucuses where blacks were not allowed to vote.

Led by Fannie Lou Hamer,* they staged a credentials floor fight at the convention in Atlantic City. It was an embarrassment to Lyndon B. Johnson,* who was desperate to win the presidency in his own right. Democratic liberals, anxious about defeating Barry Goldwater* in the presidential election of 1964,* tried to compromise their way out of the controversy. They offered to seat two members of the Freedom Democratic Party in the Mississippi delegation, formally declared the rest of the Freedom Democratic delegates as "honored guests" of the convention, and agreed to outlaw segregated delegations at the 1968 Democratic convention. Hamer refused to accept the compromise, calling it a token of which Democratic leaders should be ashamed. The convention voted not to recognize the Freedom Democratic Party's credentials. Hamer may have lost the battle, but she won the war. In 1968, the Democratic Party banned segregated delegations from its convention.

Historians today look back on the Freedom Democratic Party experience as a watershed in the civil rights movement.* Party members felt betrayed by the willingness of Democratic liberals, including such high-profile civil rights activists as Senator Hubert Humphrey,* to compromise so readily on a moral issue. After 1964, nonviolent civil disobedience began to give way to black power* as the ideological focus of the civil rights movement.

REFERENCE: Frank Parker, *Black Votes Count: Political Empowerment in Mississippi after 1965*, 1990.

FREEDOM RIDES. Although the U.S. Supreme Court had already outlawed segregation in interstate transportation facilities, a number of southern states defiantly maintained the practice of segregating blacks and whites in airports, bus terminals, and train stations. In May 1961, the Congress of Racial Equality* (CORE) decided to demonstrate the continuing discrepancy between practice and the law. CORE selected thirteen young people—seven blacks and six whites—to board a bus in Washington, D.C., and travel through the South to New Orleans. Along the way they were to peacefully resist attempts to segregate them. CORE widely publicized the so-called freedom rides, and southern racists were ready for them. In Anniston, Virginia, mobs stoned and firebombed one bus, and a second bus was attacked in Birmingham, Alabama, when a racist mob stopped the vehicle, pulled out the freedom riders, and savagely beat them. CORE achieved exactly what it had hoped to achieve in sponsoring the freedom rides—focus national attention on southern racism and Jim Crow* practices. The freedom rides and the attacks against them galvanized the civil rights movement* and exposed southern racists to national condemnation.

REFERENCES: David Burner, *Making Peace with the Sixties*, 1996; David J. Garrow, *Bearing the Cross: Martin Luther King, Jr. and the Southern Christian Leadership Conference*, 1986; Frank Parker, *Black Votes Count: Political Empowerment in Mississippi after 1965*, 1990.

FREEDOM SUMMER. The term "Freedom Summer" is used by historians to describe the summer of 1964, when civil rights activists staged a series of demonstrations in Mississippi to increase the number of registered black voters. Robert Parris Moses of the Student Nonviolent Coordinating Committee* organized the program. After an initial period of training in Ohio, more than 900 white college student volunteers from the North descended on Mississippi to help register African Americans. Nine civil rights workers were murdered that summer. The most infamous of the killings took the lives of Michael Schwerner, Andrew Goodman, and James Chaney, who were killed by local Ku Klux Klan (KKK) terrorists after a local sheriff had arrested them.

J. Edgar Hoover,* head of the Federal Bureau of Investigation (FBI), had been reluctant to get involved in a state matter, because he had long argued, "I consider the local police officers to be our first line of defense.'' But Mississippi was another matter. Hoover also despised the KKK, and its ties to local criminal justice officials made justice and the law impossible to enforce. Hoover set up an FBI office in Jackson, Mississippi, sent more than 400 FBI agents into the state, and eventually developed more than 2,000 Klan informants. Because of his superpatriotism and anticommunism, Hoover had long been admired in the South, and his crusade to get the killers of black civil rights workers in 1964 enjoyed substantial credibility among many Mississippi whites. Because of the FBI's efforts during Freedom Summer, dozens of local Klansmen were arrested for the murder, beating, and intimidation of Mississippi blacks.

The presence of the Freedom Summer civil rights workers also brought the voter registration of tens of thousands of African Americans and inspired the activities of the Freedom Democratic Party,* which challenged the credentials of the regular Mississippi delegation at the Democratic presidential convention in August 1964. The summer of 1964 is also known as Freedom Summer because Congress passed the Civil Rights Act* in June.

REFERENCES: David Burner, *Making Peace with the Sixties*, 1996; David J. Garrow, *Bearing the Cross: Martin Luther King, Jr. and the Southern Christian Leadership Conference*, 1986; Frank Parker, *Black Votes Count: Political Empowerment in Mississippi after 1965*, 1990.

FRIEDAN, BETTY. Betty Friedan was born Betty Goldstein on February 4, 1921, in Peoria, Illinois. She grew up in a prosperous Jewish family and exhibited keen intellectual strengths even as a child. She majored in psychology at Smith College (an all-women's college in Massachusetts), and upon graduation she accepted a fellowship at the University of California at Berkeley, where she intended to pursue graduate studies in psychology. Before going to Berkeley, however, she met and then married Carl Friedan. She then became a homemaker, busying herself with three children and life in the suburbs.

Friedan soon grew disenchanted with her life. Something seemed to be missing, and as she shared her feelings with college friends, she learned that she was not alone. Using formal questionnaires and interviews, Friedan explored the issue in more depth, and in 1963 she wrote her book *The Feminine Mystique*. It soon became a best-seller, striking a responsive chord in the hearts and minds of millions of American women. A malaise blanketed American women, she argued, because they had long been taught and trained to subordinate their own emotional and intellectual needs to the needs of the men in their lives. But the twin goals of becoming great housewives and husband-pleasers bore no long-term satisfaction, only eventual feelings of worthlessness and emptiness.

The solution to the malaise, Friedan argued, was quite simple—go back to work and make a career. In the process of earning their own money and stimulating their own minds, women could find happiness again. Betty Friedan founded the National Organization of Women* (NOW) in 1966 and served as its first president. She called for true equality—equal partnership between men and women. Friedan also campaigned for ratification of the Equal Rights Amendment, national child care centers, reproductive freedom, and paid maternity leave.

Since then, Friedan has emerged as the founding mother of the modern feminist movement in the United States. She continues to write, and her most recent efforts include *The Second Stage* (1991) and *The Fountain of Age* (1993). Friedan lives in New York City.

REFERENCES: Justine Blau, *Betty Friedan*, 1990; Betty Friedan, *The Feminine Mystique*, 1963.

FRIENDLY FIRE. "Friendly fire" was a euphemism used during the war in Vietnam to describe air, artillery, or small-arms fire from American forces mistakenly directed at American positions. The term gained national prominence as the title of C. D. B. Bryan's 1976 book, *Friendly Fire*, describing the death of Michael E. Mullen in Vietnam on February 18, 1970. Mullen was killed by an accidental American artillery strike, and the telegram to his parents said he had been "at a night defensive position when artillery fire from friendly forces landed on the area." In 1983 a television movie starring Carol Burnett further emphasized the term in the public consciousness.

REFERENCE: James S. Olson, ed., *Dictionary of the Vietnam War*, 1988.

FRISBEE. The "Frisbee"—a flat, aerodynamically sound plastic saucer—was invented by the Wham-O Company of California in 1957, and within a decade it had become a fad among young people around the country. In 1967, the International Frisbee Association was formed, signifying the arrival of the toy as a national craze. In parks, beaches, school playgrounds, and university commons, throwing the Frisbee had become a ubiquitous activity among American young people.

REFERENCE: Jane Stern and Michael Stern, *Encyclopedia of Pop Culture*, 1992.

FROMM, ERICH. Erich Fromm was born in Frankfurt-am-Rhein, Germany, in 1900. He studied at the universities of Heidelberg and Frankfurt and then at the Berlin Psychoanalytic Institute. He fled Germany in 1933 because of Nazi anti-Semitism, settled in the United States, and worked at the New School for Social Research in New York City. He later taught at Columbia, Yale, and Bennington. A classical Freudian as well as a Marxist, he wrote *Escape from Freedom* in 1941, in which he argued that human society, in moving from feudalism to capitalism, had lost touch with the land and with its sense of community. As a result, people became insecure and more likely to turn to totalitarian political systems. He wrote *Man for Himself* in 1947 and *The Sane Society* in 1951, both of which elaborated on that primary theme.

Fromm abandoned the United States for Mexico in 1949, although he continued to write, lecture, and engage in social activism here, even though he was a faculty member at the National University of Mexico. As an early promoter of democratic socialism and individual liberty and a critic of consumer society, Fromm was a precursor of 1960s values. During the 1950s and 1960s, Fromm opposed the proliferation of nuclear weapons and the war in Vietnam. Although some New Left* critics believed his concerns for the human potential were too personal—that he de-emphasized political action and revolution—Fromm became during the 1960s one of America's most powerful intellectual voices opposing consumerism, capitalism, fascism, and violence. His other writings include *The Art of Loving* (1956), *The Crisis of Psychoanalysis* (1970), and *The Anatomy of Human Destructiveness* (1973). Fromm moved to Switzerland in 1971 and died there in 1980.

REFERENCES: Erich Fromm, *To Have or to Be?*, 1976; Rainer Funk, *Erich Fromm: The Courage to Be*, 1982; John H. Schaar, *Escape from Authority: The Perspectives of Erich Fromm*, 1961.

THE FUGITIVE. *The Fugitive* was one of the 1960s most popular television* dramatic series. ABC broadcast the first episode on September 13, 1963. It starred David Janssen as Dr. Richard Kimble, a physician falsely accused of murdering his wife. He is tried, convicted, and sentenced to death, but on his way to death row he escapes. Kimble then tries to find a mysterious, one-armed man, who was the real killer. The good doctor has a heart of gold, and each weekly episode focuses on the good deeds he accomplishes while being pursued by the relentless Lieutenant Philip Gerard, played by Barry Morse. The last episode of *The Fugitive*—the one in which Kimble catches up with the guilty man and exonerates himself—was broadcast on August 29, 1967. It played to the largest audience in American television history.

REFERENCE: John Cooper, *The Fugitive: A Complete Episode Guide, 1963–1967*, 1994.

FULBRIGHT, JAMES WILLIAM. J. William Fulbright was born in Sumner, Missouri, April 9, 1905. A very bright young man, he won a Rhodes Scholarship to Oxford University in Great Britain after graduating from the University of Arkansas. Upon his return to the United States, he enrolled in the George Washington University Law School, earning his degree in 1934. Fulbright then began a brilliant academic career that carried him to the presidency of the University of Arkansas in 1939. It was a high-profile position that networked him into the state Democratic Party. In 1942, Fulbright was elected to Congress, and in 1944 he won a seat in the U.S. Senate, where he specialized in foreign affairs and in 1959 became head of the Senate Foreign Relations Committee. From that post, he became an early critic of the Vietnam War.* The political dynamic at work in Vietnam, Fulbright believed, was nationalism, not communism, and a military solution would never work. The Vietnam War was futile and misguided. In 1967 and 1968, when he convened public hearings of the Senate Foreign Relations Committee to express such concerns, he earned the enmity of President Lyndon Johnson.* Fulbright became the most prominent opponent of the war. He was defeated for reelection in 1974 and spent the rest of his life practicing law. Fulbright died February 10, 1995.

REFERENCES: Tristam Coffin, *Senator Fulbright: Portrait of a Public Philosopher*, 1966; Hoyt Purvis, "J. William Fulbright," in James S. Olson, *Dictionary of the Vietnam War*, 1988; Randall Bennett Woods, *Fulbright: A Biography*, 1995

G

GALBRAITH, JOHN KENNETH. John Kenneth Galbraith was born near Ontario, Canada, October 15, 1908. In 1931, he graduated from the University of Tornoto, specializing in economics, after which he earned a Ph.D. at the University of California at Berkeley. He spent his entire career at Harvard, except for two years at Princeton (1939–1940), four years in Washington, D.C., as a government economist (1941–1945), and three years as ambassador to India (1961–1963). A Keynesian economist who urged the federal government to manage the economy through spending and taxation policies, he gained near celebrity status in 1958 with his bestselling book *The Affluent Society*, a critique of consumer culture and poverty in America. A prolific writer, his other books include *American Capitalism* (1952), *The Great Crash* (1955), *The New Industrial State* (1967), *Economics, Peace, and Laughter* (1971), and *The Age of Uncertainty* (1977).

During the 1960s, Galbraith served as an economic advisor to Presidents John Kennedy* and Lyndon Johnson.* From that vantage point, he urged them to make the government an instrument of macroeconomic policy. He also pushed both presidents to be more proactive on civil rights. As for the Vietnam War,* he was an early opponent who realized that a military solution to a political problem would never work. He told Kennedy to avoid escalating the war, and he urged Johnson to withdraw U.S. troops. Since leaving politics and retiring from Harvard, Galbraith has continued to write and advocate, ever faithful to his liberal interpretation of politics and economics. His most recent books include *Capitalism, Communism, and Coexistence* (1988), *The Culture of Contentment* (1992), and *The Good Society: The Humane Agenda* (1996). In 1998, at the age of ninety, Galbraith was still writing and being interviewed.
REFERENCE: John Kenneth Galbraith, *A Life in Our Times*, 1981.

GARCÍA, HÉCTOR PEREZ. Héctor Perez García was born January 17, 1914, in rural Tamualipas, Mexico. Fleeing the Mexican revolution, his family came

to Texas in 1917. Perez graduated from the University of Texas in 1936 and took his degree as a physician there in 1940. After a surgical residency in Omaha, Nebraska, he joined the army and served in the European theater. After World War II, García set up a medical practice in Corpus Christi, Texas. Outraged over the refusal—because he was a Mexican American—of city officials in Three Rivers, Texas, to bury the remains of Felix Longoria, a veteran who had died in battle, in the city cemetery, García established the American G.I. Forum in 1948. The forum's mission was to defend the civil rights* of Mexican Americans.* Ten years later, García was a founding member of the Political Association of Spanish-Speaking Organizations.* In the presidential election of 1960,* García led the movement to establish Viva Kennedy Clubs* throughout Texas. In 1968, President Lyndon B. Johnson* appointed García to the U.S. Civil Rights Commission, a post never before held by a Mexican American. He continued his activism and his medical practice in the 1970s and 1980s, and in 1984 President Ronald Reagan* awarded him the Medal of Freedom.
REFERENCE: "President Honors G.I. Forum Founder," *Nuestro* 8 (May 1984).

GARMENT, LEONARD. Born in 1924, Leonard Garment graduated from the Brooklyn Law School in Brooklyn, New York, in 1949. He went on to become special counsel and adviser on minority affairs to President Richard Nixon.* Leonard Garment was sympathetic to the needs of American Indian people, a feeling shared by President Richard Nixon, and used his position as special counsel to the president to support Indian people. Garment was instrumental in the drafting of President Nixon's 1970 message setting forth his American Indian policy of "self-determination* without termination."* In this statement, drafted by Garment and his assistant Bradley H. Patterson, Jr., Nixon told the American people, "[I]t is long past time that the Indian policies of the Federal government began to recognize and build upon the capacities and insights of the Indian people."

In addition to his drafting of this statement of support for American Indian people, Garment was the central figure in three significant events that changed forever the lives of American Indian people and the perception of Indian people by the American public at large: the 1969 occupation of Alcatraz Island,* the 1972 occupation of the Bureau of Indian Affairs building in Washington, D.C., and the 1973 occupation of Wounded Knee Village, South Dakota. On November 20, 1969, eighty-nine American Indians landed on Alcatraz Island in San Francisco Bay. Identifying themselves as "Indians of All Tribes,"* this group of young urban Indian college students claimed the island by "right of discovery." The occupiers demanded clear title to Alcatraz Island and the establishment of an American Indian University, an American Indian Cultural Center, and an American Indian Museum on Alcatraz Island. When U.S. marshals were ordered to remove the Indians from the island at gunpoint, Garment recognized the danger of use of excessive force and the public relations problems faced by the Nixon administration if blood was shed in an attempt to remove the Indians from Alcatraz Island. Garment instructed the Washington, D.C., Government Services Administration Office (GSA) to call off the marshals and issued instructions that the White House would coordinate all future actions with the Indian occupiers directly with the San Francisco GSA office. Garment and Patterson orchestrated the government's actions, reactions, and negotiations, which took place over a nineteen-month period, ending on June 11, 1971, when the few remaining occupiers were removed from the island. Garment was sympathetic to Indian issues and felt that his feelings mirrored those of President Nixon and recognized that the Alcatraz occupation was an attempt on the part of urban Indian people to focus the attention of the American people, particularly politicians in Washington, D.C., on their needs.

In the fall of 1972, Indian leaders from the American Indian Movement* (AIM) planned a civil rights march to Washington, D.C., which became known as the "Trail of Broken Treaties." The march was a cross-country caravan starting at three separate points on the West Coast, picking up Indian people from reservations as it went along, arriving in Washington, D.C., just prior to the 1972 presidential election. Several hundred Indian people arrived in Washington, D.C., on November 2; however, no arrangements had been made to provide housing or meals. A few Indians were housed with the assistance of the Department of the Interior. Many, however, had no place to stay and nothing to eat. The Indian people met at the Bureau of Indian Affairs (BIA) building on Constitution Avenue, awaiting word on housing. When shelter could not be found, the Department of Interior offered the use of the BIA building auditorium. The Indians accepted, and as BIA employees left the building at the end of the workday, some young Indians were shoved out the door by guards. The Indians believed that they were being shoved outside into a waiting District of Columbia riot squad. They stopped, turned around, and then seized the BIA building. They barricaded the doors, blocked the windows, upended desks, and piled metal chairs against doors to prevent forcible removal.

On November 6, 1972, a judge ordered the forcible removal of the Indians by 6:00 P.M. that day. The situation inside the BIA building worsened as tensions grew. The Indians decided to wait until 5:45 P.M. for the government to respond to their demands, and if they had not heard anything positive or seen any police withdrawal, they would set the building on fire. Leonard Garment, along with Office of Management and Budget (OMB) director Frank Carlucci, Secretary of the Interior Rogers Morton, and Commissioner of Indian Affairs Louis Bruce, agreed to negotiate with the Indian people on behalf of the president. On election morning, Garment, Carlucci, and Bruce met with the Indians. A federal task force was agreed upon to review the complaints of the Indian people. It would examine wide issues in Indian country. Amnesty was promised. Negotiations were conducted under direct White House auspices with Leonard Garment in charge. A settlement was reached whereby the government would provide $66,500 in travel expenses to get the Indians home, and in return the Indian people would leave the BIA building. They left the building before a 9:00 P.M. November 8, 1972, deadline.

On the evening of February 27, 1973, some 200 Indian people occupied the Village of Wounded Knee, South Dakota, the site of the 1890 Wounded Knee massacre of 150 Lakota Indians, to protest against the corrupt tribal government headed by Richard "Dicky" Wilson and numerous uninvestigated murders of Indian people on the Pine Ridge Indian Reservation. The White House was immediately notified of the occupation, and Leonard Garment once again became the federal government point man for the negotiations. Keenly aware of the president's views and concerns for American Indian people, Garment established the initial policy against the use of violence to remove the Indian occupiers from the village. The Indian occupiers, however, had various weapons with them, and the 300 federal police aligned against them had in their possession fifteen armored personnel carriers and over 100 M-16 rifles. Soon rifle fire was exchanged, two Indian occupiers were killed, fourteen Indian occupiers were injured, and one Federal Bureau of Investigation (FBI) agent was wounded.

During the occupation of Wounded Knee 300 newspeople, including representatives from twelve foreign countries, converged on Wounded Knee. The attention of the nation was focused on Wounded Knee. In Washington, D.C., the decision-making machinery was totally under White House direction, specifically Leonard Garment. Despite the urgency of the situation and the involvement of the assistant attorney general, Garment's decisions carried the most weight, that of the president of the United States. The occupation of Wounded Knee lasted seventy-one days and required patient, persistent, trying negotiations, a task at which Leonard Garment had become a master.

REFERENCE: Leonard Garment, *Crazy Rhythm: Richard Nixon and All That Jazz*, 1997.

Troy Johnson

GASTON COUNTY V. UNITED STATES. Throughout the 1960s, the Supreme Court continued the trends launched when Earl Warren* became chief justice in 1953. Very consistently, the Court struck down all forms of de jure segregation, expanded the rights of individuals, narrowed the powers of government, and labored to make sure that the Fifteenth Amendment's protection of voting rights* was expanded. One of the most important of the voting rights decisions of the Warren Court was *Gaston County v. United States*, decided on June 2, 1969, by a 7 to 1 vote. Justice John Harlan* wrote the majority opinion. In response to the Voting Rights Act* of 1965, a number of counties in the South tried to implement new literacy tests for voters. The Court overturned the literacy tests, arguing that such tests, because of the long history of depriving African Americans of educational opportunities, constituted a violation of the Fifteenth Amendment right to vote.

REFERENCE: 395 U.S. 285 (1969).

GAVIN, JAMES MAURICE. James Gavin was born in New York City March 22, 1907. In 1924, he joined the U.S. Army and impressed his superiors enough to secure an appointment to West Point. Gavin graduated there in 1929. During World War II, he became an expert on airborne warfare and earned a silver star and the rank of lieutenant general. President John F. Kennedy* named him U.S. ambassador to France in 1961. Gavin remained in Paris until 1963, and during those years the French gave him a deep perspective about Indochina. He was soon one of the few U.S. military figures voicing serious misgivings about American policy there. When Senator J. William Fulbright opened hearings about Vietnam by the Senate Foreign Relations Committee in 1966, Gavin testified, urging the Johnson adminstration to adopt an "enclave strategy,"* which would allow U.S. troops to defend major towns and cities without escalating the war. In 1968, Gavin wrote *Crisis Now* and toyed with the idea of running for the presidency, but his campaign was stillborn. He died on February 23, 1990.

REFERENCES: Michael T. Booth, *Paratrooper: The Life of General James M. Gavin*, 1994; *New York Times*, February 24, 1990.

GAY LIBERATION FRONT. See STONEWALL INN RIOTS.

GAY POWER. See STONEWALL INN RIOTS.

GAYE, MARVIN PENZ, JR. Marvin Gaye was born in Washington, D.C., April 2, 1939. As a child he played the organ and sang in church, and then as a teenager he performed with a variety of local doo-wop* groups. He did a tour in the air force after leaving high school, and when he returned home, Gaye formed his own vocal group, known as the Marquees. The ensemble changed names frequently, but in 1961 Berry Gordy of Motown Records* heard them perform and signed them to a contract. Gaye's first hit came a year later with "Stubborn Kind of Fellow." He followed that with twenty more hits during the next decade, including "Hitch Hike" (1963), "Can I Get a Witness?" (1963), "Baby Don't You Do It" (1964), "I'll Be Doggone" (1965), and "How Sweet It Is to Be Loved by You" (1965). During the course of his career, Gaye moved from romantic black pop music to more sophisticated themes that included sexual politics and social concern. He was murdered by his father in 1984.

REFERENCE: David Ritz, *Divided Soul: The Life of Marvin Gaye*, 1991.

GEMINI PROGRAM. See NATIONAL AERONAUTICS AND SPACE ADMINISTRATION.

GENERAL AGREEMENT ON TRADE AND TARIFFS. See KENNEDY ROUND.

GENERATION GAP. The term "generation gap" was commonly used during the 1960s and 1970s to describe the philosophical and cultural differences between the people who came of age during the Great Depression and World War

II and the post–World War II baby boom generation. Stereotypically, the "generation gap" argued that the older generation was conservative, materialistic, and traditional, while the baby boomers were liberal, innovative, and less concerned with the consumer culture.

REFERENCE: Christopher Bone, *The Disinherited Children: A Study of the New Left and the Generation Gap*, 1977.

GENEVA CONFERENCE (1961–1962). The history of Laos as a quiet, backwater outpost of the French colonial empire came to an end after World War II. In 1945 the Lao Issara (Free Lao), a nationalist movement, declared Laos independent of France. Eventually, what began as jockeying for political influence between rival branches of the Laotian royal family gradually became transformed into a Cold War* struggle between left-wing nationalists and a right-wing military.

Prince Boun Khong fathered twenty children, including Prince Souvanna Phouma and his half brother Prince Souphanouvong. They were both raised, after their father's death, by Prince Phetsart, the eldest brother. All three sons received French educations, and all three were committed nationalists. Prince Souphanouvong, however, was the most radical of the brothers, and Prince Souvanna Phouma the most conservative. Phetsart charted a middle course. In August 1945, Souphanouvong expelled the French from Laos and established an independent government with Phetsart and Souvanna Phouma serving as ministers.

But the French soon reasserted themselves and defeated royal Laotian forces. Souphanouvong retreated into the jungles and began forming anti-French resistance forces, while Souvanna Phouma and Phetsart went into exile in Thailand. Eventually, the French talked Souvanna Phouma into returning and establishing a provisional government, but Phetsart stayed in Bangkok, refusing to have anything to do with the French. Souphanouvong stayed in the countryside forming a guerrilla army, which he called the Pathet Lao, and he began to cooperate closely, militarily, and ideologically with Ho Chi Minh's Vietminh forces.

The emergence of a communist guerrilla movement in Laos was not unlike Ho Chi Minh's* development of the Vietminh in Vietnam. During the late nineteenth and early twentieth centuries, there was a variety of anti-French, nationalist movements in Indochina. Because of his own charisma, Ho Chi Minh emerged as one of the leading figures. While his intense nationalism addressed the problem of French imperialism, his communist ideology seemed to address the poverty of the region. Ho Chi Minh's Lao Dong Party became the political vehicle of communism, and the Pathet Lao emerged from it. Communism and nationalism fused in Laos as they had in Vietnam. That nationalism had an anti-French flavor to it until 1954 and then an anti-American flavor throughout the 1950s, 1960s, and 1970s.

The internal struggle for power in Laos became a much broader conflict when the United States, France, the Soviet Union, and the People's Republic of China became intimately involved in it. After the fall of China to Mao Zedong* in 1949 and the outbreak of the Korean War in 1950, American policymakers began to apply the containment* doctrine to Asia as well. In Laos, American policymakers focused on the communism in Souphanouvong's ideology, not on his anti-French, pro-Laotian nationalism. The United States began to see both Souphanouvong and Souvanna Phouma as ''bad guys''—Souphanouvong because of his ties to the Vietminh and Souvanna Phouma because of his increasing neutrality. France set up a puppet regime in Laos under a right-wing collaborator—Phoumi Nosovan. France, of course, was intent on maintaining its imperial outpost in Laos and similarly saw Souphanouvong as a real threat and Souvanna Phouma as a potential threat. The early U.S. decision to provide financial support to the French in Laos was based on the Eisenhower* administration's desire to stop the spread of communism in Asia. During the Kennedy* and Johnson* administrations, that Cold War interpretation of the struggle in Indochina prevailed.

The interest became even more compelling after the Geneva Accords of 1954. At the battle of Dien Bien Phu in 1954, Souphanouvong's Pathet Lao had assisted the Vietminh in the defeat of French forces, and at the Geneva Conference on Indochina the United States made sure that the Pathet Lao did not have representation. The United States had no intention of allowing either Souvanna Phouma or Souphanouvong to take control of an independent Laos. Eventually, the Geneva Accords called for negotiations between all three factions in Laos— the right-wingers under Phoumi Nosovan, the neutralists under Souvanna Phouma, and the leftists under Souphanouvong.

For North Vietnam, which had become independent in 1954, Laos suddenly had an even greater significance. When it became increasingly clear in the 1950s that there would be no free elections to reunite North Vietnam and South Vietnam, Ho Chi Minh realized that Laos would be strategically critical in order to ship troop supplies into South Vietnam. What became known as the Ho Chi Minh Trail* traversed hundreds of miles through Laos and from there into the northern regions of South Vietnam; in the late 1950s the North Vietnamese began providing resources and training to the Pathet Lao, and that relationship became closer and firmer during the years of the Vietnam War.

Throughout the 1950s and into the 1960s, Souvanna Phouma and Souphanouvong tried to establish and maintain a united coalition government, but superpower involvement in Laos really prevented that. The United States was dead set opposed to any Pathet Lao participation in the national government and sabotaged all attempts to establish a coalition government in Laos. The United States was frustrated with Souvanna Phouma's unwillingness to use the Royal Laotian Army to attack the Pathet Lao troops of Souphanouvong. The Eisenhower administration had the Central Intelligence Agency* (CIA) fund a right-wing mercenary army under the corrupt Phoumi Nosovan in an attempt to take over the country. Souvanna Phouma and Souphanouvong then joined hands and defeated Nosovan's troops. The defeat of Nosovan's mercenaries precipitated the "Laotian crisis" of 1962 and the Geneva agreements that year.

The Geneva Conference has been of some controversy among historians. The Kennedy administration portrayed the conference as a major foreign policy achievement, as if the United States orchestrated a great triumph by establishing a neutral government under Souvanna Phouma. The agreements did give the Pathet Lao a minor voice in the new government, called for neutrality, provided for an end of CIA-based military activities, insisted on the expulsion of all foreign military personnel (meaning any North Vietnamese troops), prohibited Laos from entering into any military alliances, and arranged for the election of a national legislature. But the ink on the Geneva documents was hardly dry before the CIA was back in business subverting the Laotian government. The Pathet Lao were essentially driven into the two northern provinces and the eastern border of the country, where they became even more closely connected with the North Vietnamese army* in protecting the Ho Chi Minh Trail. The CIA began a campaign of assassinations against left-wing and even neutralist political officials in Laos, while U.S. Special Forces teams began recruiting and training an army of 12,000 Meo tribesmen to go to war against the Pathet Lao. Late in 1964, under the pretext of bombing the supplies moving south down the Ho Chi Minh Trail, the United States began a concerted bombing campaign against the Pathet Lao that lasted for the next decade. Eventually, the United States unloaded more than 2 million tons of explosives on Laos during the Vietnam War.

REFERENCES: James S. Olson, ed., *The Vietnam War: Handbook of the Literature and Research*, 1993; John Prados, *Presidents' Secret Wars: CIA and Pentagon Covert Operations since World War II*, 1986; R. R. Randall, *Geneva, 1954*, 1969; Perala Ratnam, *Laos and the Super Powers*, 1980; William J. Rust, *Kennedy in Vietnam: American Foreign Policy, 1960–1963*, 1987.

GENOVESE, EUGENE DOMINICK. Eugene Genovese was born in Brooklyn, New York, on May 19, 1930. He graduated from Brooklyn College in 1955 and then earned an M.A. and Ph.D. in history from Columbia University. Genovese began his academic career at Brooklyn Polytechnic Institute, teaching there from 1958 to 1963. During those years, he also completed research and writing on his first book—*The Political Economy of Slavery* (1965). By that time he was teaching at Rutger's University.

Genovese described himself as a "neo-Marxist historian," and he was an early critic of the Vietnam War.* In 1965, he came to national attention for remarking that he would "welcome a Vietcong ascendancy in Vietnam." Vilified throughout the country, he moved to Canada in 1967, taking a faculty post at Sir George Williams University in Montreal. Two years later, he returned to the United States to teach at the University of Rochester, where he became a highly respected historian because of his research. His most important books were *The World the Slaveholders Made* (1969) and *Roll, Jordan, Roll* (1974),

both of which helped reshape the way historians viewed slavery and the South. In more recent years, Genovese's politics have become decidedly more conservative.
REFERENCE: *New York Times*, February 28, 1967.

GENOVESE, KITTY. Kitty Genovese's tragic death in 1964 became a metaphor for the problem of urban crime and apathy in the United States. Kitty Genovese lived in a middle-class apartment complex in Queens, New York. On March 13, 1964, thirty-eight people either heard or saw Genovese being attacked by a knife-wielding assailant. Although she screamed and moaned for nearly ninety minutes, none of the witnesses called police until the attack was over. By that time, Genovese was dead. Most of the witnesses, when interviewed later by police and journalists, simply said that they "did not want to get involved." The incident became headlines on newspapers across the country and the lead story on television news broadcasts as Americans wondered what had happened to them as a people.
REFERENCES: *New York Times*, March 14–17, 1964.

GET SMART. *Get Smart* was a popular television series of the 1960s. First broadcast by NBC on September 18, 1965, the series spoofed the James Bond spy movies and novels that were so popular. *Get Smart* starred Don Adams as Maxwell Smart, Agent 86, and Barbara Feldon as Agent 99. Both worked for CONTROL, the U.S. intelligence agency, and tried to foil the attempts of KAOS, an evil conspiracy, to take over the world. *Get Smart* was a sophomoric, but popular, situation comedy. CBS picked up the series in 1969, and the last episode was broadcast on September 10, 1970.
REFERENCE: Joey Greene, *The* Get Smart *Handbook*, 1993.

G.I. COFFEE HOUSE MOVEMENT. The G.I. Coffee House first opened in Columbia, South Carolina, in 1968, when Fred Gardner hoped to attract soldiers at the nearby Fort Jackson army base and convince them to abandon the Vietnam War.* Gardner soon learned that there was already considerable antiwar* sentiment among G.I.s. He soon established the U.S. Servicemen's Fund, which organized thirty-four G.I. coffeehouses near major military bases around the country. The U.S. Servicemen's Fund also helped finance dozens of underground G.I. newspapers throughout the United States. The coffeehouse movement was not just an antiwar organization. Soldiers also joined civil rights* demonstrations, organized against merchants who exploited servicemen, canceled their U.S. savings bonds, and had various radical groups named as the beneficiary of their military life insurance policies.
REFERENCES: Dick Cluster, ed., *They Should Have Served That Coffee*, 1979; David Cortright, *Soldiers in Revolt*, 1975.

G.I. JOE. Trying to take advantage of Mattel's phenomenal success in marketing "Barbie," a plastic doll portraying a teenaged American young woman, Hasbro Toys released G.I. Joe in 1964, a plastic male counterpart. A toy soldier, G.I. Joe was the first doll aimed at boys, and its various accessories included uniforms, weapons, assault vehicles, and medical supplies. It was a huge success among boys and girls. Sales of G.I. Joe had peaked by 1967, however, because of the growing unpopularity of the military in general and the Vietnam War* in particular. Antiwar critics took on G.I. Joe as an example of the militarism and violence inherent in American popular culture, and Hasbro changed G.I. Joe from a soldier to an adventure hero.
REFERENCE: Jane Stern and Michael Stern, *Encyclopedia of Pop Culture*, 1992.

GIAP, VO NGUYEN. See **VO NGUYEN GIAP**.

GIDEON V. WAINWRIGHT. During the tenure of Chief Justice Earl Warren* (1953–1960), the Supreme Court assumed the most liberal constitutional profile in U.S. history, narrowing the powers of government officials and broadening the rights of individuals. A series of decisions revolving around the right-to-counsel clause of the Sixth Amendment substantially increased the rights of criminal defendants. One such case was *Gideon v. Wainwright*, decided on March 18, 1963, by a unanimous vote. Justice Hugo Black* wrote the majority opinion. The Court overturned the *Betts v. Brady* decision of 1942. The question at hand was whether the Sixth Amendment right to counsel applied to state governments as well as to the federal government. The Court decided that because of the Fourteenth Amendment to the Constitution, state governments fell under Sixth Amendment requirements to provide counsel to indigent defendants.
REFERENCE: 372 U.S. 335 (1963).

GINSBERG, ALLEN. Allen Ginsberg was born in New York City June 3, 1926. He enrolled at Columbia College in 1943 and soon found himself in trouble. An avowed homosexual at a time when homosexuality was illegal and socially unacceptable, Ginsberg had no respect for social convention, authority, or bureaucratic institutions. He was suspended from the university and did not return until 1949. Still unrepentant, Ginsberg allowed friends to store stolen goods in his apartment, and police eventually arrested him. Several prominent faculty members—including Lionel Trilling, Meyer Schapiro, and Herbert Weschler—rallied to him, and on their advice, Ginsberg pleaded insanity. Instead of a penitentiary, Ginsberg ended up in the mental ward of Columbia Presbyterian Hospital. After several months there, he promised to live a conventional life and was released. He tried to settle down to a life of work and women, but he was frustrated. In 1954 he moved to Berkeley, California.

There Ginsberg flowered into the poet laureate of the beat* generation. He experimented with drugs as a means of exploring sensory experience and inner feelings, worked to protect the underdogs in American society, promoted individual faithfulness to sexual identity—whether homosexual or heterosexual—and called for a rejection of all individual-limiting social conventions. By the 1960s, Ginsberg had become an icon to the counterculture,* the original precursor to all that they wanted to become. He gave away his money to the antiwar movement,* to underground newspapers, and to legal defense groups representing whom he thought to be political prisoners. Ginsberg rejected the recreational use of drugs in the 1960s. Responsible drug use, he believed, should be designed to explore feelings and expand experience, not simply to party. His own drug use declined in the later 1960s, when political protest became so central to the counterculture.

During the 1970s and 1980s, Ginsberg kept the faith, remaining loyal to his own vision of the world. He aged well, maintaining his reputation as an artist of enormous talent and a man of great integrity. In 1996, Ginsberg was teaching at Brooklyn College and commenting on the presidential election between Bill Clinton, Bob Dole, and Ross Perot. He died on April 5, 1997.

REFERENCES: Barry Miles, *Ginsberg: A Biography*, 1989; Michael Schumacher, *Dharma Lion: A Critical Biography of Allen Ginsberg*, 1992.

THE GINZBURG CASE. Steadily during the 1950s and early 1960s, federal courts relaxed their definition of pornography, making it more difficult for state and local governments to engage in censorship. Ralph Ginzburg was a publisher of soft-core pornography, material that was considered well within federal court guidelines. To increase subscriptions to his magazines *Eros, Liaison Newsletter*, and *Documentary Books*, Ginzburg purchased extensive national mailing lists, and to sensationalize the advertisements, he mailed them from Blue Ball and Intercourse, Pennsylvania. Unfortunately for his business career, Ginzburg neglected to screen the mailing list and eliminate the names of ministers, priests, rabbis, and other individuals concerned about public morality.

Dozens of those people found the mail-outs obscene and filed suit against Ginzburg. He was convicted of ''pandering'' obscene material and sentenced to five years. Ginzburg was confident that the Warren Court would throw out the conviction on First Amendment freedom of expression grounds. The Court, however, ignored the actual content of his publications and instead ruled on his methods of distribution and upheld, by a narrow 5 to 4 vote, the conviction on pandering. Civil liberties advocates came to his defense, and a federal court in May 1970 reduced the sentence to three years. In February 1972, Ginzburg entered a federal penitentiary. He was paroled eight months later.

REFERENCE: Gay Talese, *Thy Neighbor's Wife*, 1980.

GLENN, JOHN HERSCHEL, JR. John Glenn was born in Cambridge, Ohio, July 18, 1921. After graduating from Muskingum in 1942, he joined the Marine Corps and became a test pilot. Glenn remained in the marines until 1965. His fame during the 1960s came from his selection as one of the original seven Mercury program astronauts. On February 20, 1962, Glenn was launched into

space, and in his Mercury capsule he became the first American astronaut to orbit the earth. He almost died during the return to earth when the heat shield of his capsule malfunctioned. Glenn lost a bid for the U.S. Senate from Ohio in 1964, but in 1976 he finally won the seat, and he was reelected in 1982, 1988, and 1994. In 1997, he announced that he would not stand for election to another term. In 1998 Glenn returned to space as an astronaut on the shuttle *Discovery.*
REFERENCE: Michael Cole, *John Glenn: Astronaut and Senator*, 1993.

"GOD IS DEAD." See **ALTIZER, THOMAS JONATHAN JACKSON**.

GOLDBERG, ARTHUR JOSEPH. Arthur Goldberg was born August 8, 1908, in Chicago, Illinois. A brilliant young man, he graduated from Northwestern University and then took a law degree there. In 1929, he went into private practice, specializing in corporate and labor law. When World War II erupted, Goldberg joined the Office of Strategic Services (OSS), a forerunner of the Central Intelligence Agency* (CIA); after the war, his acquaintances in the CIA helped provide him access to important government officials. In 1946, the United Steelworkers Union hired him as its general counsel. From that post, Goldberg became a prominent figure in the American Federation of Labor-Congress of Industrial Organizations (AFL-CIO). As a prominent labor leader, he also became wired into the Democratic Party establishment in Washington, D.C.

In 1961, President John F. Kennedy* appointed him to the U.S. Supreme Court. He voted consistently with the liberal wing, led by Chief Justice Earl Warren.* In 1965, Goldberg resigned from the court when Lyndon Johnson* appointed him U.S. ambassador to the United Nations. It proved to be a frustrating job, since Johnson kept him in the dark about foreign policy issues and because Goldberg soon harbored serious opposition to the Vietnam War.* Goldberg later regretted having given up his justiceship on the Supreme Court. As one of the so-called "Wise Old Men"* senior statesmen, he urged Johnson to de-escalate the war. In April 1968, Goldberg resigned from the UN ambassadorship and became active in the antiwar* movement. Among his publications are *Defense of Freedom* (1966) and *Equal Justice: The Warren Era of the Supreme Court* (1972). Arthur Goldberg died January 19, 1990.
REFERENCES: *New York Times*, January 20, 1990; David Stebenn, *Arthur J. Goldberg: New Deal Liberal*, 1996.

GOLDWATER, BARRY MORRIS. Barry Goldwater was born in Phoenix, Arizona, January 1, 1909. He attended the University of Arizona for a year but then went to work in the family department store business. During World War II, he was a pilot in the army air corps. A conservative Republican, Goldwater was elected to the U.S. Senate in 1952, and in 1964, he won the Republican presidential nomination. He lost in a landslide to Lyndon B. Johnson.* While most of the country hoped to avoid war in Vietnam, Goldwater took a very

aggressive position. In terms of domestic policy, he advocated drastic cuts in federal spending for all programs and severe reductions in social security benefits. Most Americans were then still enamored of the New Deal. Goldwater's brand of political and economic conservatism would not receive widespread support until the 1980s, when Ronald Reagan* took advantage of it. Because of the presidential nomination, Goldwater did not run for reelection to the Senate in 1964, but he was reelected in 1968, 1974, and 1980. He retired from the Senate in 1987 and returned to Arizona, where he lives today and serves as the elder statesman of the Republican Party. Barry Goldwater died May 29, 1998.
REFERENCE: Robert Alan Goldberg, *Barry Goldwater*, 1995.

GOMER PYLE, U.S.M.C. *Gomer Pyle, U.S.M.C.* took the popular rural situation comedy of CBS from the country to the city and from the South to California. However, its popularity was concentrated in the rural South. The series, a spin-off from the popular *Andy Griffith Show,** took a naive North Carolina country boy from the sticks and stationed him at Fort Henderson, California, in the U.S. Marine Corps. *Gomer Pyle* first aired September 25, 1964, and starred Jim Nabors as Gomer Pyle and Frank Sutton as Sergeant Vince Carter, his nemesis and, later, fatherly friend.

Gomer Pyle, U.S.M.C. maintained its popularity by offering the familiar rural-based sitcom successfully transferred to an urban setting. When the audience desired greater family-oriented viewing, the familial relationship between Gomer and Sergeant Carter improved. *Gomer Pyle* survived six seasons during a time in the 1960s of profound disillusionment with war and the military. The series achieved this by avoiding war themes completely and focusing on Gomer's innocent simplicity, Sergeant Carter's frustration and later concern for Gomer's well-being, and the continued appeal of the rural genre.

The series became an early victim of a CBS cancellation decision. The network was ranked in the number one position by viewers. In the early 1970s, however, CBS decided to move away from rural-oriented comedy. This decision was a gamble based on demographic studies indicating the show's popularity with older rural audiences but lack of support among higher-income, younger urban audiences. The show's last telecast was on September 9, 1970.
REFERENCES: Tim Brook and Earle Marsh, *The Complete Directory to Prime Time Network Shows: 1946–Present*, 1992; David Marc, *Demographic Vistas: Television in American Culture*, 1984.

Christopher Gore

GOMILLION V. LIGHTFOOT. Throughout the 1960s, the Supreme Court continued the trends launched when Earl Warren* became chief justice in 1953. Very consistently, the Court struck down all forms of de jure segregation, expanded the rights of individuals, narrowed the powers of government, and labored to make sure that the Fifteenth Amendment's protection of voting rights was expanded. One of the most important of the voting rights decisions of the

Warren Court was *Gomillion v. Lightfoot,* decided on November 4, 1960, by a unanimous vote. In cooperation with the city of Tuskegee, Alabama, the state legislature had approved a city redistricting plan whose effect excluded nearly all black voters from city elections. The Court declared the plan an unconstitutional violation of the Fifteenth Amendment.
REFERENCE: 364 U.S. 339 (1960).

GONZALES, RODOLFO "CORKY." Rodolfo "Corky" Gonzales was born in Denver in 1929 to a migrant worker family. As a child he made the annual journeys to fields throughout the western states. After a stint as a professional boxer, Gonzales started his own business and became active in Democratic politics. Frustrated with the conservatism of the mainstream political parties, he abandoned the Democrats in 1965 and established his Crusade for Justice,* a Chicano* activist and civil rights* group. The Crusade for Justice sponsored school walkouts to dramatize the problems in Hispanic education, marches against police brutality, and demonstrations for the civil rights of Chicano criminal defendants. Gonzales also opposed and demonstrated against the Vietnam War.*

Gonzales was a leader in the Chicano delegation in the Poor People's Campaign* of 1968, and while camped on the mall in Washington, D.C., he issued his formal "Plan of the Barrio," a demand for civil rights for Mexican Americans,* improved housing, return of stolen lands in the Southwest, and better-funded and improved public schools. Gonzales also founded the Chicano Youth Liberation group, which promoted the ideas of Chicano ethnic nationalism and self-determination. As the author of the stirring poem "Yo Soy Joaquín," Corky Gonzales remains today an important figure in the history of Chicano activism. He has remained an active supporter of Chicano causes, and since the late 1970s he has returned to boxing as a trainer and promoter.
REFERENCE: Christine Marin, *A Spokesman of the Mexican American Movement: Rodolfo "Corky" Gonzales and the Fight for Chicano Liberation, 1966–1972,* 1977.

GOODMAN, PAUL. Paul Goodman was born in 1911 and educated at the City College of New York and the University of Chicago, where he specialized in philosophy and psychology. Many historians now consider Goodman the intellectual godfather of the New Left* movement during the 1960s. An avowed homosexual who was out of the closet before that was acceptable anywhere in America, Goodman was fired several times from teaching jobs because of his sexual orientation. Goodman's genius spread across several disciplines. In 1947, with his architect brother Percival, he wrote *Communitas,* a highly regarded book on community planning. With Fritz Stern, he wrote *Gestalt Therapy* in 1951, and the book became the theoretical backbone of that therapeutic movement. His *The Structure of Language* in 1954 was brilliant literary criticism, and his 1957 book, *Speaking and Language,* was a brilliant exposition of philosophical linguistics. Goodman also wrote plays, social criticism, short stories, and poems. He was a philosophical anarchist who did not trust established political institutions. During the 1960s, Goodman served on the editorial board of *Liberation* magazine. His book *Growing Up Absurd* (1960) earned him his place as an intellectual leader of the 1960s youth rebellion and counterculture.* In the book he called on young people to rise up in America and bring to a completion the "unfinished revolutions." He died August 2, 1972.

REFERENCES: George Dennison, "A Memoir," in Paul Goodman, *Collected Poems*, 1973; *New York Times*, November 3, 1972; Widmer Kingsley, *Paul Goodman*, 1980.

GOOK. The term "gook" was a racist term brought to Vietnam by U.S. veterans of the Korean War. It is a derogatory reference to people of Asian extraction.

REFERENCE: James S. Olson, ed., *Dictionary of the Vietnam War*, 1988.

GORE, LESLIE. Leslie Gore was born in New York City May 2, 1946. While she was attending a private school in New Jersey and singing locally, she was discovered by Quincy Jones, who signed her with Mercury Records. Gore enjoyed a spectacular, but brief, career as a pop singer in the early 1960s. When she turned seventeen, Mercury released her "It's My Party," which shot to number one on the pop charts. Later in 1963, "Judy's Turn to Cry," "She's a Fool," and "You Don't Own Me" all reached the top five. During the next two years, Gore had four more hits: "That's the Way Boys Are," "Maybe I Know," "Sunshine, Lollipops and Rainbows," and "California Nights." Her heyday as a performer then ended. Gore graduated from Sarah Lawrence College and went into the songwriting and music production business.

REFERENCE: Patricia Romanowski and Holly George-Warren, eds., *The New Rolling Stone Encyclopedia of Rock and Roll*, 1996.

THE GRADUATE. *The Graduate* was one of the most popular and symbolic films of the 1960s. Directed by Mike Nichols, the film starred Dustin Hoffman as Benjamin Braddock, a recent college graduate who comes from a neighborhood of self-absorbed, upper-middle-class snobs whose lives revolve around money and things. Full of confusion and angst about the meaning of life and the irrelevancy of all those things his parents value, Braddock searches for what life means to him. He is seduced by middle-aged Mrs. Robinson (Anne Bancroft) but then falls in love with her daughter Elaine (Katherine Ross). Young people identified closely with Braddock's sense of ennui and antimaterialism. At the end of the film, he races all the way from northern to southern California to rescue Elaine from her own wedding and finds the meaning of life in his love for her. Simon and Garfunkle's song "Here's to You, Mrs. Robinson" went to the top of the charts and became the first time that a rock-and-roll number was used as a cinematic theme song.

REFERENCE: *New York Times*, December 22, 1967.

GRAHAM, WILLIAM FRANKLIN, JR. Billy Graham was born November 7, 1918, in Charlotte, North Carolina. He was the son of a dairy farmer, William Franklin Graham, and Morrow Graham. He received a Th.B. from Florida Bible Institute in 1940 and a B.A. from Wheaton College in 1943. He was ordained to the Baptist ministry in 1940 and became a pastor and radio personality during the early 1940s. He was an innovator in using many forms of media to get the gospel message to the world. He has written many books and articles, led mass evangelistic crusades, produced motion pictures and television programs, and started schools. His multimedia approach has earned him international recognition and awards. *Time* magazine has labeled him "America's premier evangelist." Graham gained "notoriety through his association with Richard Nixon* before and during the Watergate years."

Graham's popularity has made him the subject of many controversies. Fundamentalist theologians think that he is too liberal, while others think that his theology is too simplistic. Although controversial, he is still popular in international crusades, which draw hundreds of thousands each year. His writings are often criticized as being nothing more than transcripts of his sermons. Even Graham has admitted: "I'm not an accomplished writer in any sense. I usually send my manuscripts off to the publishers to have them edited. I like to write, though, because I have many things in my heart to say before I get to heaven."
REFERENCE: John Pollock, *To All the Nations of the World: The Billy Graham Story*, 1985.

Bobby J. James

GRAPE BOYCOTT. See **DELANO GRAPE STRIKE** and **UNITED FARM WORKERS**.

THE GRATEFUL DEAD. The Grateful Dead enjoy the reputation as the psychedelic rock-and-roll band with the most longevity. Formed in San Francisco in 1965, the group included Jerry Garcia, Bob Weir, Ron McKernan, Phil Lesh, and Bill Kreutzmann. Although they never really had huge commercial success on the pop charts, they created a virtual movement of "Deadheads"*—fans who followed them from concert to concert and preserved the 1960s culture of tie-dyed clothing and hallucinogenic drug use. Their music was highly improvised and a mix of country, blues, and rock. The Grateful Dead are one of the most extraordinary phenomena in the history of modern American rock-and-roll and popular culture. They became a permanent time warp for Americans back to the 1960s, and their hippie concert following was more of a "happening" than an event. Deadheads followed the band everywhere, showing up at every concert possible, and became a sort of communal tribe drawing the meaning for their lives from their association with the Grateful Dead. The band kept ticket prices low, permitted fans to tape concerts, tended to stay away from recording studios, refused to become involved with any political candidate, and performed a freestyle, jazz-style music. Throughout the 1970s, 1980s, and early 1990s, the

Grateful Dead focused their energies on live performances rather than recording, and in doing so they became one of the world's most profitable bands. Jerry Garcia's death in 1995, however, seems to have marked the end of the group's spectacular popularity.
REFERENCE: Carol Brightman, *Dead Reckoning: The Life and Times of the Grateful Dead*, 1999; Robert Weiner, *Perspectives on the Grateful Dead: Critical Writings*, 1999.

THE GREAT BLACKOUT OF 1965. On November 9, 1965, because of an enormous power surge, 30 million people suddenly found themselves without electricity. The utility companies did not possess at the time any sophisticated backup systems, and the power surge spread across the northeastern United States like falling dominos. From Ontario, Canada, through New England and New York State and out as far west as Michigan, the blackout kept millions of people trapped in subways and high-rise buildings, where elevators would not work, and everything was in complete darkness. In New York City, the blackout lasted more than thirteen hours, and in American popular culture, the question "Where were you during the blackout?" evoked both fond and frightening memories. The utility companies eventually constructed sophisticated backup systems to prevent another regional blackout.
REFERENCES: *New York Times*, November 10–11, 1965.

GREAT SOCIETY. During the twentieth century, journalists have created catchy phrases to describe the administrations of activist U.S. presidents. Theodore Roosevelt's became known as the "Square Deal," Franklin D. Roosevelt's the "New Deal," and Harry Truman's the "Fair Deal." Journalists used the term "New Frontier" to describe the John F. Kennedy* administration, and the "Great Society" became the phrase associated with President Lyndon B. Johnson.* The phrase came from a speech Johnson delivered at the University of Michigan in May 1964, in which he promoted the "opportunity to move not only toward the rich society and the powerful society but upward to the Great Society." The president defined the Great Society as one which "rests on abundance and liberty for all. It demands an end to poverty and racial injustice." Eventually, the Great Society found expression in the Civil Rights Act of 1964,* the Voting Rights Act of 1965,* and the "war on poverty."* But it also died in the jungles of Vietnam, since it became impossible to sustain a reform agenda when the war sapped so many national resources and bred such political infighting at home.
REFERENCE: Irwin Unger, *The Best of Intentions: The Triumph and Failure of the Great Society Under Kennedy, Johnson, and Nixon*, 1996.

THE GREAT WHITE HOPE. *The Great White Hope* was one of the decade's most popular Broadway plays. Written by Howard Sackler, *The Great White Hope* opened at the Alvin Ailey theater in New York City on October 3, 1968. It starred James Earl Jones as boxer Jack Jefferson and Jane Alexander as

Eleanor Bachman. The play was loosely based on the life of Jack Johnson, the proud, outspoken African-American heavyweight champion who, in the years before World War I, experienced racism, discrimination, and oppression at the hands of a white America more used to Irish boxing champions. Johnson married a white woman, and the play openly dealt with questions of race, gender, sexuality, and pride. *The Great White Hope* enjoyed a Broadway run of 556 performances.
REFERENCE: *New York Times*, October 4, 1968.

GREEN ACRES. *Green Acres* was the last of the rural-oriented situation comedies created by Paul Henning for CBS during the 1960s. The series was a spinoff from *Petticoat Junction** and ran for six years after it first aired September 15, 1965. It starred Eddie Albert as Oliver Douglas, Eva Gabor as Lisa Douglas, Pat Buttram as Mr. Haney, Tom Lester as Ed Dawson, and Frank Cady as Sam Drucker.

The *Green Acres* story line was basically *The Beverly Hillbillies** in reverse. This series was more outlandish than any of the other Henning creations. In *Green Acres* Henning used the humorous extreme to show culture clash and to demonstrate cultural acceptance. *Green Acres* also provided the same basic comic relief from other national tensions as exemplified in *Petticoat Junction* and *The Beverly Hillbillies*. Though it was still successful for CBS, *Green Acres* was canceled with other rural comedies in the early 1970s. The final telecast aired September 7, 1971.
REFERENCES: Tim Brooks and Earle Marsh, *The Complete Directory to Prime Time Network Shows: 1946–Present*, 1992; David Marc, *Demographic Vistas: Television in American Culture*, 1984.

Christopher Gore

GREEN BERETS. See SPECIAL FORCES.

THE GREEN BERETS (Book). One of the bestselling books of 1965 was Robin Moore's novel *The Green Berets*, a fictionalized account of U.S. Special Forces* in Vietnam. Moore worked closely with the Green Berets in researching the novel, so closely, in fact, that the Defense Department became uneasy about its accuracy in describing counterinsurgency* tactics in the Vietnam War.* The novel is highly ideological. The Special Forces are portrayed as sincere, highly motivated soldiers willing to risk their lives to rescue South Vietnam from Communism, while the South Vietnamese are seen as venal and incompetent. The North Vietnamese and Vietcong are portrayed as evil aggressors willing to commit murder, torture, and any manner of atrocity to achieve their goals of dictatorship and oppression. The Green Berets quickly lost caché, however, as the antiwar movement* gained momentum in the United States. Critics charged it with being irrelevant, a "World War II novel about Vietnam."

REFERENCES: Robin Moore, *The Green Berets*, 1965; James S. Olson and Randy Roberts, *Where the Domino Fell: America and Vietnam 1945–1995*, 1995.

THE GREEN BERETS (Film). Written in 1965, when the Vietnam War* was just under way at its escalated level, but released in 1968, when the antiwar movement* was at its peak, *The Green Berets* starred John Wayne* as the Green Beret colonel, David Janssen as a jaded journalist, and Jim Hutton as the naive, big-hearted American GI out to save the world. The film was loaded with World War II clichés, with the Vietcong* portrayed as universal savages and the Americans and South Vietnamese characterized as the epitome of goodness and mercy.

The Green Berets tells two completely unrelated stories. The first part of the film features "Dodge City," a base camp near the Cambodian and Laotian borders where Green Beret* advisers teach the South Vietnamese how to defend themselves. Eventually, a huge battle ensues in which the Vietcong, using human wave assaults, attack and overrun the camp. The battle scenes are part *Alamo*,* part *Fort Apache*, part *Fighting Seabees*. Vietcong troops hoist ladders against the base camp walls as Mexican soldiers did at the Alamo, and Patrick Wayne (John Wayne's son), playing a navy engineer, drives a bulldozer against the Vietcong, just as Duke had done to the Japanese in *Fighting Seabees*. American airpower eventually saves the day, with "Puff the Magic Dragon" C-47 gunships cutting the Vietcong to pieces and allowing the Green Berets to retake the base camp, but not before the Vietcong have systematically murdered all of the Vietnamese civilians there.

The Green Berets then shifts into a *Dirty Dozen* mode. A team of Green Berets parachutes into Vietcong country to capture an enemy general. A beautiful young Vietnamese woman who hates the Vietcong and secretly spies for the Americans seduces the general, luring him into her boudoir at a secluded villa. As he is making love to her, the Green Berets kill his bodyguards and capture him. They then make their way back through the jungle to friendly territory. Along the way, Sergeant Peterson, a beloved scrounger who has befriended a Vietnamese orphan, steps into a Vietcong booby trap and is impaled on dozens of punji* stakes. The film ends with Colonel Mike Kirby (John Wayne) comforting Hamchunk, the Vietnamese orphan, and reassuring him that all will be well because "you're what this war is all about."

The unifying focus of the movie is the awakening of George Beckwith (David Janssen), a liberal journalist, to the real nature of American involvement. At first Beckwith is skeptical; he doubts the domino theory,* the threat of communism, and the viability of the government in South Vietnam. But after observing a series of heinous Vietcong atrocities and following the activities of Green Beret colonel Kirby, he reverses his earlier opinions. Beckwith abandons civilian clothes for army fatigues and picks up the slack during battle scenes, readily helping the Americans to fight off the Vietcong. Nevertheless, even the journalist realizes that it will be difficult to tell the true story of the war in

Vietnam because of the liberal bias of the American press. ''If I say what I feel,'' he informs Kirby, ''I may be out of a job.'' The film suggests that the United States' biggest fight is not against the North Vietnamese but rather against the liberal establishment that threatens the war effort by its opposition. Of all the films of the Vietnam era, none was a better reflection of American policies in 1965, at the beginning of the conflict.
REFERENCE: Randy Roberts and James S. Olson, *John Wayne, American*, 1995.

''GREEN BERETS'' (Song). In March 1966, the song ''Ballad of the Green Berets'' reached number one on the *Billboard* pop music charts and remained there for five weeks. Its success was certainly a unique phenomenon, given the success of rock and roll in popular music. Written and performed by Sergeant Barry Sadler, a real-life Green Beret,* the song had been recorded solely for military audiences, but RCA Records picked it up and sold more than 1.5 million copies. Antiwar critics, of course, panned the record, but for a few months at least, Barry Sadler was a military hero in a war that badly needed heroes.
REFERENCE: Jane Stern and Michael Stern, *Encyclopedia of Pop Culture*, 1992.

GRIFFIN V. CALIFORNIA. During the tenure of Chief Justice Earl Warren* (1953–1960), the Supreme Court assumed the most liberal constitutional profile in U.S. history, narrowing the powers of government officials and broadening the rights of individuals. A series of decisions revolving around the self-incrimination clause of the Fifth Amendment particularly revealed the Court's liberal bent. One such case was *Griffin v. California*, decided by a 7 to 1 vote on April 28, 1965. Justice William Douglas* wrote the majority opinion. The question at hand involved whether a judge in a criminal case had violated a defendant's Fifth Amendment right by commenting negatively to the jury about the defendant's decision not to testify. The Court decided that such comments, because they may bias the jury, are unconstitutional.
REFERENCE: 380 U.S. 479 (1965).

GRIFFIN V. COUNTY SCHOOL BOARD OF PRINCE EDWARD COUNTY.
With its *Brown v. Board of Education of Topeka, Kansas*, decision in 1954, the Supreme Court had outlawed racial segregation in public schools. Although the Court ordered desegregation to occur ''with all deliberate speed,'' southern politicians launched what came to be known as ''massive resistance,'' a concerted political and legal campaign to postpone or prevent implementation of the *Brown* decision. A decade after the decision, the Court found itself still dealing with massive resistance. One such instance was *Griffin v. County School Board of Prince Edward County*, decided by a 7 to 2 vote on May 25, 1964. To prevent desegregation, school officials in Prince Edward County, Virginia, had ordered the closing of all public schools. The Court said such a decision was a violation of equal protection clause of the Fourteenth Amendment.
REFERENCE: 377 U.S. 218 (1964).

GRISSOM, VIRGIL ("GUS"). Born April 3, 1926, in Mitchell, Indiana, Virgil "Gus" Grissom paved the way for future space exploration with his 1961 suborbital flight in the Mercury spacecraft. A distinguished air force pilot, he flew more than 100 missions during the Korean War, for which he received the Distinguished Flying Cross. During the later 1950s, Grissom worked as an air force test pilot before being selected as one of the country's original seven astronauts.

Astronaut Alan Shepard made the first suborbital flight in a Mercury spacecraft, and Grissom made the second. But upon his reentry aboard the spacecraft *Liberty Bell*, Grissom nearly drowned when a detonator malfunction blew off the hatch cover prematurely, before the navy's rescue team arrived on the scene. Seawater filled the capsule. Due to the additional weight of the seawater, the rescue helicopter was unable to retrieve the capsule. Fortunately, Grissom was unharmed. He later remarked, "In all of my years of flying—including combat in Korea—this was the first time that my aircraft and I had not come back together." His suborbital flight and near fatal accident proved crucial in developing a new life vest for astronauts and a new survival kit that included such things as shark repellent. It also set the stage for John Glenn's* orbital flight.

On June 27, 1967, Virgil Grissom, Edward H. White, and Roger B. Chaffee of the Apollo 1 crew became the first casualties of the American space program. During a practice session in the Apollo 1 capsule, the crew experienced a number of problems. When the capsule was pressurized with pure oxygen at thirty-six pounds per square inch to simulate flight conditions, the crew noticed a strange, faint odor. Scientists stopped the simulation and took samples of the air in the capsule, but they detected nothing unusual. The capsule was repressurized, and the simulation continued. But at 6:30 P.M., an electrical spark ignited the oxygen. Due to the pressurization of the cabin, the heat reached nearly 2,000 degrees; heat-resistant materials melted, and the crew died in a matter of seconds. After the Apollo 1 tragedy, the National Aeronautic and Space Administration* developed elaborate new safety procedures, and the Apollo capsule had to be redesigned.

REFERENCES: *New York Times*, June 28–30, July 1–8, 1967.

Alexander Pinh Vilaythong

GRISWOLD V. CONNECTICUT. During the 1950s and 1960s, the Supreme Court under Chief Justice Earl Warren* pursued a consistent legal goal of undermining de jure segregation, restricting the powers of the state, and expanding the rights of individuals. They were especially concerned with issues of personal privacy, which found expression in *Griswold v. Connecticut*, decided by a 7 to 2 vote on June 7, 1965. Connecticut state law prohibited the sale of contraceptives, even to married adults. The Court overturned the law, arguing that there is a right of personal privacy inherent in the Constitution.

REFERENCE: 381 U.S. 479 (1965).

GROOVY. The term "groovy" first emerged among beatniks* during the 1950s as a positive adjective for something that was pleasing to the mind or to the senses. During the 1960s, the counterculture* picked up on the term, and by the late 1960s and early 1970s it was widely used by young people throughout the United States.

REFERENCE: Ruth Bronsteen, *The Hippy's Handbook—How to Live on Love*, 1967.

GRUENING, ERNEST HENRY. Born in New York in 1887, Ernest Gruening began his professional life studying medicine, but his heart was in public affairs and he crossed over into journalism. He wrote well, had excellent instincts for ferreting out good stories, and eventually became an editor for *Nation* magazine. He specialized in Latin American affairs and developed an antipathy for U.S. policy there, especially dollar diplomacy, through which the United States government backed private corporations in financially exploiting the resources of Central and South American countries. He expressed some of those views in his 1928 book *Mexico and Its Heritage*. In 1934, Gruening joined the Department of the Interior, and in 1939 President Franklin D. Roosevelt appointed him governor of Alaska Territory. He served as governor until 1953. When Alaska achieved statehood in 1959, Gruening proclaimed his candidacy and became one of its first two U.S. senators.

A liberal Democrat loyal to New Deal values, Gruening supported Lyndon B. Johnson's* Great Society* programs, but he broke with the administration over Vietnam. For Gruening, the Vietnam War* smacked of Latin American adventurism because the United States was throwing its political and economic support behind a hopelessly corrupt, elitist regime. In his view, the war was completely misguided and unwinnable. On March 10, 1964, he asked President Johnson to de-escalate the war and withdraw U.S. troops. "All Vietnam," Gruening contended, "is not worth the life of a single American boy." After the Gulf of Tonkin incident in August 1964, Gruening was one of only two senators to oppose the Gulf of Tonkin Resolution.* In doing so, he earned the lasting enmity of Lyndon Johnson. Gruening's opposition to the war cost him his Senate seat. In 1968, he lost the Democratic primary to Mike Gravel. Gruening spent the next several years writing his book *Vietnam Folly* (1972). He died June 26, 1974.

REFERENCES: Robert David Johnson, *Ernest Gruening and the American Dissenting Tradition*, 1998; Hoyt Purvis, "Ernest Gruening," in James S. Olson, ed., *Dictionary of the Vietnam War*, 1988.

GUERNICA. Spain's leader Francisco Franco ordered German planes to attack the Basque town of Guernica on April 26, 1937, during the Spanish civil war. Shortly after this, Pablo Picasso painted the huge mural *Guernica*. Completed in less than two months, *Guernica* was hung in the Spanish Pavilion of the Paris International Exposition of 1937. The painting does not portray the event; rather, Picasso expressed his outrage by employing such imagery as the bull, the dying horse, a fallen warrior, a mother and dead child, a woman trapped in a burning building, another rushing into the scene, and a figure leaning from a window and holding out a lamp. Despite the complexity of its symbolism, *Guernica* made an overwhelming impact in its portrayal of the horrors of war. It was on extended loan at New York City's Museum of Modern Art from 1939 to 1981.

In 1968, Franco himself launched the movement to secure *Guernica* for Spain. By that time it had been associated with the Museum of Modern Art in New York. It had been integrated into the collections of the museum, extensively studied, widely published, given excellent conservation treatment, and seen by more viewers than it might have been in any other museum all over the world. Spain's request for the painting came as a surprise.

During the 1960s *Guernica* depicted a threatening image of nuclear warfare that haunted the minds of everyone. When the government's request for *Guernica* was made public, Picasso, through his lawyer, Roland Dumas, issued a written response, that for the moment the answer was no, although both Picasso and Dumas made clear the artist's intention that *Guernica* should eventually go to Spain. Dumas wrote that "the painting shall be returned when the Republic shall be restored in Spain." On December 5, 1975, Picasso gave *Guernica* to the Spanish republic.

REFERENCE: Eberhard Fisch, *Guernica by Picasso*, 1988.

Emily Cason

GUERRILLAS. See VIETCONG.

GUEVARA, ERNESTO (CHE). Ernesto "Che" Guevara was born to a prosperous family in Rosario, Argentina, July 14, 1928. As a young college student, he developed revolutionary ideas while opposing the regime of Juan Perón. After receiving his medical degree in 1953, Guevara went first to live in Guatemala and then to Mexico City, where he met Fidel Castro.* He returned with Castro to Cuba and became the tactical mastermind of the Cuban revolution, overthrowing the Batista regime in 1959. In the process, Guevara became a close personal friend and leading political adviser to Castro.

Guevara came to world attention when he wrote *Guerrilla Warfare* shortly after the Cuban revolution. The book was a political and military handbook on how Third World people could throw off their colonial and upper-class masters. The book found a ready audience among middle-class, left-wing college students in the United States. Posters of Che Guevara—his beret-topped, long-haired, bearded face with red background—adorned tens of thousands of dormitory rooms in the United States in the late 1960s.

Suddenly, in 1965, Guevara dropped out of sight, and his whereabouts intrigued the world. Actually, he spent a good deal of time in the Congo organizing Marxist guerrilla military and political groups, and then he moved to Latin America, where he thought the potential for revolutionary upheaval was excellent. On October 8, 1967, however, Bolivian troops, backed with Central Intel-

ligence Agency* (CIA) money and information, captured and executed Che Guevara, ending his reign as the most popular radical icon of the 1960s.
REFERENCES: Anne Neimer, *Che! Latin America's Legendary Guerrilla Leader*, 1989; Gary Prado Salmon, *The Defeat of Che Guevara: Military Response to Guerrilla Warfare in Bolivia*, 1990.

GULF OF TONKIN INCIDENT (1964). On August 1, 1964, the USS *Maddox*, an American destroyer, was patrolling within a range of ten to twenty miles off the North Vietnamese coast, collecting electronic data on North Vietnamese radar signals and ship movements. The ship was also monitoring four South Vietnamese gunboats, which the night before had left Danang and attacked North Vietnamese coastal sites as part of Oplan 34-A. North Vietnamese patrol boats approached the *Maddox*. In just a few moments, the *Maddox* opened fire, and the patrol boats launched several torpedoes. Jets from the USS *Ticonderoga* attacked the North Vietnamese ships, damaging all of them. The next day the *Maddox* was joined by another destroyer, the USS *C. Turner Joy*. President Lyndon B. Johnson* ordered the ships to continue their patrols.

More South Vietnamese gunboats left Danang for Oplan 34-A attacks. On August 4 the *Maddox* and the *C. Turner Joy* picked up radio traffic from confused and enraged North Vietnamese naval vessels. Tension was running high on both the *Maddox* and the *Turner Joy*. Men on both ships saw blips on the radar they believed represented PT boats, and the sonar man on the *Maddox* reported underwater noises that he believed to be the sounds of incoming torpedoes. Both ships commenced evasive actions and began firing into the dark at the direction of the radar blips, although they made no visual sightings of North Vietnamese patrol boats. Several hours later, Captain John Herrick, head of the DeSoto Mission on board the *Maddox*, concluded that there probably had been no attack, that rough seas and atmospheric conditions generated spurious radar blips, and that the evasive movements of the ships had created torpedo-like sonar sounds. In a cable to the Pentagon, Herrick reported that conclusion. By the time Herrick sent the cable, it was too late. The Pentagon and White House were like hornets' nests, and Admiral Ulysses S. Grant Sharp, Jr., the commander of American naval forces in the Pacific, confirmed to Robert McNamara* that a "bona fide ambush has occurred."

The evidence at the time as to whether an attack had really occurred was contradictory, but the Johnson administration decided nonetheless to retaliate. Late that afternoon, the USS *Ticonderoga* and the USS *Constellation* sent aircraft to attack torpedo boat bases and oil storage facilities in North Vietnam. While the attack was going on, Johnson spoke live over all three major television networks: "Aggression by terror against peaceful villages of South Vietnam," he said, "has now been joined by open aggression on the high seas against the United States of America." He then reassured the country: "We know, although others appear to forget, the risks of spreading conflict. We seek no wider war."

The next day Johnson met with congressional leaders to explain the air strike and seek their support for the joint resolution William Bundy* had drafted. At the meeting Senator Mike Mansfield* reminded Johnson of his long-standing opposition to American military involvement in Indochina. Johnson asked Senator J. William Fulbright,* an Arkansas Democrat, to serve as floor manager for the resolution. An old friend and veteran of many Senate battles, Fulbright agreed. Senator George Aiken,* a Republican from Vermont, did not like the resolution, telling Johnson, "By the time you send it up, there won't be anything for us to do but support you." He saw the resolution as open-ended permission by Johnson to wage war without a formal declaration. But Johnson gave Mansfield and Aiken what other senators called the "full Johnson"—his arm tightly around their shoulders, his face nose-to-nose with theirs, and his voice pleading, cajoling, begging, whining, promising, and threatening. Before the meeting ended, they agreed to support the resolution.

At a joint session of the Senate Armed Services and Foreign Relations Committees, Senator Wayne Morse,* the renegade Democrat from Oregon, wanted to know if the United States had provoked the North Vietnamese patrol boat attack. Robert McNamara assured him that the "navy played absolutely no part in, was not associated with, was not aware of any South Vietnamese actions, if there were any. . . . This is the fact." It was, of course, a bald-faced lie. On August 7 the administration submitted to Congress the resolution William Bundy had written. Its wording was simple and direct, with enormous potential consequences:

The Congress . . . supports the determination of the President . . . to take all necessary measures to repel any armed attack against the armed forces of the United States and to prevent further aggression. . . . The United States is, therefore, prepared, as the President determines, to take all necessary steps, including the use of armed force, to assist any member or Protocol state of the Southeast Asia Collective Defence treaty requesting assistance in defense of its freedom.

The House of Representatives passed the resolution by voice vote, but a debate developed in the Senate. Senator George McGovern* of South Dakota stated that he did not wish his vote for the resolution "to be interpreted as an endorsement of our long-standing and apparently growing military involvement in Vietnam." Daniel Brewster of Maryland worried that the resolution might "authorize or recommend or approve the landing of large American armies in Vietnam or in China." The strongest opposition came from Senators Ernest Gruening* of Alaska and Wayne Morse,* who both refused to endorse the administration position. They voted against the resolution.

For President Lyndon B. Johnson, the Gulf of Tonkin Resolution gave him the authority to escalate U.S. military activity in Vietnam without going back to Congress for permission, and it gave him a real advantage in his reelection campaign in the fall of 1964. Republican candidate Barry Goldwater* had been accusing the Johnson administration of being soft on communism, but when the president began bombing North Vietnam in the wake of the Gulf of Tonkin Resolution, much of Goldwater's critique lost credibility.

REFERENCE: Joseph C. Goulden, *Truth Is the First Casualty: The Gulf of Tonkin Affair—Illusion and Reality*, 1969.

GULF OF TONKIN RESOLUTION. See GULF OF TONKIN INCIDENT (1964).

GUNS AND BUTTER. When President Lyndon B. Johnson* entered the White House in the wake of John F. Kennedy's* assassination, he had visions of using the federal government to address the problems of poverty and discrimination in the United States. For the most part, foreign affairs bored the president, and he concentrated all his attention on achieving his Great Society* programs. His huge reelection victory in 1964 over conservative Republican Barry Goldwater* further convinced him that he had a mandate from the American people. Gradually, however, the Vietnam War* loomed larger and larger in his administration, diverting his attention from domestic issues and reallocating the nation's financial resources as well. Vietnam was expensive, in dollars and in the lives, and the president found himself trying to balance the demands of the war with his own passion for the Great Society. Journalists employed the terms "guns and butter" to describe his dilemma. By "guns" they meant the military effort in Vietnam, and "butter" was a metaphor for his Great Society domestic programs. Johnson's challenge, they claimed, was to simultaneously provide "guns and butter" to the American people.

It proved an impossible challenge. First, there simply was not enough money to do both. The Vietnam War consumed hundreds of billions of dollars during Lyndon Johnson's term in office. The federal government's annual budget soared, and so did the deficit. Interest rates spiked, and the economy entered an inflationary spiral. For macroeconomic reasons, constraints had to be imposed on the federal budget, but, with U.S. soldiers in the field, those contraints could not come in military spending. Domestic programs took the cuts. Equally important, the president could not politically sustain "guns and butter." The Great Society programs had never attracted much support from Republicans, and the president relied on Democrats to push them through Congress. But the antiwar movement* alienated many liberal Democrats from the administration, all but wiping out the political coalition upon which the Great Society depended. In 1968, a disappointed president complained, "That bitch of a war has ruined my true love—the Great Society."

REFERENCES: Anthony S. Campagna, *The Economic Consequences of the Vietnam War*, 1991; Kathleen J. Turner, *Lyndon Johnson's Dual War: Vietnam and the Press*, 1985.

GUNSMOKE. *Gunsmoke* was the most successful adult western in television* history. It was adapted to television from the 1952 CBS radio serial, which starred William Conrad. Originally, CBS offered John Wayne* the leading role. Wayne declined but directed CBS to his friend James Arness. The television series aired September 10, 1955, and produced 640 episodes. The main cast was composed of James Arness as Marshal Matt Dillon, Milburn Stone as Dr. Galen ''Doc'' Adams, Amanda Blake as saloon owner Miss Kitty Russell, Dennis Weaver as deputy Chester Goode, Ken Curtis as deputy Festus Haggen, and Buck Taylor as gunsmith Newly O'Brien. Notable directors of the series were Andrew McLaglen and Sam Peckinpah.

The successful life of *Gunsmoke* can be attributed to the attachment of viewers to the main characters and the ability of the producers and writers to provide continuing entertainment by offering escape from the everyday life of the 1960s. The characters had believable and relatable human shortcomings. Marshal Dillon was occasionally full of doubts and rarely had all the right answers. This form of fantasy entertainment, however, was directed toward adults. Westerns represented freedom to the viewers of the 1960s. *Gunsmoke* offered escape from conformity. Westerns also venerated firearms for a society that felt itself held captive during the Cold War.*

Gunsmoke adapted with the changing interests of the national viewers during the 1960s. It is significant to note the effects of society on television. The 1960s changed not only the image seen but the way it was seen. *Gunsmoke*'s ability to conform to the desires of its viewing audience ensured longevity. As the nation became increasingly aware of, and sympathetic to, ethnic minorities, so did the western series. When the nation wanted family-oriented and more compassionate viewing, the writers and producers developed a more domestic western. This conformity saved *Gunsmoke* from early demise in 1967. Nielsen showed *Gunsmoke* improved from the thirty-fourth position to the fourth in its ratings.

The ability to adapt kept *Gunsmoke* on the air for two decades. The later decline and demise during the 1970s was the result of the change in interest from the western to other types of programming and the reevaluation of American attitudes toward women, politics, and war. The western series could attempt to conform to the social and cultural desires of the viewers, but it could not change its genre. The women's movement reappraised the role of the American woman, which the western ignored or avoided. Watergate damaged the unquestionable authority of government demonstrated in westerns. News reports of the Vietnam War* showed frightening images of violence and death, which westerns romanticized. The ability of westerns such as *Gunsmoke* to adapt during the 1960s made them fit for survival. These changing tastes in the 1970s created an environment so harsh it drove the western to extinction. *Gunsmoke* died peacefully on September 1, 1975, after twenty years of production.

REFERENCES: Tim Brook and Earle Marsh, *The Complete Directory to Prime Time Network TV Shows: 1946–Present*, 1992; J. Fred MacDonald, *Who Shot the Sheriff?*, 1987.

Christopher Gore

GUTIÉRREZ, JOSÉ ANGEL. José Angel Gutiérrez was born in Crystal City, Texas, in 1944 to a well-to-do Mexican immigrant family. During his public school career in Crystal City, he became an excellent debater, and he went on to an undergraduate degree at Texas A & I University in Kingsville. He then earned a master's degree in political science at St. Mary's University in San Antonio. Gutiérrez completed his formal education with a Ph.D. in political science from the University of Texas in 1976.

In the history of the 1960s, Gutiérrez is best remembered for his activism on behalf of the Mexican-American community. Along with Mario Compeán, he formed the Mexican American Youth Organization (MAYO) in 1967. After two years as MAYO's president, Gutiérrez returned to Crystal City and organized La Raza Unida party to contest local elections. He was elected to the Crystal City city council and as president of the school board. The school board then launched a new bilingual and bicultural curriculum designed to improve the educations of all children, but especially Tejano children. Early in the 1970s, Gutiérrez went national with La Raza Unida, becoming its president and endorsing political candidates sympathetic to Mexican-American concerns. He was elected judge of Zavala County, Texas, in 1974, a position he held for the next seven years. Since then, Gutiérrez has returned to academe, first as a professor of political science at Colegio César Chávez in Mount Angel, Oregon, and then at Western Oregon State University.

REFERENCE: John S. Shockley, *Chicano Revolt in a Texas Town*, 1974.

H

HAIR. *Hair* was an extraordinarily popular tribal-rock musical of the late 1960s and 1970s. It was written by Gerome Ragni and James Rado, with music by Galt MacDermot. *Hair* opened originally at the Anspacher Theater in New York on October 17, 1967, and a revised version premiered at the Biltmore Theater on April 29, 1968. Basically, *Hair* was a celebration of the values of the hippie,* "make-love-not war"* generation of the 1960s. Members of the group "Hair" are a hedonistic bunch who want a life without responsibilities or rules. Sex, drugs, and doing anything one wants whenever one wants are the group's values. *Hair* eventually had a run of 1,742 performances and became the Broadway version of the 1960s counterculture.
REFERENCE: Kurt Ganzl, *The Encyclopedia of the Musical Theater*, 1994.

HALBERSTAM, DAVID. David Halberstam was born in New York City in 1934. He graduated from Harvard in 1956. Determined to become a journalist, and blessed with an engaging writing style and fertile mind, he joined the staff of the *New York Times* in 1960. He soon found himself working as a war correspondent in South Vietnam, covering the deepening involvement of the United States there. At first he agreed with the U.S. military commitment, accepting the policy rhetoric that South Vietnam had to be saved from Communist aggression. But he soon realized that the regime of President Ngo Dinh Diem* of South Vietnam was hopelessly corrupt and that most South Vietnamese identified more closely with Ho Chi Minh,* leader of North Vietnam and Communist forces. The most powerful force in South Vietnam, Halberstam concluded, was nationalism, not communism, and most Vietnamese wanted to be rid of foreigners, including Americans. He won a Pulitzer Prize in 1964 for his reporting. Halberstam left South Vietnam in 1964 and wrote *The Making of a Quagmire: America and Vietnam During the Kennedy Era*, which was published in 1965. The book predicted a continuing deterioriaton of the U.S. political position in

South Vietnam and all but concluded that the war was unwinnable. Historians looking back on the war find Halberstam's views remarkably prescient.

Halberstam left the *New York Times* in 1967 and embarked on a freelance writing career, which has been extremely successful. He ventured into fiction with *One Very Hot Day** (1968), a novel about combat in Vietnam, but his forte was nonfiction. His short biography of Ho Chi Minh—*Ho*—appeared in 1971, and in 1972 his classic *The Best and the Brightest* (1972) was published, which demonstrated just how U.S. policymakers in the 1960s had gotten the United States so deeply involved in Vietnam. Among his other books are *The Powers That Be* (1979), *The Reckoning* (1986), *The Summer of '49* (1989), and *The Fifties* (1993).

REFERENCES: David Halbertsam, *The Making of a Quagmire*, 1965, and *The Best and the Brightest*, 1972; William Prochnau, *Once Upon a Distant War*, 1995.

HALPERIN, MORTON. Morton Halperin was born in 1938 in Brooklyn, New York. He majored in political science at Columbia and received a Ph.D. from Yale in 1961. At Yale, Halperin focused his attention on international relations in general and defense and national security policy in particular. Halperin then spent six years working for the Harvard University's Center for International Affairs. Late in 1967, he was appointed deputy assistant secretary of defense in the Lyndon B. Johnson* administration. A renowed expert in arms control, Halperin wrote *Nuclear Weapons and Limited War* (1960), *Strategy and Arms Control* (1961), *A Proposal for a Ban of the Use of Nuclear Weapons* (1961), *Arms Control and Inadvertent General War* (1962), and *Limited War in the Nuclear Age* (1963).

At the Pentagon, Halperin quickly earned a reputation as a critic of the Vietnam War.* He was convinced that politicians had gotten too deeply involved in Vietnam out of fear of being labeled "soft on communism," and the result had been a steady escalation of the American commitment. He did not believe that South Vietnam was strategically critical to U.S. national security. He also argued that too much secrecy surrounding the commitment had produced the "credibility gap"* and undermined political support for the war effort. In addition, Halperin insisted that the use of herbicides and indiscriminate artillery and aerial bombardment only undermined the U.S. political position in South Vietnam and made winning the war even more unlikely. In 1969, Halperin was appointed to the staff of the National Security Council and as a senior fellow at the Brookings Institution, a Washington, D.C., think tank. Since then, he has continued to function as a consultant on arms control and defense policy issues.

REFERENCES: *American Men of Science: The Social and Behavioral Sciences*, vol. 7, 1968; Joanna D. Cowden, "Morton Halperin," in James S. Olson, *Dictionary of the Vietnam War*, 1988; *Contemporary Authors*, vols. 9–12, 1974; Morton H. Halperin, *Bureaucratic Politics and Foreign Policy*, 1974.

HAMBURGER HILL. Because of its guerrilla nature and complicated political contours, the Vietnam War* generated unprecedented opposition in the United

States and around the world. Many antiwar* activists concluded that the United States was applying a military solution to what was essentially a political problem, and as such, the war was futile. Few battles of the Vietnam War better illustrated that futility than "Hamburger Hill," or the battle for Dong Ap Bia in May 1969.

Dong Ap Bia was a mountain in the A Shau Valley of South Vietnam, near the Laotian border. North Vietnamese troops had infiltrated down the Ho Chi Minh Trail,* occupied positions on Dong Ap Bia, and then dug in, correctly anticipating a U.S. infantry assault. The North Vietnamese also departed from their typical tactics, which traditionally revolved around surprise hit-and-run assaults on U.S. and South Vietnamese forces. This time, they decided to hold the position and defend it against attack.

To attack and dislodge the North Vietnamese forces from Dong Ap Bia, the United States launched Operation Apache Snow, a combined offensive by South Vietnamese troops and the 101st Airborne Division. The battle commenced on May 10, 1969, and lasted ten days. For several days before the attack, U.S. B-52 bombers pulverized Dong Ap Bia, and there were also heavy artillery bombardment and napalm* raids. But the North Vietnamese had created elaborate tunnels and bunkers all over the hill, and they survived the air campaign. In the end, 101st Airborne troops had to ascend the hill in an infantry assault. Fierce combat, characterized by hand-to-hand fighting, ensued during the next several days. Then, suddenly, on the eleventh day of combat, the North Vietnamese secretly abandoned Dong Ap Bia and retreated back across the Laotian border. By the time U.S. soldiers reached the summit, they had lost 56 men. The North Vietnamese, in contrast, had lost 630 men. Casualties were so heavy and the carnage so great that U.S. troops renamed Dong Ap Bia "Hamburger Hill."

Although General Creighton Abrams* hailed it as a great U.S. victory, "Hamburder Hill" was a political disaster at home. One week after the battle, Abrams withdrew U.S. forces from Dong Ap Bia, and the North Vietnamese just as promptly reoccupied it. In Congress, Senator Edward Kennedy,* a leading antiwar figure, complained, "President Nixon has told us, without question, that we seek no military victory, that we seek only peace. How then can we justify sending our boys against a hill a dozen times, finally taking it, and then withdrawing a week later?"

REFERENCES: Shelby L. Stanton, *The Rise and Fall of an American Army: U.S. Ground Troops in Vietnam, 1965–1973,* 1985; Stafford T. Thomas, "Hamburger Hill," in James S. Olson, ed., *Dictionary of the Vietnam War,* 1988; Samuel Zaffiri, *Hamburger Hill, May 11–20, 1969,* 1988.

HAMILTON, WILLIAM, JR. William Hamilton was born March 9, 1924, in Evanston, Illinois. He was educated at Oberlin College (B.A., 1943), Union Theological Seminary (B.D., 1949), and the University of St. Andrews (Ph.D., 1952). He described himself in politics as "[c]onventionally left, though tempted to a post-political irony." In religion, he was "Protestant: Death of God* variety.'' Although he was a coauthor of *Radical Theology and the Death of God* with Thomas J. J. Altizer, he meant something quite different than did Altizer. For Hamilton, the real transcendence of God had disappeared for modern man. ''Death of God'' was a metaphor for that lack of transcendence. Secular man is ''led into the affairs of the world and into solidarity with his neighbor, in whom he encounters Jesus and where alone he can become Jesus to the world.'' By 1975, Hamilton had written or contributed to eleven books and written scholarly articles to more than fourteen journals. He has also written several television scripts. He was active in the antiwar movement* of the 1960s.

REFERENCES: *The Encyclopedia of Religion*, vol. 1, 489; *Contemporary Authors*, 1975, 264.

Bobby J. James

HANDLER, RUTH. Ruth Handler was born Ruth Mosko November 4, 1916, the tenth child of Jewish immigrants from Poland. After graduating from high school, she attended the University of Denver and then went to Hollywood, where she worked as a stenographer for Paramount Studios. She married Elliott Handler in 1938, and six years later they founded the Mattel Toy Company. Within a decade—on the backs of such toys as Chuck Wagon, Lullabye Crib, Peek-a-Boo Egg, Jack-in-the-Box, and Musical Merry-Go-Round—Mattel sales reached $14 million a year. Ten years later, the annual sales exceeded $100 million, making the company the top toy maker in the country.

Barbie explained Mattel's phenomenal success. In the late 1940s and early 1950s, research and development at Mattel were quite simple: the Handlers watched children play. Ruth became fascinated with her daughter Barbie's affection for paper dolls. Although Barbie and her little girlfriends spent some time with traditional baby dolls, they pretended to be adults when they played with paper dolls, dressing and undressing the cardboard figures for hours on end, creating a make-believe world of dates, proms, weddings, and outings. But when Handler broached the idea of creating an adult plastic doll, complete with different outfits, the men at Mattel brushed her off, claiming that the doll would require an Asian manufacturer to keep costs down. ''That was the *official* reason,'' she later wrote. ''But I really think that the squeamishness of those designers—every last one of them male—stemmed mostly from the fact that the doll would have *breasts*. . . . Elliott claimed that 'no mother will ever buy her daughter a doll with a chest.' ''

She promoted her idea unsuccessfully until 1956, when she returned home from a family vacation in Lucerne, Switzerland. During an afternoon of shopping, Ruth and Barbara noticed Lilli—an eleven-inch adult doll dressed in a European ski outfit—adorning the window of a Lucerne shop. Six versions of Lilli in the window each had a different outfit. Handler purchased one of the Lilli dolls for Barbara and then asked about buying just the outfits from the other dolls. When the clerk informed her that each doll and each outfit were a single unit, Handler had a brainstorm. Millions of little girls in America, she

was convinced, would want one of the dolls and dozens of outfits—wedding gowns, nightgowns, prom dresses, sports ensembles, casual fashions, school clothes. There was a fortune to be made, and Handler made it. By 1993, Barbie sales in 140 countries exceeded $1 billion.
REFERENCE: Ruth Handler, *Dream Doll*, 1994.

HANG-UP. The term "hang-up" emerged as a slang expression in the 1960s to refer to a traditional value that prevented an individual from engaging in rebellion. Opposition to premarital sex, for example, was termed a "hang-up," as was resistance to the use of psychedelic drugs.
REFERENCE: Ruth Bronsteen, *The Hippy's Handbook—How to Live on Love*, 1967.

HANOI. The city of Hanoi, which is situated on the Red River approximately seventy-miles from the coast of the South China Sea, has been the site of a Vietnamese settlement for thousands of years and today serves as the capital of the Socialist Republic of Vietnam. During the years of French rule, from the 1850s to 1954, Hanoi was also the capital city of the colony of Tonkin and later the capital of all of French Indochina. The Red River, which drains a rich, rice-producing region known as the Red River Delta, has long been the primary commercial avenue of northern Indochina. Travelers to Hanoi today can still see the French influence in the city's wide-tree-lined streets and French architecture.

In 1945, Ho Chi Minh* declared Hanoi the capital city of his new Democratic Republic of Vietnam. However, when the French returned to Hanoi and re-imposed their imperial will, Ho Chi Minh and his Vietminh engaged in guerrilla attacks on the city. As the Vietminh war against the French proceeded between 1946 and 1954, French influence in Vietnam was increasingly confined to Hanoi and the port city of Haiphong. After the French surrender at Dien Bien Phu in 1954, Ho Chi Minh once again proclaimed Hanoi as the capital city of the Democratic Republic of Vietnam.

Under Presidents Lyndon B. Johnson* and Richard M. Nixon,* Hanoi sustained severe aerial bombardment from U.S. forces. Both presidents hoped that the bombing* would disrupt the North Vietnamese economy and break the morale of the population. It did neither. North Vietnam all but depopulated the city, reducing its population from more than one million people in 1964 to only 250,000 in 1972. Factories were also relocated outside the city. As a result, U.S. bombing* campaigns never achieved the desired objectives.
REFERENCES: Paul Burbage et al., *The Battle for the Skies over North Vietnam, 1964–1972*, 1976; Lou Drendel, *Air War over Southeast Asia*, 1984; Samuel Freeman, "Hanoi," in James S. Olson, ed., *Dictionary of the Vietnam War*, 1988; Danny J. Whitfield, *Historical and Cultural Dictionary of Vietnam*, 1976.

HANOI HANNAH. During the Vietnam War,* North Vietnam's propaganda campaign included radio broadcasts into South Vietnam, planned to destroy GI morale. One of the personalities doing the broadcasts was nicknamed "Hanoi

Hannah'' by U.S. soldiers. They took their cue from the ''Tokyo Rose'' of World War II fame. ''Hanoi Hannah'' exaggerated U.S. casualties and was treated with contempt by most American troops, but she no doubt had an affect on some, especially after 1969 when the U.S. troop withdrawals began. She kept posing to U.S. soldiers the question, ''Do you want to die for nothing?'' She also worked on increasing racial animosity among American soldiers by telling African-American troops that they were being exploited by a white-dominated military.

REFERENCES: Terrence Maitland and Peter McInerney, *The Vietnam Experience. A Contagion of War*, 1983; Samuel Freeman, ''Hanoi Hannah,'' in James S. Olson, ed., *Dictionary of the Vietnam War*, 1988.

HANOI HILTON. One of the numerous prisons that ultimately housed over 700 American prisoners of war (POW) between August 1964 and February 1973, the Hanoi Hilton (Hoa Lo Prison) was built by the French near the center of Hanoi.* Sections of the Hilton were dubbed ''New Guy Village,'' ''Heartbreak Hotel,'' ''Little Las Vegas,'' and ''Camp Unity.'' These sections were further subdivided and named. It is an imposing facility, occupying a city block. Walls are four feet thick and twenty feet high and extend another five feet by electrified strands of barbed wire. Shards of glass are embedded on the wall's top. Other prisons located in or near Hanoi included the Zoo, Alcatraz, the Plantation, and the Powerplant. The Briarpatch, Camp Faith, and Camp Hope (Son Tay) were located within about thirty-five miles of Hanoi.

Jeremiah Denton's* cell in New Guy Village consisted of ''two solid concrete beds . . . with metal-and-wood stocks at the foot of each. The one amenity was a small honey bucket (a pail that served as a toilet). . . . The concrete bunks were about 3 ½ feet high and 2 ½ feet apart. The cell was 9 feet by 8 feet. The door had a small peephole and was flanked by windows which had been covered over by a thin layer of concrete.'' Sanitation was poor. Cells were infested with insects and rodents. The food, by normal standards, was not fit to eat. Medical treatment was poor to nonexistent and was provided only when a captive's condition became serious, or the captive became cooperative.

The North Vietnamese constantly utilized various methods to break captives psychologically, primarily to elicit confessions or information of propaganda value. Captives were not permitted to organize with a recognized chain of command, as POWs generally do. Efforts were made to isolate prisoners and prohibit communications. Consequently, captives developed unobtrusive communication networks employing Morse and ''tap'' codes. Transmission methods included whistling softly, scratching sounds, even the cadence of sweeping with a broom. As communications networks and chains of command were established and ultimately discovered, prisoners were moved to different units and even to different prisons to break them up or punish the uncooperative. Prisoners were subjected to torture, but not for military information until later in the war. Sometimes this occurred in their cells, but the Hilton and other prisons also had rooms especially for interrogation and torture. Torture took many forms, from various deprivations such as not being permitted to bathe, to beatings, extended darkness, isolation, shackling (often in contorted positions), and psychological torture.

While U.S. commanders were concerned that prisons inadvertently might be hit during the 1972 Christmas bombing, prisoners welcomed the bombing and its attendant risks. As a peace settlement neared, conditions at the Hilton and other prisons improved markedly. Captives were given new clothes, were permitted to organize and to bathe and exercise regularly, and were given much-improved medical attention and food.

REFERENCES: Jeremiah Denton, *When Hell Was in Session*, 1982; Benjamin F. Schemmer, *The Raid*, 1976.

Samuel Freeman

HARGIS, BILLY JAMES. Billy James Hargis was born in Texarkana, Texas, August 3, 1925. He was converted to Christianity as a teenager, attended Ozark Bible College for two years, and in 1943 was ordained to the ministry at the Rose Hill Christian Church of the Disciples of Christ in 1943. In 1948, after several pastorates, he settled in Tulsa, Oklahoma, and founded the Christian Echoes National Ministry, a Christian anticommunist organization. By the mid-1950s, his group had targeted communism, socialism, liberalism, the United Nations, and the National Council of Churches as enemies of America, as well as Martin Luther King, Jr.,* John F. Kennedy,* and Lyndon B. Johnson.* He enjoyed a considerable following in Oklahoma, Arkansas, Missouri, and Texas and was one of the leading Cold War* anticommunists in the United States during the 1960s.

In 1966 Billy James Hargis decided to leave the Disciples of Christ. He founded an independent ministry—the Church of the Christian Crusade—in 1966 in Tulsa. He sponsored Christian Anti-Communist Crusade rallies and mass meetings throughout the South and Southwest. In 1970 Hargis established the American Christian College in Tulsa to provide an opportunity for college students to study "anti-communist patriotic Americanism." After the Supreme Court's *Roe v. Wade* decision in 1973, he founded Americans for Life to oppose abortion.

His ministry crumbled, however, in 1974, when several students at American Christian College accused him of sexual misconduct. He resigned as president of the college and retired. Hargis came out of retirement a year later, but he no longer had anywhere near the influence he possessed during the 1960s and early 1970s.

REFERENCES: Richard Durham, *Men of the Far Right*, 1962; John Redekop, *The American Far Right: A Case Study of Billy James Hargis and Christian Crusade*, 1968.

HARKINS, PAUL DONÁL. Paul Donál Harkins was born May 15, 1904, in Boston, Massachusetts. He graduated from West Point in 1929 with a specialty in cavalry, but he switched to tanks when horses were phased out. The decision to specialize in armored warfare allowed Harkins to rise quickly through the ranks. During World War II, he served as deputy chief of staff to General George Patton, commander of the Third Army in Europe. During the Korean War, Harkins became chief of staff to the Eighth Army. In 1962, as the U.S. commitment in South Vietnam began to escalate, General Paul Harkins became commander of Military Assistance Command, Vietnam. He remained in that post until June 1964. In South Vietnam, Harkins supported the regime of Ngo Dinh Diem* and bragged continually that his forces were winning the war against the Communists. Ironically, he kept begging for more U.S. troops. American journalists covering the war knew that the communists were steadily gaining ground, and they nicknamed Harkins ''Blimpie'' because of his exaggerated success stories. Upon leaving South Vietnam, Harkins retired from active duty. He died on August 21, 1984.

REFERENCES: *New York Times*, August 22, 1984; David Halberstam, *The Best and the Brightest*, 1972; George S. Eckhardt, *Command and Control, 1950–1969*, 1974; Sean Kelleher, ''Paul Donal Harkins,'' in James S. Olson, ed., *Dictionary of the Vietnam War*, 1988.

HARLAN, JOHN MARSHALL. John Marshall Harlan was born May 20, 1899, in Chicago. He graduated from Princeton in 1920, was a Rhodes Scholar at Oxford University, and took his law degree at the New York Law School in 1925. Upon graduation from law school, Harlan accepted a position in a prominent Wall Street law firm, periodically accepting leaves of absence for such public positions as assistant U.S. attorney for the southern district of New York (1925–1927) and special assistant attorney general of New York (1928–1930). During World War II, he headed the operational analysis section of the Eighth Air Force in Europe. He returned to Wall Street in 1946, and from 1951 to 1953 he served as special counsel to Governor Thomas Dewey's New York State Crime Commission, which was investigating the connections between organized crime and state and local government. President Dwight D. Eisenhower* appointed Harlan to the U.S. Court of Appeals for the Second District in 1954 and to the U.S. Supreme Court in 1955.

Although the Warren Court earned a reputation as the most liberal Supreme Court in U.S. history, Harlan was prominent because of his dissents. He was widely known for his rational, conservative opinions, favoring a limited role for the federal government in American life but also protecting civil liberties. He opposed most government antitrust programs, opposed reapportionment of state legislatures in the name of ''one-man, one-vote,'' opposed outlawing state poll taxes, favored government censorship of pornography, and dissented in the *Miranda** ruling, but he also upheld the right of indigent defendants to have counsel and believed the wearing of clothing bearing obscene statements was protected by the First Amendment. He was also a thoughtful historian, always working to de-emotionalize issues by finding statutory precedents. In failing health, he resigned his position on the Court September 23, 1971. John Harlan died December 29, 1971.

REFERENCE: Tinsley E. Yarbrough, *John Marshall Harlan: Great Dissenter of the Warren Court*, 1992.

HARLEM REBELLION. See RIOTS IN THE 1960S.

HARMAN V. FORSENNIUS. Throughout the 1960s, the Supreme Court continued the trends launched when Earl Warren* became chief justice in 1953. Very consistently, the Court struck down all forms of de jure segregation, expanded the rights of individuals, narrowed the powers of government, and labored to make sure that the Fifteenth Amendment's protection of voting rights was expanded. One of the most important of the voting rights decisions of the Warren Court was *Harman v. Forsennius*. The Virginia state legislature had passed a law elaborating voter registration requirements for individuals not able to pay the poll tax. The law was a blatant attempt to keep large numbers of African Americans from the polls. The Court overturned the law, declaring it an unconstitutional violation of the Twenty-Fourth Amendment,* which outlawed poll taxes.

REFERENCE: 380 U.S. 528 (1965).

HARRIMAN, WILLIAM AVERELL. William Averell Harriman was born in New York City November 15, 1891, to one of America's best-known families. After graduating from Yale in 1913, he went to work for the Union Pacific Railroad. In 1917 he organized the Merchant Shipbuilding Company, made a fortune during World War I, and by the mid-1920s owned the largest fleet in the country. He became chairman of the board of the Illinois Central Railroad in 1931 and the Union Pacific Railroad in 1932. During World War II, Harriman represented the Lend Lease program to the British and the Soviets, and he became ambassador to the Soviet Union in 1943. He served briefly as ambassador to Great Britain in 1946 before being named secretary of commerce in President Harry S Truman's cabinet. In 1948 Harriman was named the official U.S. representative in Europe for the Marshall Plan. He was the U.S. representative to the North American Treaty Organization (NATO) in 1951, elected governor of New York in 1954, and during the Kennedy* administration served as an ambassador at large and assistant secretary of state for Far Eastern affairs. Between 1963 and 1965, Harriman was undersecretary of state for political affairs.

In 1962 he played a key role in negotiating the settlement in Laos, and he had serious doubts about the efficacy of any military solution in Vietnam. Harriman had been a supporter of the containment policy* in Europe, but he saw Asia in different terms. By 1963 Harriman was privately condemning the corruption of the Ngo Dinh Diem* regime and urging Kennedy to disassociate the United States from him. President Lyndon B. Johnson* appointed Harriman ambassador at large in 1965 with responsibility for Southeast Asia. Harriman traveled throughout the world in 1965 and 1966, trying to gather support for the American war effort in Vietnam and trying to work out the details for peace talks. By that time his own faith in the war was dead. Early in 1968 Harriman took an active part in the ''Wise Old Men''* group, which advised President Johnson to negotiate a settlement to the war and withdraw American troops. In May 1968, when the Paris peace talks* began, Harriman went there as the chief American negotiator. He remained in Paris until Henry Cabot Lodge* replaced him in January 1969. Throughout the Nixon* administration, Harriman urged American fidelity to a strict withdrawal timetable. W. Averell Harriman died July 26, 1986.

REFERENCES: Lee H. Burke, *Ambassador at Large: Diplomat Extraordinary*, 1972; *New York Times*, July 27, 1986; Walter Isaacson and Evan Thomas, *The Wise Men: Six Friends and the World They Made*, 1986.

HARRINGTON, MICHAEL. Michael Harrington was born in St. Louis, Missouri, in 1928. Of Irish Catholic ancestry, he received a Jesuit education at Holy Cross College and then a law degree at Yale. When he left Yale, he was an avowed socialist. After getting a master's degree in English at the University of Chicago, Harrington moved to Greenwich Village and lived as a bohemian for several years. From 1951 to 1953, he served as a volunteer at the Catholic Worker House on the Lower East Side of Manhattan, where he found plenty of sympathy for his pacifism and anarchism. He supported himself as associate editor of *The Catholic Worker*. He then worked as a researcher and writer for the Fund for the Republic.

Harrington came to national attention in 1962, when he wrote *The Other America*, a best-selling description of poverty in the United States. The book had enormous influence, especially on such political figures as John F. Kennedy,* Lyndon B. Johnson,* and Robert F. Kennedy,* and it inspired the antipoverty* programs of the 1960s. Many historians attribute medicaid,* medicare,* food stamps,* and increased social security benefits in the 1960s to *The Other America*.

During the late 1960s, however, because of his rigid anticommunism, Harrington would not demand the withdrawal of American troops from Vietnam and became alienated from many of his colleagues on the American Left. From 1968 to 1972 he served as chairman of the Socialist Party. He wrote *The New American Poverty* in 1982 and began teaching political science at Queen's College. Harrington's last book—*Socialism: Past and Present*—was published in 1989. Michael Harrington died July 31, 1989.

REFERENCE: *New York Times*, August 1, 1989.

HARRIS, LaDONNA. LaDonna Harris was born February 15, 1931, in Temple, Oklahoma. She was raised in a conservative, traditional Comanche home, speaking only Comanche until she attended public schools. She married Fred

Harris, who became the Democratic U.S. senator from Oklahoma, and soon emerged as a political leader in her own right, championing the rights of Indian peoples. In 1965, Harris founded Oklahomans for Indian Opportunity, which soon became a nationally prominent Indian self-help group. Five years later, she established Americans for Indian Opportunity,* a similar organization that functioned on a national level and promoted Indian self-determination.* Today, LaDonna Harris is active in the world peace movement.

REFERENCE: Duane Champagne, ed., *The Native North American Almanac*, 1994.

HARTKE, VANCE. Vance Hartke was born in Stendal, Indiana, on May 31, 1919. After graduating from Evansville College, he earned a law degree at Indiana University and then practiced law privately between 1948 and 1958. He also dabbled in local Democratic politics, serving as mayor of Evansville from 1956 to 1958. Beginning in 1958, he served for twenty years in the United States Senate. A liberal Democrat, Hartke enthusiastically supported President John Kennedy's* New Frontier* and President Lyndon Johnson's* Great Society.* He believed passionately in the civil rights movement* and in the war on poverty.*

In 1966, Hartke broke with the Johnson administration over the Vietnam War.* He was convinced that the war was misguided and unwinnable. Along with several Senate colleagues, he signed and then released for publication a letter to President Johnson calling for an end to the bombing* of North Vietnam and a diplomatic solution to the war. Such actions earned him the enduring wrath of Lyndon Johnson, but Hartke persisted in his opposition to the war, later becoming a thorn in the side of President Richard Nixon* as well. In 1976, Hartke retired from public life.

REFERENCES: *Who's Who in American Politics, 1985–1986*, 1986; Stanley Karnow, *Vietnam: A History*, 1983.

HATFIELD, MARK ODUM. Mark Hatfield was born July 12, 1922, in The Dalles, Oregon. After graduating from Willamette University in 1943, he earned a master's degree in political science at Stanford. Between 1950 and 1956, Hatfield taught political science at Willamette and dabbled in state Republican Party politics. He proved to be especially good at legislative maneuvering. He served as a state legislator from 1951 to 1957, secretary of state from 1957 to 1959, and state governor from 1959 until 1967. He then moved to Washington, D.C., as a U.S. Senator, having won the Republican primary and then the general election in 1966.

An outspoken opponent of the Vietnam War,* Hatfield became a thorn in the side of President Lyndon B. Johnson* and especially of fellow Republican Richard M. Nixon.* He accused Nixon and national security advisor Henry Kissinger* of intentionally postponing U.S. withdrawal. He condemned the invasion of Cambodia in 1970 and jointly sponsored, with Senator George McGovern* of South Dakota, a Senate amendment to eliminate funding for the war after

December 31, 1971. The amendment never passed, but it did reveal the depth of antiwar sentiment in the United States. Hatfield was also an outspoken critic of the military draft* and an advocate of the all-volunteer army. He was re-elected in 1972, 1978, 1984, and 1990, becoming the most senior Republican in the Senate. He officially retired from the Senate in January 1997.

REFERENCES: Robert Eells, *Lonely Walk: The Life of Senator Mark Hatfield*, 1979; Mark Hatfield, *Conflict and Conscience*, 1971, and *Amnesty: The Unsettled Question of Vietnam*, 1973.

HAVE GUN WILL TRAVEL. *Have Gun Will Travel* was an extremely popular television* western during the late 1950s and early 1960s. It was a staple of Saturday night viewing in America, appearing each week in the time slot just before *Gunsmoke*. It starred Richard Boone as Paladin, a hired gun with an education and a sense of taste, drama, and justice. Paladin dressed in black and righted wrongs with violence, but his sense of ethics was fine-tuned. *Have Gun Will Travel* first aired on September 14, 1957, and the last episode was broadcast on September 21, 1963.

REFERENCE: Tim Brooks and Earle Marsh, *The Complete Directory to Prime Time Network and Cable TV Shows*, 1995.

HAWK. During the 1960s and early 1970s, the term "hawk" was used to refer to those individuals in the United States who supported the war in Vietnam and wanted to see more military power expended there.

REFERENCE: James S. Olson, ed., *Dictionary of the Vietnam War*, 1988.

HAYDEN, THOMAS EMMETT. Thomas Hayden was born in Royal Oak, Michigan, on December 12, 1940. Growing up, he absorbed the values of his working-class, Catholic parents and considered himself a liberal Democrat, but as a student at the University of Michigan, his politics became more left-wing. In December 1961, he became a charter member of Students for a Democratic Society (SDS) and drafted the Port Huron Statement.* Steadily during the early 1960s, galvanized by the civil rights movement* and the antiwar* movement, SDS became increasingly radical. By 1966, SDS activists were organizing antiwar demonstrations and antidraft protests on college campuses across the country, and Hayden had become a popular speaker on the lecture circuit.

Hayden's opposition to the Vietnam War* soon rendered him a very controversial figure in American politics. In 1967, he flew to Prague, Czechoslovakia, to negotiate with representatives from North Vietnam the release of several U.S. prisoners of war* (POWs). Two months later, he flew to Cambodia and brought home three U.S. POWs. His efforts did not make him very popular in the U.S. military. Critics charged Hayden with treason, fraternizing with the enemy, and actually making life more dangerous for U.S. soldiers. Hayden's status among antiwar activists, however, could not have been higher, and in 1968 he helped plan the National Mobilization Committee's mass protests in Chicago at the

Democratic National Convention.* Arrested for his role in the demonstrations, Hayden later became one of the famous, or infamous, Chicago 8* defendants. He was convicted of conspiracy, but the verdict was appealed and overturned.

In 1973, Hayden married actress Jane Fonda,* whose antiwar activities had also earned her the ire of the military community. They settled in California. By the late 1970s, with the war over and the U.S. political atmosphere becoming more conservative, Hayden became interested in a political career. It required him to alter his radical image. In 1976, he surprised most observers by staging a close primary race against U.S. Senator John Tunney. In 1979, Hayden and Fonda founded the Campaign for Economic Democracy, a group committed to establishing worker and consumer control over major corporations. Columnist George Will ridiculed them as the "Mork and Mindy" of the American left. Still, Hayden won a seat in the state legislature in 1980. Since then, he has continued to remain active in economic and environmental concerns.

REFERENCES: John Bunzel, *New Force on the Left: Tom Hayden and the Campaign Against Corporate America*, 1983; Frances Frenzel, "Thomas Hayden," in James S. Olson, ed., *Dictionary of the Vietnam War*, 1988; Tom Hayden, *The American Future: New Visions Beyond Old Frontiers*, 1980, and *Reunion*, 1988.

HEAD START. Head Start was arguably the most successful of Lyndon B. Johnson's* "War on Poverty"* programs. Part of the Economic Opportunity Act* of 1964, Head Start was designed to prepare poor, underprivileged preschool children for school. By August 1965, after its first summer of operation, most observers judged Head Start a success. More than 500,000 four-year-old children were enrolled in 2,500 community Head Start programs throughout the country. The program also provided badly needed employment for teachers' aides, cooks, and janitors in the Head Start preschools. The summer 1965 program had been only a pilot, but late in August 1965, the president announced that Head Start would continue during the school year for all preschool children three years old and up. Critics eventually charged that the program was laced with waste, that the children did not really benefit, and that the government should not be in the baby-sitting business. Nevertheless, the program continued to enjoy widespread support from the American public, and its budget steadily increased during the decade.

REFERENCE: David Burner, *Making Peace with the Sixties*, 1996.

HEART OF ATLANTA MOTEL V. UNITED STATES. One of the most important elements of the Civil Rights Act of 1964* was its provision that privately owned businesses serving the general public could not discriminate on the basis of race. Opponents charged, of course, that the law was an unconstitutional violation of Fifth Amendment property rights, while proponents claimed the law protected Fifth Amendment liberty rights. *Heart of Atlanta Motel v. United States* was a test case of the Civil Rights Act of 1964. In its decision, rendered on December 14, 1964, by a unanimous vote, the Court overturned its own

decision in *Civil Rights Cases* (1883). Congress could prohibit discrimination on the basis of race, religion, and national origins in public accommodations that served interstate travelers or provided food and entertainment that had been shipped or transmitted across state lines. Such powers, the Court argued, are implied in the commerce clause of the Constitution.
REFERENCE: 379 U.S. 241 (1964).

"HEARTS AND MINDS" SPEECH. In 1965 Lyndon B. Johnson* paraphrased John Adams description of the American Revolution: ''The Revolution was effected before the war commenced. The Revolution was in the minds and hearts of the people.'' About Vietnam, Johnson said: ''So we must be ready to fight in Vietnam, but the ultimate victory will depend on the hearts and minds of the people who actually live out there.'' Eventually, however, the United States did not win the hearts and minds of the Vietnamese people, and the war became a conflict over the hearts and minds of the American people.

Military apologists argue that the war was lost because Washington misperceived it as a guerrilla/civil war rather than conventional war instigated, directed, and ultimately fought by North Vietnam. To them the emphasis on pacification was misplaced, resulting in misallocation of resources away from fighting the war, inappropriate strategy aimed at ferreting out guerrilla bands when main-force, hard-core North Vietnamese army units were the real problem, allowing invading forces sanctuaries that guaranteed they could never be defeated and a media focus that caused Americans to misunderstand and lose patience with the war. According to Harry G. Summers, the war was not in ''the hearts and minds of the . . . people but the guns and bullets of the North Vietnamese Army.''

Most observers, however, accepted the counterarguments of military and pacification professionals like William Sorson (*The Betrayal*, 1968) and Cincinnatus (*Self-Destruction*, 1981), who argued that ''every strike that levels a village or cuts a road or kills innocent civilians contributes to the ultimate victory even if . . . the guerrillas lose both ground and men. For all such military operations, by their very nature and destructiveness, alienate the people among whom they occur.'' That sentiment was shared by people like Central Intelligence Agency (CIA) director William Colby* and pacification expert Robert Komer.* Robert Taber (*The War of the Flea*, 1965) said there ''is only one way of defeating an insurgent people who will not surrender, and that is extermination. There is only one way to control territory that harbours resistance, and that is to turn it into a desert. Where these means cannot, for whatever reason, be used, the war is lost.''

But unwillingness to understand, much less respect, either pacification or the Vietnamese people permeated the American structure. American military personnel were either paternalistic or racist in their attitudes toward the Vietnamese; if U.S.–Army of the Republic of Vietnam (ARVN) military violence did not turn the Vietnamese peasants against the United States, those attitudes surely did. Ultimately, the war would become a battle for the American people's

"hearts and minds." The Vietnamese could refuse defeat. They understood that Americans would tire of a war they did not and could not understand, that eventually enough body bags would return, and that there were limits to the resources the United States could squander in Vietnam. When that day came, the Americans would leave, just as had the Chinese and French before them.
REFERENCES: Larry E. Cable, *Conflict of Myths: The Development of American Counterinsurgency Doctrine and the Vietnam War*, 1986; Andrew F. Krepinevich, Jr., *The Army and Vietnam*, 1986; Frances FitzGerald, *Fire in the Lake: The Vietnamese and the Americans in Vietnam*, 1972.

Samuel Freeman

HEFNER, HUGH MARSTON. Hugh Hefner was born in Chicago April 9, 1926. His parents were devoutly religious, churchgoing Methodists. He graduated from the University of Illinois with a strong interest in writing and publishing. After a stint in the army during World War II, Hefner tried his hand at a number of jobs, including copyediting, but he was frustrated, feeling trapped working for other people. He decided to try his own hand at publishing. The country was ready, Hefner thought, for a glossy men's magazine. In 1953, for $500, he purchased the rights to a nude photograph of Marilyn Monroe.* Originally, he was going to call his magazine *Stag Party*, but at the last minute, before the printer ran 60,000 copies of the magazine, he changed its name from *Stag Party* to *Playboy*. With Marilyn Monroe on his first centerfold, he sold 53,000 copies. One year later, *Playboy*'s monthly circulation topped 100,000. In December 1956, after only three years in publication, *Playboy*'s circulation topped 600,000 copies. Hefner was a rich man, and the *Playboy* empire—complete with mansions, clubs, and nude, willing women—was born.

Hefner carefully selected the *Playboy* models. He had a particular look in mind—young, wholesome, and innocent women without trashy lines or tawdry looks, not really virgins but not too sexually experienced either. Rebelling against his Calvinist upbringing, he marketed sex and pleasure as positive pursuits for men and women, not dirty or even inappropriate. Compared to the sleazy, nasty competition in the market of men's magazines, *Playboy* seemed almost wholesome to many American men, a vehicle for the free, unencumbered expression of their fantasies. By the mid-1960s, *Playboy*'s monthly circulation had reached 6 million, and he had almost single-handedly launched the soft-core pornography industry in the United States.

In subsequent years, *Playboy*'s circulation would decline significantly, primarily because of criticism from the women's movement and increased competition in what is certainly a limited market. Nevertheless, if the terms "sexual revolution" and "the 1960s" go together, so do "Hugh Hefner" and "the 1960s." During the 1960s, he became the American icon of the sexual revolution.* Late in the 1980s and early in the 1990s, Hefner finally "settled down," turning over management of the *Playboy* business empire to his daughter, marrying a former *Playboy* bunnie, and becoming the devoted father of two children.
REFERENCE: Frank Brady, *Hefner*, 1974.

"HELICOPTER VALLEY." The greatest tactical innovation of the Vietnam War* was the helicopter, which allowed for the rapid deployment and rescue of U.S. soldiers in the field. It was the most visible symbol of the war. A battle at Song Ngan Valley on July 15, 1966, involving helicopters, became a powerful illustration of the futility of the war. A squadron of CH-46 helicopters delivered a battalion of U.S. marines into battle in the Song Ngan Valley in Quang Tri Province. But during the battle, two of the CH-46s collided and crashed. A third one crashed trying to avoid the collision, and North Vietnamese snipers brought down another CH-46. Photojournalists quickly relayed pictures of the CH-46 crash sights and wreckage to wire services, which published them widely. U.S. marines nicknamed Song Ngan Valley "Helicopter Valley" after the battle.
REFERENCES: Edward Doyle and Samuel Lipsman, *The Vietnam Experience: America Takes Over, 1965–1967*, 1985; Willard Pearson, *The War in the Northern Provinces, 1966–1968*, 1975; David Wragg, *Helicopters at War: A Pictorial History*, 1983.

HELLER, WALTER. Walter Heller, a premier American economist during the 1960s and 1970s, received a Ph.D. from the University of Wisconsin in 1941, where he specialized in finance and taxation. During World War II, he worked as an economic analyst for the Treasury Department. After the war, he took an academic post at the University of Minnesota. In December 1960, President John F. Kennedy* appointed Heller chairman of the Council of Economic Advisers. Heller immediately advocated deficit government spending as a means of stimulating the economy and addressing the 7 percent unemployment rate. During the last year of the Kennedy administration, Heller drafted the legislation that became the antipoverty program under Lyndon B. Johnson.* He left the administration in 1964 and returned to academe, but he continued to serve as a consultant, always from the perspective of Keynesian economics. Walter Heller died June 15, 1987.
REFERENCE: *New York Times*, June 16, 1987.

HELMS, RICHARD McGARRAH. Richard Helms was born in St. Davids, Pennsylvania, March 30, 1913. After graduating from Williams College in 1935, he became a staff correspondent for UPI and joined the *Indianapolis Times* in 1937. Helms stayed with the *Times* until 1942, when he was assigned by the United States Navy to work with the Office of Strategic Services (OSS). After the war Helms stayed on with the OSS when it became the Central Intelligence Agency* (CIA). Between 1965 and 1973, during the years of the Vietnam War,* Helms was deputy director and then director of the CIA. When the war reached its late stages in the early 1970s, he came under siege from critics protesting clandestine CIA activities in Indochina—secret armies, assassination squads, sponsored coup d'etats, and domestic surveillance. As a result of congressional hearings, new legislation required the CIA to secure presidential approval of all covert operations, surrender documents to public scrutiny as long as it did not compromise agents in the field, stop surveillance of Americans abroad unless national security required it, and cease domestic surveillance. Helms was forced to appear before a number of House and Senate committees in the mid-1970s as the legislation was evolving. Between 1973 and 1976, he also served as ambassador to Iran. Since leaving Teheran, Helms has worked as president of Safeer Corporation and as a consultant to international business and political concerns.

SUGGESTED READING: Thomas Powers, *The Man Who Kept the Secrets: Richard Helms and the CIA*, 1979.

HENDRIX, JAMES MARSHALL "JIMI." James Marshall Hendrix was born November 27, 1942, in Seattle. He quit high school to join the army in 1958. When he got out of the army, he traveled all over the country finding work as a backup guitarist in clubs and recording studios. While playing in Greenwich Village in 1966, Hendrix was noticed by the manager of the British rock group the Animals, who persuaded him to come to London and form his own band. In May 1966, the Jimi Hendrix Experience debuted. Their first number—"Hey, Joe"—was a hit in Great Britain. In 1967, Jimi Hendrix returned to the United States and played to huge concert audiences. Among his most memorable songs were "Purple Haze," "Foxy Lady," "Let Me Stand Next to Your Fire," and "The Wind Cries Mary." At the Woodstock* Festival in 1969, Hendrix concluded the concert with a highly personalized guitar rendition of "The Star Spangled Banner." A live Jimi Hendrix concert was known for its overt sexuality, his pulsating guitar rhythms, enormous energy, and the sultry, moaning tones of his voice. On September 18, 1970, Hendrix died of a drug overdose in London, his death symbolic of how some elements of 1960s popular culture soured and deteriorated into dysfunctionality.

REFERENCE: *New York Times*, September 19, 1970.

HERMAN'S HERMITS. Herman's Hermits enjoyed spectacular rock-and-roll success in the United States between 1964 and 1967. Composed of Peter "Herman" Noone, Karl Green, Keith Hopwood, Derek Leckenby, and Barry Whitman, Herman's Hermits were formed in Manchester, England, in 1963. They were part of the so-called British invasion of American popular music in the 1960s. Their first hit—"I'm into Something Good"—was a hit on the British pop charts and sold more than a million copies around the world. They came to the United States in 1964 and the next year had six singles reach the top ten: "Mrs. Brown, You've Got a Lovely Daughter," "I'm Henry the Eighth, I Am," "Can't You Hear My Heartbeat," "Wonderful World," "Silhouettes," and "Just a Little Bit Better." Herman's Hermits followed that up in 1966 with four more top ten hits: "Listen People," "Dandy," "A Must to Avoid," and "Leaning on the Lamp Post." Their last hit—"There's a Kind of Hush"—was released in 1967. The group disbanded in 1971.

REFERENCE: Patricia Romanowski and Holly George-Warren, eds., *The New Rolling Stone Encyclopedia of Rock and Roll*, 1996.

HESCHEL, ABRAHAM JOSHUA. Abraham Heschel was born in Warsaw, Poland, in 1907. He received the Ph.D. from the University of Berlin in 1933, lived a miserable existence at the hands of the Nazis for several years in the 1930s, and came to New York as a professor of philosophy at Hebrew Union College in 1940. In 1945, Heschel joined the faculty of the Jewish Seminary of America in New York, where he remained for the rest of his career. During the next quarter of a century, he became known as one of the greatest Jewish theologians in the United States. He wrote *Man Is Not Alone: A Philosophy of Religion* (1951), *Man's Quest for God* (1954), *God in Search of Man: A Philosophy of Judaism* (1955), *The Prophets* (1962), *The Insecurity of Freedom* (1965), and *Israel: An Echo of Eternity* (1969). When Heschel wrote of God, he described a living God who functioned in reality and was deeply concerned about the welfare of his children. The central dynamic in Jewish history, according to Heschel, was the alternating success and failure of human beings in making contact with God. Heschel also found God's wishes expressed in the civil rights movement,* ecumenism, and the founding and survival of Israel. He died on December 23, 1972.

REFERENCES: *New York Times*, December 24, 1972; Franklin Sherman, *The Promise of Heschel*, 1970.

HILSMAN, ROGER. Roger Hilsman was born November 23, 1919, in Waco, Texas. He graduated from the U.S. Military Academy at West Point in 1943 and joined the Office of Strategic Services (OSS), the forerunner of the Central Intelligence Agency* (CIA). Hilsman spent much of the war behind the lines in Asia fighting the Japanese. He remained with the CIA after World War II, and in 1951 he received a Ph.D. in international relations from Yale. From 1953 to 1956, Hilsman worked for the Center for International Studies at Princeton, and in 1956 he signed on with the Library of Congress. A prolific writer, he wrote *Strategic Intelligence and National Decisions* in 1956 and *Alliance Policy in the Cold War* in 1959. In 1961, he was apointed director of the Bureau of Intelligence and Research in the State Department.

He became an early critic of United States policy in Vietnam, warning that a military solution would never solve what was essentially a political problem. The United States, he argued, should not underestimate the power of nationalism and should be engaged in building the political loyalties of the South Vietnamese through economic reform and political security. Hilsman became assistant secretary of state for Far Eastern affairs in 1963 and accompanied Michael Forrestal* on a fact-finding mission to Vietnam that year. Both men returned from Indochina convinced that Vietnam would become a quagmire for the United States. After John Kennedy's* assassination in November 1963, Hilsman resigned from government and retuned to academe, accepting a faculty position at Columbia University.

Since joining Columbia, Hilsman has become one of the country's premier figures in defense policy. Among his many books are *To Move a Nation* (1967),

To Govern America (1979), *The Problem of Governing America* (1985), *The Politics of Policymaking in Defense and Foreign Affairs* (1992), *The Cuban Missile Crisis* (1996), and *From Nuclear Military Strategy to a World Without War*, 1999.
REFERENCES: *Current Biography*, 1964; *Current Authors*, 1969; Roger Hilsman, *To Move a Nation*, 1967; Joseph M. Rowe, Jr., "Roger Hilsman," in James S. Olson, ed., *Dictionary of the Vietnam War*, 1988.

HILSMAN-FORRESTAL REPORT. By 1963, President John F. Kennedy* was thoroughly frustrated with events in South Vietnam, primarily because of the optimistic reports he received from U.S. military officials there and the negative reports from Saigon-based journalists. In 1963, he asked White House staffer Michael Forrestal* and assistant secretary of state Roger Hilsman* to go on a fact-finding mission to South Vietnam. Their report to the president warned that the government of President Ngo Dinh Diem* was dangerously isolated from his own people, that the South Vietnamese army was hopelessly corrupt and inefficient, and that the Vietcong* were steadily gaining ground there. Nevertheless, the Hilsman-Forestal Report urged President Kennedy to stay the course in Vietnam. Otherwise, Southeast Asia would be threatened with a Communist takeover.
REFERENCE: George C. Herring, *America's Longest War: The United States in Vietnam*, 1950–1975, 1986.

HIPPIES. The so-called hippies, or flower children, have become one of the most ubiquitously remembered icons of the 1960s. The word originally came from "hip," an African-American expression in the urban North that referred to an individual who was in tune with currently changing social values, whatever they happened to be at the time. "Hip" was the opposite of being "square." The term "hippies" was coined by members of the beat* generation as a pejorative reference to the newly emerging counterculture.* The reference to hippies first came into the national consciousness when Michael Fallon, a reporter for the *San Francisco Examiner*, wrote an article in 1965 about a new group of young people who gathered in the Haight-Ashbury section of San Francisco and championed the virtues of peace, free love, recreational drug use, rock and roll, and absolute individual freedom to do "your own thing." They sported long, disheveled hairdos, baggy, thrift-shop clothes, and paisley colors. LSD* was their drug of choice. The New York City hippie community first appeared in Tompkins Square Park.

Hippie culture rejected the materialism of capitalist society, sexual monogamy, war and militarism, and all varieties of hard work and social climbing. In doing so, they claimed to be ushering in a new era in world history, the beginning of an age of peace, love, equality, and hedonistic pleasure. Their new era proved to be tragically short-lived. Crime, prostitution, venereal disease, and drug addiction had become more common in Haight-Ashbury by 1968 than peace, love, and brotherhood. The flower children had left by then, replaced by purveyors of heroin and speed. By the early 1970s, all that was left of the hippie phenomenon was a bit of nostalgia, another Grateful Dead* concert, and a lexicon of hippie phrases that had permanently entered American slang: "bag," "beautiful," "blow your mind," "freak," "groovy," "out of sight," "rapping," "scene," "super," "thing," and "zap."

REFERENCES: Ruth Bronsteen, *The Hippy's Handbook—How to Live on Love*, 1967; Lewis Yablonsky, *The Hippie Trip*, 1968.

HO CHI MINH. Ho Chi Minh, who used many other aliases during his political career, was born on May 19, 1890, in Nghe An Province of central Vietnam. His birth name was Nguyen Sinh Cung. His father was a teacher who hated the French domination in Indochina and inculcated his own Vietnamese nationalism into his children. Ho received his education in Hue,* where his sense of nationalism and Vietnamese patriotism only intensified. In 1909, he changed his name, informally at least, to Van Ba and moved south, teaching school in a number of villages before settling in Saigon.

In 1911, he signed on with a French freighter as a cook and left Vietnam, not returning for nearly thirty years. He spent three years making his way to Europe, spending time in India, South Africa, and New York City. During his year in Brooklyn, he called himself Nguyen Tat Thanh. From there, he went on to London, finally settling in Paris. He became part of the Vietnamese emigré community, further developing his own nationalist ideas. He attended the Versailles Peace Conference in 1919 and electrified Vietnamese everywhere by calling for independence. That pronouncement made him the *de facto* leader of Vietnamese nationalists. During those years he also became a devoted communist, since he was convinced that imperialism and capitalism were just different sides of the same coin. In 1920, Ho Chi Minh founded the French Communist Party.

French police began keeping track of Ho Chi Minh, whom they considered a dangerous revolutionary, and in 1924 he fled to Moscow to study at the University of Oriental Workers. In 1925, he moved to Canton, China, and founded the Thanh Nien Cach Menh Dong Chi Hoi (Revolutionary Youth League) to push for Vietnamese independence. In 1930, he established the Indochinese Communist party. During the 1930s, Ho spent time in China, Thailand, Burma, and the Soviet Union, always preaching the same message—Vietnamese independence.

When World War II erupted and the Japanese occupied Indochina, Ho returned to Vietnam. He considered Japanese control of Vietnam no more tolerable than French control. It was at this time that he assumed the name Ho Chi Minh. In May 1941, he established the Viet Nam Doc Lap Dong Minh Hoi (League for Vietnamese Independence), also known as the Vietminh. The Vietminh allied themselves with the United States during the war. On September 2, 1945, with World War II over, Ho Chi Minh proclaimed the independence of Vietnam.

France did not agree, and for the next nine years a bloody conflict ensued for control of Indochina, culminating finally in 1954, when the Vietminh defeated French forces at Dien Bien Phu. At the Geneva Conference of 1954, Ho agreed to the division of Vietnam at the seventeenth parallel into North Vietnam and South Vietnam, as long as free unification elections would be held in 1956.

But in 1956, the U.S. cancelled the elections when it became obvious that Ho Chi Minh would win in North Vietnam and South Vietnam. At that point, Ho began the war to overthrow the U.S.-backed government of South Vietnam and reunite the country. He formed the National Liberation Front, or Vietcong,* in 1960, started work on the Ho Chi Minh Trail through Laos and Cambodia to ferry supplies to South Vietnam, and by 1964 was infiltrating North Vietnamese troops south. He was an indefatigable nationalist and dedicated Communist intent on reunifying the two Vietnams and creating a Marxist state. Most Vietnamese, both northerners and southerners, identified him as ''Uncle Ho'' and considered him the father of their country. In spite of massive U.S. military power, Ho Chi Minh and his supporters steadily gained ground in Vietnam during the 1960s, making it clear that war was unwinnable. Ho Chi Minh died on September 2, 1969.

REFERENCES: Charles Fenn, *Ho Chi Minh: A Biographical Introduction*, 1973; David Halberstam, *Ho*, 1971; *New York Times*, September 3–7, 1969.

HO CHI MINH TRAIL. During the 1960s, Americans heard a great deal about the Ho Chi Minh Trail. In May 1959, the leaders of North Vietnam began investigating ways of smuggling supplies and troops into South Vietnam. Eventually, they constructed the so-called Ho Chi Minh Trail, a series of roads and paths from North Vietnam through Laos and Cambodia into South Vietnam. As the American escalation took place beginning in 1965, the North Vietnamese began improving the path from a primitive series of trails to what eventually became, by the early 1970s, a sophisticated, 12,000-mile system of roads, pipelines, fuel depots, and warehouses. Americans conducted enormous, long-term bombing campaigns over the Ho Chi Minh Trail in an attempt to stop the flow of supplies, but the effort was unsuccessful.

REFERENCE: James S. Olson and Randy Roberts, *Where the Domino Fell: America and Vietnam 1945–1995*, 1995.

HOFFMAN, ABBIE (ABBOTT HOWARD). Abbie Hoffman was born in Worcester, Massachusetts, November 30, 1936. He received a degree in psychology from Brandeis University in 1959 and then a master's degree at the University of California at Berkeley. Hoffman returned to Worcester in 1960 and found work as a hospital psychologist. He was soon active in the civil rights* and peace movements, working to raise money in the North for the Student Nonviolent Coordinating Committee* (SNCC). When SNCC purged all of its white leaders in 1966, Hoffman emerged as the leader of the countercultural anti-Vietnam War* movement. He produced several antiwar street theater productions, and in 1967 he threw money from a balcony onto the floor of the New York Stock Exchange. A number of newspaper photographers and television correspondents had been tipped off in advance, and the next day the press was full of pictures of stockbrokers groveling for every bill they could get their hands on.

Hoffman joined Jerry Rubin* in 1968 to form the Youth International Party,* or "yippies." Along with other antiwar groups, they staged the demonstrations in Chicago at the Democratic National Convention* in 1968 that became the famous "police riot." Hoffman was charged with conspiracy to commit violence, and, during the famous "Chicago Eight"* trial in 1969, he was convicted on that charge as well as for contempt of court. Both charges were later overturned on appeal.

In 1973, Hoffman was arrested for selling cocaine. He was convicted and received a ten-year sentence. Rather than serve his time, he jumped bail and went underground, living as Barry Freed. Even then, he could not keep himself out of the political limelight. In 1978, as Barry Freed, he led the "Save the River" campaign to keep the Hudson River from being dredged. He wrote his autobiography—*Soon to Be a Major Motion Picture*—in 1980 and came out of hiding to promote it. He resolved his legal problems and in 1984 led the campaign against construction of a power plant at Point Pleasant on the Delaware River. By that time, Hoffman was suffering from a serious bout with depression, an illness that had frequently plagued him during his life. He committed suicide on April 12, 1989.

REFERENCES: Abbie Hoffman, *Soon to Be a Major Motion Picture*, 1980; Marty Jezer, *Abbie Hoffman: American Rebel*, 1992.

HOGAN'S HEROES. *Hogan's Heroes* was a popular situation comedy of the 1960s. Loosely based on the films *Stalag 17* and *The Great Escape, Hogan's Heroes* made a comedy of a Nazi prisoner of war camp during World War II. CBS first broadcast *Hogan's Heroes* on September 17, 1965, with Bob Crane starring as Colonel Robert Hogan, Werner Klemperer as Colonel Wilhelm Klink, and John Banner as Sergeant Hans Schultz. The Nazis are portrayed as incompetent oafs and the Americans as brilliant schemers who control the camp, provide espionage information to the Allies, escape at will, and counterfeit money whenever necessary. The last episode was broadcast on July 4, 1971.

REFERENCE: Brenda Royce, Hogan's Heroes: *Behind the Scenes at Stalag 13*, 1998.

HOOK, SIDNEY. Sidney Hook was born in New York City in 1902. He took a Ph.D. in philosophy under John Dewey at Columbia and then studied in Berlin, Munich, and Moscow. When he returned to the United States and took a faculty position at New York University, Hook was a confirmed Marxist. His early works included *Towards an Understanding of Karl Marx* (1933) and *From Hegel to Marx* (1936). He joined the American Communist Party. But even then, Hooks' Marxism was not ideological and determinist. He was passionate in his belief that philosophy is not an abstraction and can be used as an important tool in the scientific analysis of social problems and that no ideology can explain all social, political, cultural, and political phenomena in all times. Such pragmatism inevitably doomed his Marxism. By 1940, Hooks was doing an about-face philosophically. He wrote *Reason, Social Myths, and Democracy* in 1940 and proclaimed his abandonment of Marxism for Dewey's pragmatism. He soon became a fanatical anticommunist and conservative, endorsing Republican candidates in the 1960s and 1970s. Sidney Hook died in 1989.

REFERENCES: Richard H. Pells, *Radical Visions and American Dreams*, 1973; Alan Wald, *The New York Intellectuals*, 1987.

HOOVER, J. EDGAR. Born in Washington, D.C., in 1895, J. Edgar Hoover grew up in Seward Square, an all-white, middle-class neighborhood in Washington, D.C., where he developed a value system committed to evangelical education, protection and transmission of a culture under siege, promotion of middle-class respectability, and support for tradition and conservatism. After graduating from college and law school in 1913 at George Washington University, Hoover secured employment with the Library of Congress. Four years later his uncle, William Hitz of the Justice Department, called Hoover into service in "Uncle Bill's" branch. Hoover worked for the Alien Enemy Department and the Labor Department's Immigration Department. He reviewed cases of individuals charged with being pro-German or alien. After the war, during the red scare, Hoover formed the Radical Division of the General Intelligence Division (GID). He concluded that 60,000 communist reds lived in America and that most of them were aliens. The answer was simple: deportation. A twenty-state sweep for radicals netted suspects and charges from the American Civil Liberties Union for violations of civil rights for the arrests and bureaucratic deportations of aliens. The experience reinforced Hoover's belief that communism represented the greatest evil to American society.

Hoover became assistant director of the new Federal Bureau of Investigation (FBI) under the Justice Department. While in this position he destroyed Ed Clark, leader of the Louisiana Ku Klux Klan, through wiretaps and disclosures of Clark's sexual behavior. In 1924, President Calvin Coolidge appointed him director of the FBI. He recruited college-educated men for agents and required the presentation of a gentlemanly image. Uniform moral discipline became a high priority within the bureau. Agents received the most modern police training and absorbed lessons in motivation and self-esteem.

In the 1930s the FBI and Hoover enjoyed widespread popularity as America's leading gangbusters, and the reputation he gained, as well as widespread political support, made him the absolute master of the FBI. Late in the 1930s, Hoover returned to his crusade against communists, a campaign that lasted well into the early 1960s. During the decade, Hoover had problems with all three American presidents. He got along best with Lyndon B. Johnson,* who once said, "I'd rather have him inside the tent pissing out than outside pissing in." They counted on one another for legal and extralegal assistance. Hoover hated John F. Kennedy* and Robert F. Kennedy.* He felt slighted when the Kennedys cavalierly dismissed his intelligence work, particularly in regard to Martin Luther King, Jr.* He never forgave the Kennedys, nor did he forget his belief that the communist menace lurked behind civil rights and other forms of social change.

Hoover believed that the unrest over civil rights originated from some Moscow connection. Martin Luther King, Jr., received a great deal of Hoover's attention, especially after King received the Nobel Prize. False letters, disinformation, electronic bugging, and planting informers in the Southern Christian Leadership Conference (SCLC) were employed to discredit King or find the elusive Moscow connection. Hoover also formed the FBI's Black Hate Division to investigate such black power* groups as the Student Nonviolent Coordinating Committee* and the Black Panthers.* The FBI also targeted New Left student groups during the 1960s. Although Presidents Kennedy, Johnson, and Nixon at one time or another contemplated firing Hoover, they never decided once and for all to confront him. J. Edgar Hoover was simply one of the most powerful individuals in the United States. He died May 2, 1972.

REFERENCES: Curt Gentry, *J. Edgar Hoover: The Man and the Secrets*, 1991; Ovid Demaris, *The Director: An Oral Biography of J. Edgar Hoover*, 1975.

Michael Hall

"HOT PURSUIT" POLICY. One of the most frustrating problems facing U.S. military leaders during the Vietnam War* was the ability of Vietcong* and North Vietnamese forces to escape across the border of South Vietnam into Cambodia, where American troops could not attack them. Critics of U.S. military policy charged that the presence of "sanctuaries" in Cambodia made it very extremely difficult for the United States to achieve a military victory, and insisted that the sanctuaries cost the lives of many U.S. troops. General William Westmoreland* proposed implementing a "hot pursuit policy," which would allow U.S. troops to follow retreating enemy troops into Cambodia and engage them there. Because Cambodia was officially neutral, however, President Lyndon B. Johnson* refused to approve "hot pursuit" for fear of widening the war and generating even more opposition in the international community. The whole "hot pursuit" issue became moot, however, in 1970 when President Richard Nixon* authorized the U.S. invasion of Cambodia.

REFERENCE: William Shawcross, *Sideshow: Kissinger, Nixon, and the Destruction of Cambodia*, 1979.

HOUSING ACT OF 1968. One of the major goals of Lyndon B. Johnson's* "War on Poverty"* was to improve the housing of poor people. The Housing Act of 1968 was designed to achieve the goal of providing better housing for the urban and the rural poor. During the law's lifetime—1968 to 1973—the federal government provided funds for the construction of more than 1 million

new housing units. When the dust settled around the program, however, relatively few poor people benefited from it. Only 13 percent of the families who bought homes under the program could be considered poor, as could only 43 percent of the renters. Middle-class consumers and home construction companies were the real beneficiaries of the Housing Act of 1968.
REFERENCE: David Burner, *Making Peace with the Sixties*, 1996; James S. Olson, ed., *Dictionary of United States Economic History*, 1992.

HOUSING AND URBAN DEVELOPMENT, DEPARTMENT OF. On September 9, 1965, as part of his Great Society* program to end urban poverty, President Lyndon B. Johnson* signed into law the bill establishing the Department of Housing and Urban Development (HUD) as a cabinet-level federal agency. Robert C. Weaver, an African American who headed the Housing and Home Finance Agency in the Department of Health, Education, and Welfare, was named to head HUD. In doing so, he became the first African American in the United States to serve as a member of the president's cabinet. The Department of Housing and Urban Development symbolized the fact that America was no longer a rural, farming country.
REFERENCE: M. Carter McFarland, *Federal Government and Urban Problems: HUD*, 1978.

HUD. *Hud* was one of the 1960s most important films. Directed by Martin Ritt and released in 1963, *Hud* starred Melvyn Douglas as Homer Bannon, Paul Newman as Hud Bannon, Patricia Neal as Alma, and Brandon de Wilde as Lon Bannon; the film was set in a Texas cattle town of the 1950s. Homer Bannon is an aging cattleman who has earned a reputation in his community for honesty, integrity, hard work, and common sense. His son Hud, however, is an arrogant, contemptuous, materialistic, self-centered, ''I'm gonna-get-mine'' louse who is a disgrace to his father. All Hud cares about is himself. Lon Bannon is Hud's impressionable seventeen-year-old son, who must observe the struggle between father and grandfather and determine his own identity.
REFERENCE: *New York Times*, May 29, 1963.

HUE. The city of Hue in central Vietnam served as the country's capital between 1802 and 1945. It was, and remains today, the cultural center of Vietnam and the seat of the Roman Catholic Church there. Hue straddles Highway 1, approximately 670 miles north of Ho Chi Minh City and 420 miles south of Hanoi.* During the Vietnam War,* the city was badly damaged, especially during the Tet Offensive,* when it suffered the loss of tens of thousands of its citizens. When the Vietnam War ended in 1975, Hue had a population of 205,000 people.
REFERENCE: Joseph Buttinger, *Vietnam: A Dragon Embattled*, vol. 2, *Vietnam at War*, 1967.

HUE, BATTLE OF. Between 1802 and 1945, the city of Hue* in Thua Thien Province of central Vietnam served as the imperial capital of Vietnam, the seat of the Vietnamese imperial family and site of the Imperial Citadel. It was also the provincial capital of Thua Thien Province. As such, it was a significant target for the Vietcong* and the North Vietnamese Army* (NVA) troops during the Vietnam War.* Capturing Hue would be worth its weight in propaganda gold. Its location made it even more tempting. The city was situated just south of the Demilitarized Zone* (DMZ) and isolated from Laos by the Annamese Mountain chain. It also had no port city nearby to keep it in supplies. Goods and people arriving in and leaving from Hue had to travel along Highway 1, which was vulnerable to military blockades and attack.

At the end of January 1968, during the Tet Offensive,* the North Vietnamese and Vietcong launched a concerted military offensive to conquer Hue. Early in the morning of January 31, 1968, North Vietnamese troops blocked Highway 1 north and south of the city, and combined North Vietnamese and Vietcong soldiers invaded the city, attacking it simultaneously in hundreds of places. When the sun rose that morning, the Vietcong flag was fluttering from atop the Citadel.

Later that morning, the United States counterattacked, using troops from the 1st Air Cavalry Division, the 101st Airborne Division, the Army of the Republic of Vietnam (ARVN) 1st Division, the U.S. 1st Marines, and ARVN Rangers and Marines. The fighting was fierce, often involving house-to-house, hand-to-hand combat with NVA troops and Vietcong. It took more than three weeks before U.S. and ARVN troops had retaken the Citadel, and enemy soldiers caused troubles for several weeks after that.

When the fighting ended, the city lay in ruin and bodies littered the streets. More than 50 percent of the buildings and houses in the city had been leveled by artillery and aerial bombardment, leaving 116,000 of the city's 140,000 residents homeless. More than 6,000 civilian noncombatants were killed in the fighting, and the Vietcong executed thousands more during the first few days of their occupation, when they systematically eliminated much of Hue's political and economic elite. More than 5,000 Vietcong and North Vietnamese troops had been killed in the fighting, compared to 216 American and 384 South Vietnamese troops.

REFERENCES: Eric Hammel, *Fire in the Streets: The Battle for Hue, Tet, 1968*, 1991; Don Oberdorfer, *Tet!*, 1971; Keith W. Nolan, *The Battle for Hue: Tet, 1968*, 1973.

HUMPHREY, HUBERT HORATIO. Hubert Humphrey was born in Wallace, South Dakota, May 27, 1911. He graduated from the Denver College of Pharmacy in 1933 and then opened the Humphrey Drug Company in Huron, South Dakota. Between 1937 and 1938, he earned a bachelor's degree at the University of Minnesota and then went on to earn a master's degree in political science at Louisiana State University in 1940. Humphrey worked briefly on a Ph.D. in political science, but in 1942, when color blindness and a double hernia kept him out of the army, he became head of the Minnesota state war production training program. In 1943, he served as assistant director of the War Manpower Commission. Active politically, he also played a key role in the merger of the Democratic Party and the Farmer–Labor Party in Minnesota in 1944.

Humphrey's political career began in 1945, when he won a landslide victory as mayor of Minneapolis. A true liberal, he established a fair employment practices commission in Minneapolis, launched an ambitious housing program for low-income families, and helped found the Americans for Democratic Action. At the 1948 Democratic National Convention, Humphrey earned a national profile by delivering a powerful speech calling for full civil rights for African Americans. That same year, he won a seat in the U.S. Senate. He was reelected in 1954 and 1960.

During his time in the Senate, Humphrey built on his reputation as a liberal who favored increased social security benefits, medicare* for the elderly, antipoverty job training programs, and civil rights for minority groups. He made a run for the 1960 presidential nomination but lost out in the primaries to John F. Kennedy.* In 1964, Humphrey accepted President Lyndon B. Johnson's* offer to become his vice presidential running mate. It was a difficult position for Humphrey. He enthusiastically supported the administration's Great Society* programs, but as his doubts about the Vietnam War* increased, he was unable to speak out against the American commitment there.

He was not able to chart an independent course on Vietnam until October 1968, when he ran for president of the United States. President Johnson had withdrawn from the race in 1968, and Humphrey won the nomination. But he lost to Richard Nixon* in the general election. From 1968 to 1970, Humphrey taught at the University of Minnesota and made some money on the lecture circuit. He was reelected to the U.S. Senate from Minnesota in 1970. Humphrey died January 13, 1978.

REFERENCES: Dan Cohen, *Undefeated: The Life of Hubert H. Humphrey*, 1978; Carl Solberg, *Hubert Humphrey: A Biography*, 1984.

I

I AM CURIOUS (YELLOW). *I Am Curious* (*Yellow*), a Swedish film directed by Vilgot Sjoman, caused enormous controversy when it was released in the United States in 1968. In the broadest sense, *I Am Curious* (*Yellow*) is about Lena, a young woman who travels around Stockholm trying to find answers to the cultural, sexual, and social dilemmas of the modern era. A troubled, but liberated, woman, Lena has sex with her friend Borje all over Stockholm, and the scenes were explicit enough for the U.S. Customs Service to seek a federal court opinion before allowing its distribution in the United States. A U.S. District Court labeled it pornographic, which stalled its distribution but provided the film with enough free media coverage to guarantee its box office success.
REFERENCE: *New York Times*, January 19, 1968.

I DREAM OF JEANNIE. *I Dream of Jeannie* was a popular situation comedy of the late 1960s. First broadcast by NBC on September 18, 1965, it starred Barbara Eden as Jeannie, a real-life genie whom astronaut Captain Tony Nelson (Larry Hagman) had discovered in a bottle on a deserted island where he had crash-landed. Jeannie is capable of giving him any wish he wants and some he does not want, and her escapades in complicating his social and professional life are the heart of the program. The last episode of *I Dream of Jeannie* was broadcast on September 1, 1970.
REFERENCE: Leon Adams, *Larry Hagman: A Biography*, 1987.

"I HAVE A DREAM" SPEECH. See **MARCH ON WASHINGTON (1963).**

IA DRANG VALLEY, BATTLE OF (1965). The Ia Drang Valley is located near Plei Me in the Central Highlands of southern Vietnam. In 1965, a famous battle of the Vietnam War* took place there. On October 19, 1965, North Vietnamese troops attacked an encampment of U.S. Special Forces* at Plei Me.

Soldiers from the 1st Cavalry Division counterattacked and relieved the American soldiers there. North Vietnamese troops fled for sanctuaries in the Chu Phong mountains just over the border in Cambodia. Early in November, the 1st Cavalry then headed out on a massive search and destroy* mission to clear all enemy troops out of the Ia Drang Valley. On November 14, however, North Vietnamese soldiers ambushed the 1st and 2nd battalions of the 7th Cavalry there. In three days of bloody fighting, complete with B-52 bombers providing tactical air support to the Americans, the United States lost nearly 300 dead while killing 1,770 enemy troops. Although William Westmoreland* interpreted Ia Drang as a military victory for the United States, the staggering number of American casualties was a somber warning to President Lyndon B. Johnson* and Secretary of Defense Robert McNamara* that the war in Indochina would be a difficult one.

REFERENCE: Harold G. Moore, *We Were Soldiers Once—and Young: Ia Drang, the Battle That Changed the War in Vietnam*, 1992.

IAN, JANIS. Janis Ian was born May 7, 1951, in New York City. A singer and songwriter, Ian had only one hit in the 1960s, but its theme carved out a permanent place for her in the culture of the decade. The song was entitled "Society's Child." Its theme was interracial love, and most radio stations blackballed the recording when it was first released in 1966. But conductor Leonard Bernstein featured Ian on his CBS-TV special "Inside Pop: The Rock Revolution." The New York Philharmonic accompanied her, and the song reached number fourteen on the pop charts. It was her only hit of the 1960s, although she managed to record several hits during the 1970s.

REFERENCE: Janis Ian, *Who Really Cares*, 1969.

IMMIGRATION AND NATIONALITY ACT OF 1965. During the heyday of the civil rights movement* in the 1960s, federal immigration policy came under increasingly close scrutiny, particularly the quota system, which had been first instituted with the National Origins Act of 1924. The National Origins Act had turned ethnic bias into policy, favoring immigrants from Western Europe over those from other parts of the world. In the heightened ethnic consciousness of the 1960s, such a blatant example of racism and ethnocentrism could not survive. Congress responded to mounting pressure with the Immigration and Nationality Act of 1965, which ended the forty-year-old system of ethnic quotas based on national origins. The United States would permit a total of 170,000 people from the Eastern Hemisphere to immigrate each year on a first-come, first-served basis, except that no more than 20,000 people could come from any one country. Preferences went to refugees, those with family members already in the United States, and professional and skilled workers. The act also, for the first time in U.S. history, limited immigration from the Western Hemisphere to 120,000 people per year, and they were allowed to enter on a first-come, first-served basis without categorical preference or limits from any given country.

REFERENCES: E. P. Hutchinson, *Legislative History of American Immigration Policy, 1798–1965*, 1981; James S. Olson, *The Ethnic Dimension in American History*, 1995.

IN COLD BLOOD. *In Cold Blood* was the title of Truman Capote's riveting, so-called nonfiction novel, which was released in 1966. The book dealt with the grisly murder of the Clutters, a Kansas farm family, by two psychopathic killers—Dick Hickman and Perry Smith. Capote had access to Clutter family records and diaries, and he conducted exhaustive interviews with Hickman and Smith before their executions. The book was a runaway best-seller that was made into a successful 1968 film starring John Forsythe as Detective Alvin Dewey. The book and film illustrated a dark side of the 1960s.
REFERENCES: Truman Capote, *In Cold Blood*, 1966; *New York Times*, January 28, 1968.

INDIAN CIVIL RIGHTS ACT OF 1968. In 1968, Congress passed the Indian Civil Rights Act (ICRA). Because this act authorizes federal courts to intervene in intratribal disputes and expressly limits the power of tribes to regulate internal affairs, many Native Americans perceive it to be a threat to their self-determination* and have characterized it as an attempt by the federal government to preempt overall sovereignty. Their dissent implies a genuine suspicion and skepticism, both of which have resulted in extensive criticism of this statute.

In 1896, the Supreme Court decided the *Talton v. Mayes* case, which stressed that Indian tribes possessed the inherent right to govern themselves. The decision stated that the Bill of Rights applied to actions of federal and state governments, not tribal governments, since tribes are not subordinate bodies of those governments. Tribal sovereignty, the Court argued, flows from their aboriginal independence, which preceded the writing of the Constitution. Talton had murdered a Cherokee Indian on the Cherokee reservation. A five-man Cherokee grand jury indicted him for murder, and a Cherokee court convicted him. He appealed to the federal courts, arguing that his Fifth Amendment rights had been violated because a proper, six-man grand jury had not been impaneled. The Supreme Court rejected his argument. The U.S. Constitution placed no limits or restrictions on the manner in which this right manifested itself. In the absence of such limitation, intratribal disputes and complaints against tribal officials had to be resolved within the tribe; the net result was a system that denied tribal members the opportunity to challenge those decisions that they felt were arbitrary and unfair. Because Indian tribes were recognized as independent nations within a nation, the U.S. Supreme Court argued that they enjoyed the same "sovereign immunity" from suit that the state and federal governments enjoy.

In the early 1960s, Congress began to respond to numerous complaints by individual tribal members who contended that tribal officials were abusive and tyrannical. They appealed to Congress to pass legislation that would protect them from such mistreatment. Congressional hearings convened in 1962 to investigate their complaints of misconduct, and several congressmen concluded that individual Indians needed "some guaranteed form of civil rights against the actions of their own governments."

According to congressional records, the ICRA was passed to "ensure that the American Indian is afforded the broad Constitutional rights secured to other Americans . . . [in order to] protect individual Indians from arbitrary and unjust actions of tribal governments." Legislatively, it confers certain rights on all persons who are subject to the jurisdiction of a tribal government, and the act authorizes federal courts to enforce these rights. The purpose and scope of the Indian Civil Rights Act are similar to those of the U.S. Constitution; however, Congress did deny certain individual rights, which they felt were inherently dangerous to the survival of tribal self-government. Consequently, the ICRA guarantees almost all the fundamental rights enumerated in the U.S. Constitution, with the exception of four. Tribal governments are not subject to the Establishment Clause of the First Amendment, do not have to provide legal counsel (free of charge) to indigent defendants, and do not have to provide a trial by jury in civil cases or provide grand jury indictments in criminal cases. These amendments or protections were not included because Congress surmised that they would be a potential threat to political stability within tribal governments.

The Indian Civil Rights Act has fundamentally changed the procedural aspects of the tribal judicial system. Prior to its enactment, procedural uniformity was nonexistent. Tribes would invariably employ their own methods of conflict resolution. The Indian Civil Rights Act, however, requires that all tribes adhere to certain procedural standards. In particular, federal courts mandate that tribal courts advise criminal defendants of their right to a trial by jury, write their criminal laws in clear and certain language, honor a criminal defendant's right against self-incrimination, prohibit the trial judge from also being the prosecutor, and maintain complete records of judicial proceedings. Some Native Americans have considered these changes a direct threat to their conventional notions of self-determination and tribal sovereignty. The ICRA, they contend, by implication suggests that the rights of individual Indians are more important than the survival of the tribe itself. Consequently, many Native Americans have expressed continued opposition to the Indian Civil Rights Act of 1968.

REFERENCES: Marjane Ambler, *Breaking the Iron Bonds: Indian Control of Energy Development*, 1990; Donald L. Burnett, "An Historical Analysis of the 1968 'Indian Civil Rights Act,' " *Harvard Journal of Legislation* 9 (1972); Vine Deloria, Jr., and Clifford Lytle, *The Nations Within: The Past and Future of American Indian Sovereignty*, 1984; Roxanne Dunbar Ortiz, *Indians of the Americas: Human Rights and Self-Determination*, 1984; Hurst Hannum, *Autonomy, Self-Determination and Sovereignty: The Accommodation of Conflicting Rights*, 1990.

Carlos Rainer

INDIANS. See **RED POWER**.

INDIANS OF ALL TRIBES. In the early morning hours of November 20, 1969, eighty-nine American Indians landed on Alcatraz Island* in San Francisco

Bay. Identifying themselves as "Indians of All Tribes," this group of young, urban, Indian college students claimed the island by "right of discovery" and by the terms of the 1868 Sioux Treaty of Fort Laramie, which they interpreted as giving Indians the right to claim unused federal property that had been Indian land previously. The occupiers demanded clear title to Alcatraz Island and the establishment of an American Indian University, an American Indian Cultural Center, and an American Indian Museum on Alcatraz Island.

The Indian group initially used the name of United Native Americans but recognized that the name was not representative of the large number of Indian tribes that participated in the occupation. While casting about for a name, Belvia Cottier, a Lakota Indian woman who had been instrumental in the planning of a brief 1964 occupation of Alcatraz Island as well as the 1969 occupation, suggested the name "Indians of All Tribes." The name was more appropriate because Indian people from tribes from all across the United States participated in the planning and carrying out of the occupation. The name was adopted and remained unchanged until January 15, 1970, at which time the group filed legal articles of incorporation with the state of California and became a legal entity, "Indians of All Tribes, Inc." The corporation's principal office was listed as Alcatraz Island in San Francisco.

The specific and primary purpose of the incorporated group was to promote the welfare of all Indians on Alcatraz Island and elsewhere. The general purposes and powers were listed as (1) to administer Alcatraz Island; (2) to promote the welfare of residents of Alcatraz Island; (3) to negotiate with the federal government for the purpose of obtaining title to Alcatraz Island and other demands; (4) to establish Indian educational and cultural centers on Alcatraz Island and elsewhere; (5) to enter into and perform contracts, agreements, and other transactions of any description; and (6) to receive, own, possess, administer, and dispose of money and property of any description, individually in its own name, as trustee, or fiduciary, jointly with others or in any other manner. The corporation was organized pursuant to the California General Nonprofit Corporation Law, and the board of directors, known as council members, were all Indian people: Stella Leach (Colville/Sioux), Alan Miller (Seminole), Judy Scraper (Shawnee), David Leach (Colville/Sioux), Denis Turner (Luiseño), Richard Oakes (Mohawk), and Ray Spang (Northern Cheyenne).

Criteria for membership in Indians of All Tribes, Inc. was set forth in the bylaws of the organization. "Every Indian on Alcatraz Island in San Francisco Bay is a member of the corporation if he or she (a) is registered with the coordinator's office as a resident, and (b) has lived continuously on Alcatraz for at least seven days. An Indian loses his membership if (a) he leaves Alcatraz for more than seventy-two hours in any calendar week, without permission from Council; or (b) a majority of the Council votes to revoke his membership for violation of the security rules. If membership was lost by leaving Alcatraz for more than seventy-two hours, it could be regained by re-registering as a resident and living continuously on Alcatraz for at least seven (7) days."

The members of the island council established by Indians of All Tribes, Inc. changed numerous times during the nineteen-month occupation of Alcatraz Island, which ended on June 11, 1971. Provisions in the bylaws called for regular elections so that the island leadership would reflect the choice of leadership of the Indian people on the island. Throughout much of the occupation, Indians of All Tribes, Inc. provided a sound framework for the diverse groups of Indian occupiers on Alcatraz Island. The council subcommittees provided for housing, security, finance, public relations, sanitation, cooking, day care, and medical care, as well as a negotiation team to meet with federal officials during the occupation. Every resident of Alcatraz Island was assigned duties in one of these areas. Indians of All Tribes, Inc. ceased to exist following the Alcatraz occupation; however, the name remains today as part of the United Indians of All Tribes Foundation in Seattle.

REFERENCE: Troy R. Johnson, *The Occupation of Alcatraz Island: Indian Self-Determination and the Rise of Indian Activism*, 1996.

Troy Johnson

INNIS, ROY. Roy Innis was born in St. Croix, Virgin Islands, June 6, 1934. His family immigrated to New York City in 1946. After a two-year stint in the army, Innis returned to New York City and earned a degree in chemistry at City College. He was drawn gradually into the civil rights movement,* primarily out of his conviction that black men needed to be more assertive and that integration was a mixed blessing for African Americans. Innis was also convinced that economic competitiveness and education would be as important to black liberation as political change.

By the late 1950s, Innis was active in James Farmer's Congress of Racial Equality* (CORE). In 1965, Innis became head of the Harlem chapter of CORE, and in 1968 he succeeded Floyd McKissick* as national director of the organization. At the time, CORE's membership exceeded 70,000 people. Consistent with the new emphasis on black power* in the civil rights movement, Innis completely abandoned his support of nonviolent civil disobedience and began advocating what he called black self-defense—answering violence with violence to protect one's family and people.

Under Innis' leadership, CORE declined rapidly, losing membership and its charitable financial base. He was charged with misusing CORE funds for personal use, and critics inside the organization accused Innis of being dictatorial. After a decade of having Roy Innis at the helm, CORE had for the most part ceased to function. He remained at the helm of the Congress of Racial Equality until 1982, when he stepped down. Since then Innis has continued to serve as a vocal spokesman and advocate for African-American civil rights.

REFERENCE: August Meier and Elliott Rudwick, *CORE: A Study in the Civil Rights Movement, 1942–1968*, 1975.

IRON TRIANGLE (WAR ZONE D). The Iron Triangle was a National Liberation Front (NLF) stronghold twenty miles northwest of Saigon that had been built by the Vietminh twenty years before in the war against the French colonialism. Serving as a supply depot and staging area with a vast underground complex including command headquarters, dining halls, hospital rooms, munitions factories, and living quarters, it was never cleared by the French, nor was it successfully neutralized by the United States or the Army of the Republic of Vietnam (ARVN). Located between Saigon,* Tay Ninh, and Song Be cities, the triangle comprised about 125 square miles and included portions of Bien Hoa, Binh Duong, Phouc Long, Long Khanh, and Hau Nghia Provinces. It was generally bounded by the Saigon River, the Song (river) Thi Thinh north of Bien Hoa, and the Than Dien Forest in Binh Duong Province. The area was heavily forested, consisting of jungle and rubber plantations and containing a few small villages and hamlets, the most strategic being Ben Suc, which had been under NLF control since 1964.

In January 1967 the United States and ARVN mounted the war's first major combined operation and the first U.S. corps-size operation. Operation Cedar Falls deployed 32,000 troops against the triangle. Its "search and destroy"* objective was to engage and eliminate enemy forces, destroy base camps and supplies, remove all noncombatants along with possessions and livestock to strategic hamlets, and completely destroy four principal villages. Extensive underground complexes were found, and large quantities of papers were captured. The complete U.S. arsenal was employed—intensive bombing, flamethrowers, chemical warfare (defoliants and the first authorized major use of CS, or tear, gas), and land-clearing Rome plows. Units participating in Cedar Falls included the 173d Airborne Brigade, the 196th and 199th Infantry brigades, elements of the 1st and 25th Infantry divisions, the 11th Armored Cavalry Regiment, and the ARVN 5th Ranger Group.

There was little fighting as the NLF fled to sanctuaries in Cambodia until the operation was finished. However, the destruction, chronicled in Jonathan Schell's *The Village of Ben Suc*, was considerable. About 700 refugees were created, and the region was made uninhabitable to anyone other than the NVA-NLF forces. The operation's magnitude increased NLF utilization of Cambodian sanctuaries; however, they did return to rebuild camps, which became springboards for the assault on Saigon during the Tet Offensive* in 1968. Subsequent operations against the Iron Triangle included Uniontown, Atlas Wedge, and Toan Thang.

REFERENCES: Jonathan Schell, *The Village of Ben Suc*, 1969; William Shawcross, *Sideshow: Nixon, Kissinger, and the Destruction of Cambodia*, 1979.

Samuel Freeman

J

JACKSON, JESSE. Jesse Jackson, the son of an Alabama sharecropper, was born October 8, 1941. A gifted athlete, he received a football scholarship to the University of Illinois in 1959, but he experienced what he considered unacceptable racist treatment in Urbana and transferred to North Carolina A&T College in Greensboro. It was an auspicious decision. He became the leader of the famous "sit-ins"* at Greensboro lunch counters. Jackson would enter the restaurant and ask to be served. When the proprietors denied him service, students set up picket lines, occupied the other seats in the establishment, and refused to leave.

After graduating from North Carolina A&T, where he had decided to go into the ministry, Jackson moved back to Illinois to attend the Chicago Theological Seminary. He joined the Southern Christian Leadership Conference* in 1963 and managed to organize most of the black clergymen in Chicago in support of Martin Luther King, Jr.* Jackson also founded Operation Breadbasket, a program in Chicago that called on black people to boycott stores and businesses that would not hire black workers. He came to Martin Luther King's attention, and he was in Memphis, Tennessee, with the civil rights leader when the assassination occurred. In 1971, Jackson left the Southern Christian Leadership Conference and formed Operation PUSH, an advocacy group dedicated to promoting black education and the hiring of black workers.

In subsequent years, Jackson emerged as the most prominent civil rights leader in the country. He spoke of black pride and black responsibility and of the need for compassion for the poor and downtrodden, with passion and inspiration. In the 1980s, Jackson turned to more traditional political action. He decided to run in the Democratic presidential primaries in 1984 and 1988 under the aegis of what he called the Rainbow Coalition, an alliance of minority groups. Although he did not win the nomination, he became a power broker in the Democratic Party because of the support he had among African-American voters. During the 1990s, Jackson kept the faith, maintaining his role as spokesman for the poor and weak, even as the Democratic Party and much of the American electorate grew more conservative.

REFERENCES: Teresa Noel Celsi, *Jesse Jackson and Political Power*, 1991; Adolph Reed, *The Jesse Jackson Phenomenon*, 1986.

TOMMY JAMES AND THE SHONDELLS. The rock group known as Tommy James and the Shondells was formed in Niles, Michigan, in 1960. Tommy James had recorded "Hanky Panky" in 1963, but it did not become a hit until 1966, when it reached number one on the pop charts and sold a million copies. James then formed a new Shondells group. During the next four years, they put together thirteen top forty hits. Among the most memorable are "I Think We're Alone Now," "Mirage," "Mony, Mony," "Crimson and Clover," "Sweet Cherry Wine," and "Crystal Blue Persuasion." Critics classified it as "bubble-gum rock," but "Crystal Clear Persuasion" sold nearly 6 million copies. The group then declined in popularity, and James turned to record production.

REFERENCE: Patricia Romanowski and Holly George-Warren, eds., *The New Rolling Stone Encyclopedia of Rock and Roll*, 1996.

JASON STUDY. Although Secretary of Defense Robert M. McNamara* had forcefully supported escalation of the U.S. commitment in Vietnam during the administration of President John F. Kennedy* and the first years of the Lyndon B. Johnson* administration, he had serious doubts about the conflict by 1966. That year, John McNaughton and Adam Yarmolinsky, two of McNamara's aides, asked the Institute of Defense Analysis to convene a conference of leading scholars to evaluate U.S. policy in Indochina, especially the efficacy of U.S. bombing* raids. They met at Wellesley, Massachusetts, during the summer of 1966. The conference report became known as the Jason Study. The Jason Study concluded that U.S. bombing of North Vietnam and the Ho Chi Minh Trail* had not seriously compromised the enemy's ability to wage war, and that it had actually stiffened the resolve of North Vietnamese civilians to continue the struggle. North Vietnam, with its subsistence, agricultural economy and already poor infrastructure, was not really vulnerable to air strikes, and the Soviet Union and China provided them all the weapons and ammunition they needed. The Jason Study helped change Robert M. McNamara's thinking about the war and transformed him into an advocate for a diplomatic solution as opposed to pursuing a military victory.

REFERENCE: Robert S. McNamara, *In Retrospect: The Tragedy and Lessons of Vietnam*, 1994.

JAVITS, JACOB KOPPEL. Jacob Javits was born May 18, 1904, in New York City. He practiced law for several years after earning a law degree from New York University and joined the army during World War II. A liberal Republican, he was elected to Congress in 1946, served five terms, and won a seat in the U.S. Senate in 1966. No sooner had he taken the oath of office than he condemned the Vietnam War* and called for the withdrawal of U.S. troops and an end to U.S. bombing raids over North Vietnam. He became the leading Republican opponent of the Vietnam policies of Presidents Lyndon Johnson* and Richard Nixon.* In 1973, he was the sponsor of the War Powers Resolution, which forbade the president from conducting war without congressional approval. Javits lost the Republican primary election in 1980 and retired from the Senate in 1981. He died of Lou Gehrig's disease five years later on March 7, 1986.

REFERENCES: Jacob Javits, *Javits: The Autobiography of a Public Man*, 1981; *New York Times*, March 8, 1986.

THE JEFFERSON AIRPLANE. Formed in San Francisco in 1965, the Jefferson Airplane was a rock group that epitomized the hippie* culture of Haight-Ashbury. Its original members included Marty Balin, Paul Kantner, Jorma Kaukonen, Skip Spence, Signe Anderson, and Bob Harvey. Jack Casidy replaced Bob Harvey late in 1965, and Grace Slick replaced Anderson in 1966. In 1967, the Jefferson Airplane had two top ten hits—"Somebody to Love" and "White Rabbit." Their 1968 album *Crown of Creation* went gold. In the name of artistic control, they managed to secure the right to use whatever lyrics they wanted, and both *Bless Its Pointed Little Head* in 1968 and *Volunteers* in 1969 were raw, scatological, and, in the minds of some critics, obscene. The Jefferson Airplane, with shifting personnel over the years, continued to perform and record in the 1970s, 1980s, and 1990s.

REFERENCE: Ralph J. Gleason, *The Jefferson Airplane and the San Francisco Sound*, 1969.

JET SET. By the 1960s, the term "jet set" had emerged to describe the lifestyles of the rich and powerful around the world. During the nineteenth and early twentieth centuries, the rich and powerful had often exhibited their wealth in elaborate railroad cars and fancy yachts and cruisers. But the advent of the commercial jet aircraft in the late 1950s gave birth to the term "jet set" to describe well-to-do people who could crisscross the globe at a moment's notice for work and pleasure. The term "jet set" remains a part of popular English today.

REFERENCE: Carl Solberg, *Conquest of the Skies*, 1979.

JEWISH DEFENSE LEAGUE. The Jewish Defense League (JDL) was founded in 1968 in New York City by Rabbi Meir Kahane. Militantly committed to promoting Jewish power and the state of Israel and opposing, violently if necessary, all forms of anti-Semitism, Kahane was the Jewish equivalent of black power* activists like Stokely Carmichael* and H. Rap Brown.* Kahane organized "Jewish Is Beautiful" rallies, engaged in civil disobedience to protest black anti-Semitism, and called for all Jews to return to traditional religious practices and to consider emigrating to Israel. More moderate Jewish organizations opposed Kahane's militant radicalism, and JDL membership never exceeded 7,000 people. In 1971, Kahane emigrated to Israel.

REFERENCE: Meir Kahane, *The Story of the Jewish Defense League*, 1975.

JIM CROW. The term "Jim Crow" refers to the system of de jure, or legal, racial segregation that descended on southern states after Reconstruction. African Americans found themselves segregated by law in every dimension of public life and unable to exercise their Fifteenth Amendment right to vote because of poll taxes, literacy tests, white primaries, and grandfather clauses. But after World War II and into the 1960s, formal, legal segregation was outlawed in the United States.

In 1945, as never before, African Americans were ready for changes. Of all the approaches of the past, the National Association for the Advancement of Colored People (NAACP) had been the most successful. Thurgood Marshall,* leader of the NAACP Legal Defense Fund, had always argued in the federal courts that racial discrimination was unconstitutional, a violation of the First, Fifth, Fourteenth, and Fifteenth Amendments. Under Chief Justices Harlan Stone* (1941–1946), Fred M. Vinson* (1946–1953), and Earl Warren* (1953–1969), the Supreme Court proved surprisingly consistent in condemning segregation. Between 1941 and 1964 the Court invalidated virtually every form of de jure segregation.

The *Plessy v. Ferguson* decision of 1896 had upheld "separate but equal" facilities, but after 1940 the whole constitutional edifice of Jim Crow collapsed. In *Mitchell v. United States* (1941) the Court declared that the denial of a Pullman berth to an African-American traveler violated the Interstate Commerce Act, and in *Morgan v. Virginia* (1946) the Court prohibited segregation in public buses crossing state lines. Subsequent decisions invalidated racial segregation in other interstate transportation as well. With *Shelley v. Kraemer* and *Hard v. Hodge* in 1948, the Court also prohibited restrictive covenants excluding blacks from housing developments. Other Court orders integrated parks, theaters, and private businesses operating on public property, and in 1964, in *McLaughlin v. Florida*, the Court outlawed a Florida statute prohibiting interracial sexual relations. Finally, in an assault on political discrimination, the Court declared that white primaries (*Smith v. Allwright*, 1944) and literacy tests (*Schnell v. Davis*, 1949) were violations of the Fifteenth Amendment. The Twenty-Fourth Amendment to the Constitution, which was ratified in 1964, outlawed the poll tax.

But if these Court decisions irritated white southerners, desegregation of the schools enraged them and led to "massive resistance" in the 1950s and 1960s. Arguing that "separate but equal" was inherently discriminatory and unconstitutional, the Supreme Court dismantled the central institution of Jim Crow. The outline of the future had appeared in 1938, when the Court declared, in *Missouri rel. Gaines v. Canada*, that by refusing to admit an African-American student to the state law school, Missouri had violated the equal protection clause of the Fourteenth Amendment. After World War II, the NAACP continued to set its sights on higher education, and in *Sweatt v. Painter* (1950) the Supreme Court decided that a separate law school for Texas blacks was unconstitutional. Shortly thereafter, in *McLaurin v. Oklahoma State Regents* (1950), the Court outlawed University of Oklahoma regulations segregating an African-American graduate student to special desks and tables. Then, in *Brown v. Board of Education* (1954), the Court unanimously declared that de jure segregation of schools, by imposing inferior status on African-American children, denied them equal protection of the law. In one stroke the Court had destroyed the legal foundation of de jure segregation.

REFERENCE: James S. Olson, *The Ethnic Dimension in American History*, 1979.

JOB CORPS. The Job Corps was the brainchild of Senator Hubert Humphrey* of Minnesota. Humphrey wanted to do something for disadvantaged urban youth, and he wanted to model the federal program after the Civilian Conservation Corps of the New Deal, when unemployed young men by the tens of thousands went to work in rural areas building roads, fighting fires, and cleaning state and national parks. He submitted legislation to Congress several times during the late 1950s and early 1960s but could never manage to muster the votes needed to implement it. The increasing awareness of the serious problem of urban unemployment, however, gave the proposal more visibility. In 1964, President Lyndon B. Johnson* decided to back the idea and included it as part of the Economic Opportunity Act* of 1964. The legislation created centers where poor, teenaged young men and women could learn job skills and become self-supporting.

Job Corps centers were established throughout the country. It was a residential program of vocational and basic literacy education for disadvantaged young people between the ages of sixteen and twenty-one. The program was soon enveloped in enormous controversy. Because its objectives were poorly defined, and implementation was too rapid, the program became the object of intense criticism and negative publicity. Although it tried to train the students in job skills and literacy, it proved to be extremely costly for the results achieved— more than $500,000 for each young person placed in a job. Racial tensions at the camps—between urban black and rural white youths—ran high, and people in the communities where Job Corps centers were established often complained about the unruliness of the participants. Problems associated with youth gangs, drugs, crime, and alcohol abuse plagued many Job Corps centers. Instead of the 100,000 enrollees as originally conceived, Congress capped it at 45,000 in 1965. In 1969, President Richard Nixon* reduced it even more. By the mid-1970s, there was a total of sixty-four Job Corp centers training approximately 20,000 young people, but the Job Corps was seen widely as one of the least successful of the Great Society's* ''war on poverty''* programs.

REFERENCES: David Burner, *Making Peace with the Sixties*, 1996; James S. Olson, ed., *Dictionary of United States Economic History*, 1992; Sar Levitan and Benjamin Johnston, *The Job Corps: A Social Experiment That Works*, 1975.

JOGGING. See **AEROBICS**.

JOHN BIRCH SOCIETY. John Birch serves as the namesake of the John Birch Society, which is an organization founded by Robert Welch in 1958 to combat communism. Welch chose the name because John Birch, a Korean War casualty, exemplified an image of ''the ideal Americanist . . . a perfect fusion of rural virtues, fundamentalist faith, and dedicated patriotism.'' John Birch was born May 18, 1918, in India, to fundamentalist Methodist missionary parents. He was raised in Georgia. Birch graduated from Mercer University in 1939 and from the Bible Baptist Seminary in Fort Worth, Texas, in 1940. He then left for China to become a missionary. During World War II, Birch served in the army air corps. Ten days after V-J Day, however, he was killed by Chinese communists. As a reward for his service, Birch received two decorations, although one was awarded posthumously.

Robert Welch chose to name his anticommunist organization after John Birch for several reasons. Birch died serving his country, therefore making the ultimate sacrifice for patriotism. He held strong fundamentalist beliefs and upheld virtues that Welch saw as important. Finally, Birch was killed by a communist. Welch, therefore, believed that Birch was the first victim of the Cold War* and would serve as a worthy symbol of his organization's war against communism.

During the 1960s, the John Birch Society became one of the country's most influential, ultra right-wing political organizations. The John Birch Society gained national attention and had a peak membership estimated at about 100,000 people. They saw conspiracies everywhere, all of them orchestrated by international communism. For the John Birch Society, the red scare of the early 1950s never ended. They even accused people like President Dwight D. Eisenhower* of promoting an international communist conspiracy.

REFERENCE: J. Allen Broyles, *The John Birch Society: Anatomy of a Protest*, 1964.

John Hinson

JOHNSON, LYNDON BAINES. Lyndon B. Johnson was born in Stonewall, Texas, August 27, 1908. He was raised in the Hill Country town of Johnson City. His father speculated in cattle and real estate and served in the state legislature. The younger Johnson graduated from Southwest Texas State Teachers College in 1930, where he had been very active in student politics. From 1930 to 1932 he taught school in Cotulla, Texas, where he became acquainted with the challenges facing Mexican-American people. Johnson then left teaching for politics, becoming legislative secretary to Congressman Richard Kleberg, a Texas Democrat. Tireless and indefatigable, Johnson became the most influential legislative secretary in Congress, dutifully responding to constituent needs. In 1934, President Franklin D. Roosevelt appointed him head of the state office of the National Youth Administration. Johnson used the post to provide tens of thousands of jobs to Texas young adults and build up his own political constituency.

In 1937, he was elected to Congress on a platform that strongly endorsed the New Deal of Franklin D. Roosevelt. Johnson served in the navy during World War II, and in 1948 he won a seat in the U.S. Senate. The election was perilously close and remains cited as one of the most corrupt in Texas history. His success in moving up through the Senate ranks was unprecedented. Midway into his first term, Johnson was named majority whip of the Senate, the youngest man ever to hold the post. Two years later, still in his first term, Johnson won election as the minority leader and became majority leader after the Democrats retook control of the Senate in 1954. His tenure there was marked by his success in seeing to the passage of the Civil Rights Act of 1957.

In 1960, Johnson made a run for the Democratic presidential nomination, but he lost to Senator John F. Kennedy* of Massachusetts in the primary elections. Kennedy then named Johnson as his vice presidential running mate. The Kennedy–Johnson ticket narrowly edged out the Richard Nixon*–Henry Cabot Lodge* ticket, and Johnson became vice president in 1961. When Kennedy was assassinated on November 22, 1963, Lyndon B. Johnson became president of the United States.

He dreamed of being another Franklin D. Roosevelt and passing a comprehensive reform package to improve the American economy and fulfill the true meaning of the U.S. Constitution. Johnson's record in the area of civil rights was the most enlightened in U.S. history. The Civil Rights Act of 1964 outlawed discrimination in employment and segregation in public facilities, and the Voting Rights Act* of 1965 sent federal marshals into the South to make sure that African Americans and Mexican Americans were allowed to register and to vote without intimidation. The Civil Rights Act of 1968* prohibited discrimination in housing. Johnson also launched his ''war on poverty''* with the Economic Opportunity Act of 1964. Johnson labeled his civil rights and antipoverty legislation as part of his ''Great Society,''* and on that basis he won reelection in 1964 over Senator Barry Goldwater* of Arizona by a landslide.

But he never really was able to fulfill the vision of the Great Society. The Vietnam War* eventually destroyed Johnson's presidency. Early in 1965, he deployed 3,000 U.S. ground troops to augment the 25,000 U.S. military advisers already there. The troops never proved enough to defeat the communist enemy in South Vietnam, and the Pentagon kept asking for more soldiers. By early 1968, Johnson had raised the troop limit to more than 500,000 soldiers, but it was still not enough. The antiwar movement* within the United States steadily gained momentum. The Tet Offensive* that began on January 31, 1968, demonstrated that the enemy was still highly committed and militarily strong and that the war would continue indefinitely. Senator Eugene McCarthy* of Minnesota, an antiwar Democrat, decided to run for the 1968 Democratic presidential nomination, and he almost defeated Johnson in the February New Hampshire primary. When Senator Robert F. Kennedy* then proclaimed his candidacy for the nomination, Johnson knew that his presidency was doomed. At the end of March 1968, he announced over national television that he would not seek another term in the White House.

Johnson retired from public life when he left the White House on January 20, 1969, and returned to his ranch in the Hill Country. He spent the remaining years of his life helping build the Lyndon B. Johnson Library at the University of Texas in Austin. Johnson died of a heart attack January 22, 1973.

REFERENCES: Vaughn Davis Bornet, *The Presidency of Lyndon B. Johnson*, 1983; Robert Caro, *The Years of Lyndon Johnson: The Path to Power*, 1992; Eric F. Goldman, *The Tragedy of Lyndon Johnson*, 1969; Doris Kearns, *Lyndon Johnson and the American Dream*, 1976.

JOPLIN, JANIS. Janis Joplin was born in Port Arthur, Texas, in 1943. In her music, which she delivered in a raspy, shrieking voice, she epitomized the youth rebellion of the 1960s. She performed the song ''Love Is Like a Ball and Chain'' at the 1967 Monterey Rock Festival and subsequently rose to fame among hard rock fans just a year after her first booking as a professional singer. She went to San Francisco to sing in an old friend's band—Big Brother and the Holding Company—and lived among the hippies* in Haight-Ashbury. Her subsequent album *Cheap Thrills* sold more than 3 million copies. Joplin drank Southern Comfort from bottles at her concerts and celebrated booze, drugs, getting stoned, and rebellion. She lived hard and self-destructed, as did the youth rebellion of the 1960s. Janis Joplin died of a heroin overdose October 4, 1970.

REFERENCE: *New York Times*, October 5, 1970.

JULIA. The television series *Julia* was first broadcast by NBC on September 17, 1968. It was a situation comedy with a serious tone. Julia was a widowed nurse whose husband had been killed in Vietnam. Although the series lasted only until May 25, 1971, when the last episode was broadcast, it is important in television because it was the first regular television series whose star was an African-American woman—Diahann Carroll.

REFERENCE: Diahann Carroll, *Diahann: An Autobiography*, 1986.

K

KAHN, HERMAN. Herman Kahn was born in Bayonne, New Jersey, February 15, 1922. He graduated from the University of California at Los Angeles (UCLA) in 1945 and then completed a master's degree at the California Institute of Technology. Kahn worked as a mathematician for Northrop Aviation until 1948, when he joined the Rand Corporation as a physicist, mathematician, and military analyst. In 1961, he established his own think tank—the Hudson Institute—at Croton-on-Hudson, New York. Among political liberals, Kahn became infamous with the publication of his books *On Thermonuclear War* (1960), *Thinking about the Unthinkable* (1962), and *On Escalation Metaphors and Scenarios* (1965), three books that viewed nuclear war as a reasonable strategic option to protect American national security interests. Critics believed Kahn vastly underestimated the impact of global thermonuclear war. Later in his career, Kahn defined himself as a futurist whose Hudson Institute could advise clients on emerging economic, military, and political trends. He subsequently wrote dozens of other books and studies, including *Can We Win in Vietnam?* (1968), *Why ABM?* (1969), *The Emerging Japanese Superstate* (1970), *Things to Come* (1972), *The Future of the Corporation* (1974), and *The Next Two Hundred Years* (1976). Herman Kahn died July 7, 1983.
REFERENCE: *New York Times*, July 8, 1983.

KATZ V. UNITED STATES. During the 1960s, the Supreme Court under the leadership of Chief Justice Earl Warren* continued its program of broadening individual rights while narrowing those of federal, state, and government officials, particularly in the area of searches and seizures. *Katz v. United States* was decided on December 18, 1967, by a 7 to 1 vote, with Justice Potter Stewart* writing the majority opinion. The decision overturned the Court's earlier opinion in *Olmstead v. United States* (1928), which had declared that electronic surveillance and wiretaps were not technically "searches and seizures" and

therefore not subject to Fourth Amendment search warrant laws. Essentially, the Court determined that the purpose of the Fourth Amendment is to protect people, not places, including voice messages they intend to keep private.
REFERENCE: 389 U.S. 347 (1967).

KATZENBACH, NICHOLAS. Nicholas Katzenbach was born in Philadelphia in 1922. He attended Princeton until joining the army in 1942 and spent most of the war in Italian and German prisoner of war (POW) camps. When the war was over, he returned to Princeton and was allowed to graduate in 1945 by taking special examinations. Katzenbach then received a law degree from Yale in 1947. A Rhodes Scholarship took him to Oxford between 1947 and 1949, and he then returned to the United States to practice law. In 1952 Katzenbach joined the law faculty at Yale, and between 1956 and 1960 he was professor of law at the University of Chicago Law School. With the election of John F. Kennedy* in 1960, Katzenbach came to Washington as an assistant attorney general and he specialized in civil rights issues. He helped draft the Civil Rights Acts of 1964* and 1965.* Katzenbach's reputation for composure under pressure was enhanced in December 1962, when he negotiated the release of prisoners captured by Cuba during the Bay of Pigs* invasion in 1961.

When he became undersecretary of state in 1966, Katzenbach, who had no direct experience with foreign policy, spent his early months reading files and briefs and talking with his colleagues. Yet his experience in the Department of State was less successful than in the office of the attorney general. In an early session with the Senate Foreign Relations Committee, Katzenbach provoked dismay among those who believed that he would continue in the tradition of his predecessor, George Ball,* who did not favor the escalation of the war. Katzenbach, when asked by the committee to interpret the 1964 Gulf of Tonkin Resolution,* argued that in its wording, it supported President Lyndon B. Johnson's* right to escalate the war as he saw fit. In this and other situations, Katzenbach's analytical approach and propensity to reconcile opposing viewpoints led his former admirer to see him as a mere functionary, unwilling to argue against a doubtful policy. Katzenbach was a senior vice president and general counsel for IBM from 1969 to 1981, when he returned to private law practice.
REFERENCE: U. S. Navasky, "No. 2 Man at State Is a Cooler-Downer," *New York Times Magazine*, December 24, 1967.

Joanna Cowden

KENNAN, GEORGE FROST. George Kennan was born February 16, 1904, in Milwaukee, Wisconsin. After graduating from Princeton in 1925, he landed a position with the Foreign Service. Kennan filled a variety of State Department posts, and in 1947 he wrote a highly influential article outlining the "containment* policy" in the journal *Foreign Affairs*. An expert in Soviet affairs, he argued that the United States should accept the political alignment of Europe as it existed at the end of World War II, with the Soviet Union dominating Eastern

Europe, but that any attempts by the Soviets to expand beyond those 1945 political and military boundaries should be "contained." The idea became the backbone of post–World War II U.S. foreign policy and was reflected in the Truman Doctrine, the Marshall Plan, the Berlin Airlift, and the North Atlantic Treaty Organization. After a tour as U.S. ambassador to the Soviet Union in the 1950s, Kennan accepted a position as professor of historical studies at the Institute for Advanced Studies at Princeton. A prolific writer, Kennan was the author of many books, including *American Diplomacy 1900–1950* (1951), *Soviet–American Relations, 1917–1941* (1956), *Soviet Foreign Policy under Lenin and Stalin* (1961), *Realities of American Foreign Policy* (1966), and *Memoirs, 1925–1950* ((1968).

During the Vietnam War,* it was only natural that supporters and opponents of American policy there would seek out Kennan's opinion. The domino theory* when applied to Asia was essentially an extrapolation from Kennan's containment notions. But Kennan disagreed with such an application of his ideas and believed that American policies in Vietnam were misguided. The dominating force in Asia, he believed, was nationalism, not communism. The Kennedy* and Johnson* administrations had erred in committing themselves to a hopelessly corrupt regime in South Vietnam. It would be difficult, if not impossible, for the United States to defeat the Vietcong* militarily and politically, and in any event such a victory would mean little, since the region was not directly connected to America's national security. In February 1966, Kennan said as much before the Senate Foreign Relations Committee, which was investigating U.S. policies in Indochina. He recommended withdrawal of American forces as soon as possible.

Since then, Kennan has continued to lecture and teach. Among his most recent books are *The Nuclear Delusion: Soviet-American Relations in the Atomic Age* (1982), *Soviet-American Relations, 1917–1920* (1984), *Sketches From a Life* (1989), and *Around the Cragged Hill* (1993).

REFERENCES: John L. Harper, *America's Vision of Europe: Franklin D. Roosevelt, George F. Kennan, and Dean C. Acheson*, 1994; George F. Kennan, *Memoirs, 1925–1950*, 1968, *George F. Kennan and the Origins of Containment*, 1997, and *At the Century's End: Reflections*, 1996.

KENNEDY, EDWARD MOORE "TEDDY."

Edward Moore "Teddy" Kennedy was born on Washington's birthday in 1932, the ninth and final child of Joe Kennedy's family. Young Teddy, like his brothers, attended several prestigious New England preparatory schools. During the fall of 1950, he entered Harvard, but he was expelled in 1951 for allowing another student to take a Spanish final for him. Subsequently, he joined the army and spent sixteen months in Europe as a private. In 1953 he was readmitted to Harvard, where he graduated; however, he was rejected by Harvard Law School. Thereupon, he entered the University of Virginia Law School in the autumn of 1957 and graduated in 1959. In 1962 he ran for John F. Kennedy's* vacant Senate seat from

Massachusetts and won by a landslide. Two years later, after a near fatal plane crash, he won reelection, and in 1969 he defeated Russell Long of Louisiana for the majority whip position, which allowed him to push his own legislative agenda.

On July 18, 1969, came the incident that ended Kennedy's chances at the White House and almost cost him his political career—Chappaquiddick.* The incident occurred on the island resort of Martha's Vineyard in Massachusetts around midnight. Kennedy lost control of his car and plunged off a bridge. He managed to escape, but his passenger, Mary Jo Kopechne, drowned. He neglected to report the accident and instead returned to the party the two had been attending and secured the assistance of a former U.S. attorney for the state of Massachusetts, Paul Mackham, and his cousin, Joseph Gargan. They returned to the scene of the accident, but belated attempts to rescue Kopechne failed. Kennedy reportedly swam the channel to the mainland, while his two companions returned to the party, leaving her in the water. Neither Kennedy nor the two men reported the accident to the police.

The wrecked car was spotted the following morning and reported to Edgartown Police Chief Diminich Arena. The vehicle was later identified as belonging to Kennedy. Police launched a search for him, but around 8:30 A.M. Kennedy and his two assistants reported to Edgartown police headquarters. On July 25, 1969, Kennedy pleaded guilty to leaving the scene of an accident and was given a two-month suspended sentence and a one-year probation. The apparent miscarriage of justice gave rise to a widespread belief that a massive cover-up was taking place.

The incident forever tarnished Edward Kennedy's political reputation. He had been partying with a single woman, and when his own driving caused the accident, he had apparently been more worried about his own political career than her life. Although Kennedy survived the incident in the state of Massachusetts and is now serving his sixth term in the U.S. Senate, his chances for national office were forever doomed. In 1972 and again in 1980 he made a run for the Democratic presidential nomination, but in each instance the legacy of Chappaquiddick undermined his campaigns. After Chappaquiddick he lost his majority whip position, but he became the chairman of a Senate subcommittee on health policy, where he used his power to advance a national health plan for all Americans. He has continuously been reelected to his senatorial position and is still a leading senior senator for the Democratic Party.

REFERENCES: James E. T. Lange, *Chappaquiddick: The Real Story*, 1993; Joe McGinniss, *The Last Brother*, 1993.

Jerry Jay Inmon

KENNEDY, JOHN FITZGERALD. John Fitzgerald Kennedy was born in Brookline, Massachusetts, May 29, 1917. His father, Joseph, was a prominent Boston banker, and his mother, Rose Fitzgerald, the daughter of one of Boston's most powerful political families. Obsessive in his desire for his children to be accepted as equals in elite Boston society, Joseph Kennedy decided to groom his oldest son and namesake, Joseph Kennedy, Jr., for the presidency. Surely having his bright, Irish Catholic son in the White House would bring the family respectability. He sent all four of his sons—Joseph, John, Robert, and Edward— to Harvard. John graduated in 1938 with a degree in history.

When World War II broke out, Joseph joined the Royal Canadian Air Force, and John volunteered for PT-boat duty in the U.S. Navy. John's boat was destroyed in the South Pacific, and he earned medals for bravery in rescuing his crew. When brother Joe died in an aircraft explosion over the English Channel, John became the heir apparent, and his father began scheming to build his political career. After the war, John F. Kennedy campaigned for Congress as a war hero, and he won easily as a Democrat. The Kennedy and Fitzgerald names were as good as gold in Massachusetts. In 1950 he defeated Republican Henry Cabot Lodge* for a seat in the U.S. Senate.

Young, handsome, and politically ambitious, Kennedy played it carefully in the Senate, rarely taking a firm political position on any domestic or foreign policy issue. He tried, but failed, to win the Democratic vice presidential nomination in 1956, but in 1960, with Dwight D. Eisenhower* completing his second term in the White House, Kennedy decided to make his own run for the Democratic presidential nomination. In the Democratic primaries, he defeated Lyndon B. Johnson* of Texas and Hubert H. Humphrey* of Minnesota. Vice President Richard Nixon* ran against him on the Republican ticket, and the election was one of the closest in U.S. history. Kennedy did well in the televised debates, which gave him the narrowest margin of victory. On January 20, 1960, John F. Kennedy became the thirty-fourth president of the United States.

During his administration, Kennedy walked a political tightrope on civil rights, trying to appease northern white and African-American Democrats without alienating southern Democrats. Eventually, the civil rights movement* of Martin Luther King, Jr.,* combined with the violent southern reaction to it, pushed Kennedy farther toward the left. By late 1963, he was preparing to submit to Congress a broad-based civil rights bill designed to end racial discrimination in government, public facilities, and employment.

On the foreign policy front, Kennedy was the coldest of cold warriors. After the disastrous Bay of Pigs* fiasco in April 1961, in which a Central Intelligence Agency* (CIA)–backed Cuban exile army invaded Cuba and was quickly defeated by Castro's army, Kennedy assumed an even more aggressive stance. When the Soviets tried to introduce nuclear warheads into Cuba in 1962, the president went to the brink of war, forcing the Russians to back down and withdraw their missiles. He was more circumspect about Vietnam, gradually escalating the U.S. commitment there while hoping to find a way out of the quagmire. In 1963, somewhat alarmed about how close the world had come to nuclear war, Kennedy negotiated the Nuclear Test Ban Treaty* with the Russians, outlawing the atmospheric testing of nuclear weapons. Many historians consider the treaty the beginning of the period of detente between the United States and the Soviet Union.

Because of his youth, charisma, beautiful wife Jacqueline, and two adorable small children, Kennedy was a very popular president, earning almost a cult following in many circles. He radiated an image of confidence, ability, and optimism, and in doing so he defined the values of a generation, calling on his fellow Americans to create a "new frontier."* His assassination on November 22, 1963, shocked the nation and serves as a historical dividing line between the optimism of the early 1960s and the pessimism of the later 1960s. Since then, history has been harsh on Kennedy, emphasizing his marital infidelities and political shortcomings.

REFERENCES: David Burner, *John F. Kennedy and a New Generation*, 1992; Christopher Matthews, *Kennedy and Nixon: The Rivalry That Shaped Postwar America*, 1996; Bruce Miroff, *Pragmatic Illusions: The Presidential Politics of John F. Kennedy*, 1976.

KENNEDY, ROBERT FRANCIS. Robert Kennedy was born in Brookline, Massachusetts, on November 20, 1925. He graduated from Harvard in 1948 and then earned a law degree at the University of Virginia in 1951. During the late 1950s, he served as a staff member during Senator John McClellan's investigation into labor union corruption. In 1959–1960, Kennedy managed his elder brother John F. Kennedy's* successful presidential campaign against Republican Richard M. Nixon.* The new president then appointed his brother to the cabinet as attorney-general. After John F. Kennedy's assassination in November 1963, Robert Kennedy remained in President Lyndon Johnson's* cabinet, but the two men viewed themselves as political rivals. Kennedy resigned in 1964 and won election as U.S. Senator from New York.

Between 1965 and 1967, Kennedy became increasingly concerned about the escalation of the Vietnam War,* even though he had been influential in expanding the U.S. commitment there during his brother's presidential administration. In 1966, he began publicly expressing some of his concerns. On March 16, 1968, he openly broke with Johnson, announced his own candidacy for the upcoming Democratic presidential nomination, and said: "In private talks and in public I have tried in vain to alter our course in Vietnam before it further saps our spirit and our manpower, further raises the risks of wider war, and further destroys the country and the people it was meant to save." He called for an end of the bombing* of North Vietnam and de-escalation. His presidential campaign got a boost when President Johnson decided not to seek reelection. Kennedy vigorously promoted civil rights* and antipoverty legislation as well and soon rivaled Vice-President Hubert Humphrey* as the frontrunner for the nomination. On June 6, 1968, after winning the California Democratic presidential primary, Robert F. Kennedy was assassinated by Sirhan Sirhan.*

REFERENCES: Hoyt Purvis, "Robert F. Kennedy," in James S. Olson, ed., *Dictionary of the Vietnam War*, 1988; Arthur M. Schlesinger, Jr., *Robert F. Kennedy and His Times*, 1979.

THE KENNEDY ASSASSINATION. In preparation for his 1964 bid for re-election, President John F. Kennedy* decided to make a precampaign visit to Texas, primarily to shore up his political position in the conservative state, where right-wing radicals in such groups as the John Birch Society* bitterly attacked him. First Lady Jacqueline Kennedy accompanied the president on his visit to Dallas. They flew into Dallas on the morning of Friday, November 22, 1963, toured the world trade center, and then embarked on a motorcade through the city. A black Lincoln convertible carried the president and his wife.

As the car entered Dealey Plaza, large, enthusiastic crowds greeted the president. The Kennedys were gratified by the reception and stopped worrying about the vitriol being published by far right-wing Texas conservatives. But at precisely 12:30 P.M., shots rang out, apparently coming from a sixth-floor window of the Texas School Book Depository Building. Time seemed to stand still. President Kennedy at first tried to grasp his throat as an assassin's bullet sliced through his neck, but no sooner had he lifted his hand than a second bullet struck the back of his skull. Blood, brain, and bone fragments exploded in a reddish mist, and the president slumped into his seat. Jacqueline Kennedy, in a moment of panic, tried to climb on the trunk of the car in an apparent effort to recover some of the president's brain tissue. Texas governor John Connelly, who was riding in the front seat of the car, was wounded, apparently by the bullet that had passed through the president's neck. The Lincoln then accelerated and took the dying president to Parkland Memorial Hospital, where he was pronounced dead at 1:00 P.M.

A home movie taken by Abraham Zapruder, known as the Zapruder film,* is the only existing camera footage of the tragedy.

Vice President Lyndon B. Johnson,* who had been behind the president in another car, immediately received Secret Service protection and was hustled from Parkland Hospital back to Air Force One. The body of the president, accompanied by the First Lady, soon arrived in a casket and was loaded aboard the jet. There, three hours after Kennedy's death, Johnson took the oath of office as thirty-sixth president of the United States. Mrs. Kennedy, still dressed in her blood-soaked pink suit, witnessed the rapid-fire inauguration. Air Force One then lifted off for its return flight to Washington, D.C.

Later in the afternoon, Dallas police arrested Lee Harvey Oswald,* a twenty-four-year-old employee of the Texas School Book Depository, and charged him with the assassination. Two days later, on Sunday, November 24, Dallas police were moving Oswald from the city jail to a county jail. Millions of television viewers were watching the transfer. While the United States mourned the death of its president and prepared for his funeral, Lee Harvey Oswald was shot and killed by Jack Ruby,* a local Dallas nightclub owner. At the time of his death, Oswald was in police custody at the city jail.

Speculation about the assassination began immediately. Lee Harvey Oswald had a politically checkered past, having spent time in Cuba and the Soviet Union after an unsuccessful stint in the Marine Corps. In the Cold War* climate of the

United States in 1963, the fact that Oswald had communist connections only stimulated the American inclination to start looking for conspiracies. Oswald's murder while in police custody by a shady character with links to organized crime in Dallas only fueled the speculation. That Kennedy's death occurred in superconservative Dallas and that the vice president was a Texan provided conspiracy afficionados with another conspiracy theory. Suspected Communist sympathizers ("Commies"), Texans, and organized crime all became objects of conspiratorial speculation.

President Lyndon B. Johnson moved quickly against the rumor mongering and appointed a special commission headed by Earl Warren,* chief justice of the U.S. Supreme Court, to investigate the murder of the president. Johnson was anxious to put the assassination behind him and get on with his own presidency.

The Warren Commission conducted its investigation with dispatch, perhaps too much dispatch, and reached its conclusions late in 1964. Lee Harvey Oswald, they concluded, had acted alone, in spite of questions that he could not have fired three shots so rapidly and that some witnesses claimed to have heard shots fired from a grassy knoll in front of the motorcade. Jack Ruby was not part of the conspiracy, the commission claimed, but had killed Oswald in a rage over the death of the president.

Few Americans were satisfied with the report of the Warren Commission. Throughout the rest of the century, a host of books, films, and articles examined the assassination, but nobody ever came up with a theory that explained the tragedy consistent with the forensic evidence. Since then, Americans have never tired of wondering whether Fidel Castro,* the Central Intelligence Agency* (CIA), communists, right-wing fascists, the Soviet KGB, Lyndon Johnson, or the Mafia had anything to do with Kennedy's death.

REFERENCES: William Manchester, *The Death of a President*, 1965; Gerald L. Posner, *Case Closed*, 1994.

KENNEDY REPORT. By the late 1960s, the movement against termination* and for Indian civil rights was gaining momentum, and a number of prominent political liberals took up the Indian cause. One of these liberals was Senator Edward (Ted) Kennedy,* Democrat from Massachusetts. Late in 1968, several months after the assassination of his brother, Senator Robert F. Kennedy* of New York, Ted Kennedy inherited his brother's crusade for Indian rights. The Indian Education Subcommittee of the U.S. Senate had been conducting a study of Indian education, and in 1969, they published their findings as *Indian Education: A National Tragedy—A National Challenge*.

Also called the Kennedy Report, the document argued that the basic conditions of Indian education had not changed since the 1920s. In many ways, there had been little progress since the Meriam Report of 1928. The Kennedy report stated that racism, poverty, discrimination, cultural oppression, absenteeism, and academic underachievement still plagued Native American education. The report condemned the termination* program, called for the addition of Native American history, culture, and language to school curricula, and insisted that Indian parents and tribal leaders should be intimately involved in local school decision making. Many of the recommendations of the Kennedy Report were implemented in the Indian Education Act of 1972.

REFERENCES: David H. DeJong, *Promises of the Past: A History of Indian Education in the United States*, 1993; Margaret Connell Szasz, *Education and the American Indian: The Road to Self-Determination since 1928*, 1977.

KENNEDY ROUND. The term ''Kennedy Round'' refers to a series of tariff negotiations among the prominent economic powers of the world. The General Agreement on Tariffs and Trade (GATT) in 1947 had provided for periodic tariff negotiations, and the Kennedy Round was the sixth of those meetings. It began after Congress passed the Trade Expansion Act of 1962.* U.S. trade with Europe was languishing, and in 1957 France, Italy, Germany, Belgium, Luxembourg, and the Netherlands had created the European Economic Community. American policymakers wanted to make sure that European markets remained open to U.S. products. The Kennedy Round began in Geneva with the goal of achieving mutual tariff reductions. Fifty-three nations participated in the talks, and they eventually agreed to mutual tariff reductions averaging 35 to 40 percent.

REFERENCE: John W. Evans, *The Kennedy Round in American Trade Policy*, 1971.

KERNER REPORT. Because of the deadly urban riots that erupted in the mid-1960s in Harlem, Los Angeles, Newark, and Detroit, President Lyndon B. Johnson* established a Commission on Civil Disorder in 1967. Governor Otto Kerner of Illinois chaired the commission. In March 1968, the Kerner Report was issued. It denied that communist subversion had anything to do with the riots and instead looked to domestic economic and social problems. Most rioters were unemployed young men who had dropped out of high school and who feared and/or hated the police. The report identified high urban crime rates, poverty, lack of educational opportunity, lack of health facilities, poor ghetto services, and extremely high unemployment as the real causes of urban discontent. America could not expect an end to rioting until the causes of urban blight had been addressed. The commission also agreed, however, that the media had grossly exaggerated the extent of the rioting. The Kerner Report identified 164 ''racial disorders,'' of which eight were deemed ''major'' and thirty-three ''serious.'' There was no evidence of a nationwide conspiracy to incite the riots. They were, on the other hand, spontaneous rebellions growing out of severe economic, social, and political problems in urban America. One month after the Kerner Report was issued, Martin Luther King, Jr.,* was assassinated. Spontaneously, arson, rioting, and looting erupted in 125 American cities.

REFERENCE: Kerner Commission, *The Kerner Report*, 1968.

KEROUAC, JACK. Jack Kerouac was born March 12, 1922, to a French Canadian family in Lowell, Massachusetts. He was a free spirit from the very beginning. Kerouac got a football scholarship to Columbia University in 1940, but he quit after two years. Academe was too stifling. He then joined the navy but did not last long. If Columbia was stifling to him, the navy was absolutely repressive. Kerouac was also too much for the navy. They discharged him when he kept marching off in whatever direction suited him during close-order drill. Kerouac spent the next eight years living around Columbia in the Morningside Heights neighborhood, where the urban literary community seemed full of vitality and energy. There he became part of the emerging "beat* generation" of writers and iconoclasts.

His most famous work and the one that cemented his reputation as a leading light of the beat movement was *On the Road* (1957). The leading characters are Sal Paradise and Dean Moriarty, who drive back and forth across America, living a life somewhere between that of hoboes and that of Bohemians. They visited a host of beat friends along the way, and in a stream of consciousness dialogue they promoted a culture of rebellion and the importance of individual liberation in a society of rigid social convention, conformity, and private property.

Like other writers of the beat generation, Kerouac helped prepare America for the counterculture* of the 1960s, even if that counterculture eventually eclipsed his literary and cultural influence. Before the free speech movement* at Berkeley, the hippies,* and the civil rights* crusade, there was Jack Kerouac's *On the Road*, a beat novel celebrating the individual over the group, rebellion over conformity, and freedom over conventional discipline.

Kerouac also delved into Buddhism, an interest that found expression in his 1959 novel *The Dharma Bums*. Kerouac shunned New York literary society, preferring the seclusion of rural homes in Northport, Long Island, New York, and Lowell, Massachusetts. Kerouac died October 21, 1969.

REFERENCES: Ann Charter, *Kerouac: A Biography*, 1973; Dennis McNally, *Desolate Angel: Jack Kerouac, the Beat Generation, and America*, 1979; Michael White, ed., *Safe in Heaven Dead: Interviews with Jack Kerouac*, 1990.

KESEY, KENNETH. Kenneth Kesey was born September 17, 1935, in La Junta, Colorado. He became famous on the merits of his novel *One Flew over the Cuckoo's Nest*, which was published in 1962. The book featured Randall McMurphy, a petty criminal who has faked his way into a mental hospital to avoid hard time at the penitentiary. The setting is a mental hospital ward, presided over by the sinister, passive-aggressive nurse Ratchet, who is more interested in controlling, than in curing, her patients.

The real enemy in *Cuckoo's Nest* is what Kesey called "the Combine," an amorphous, institutional entity in charge of modern industrial, bureaucratic society and responsible for the social and political conventions that inhibit individual freedom. Nurse Ratchet and the mental hospital are symbols of that new world order, which denies individual freedom and responsibility. McMurphy is a rebel bent on liberating his fellow patients from the nurse's malignant manipulations. He becomes especially close to Chief Broom, a six-foot-eight-inch Indian who also understands, as does McMurphy, that the enemy of individual happiness is "the Combine." When McMurphy's rebelliousness eventually earns him a lobotomy, Broom liberates him from this new imprisonment through death. After killing McMurphy, Broom escapes from the hospital and inspires the other patients to their own individual forms of rebellion.

In other novels, like *Sometimes a Great Notion* (1964), Kesey kept up the same refrain: individuals should follow their own personal instincts and not be forced into conformity by social convention or interest group coercion. Literary historians today look back on Kesey's work as a transitional link between the "beat* generation" of the 1950s and the counterculture* of the 1970s. Among Kesey's other works are *Garage Sale* (1973), *Demon Box* (1986), *Little Trickler the Squirrel Meets Big Double Bear* (1988), *The Further Inquiry* (1990), and *The Sea Lion* (1991). Since 1974, Kesey has also served as editor and publisher of the magazine *Spit in the Ocean*.

REFERENCES: Barry H. Leeds, *Ken Kesey*, 1981; M. Gilbert Porter, *The Art of Grit: Ken Kesey's Fiction*, 1982; Stephen L. Tanner, *Ken Kesey*, 1983; Tom Wolfe, *The Electric Kool-Aid Acid Test*, 1968.

KEYISHIAN V. BOARD OF REGENTS. The Supreme Court under Chief Justice Earl Warren* earned a reputation for limiting the powers of the state and enhancing the rights and freedoms of individuals. That was especially true in how the Court interpreted First Amendment issues during the 1960s, including the freedom of association clause. New York had enacted legislation disqualifying members of the Communist Party from teaching in the public schools. The Court decided *Keyishian v. Board of Regents* on January 23, 1967, by a 5 to 4 vote. Justice William Brennan* wrote the majority opinion, overthrowing the law as an unconstitutional violation of the freedom of association clause of the First Amendment.

REFERENCE: 385 U.S. 589 (1967).

KHE SANH, BATTLE OF (1967–68). The Battle of Khe Sanh, one of the pivotal confrontations between U.S. and North Vietnamese forces during the Vietnam War,* was actually a decoy on the part of North Vietnam, an attempt to confuse American military officials on the eve of the Tet Offensive* of January 1968. Khe Sanh was located in Quang Tri Province of South Vietnam, approximately eight miles east of the Laotian border and eighteen miles south of the Demilitarized Zone* (DMZ). The United States had maintained a Special Forces* base there since 1962, but in 1967 General William Westmoreland* decided that Khe Sanh had acquired a new strategic significance. With an increase in the U.S. military contingent there, Westmoreland intended to launch secret U.S. missions into Laos, conduct reconaissance flights over the Ho Chi Minh Trail* to interrupt the flow of North Vietnamese supplies into South Vietnam, and stop the infiltration of North Vietnamese troops into South Vietnam. He even considered using Khe Sanh as a staging area for a possible U.S. invasion of Laos, if President Lyndon B. Johnson* would approve such an escalation of the war. Westmoreland's plans became even more compelling in 1966 when U.S. intelligence reported an increase in the infiltration of North Vietnamese troops into the area. Westmoreland had the airstrip at Khe Sanh extended so that it could handle larger aircraft, and he deployed the two marine battalions to the region. By mid-1967, army intelligence learned of massive increases of troop movements along the Ho Chi Minh Trail, and Westmoreland decided that the enemy was planning a major offensive, with Khe Sanh as a key to the line of attack.

Actually, it was all a North Vietnamese ploy. As a preliminary to the upcoming Tet Offensive,* in which Vietcong* troops would attack cities and towns throughout South Vietnam, they wanted Westmoreland to pull U.S. troops out of major cities and relocate them to border areas like Khe Sanh. By November 1967, the North Vietnamese had put three full divisions of troops—25,000 to 35,000 soldiers—into the environs surrounding Khe Sanh, and Westmoreland was certain that the invasion was imminent. Westmoreland then launched Operation Niagara, deploying 6,000 more marines to Khe Sanh and subjecting the North Vietnamese to a pulverizing artillery and aerial bombardment. The so-called siege of Khe Sanh commenced on January 21, 1968.

But the attack on Khe Sanh and the anticipated North Vietnamese invasion of South Vietnam along Route 9 never took place. Ten days after the siege of Khe Sanh began, the Vietcong launched the Tet Offensive throughout South Vietnam, and Khe Sanh was suddenly swallowed up in that much larger conflict. Early in March 1968, the North Vietnamese troops simply withdrew from Khe Sanh, their mission accomplished. They had tricked Westmoreland into thinking that a major invasion was underway and left him less prepared to handle the Tet Offensive.

The Tet Offensive did not achieve all the results that North Vietnam and the Vietcong had hoped to achieve. It did not lead to a popular uprising of the South Vietnamese against their own government or to massive defections among South Vietnamese military forces. Worse yet, the Vietcong sustained more than 70,000 deaths, all but eliminating them as a military factor in the war. However Tet had been a huge political victory for North Vietnam because back in the United States, the antiwar movement* gained a tremendous boost, and pressure mounted for U.S. withdrawal from the conflict.

REFERENCES: Eric M. Hammel, *Khe Sanh: Siege in the Clouds: An Oral History*, 1989; Andrew F. Krepinevich, Jr., *The Army in Vietnam*, 1986; Robert Pisor, *The End of the Line: The Siege of Khe Sanh*, 1982; William Westmoreland, *A Soldier Reports*, 1976.

KHRUSHCHEV, NIKITA. Nikita Khrushchev was born in Ukraine, Russia, in 1894 to a family of very poor pig farmers. He joined the Communist Party in 1918, proved adept at party politics, rising through the party ranks by demonstrating constant loyalty to Joseph Stalin, premier of the Soviet Union, and by exhibiting considerable political and administrative abilities. In 1934, Khrushchev was appointed to the central committee, and in 1939 he became a member of the politburo. After Stalin's death, Khrushchev maneuvered his way to the top of the power structure, becoming first secretary of the Communist Party in 1953 and then premier in 1958. Khrushchev was premier of the Soviet Union during the crises over the U-2* flight in 1960, the city of Berlin* in 1961, and the Cuban missile crisis* in 1962. The increasing American commitment in Indochina troubled Khrushchev because he did not know how the People's Republic of China would respond. Khrushchev did not want to see another Korea in Southeast Asia. In 1964, Khrushchev was removed from the premiership. Political rivals believed that he had handled the Cuban missile crisis poorly, and terrible agricultural harvests, as well as increasing tensions with China, undermined him politically. He lived out the rest of his life in obscurity, dying in 1971.
REFERENCES: Michael Beschloss, *The Crisis Years: Kennedy and Khrushchev*, 1991; Nikita Khrushchev, *Khrushchev Remembers*, 1970.

KING, MARTIN LUTHER, JR. Martin Luther King, Jr., was born January 15, 1929, in Atlanta, Georgia. His parents first named him Michael Luther King, but when he was six, they changed it to Martin Luther King, Jr., after his father, Martin Luther King, who was pastor of the Ebenezer Baptist Church in Atlanta. The younger King graduated from Morehouse College in 1948 and the Crozer Theological Seminary in 1951 and then took a Ph.D. in theology from Boston University in 1955. King rocketed into the national consciousness as leader of the Montgomery bus boycott in 1955 and 1956, and in 1957 he established the Southern Christian Leadership Conference* to fight segregation. In 1960, King was one of the founding members of the Student Nonviolent Coordinating Committee.* Inspired by the passive disobedience of Mohandas Gandhi in India, he applied those same tactics to the American South, leading demonstrations, sit-ins,* boycotts, and protest marches. His speech in 1963 in front of the Lincoln Memorial during the civil rights movement's* March on Washington* was among the most eloquent in U.S. history. When Congress passed the Civil Rights Act of 1964* and the Voting Rights Act of 1965,* it was largely in response to the moral crusade Martin Luther King, Jr., had generated in the United States.

Beginning in 1965, King's leadership of the civil rights movement was challenged by the rise of black power* advocates, who had little patience for his nonviolent civil disobedience philosophy. At about the same time, King developed serious misgivings about the Vietnam War,* seeing it as a misguided effort on the part of the United States that the Third World would interpret as simply another attempt by the white, industrialized West to colonize the rest of the world. King was also disturbed by the effect of the draft* on the black community and the inordinately large numbers of casualties* black soldiers* were sustaining in 1965 and 1966. In 1967, he openly protested the Vietnam War and linked the civil rights and antiwar movements* together, a step that earned him the ire of President Lyndon Johnson* and most civil rights leaders. Other civil rights leaders, both black and white, worried that linking the two movements would only dissipate the force of the campaign for equality. But King was convinced that the Vietnam War was diverting financial and emotional resources away from domestic programs and into a futile effort abroad. By 1968 the rest of the country was slowly coming around to King's point of view, but his voice was stilled by an assassin on April 4, 1968.

REFERENCE: Stephen B. Oates, *Let the Trumpet Sound: The Life of Martin Luther King, Jr.*, 1982.

THE KING ASSASSINATION. Rev. Martin Luther King, Jr., first emerged on the national scene in 1955, when he took over leadership of the Montgomery, Alabama, bus boycott. During the next thirteen years, he became one of the most influential and controversial men in the United States. White liberals and African Americans viewed him as the man of the century—a gifted, visionary leader responsible for bringing to an end more than a century of the rankest forms of formal racial discrimination in the United States. Critics accused him of being a communist, a philanderer, and a black radical intent on overthrowing the social structure of the South.

King became even more controversial after 1965, when he began addressing other issues. He came out against the war in Vietnam, and he called for a national crusade to eliminate poverty in America. He was preparing for the Poor People's March* on Washington, D.C., for the spring of 1968. King also decided to travel to Memphis, Tennessee, to lend support to a strike by garbage collectors who wanted better pay. Early in April, he arrived in Memphis and delivered several impassioned speeches to garbage workers, civil rights groups, and black church congregations.

But King was being stalked in Memphis by a violent white racist intent on killing him. James Earl Ray* was a poor drifter who blamed Martin Luther King, Jr., for all of the problems in his personal life. On the afternoon of April 4, 1968, while King was relaxing on a balcony at his Memphis hotel, Ray took careful aim and put a bullet through the civil rights leader's neck. King died quickly, and Ray fled.

News of King's assassination spread within minutes across the United States. For tens of millions of African Americans, he had been the greatest leader of all time, and his death came first as a shock and then as a source of rage. Riots erupted spontaneously in cities throughout the country as black people took their anger to the streets. Ray fled the country but was apprehended later. In a subsequent trial, he was convicted of murder and sentenced to life in prison. Since his assassination, King has become a martyred hero in the black community, his life symbolic of the suffering and triumph of African America.

James Earl Ray continues to deny that he murdered Martin Luther King, Jr. In 1997, when Ray was facing death because of advanced liver disease, he again pleaded for another trial. He received support for his request from members of Martin Luther King's family, who worried that an official conspiracy to cover up details of the killing might have originated at the highest levels of the U.S. government. Although a federal judge did authorize new ballistics tests on the alleged murder weapon, Ray was not granted a new trial.

REFERENCES: Joan Turner Beifuss, *At the River I Stand: Memphis, the 1968 Strike, and Martin Luther King*, 1989; Michael K. Honey, *Southern Labor and Black Civil Rights: Organizing Memphis Workers*, 1993; *New York Times*, April 5–10, 1968; Stephen B. Oates, *Let the Trumpet Sound: The Life of Martin Luther King, Jr.*, 1982.

KISSINGER, HENRY ALFRED. Henry Kissinger was born May 27, 1923, in Furth, Germany. Life during the 1930s in Hitler's Germany was difficult for Jews, and in 1938 the Kissinger family decided to emigrate to America. Henry was a brilliant child, intellectually and politically, but instead of going to college, he joined the U.S. Army during World War II. He was assigned to the European theater, where he worked as a translator and in military intelligence. Kissinger enrolled at Harvard in 1946 and received his degree there in 1950. Determined to pursue an academic career, he went on to graduate school at Harvard, receiving a master's degree in 1952 and a Ph.D. in international relations in 1954. His doctoral dissertation was a study of the Congress of Vienna in 1815, which brought about the European peace settlement following the Napoleonic Wars.

At Harvard, Kissinger had a distinguished, indeed brilliant, academic career, so impressing his professors that they decided to add him to the faculty as soon as he received his Ph.D. By the late 1950s and early 1960s, Kissinger had become a leading figure in what became known as the ''nuclear strategy'' movement—a group of professors and intellectuals who viewed thermonuclear war as a key element in any rational defense policy. In 1957, Kissinger wrote *Nuclear War and Foreign Policy*, a book that defended the notion that nuclear weapons could be employed to the nation's advantage. It was an extremely controversial book and subjected Kissinger to intense criticism from those opposed to the arms race. Between 1960 and 1967, Kissinger worked as a defense consultant to the Kennedy and Johnson administrations and as a foreign policy advisor to Nelson Rockefeller,* the Republican governor of New York, who was considering a presidential bid. In 1969, newly elected President Richard M. Nixon* appointed Kissinger as his special assistant for national security affairs.

From the outset of the Nixon administration, Kissinger knew that a military victory in Vietnam was impossible. At the same time, he believed that unilateral withdrawal was out of the question because it would undermine American credibility around the world. Instead, he wanted to find a way to return the war to the South Vietnamese and gradually disengage the United States, a process that became known, in June 1969, as "Vietnamization."* Nixon announced a phased withdrawal of U.S. troops. At the same time, Kissinger felt that the government of South Vietnam was so corrupt that even with billions of dollars and unlimited amounts of war matériel, South Vietnam would not be able to defeat the Vietcong* and North Vietnamese. So Kissinger decided to convince North Vietnam, with the threat of military escalation and promises of U.S. economic assistance, to end the war diplomatically.

During the first term of the Nixon administration, Kissinger's convictions produced an intense diplomatic effort to find a credible way out of the war, but he had underestimated the intransigence, or the commitment, of the Vietcong* and North Vietnamese. They insisted on cessation of U.S. bombing* raids over North Vietnam, complete withdrawal of all U.S. forces from the theater of operations, removal from power of President Nguyen Van Thieu* of South Vietnam, and formal installation of the National Liberation Front (the political arm of the Vietcong) as a part of the new government of South Vietnam. Kissinger found those terms unacceptable. Instead, he wanted a mutual withdrawal of U.S. and North Vietnamese forces, refused to incorporate the National Liberation front into the South Vietnamese government, and insisted on leaving Nguyen Van Thieu in power.

For the next four years, Kissinger found himself mired in diplomatic negotiations with North Vietnam, and little progress was made. He also worked hard at exploiting strategic rivalries between the Soviet Union and the People's Republic of China, hoping to improve U.S. relations with both by increasing each country's fear of a U.S. rapprochement with the other. As part of that scheme, President Nixon visited Beijing in February 1972 and Moscow in May 1972.

By early 1971, it was clear to everyone that the United States' negotiating position had to change. The antiwar movement* at home had dramatically increased political pressures to get out of Vietnam, while North Vietnam's success in pursuing the war only encouraged it to greater resistance. Also, it had become obvious, with the withdrawal of so many U.S. troops, that it was only a matter of time before the United States was out of the war altogether. To avoid images of a U.S. military defeat, Kissinger began modifying the U.S. diplomatic position. In the summer of 1972, the negotiations began to produce results because the United States agreed to a unilateral withdrawal of its forces from the war and allowed North Vietnam to leave its troops in place in South Vietnam. In October 1972, the agreement was set, although it almost unraveled in December. A massive bombing* campaign by the United States brought North Vietnam back to the diplomatic table, and the Paris Peace Accords* were signed in January 1973. The war was over, at least as far as the United States was concerned.

Henry Kissinger became secretary of state in September 1973, but he spent much of the next eleven months trying to maintain U.S. foreign policy during the Watergate crisis. He remained in office after Nixon resigned in August 1974, and served as secretary of state until Jimmy Carter, a Democrat, took office as president in January 1977. Since that time, Kissinger has written and lectured widely on foreign policy issues.

REFERENCES: Seymour Hersh, *The Price of Power: Kissinger in the Nixon White House*, 1983; Walter Isaacson, *Kissinger: A Biography*, 1992; Henry A. Kissinger, *White House Years*, 1979, and *Years of Upheaval*, 1982; Robert D. Schulzinger, *The Doctor of Diplomacy: Henry Kissinger*, 1989; William Shawcross, *Sideshow: Kissinger, Nixon, and the Destruction of Cambodia*, 1979.

KOMER, ROBERT WILLIAM. Robert Komer was born in Chicago, Illinois, on February 23, 1932. He graduated from Harvard in 1942 and then joined the U.S. Army, where he was assigned to military intelligence. After the war, he earned an MBA at Harvard and then signed on the with fledgling Central Intelligence Agency (CIA). He became a Middle East expert, and in 1960 he was appointed to the National Security Council. In 1965, Komer became deputy special assistant to President Lyndon B. Johnson,* focusing his attention on the Vietnam War,* and in 1966 Johnson named him special assistant to the president.

Komer felt that the United States could prevail in Vietnam if counterinsurgency* was emphasized and if U.S. military planners respected to the political dimensions of the war. He was also certain that a military approach to the war, without large-scale social and economic development, was doomed. Victory in Vietnam depended upon the United States winning the support of the South Vietnamese people, and too much artillery, napalm,* B-52s, chemical defoliation, and destruction of ancestral villages would only alienate them further.

In May 1967, President Johnson sent Komer to Saigon as civilian deputy to General William Westmoreland,* commander of U.S. forces in Vietnam. Komer founded the Civil Operations and Revolutionary Development Support (CORDS) program to generate Vietnamese support for the war. It was a failure. The antiwar movement* was eroding political support for the war at home, and the president was anxious for a quick solution. Social and economic development was long term, so the military solution prevailed. But increased bombing and battles only left Vietnamese more resentful of the U.S. presence in their country. In 1968, Komer left South Vietnam to become ambassador to Turkey.

When Richard Nixon* and the Republicans took over the White House in 1969, Komer joined the Rand Corporation as an intelligence analyist. He remained there until 1977, when Democratic President Jimmy Carter appointed him as an advisor to NATO. In 1979, Komer became undersecretary for policy in the Defense Department. In 1981, he joined the faculty of George Washington University. He is the author of *Maritime Strategy or Coalition Defense?* (1984) and *Bureaucracy at War* (1986).

REFERENCES: David Halberstam, *The Best and the Brightest*, 1972; Robert W. Komer, *Bureaucracy Does Its Thing: Institutional Constraints on US-GVN Performance*, 1972.

KUHLMAN, KATHRYN. Kathryn Kuhlman was born in Concordia, Missouri, May 9, 1907. When she was sixteen years old, she joined an itinerant tent revival campaign and spent the next ten years preaching on the road. She studied for a time under the healing evangelist Charles S. Price in Oregon, where she developed her own telltale style: baptism of the Holy Spirit and the miraculous healing of the sick. She received ministerial credentials from the Evangelical Church Alliance in 1934. That same year, she built the Kuhlman Revival Tabernacle in Denver, which attracted huge crowds. In 1938, her ministry began to disintegrate under the cloud of sexual scandal. Evangelist Burroughs Waltrip had left his own wife and two children to marry Kuhlman.

They moved to Los Angeles for several years, but Kuhlman left Waltrip in 1944 and returned to the itinerant circuit, where she rebuilt her reputation. Two years later, she constructed the Gospel Revival Tabernacle and gained a large following in western Pennsylvania. She added radio to her preaching, and by the early 1950s she was well known in Ohio, Pennsylvania, West Virginia, and Indiana. In her services, she emphasized healing. In 1962, her book *I Believe in Miracles* became a best-seller. Five years later, Kuhlman's CBS weekly religious program was carried by sixty major television stations, and she had become one of the best-known evangelists in the United States. She went on to write ten more books. Kathryn Kuhlman died February 20, 1976.

REFERENCE: Jamie Buckingham, *Daughter of Destiny: Kathryn Kuhlman, Her Story*, 1976.

KUNTSLER, WILLIAM. William Kuntsler was born July 7, 1919, in New York City and grew up in Manhattan. He graduated from Yale in 1942 and then joined the U.S. Army, winning a Bronze Star for combat in the Pacific theater. When Kuntsler returned home after the war, he earned his law degree at Columbia. He practiced law during the 1950s, but the civil rights movement* radicalized him, and he became legal adviser to Rev. Martin Luther King, Jr.,* during the mid-1960s. Kuntsler then spent the rest of his career defending politically and sometimes socially unpopular clients. "My purpose," he once told a reporter, "is to keep the state from becoming all-domineering." In 1969, he defended the Chicago Eight* in their trial for conspiracy to riot and disrupt the 1968 Democratic National Convention* in Chicago. Subsequently, he accepted as clients El Sayyid Nosair, the man accused of murdering Jewish militant Meier Kahane; Ibrahim El-Gabrowney, accused in the 1993 bombing of the World Trade Center; and Qubilah Shabazz, the daughter of Malcolm X,* when she was accused of conspiracy to murder Nation of Islam leader Louis Farrakhan. William Kuntsler died September 3, 1995.

REFERENCE: *New York Times*, September 4, 1995.

L

LAIRD, MELVIN. Melvin Laird was born September 1, 1922. After eight terms as a U.S. congressman from Wisconsin, Laird became secretary of defense in the Richard Nixon* administration. He kept the post until 1972. Laird was the chief architect of Nixon's "Vietnamization"* program of phased troop withdrawals beginning in the spring of 1969. He often reminded Nixon of the campaign promise to bring the war to an honorable conclusion. Otherwise, Nixon would lose all of his goodwill with Congress and the American people, who were anxious to put an end to the Vietnam War.* Frequently, Laird found himself debating the issue with national security adviser Henry Kissinger,* who feared that rapid troop withdrawals would undermine his negotiating position with North Vietnam. Laird also opposed widespread bombing* of North Vietnam. Laird retired from public life after Nixon's reelection in 1972.
REFERENCE: John S. Lieby, "Melvin Laird," in James S. Olson, ed., *Dictionary of the Vietnam War*, 1988.

LASER. The first operational laser appeared in 1960. Theodore Maiman was a physicist with the Hughes Research Laboratories in Miami, Florida. Maiman managed to stimulate the chromium atoms within a ruby crystal, from which a narrow beam of light emerged with a temperature equal to that of the sun. It was a scientific development of extraordinary significance, because it opened up a technological world that would eventually include fiberoptic cable, compact discs, radar detectors, bar-code scanners, and a host of other technologies.
REFERENCE: Lorraine Glennon, ed., *Our Times: The Illustrated History of the 20th Century*, 1995.

LASSIE. *Lassie* was one of television's* longest-running and most successful regular series. CBS first broadcast the show on September 12, 1954, with Lassie, a male collie, starring as the female Lassie and Tommy Rettig as Jeff Miller,

Jan Clayton as his mother, Ellen, and George Cleveland as Gramps. Since the show lasted until 1971, the cast changed over the years, but the themes did not. *Lassie* was a boy-loves-smart-dog and smart-dog-loves-boy adventure series set in rural, 1950s America. The Miller family was poor but hardworking, quintessential yeoman farmers in Jeffersonian terms, the backbone of America. *Lassie* survived the rancor of the 1960s because of its rural, homespun quality. The last episode was telecast on September 12, 1971.

REFERENCE: Ace Collins, Lassie: *A Dog's Life: The First Fifty Years*, 1993.

LAUGH-IN. See **ROWAN AND MARTIN'S** *LAUGH-IN*.

THE LAWRENCE WELK SHOW. *The Lawrence Welk Show* was a weekly musical variety program produced by ABC. Hosted by Lawrence Welk, it was first broadcast on July 2, 1955. Welk offered the old-fashioned to his viewers— old-fashioned music in an era of rock and roll, old-fashioned ballroom dancing, square dancing, and polkas in the age of the stomp and the twist, and old-fashioned homilies in an age of rebellion. Over the years the audiences became steadily older, but they were faithful. ABC canceled the show after its last broadcast on September 4, 1971, but it continued in syndication until 1982.

REFERENCE: Tim Brooks and Earle Marsh, *The Complete Directory to Prime Time Network and Cable TV Shows*, 1995.

LE DUC THO. Born in 1910 in Nam Ha Province in Tonkin, Le Duc Tho was North Vietnam's principal negotiator at the Paris peace talks.* The son of a French functionary in the Vietnamese colonial government, Le was educated in French schools before joining the revolution. He spent years in jail and in hiding because of his revolutionary activities and helped found both the Indochinese Communist Party and the Vietminh. During the French Indochina War he was chief commissar for southern Vietnam and maintained primary responsibility for the region after U.S. intervention ended.

The Paris peace talks formally began on May 13, 1968, and deadlocked immediately. Le insisted that U.S. bombing* of North Vietnam must stop before anything else could be negotiated. While his position was firm, Le apparently had considerable discretion in how to pursue negotiations until Ho Chi Minh's* death in September 1969. After that, North Vietnamese decision making became collegial, and Le reported to the collective leadership. Beginning February 21, 1970, Le met secretly with Henry Kissinger* for two years. Seeing the military and political struggles as part of the same overall conflict, Le maintained a negotiating position throughout that any agreement must simultaneously resolve both issues. Furthermore, any armistice must include replacement of Nguyen Van Thieu's* government with a coalition that included the Vietcong.*

In order to effect American withdrawal from Vietnam, Le ultimately made concessions on these points. The principal provision of the October 1972 agreement allowed Thieu to remain in power, with 150,000 North Vietnamese army* troops remaining in South Vietnam. Thieu angrily rejected the agreement, and all sides sought "modifications." Renewed negotiations stalled in December. They were soon back on track, however, and an agreement almost identical to the October agreement was signed in Paris on January 27, 1973. Although the cease-fire never took place, President Richard Nixon* proclaimed "peace with honor." The settlement really provided only a face-saving "decent interval" before the Vietnamese finally settled the issue among themselves. With the agreements being roundly violated by all parties, Le Duc Tho and Henry Kissinger attempted in June 1973 to effect better observance of them, but there were no substantive results. Both men were awarded the Nobel Peace Prize, but Tho refused to accept, contending it would be inappropriate until there was genuine peace in Vietnam. In 1975, Le Duc Tho returned to South Vietnam to oversee the final assault on Saigon.* Between 1975 and 1986, he served on the politburo in Hanoi* and as the Lao Dong Party's* chief theoretician, but he resigned his post in December 1986 because of continuing economic troubles in the Socialist Republic of Vietnam. Le Duc Tho died October 13, 1990.

REFERENCES: Stanley Karnow, *Vietnam: A History*, 1983; *Washington Post*, December 18, 1986, and October 14, 1990.

Samuel Freeman

LEAGUE OF UNITED LATIN AMERICAN CITIZENS. The League of United Latin American Citizens (LULAC) was established in 1929 to promote civil rights for Mexican Americans* in the United States. After World War II, LULAC focused its attention on desegregation and voting rights, goals that were consistent with those of the African-American civil rights movement.* By the late 1960s, with a membership approaching 100,000 people, most of whom were middle- and upper-class Mexican Americans, and more than 235 organized chapters, LULAC was the most influential Mexican-American advocacy group in the United States.

REFERENCE: Matt S. Meier and Feliciano Rivera, *Dictionary of Mexican American History*, 1981.

LEARY, TIMOTHY. "Tune in. Turn on. Drop out." Those are the words most people recall when they think of Dr. Timothy Leary. Leary was born in Springfield, Massachusetts, in 1920. He entered the U.S. Military Academy at West Point in 1940, but the military regimen did not suit him. After being implicated in a drunken party on a troop train, he left the academy in 1941. He switched to psychology and eventually earned a Ph.D. from the University of California at Berkeley. Brilliant and innovative, Leary brought a new perspective to the discipline. He was convinced that what most people considered abnormal behavior was only an exaggeration of a normal personality. In 1957, Leary's book *The Interpersonal Diagnosis of Personality* was a huge intellectual success and established his reputation as one of the leading lights in American psychology. He joined the Harvard faculty in 1959.

In 1960, while on a trip to Mexico, a colleague suggested that he eat a fungus known locally as "magic mushrooms," and he did. The experience changed his life. That day, he later wrote, "I learned that consciousness and intelligence can be systematically expanded. The brain can be reprogrammed." Leary became the most prominent of a group of Harvard psychologists conducting experiments concerning the usefulness of psychoactive drugs like psilocbyin and LSD. What was unusual about the scientific protocol was the fact that Leary was testing the drugs on himself and graduate students. He also conducted experiments and "turned on" such individuals as Aldous Huxley, Allen Ginsberg,* Jack Kerouac,* and Neal Cassady. As soon as their involvement with Leary became known, public interest in his work grew rapidly. Leary began traveling around the country lecturing, praising the virtues of drug use. The lectures introduced him to the Hollywood crowd and gave him the opportunity of having drug experiences with Marilyn Monroe* and Cary Grant.

By that time, some of his colleagues at Harvard were criticizing his research, arguing that experimental drugs like LSD should be administered by physicians in controlled medical settings, not by psychologists at late-night parties. Leary was unrepentant, claiming that "control of the mind through drugs, which we call internal politics, will be the leading civil rights issue in the coming decades." He also claimed that for him, "LSD use is a sacramental ritual." In 1963, he was fired from Harvard at a time when the dean, who was one of his supporters, was out of town, and Leary's most adamant opponent was in charge. The "official" reason was that he had failed to show up for his classes, even though all class work had ceased for the summer break.

At this point Leary began to make his effect on the 1960s. When he was fired by Harvard, his credibility with the counterculture* expanded exponentially. He campaigned for the legalization of marijuana, and in 1966 he testified before a Senate committee to support "legislation which will license responsible adults to use psychedelic drugs for serious purposes." However, at this time, more and more reports began surfacing of people having "bad trips," which made Leary a visible target for antidrug forces. In 1965, he was arrested and charged with trying to smuggle marijuana into the United States. His lawyer urged him to accept a plea bargain, but Leary wanted to use the trial as a forum for challenging existing drug laws. As a result, he was convicted and sentenced to thirty years in prison and a fine of $30,000.

The conviction was later overturned, but upon retrial he was sentenced to ten years for possession and was termed a "menace to the country" by the presiding judge. In 1966, Leary was arrested again for possession in Dutchess County, New York. He dodged going to jail until 1970, when he was sent to the state prison in San Luis Obispo, California. He escaped and remained on the run until 1973, when he was apprehended trying to enter Afghanistan. This time he remained in prison until 1976, when he was paroled. Leary then began traveling around the country giving more speeches. He finally settled in Hollywood. Leary

disclosed in 1995 that he had inoperable prostate cancer, and he died May 31, 1996. His last words were "Why? . . . Why not?"
REFERENCES: Timothy Leary, *Flashbacks*, 1983; *New York Times*, June 1, 1996.

Brad Wuergler

LEAVE IT TO BEAVER. *Leave It to Beaver* was a fantastically popular situation comedy first broadcast by CBS on October 4, 1957. ABC then picked it up from October 1958 to the last episode, which was broadcast on September 12, 1963. The series revolved around the life of Theodore "Beaver" Cleaver (Jerry Mathers), an adolescent boy living in an upscale, middle-class neighborhood. His older brother, Wally, was played Tony Dow, his father, Ward, by Hugh Beaumont, and his mother, June, by Barbara Billingsley. The series had an endearing innocence to it, perfect for an America before Vietnam, urban riots, and civil disobedience.
REFERENCE: Jerry Mathers, *And Jerry Mathers as "The Beaver,"* 1998.

LeMAY, CURTIS EMERSON. Curtis E. LeMay was born November 15, 1906, in Columbus, Ohio. He joined the army air corps in 1928 and was commissioned a second lieutenant in 1930. He rose to the rank of major general in 1943, when he commanded the 305th Bomber Group and 20th Bomber Command in the European theater during World War II. He received command of the 21st Bomber Command in the Marianas in 1945 and advanced to commanding general of the 20th Air Force at Guam. LeMay became a legend because of his unorthodox methods. In Europe he had his bombers abandon the usual zigzag pattern of flight to avoid flak so they could have more accurate runs, and in the Pacific he removed the guns from the bombers in order to carry heavier payloads. In Japan, LeMay opposed dropping the atomic bombs because he believed more firebomb raids would secure a surrender. After World War II, LeMay rose through the ranks of the air force, becoming head of the Strategic Air Command in 1957 and air force chief of staff in 1961, a position he held until his retirement in 1965.

LeMay came out of retirement to serve as George Wallace's* vice presidential running mate in the election of 1968,* and his position on Vietnam was hardline. He urged the United States to bring all of its firepower to bear, even nuclear weapons if necessary, on North Vietnam to end the war quickly. He said that the United States was capable of "bombing Vietnam back into the stone age" and that the North Vietnamese should be aware of such power. LeMay felt any settlement in the Far East should protect free governments from communist takeovers. Curtis LeMay died October 1, 1990.
REFERENCE: Thomas M. Coffey, *Iron Eagle: The Times and Life of General Curtis LeMay*, 1986.

GARY LEWIS AND THE PLAYBOYS. The rock-and-roll group Gary Lewis and the Playboys was formed in Los Angeles in 1964. Gary Lewis was the son

of comedian Jerry Lewis, and the band enjoyed spectacular, but brief, success in the late 1960s. Their first number one hit appeared in 1965—"This Diamond Ring"—and in the next two years, they recorded six other top ten hits, including "Count Me In," "Save Your Heart for Me," "Everybody Loves a Clown," "She's Just My Style," "Sure Gonna Miss Her," and "Green Grass." Lewis was then drafted into the army, and when he was discharged two years later, he tried to reform the band, but they never recovered their earlier popularity.
REFERENCE: Patricia Romanowski and Holly George-Warren, eds., *The New Rolling Stone Encyclopedia of Rock and Roll*, 1996.

USS *LIBERTY*. On June 8, 1967, a U.S. naval intelligence-gathering ship was attacked by Israeli fighters off the coast of Egypt. The *Liberty* was classified as a "technical research ship" whose mission was to conduct research in communications and electromagnetic radiation. The mission was a cover; the *Liberty* was actually used for intelligence gathering. *Liberty* was a transformed merchant ship that was chosen specifically for this type of mission. It was fitted with extensive communication technology to fulfill its role as a "spy" ship. The ship had a crew of 400, of whom 100 were communications specialists. During the Six-Day War between Israel and several Arab nations, the *Liberty* had been deployed to the eastern Mediterranean to observe the fighting and collect intelligence.

Israeli aircraft conducted daily reconnaissance missions over the *Liberty*. At 2:00 P.M. on June 8, Israeli planes and torpedo boats attacked the *Liberty*. A total of thirty-five U.S. sailors were killed. Israel apologized and claimed that it had mistaken the *Liberty* for an Egyptian ship, the *El Quseir*. The *Liberty*, however, was flying the American flag constantly during the reconnaissance and the attack. Also, the *El Quseir* was an older and slower ship than the *Liberty*, and Israeli pilots and patrol boat skippers should have known the difference. The United States officially accepted the apology; Israel was too close an ally to risk a diplomatic crisis. But few American officials believed the Israeli explanation. Unofficially, most American policymakers believed the attack had been intentional—that the Israelis had feared that the *Liberty* was passing on Israeli intelligence information to the Egyptians.
REFERENCE: James M. Ennes, Jr., *Assault on the Liberty*, 1979.

William Wooten

LIGHT AT THE END OF THE TUNNEL. On November 17, 1967, at a televised press conference in Washington, D.C., General William Westmoreland* said that he could see the "light at the end of the tunnel" in Vietnam, meaning that a U.S. victory there was imminent. When the Tet Offensive* two months later demonstrated just how wrong Westmoreland had been, journalists began using the term sarcastically to describe the futility of U.S. policies there. During the next eight years, the phrase appeared hundreds of times in television broadcasts and newspaper and magazine articles. A play on words also emerged in the press: "I see the light at the end of the tunnel, and it's the train." In 1975, newspapers widely published a photo of a GI leaving Vietnam during the final withdrawal of U.S. forces. He had made a poster which showed a lightbulb shining from a tunnel.

REFERENCE: James S. Olson, ed., *Dictionary of the Vietnam War*, 1988.

LIMITED NUCLEAR TEST BAN TREATY. See NUCLEAR TEST BAN TREATY (1963).

LINDSAY, JOHN VLIET. John V. Lindsay was born in New York City November 24, 1921. He graduated from Yale in 1944 and then took a law degree there in 1948. Lindsay then joined the staff of the U.S. attorney's office for the southern district of New York. In 1953, he went into private practice with the New York City firm of Webster and Sheffield. In 1960, running as a liberal Republican, Lindsay won a seat in Congress and served there until 1965, when he became mayor of New York City. Along with people like Governor Nelson Rockefeller* of New York, Senator Jacob Javits* of New York, Senator Charles Percy* of Illinois, and Senator Edwin Brooke* of Massachusetts, Lindsay became one of the most prominent liberal Republicans in the United States, speaking out against American involvement in the Vietnam War* and in favor of using the federal government to deal with social problems.

Lindsay left politics in 1973 and returned to Webster and Sheffield. His influence in the Republican Party, however, steadily diminished because of the growing strength of conservatives. Lindsay eventually left the Republican Party and declared himself a Democrat. He retired in 1991.

REFERENCES: Nat Hentoff, *A Political Life*, 1969; John V. Lindsay, *Journey into Politics*, 1966.

LITTLE, MALCOLM. See MALCOLM X.

LOC NINH, BATTLE OF (1967). Loc Ninh is located in Binh Long Province of what was, in 1967, South Vietnam, approximately nine miles east of the border with Cambodia. Late in 1967, General Vo Nguyen Giap* of North Vietnam used Loc Ninh as part of his strategic preparation for the Tet Offensive* of 1968. On October 29, 1967, troops of the Vietcong* 9th Division left their Cambodian sanctuaries and attacked Loc Ninh, which was defended by several hundred local South Vietnamese militia. Regular U.S. and South Vietnamese soldiers were airlifted in, and they managed to repulse the attack. The Vietcong gave up the fight on November 7, 1967, and retreated, leaving behind 850 dead comrades. The Battle of Loc Ninh, along with similar battles at Dak To* and Song Be, convinced General William Westmoreland,* commander of U.S. forces in Vietnam, that the enemy was finally abandoning guerrilla tactics and planning a conventional offensive. In reality, Giap was using the battles to draw U.S. troops out of the major cities, so that the Tet Offensive of 1968 would be even more effective. His strategy worked. At the end of January 1968, with U.S. troops widely scattered, the Tet Offensive caught the United States completely off guard.

REFERENCE: Shelby M. Stanton, *The Rise and Fall of an American Army: U.S. Ground Forces in Vietnam, 1965–1973*, 1985.

LODGE, HENRY CABOT, JR. Henry Cabot Lodge, Jr., was born in Nahant, Massachusetts, on July 5, 1902, to a distinguished family. His father, Henry Cabot Lodge, had long served in the U.S. Senate and had been a leading figure in shaping early twentieth-century U.S. foreign policy. The younger Lodge attended Harvard and graduated in 1924. He worked as a journalist for the *Boston Transcript* before joining the staff of the *New York Herald Tribune*. During the 1920s, Lodge traveled throughout the world and spent a considerable amount of time in Vietnam, where he wrote about French control there. He won a seat as a Republican in the state legislature in 1932, and in 1936 he won his father's old seat in the U.S. Senate. Lodge spent two years in the U.S. Army during World War II and then returned to his Senate seat. In 1952, however, he lost his reelection bid to Democratic Senator John F. Kennedy.*

In 1953, President Dwight Eisenhower* appointed Lodge as U.S. ambassador to the United Nations. Lodge remained in that post until 1960, when Richard M. Nixon* selected him as his vice-presidential running mate. They lost the election to John F. Kennedy.* As the situation deteriorated in Vietnam, Kennedy called on Lodge's expertise. Lodge was fluent in French, and in June 1963 he became U.S. ambassador to South Vietnam. Kennedy also hoped that Lodge's presence in Vietnam would deflect Republican criticism of administration policies there.

Within a few weeks of his arrival in Saigon, Lodge decided that the government of Ngo Dinh Diem* was hopelessly corrupt. Preventing a Vietcong* triumph would be difficult anyway, and Diem's arrogance and greed rendered him the wrong man to preside over the country. In August 1963, when Diem launched his repressive attacks on South Vietnam's Buddhists, Lodge became incensed and urged President Kennedy to the overthrow the regime. The Central Intelligence Agency* (CIA) began working with the South Vietnamese military to bring it about, but Lodge was horrified when the coup resulted in Diem's assassination.

Lodge became more and more frustrated as the political and military situation deteriorated in Vietnam, and in the spring of 1964 he resigned. One year later, President Lyndon Johnson* sent Lodge back to South Vietnam as U.S. ambassador, and Lodge remained there until 1967. Between 1967 and 1970, Lodge served as U.S. ambassador to West Germany and as head of the U.S. delegation to the Paris peace talks. He resigned from the post in 1970 to become U.S. envoy to the Vatican. Lodge retired in 1970 and died on February 27, 1985.

REFERENCES: Anne Blair, *Lodge in Vietnam: A Patriot Abroad*, 1995; *New York Times*, February 28, 1985.

LOMBARDI, VINCENT THOMAS. Vincent Thomas Lombardi was born in Brooklyn, New York, June 11, 1913. He attended Fordham University and played lineman on the football team. Lombardi graduated from Fordham in 1937, and after studying law and playing semiprofessional football for two years, he became an assistant high school football coach. Soon afterward, he became an assistant coach at Fordham. He later accepted the head coaching job at the U.S. Military Academy at West Point.

In 1959, after a successful collegiate career, Lombardi was named head coach and general manager of the Green Bay Packers, and his success and coaching philosophy there made him an American sports legend. Lombardi took the Packers in two years from an embarrassing losing season to a league championship. In his nine years as head coach, the Packers won five league championships (1961, 1962, 1965, 1966, and 1967) and defeated the Kansas City Chiefs (1966) and the Oakland Raiders (1967) in the first two Super Bowls. He left Green Bay in 1968 to become head coach and executive vice president of the Washington Redskins, and he led them to their first winning season in fourteen years. By that time, however, Lombardi's health was already failing, and he died of cancer September 3, 1970.

Vince Lombardi was a true spartan—some say the meanest and most strict man ever to coach American football. When he took over the Green Bay Packers in 1959, he imposed a fanatical regimen on his players, forcing them to adopt his trademark motto, ''Winning isn't everything; it's the only thing.'' He was a special breed of coach—the taskmaster who could scream and spit in a player's ear one minute and give him a hug the next. If a player made a mistake, Lombardi's wrath appeared immediately, but if, on the other hand, a player performed particularly well, Lombardi was the first one to slap his helmet or his behind. His players grew to adore him, despite his austere coaching style, and they transposed their fear of him to respect and dedication, which elevated their play to another level. Lombardi paved the way for such other professional football coaches as Mike Ditka and George Allen.

Historians surmise that Lombardi became an American icon in the 1960s because his coaching philosophy seemed so out of step with prevailing values. At a time of protests against the Vietnam War,* Lombardi demanded absolute loyalty. In an era of free love and youthful rebellion, Lombardi insisted on dedication and discipline. While much of America looked down upon competition, Lombardi praised the virtues of victory. When a reporter asked one of Lombardi's African-American linemen if the coach discriminated against blacks, the player replied, ''Oh no. He hates everybody.''

REFERENCES: Vince Lombardi, *Run to Daylight*, 1963; Michael O'Brien, *Vince: A Personal Biography of Vince Lombardi*, 1989.

Bradley A. Olson

LOTTERY. Throughout the 1960s, the Selective Service System drafted millions of young men to fill the country's military personnel needs. Eventually, the Selective Service's method of choosing young men became highly controversial. Because the system provided for educational deferments to young men attending college, the system discriminated against minorities and the poor. Poor whites, Hispanics, and African Americans were far more likely to be drafted into military service than young men from middle- and upper-class families. Part of the civil rights movement's* opposition to the Vietnam War* was that minority youth carried a disproportionate share of the fighting and the dying.

In November 1969, President Richard M. Nixon* responded to those criticisms by signing legislation creating a lottery system. The Selective Service System, through a lottery, randomly selected birthdates and assigned to each day of the year a number from 1 to 365. Young men would then be drafted into the military based on their lottery number rather than their age or educational status. The lottery system went a long way in addressing the criticism that the Selective Service System was biased against minorities and the poor.

REFERENCE: Andrew O. Shapiro and John M. Striker, *Mastering the Draft*, 1970.

LOVING V. VIRGINIA. During the 1950s and 1960s, the Supreme Court under Chief Justice Earl Warren* pursued a consistent legal goal of undermining de jure segregation, restricting the powers of the state, and expanding the rights of individuals. They were especially concerned with issues of personal privacy, which found expression in *Loving v. Virginia*, a case decided by unanimous vote on June 12, 1967. Virginia state law prohibited interracial marriages, but the Court overturned the law, arguing that it violated the equal protection and due process clauses of the Fifth and Fourteenth Amendments. The right to choose a marriage partner, the Court concluded, could not be infringed upon by the state.

REFERENCE: 388 U.S. 1 (1967).

LOWENSTEIN, ALLARD KENNETH. Allard Lowenstein was born in Newark, New Jersey, on January 16, 1929. A very bright student, he received a bachelor's degree from the University of North Carolina in 1949 and a law degree from Yale in 1954. As an undergraduate at North Carolina, Lowenstein developed decidedly liberal political views, and in 1951 he became president of the National Student Organization (NSO). He remained active in the NSO througout the decade, and when student unrest over civil rights* and the Vietnam War* developed in the early 1960s, he found himself in the forefront of a budding political movement. He used his legal talents to assist jailed civil rights workers in the South and offered free legal advice to Martin Luther King, Jr.,* the Southern Leadership Leadership Conference,* and the Student Nonviolent Coordinating Committee.*

In 1967, Lowenstein was appointed to a commission dispatched to South Vietnam to observe the presidential elections there and to certify that the elections had been conducted fairly. Rather than convincing him to support U.S. policies, the visit had exactly the opposite effect on Lowenstein, who came back to the United States and promptly formed the Conference of Concerned Democrats and the Coalition for a Democratic Alternative. The group was committed to ending the Vietnam War and convincing President Lyndon B. Johnson* not to seek reelection in 1968. The "Dump Johnson" campaign gathered momentum in 1967 and early 1968 and played an important role in Johnson's decision not to seek another term.

At the Democratic National Convention in Chicago in 1968, Lowenstein founded the Coalition for an Open Convention, which opposed the presidential candidacy of Vice-President Hubert H. Humphrey.* That same year, Lowenstein won a seat in Congress, representing voters on Long Island, New York. For his antiwar* position, he soon earned the wrath of President Richard M. Nixon,* who listed Lowenstein as an "enemy" of the administration. Lowenstein failed in his bid for reelection in 1970 but continued to support liberal causes. He was assassinated on March 14, 1980.

REFERENCE: William Chafe, *Never Stop Running: Allard Lowenstein and the Struggle to Save American Liberalism*, 1998.

LSD. See **LYSERGIC ACID DIETHYLAMIDE**.

THE LUCY SHOW. In 1962, after her unprecedented success with the *I Love Lucy* show, Lucille Ball abandoned her association with Desi Arnaz and launched *The Lucy Show*. It starred Lucille Ball as Lucy Carmichael and Vivian Vance as Vivian Carmichael, a widow and divorcée who live together, share expenses, raise their children, and try to land husbands. Like *I Love Lucy, The Lucy Show* is full of pranks, pratfalls, practical jokes, and the physical humor at which Lucille Ball was so adept. *The Lucy Show* became known as *Here's Lucy* in 1968. CBS broadcast the last episode on September 2, 1974.

REFERENCE: Lucille Ball, *Love, Lucy*, 1996; Ric Wyman, *For the Love of Lucy*, 1995.

LUNAR LANDING. In 1961, when President John F. Kennedy* announced his intention to put a man on the moon "in this decade," few Americans took him seriously, but the National Aeronautics and Space Administration* (NASA) did. Through the Mercury, Gemini, and Apollo programs, NASA steadily closed in on a manned landing on the moon, and their crusade came to fruition on July 21, 1969, when astronaut Neil Armstrong walked on the moon. The Apollo 11 spacecraft *Columbia* had taken Armstrong, Edwin "Buzz" Aldrin, and Michael Collins into a lunar orbit, and then Armstrong and Aldrin took a lunar landing vehicle named *Eagle* to the surface of the moon. Armstrong was the first to step out of the *Eagle* and onto the moon, remarking as he did so, "That's one small step for man, one giant leap for mankind." A few minutes later, Aldrin joined Armstrong, and they planted a U.S. flag on the moon. The two astronauts collected rock samples for more than two hours, took hundreds of photographs, and then got back aboard the *Eagle*.

Back at home, hundreds of millions of people watched live video of the visit

to the moon, and most of the world viewed the event as a triumph of American technology, and a victory over the Soviet Union in the space race. The *Eagle* left the moon after twenty-one hours and rendezvoused with *Columbia*, where Collins was awaiting the return of Armstrong and Aldrin. The astronauts returned to earth on July 24, splashing down safely in the Pacific Ocean.
REFERENCES: *New York Times*, July 21–25, 1969.

LYND, STAUGHTON. Staughton Lynd was born in 1929 to Robert and Helen Lynd, the world-famous sociologists. He graduated from Harvard in 1951, and when faced with the military draft during the Korean War registered as a conscientious objector. The Selective Service then classified him as noncombatant. He taught history at Spellman College in Atlanta for several years, and in 1965 he earned a Ph.D. in history from Columbia. During his years in Atlanta, he became active in the Student Nonviolent Coordinating Committee (SNCC), which was active registering black voters in the South. Lynd left Atlanta in 1965 to accept aln assistant professorship at Yale.

When the United States escalated its military commitment in Vietnam in 1965, Lynd became an early antiwar protestor. In 1965, he refused to pay $300 in federal income taxes, which he argued would be used to fight an immoral war, and late in 1965 he visited Hanoi* with Tom Hayden,* leader of the Students for a Democratic Society (SDS).* The trip was enormously controversial. Kingman Brewster, president of Yale, publicly denounced Lynd's visit, accusing him of "aiding and abetting the enemy." Lynd took a leave of absence from Yale and then abandoned his academic career. In 1976, he earned a law degree from the University of Chicago. He practices law today and specializes in the needs of working-class people.
REFERENCES: John Corry, " 'We Must Say Yes to Our Souls': Staughton Lynd: Spokesman for the New Left," *New York Times Magazine*, January 23, 1966; Joanna Cowden, "Staughton Lynd," in James S. Olson, ed., *Dictionary of the Vietnam War*, 1988; Joseph Lelyveld, "A Touch of Class," *New York Times Magazine*, August 14, 1977.

LYSERGIC ACID DIETHYLAMIDE (LSD). Lysergic Acid Diethylamide, or LSD, is one of the most potent hallucinogenic drugs in the world. It is taken from a fungus that grows on rye and from lysergic acid amide, a naturally occurring pharmaceutical found in morning glory seeds. Among its hallucinogenic effects are a false sense of heightened clarity or understanding, intense but unreal images, and decreased levels of emotional and physical control. During the 1960s, LSD was frequently the "drug of choice" for youthful rebels. Among its pseudonyms were "acid," "blotter acid," "California sunshine," and "micro-dots." People like Timothy Leary* helped popularize LSD as a recreational drug, as did the Beatles* in their hit song "Lucy in the Sky with Diamonds."
REFERENCE: Albert Hoffman, *LSD: My Problem Child*, 1979.

M

MacARTHUR, DOUGLAS. Douglas MacArthur was born on an army base near Little Rock, Arkansas, on January 26, 1880. He came from a distinguished American military family. After graduating from West Point in 1903, he saw action in Mexico and the Philippines and was assigned to the Rainbow Division during World War I. He made general in 1930, and five years later he was assigned to the Philippines. MacArthur was in Manila when Japan attacked Pearl harbor and the Philippines in December 1941. President Franklin D. Roosevelt named him commander-in-chief of U.S. army forces in the Pacific. After the war, President Harry Truman named MacArthur to command U.S. occupation forces in Japan, and in that position the general created a democratic government for Japan and built the foundation for economic revival there.

When North Korea attacked South Korea in 1950, MacArthur was named commander of United Nations forces. In 1951, however, Truman relieved him of his command for insubordination because MacArthur had refused to endorse the president's definition of the war as a ''limited conflict.'' MacArthur then retired. Early in the 1960s, MacArthur repeatedly warned President John F. Kennedy* that the United States should not become involved in a protracted guerrilla war in Southeast Asia. Kennedy heeded the advice, but President Lyndon Johnson* did not. MacArthur died on April 5, 1964, just three weeks after the United States deployed regular combat troops to South Vietnam.
REFERENCE: William Manchester, *American Caesar: Douglas MacArthur, 1880–1964*, 1978.

MADDOX, LESTER. Lester Maddox was born in Atlanta, Georgia, September 30, 1915. Maddox ran a prosperous chicken restaurant in Atlanta, Georgia, and he headed a local white racist group known as Georgians Unwilling to Surrender (GUTS). A close associate of many Ku Klux Klan members, Maddox denounced the civil rights movement* and demanded that whites make sure that blacks remain "in their place." By the mid-1960s, Maddox had emerged in Atlanta as the leading white racist. He won the Democratic gubernatorial primary in 1966 and became governor of Georgia. Maddox remained governor of Georgia until 1974. Since then he has been engaged in the real estate business.

REFERENCE: Lester G. Maddox, *Speaking Out: The Autobiography of Lester Garfield Maddox*, 1975.

MAHARISHI MAHESH YOGI. Maharishi Mahesh Yogi was born in 1918 in Jubbulpore, India. In 1940, he graduated from Allahabad University with a degree in physics and then studied for the next thirteen years with Swami Brahmananda Saraswati Maharaj, the founder of transcendental meditation (TM). When Maharaj died in 1953, Maharishi Mahesh Yogi inherited the burden of teaching transcendental meditation to the world. In 1959, he founded the Sonorama Society, an American branch of the movement. He taught and labored in obscurity until 1967, when the Beatles* decided to take lessons from Maharishi. He quickly developed a cult following in the United States. Transcendental meditation revolves around the use of a mantra while sitting quietly. Daily meditation and the chanting, silent repetition of the mantra were believed to generate intelligence, harmony, and health. If the people of the world could be converted to TM, advocates believed, an indefinite period of peace and harmony would descend on the earth. TM was the leading New Age religion of the late 1960s and early 1970s. By the late 1970s, it rapidly began losing followers.

REFERENCE: John R. Hinnells, *Who's Who of World Religions*, 1992.

MAILER, NORMAN. Norman Mailer was born in Long Branch, New Jersey, January 31, 1943. He graduated from Harvard University in 1943, did postgraduate work at the Sorbonne in Paris, and then worked briefly as a columnist for the *Village Voice*. A gifted writer, Mailer's first book—*No Percentage*—was published in 1941, when he was still an undergraduate. He burst upon the American literary scene in 1948 with his World War II novel, *The Naked and the Dead*. Mailer continued to write in the 1950s, producing *Barbary Shore* (1951), *The Deer Park* (1955), *The White Negro: Superficial Reflections on the Hipster* (1957), and *Advertisements on Myself* (1959).

During the 1960s, an extraordinarily prolific period in Mailer's career, he emerged as the country's leading literary figure, a political liberal willing to take a stand on the major issues facing the country. In addition to such works as *Deaths for the Ladies and Other Disasters* (1962), *The Presidential Papers* (1963), *An American Dream* (1965), *Cannibals and Christians* (1966), and *The Bullfight* (1967), Mailer wrote *Miami and the Siege of Chicago* (1968) and *The Armies of the Night* (1968), books about the counterculture* and its political impact on the United States. *The Armies of the Night* won Mailer his first Pulitzer Prize. His 1967 novel *Why Are We in Vietnam?*, an allegorical tale about a hunting trip to Alaska, was a powerful critique of American military policy in Southeast Asia.

During the 1970s and 1980s, Mailer continued to earn his reputation as one of the most productive writers in the history of American letters. His 1972 biography of Marilyn Monroe—*Marilyn*—was a best-seller, and he won his second Pulitzer for *Executioner's Song* (1979), a book about the crimes and the execution of Gary Gilmore. Since then, he has written more than a dozen new books.

REFERENCE: Michael K. Glenday, *Norman Mailer*, 1995.

MAKE LOVE, NOT WAR. During the 1960s, the phrase "Make love, not war" emerged among the counterculture* and antiwar* communities to celebrate a repudiation of middle-class sexual mores and the military-industrial complex.* Most Americans associated the phrase with hippies.*

REFERENCE: David Lee Stein, *Living the Revolution: The Yippies in Chicago*, 1969.

MAKE ROOM FOR DADDY. *Make Room for Daddy*, later known as *The Danny Thomas Show*, was a popular situation comedy of the 1950s and 1960s. It was first telecast by ABC on September 29, 1953, and in 1957 CBS picked up the series and continued to broadcast until September 1965. During the 1971 television season, ABC tried to reprise the series, but it did not succeed in the ratings. *Make Room for Daddy* starred Danny Thomas as Danny Williams, a loudmouth, heart-of-gold nightclub entertainer trying to support his family in New York City. During the twelve-year run of *Make Room for Daddy*, the character of Danny Williams raised his family, became a widower, remarried, and saw his children get married. *Make Room for Daddy* was one of the most popular situation comedies in television history.

REFERENCE: Danny Thomas, *Make Room for Danny*, 1991.

MALAMUD, BERNARD. Bernard Malamud was born April 26, 1914, in New York City. A gifted novelist, he wrote *The Assistant* (1957), *The Magic Barrel* (1958), *A New Life* (1961), *The Fixer* (1966), and *Dubin's Lives* (1979). *The Fixer* won him the 1967 Pulitzer Prize. Malamud's characters, like America in the 1960s, are perpetually engaged in a search for meaning in their lives. He always deals in Jewish people, Jewish questions, Jewish themes, and Jewish suffering. Although his characters often find that search difficult, he rejects nihilism for a faith that there is an ultimate meaning in the universe. Bernard Malamud died March 18, 1986.

REFERENCES: Harold Bloom, ed., *Bernard Malamud*, 1986; Leslie Field and Joyce W. Field, eds., *Bernard Malamud and His Critics*, 1970.

MALCOLM X. Malcolm Little, who took the name Malcolm X after his conversion to Islam, was born in Omaha, Nebraska, May 19, 1925. His father was a Baptist preacher in the 1920s and a follower of Marcus Garvey, and as such he attracted the violent attention of local white racists. He moved to Boston as a teenager and soon found himself in the midst of prostitution, drugs, gambling, and petty crime. He eventually drew a ten-year prison sentence for burglary. In the penitentiary, he came upon the religious teachings of the Nation of Islam, and he soon converted. The conversion was deep and sincere.

Upon his release from prison in 1952, Malcolm X moved to Detroit and became a follower of Elijah Muhammad.* The last name "X" was symbolic of the family name of his ancestors, whom he would never know because slavery had ripped his people from their African home. He was a charismatic preacher, telling black people to discard the ghetto mentality, build strong marriages and families, and avoid pork, narcotics, alcohol, gambling, fornication, and adultery. By 1961, Malcolm X was named national minister in the Nation of Islam.

In contrast to the nonviolent civil disobedience teachings of Martin Luther King, Jr.,* Malcolm urged black people to defend themselves and their families when necessary. He called King just "another Uncle Tom." When President John F. Kennedy* was assassinated, Malcolm called it a case of "the chickens coming home to roost." To most white people, he appeared to be a dangerous firebrand.

By that time, many Black Muslims* believed Malcolm X was becoming too powerful, a rival to Elijah Muhammad. He began receiving death threats. When he learned that Elijah Muhammad was guilty of adultery with two of his secretaries, Malcolm broke with the Nation of Islam, founding his own organization—Muslim Mosque, Inc. In 1964, Malcolm X's life changed again when he made the Muslim pilgrimage to Mecca. There he discovered that Islam was color-blind and eschewed the racist teaching of the Nation of Islam. Malcolm returned to the United States as El-Hajj Malik El-Shabazz and founded the Organization for African Unity, a group promoting black nationalism regardless of religious persuasion. Malcolm X was assassinated February 21, 1965.

REFERENCES: Peter Goldmam, *The Death and Life of Malcolm X*, 1979; Alex Haley, *The Autobiography of Malcolm X*, 1965; E. Victor Wolfenstein, *The Victims of Democracy: Malcolm X and the Black Revolution*, 1981.

THE MAMAS AND THE PAPAS. The Mamas and the Papas rock group was formed in New York City in 1965. Even though they had their beginnnings on the East Coast, they gained their fame as a psychedelic California folk pop group. The group included John Phillips, Dennis Doherty, Michelle Phillips, and "Mama" Cass Eliot. They produced six hits in 1966 and 1967 that reached the top five in the pop charts—"California Dreamin'," "Monday, Monday," "I Saw Her Again," "Words of Love," "Dedicated to the One I Love," and "Creeque Alley." Their 1967 hit "San Francisco" became a landmark song of the countercultural era. Soon after, the group disintegrated because of personal and professional difficulties.

REFERENCE: Michelle Phillips, *California Dreamin': The True Story of the Mamas and the Papas*, 1986.

MAME. *Mame* was one of the 1960s most popular Broadway musicals. Written by Jerome Lawrence and Robert E. Lee, it was based on Patrick Dennis'

novel *Auntie Mame*. It premiered at the Winter Garden Theater in New York on May 24, 1966. Starring Angela Lansbury, the play revolved around Auntie Mame, a freethinking woman charged with raising her orphaned nephew Patrick, played by Jerry Lanning. Mame wants nothing to do with a conventional, middle-class American lifestyle, and she raises her nephew to think the same way. *Mame* enjoyed a run of 1,508 performances at the Winter Garden Theater.
REFERENCE: Kurt Ganzl, *The Encyclopedia of the Musical Theater*, 1994.

THE MAN FROM U.N.C.L.E. *The Man from U.N.C.L.E.* was a spoof on the James Bond* novels and movies of the 1960s. First broadcast by NBC on September 12, 1964, the series starred Robert Vaughn as Napoleon Solo and David McCallum as Illya Kuryakin. Headquartered in New York, U.N.C.L.E. (United Network Command for Law and Enforcement) worked weekly to foil the conspiracies of THRUSH, an international crime syndicate. The plots were outlandish, designed as much for humor as for suspense. The last episode of *The Man from U.N.C.L.E.* was broadcast on January 15, 1968.
REFERENCE: Tim Brooks and Earle Marsh, *The Complete Directory to Prime Time Network and Cable TV Shows*, 1995.

MAN OF LA MANCHA. *Man of La Mancha* was one of the most popular musicals in Broadway history. Written by Dale Wasserman, with music by Mitch Leigh and lyrics by Joe Darion, *Man of La Mancha* was based loosely on Miguel de Cervantes' famous novel *Don Quixote*. The play opened at the Washington Square Theater in New York on November 22, 1965. Richard Kiley starred as Cervantes, an over-the-hill knight in sixteenth-century Spain who is still loyal to the code of chivalry and still chasing "the impossible dream." *Man of La Mancha* enjoyed a Broadway run of 2,328 performances, one of the longest in the history of the American stage.
REFERENCE: Kurt Ganzl, *The Encyclopedia of the Musical Theater*, 1994.

THE MANCHURIAN CANDIDATE. *The Manchurian Candidate*, an important film of the 1960s, was released by United Artists in October 1962. The film starred Frank Sinatra as Bennett March, Laurence Harvey as Raymond Shaw, and Janet Leigh as Rosie and was directed by John Frankenheimer. It was based on the novel of the same name by Richard Condon. Shaw is a Korean War veteran who was captured and became a prisoner of war, during which the communists trained him to be a hypnotic assassin ready to kill on command. Bennett March is the army major who breaks the case before Shaw can do any real damage. *The Manchurian Candidate* generated real interest among Americans because United Artists released it right in the middle of the Cuban missile crisis,* when fear of communism and nuclear war had reached a fever pitch.
REFERENCE: *New York Times*, October 25, 1962.

MANSFIELD, MICHAEL JOSEPH. Michael Mansfield was born in New York City on March 16, 1903. His family soon moved to Montana, where he was raised. He quit school in 1918 to join the U.S. Navy and he ended up serving his tour of duty as a marine. His naval career allowed him to travel extensively in East Asia, and he developed a love and respect for the region. He earned a B.A. degree at Montana State University in 1933 and a master's degree there in 1934. From 1933 to 1942, he taught history at the University of Montana. In 1942, Mansfield was elected as a Democrat to the House of Representatives and appointed to the House Foreign Affairs Committee. After five terms in the House, he won a U.S. Senate seat in 1952, where he was appointed to the Senate Foreign Relations Committee. When Lyndon B. Johnson* was elected vice-president in 1960, Mansfield succeeded him as Senate majority leader.

During the 1950s, Mansfield became an early supporter of Ngo Dinh Diem* and the cause of South Vietnam. In 1962 President John Kennedy* asked Mansfield to visit South Vietnam, and he came home with decidedly negative views on the progress of the war. The government was riddled with corruption, and the Diem family was largely responsible. When Lyndon Johnson was president, Mansfield returned to South Vietnam many times, and each time he grew increasingly skeptical and urged de-escalation on the president. When Johnson continued to escalate the conflict, Mansfield in 1965 went public with his criticism.

When Richard M. Nixon* entered the White House, Mansfield's criticism became even more intense, and he launched a movement to regain congressional authority over the war-making process. He endorsed the Cooper-Church Amendment and the Hatfield-McGovern Amendment in 1970, and in 1971 he sponsored a Senate resolution requiring complete withdrawal of all U.S. troops from Vietnam within nine months. The resolution passed the Senate but died in the House. Mansfield retired from the Senate in 1977 to become U.S. ambassador to Japan, and he remained there until 1993. Since then he has lectured widely on foreign affairs.

REFERENCES: Louis Baldwin, *The Honorable Politician: Mike Mansfield of Montana*, 1979; Gregory Olson, *Mansfield and Vietnam: A Study in Rhetorical Adaptation*, 1995; Hoyt Purvis, "Michael Joseph Mansfield," in James S. Olson, ed., *Dictionary of the Vietnam War*, 1988.

MANSON, CHARLES. See **THE MANSON FAMILY**.

THE MANSON FAMILY. In 1969, Charles Manson became a household name in the United States. A career criminal who fancied himself a talented songwriter, Manson sank deep into the drug culture in the 1960s and became obsessed with Beatles* music, even reading the lyrics as scripture and the music as liturgy. He developed a small following and established a tiny commune outside Los Angeles. A convoluted combination of hippie,* priest, drug addict, and megalomaniac, Manson convinced five of his followers that in murder and mayhem they could achieve eternal redemption. On August 9, 1969, they made their way into the Los Angeles home of actress Sharon Tate,* the wife of director Roman Polanski, and brutally murdered her and four of her friends. They shot and stabbed the victims dozens of times and then smeared the word ''Pig'' in blood across the front door. One day later, the Manson ''family'' struck again, murdering Leno and Rosemary LaBianca in their own home and using their blood to write such messages as ''Death to Pigs'' and ''Helter Skelter'' on the walls.

The trial of the so-called Manson family was pure theater. Manson's behavior was erratic at best, and his groupie followers all but worshiped him. They were all convicted of murder and sentenced to death, but when California outlawed the death penalty in 1972, their sentences were commuted to life in prison. For many Americans, the Manson family came to represent the darkest side of a drug-sex-hippie-rock-and-roll culture. Although he annually appears before a parole board hoping to get out of prison, Charles Manson remains incarcerated today.

REFERENCES: Vincent Bugliosi, *Helter Skelter: The True Story of the Manson Murders*, 1974; Ed Sanders, *The Family: The Manson Group and Its Aftermath*, 1989.

MAO ZEDONG. Mao Zedong, the legendary communist leader of the People's Republic of China, was born in 1893. As a teenager, he moved to Beijing and worked in the national library there. Radical politics intrigued him as a student, and he converted to the Communist Party soon after the Bolshevik Revolution in Russia. But he soon departed from the Russian model, which envisioned industrial workers as the vanguard of revolution. Mao saw peasants in the vanguard instead, and during the 1920s he began writing about his theory. He emerged as the leader of Chinese communism, and after the famous Long March of 1934–1935, Mao used Yenan in northwest China as his base of operations. During World War II, Mao Zedong led communist forces in a series of bloody, successful battles against Japanese occupation forces, and in the process he became a folk hero in China. Four years after the end of the war, Mao and his communist forces seized political control of China.

For Americans, Mao Zedong became an evil icon, proof that the international communist conspiracy was succeeding. He posed a threat to all of Asia, and the domino theory* developed in the 1950s because of Mao's victory. American policymakers viewed him as just another facet of the Soviet Union's plan for global revolution. Actually, Mao's fear of the Soviets was greater than his worries about the United States, but not until the late 1960s did prominent Americans begin to realize it. By that time, Mao had launched the disastrous Cultural Revolution—an attempt to reeducate the Chinese people into a greater respect and belief in ideological purity—which made China a land of political turmoil and economic collapse. In 1972, President Richard Nixon* began an American rapprochement with China. Mao Zedong died in 1976.

REFERENCES: Hedda Garza, *Mao Zedong*, 1988; Rebecca Stefoff, *Mao Zedong: Founder of the People's Republic of China*, 1996.

MAPP V. OHIO. During the 1960s, the Supreme Court under the leadership of Chief Justice Earl Warren* continued its program of broadening individual rights while narrowing those of federal, state, and local government officials. *Mapp v. Ohio* was decided on June 19, 1961, by a narrow 5 to 4 margin. Justice Tom Clark* wrote the majority opinion. The Court overturned its *Wolf v. Colorado* decision of 1942 and concluded that evidence obtained illegally in violation of the Fourth Amendment had to be excluded from state trials as well as from federal trials.
REFERENCE: 367 U.S. 643 (1961).

MARCH ON WASHINGTON (1963). Early in 1963, civil rights activist and socialist Bayard Rustin* began planning a "March on Washington" to dramatize the need to end job discrimination in the United States. During the year, white liberals worked to broaden the march into an event to support passage of the civil rights bill then pending in Congress. On August 28, 1963, more than 200,000 people gathered in front of the Lincoln Memorial in Washington, D.C., to listen to speeches and to demand passage of the civil rights act. Among the speakers was Martin Luther King, Jr.,* who mesmerized the crowd and a national television audience with his "I Have a Dream"* speech. Tens of millions of white Americans recalled the speech as a spiritually defining event in their lives. President John F. Kennedy,* who had expressed only the most lukewarm support for the march, called it an event of which "the nation could be justly proud." Civil rights historians remember the March on Washington as the high point of the nonviolent civil rights movement.*
REFERENCE: David J. Garrow, *Bearing the Cross: Martin Luther King, Jr. and the Southern Christian Leadership Conference*, 1986.

MARCH TO AUSTIN. On July 4, 1966, emboldened by the National Association of Farm Workers (NAFW) success in the March to Sacramento against Schenley Industries, NAFW workers scheduled a "March to Austin" to convince Governor John Connolly to call a special session of the state legislature and include farmworkers in the $1.25 minimum wage law. They arrived at the state capitol on Labor Day in September, but the governor refused to call a special session.
REFERENCE: Matt S. Meier and Feliciano Rivera, *Dictionary of Mexican American History*, 1981.

MARCH TO SACRAMENTO. In 1966, the National Farm Workers Association (NFWA) launched a boycott against Schenley Industries in California, demanding that the agribusiness company recognize them as the bargaining agent for farmworkers, most of whom were Mexican Americans.* NFWA then sponsored the "March to Sacramento," a protest demonstration in which union advocates spent nearly a month walking from Delano to Sacramento, California, holding rallies along the way and urging supporters to join them. On the eve of their arrival in Sacramento, Schenley Industries recognized the union. With that victory, César Chávez* announced that the Di Giorgio Corporation would be the union's next target.

REFERENCE: Matt S. Meier and Feliciano Rivera, *Dictionary of Mexican American History*, 1981.

MARCUSE, HERBERT. Herbert Marcuse was born in Berlin, Germany, July 19, 1898, to a prosperous German-Jewish family. After World War I, Marcuse became a socialist and attended the University of Frieburg. There he became interested in a kind of romantic anticapitalism and tried to develop alternatives to bourgeois industrialism. During the mid-1920s, Marcuse worked closely with Martin Heidegger and delved deeply into Hegelianism and Marxism. Soon after the Nazi triumph in Germany in 1933, he emigrated and ended up in New York City.

He spent his academic carer at Columbia, Harvard, and Brandeis, and among his most brilliant writings were *Eros and Civilization: A Philosophical Inquiry into Freud* (1955), *Soviet Marxism: A Critical Analysis* (1958), and *One-Dimensional Man: Studies in the Ideology of Advanced Industrial Society* (1964). Later books included *Essays on Liberation* (1969), *Counter-Revolution and Revolt* (1972), and *The Aesthetic Dimension* (1978). Marcuse ended his career at the University of California at San Diego, where throughout the rest of the 1960s and 1970s he continued to speak out about the evils of modern technology, industrialism, consumerism, and bourgeois values. He was widely considered to be the reigning guru of the New Left.* Herbert Marcuse died July 29, 1979.

REFERENCES: Vincent Geoghegan, *Reason and Eros: The Social Theory of Herbert Marcuse*, 1981; Barry Katz, *Herbert Marcuse: Art of Liberation*, 1982.

MARIJUANA. Marijuana, a drug derived from the hemp plant, has depressant and hallucinogenic properties. Since the 1960s, it has been a popular but illegal drug. Today, economists estimate that it is the country's largest cash crop. In the 1990s, marijuana once again became a political issue when several states legalized its use for medicinal purposes when prescribed by a physician. Cancer patients undergoing chemotherapy find the drug an antidote for nausea. Critics charged that medical use would soon lead to decriminalization of the drug.

REFERENCE: Kevin Scheel, *Drugs of Abuse*, 1991.

MARIS, ROGER. Roger Maris was born in Hibbing, Minnesota, on September 10, 1934. He was raised in Fargo, North Dakota. An outstanding high school athlete, Maris signed a professional baseball contract in 1952 with the Cleveland Indians. After several years moving up through the ranks of the minor leagues,

Maris was called up to the majors in 1957. He was traded to the Kansas City Athletics in 1958 and to the New York Yankees in 1959, where he consistently hit for power. In the 1960 season, Maris had thirty-nine home runs. But he is best remembered as a sports icon of the 1960s for the 1961 season. Maris and teammate Mickey Mantle both made a run at Babe Ruth's record of sixty home runs in a single season, and America watched the competition with extraordinary interest. During the last two weeks of the season, Maris pulled ahead of Mantle. When the year ended, Maris had sixty-one home runs to Mantle's fifty-four. Maris also owned the record for most home runs in a season.

Controversy, however, surrounded the accomplishment. Babe Ruth had hit sixty home runs in a 154-game season, while in Maris's time, the major league season had expanded to 162 games. Some people insisted that he had not really broken Babe Ruth's record, and in official major league record books, an asterisk was placed next to Maris's name, explaining the difference in the number of games. Maris never again had a season as good as 1961. In 1966, the Yankees traded him to the St. Louis Cardinals. Maris retired from professional baseball after the 1968 season. He then ran a beer distributorship in Gainesville, Florida. Roger Maris died on December 14, 1985.
REFERENCE: *New York Times*, December 15, 1985.

MARSHALL, THURGOOD. Thurgood Marshall was born July 2, 1908, in Baltimore. He graduated from Lincoln University in 1930 but was denied admission to the University of Maryland Law School because of his race. He then took a law degree at Howard University in 1933. He went to work for the National Association for the Advancement of Colored People (NAACP) and in 1940 became head of its legal defense and education fund. During his years with the NAACP, Marshall put 50,000 miles a year on his car, driving throughout the South to defend black clients. He was a gifted specialist in civil rights issues, and he led the NAACP's campaign against de jure segregation in education, public facilities, housing, and voting. He was the NAACP's chief counsel in the famous *Brown v. Board of Education* case, in which the Supreme Court ended school segregation in 1954. President John F. Kennedy* named Marshall to the Court of Appeals for the Second Circuit in 1961, and in 1965 President Lyndon B. Johnson* appointed him solicitor general of the United States. Marshall was the first African American to hold the office. In 1967, Johnson made Marshall the first African-American justice of the U.S. Supreme Court.

His reputation as a Supreme Court justice, however, was made in the area of dissent. During Marshall's tenure, the Supreme Court gradually retreated from its liberal position during the Earl Warren* years. Marshall consistently dissented from any decision upholding the death penalty and vociferously upheld the need for continuing affirmative action* programs, even when public and judicial sentiment went against him. On civil liberties issues, Marshall could be counted on to uphold the protections of individual rights existing in the First, Fourth, Fifth, Sixth, Eighth, and Fourteenth Amendments to the Constitution.

His health failing, Marshall retired from the Supreme Court in 1991. He died January 24, 1993.
REFERENCE: Mark V. Tushnet, *Making Constitutional Law: Thurgood Marshall and the Supreme Court, 1961–1991*, 1997.

MARTHA AND THE VANDELLAS. Martha and the Vandellas were a rock group that produced some of the decade's most memorable dance tunes. The group was formed in Detroit in 1962 by Martha Reeves, Annette Beard, and Rosalind Ashford. They worked for Motown* before signing a recording contract with the Detroit company, and their first hit record appeared in 1963— "Come and Get Those Memories." Later in the year, their "Heat Wave" and "Quicksand" broke into the top ten on the pop music charts. Their biggest hit was "Dancing in the Street," which was released in 1964 and went to number two on the charts. Their other major hits included "Jimmy Mack," "Nowhere to Run," "I'm Ready for Love," and "Honey Chile." Martha and the Vandellas broke up after 1967.
REFERENCES: Martha Reeves, *Dancing in the Street*, 1994; Patricia Romanowski and Holly George-Warren, eds., *The New Rolling Stone Encyclopedia of Rock and Roll*, 1996.

MASTERS, WILLIAM HOWELL. William H. Masters was born in Cleveland, Ohio, December 27, 1915. He graduated from Hamilton College in 1938 and then earned his medical degree at the University of Rochester in 1943. He completed residencies in obstetrics/gynecology and pathology and then joined the faculty of the Washington University Medical School in St. Louis. Masters rose through the academic ranks, and over the years he became increasingly interested in human sexuality, particularly in its physiological and psychological pathologies. In 1964, he became director of the Reproductive Biology Research Foundation, which subsequently became known as the Masters and Johnson Institute, named also after his collaborator, Virginia E. Johnson.

In 1966, the laboratory and clinical work of Masters and Johnson left the ivory towers of academe and became headlines when they published the results of their research—*Human Sexual Response*. For an academic publication, it received unprecedented media attention, not just because its topic was human sexuality but because Masters and Johnson had studied, in laboratory settings, human sexual activity in an attempt to determine methods to deal with such problems as premature ejaculation and impotence in men and inability to reach orgasm in women. Masters and Johnson also began treating people with sexual dysfunctions, using surrogate sexual partners. The fact that they discussed their scientific work candidly and matter-of-factly scandalized more conservative elements of American society, who viewed them as part of the so-called sexual revolution.* Masters' other works, which were equally controversial, included *Human Sexual Inadequacy* (1970), *The Pleasure Bond* (1975), and *Homosexuality in Perspective* (1979).

REFERENCE: Paul A. Robinson, *The Modernization of Sexuality: Havelock Ellis, Alfred Kinsey, William Masters, and Virginia Johnson*, 1989.

McCARTHY, EUGENE JOSEPH. Eugene McCarthy was born in Watkins, Minnesota, on March 29, 1916. McCarthy graduated from St. John's University in 1935 and earned a master's degree at the University of Minnesota in 1939. He taught at the public school and college level before winning election to the House of Representatives as a Democrat in 1948, where, after five terms, he was elected as one of Minnesota's U.S. Senators. He soon earned a reputation as one of the Senate's most liberal Democrats and was appointed to the Senate Foreign Relations Committee. Although McCarthy supported the Lyndon Johnson* adminstration in the Gulf of Tonkin Resolution,* he grew more and more frustrated with the war, and by 1967 he had become an outspoken critic.

On November 30, 1967, McCarthy announced his candidacy for the 1968 Democratic presidential nomination, a move that stunned Democrats, who hoped to avoid an intraparty nomination battle. Antiwar* Democrats rallied around McCarthy, and he did surprisingly well in the March 1968 New Hampshire primary, almost defeating President Johnson. McCarthy's success played a key role in the president's decision not to seek another term in the White House. McCarthy stayed in the race, but Senator Robert F. Kennedy* soon upstaged him, and after Kennedy's assassination, Vice-President Hubert Humphrey* won the nomination. Eugene McCarthy then retired from the Senate in 1970. Since then he has lectured widely about American politics.

REFERENCES: Hoyt Purvis, "Eugene McCarthy," in James S. Olson, ed., *Dictionary of the Vietnam War*, 1988; George Rising, *Clean for Gene: Eugene McCarthy's 1968 Presidential Campaign*, 1997.

McGOVERN, GEORGE STANLEY. George Stanley McGovern was born July 19, 1922, in Avon, South Dakota. During World War II he flew as a pilot with the U.S. Army Air Corps, and he received a bachelor's degree from Dakota Wesleyan University in 1945. He went to graduate school at Northwestern University, earning a Ph.D. there in 1953. During graduate school, he also taught at Dakota Wesleyan. Between 1953 and 1955, McGovern worked as executive secretary to the South Dakota Democratic Party and positioned himself in the state political network. He was elected to Congress in 1956, retired in 1961 to accept President John F. Kennedy's* appointment as head of the Food for Peace program, and then won a U.S. Senate seat in 1963.

After Senator Robert F. Kennedy's* assassination in June 1968, McGovern emerged as the leader of the antiwar* Democrats, but he could not wrest the presidential nomination from Vice-President Hubert Humphrey.* McGovern did win the party's nomination in 1972 and staged a liberal campaign based on an immediate, unilateral U.S. withdrawal from Vietnam, increases in government social programs, and new political power for women and minorities. But his campaign was badly flawed. When journalists revealed that his running mate,

Senator Thomas Eagleton, had a history of chronic depression, McGovern dumped him, a move that smacked of disloyalty. Also, McGovern's liberal principles were out of touch with most voters. President Richard M. Nixon* won a landslide victory over McGovern. McGovern remained in the Senate until his retirement in 1981. Since his retirement, McGovern has continued to lecture, consult, and write. He is the author of *The Colorado Coal Strike, 1913–14* (1953), *War Against Want* (1964), *Agricultural Thought in the Twentieth Century* (1967), *A Time of War, A Time of Peace* (1968), *The Great Coalfield War* (1972), *An American Journey* (1974), and *Grassroots* (1978). Most recently, he wrote *Terry* (1996), the poignant story of his daughter's struggle with and death from alcoholism.

REFERENCE: Norman Mailer, *St. George and the Godfather*, 1983.

McHALE'S NAVY. McHale's Navy was a popular television* situation comedy in the 1960s. First broadcast by ABC on October 11, 1962, it starred Ernest Borgnine as Lieutenant Commander Quinton McHale, Joe Flynn as Captain Wallace Binghamton, and Tim Conway as Ensign Charles Parker. The setting is a P.T. boat group in World War II. McHale is an easygoing, break-any-rule officer, but his superior, Captain Binghamton, is an anal-retentive, by-the-book commander. The conflict between those two personalities provided most of the show's humor. The last episode of *McHale's Navy* was broadcast on August 30, 1966.

REFERENCE: Tim Brooks and Earle Marsh, *The Complete Directory to Prime Time Network and Cable TV Shows*, 1995.

McINTIRE, CARL. Carl McIntire was born May 17, 1906, in Ypsilanti, Michigan. He was raised in Oklahoma. After taking a teaching certificate at Southeastern State Teachers College in Oklahoma, McIntire went on to earn a bachelor's degree at Park College in Missouri. In 1927, he entered the Princeton Theological Seminary, and his experiences there shaped the rest of his life. Late in the 1920s, the Princeton Theological Seminary was embroiled in a bitter struggle between liberals and fundamentalists, and McIntire came under the influence of J. Gresham Machen, a New Testament scholar who wanted to purge the Presbyterian church of all liberals. He accepted absolutely the inerrancy of the Bible, the Virgin birth, and the Resurrection of Jesus Christ.

In 1929, McIntire left Princeton, which he thought was becoming too liberal. He founded the Westminster Seminary. Seven years later, McIntire and Machen founded the Presbyterian Church of America, insisting that only they were truly faithful to the original Westminster Confession. The Presbyterian Church of America was soon divided by factionalism, and McIntire came to head the Bible Presbyterian Church.

During the 1950s, McIntire was a bitter opponent of the ecumenical movement. He would tolerate no overtures to Jews and Roman Catholics. He was also one of America's most outspoken anticommunists. The Bible sanctioned, he believed, the free enterprise system, democracy, and economic competition and opposed all forms of collectivism, including the welfare state. During the 1960s, McIntire was a leading exponent of the radical right, openly endorsing the presidential candidacy of Barry Goldwater* in 1964 and calling the Vietnam War* a "righteous crusade." Carl McIntire was a harbinger of the rise of the far right in American politics, although the likes of Jerry Falwell and Pat Robertson eclipsed him in influence in the 1980s.

REFERENCES: Gary Clabaugh, *Thunder on the Right: The Protestant Fundamentalists*, 1974; Erling Jorstad, *The Politics of Doomsday: Fundamentalists of the Far Right*, 1970.

McKISSICK, FLOYD. Floyd McKissick was born in Asheville, North Carolina, March 9, 1922. He served in the army during World War II and did his undergraduate studies at Morehouse College and the University of North Carolina. McKissick then completed a law degree at North Carolina. He practiced law privately, taking on public school integration cases and becoming embittered at what black children had to endure when a previously white public school was desegregated. He also defended sit-in* protesters and black members of labor unions. McKissick became active in the Congress of Racial Equality* (CORE), and in 1966 he replaced James Farmer* as head of CORE.

Under McKissick's direction, CORE abandoned its liberal, interracial, integrationist philosophy for a militant, black power* point of view. He also rejected Martin Luther King, Jr.'s* emphasis on nonviolent civil disobedience. McKissick left CORE in 1968 to focus his attention on economic and political empowerment for African Americans. More specifically, he invested his energies into constructing Soul City, a new community in Warren County, North Carolina. He hoped to build there an integrated community of 55,000 people with an industrial economy. Although the Department of Housing and Urban Development eventually poured millions into the project, it never really got off the ground. Floyd McKissick died April 2, 1991.

REFERENCE: *New York Times*, April 3, 1991.

McLUHAN, HERBERT MARSHALL. Marshall McLuhan was born in Edmonton, Alberta, Canada, July 21, 1911. He was raised in Winnipeg, Manitoba, and graduated from the University of Manitoba in 1933. McLuhan earned his Ph.D. at Cambridge University in 1936. He taught English at St. Louis University from 1937 to 1944, and he then spent two years at Assumption University in Windsor, Ontario. In 1946, McLuhan joined the faculty of the University of Toronto. By that time, however, his scholarly focus was shifting from English literature to mass culture, marked by his 1952 book, *The Mechanical Bride: Folklore of Industrial Men*. His prizewinning book *The Gutenberg Galaxy* in 1962 argued that the development of movable type actually led to the development of linear thinking in the humanities and sciences. He theorized that as oral communication gave way to print, the eye became more important than the ear as a sensory organ, leading to self-centeredness in human beings and social disintegration. Thought and action became separate functions.

In the mid-twentieth century, McLuhan argued, the electronic age had created what he called a "global village," which he discussed in his 1962 book, *Understanding Media*. The separation of thought and action ended because television had intensified and redistributed sensory awareness. In 1967 he wrote the book *The Medium Is the Message*. By that time, McLuhan had become the reigning intellectual guru of the television age. He died December 30, 1981. REFERENCE: *New York Times*, January 1, 1981.

McNAMARA, ROBERT STRANGE. Robert S. McNamara was born in San Francisco, California, on June 9, 1916. He received an undergraduate degree from the University of California at Berkeley in 1937 and an MBA from Harvard in 1939. McNamara served in the U.S. Army Air Corps during World War II, primarily in influential administrative positions, where he demonstrated his expertise in statistics and management and showed his ability in dealing with large bureaucracies. After the war, he pioneered the field of management systems at Ford Motor Company, rising rapidly through company as one of its "Whiz Kids." In 1960, at the age of forty-four, McNamara was named president of Ford and hailed as one of America's business geniuses. The next year, he accepted President John F. Kennedy's* appointment as secretary of defense. He remained at the Pentagon until his resignation in 1968.

Full of faith and naïveté, McNamara became an early architect of U.S. policy in Vietnam. Supremely confident of the efficacy of modern technology and of the ability of systems managers, he was certain that the United States would prevail in Vietnam, just as it had against the Germans and Japanese during World War II. In 1964 and 1965, McNamara was the power behind the throne, orchestrating early counterinsurgency* efforts, the Gulf of Tonkin Resolution,* the bombing* of North Vietnam, and the introduction of large numbers of U.S. ground troops in Vietnam. To stop the infiltration of North Vietnamese troops and supplies across the Demilitarized Zone* (DMZ) into South Vietnam, he even proposed what journalists sarcastically dubbed "McNamara's Wall"—a system of electronic devices to alert monitors of any breach of the DMZ. The proposal was never implemented.

But as the war ground to a stalemate, McNamara gradually lost his confidence. The resilience of the North Vietnamese, and their willingness to accept such punishment, astonished him. So did their ability to move huge volumes of troops and supplies down the Ho Chi Minh Trail* into South Vietnam in spite of massive U.S. aerial bombing* campaigns. His strategy of attrition,* based on the assumption that North Vietnam would give up the fight because of heavy losses of men and matériel, virtually unraveled in 1966 and 1967. McNamara visited South Vietnam many times trying to get a handle on the conflict, and each time he came away more disgusted with the political corruption endemic in the South Vietnamese government. U.S. casualties* were too high, the North Vietnamese and Vietcong* too determined, and the South Vietnamese too venal.

By 1967, McNamara was urging President Lyndon B. Johnson* to halt the bombing of North Vietnam, seek a diplomatic solution, and a negotiate a settlement to the war. It was unwinnable. Johnson considered McNamara's change of heart a betrayal. For seven years, the secretary of defense had preached the virtues of the war and the attainability of its goals, and now, with more than 500,000 U.S. soldiers in Vietnam and more than 30,000 others dead, he had changed his mind. Late in 1967, Johnson asked for McNamara's resignation. By that time, McNamara was only too willing to go. The war had sapped him of his energy, his optimism, and his emotional reserves. Upon leaving the Pentagon, McNamara assumed the presidency of the World Bank. He retired from the bank in 1983.

McNamara remained silent about Vietnam, refusing all interviews until 1994, when he wrote his memoirs. The book—*In Retrospect: The Tragedy and Lessons of Vietnam*—ignited a firestorm of controversy upon its release and became a national bestseller. Although McNamara admitted in the book that he had been wrong about Vietnam, that the United States should never have become involved there, his belated confession did little to endear him to the American people. The book raised the ire of veterans' groups, who accused McNamara of trying to profit from a war that, in their minds, he had started and that had caused so much suffering. Too much blood was on his hands, they said, for him to try to make money off the war. McNamara maintained his traditionally cool reserve throughout the entire controversy.

REFERENCE: Robert S. McNamara, *In Retrospect: The Tragedy and Lessons of Vietnam*, 1994.

MEAD, MARGARET. Born in Philadelphia in 1901 to a liberal family, Margaret Mead became America's leading anthropologist. Educated at Barnard and Columbia University, she eventually became curator of ethnology at the American Museum of Natural History. Mead's fieldwork was concentrated in the Pacific Islands. In Micronesia, adolescents are sexually active much sooner than in the United States. Premarital sex is socially acceptable in their culture. The stigma lies in social dating or showing affection in public. She wrote about her experiences in her most influential book, *Coming of Age in Samoa*. When published, it was deemed a "sex book" by many critics; some even labeled Mead "a dirty old woman." Critics have also claimed that her work was biased by an American point of view, and many Micronesians themselves felt her writings were stereotypical and only partially informed about their culture.

Even Mead's greatest critics cannot deny, however, her influential legacy. A prominent anthropologist claimed, "Her achievement was to show that the findings of anthropologists about remote people were highly relevant to the concerns of Americans about their own society." Mead compared how much easier it was for Samoan youths to enter adulthood than those in the restrictive Victorian environment of twentieth-century America.

In the 1960s, Mead's studies became a significant intellectual dimension of the counterculture's* attitudes toward sexuality. Free love, many of them argued, was natural and acceptable. The idea that another remote and uncorrupted culture had long ago implemented counterculture values proved that "their way was nature's way." Hippies embraced Mead as a counterculture icon. Sex, no longer taboo, became a topic that was discussed in social circles. It was seen as a healthy, fun activity that should be used for pleasure and communication. The 1960s sexual revolution* also had a great impact on the women's movement, in which Mead was an active participant. Her studies demonstrated that women and men could have equal or unequal roles depending on the environment in which they were raised, not their gender. Margaret Mead died in 1978.
REFERENCE: Jane Howard, *Margaret Mead: A Life*, 1984.

Laurie Pierce

MEDICARE. In 1946, President Harry Truman first called for a system of national health insurance, and in 1953 his Commission on the Health Needs of the Nation made a similar recommendation. By that time the nation was entering a more conservative period in terms of public policy, and the Dwight D. Eisenhower* administration was not inclined to act on the recommendation. Twelve years later President Lyndon B. Johnson* picked up on the idea as part of his Great Society* program. On July 30, 1965, Congress amended the Social Security Act by adding the Medical Care for the Aged Program. Medicare provided for a basic hospital insurance program for individuals over the age of sixty-five who were part of the social security system. It also provided for a supplementary, voluntary medical insurance program to cover physicians, surgeons, and home health care costs. Finally, it included the medicaid program to provide basic medical services to the needy and disabled who were not part of social security. Medicaid was designed to be a state aid program, with the federal government providing half of the funds to cover costs.
REFERENCE: *The Complete Medicare Handbook*, 1990.

MERCURY PROGRAM. See **NATIONAL AERONAUTICS AND SPACE ADMINISTRATION.**

MEREDITH, JAMES. James Meredith was born in Kosciusko, Mississippi, June 25, 1933. After graduating from high school, he joined the U.S. Air Force and rose to the rank of sergeant during his ten-year tour of duty. After leaving the military, Meredith attended Jackson State University and became point man in the civil rights crusade in 1962 to integrate the University of Mississippi. Governor Ross Barnett *bitterly opposed desegregation and tried to block Meredith's enrollment. Barnett continued his obstructionist stance even after President John F. Kennedy* called in federal troops to guarantee Meredith's admission. The governor earned a contempt citation for refusing to cooperate. Meredith graduated from the University of Mississippi in 1963.

He came to national attention again in 1966, when he decided to prove that an African American could march to Jackson, Mississippi, during voter registration week without harassment. One day into the march, he was wounded by a shotgun blast, and civil rights leaders from all over the country descended on Mississippi to complete the "freedom march." But while Martin Luther King, Jr.,* still spoke of nonviolent civil disobedience, Stokely Carmichael,* the young leader of the Student Nonviolent Coordinating Committee* (SNCC), startled the nation by ridiculing nonviolence and crying out for black power.* Meredith recovered from his wounds and received a law degree from Columbia University in 1968. Since then he has been president of his own business, Meredith Enterprises.

REFERENCE: Dan Elish, *James Meredith and School Desegregation*, 1994.

METHAMPHETAMINE. Methamphetamine, also known as "speed," is a powerful stimulant drug. Physicians legally prescribe it to treat obesity, fatigue, narcolepsy, and clogged nasal passages, but it is a popular illegal drug as well. During the late 1960s, intravenous injection of speed began to replace LSD as the most popular form of drug abuse. Among the physiological effects of speed are heightened senses of alertness, energy, and wakefulness, but when abused it can also lead to paranoia, aggression, impaired judgment, and altered sleep patterns. Chronic abuse of methamphetamine can cause liver and kidney damage, strokes, cardiac irregularities, convulsions, and coma.

REFERENCE: Kevin Scheel, *Drugs of Abuse*, 1991.

MEXICAN AMERICAN LEGAL DEFENSE AND EDUCATION FUND. The Mexican American Legal Defense and Education Fund (MALDEF) was founded in 1968 by Peter Tijerina, who hoped to protect Chicano* civil rights and assist prospective Chicano lawyers in getting their law degrees. At first, MALDEF concerned itself with the issues of school desegregation, voting rights, jury exclusion, and job discrimination, and in the 1970s it added bilingual education and U.S. Census undercounting of Hispanics as issues. Those issues have remained its concerns in recent years.

REFERENCE: Matt S. Meier and Feliciano Rivera, *Dictionary of Mexican American History*, 1981.

MEXICAN AMERICAN YOUTH ORGANIZATION. In 1967, José Angel Gutiérrez* founded the Mexican American Youth Organization (MAYO) in San Antonio, Texas, to promote the educational needs of Chicano* children. He became its first president. By 1974, MAYO had a membership in excess of 100,000 people. MAYO's primary concern was to raise the political consciousness of Mexican-American young people and encourage their participation in politics. The group sponsored demonstrations and walkouts at a number of Texas

public high schools in the late 1960s and helped found La Raza Unida Party in 1970.
REFERENCE: Matt S. Meier and Feliciano Rivera, *Dictionary of Mexican American History*, 1981.

MEXICAN AMERICANS. The need for farmworkers in the United States grew dramatically after the end of European immigration, the flight to the cities, and World War II job opportunities. To meet that demand, the United States established the *bracero* (work hands) program in 1942, and by 1964 more than 5 million Mexican *braceros* had worked seasonally in the Southwest, most of them on commercial farms and railroads. By American standards they were poorly paid, but they welcomed the chance to send money home to their families. After more than twenty years of lobbying between commercial farmers and labor unions, Congress finally gave in to the unions and terminated the *bracero* program in 1965. Abolition, however, only increased the flow of undocumented Mexican aliens because Mexican workers formerly admitted under the *bracero* program contacted their previous employers and went to work illegally. When the Immigration and Nationality Act of 1965* imposed a quota of 120,000 immigrants from the Western Hemisphere each year, the number of illegal aliens increased again.

But federal legislation was only a minor factor influencing the flow of undocumented aliens; traditional push-pull forces were responsible for the Mexican migration. Population growth in Mexico has been staggering, but the labor market has been unable to absorb the people. Industrial development and agricultural mechanization are breaking up the traditional hacienda society, and millions of farm laborers have been displaced from the land. In 1940 more than 65 percent of the Mexican workforce was engaged in agriculture, but that declined to less than 50 percent in 1970. In the meantime, more than 15 million new acres of irrigated land were put into production in the American Southwest, and along with industrialization there, the need for unskilled laborers greatly increased. With wages in the United States three to four times as much as Mexican wages for equivalent jobs, millions of farm laborers crossed the border.

Mexican immigrants found themselves in a uniquely difficult position in the United States. As a mestizo people despised for generations by white Mexicans of European descent, they felt a community spirit when faced with similar treatment by whites in the United States. At the same time, many Mexican Americans held similar prejudices against African Americans. They were a lower class separated from blacks by race and culture and from white Americans by race, culture, and income. The color line in America served to isolate Mexican Americans from whites while uniting them to one another.

After 1945 Mexican-American society changed somewhat, and those changes cleared the way for the more militant Chicano* spirit of the 1960s. For decades the quest for Mexican-American civil rights had been led by such groups as the League of United Latin American Citizens (LULAC) and the GI Forum, which worked to end de jure discrimination. By the late 1950s, however, Mexican-American leaders realized that legal action was ineffective without political power, and in 1958 they formed the Mexican-American Political Association (MAPA) in California, the Political Association of Spanish-Speaking Organizations (PASO) in Texas, and the American Coordinating Council on Political Education (ACCPE) in Arizona. MAPA worked for only Mexican support, and the others for a coalition with white liberals, black activists, and labor unions, but all three tried to mobilize Mexican-American political power. John F. Kennedy's* campaign in 1960 worked through MAPA, PASO, and ACCPE to form Viva Kennedy* clubs, and in 1962 MAPA and PASO ran successful candidates in the Crystal City, Texas, elections. José Gutiérrez* rose out of those elections and in 1970 formed La Raza Unida, a political party dedicated to community control of Mexican-American counties in south Texas.

Corky Gonzalez* founded the Crusade for Justice* in 1965. Schooled in local politics and Denver antipoverty programs, Gonzalez demanded reform of the criminal justice system, an end to police brutality, and good housing, schools, and jobs for Mexican Americans. Culturally nationalistic, Gonzalez also sponsored Chicanismo, a pride in being Mexican-American and in mestizo roots and a consciousness of ethnic origins that reflected an earlier Pachuco culture. A host of Chicano writers and artists—including novelists Raymond Barrio and Richard Vásquez, short story writer Daniel Garza, playwright Luis Valdez, and painter Raul Espinoza—evoked the Chicano spirit, and Chicano studies programs swept through the schools of the Southwest in the 1970s and 1980s.

Reies Tijerina* was another Mexican-American activist of the 1960s and 1970s. After traveling widely in Spain and the United States, he formed the Alianza Federal de Mercedes (Federal Alliance of Land Grants) in 1963 and demanded the return of land taken from *tejanos, californios*, and *nuevos mexicanos*. Militant and articulate, Tijerina was a charismatic leader who denounced racism and called for ethnic solidarity. In 1966, claiming millions of acres in New Mexico and urging secession, he ''occupied'' Kit Carson National Forest and assaulted several forest rangers. On June 5, 1967, Tijerina and some of his supporters raided the courthouse at Tierra Amarillo, New Mexico, shot two deputies, released eleven Alianza members, and fled the town with several hostages. Sentenced to prison, Tijerina was paroled in 1971 on the condition that he dissociate himself from the Alianza, and without his leadership the movement died.

No Mexican-American leader rivaled César Chávez in influence. A counterpart in time and philosophy to Martin Luther King, Jr.,* he too believed in nonviolence but was more committed to economic action than civil rights. In 1962, he organized the National Farm Workers (later the United Farm Workers). For two years he built the union; then he struck the Delano grape growers, demanding better pay. The growers refused, and Chávez turned the strike into a moral crusade, an appeal to the conscience of America. The growers used violence, strikebreakers, and anticommunist rhetoric; and Chávez appealed to white liberals like Robert Kennedy* and Hubert Humphrey,* labor unions like the American Federation of Labor–Congress of Industrial Organizations (AFL–CIO), black leaders like Martin Luther King, Jr., and white students on college campuses. For five years Chávez led a national boycott of California grapes, fought the growers as well as the Teamsters Union, which tried to organize a rival union, and finally, in 1970, succeeded in winning a long-term contract with the growers. Chávez had been the most successful Chicano of all.

REFERENCES: David T. Abalos, *Latinos in the United States: The Sacred and the Political*, 1987; Mario Barrera, *Beyond Aztlan: Ethnic Autonomy in Comparative Perspective*, 1988; Juan Gomez-Quinones, *Chicano Politics: Reality and Promise, 1940–1990*, 1990; Alejandro Portes and Robert L. Bach, *Latin Journey: Cuban and Mexican Immigrants in the United States*, 1985.

MIDNIGHT COWBOY. *Midnight Cowboy* was one of the darkest, most influential films of the 1960s. Released by United Artists in 1969, it was directed by John Schlesinger and based on Jerome Herlihy's 1965 novel, *Midnight Cowboy*. The film starred Jon Voight as Joe Buck and Dustin Hoffman as Ratso Rizzo. A handsome, rural, southern misfit who has come to New York City to make his fortune as a male prostitute, Joe Buck is as green in the city as any cowboy could ever be, and he eventually teams up with street-smart Rizzo, a homeless, tuberculosis-ridden Italian American, for survival. But over time, as they try to deal with a rotten world of poverty, violence, sexual perversion, drugs, and alienation, their self-serving alliance blossoms into a real friendship, redeeming a film that would otherwise be hopelessly depressing. *Midnight Cowboy* at the time carried an "X" rating because of nudity and violence, but it nevertheless earned Hoffman and Voight Best Actor nominations from the Academy of Motion Picture Arts and Sciences.

REFERENCE: *New York Times*, May 26, 1969.

MIGRANT HEALTH ACT OF 1962. During the early 1960s, concerns about poverty in America intensified. In 1960, Edward R. Murrow of CBS broadcast his documentary "Harvest of Shame," an exposé about the plight of migrant workers in the United States. One year later, Michael Harrington's* book *Poverty in America* again brought the problem to public attention. Congress responded later in 1962 with the Migrant Health Act, a piece of federal legislation that funded private and public agencies to improve health care for migrant workers.

REFERENCE: James S. Olson, ed., *Dictionary of United States Economic History*, 1992.

MILITARY-INDUSTRIAL COMPLEX. In an impassioned speech delivered in 1959, President Dwight D. Eisenhower* warned the United States about the existence of a "military-industrial complex" that was growing in power and had the potential of affecting American foreign policy. The idea that there was an important relationship between the military and private industry was not new.

During the 1930s, Senator Gerald P. Nye of North Dakota had charged that munitions manufacturers were responsible for getting the United States involved in World War I. Eisenhower argued, however, that the Cold War* with the Soviet Union had created huge and permanent defense expenditures and that the military and the industries producing the weapons had a vested interest in the continuation of international tensions. Since Eisenhower's speech, the term ''military-industrial complex'' has continued to be used by those who oppose massive defense spending.

REFERENCE: William Greider, *Fortress America*, 1998.

MILLER, ARTHUR. Arthur Miller was born in New York City October 17, 1915. His father was a successful businessman until the Great Depression, when he went bankrupt. After graduating from high school in 1933, Miller went to work in order to make enough money to go to college. He attended the University of Michigan. At Ann Arbor, Miller began to show his talent for writing, especially plays. His most celebrated work—*The Death of a Salesman*—was published in 1949. Its hero, Willy Loman, is a washed-up, elderly salesman who loses his career and his identity. The play was an indictment of middle-class American values. In 1953, Miller wrote *The Crucible*, a play allegedly about the Salem witch trials of the 1690s but actually an attack on the hysteria, innuendo, and guilt-by-association assumptions so characteristic of American society during the red scare of the early 1950s. In 1955, Miller wrote *A View from the Bridge*. In retaliation for his liberal leanings, the House Committee on Un-American Activities subpoenaed Miller in 1956 and charged him with contempt of Congress. He appealed the conviction and won. Miller's later works grew even more pessimistic. In the *Misfits* (1961), *After the Fall* (1964), and *The Price* (1968), he presents a morally ambiguous world where human beings are alienated from the universe and from themselves. People exist in hopelessly corrupt circumstances. Miller continues to serve as America's most prolific playwright. Among his most recent works are *Timebends: A Life* (1987), *Playing for Time* (1990), *The Last Yankee* (1993), and *Broken Glass* (1994). Miller wrote the screenplay for the 1996 film *The Crucible*, which was based on his earlier play of the same name.

REFERENCE: Bruce Glassman, *Arthur Miller*, 1990; James J. Martine, ed., *Critical Essays on Arthur Miller*, 1979.

MINISKIRTS. The miniskirt was a slender, tight-fitting dress whose hemline reached to between six and ten inches above the knee. A form of rebellion against traditional styles, the miniskirt became symbolic of the sexual revolution* and the youth rebellion of the 1960s. Actually, the development of panty hose really made the miniskirt possible, because it liberated women from garter belts and traditional stockings. In the winter of 1965, Parisian fashion designer Andre Courreges took an enormous risk and sent models down his runway wearing white boots and angular-lined dresses with shockingly high hemlines.

He called them miniskirts. Fashion designer Mary Quant, who worked out of the Chelsea section of London, is considered the "mother of the miniskirt." The first miniskirt debuted at Quant's boutique, known as Bazaar, on King's Road in 1965, and in a matter of months it had become the fashion craze among young people around the world. The dress seemed to challenge propriety and respectability—exactly what the 1960s generation was interested in doing. By 1966, the miniskirt had become the trendsetting fashion statement around the world, or at least in noncommunist and non-Muslim urban centers, where legal restrictions on women's dress did not really exist. It became mainstream, at least in its more modest versions, in December 1966, when Jacqueline Kennedy wore one to a restaurant opening in New York City. In the 1970s, feminists rejected the miniskirt as an overt attempt to sexually titillate men. Its long-term impact, however, could not be changed, since hemlines have generally been higher ever since the debut of the miniskirt.

REFERENCE: Joel Lobenthal, *Radical Rags: Fashions of the Sixties*, 1990.

MIRANDA V. ARIZONA. During the tenure of Chief Justice Earl Warren* (1953–1960), the Supreme Court assumed the most liberal constitutional profile in U.S. history, narrowing the powers of government officials and broadening the rights of individuals. A series of decisions revolving around the self-incrimination clause of the Fifth Amendment particularly revealed the Court's liberal bent. One such case was *Miranda v. Arizona*, decided on June 13, 1966, with Chief Justice Warren writing the majority opinion. The vote on the case was 5 to 4. The issue at hand was the right of police to question a subject about an alleged crime before he or she had spoken to an attorney. The Court decided that in all criminal arrests, the police had to inform accused people that they had the right, under the Fifth Amendment, to remain silent, that anything they told the police could be held against them in a court of law, and that they had the right, under the Sixth Amendment, to legal counsel. Each suspect had to be given this information before any police interrogation could begin.

REFERENCE: 384 U.S. 436 (1966).

MISSING IN ACTION. During the course of the Vietnam* conflict, millions of American military men and women served in the combat theater. They fought in jungles, mountains, and lowland swamps where unprecedented volumes of firepower were expended. When the war was over, however, there were far fewer soldiers listed as missing in action than in any previous American war. After the repatriation of the prisoners of war* in 1973, 2,546 American person-nel—2,505 servicemen and women and forty-one civilians—were not accounted for, only 4 percent of the 58,152 killed. This should be compared with the 78,750 who remain unaccounted for from World War II (19.4 percent) and 8,300 (15 percent) from the Korean War.

REFERENCE: Arlene Leonard, "Prisoners-of-War, Missing-in-Action," in James S. Olson, ed., *The Vietnam War: Handbook of the Literature and Research*, 1993.

MISSION IMPOSSIBLE. *Mission Impossible* was a popular CBS television series in the 1960s. First broadcast on September 17, 1966, the program revolved around a special team of covert American intelligence agents who weekly engaged in international intrigue. It starred Peter Graves as James Phelps, Barbara Bain as Cinnamon Carter, Martin Landau as Robin Hand, Greg Morris as Barney Collier, and Peter Lupus as Willie Armitage. During its first years of the series, each weekly episode had the Impossible Mission Force interfering in the internal political affairs of foreign governments, always in the name of anticommunism and democracy. As the Vietnam* protests mounted in strength, however, the idea of American agents' toppling foreign governments became less popular, and the scripts changed, with the team now attacking organized crime. The last episode was broadcast in September 1973.
REFERENCE: Patrick J. White, *The Complete* Mission: Impossible *Dossier*, 1991.

MR. ED. *Mr. Ed* was a popular, if nonsensical, situation comedy of the early 1960s. It premiered on CBS on October 1, 1961, starring Alan Young as Wilbur Post and Connie Hines as Carol Post. Its escapist humor was built upon the idea of a horse—Mr. Ed—that could talk only to Wilbur Post. The talking horse got Post into an endless series of embarrassing and confusing situations. The last episode of *Mr. Ed* was broadcast on September 8, 1965.
REFERENCE: Tim Brooks and Earle Marsh, *The Complete Directory to Prime Time Network and Cable TV Shows*, 1995.

MOD. The term ''mod'' became a slang expression in the 1960s to refer to an individual who was young, rebellious, and into the sex, drug, fashion, long hair, and rock-and-roll culture of the 1960s. The expression actually had its origins in England and came to the United States with the so-called British invasion* of rock groups in the mid-1960s. The term was immortalized in American popular culture by the successful television program *The Mod Squad*.
REFERENCE: Ruth Bronsteen, *The Hippy's Handbook—How to Live on Love*, 1967.

THE MOD SQUAD. *Mod Squad* was a popular police drama in the late 1960s and early 1970s. ABC broadcast the first episode on September 24, 1968, with Michael Cole as Pete Cochran, Clarence Williams III as Linc Hayes, and Peggy Lipton as Julie Barnes. In the era of hippies* and the counterculture,* *The Mod Squad* portrayed hippie police officers who infiltrated the youth movement to ferret out criminals. Each member of the squad had already dropped out of straight society and remained irreverent and rebellious in his or her own right. The last episode of *The Mod Squad* was broadcast on August 23, 1973.
REFERENCE: Tim Brooks and Earle Marsh, *The Complete Directory to Prime Time Network and Cable TV Shows*, 1995.

MOHAWK BLOCKADE (1968). Under Jay's Treaty, which the United States and Great Britain signed in 1794, the Mohawk Indians of upstate New York had long enjoyed the right to cross the boundary between the United States and Canada in order to visit relatives among the Canadian Mohawks. The St. Lawrence River constituted the boundary, and the Cornwall Bridge across the river was the most frequently used crossing point. During the 1950s and 1960s, however, Canadian authorities began casually, and then systematically, inhibiting the movement of Mohawks back and forth across the border, which the Indians considered a violation of solemn treaty rights. In 1968, to protest the Canadian government's regulation of their movement, a number of Mohawk activists intentionally blockaded the bridge, disrupting traffic flow and creating one of the earliest acts of insurgency in the modern red power* movement. Several Mohawks were arrested, but neither New York nor Canadian authorities were able to prosecute them. Mohawk and Canadian officials eventually negotiated a settlement that preserved Mohawk rights. In the wake of the incident, the Mohawks began publishing *Akwesasne Notes*, a journal that soon became the most widely recognized voice of Indian militancy.

REFERENCE: Alvin M. Josephy, Jr., *Red Power: The American Indians' Fight for Freedom*, 1971.

THE MONKEES. On September 8, 1965, 437 "Monkee" wanna-bes, including Danny Hutton, Paul Williams, and Charles Manson, auditioned for parts in a pilot episode of a television sitcom to be centered around a "Beatles-type group." The four selected were Davy Jones, Mike Nesmith, Peter Tork, and Mickey Dolentz. The pilot show proved to be a huge success with test audiences and was placed in NBC television's fall 1966 prime-time schedule. Although the television show experienced difficulty taking off, Monkee records were immediate hits. Their debut single, "Last Train to Clarksville," went to number one on the pop charts, and "I'm a Believer," a single written by Neil Diamond, also rocketed to number one, earning gold record status by selling more than 1 million copies, even before it was ever released. Their debut album—*The Monkees*—topped the U.S. charts for thirteen weeks, selling 3.2 million copies in only three months.

By the end of 1966, the Monkees had become phenomenally successful, manufactured pop culture icons. Up to that time, they had not even been playing the instruments on their albums. At Mike Nesmith's insistence, the group got to incorporate more of their own songs. On February 11, 1967, while visiting the United Kingdom, their public relations representative announced, "In the future, they will play on their records and not use session men." "A Little Bit Me, A Little Bit You," another Neil Diamond piece, became the third million-selling Monkees single. Then on May 16, 1967, *Headquarters* was released, becoming their third consecutive album to sell over a million copies. They also won an Emmy Award in 1967 for the outstanding television comedy series. Their concerts in the United States and around the world were sellouts. The Monkees earned a star on the Hollywood Walk of Fame, carrying with them the love and admiration of generations of Monkee listeners.

But that was the peak of their success. In 1968, after filming the fifty-eighth episode, NBC canceled *The Monkees* television comedy. That same year, they released three progressively less successful albums—*Pisces*; *Aquarius, Capricorn and Jones Ltd.*; and *The Birds, The Bees, and The Monkees*. Their feature film *Head*, released late in 1968, was a box office catastrophe. Peter Tork left the group in 1969, buying out his own contract for $160,000. In 1970, the rest of the group split, not to be reunited again until 1989, when they had become a nostalgia act for middle-aged baby boomers.

REFERENCE: Edward Reilly, *The Monkees: A Manufactured Image*, 1987.

Melissa M. Miller

MONOKINI. In 1964, with the sexual revolution* just beginning in the United States, fashion designer Rudi Gemreich introduced what he called the "monokini," a woman's bathing suit featuring a girdlelike bottom and two shoulder straps, but without a top. Since most public beaches in the United States had ordinances outlawing nudist activity, the monokini never really caught on in the marketplace, but it was a sensational introduction to the "topless" age and to the sexual revolution* in the United States.

REFERENCE: Joel Lobenthal, *Radical Rags: Fashions of the Sixties*, 1990.

MONROE, MARILYN. On June 1, 1926, in Los Angeles, Norma Jean Mortensen was born to Gladys Mortensen, a single mother and film fanatic who suffered a mental breakdown two weeks after the baby's birth and was committed to an asylum. Two weeks old, the child was placed in her first of several foster homes. At age sixteen Norma Jean married Jim Daugherty and, soon after, took a job at a war factory, where a photographer from *Yank Magazine* found her. His morale-boosting shots of women doing war work included a photo of Norma Jean that made its way to the magazine's June 1945 cover. Norma Jean thus began her modeling career, for which she dyed her hair blond. Four years after their marriage, she divorced Jim, saying that being single was an essential element in her targeted career—acting.

After auditioning at several studios, she was signed to a contract by 20th Century Fox. Her name was changed to Marilyn, and Norma Jean chose Monroe (her mother's maiden name). The new Marilyn debuted in *Scudda-Hoo! Scudda-Hay!* (1948). Soon, her contract was dropped; with no work available, Monroe resorted to posing nude to make money. After working for the Marx Brothers, she received a seven-year contract with 20th Century Fox. She appeared in *The Asphalt Jungle* and *All about Eve* (1950). The company groomed Marilyn for stardom, using her wholesomeness, innocence, and sex appeal. Monroe's more prominent films were *Niagara, Gentlemen Prefer Blondes, How to Marry a Millionaire* (1953), *The Seven Year Itch* (1955), and *Bus Stop* (1956). Marilyn's lusty voice, bravado dance style, and humor earned her footprints and handprints on Graumann's Chinese Theater's Walk of Fame.

Monroe's second and third marriages, to Joe DiMaggio in 1954 and playwright Arthur Miller in 1956, both ended in divorce. To improve her self-confidence and acting skills, she moved to New York, studying with acting coach Lee Strasberg. At this time Monroe began seeing an analyst for depression and loneliness. Her next film, *The Prince and the Showgirl*, won her the French equivalent of a Best Foreign Actress Oscar. During the filming of *The Misfits* (1960), she arrived hours late to each shooting because of a dependency on sleeping pills and alcohol. That March, she became emotionally distressed and entered the Payne Whitney Psychiatric Clinic in New York. After being released, she began *Something's Got to Give*, but due to her inability to show up for work, the film was stopped, and she was fired. During this time she ran off to Washington to sing "Happy Birthday, Mr. President" at John F. Kennedy's* birthday party. It was widely rumored that both President John F. Kennedy and his brother Attorney General Robert F. Kennedy* had had affairs with Monroe. But soon, they too began to put some distance between themselves and the actress.

Marilyn Monroe was found dead in her Brentwood home August 5, 1962. The cause of death was officially an overdose of sleeping pills, but controversy lies behind the investigation. It is not known if her death was accidental, suicide, or a Kennedy cover-up. Whatever the cause of death, Marilyn Monroe remains a lady who charmed her way into the world's heart. Her sexuality changed American films forever. Directors began using sensuality to attract moviegoers, a practice that continues today. Marilyn Monroe's life glamorized Hollywood scandals, while her death revealed the sad truth about acting stresses. "I'm trying to prove to myself that I'm a person. Then maybe I'll convince myself that I'm an actress," she once remarked.

REFERENCES: Fred Guiles, *Norma Jean: The Life of Marilyn Monroe*, 1993; Donald Spoto, *Marilyn Monroe: A Biography*, 1993.

Meaghan J. Samuels

MOON. See LUNAR LANDING.

MORATORIUM DAY DEMONSTRATIONS (1969). The Moratorium Day demonstrations on October 15, 1969, constituted the largest public protest at that time in American history. The demonstrations were organized by the Vietnam Moratorium Committee, which was founded on June 30, 1969, in order to galvanize a majority position against the war through a nationwide demonstration in October, with plans for one additional day of demonstrations in each successive month until there were satisfactory peace negotiations and a firm American commitment to withdraw from Vietnam. This timetable of demonstrations was conceived by peace campaign veterans Sam Brown, Marge Sklencar, David Hawk, and David Mixner in an effort to counter the anarchic and violent protests seen at the Democratic National Convention* in Chicago in 1968 and to take the antiwar movement* into the communities, where people who had never protested before could respectably offer their opposition to the war in Vietnam.

At the same time, the reconstituted New Mobilization Committee to End the War in Vietnam was preparing for renewed antiwar demonstrations. Working in an uneasy collaboration, the two groups developed a moderate and mainstream approach, whereby organizers generated a grassroots structure in dozens of cities across the nation, garnered bipartisan endorsements from a multitude of senators and congressional representatives, and got their message to the people through ads in the *New York Times* and through press conferences. Millions of people participated in the October 15 moratorium. The activities, in an effort to suspend "business as usual," varied. Many people, including some GIs in Vietnam, wore black armbands to show their opposition to the war; others shone their car headlights; some passed out leaflets door to door; over 100,000 people massed on the Boston Commons; New York City mayor John Lindsay* decreed a day of mourning and ordered the city's flags to be at half-staff; the two largest unions, the Teamsters and the Auto Workers, teamed up with the Chemical Workers to support the moratorium; a quarter of a million people marched in Washington, D.C.; and Coretta Scott King led a candlelight vigil through the capital. Countless speakers, from Benjamin Spock,* to former Supreme Court justice Arthur Goldberg,* to activist David Dellinger* and diplomat Averell Harriman,* all voiced their opposition to the war.

The White House attempted to dampen the sense of goodwill and unity the moratorium demonstrated by releasing a message of support for it by North Vietnam premier Pham Van Dong, but the enormous numbers and the moderate nature of the protest demonstrated overwhelming, nationwide opposition to the war. President Richard M. Nixon's* "silent majority" speech* two weeks later attempted to downplay mainstream opposition to the war, but the moratorium demonstrations in November surpassed the October 15 demonstrations in number. The Vietnam Moratorium Committee was disbanded in April 1970.

REFERENCE: Melvin Small, *Johnson, Nixon, and the Doves*, 1988.

Linda Alkana

MORSE, WAYNE LYMAN. Wayne Morse was born October 20, 1900, in Madison, Wisconsin. He graduated from the University of Wisconsin in 1923 and then took a law degree from Columbia University. He practiced law privately for several years before joining the faculty of the University of Oregon as a professor of law. He taught at Oregon for fifteen years, eventually becoming dean of the law school. He also became involved in state Republican party politics. He was elected to the U.S. Senate in 1942 as a Republican, but he increasingly found the party too conservative. In 1952, he announced himself an independent, and in 1955 he switched over to the Democratic party. By the 1960s, he enjoyed considerable power in the U.S. Senate and had earned a reputation as a senator of fierce independence.

He was also a thorn in President Lyndon B. Johnson's* side because of his early, vociferous opposition to the Vietnam War.* In 1964, Morse was one of only two U.S. senators who voted against the Gulf of Tonkin Resolution.* Morse was suspicious that the president was misleading the country about what had happened in the Gulf of Tonkin, and he believed that the resolution gave Johnson power to wage war, without a congressional declaration, against North Vietnam. He urged the president to hand Vietnam over to the United Nations rather than get the country too deeply involved there. The way to settle the war, he said, "is not by way of the proposed predated declaration of war, giving to the President the power to make war without a declaration of war. The place to settle it is around the conference tables." In 1967, he sponsored, but failed to get passed, a Senate bill to repeal the Gulf of Tonkin Resolution. Morse's opposition to the war, couched in his irascible, blunt style, eventually cost him relection in 1968. He died on July 22, 1974.

REFERENCES: *New York Times*, July 23, 1974; Hoyt Purvis, "Wayne Morse," in James S. Olson, ed., *Dictionary of the Vietnam War*, 1988; Lee Wilkins, *Wayne Morse: A Bio-Bibliography*, 1985.

MOTOWN RECORDING COMPANY. Motown Recording Company introduced the world to the silky, smooth sounds of rhythm and blues. The company, named Motown because of its base in "the Motor City" of Detroit, was established by Berry Gordy, Jr., in 1959. Gordy's musical career started off with a $700 loan from his father and the purchase of his own record store. Although Gordy was a jazz fan, customers usually requested rhythm and blues records. Before he began to stock them, his store went bankrupt. Gordy then went to work in an automobile factory. Because of the dullness of his job, he began to write songs to liven up his life. He submitted them to established record companies but had little success. Then he began to work with his sister Gwendolyn Gordy and distant relative Billy Davis. The three sent their work to the company that managed the great soul singer Jackie Wilson. When Gordy began to write songs for Wilson, Wilson's popularity soared, especially among black, middle-class listeners. Gordy believed that he would never be successful if he did not produce his own music, so he and his fiancée, Raynoma Liles, bought a tape machine and began producing acetates for about $100 each. Soon, they rented studio time, hired professional musicians, and began to attract talented singers. The first was the hit group the Miracles, headed by the great singer Smokey Robinson.

Soon after, many artists signed with Motown, including greats like May Wells, Gladys Knight and the Pips, the Four Tops, and Martha and the Vandellas.* Others included Stevie Wonder, Marvin Gaye,* the Temptations, and the Supremes.* The Supremes, led by the soulful Diana Ross, had five straight number one hits on the *Billboard* charts in 1964 and 1965. Black music had been successful before, but Motown established a consistency that lasted through the 1960s into the 1990s. In 1971, the Motown headquarters moved to Los Angeles, and by then, Motown stopped creating musical trends; they began following them. However, the hits never stopped. Songs by Stevie Wonder, the Jackson 5, Rick James, the Commodores, and Lionel Richie still topped the charts. In 1988, Motown was sold to MCA record company, and Jeryl Busby took over its presidency. Then the hit group Boyz II Men was signed. In 1992, Boyz II Men's hit song "End of the Road" set a *Billboard* record by staying in the number one spot for thirteen straight weeks, the longest of any song since the pop charts began. In 1993, MCA sold Motown to the PolyGram Group, and in 1996, Andre Harrel took over the position of president.

Berry Gordy and Motown in general had a profound effect on not only the 1960s but the entire music world. Gordy helped ease the racial tensions of the 1960s by bridging the gap between whites and blacks by introducing the world to Motown's gospel-sounding soul and rhythm and blues music. Also, with Motown's being the largest black-owned business in the 1960s, it signed many artists who otherwise would not have been given a chance. The Motown legacy, with the help of Berry Gordy and many talented artists, will last forever in the world of popular music.

REFERENCE: David Morse, *Motown and the Arrival of Black Music*, 1971.

Marcus D. LeFlore

EL MOVIMIENTO. "El Movimiento" (the Movement) is a term that first emerged in the late 1960s among Chicano* activists to refer to the flowering of the Mexican-American political and cultural consciousness in the United States. REFERENCE: Matt S. Meier and Feliciano Rivera, *Dictionary of Mexican American History*, 1981.

THE MOYNIHAN REPORT. In 1967, Daniel Patrick Moynihan, who later became a powerful Democratic senator from New York, wrote *The Negro Family: The Case for National Action*, more commonly known as *The Moynihan Report*. At the time, Moynihan was director of the Joint Center for Urban Studies at the Massachusetts Institute of Technology and Harvard University. Moynihan reported that a crisis that could become a national social disaster was emerging in the African-American urban community. The traditional nuclear family was breaking down, primarily because too many fathers were not living in their own homes and helping to support their wives and children. Moynihan blamed the disaster on the institution of slavery, which he argued had emasculated African-American men and destroyed their sense of self-worth. The effects of slavery were still being felt a century after abolition. The consequences, he argued, were potentially disastrous. As more and more single mothers were raising children, the African-American community would sink deeper and deeper into poverty.

The Moynihan Report stimulated enormous social, political, and intellectual controversy in the United States. Many black activists called Moynihan a racist for drawing such a negative portrait of the urban African-American community. Some feminists accused him of sexism, arguing that *The Moynihan Report* implied that single women were not capable of raising children. Time, however, proved Moynihan right, even if his explanation—slavery's emasculation of black men—did not survive. During the next thirty years the problem of single black mothers and poverty reached epidemic proportions in the African-American community. It is more a problem today than thirty years ago, when Moynihan first issued his warning and call for action.

REFERENCE: Lee Rainwater and William Yancey, *The Moynihan Report and the Politics of Controversy*, 1976.

MUHAMMAD, ELIJAH. Elijah Muhammad was born Elijah Poole October 10, 1897, in Georgia. He came from a family of black tenant farmers and moved to Detroit in the mid-1920s. In 1932, Poole joined the Islamic Temple, which had been founded in Detroit by Farrad Muhammad. By 1932, Poole was the chief minister of the Black Muslim* movement and headed his own temple in Chicago. He was committed to converting African Americans to Islam, and he took on the name of Elijah Muhammad. He had a number of run-ins with the law in Chicago, primarily because of his insistence on taking black children out of the public schools and educating them at the temple. By the mid-1930s, Elijah Muhammad had emerged as the national leader of the Black Muslim movement.

During World War II, he refused to obey the selective service laws and served a four-year term at the federal prison in Milan, Michigan. When he returned to Chicago after his release, he called the movement the Nation of Islam and watched it grow steadily. In the theology of the Nation of Islam, black people were seen as direct descendants of Allah, while whites were ''devils.'' They dropped white names in favor of Koranic names and frequently used the initial ''X,'' which meant ''unknown.'' Elijah Muhammad called on black men to work hard, obey the law, govern their families with authority and righteousness, make their devotions to Allah, avoid all but the most necessary contact with white people, and await for the prophetic redemption of black people.

During the 1960s, Elijah Muhammad gained notoriety because of the assassination of Malcolm X* in 1965 and the conversion of Muhammad Ali* to the movement. Ali also refused to join the army during Vietnam, just as Muhammad had done in World War II. Ali's conversion placed a national spotlight on the Black Muslims, whose ideas of racial separation offended mainstream whites and blacks. During the 1960s and early 1970s, Elijah Muhammad wrote several books defending his ideas: *Message to the Blackman* (1965), *How to Eat to Live* (1967), *The Fall of America* (1973), and *Our Savior Has Arrived* (1974). Elijah Muhammad died February 27, 1975.

REFERENCES: C. Eric Lincoln, *The Black Muslims in Chicago*, 1974; *New York Times*, February 28 and March 1, 1975.

MUSTANG. Ford Motor Company introduced the Mustang in 1964, and the automobile became the most popular vehicle of the 1960s. Low to the ground, with bucket seats, a stick shift on the floor, an elongated hood and all but nonexistent back seat, the Mustang became an immediate hit among American teenagers and young adults. Wilson Pickett recorded a famous song ''Mustang Sally,'' about a young woman behind the wheel of a Mustang. The car was also, at $2,368, eminently affordable. Ford made billions of dollars in profits off the car.

REFERENCE: Peter Collier, *The Fords: An American Epic*, 1987.

MUSTE, ABRAHAM JOHANNES. A native of the Netherlands, A. J. Muste was born on January 8, 1885. His family emigrated to the United States in 1891. After graduating from Hope College, he went into the ministry of the Dutch Reformed Church, where he was influenced by the Social Gospel movement. By 1915, he was also a confirmed pacifist who opposed U.S. involvement in World War I and an enthusiastic member of the Fellowship of Reconciliation. Between 1926 and 1929, he served as its national chairman, and between 1940 and 1953 as its executive secretary. He opposed U.S. involvement in World War II and Korea. In the late 1950s, as a founder of the Committee for Nonviolent Action, Muste fought against the development and use of nuclear weapons.

Not surprising, Muste was one of the earliest critics of U.S. involvement in Vietnam, denouncing the war at a protest demonstration in New York City in December 1964. He was a regular speaker on the antiwar* circuit in 1965 and 1966, and he became an almost ubiquitous presence at antiwar rallies, demonstrations, and teach-ins.* In November 1966, as the elder statesman of American pacifism, he assumed the chairmanship of the Spring Mobilization to End the War in Vietnam.* He also led antiwar rallies in Saigon* before being expelled. Muste visited with Ho Chi Minh* in January 1967, just one month before his death on February 11, 1967.

REFERENCES: *New York Times*, February 12, 1967; John Ricks, ''Abraham Johannes Muste,'' in James S. Olson, ed., *Dictionary of the Vietnam War*, 1988; Jo Ann Robinson, *Abraham Went Out: A Biography of A. J. Muste*, 1981.

MY FAIR LADY. My Fair Lady was one of the most successful musicals in Broadway history. Based on George Bernard Shaw's *Pygmalion*, the play was a product of the extraordinary collaboration of Alan Jay Lerner and Frederick Loewe. It opened at the Mark Hellinger Theater in New York on March 15, 1956. The play revolves around the attempt by the sophisticated professor Henry Higgins (played most famously by Rex Harrison) to educate in speech and manner the rough, cockney young woman Eliza Doolittle (Julie Andrews on Broadway). Eventually, the two fall in love and live happily ever after. *My Fair Lady* enjoyed 2,717 consecutive performances on Broadway and 2,281 in London.

REFERENCE: Kurt Ganzl, *The Encyclopedia of the Musical Theater*, 1994.

MY LAI. See CALLEY, WILLIAM.

MY THREE SONS. *My Three Sons* was among the most popular situation comedies in television* history. ABC produced the series—first broadcast on September 29, 1960—from 1960 to 1965, when CBS took it over. Fred MacMurray starred as Steve Douglas, the widower/patriarch of the Douglas clan. He was an aerospace engineer living first in a midwestern town and then in a southern California suburb, all the while trying to trying to raise three rambunctious boys. The family was squeaky-clean, and the humor came from the typical spin-offs of an all-male household. Tim Considine starred as Mike Douglas, Don Gradie as Robbie Douglas, and Stanley Livingston as Chip Douglas. The last episode of *My Three Sons* was broadcast on August 24, 1972.

REFERENCE: Tim Brooks and Earle Marsh, *The Complete Directory to Prime Time Network and Cable TV Shows*, 1995.

N

NADER, RALPH. Born in Winsted, Connecticut, on February 27, 1934, Ralph Nader went on to become the father of the consumer rights movement in the United States. He attended Princeton University as an undergraduate and then matriculated at Harvard Law, where he graduated in 1958. Nader's instincts for liberal activism were first aroused at Harvard, where he edited the *Harvard Record*, a student magazine. He had come to the conclusion that the federal government's termination* program, which ended the government's legal protection of Indian tribes and turned them over to the vicissitudes of state and local jurisdiction, was a catastrophe, and that government policies more than anything else explained the dire poverty facing so many Indians in the late 1950s. He wrote a long article expounding his point of view for the *Harvard Record*. The article gained national attention in 1956 and turned the *Harvard Record* into an important journal for political reform. The article also gave Nader a national political profile and a personal appetite for liberal political activism.

His liberal credentials firmly established, Nader turned to the issue of automobile safety in 1959, publishing an extended article in *The Nation* arguing that the major automobile manufacturers often ignored their own engineering studies and consciously overlooked major safety problems in order to improve profit margins. Consumers, he claimed, were at the mercy of cost accountants, not safety engineers, when purchasing and driving American automobiles. The article made Nader persona non grata among automobile company executives, who vehemently denied his accusations. Not about to be intimidated, Nader embarked on a meticulous examination of the safety record of automobile companies. Highly suspicious of big business, Nader wrote *Unsafe at Any Speed* in 1965, in which he attacked the automobile industry for its lack of concern with passenger safety. He singled out General Motors and its Corvair model as examples of the industry at its worst. When it became clear that industry officials were trying to harass him and put him under the surveillance of private investigators, the book became a best-seller and made Nader the leader of the consumer rights movement in the United States. Congress also responded by passing the National Traffic and Motor Vehicle Safety Act* in 1966.

In 1969, Nader established the Center for the Study of Responsive Law. The law students he hired became known as "Nader's Raiders" for the crusading zeal they brought to the task of consumer protection. They subjected a wide variety of consumer products to safety studies and then published their results widely, lobbying actively for federal, state, and local consumer protection legislation. Nader's efforts also inspired the establishment of Public Interest Research Groups (PIRGs) to investigate consumer issues and promote consumer interests. Brilliant, articulate, and indefatigable, Ralph Nader became one of the decade's most influential people. In subsequent years, he has continued his liberal activisim and expanded his reach to environmental concerns, where he again argues that big business is more concerned with the bottom line than with environmental protection. The nuclear power industry, he argues, is one of the best examples. During the 1996 presidential elections, Nader placed himself on the California ballot as a third-party environmental candidate. Although he had no chance of winning, he used the election to promote his environmentalist agenda.

REFERENCES: Hays Gorey, *Nader and the Power of Every Man*, 1975; Charles McCarry, *Citizen Nader*, 1972; Ralph Nader, *No Contest: Corporate Lawyers and the Perversion of Justice in America*, 1996.

NAMATH, JOE WILLIE. Joe Willie Namath was born May 31, 1943, in Beaver Falls, Pennsylvania. After graduating from high school, he went to the University of Alabama, where he eventually became an all-American quarterback on Bear Bryant's national championship team. When he graduated in 1965, Namath was the most sought-after athlete in the United States. He stunned the sports world when he signed an unheard-of $400,000 contract with the New York Jets, one of the teams in the recently established American Football League (AFL). Compared to the stodgy National Football League (NFL), AFL teams played a wide-open, high-scoring football that emphasized passing over the run and offense over defense. It was perfect for Namath's considerable skills. Brash, talented, and confident, he endeared himself in the hearts of all New Yorkers in 1969, when he predicted a Jets victory over the Baltimore Colts in Super Bowl III. At the time, nobody thought the best of the AFL could compete with the best of the NFL. Namath proved them wrong, and the Jets won the game.

REFERENCE: Bruce Chadwick, *Joe Namath*, 1995.

NAPALM. The term "napalm" is derived from its chemical composition—a mix of naphthenic and palmitic acids. Napalm was employed as an infantry and aerial weapon during World War II and the Korean War, where it was referred to as "jellied gasoline." It was considered a highly effective tool for dealing with enemy troops entrenched in caves, tunnels, and bunkers. During the Vietnam War,* however, its use became a source of intense criticism from antiwar advocates, who claimed that its indiscriminate use was doing untold damage to South Vietnamese civilians. The U.S. military employed napalm in three ways. First, explosive napalm canisters were dropped on enemy positions by high-speed tactical aircraft flying in support of U.S. infantry operations. Upon detonation, napalm produced intense heat and a firestorm that sucked up surrounding oxygen. Since jet aircraft travel at high speeds and fighting occurred in or around civilian villages, noncombatant casualties were common. Second, napalm was used by U.S. infantry in flamethrowers. They could kill enemy troops in tunnels and bunkers by incinerating them or by having the napalm absorb surrounding oxygen and suffocating them. Finally, napalm was a weapon of choice in the defense of base-camp perimeters. Barrels of napalm were buried under strings of concertina (barbed) wire, and when enemy troops tried to breach the wire, U.S. troops detonated the barrels, incinerating everyone in the vicinity. Burning napalm also caused severe wounds, since its chemical properties made it stick to a victim's skin. Trying to wipe it off only spread the burning gum to other body sites. Dow Chemical Company manufactured napalm, and antiwar protestors frequently targeted Dow for criticism, claiming that the company was profiting from an inhumane weapon.

REFERENCES: Samuel Freeman, "Napalm," in James S. Olson, ed., *Dictionary of the Vietnam War*, 1988; John Takman, *Napalm*, 1968.

NATIONAL ABORTION AND REPRODUCTIVE RIGHTS ACTION LEAGUE. The National Abortion and Reproductive Rights Action League (NARAL) was founded in 1969 as the country's first national pro-choice group. The leading figures in the formation of NARAL were Lawrence Lader, Ruth Proskauer Smith, Betty Friedan,* and Bernard Nathanson. During its early years, NARAL was a loose coalition of state-level pro-choice groups. By 1973 it had a membership of approximately 2,000 people. In 1996, that membership had grown to more than 525,000 people.

REFERENCE: Sarah Slavin, *U.S. Women's Interest Groups*, 1995.

NATIONAL AERONAUTICS AND SPACE ADMINISTRATION. When the Soviet Union launched the satellite *Sputnik* on October 4, 1957, the United States entered a technological identity crisis. In the wake of that crisis, Congress established in 1958 the National Aeronautics and Space Administration (NASA). During the next two years, a number of existing military space programs were transferred to the new agency, but during the John F. Kennedy* administration NASA experienced huge growth when the president announced his intention to land an American on the moon before the end of the decade. The manned spacecraft center was placed in Houston in November 1961, and over the next decade—through the Mercury, Gemini, and Apollo programs—NASA achieved the president's goal. The first lunar landing occurred in July 1969.

The rest of the Apollo flights to the moon, except the ill-fated Apollo 13, seemed somewhat anticlimactic during the 1970s, and NASA had to search for a new mission. Public support for space exploration also waned, primarily because of its expense and the apparent domestic needs of the country. NASA personnel declined in number from 37,000 in 1967 to only 24,000 in 1980. Although the emphasis on manned flight declined, improving satellite technology gave NASA a new mission in terms of commercial economics, scientific research, and military security. NASA satellite missions provided dramatic improvements in weather forecasting, resource exploration on earth, and telecommunications. The space shuttle, or Space Transportation System, became dominant in the 1980s. The *Challenger* disaster in 1986 compromised the program, however, and during the Bush administration, NASA found itself under increasing pressure to de-emphasize its scientific research program in favor of commercially profitable programs.

REFERENCES: John M. Logsdan, *The Decision to Go to the Moon: Project Apollo and the National Interest*, 1976; National Aeronautics and Space Administration, *NASA Historical Data Book*, 1988.

NATIONAL ALLIANCE OF BUSINESSMEN. In 1968, President Lyndon B. Johnson* asked Henry Ford II* to create the National Alliance of Businessmen to generate jobs for the hard-to-employ Vietnam veterans, former convicts, minority groups, and high school dropouts. Organized labor as well as the Department of Labor cooperated in the program, and Ford established the organization in 1969. He recruited business leaders from more than 150 cities to form employment teams and locate job opportunities. Participating corporations supplied 75 percent of the funding for the alliance, and the federal government provided the other 25 percent. Between 1969 and 1986, the National Alliance of Businessmen spent more than $100 million and created more than 10 million jobs.

REFERENCE: James S. Olson, ed., *Dictionary of United States Economic History*, 1991.

NAACP V. BUTTON. The Supreme Court under Chief Justice Earl Warren* earned a reputation for limiting the powers of the state and enhancing the rights and freedoms of individuals. That was especially true in how the Court interpreted First Amendment issues during the 1960s, including the freedom of association clause. On January 14, 1963, the Supreme Court decided *NAACP v. Button* by a 6 to 3 majority. Justice William Brennan* wrote the majority opinion. The decision declared unconstitutional state statutes designed to limit the activities of the National Association for the Advancement of Colored People (NAACP). A number of southern states had written laws forbidding an organization from litigating cases in which it does not have a pecuniary interest. That, of course, was exactly how the NAACP operated in deciding which cases to take. The Court termed such laws an interference by government in the right of people and organizations to associate and to advocate.

REFERENCE: 371 U.S. 415 (1963).

NCAA CHAMPIONSHIP OF 1966. The championship game in 1966 of the National Collegiate Athletic Association (NCAA) college basketball tournament proved to be a turning point in modern sports history. The game took place on March 19, 1966, in front of 14,325 people in the Cole Field House of the University of Maryland and before a national television audience. The number-one-ranked University of Kentucky was an all-white team coached by the legendary Adolph Rupp. Rupp had always refused to recruit black athletes. The opposing team was from Texas Western College, and its starting team was all black, five young men trained on the schoolboy courts of American ghettoes: "Big Daddy" David Lattin, Willie Cager, Willie Worsley, Bobby Joe Hill, and Nevil Shedd. The Texas Western Miners won the game 72 to 65, leading the game all the way. After the win, the Texas Western coaches received more than 50,000 letters from outraged white racists complaining about the game. The victory proved to be the "Emancipation Proclamation" of college basketball. Universities in the Southeast Athletic Conference began enthusiastically recruiting African-American players.
REFERENCES: *New York Times*, March 20, 1966; Randy Roberts and James S. Olson, *Winning Is the Only Thing: Sports in America since 1945*, 1989.

NATIONAL COMMITTEE FOR A SANE NUCLEAR POLICY. The National Committee for a Sane Nuclear Policy was established in New York City in 1957. Norman Cousins, editor of the *Saturday Review*, was the leading force behind the group. Cousins was joined by such luminaries as television performer Steve Allen, musician Pablo Casals, composer Leonard Bernstein,* pediatrician Benjamin Spock,* and black writer James Baldwin.* The group at first campaigned for reductions in the number of nuclear weapons and an end to the atmospheric testing of nuclear weapons and eventually endorsed universal disarmament. When John F. Kennedy* negotiated the Nuclear Test Ban Treaty* with the Soviet Union in 1963, the committee worked tirelessly to see that the Senate ratified it. In 1969, the National Committee for a Sane Nuclear policy changed its name to SANE: A Citizens' Organization for a Sane World.
REFERENCE: Milton Katz, *Ban the Bomb*, 1987.

NATIONAL CONFERENCE OF CONCERNED DEMOCRATS. The National Conference of Concerned Democrats (NCCD) was founded by Allard Lowenstein* in New York City in 1967 in order to try to force President Lyndon B. Johnson* not to seek reelection in 1968. The NCCD also voiced its opposition to the Vietnam War.* When Senator Eugene McCarthy* announced his candidacy for the Democratic presidential nomination, the NCCD backed him. But when Senator Robert Kennedy* entered the race in March, and President Johnson withdrew, the NCCD split between those supporting Kennedy and those supporting McCarthy. Lowenstein joined Kennedy. But when Kennedy was assassinated in 1968, members of the NCCD either halfheartedly supported Hubert

Humphrey* or sat out the election. The National Conference of Concerned Democrats dissolved after the election of 1968.
REFERENCE: Edward L. Schapsmeier and Frederick H. Schapsmeier, *Political Parties and Civil Action Groups*, 1981.

NATIONAL COORDINATING COMMITTEE TO END THE WAR IN VIETNAM. The National Coordinating Committee to End the War in Vietnam (NCC) was formed in August 1965 as an antiwar umbrella organization. It represented more than thirty diverse, local antiwar groups and had its headquarters in Madison, Wisconsin. President Lyndon B. Johnson's* decision in the spring of 1965 to introduce U.S. combat troops into South Vietnam galvanized the antiwar movement.* In October 1965, the NCC sponsored the nationwide International Days of Protest, in which more than 100,000 people across the country participated. The NCC also conducted a teach-in* at the Oakland Army Base and at a number of campuses in California, Wisconsin, Michigan, Ohio, Pennsylvania, New Jersey, Massachusetts, and New York. In addition, it organized a parade of 25,000 antiwar protesters down Fifth Avenue in New York City. Finally, during the October 1965 antiwar events, the NCC also sponsored a series of draft-card burning demonstrations in New York, Chicago, Washington, D.C., Los Angeles, and San Francisco. From its inception, however, the NCC included disparate groups of New and Old Leftists who argued incessantly over socialist theory. In January 1966, the NCC announced the need for another International Day of Protest in March 1966. The turnout exceeded that of the October 1965 demonstrations, indicating that the antiwar movement had taken on a life of its own. Shortly after finishing the planning for those events, the NCC disbanded.
REFERENCES: Linda Alkana, "National Coordinating Committee to End the War in Vietnam," in James S. Olson, ed., *Dictionary of the Vietnam War*, 1988; Charles DeBenedetti, *The Peace Reform in American History*, 1980; Nancy Zaroulis and Gerald Sullivan, *Who Spoke Up? American Protest Against the War in Vietnam 1963–1975*, 1984.

NATIONAL COUNCIL OF SENIOR CITIZENS. Under the auspices of the American Federation of Labor–Congress of Industrial Organizations (AFL–CIO), the National Council of Senior Citizens was organized in 1961 to promote the needs of the elderly in the United States. Senior citizens clubs were established in thousands of small towns and large cities, and members were trained in political consciousness and lobbying techniques. During the early 1960s, the National Council of Senior Citizens campaigned for medicare,* which Lyndon B. Johnson's* Great Society* implemented in 1964. After their medicare success, the council began focusing its attention on educating the elderly about retirement issues and monitoring the quality of nursing homes. By the mid-1990s, the National Council of Senior Citizens had a membership of more than 5 million people organized in more than 5,000 chapters.

REFERENCE: Loree Bykerk and Ardith Maney, *U.S. Consumer Interest Groups: Institutional Profiles*, 1995.

NATIONAL ENDOWMENT FOR THE ARTS. On September 29, 1965, President Lyndon B. Johnson* signed legislation establishing the National Endowment for the Arts (NEA). Designed to help fund artistic endeavors, the NEA enjoyed an initial annual budget of only $2.5 million. Real estate developer and theatrical producer Roger L. Stevens was named to head the agency. Funding remained quite limited during the 1960s, with the NEA's 1969 budget totaling only $7.8 million. During the 1970s and 1980s, the NEA budget exploded in growth, reaching $150 million early in the 1990s. By that time, however, the political climate in the United States had grown more conservative, and many congressmen perceived the NEA and its funding projects as far too liberal for American values. Severe budget cuts were imposed on the National Endowment for the Arts in the mid-1990s.
REFERENCE: Fraser Barron, *Government and the Arts*, 1981.

NATIONAL ENDOWMENT FOR THE HUMANITIES. On September 29, 1965, President Lyndon B. Johnson* signed the congressional bill creating the National Endowment for the Humanities (NEH), part of an initiative to increase funding for the arts and humanities in the United States. Congress provided the new NEH with an annual budget of $2.5 million to be used to promote research and teaching in the humanities. The budget grew slowly during the 1960s, increasing only to $6.1 million in fiscal 1969; but in the 1970s and 1980s, the NEH enjoyed astonishing increasings in funding, which reached $150 million in 1991. The NEH also raised the ire of conservatives, who considered many of its funding projects well outside the mainstream of American values. During the remainder of the 1990s, the NEH sustained serious budget cuts.
REFERENCES: Fraser Barron, *Government and the Arts*, 1981; Stephen Miller, *Excellence and Equity: The National Endowment for the Humanities*, 1984.

NATIONAL ENVIRONMENTAL POLICY ACT OF 1970. By 1969, the environmental movement* was making enormous political strides in the United States, and politicians as well as businessmen had no choice but to acknowledge its power. The National Environmental Policy Act, which became law on January 1, 1970, was such an acknowledgment. The law required all federal agencies to include environmental impact statements—studies of the effects of government policies and legislation on the environment in all new program proposals—and suggested that business do the same. The law also established the Council on Environmental Quality as an advisory body to the president.
REFERENCE: James S. Olson, ed., *Dictionary of United States Economic History*, 1991.

NATIONAL INDIAN YOUTH COUNCIL. The National Indian Youth Council (NIYC) was established in the wake of the Conference on American Indians in Chicago in 1961. A group of University of Chicago social scientists had organized the conference, with the intention of producing a comprehensive Indian policy proposal for the John F. Kennedy* administration, but many younger, more educated Indians found the themes of the conference too conservative. They managed to insert into the proceedings a statement that repudiated "paternalism, even when benevolent" and insisted on the "inherent right of self-government" for Indian peoples. With encouragement from some of the elder Indians at the conference, the young radicals—led by Clyde Warrior,* Shirley Hill Witt, and Mel Thom—reconvened in Gallup, New Mexico, where they drafted a constitution for the National Indian Youth Council, an organization committed to service and Indian advocacy. They headquartered the group in Albuquerque, New Mexico.

During the 1960s, the NIYC concentrated its efforts on protest and civil disobedience, particularly over hunting and fishing rights. They were especially active in the Pacific Northwest, staging "fish-ins" against Washington state fish and game officials trying to abrogate treaty rights. In 1964, they held a large protest march at the state capitol in Olympia. NIYC members also supported the civil rights drives of other American minorities. In the 1970s, their focus shifted to environmental issues. They actively opposed development projects that threatened traditional Indian habitats. As a result of their environmental activism, the NIYC has also emphasized voter registration drives and human rights issues. They have become more committed to promoting Native American participation in the political process. The NIYC has sponsored a number of voter behavior polls among Native Americans, and it has filed several lawsuits against state and local practices that make Indian participation in politics more cumbersome and difficult. During the 1980s and 1990s, that campaign has become more focused as the Indian Voting project.

REFERENCE: Marcus E. Jacobsen, *Rise Up, Make Haste: Our People Need Us! The National Indian Youth Council and the Origins of the Red Power Movement*, 1981.

NATIONAL ORGANIZATION FOR WOMEN. The National Organization for Women (NOW) was founded in 1966 to promote the civil rights of American women. The women most responsible for the establishment of NOW were Dorothy Haener, Betty Friedan,* Kathryn Clarenbach, and Pauli Murray. The formal purpose of NOW was "action to bring women into full participation in the mainstream of American society now, exercising all the privileges and responsibilities thereof in truly equal partnership with men." Within its first few years, NOW had targeted as its concerns the issues of reproductive rights, developmental child care, equal pay, limits on nuclear weapons, an end to poverty, antirape reform, and initiatives to end violence against women. The National Organization for Women became the most influential feminist group in the country. By the mid-1990s, NOW had 750 local chapters with more than 250,000 members.

REFERENCE: Sarah Slavin, *U.S. Women's Interest Groups*, 1995.

NATIONAL STATES RIGHTS PARTY. The National States Rights Party was founded by Edward Fields in 1958 in Knoxville, Tennessee. The party nominated Orville Faubus as their presidential candidate in 1960, even though he repudiated the nomination. The National States Rights Party combined Nazi and Ku Klux Klan philosophies. In 1962, the party launched a "Fire Your Nigger" campaign designed to increase African-American unemployment and drive them out of the South. A number of murders, bombings, and muggings during the civil rights crisis of 1963–1965 were traced to National States Rights Party members. They readily joined with American Nazi Party* and Ku Klux Klan rallies in the 1960s. The last time the National States Rights Party ran a candidate in a presidential election was 1964, when John Kaspar received only 6,957 votes.
REFERENCE: Michael Newton and Judy Ann Newton, *The Ku Klux Klan: An Encyclopedia*, 1990.

NATIONAL TRAFFIC AND MOTOR VEHICLE SAFETY ACT OF 1966. In 1965, Ralph Nader* wrote the book *Unsafe at Any Speed*, which became a best-seller. The book exposed dangerous design problems in the Chevrolet Corvair model and accused all of the automobile manufacturers of being more concerned with profits than with public safety. The automobile companies denied the charges and took to harassing Nader, but he was not about to be intimidated. The whole incident created a groundswell of support for consumer protection, so in September 1966, Congress passed the National Traffic and Motor Vehicle Safety Act. The legislation required the federal government to mandate basic safety standards on all automobiles* beginning with the 1968 model year and on used cars by 1970. Congress also passed the Highway Safety Act, requiring all states to develop highway safety programs by December 31, 1968. Noncompliance would mean the loss of federal highway funds.
REFERENCE: James S. Olson, ed., *Dictionary of United States Economic History*, 1991.

NATIONAL WELFARE RIGHTS ORGANIZATION. The National Welfare Rights Organization (NWRO) was founded in 1966 to represent the needs and advocate the rights of welfare recipients in the United States. Its founder was George Wiley, a professor of chemistry at Syracuse University. The NWRO called for a minimum income of $7,500 for a family of four people on welfare, as well as access to medical and legal assistance. At its peak in the late 1960s, the National Welfare Rights Organization had more than 800 chapters functioning in all fifty states. During the 1970s, however, when the political climate in the United States became more conservative, the NWRO declined, and in 1975 it closed its national office.
REFERENCE: Harry A. Ploski and James Williams, eds., *The Negro Almanac*, 1989.

NATION-WIDE COMMITTEE ON IMPORT-EXPORT POLICY. A protectionist group, the Nation-Wide Committee on Import-Export Policy was

founded in 1953 by O. R. Strackbein. Its specific objective was to oppose the General Agreement on Tariffs and Trade (GATT), which was up for renewal. In particular, the committee wanted to insert escape clauses into the GATT, permitting the United States to increase tariff rates on certain products whose importation might undermine American producers. When the GATT went before Congress in 1955, the Nation-Wide Committee on Import-Export Policy called for higher tariff rates. They succeeded in limiting the president's authority to reduce tariffs to no more than 5 percent below the level set by Congress. In 1958, the committee managed to insert into the GATT the authority for the president to impose quota restrictions when some domestic industries were being hurt by imports; quotas on oil, zinc, and lead soon followed. The committee opposed the Trade Expansion Act* of 1962, which sought to reduce tariff rates by 50 percent over five years, and secured a clause providing for federal assistance to domestic industries damaged by imported goods. During the 1970s and 1980s, the committee continued its protectionism, lobbying for restrictions on Japanese goods unless Japan opened its markets to American products.
REFERENCE: James S. Olson, ed., *Dictionary of United States Economic History*, 1991.

NATIVE AMERICANS. See **RED POWER** and **TERMINATION**.

NEUTRALIZE. During the 1950s, the term ''neutralize'' first emerged in the intelligence community, especially the Central Intelligence Agency* and the National Security Agency, to describe a policy option to eliminate an enemy's power base by destroying its resources. It also meant the targeted assassination of an individual unfriendly to U.S. national security. During the Vietnam War,* the term's meaning expanded considerably to include the destruction of enemy personnel and enemy resources. Sometimes that involved evacuating South Vietnamese from ancestral villages and completely destroying those villages to keep the Vietcong* from using them or hiding there. All too often, the consequences of ''neutralization'' were the accidental death and maiming of innocent civilians and the creation of enormous resentment among the South Vietnamese for U.S. policies there.
REFERENCES: Samuel Freeman, ''Neutralize,'' in James S. Olson, ed., *Dictionary of the Vietnam War*, 1988; Jonathan Schell, *The Village of Ben Suc*, 1967; Richard Hammer, *One Morning in the War*, 1970.

NEW FEDERALISM. During the presidential election campaign of 1968,* Republican candidate Richard M. Nixon* made much of the fact that, in his opinion, the federal government, particularly the federal bureaucracy and the federal court system, had assumed too much centralized power in the United States. He proposed that state governments be reempowered within the federal system. In particular, Nixon proposed the idea of block grants in which federal agencies would provide grants of funds to state governments, which would then administer their own social programs, rather than have them administered from

Washington, D.C. During his first administration, Nixon called this proposal the "New Federalism." Although little of it was enacted during the Nixon presidency, the idea of block grants became part of the conservative political agenda of the 1980s, and during the 1990s the block grant ideas began to be implemented.

REFERENCE: Richard M. Nixon, *RN: The Memoirs of Richard Nixon*, 1978.

NEW FRONTIER. On July 16, 1960, John F. Kennedy* accepted the nomination of the Democratic Party to run for president of the United States. During his acceptance speech at the Los Angeles Coliseum that day, Kennedy evoked the image of the frontier to launch his political campaign. "I stand tonight facing west," he told the delegates, "on what was once the last frontier. . . . The pioneers of old gave up their safety, their comfort and sometimes their lives to build a new world here in the West. . . . But the problems are not all solved and the battles are not all won, and we stand today on the edge of a new frontier— the frontier of the 1960s." The press picked up on the term "new frontier," and it became the political synonym for the Kennedy administration. Just as Franklin D. Roosevelt had his New Deal, and Harry Truman had his Fair Deal, John F. Kennedy had his "new frontier."

REFERENCE: Richard Slotkin, *Gunfighter Nation: The Myth of the Frontier in Twentieth-Century America*, 1992.

NEW LEFT. The term "New Left" was a generic description of a new group of radicals who appeared on the American scene in the 1960s. They contrasted themselves with the so-called Old Left—hard-line communists believing passionately in the Marxist dialectic, traditional socialists advocating government ownership of the means of production and distribution, and pacifists opposing war in all of its forms. The New Left of the 1960s was a much broader coalition. It first emerged out of the civil rights movement* of the early 1960s and found its most powerful base of support on college and university campuses. Unlike Old Leftists, they had little interest in labor politics or trying to make the industrial order more egalitarian. New Leftists were far more concerned with civil rights, environmentalism, and the war in Vietnam.

The New Left first appeared on British campuses. In 1960, two traditionally leftist publications merged into the *New Left Review*. New Left Clubs appeared at colleges throughout the country. In the United States, radicals at the University of Wisconsin began publishing *Studies on the Left*, which became the intellectual backbone of the New Left. In 1962, Tom Hayden* wrote the Port Huron Statement,* which eventually became a sort of constitution of the new Students for a Democratic Society* (SDS) and a plan of action for the New Left. SDS was anti-institutional and antibureaucratic, committed to local political action more than centralized power, and called for "participatory democracy,"* or the active involvement of people in policymaking, not just in voting. By 1964, the New Left included SDS as well as the Student Nonviolent Coordinating Committee,* the Southern Christian Leadership Conference,* and the free speech movement* in Berkeley. Intellectual leaders of the New Left movement included Frantz Fanon (*Wretched of the Earth*), Paul Goodman* (*Growing Up Absurd*), and Herbert Marcuse* (*One-Dimensional Man*).

By 1965, however, opposition to the Vietnam War* had galvanized all of the New Left groups. By 1969, the New Left probably included 150,000 active participants in antiwar and civil rights demonstrations as well as millions of less active sympathizers. Groups such as the Youth International Party* tried to make a farce out of respect for traditional institutions. Their protest, along with that of many other groups, at the 1968 Democratic National Convention* was one example. New Left students also took on their own universities, demanding a greater role in campus decision making and insisting that administrators sever school ties with the military and defense contractors.

By the end of the decade and early into the 1970s, however, the New Left movement came on hard times. The de-escalation of the Vietnam War, although taking place much too slowly for the radicals, nevertheless robbed them of an energizing issue. The ideological squabbles that had always plagued the left-wing movement in the United States soon asserted themselves among New Leftists, factionalizing groups and paralyzing them. New Leftists also found themselves confronting the nascent women's movement, which accused them as well as Old Leftists of being just as sexist as American conservatives.

REFERENCES: Ronald Fraser, *1968: A Student Generation in Revolt*, 1988; Todd Gitlin, *The Sixties: Years of Hope, Days of Rage*, 1987; Kirkpatrick Sale, *SDS*, 1973.

NEW YORK ATHLETIC CLUB BOYCOTT OF 1968. In the mid-1960s, the nonviolent civil disobedience tactics of Martin Luther King, Jr.,* in the civil rights movement* gave way to the black power* rhetoric of people like Stokely Carmichael.* That movement was reflected in American sports. A number of African-American leaders began to see modern athletics as simply another example of exploitation in the United States. Late in 1967, Professor Harry Edwards* of San Jose State University organized a boycott of the New York Athletic Club's annual track meet in Madison Square Garden. The club was making major preparations for its 100th meet—the centennial event and one of the major meets in track and field history. But the New York Athletic Club had a long-standing practice of excluding all African Americans from membership. Since the club would not admit blacks as members, Edwards argued that black athletes should not compete in the meet. The boycott proved to be a success. A number of major African-American track and field stars refused to compete, and the meet's attendance and television audiences declined dramatically. His success inspired Edwards to organize the 1968 boycott of the Olympic* games.

REFERENCE: Randy Roberts and James S. Olson, *Winning Is the Only Thing: Sports in America since 1945*, 1989.

THE NEW YORK CITY BLACKOUT. When the regional power pool began to fail at 5:15 P.M. on November 9, 1965, the whole Northeast from Canada to

New York City was in danger of blackout. A few local power operators did not switch to the regional grid or got off it when the failure started and managed to avoid trouble. However, within fifteen minutes, thirty million people were in the middle of the nation's greatest and longest power failure. When people with portable radios heard the radio announcers telling of the extent of the blackout, millions became scared. Was it sabotage or war or some kind of protest by the antiwar faction? Soon the military made announcements that the nation was not under attack, but this did not allay all fears. The following by Peter Grossman is appropriate: ''An extraordinary night began to unfold, a night in which only one light burned steadily for millions of people. In the clear autumn sky, a full moon glowed brightly.''

Traffic jams were unbelievable. Five hundred airline flights had to be diverted. Cars low on fuel had to be parked. All electrical devices were useless except the few that were battery-powered. Subways were filled with people. Elevators were stalled. The list of possible disasters is endless. Unbelievably, there were no disasters. People worked together and helped each other through the difficult early evening. ''As Tuesday night wore on, people began feeling good about one another, and began to celebrate. Blackout parties sprouted up everywhere.'' Throughout the area, police reported that lawbreaking was less than usual. ''In New York City, authorities arrested only one-quarter as many people as they did on an average night.'' When the blackout ended about three hours later, one woman remarked that ''they should do this more often.''

The systems failure on November 9, 1965, had taken place on a cool evening when many people had a fear of nuclear war or some kind of violent uprising. They did not expect or even think of an electrical systems failure. When the blackout of July 13, 1977, occurred, people knew that ''Con Edison had simply let the electrical system fall apart.'' This change in understanding may have given many the courage to do their worst. Due to antiproperty feelings, violence, vandalism, and looting took place throughout the night.

After these two major electrical power failures, the Federal Power Commission made several suggestions for systems improvement. ''But New Yorkers doubted that these would help much. They believed that the darkness would come again, probably soon. And they felt that the next time it came, things would likely get worse.'' This skepticism was a radical departure from the time when people had great confidence in technology.

REFERENCES: *New York Times*, November 10–13, 1965.

Bobby J. James

NEW YORK METS (1969). The New York Mets first entered the major league baseball spotlight in 1962 as an expansion team under the management of Casey Stengel. Professional baseball had been in existence for ninety-two years when the Mets entered the league, but in just seven short years, they had become the laughingstock of an entire sport. During these first seven years the youthful Mets turned gifted veteran players into clowns of the diamond. From 1962 until 1968, the Mets finished a total of 288.5 games out of first place and compiled 737 losses, compared to only 394 wins. Their best finishes in that span were ninth place in 1966 (26.5 games out of first place) and ninth place in 1968 (24 games behind pennant-winning St. Louis). During the 1968 season, the Mets put uniforms on fifty-four different players but still managed to finish with an anemic 73–89 record and a .451 winning percentage. Because of the enormous media coverage in New York City, the Mets soon became a national joke. For almost a decade, they stumbled through the league as an expansion team of absurd incompetence. The odds of the Mets' winning the pennant in 1969 were posted at 25–1.

The 1969 baseball season saw tremendous changes take place in the Mets organization, headlined by the hiring of manager Gil Hodges and signing of superstar pitcher Tom Seaver. The Mets made the 1969 season one to remember. On August 15, they were 9.5 games behind the Chicago Cubs in the National League East race; by the end of September, thanks to a record of 26–7 over a six-week period, the Mets became the divisional front-runners and never looked back. They went on to win the National League East title with ninety-six wins, and they faced the powerful Atlanta Braves in the National League Championship Series. With increasing momentum and tremendous fan support, the Mets swept the Braves in three games.

The 1969 World Series opened in Baltimore with the Mets playing the Orioles. In the first game, the underdog Mets were defeated 4–1 by a much more powerful Baltimore club. But, in the next four games, the New York Mets proved to everyone that it was their year by winning all four games and ultimately the World Series. Several key players played a huge role in the magical championship season, including outfielders Tommy Agee and Alan Swoboda, infielders Ken Boswell, Don Clendenon, and Albert Weis, and pitchers Jerry Koosman, Nolan Ryan, and Tom Seaver.

The championship created excitement in New York City and brought the national pastime back into prominence there. In fact, the annual attendance at Shea Stadium for 1969 totaled over 2 million people—a record number for that era. The Mets also proved that an expansion team could win a championship with young, determined players. Finally, the New York Mets gave hope to underdogs everywhere.

REFERENCES: Jay Jennings, *Long Shot: They Beat the Odds*, 1990; Stanley Cohen, *A Magic Summer: The '69 Mets*, 1988.

Adam Harwell

NEW YORK TIMES CO. V. SULLIVAN. The so-called Warren Court of the 1950s and 1960s justifiably earned its reputation as the most liberal Supreme Court in U.S. history. Its liberal point of view was particularly evident in civil liberties decisions, especially in First Amendment freedom of speech and freedom of the press controversies. One example is *New York Times Co. v. Sullivan*, decided by a unanimous vote on March 9, 1964. Justice William Brennan* wrote

the majority opinion. The decision expanded the protections afforded the press from libel suits initiated by public officials. The Court ordered that public officials could not sue for libel unless they could prove that the publishing unit had made false reports with ''actual malice.'' Whether the report was true or false was irrelevant.
REFERENCE: 376 U.S. 254 (1963).

NEWTON, HUEY. Huey Newton was born in Monroe, Louisiana, February 17, 1942. He was the youngest of seven children. The family moved to Oakland, California, when he was still a child. After graduating from high school, Newton attended Oakland City College, where his political consciousness developed rapidly. He founded the campus chapter of the Afro-American Society. Newton then attended the San Francisco School of Law but quit before earning a degree. By that time, in 1966, he had joined Bobbie Seale* in founding the Black Panthers.*

The Black Panthers' original mission was to stop police brutality against the African-American community in Oakland. Arming themselves with cameras and shotguns, Newton and Seale began patrolling ghetto streets, trying to document cases of police brutality and defending black victims. Oakland police went after Newton with a vengeance. In 1967, he became involved in a shoot-out with police and was charged with manslaughter. His trial lasted for more than eight weeks and became a cause célèbre in the local black community. Thousands of demonstrators appeared outside the courthouse, including 250 Black Panthers wearing their characteristic leather jackets and berets. Newton was convicted in September 1968 and sentenced to prison. The court of appeals in California subsequently overturned the conviction and ordered a retrial, but by that time Newton had fled to Cuba. He returned voluntarily to the United States in 1977 and was again convicted of manslaughter in the police officer's death, but that conviction did not survive an appeal. In 1978, Newton was put on trial twice for murdering a woman in 1974, but the charges were dropped after two hung juries.

Newton received a Ph.D. from the University of California at Berkeley in 1980, but in 1985 he was arrested and charged with embezzling money from a government nutrition and educational program he administered. In 1987, Newton was convicted of firearms possession and sentenced to three years in prison.
REFERENCE: Hugh Pearson, *The Shadow of the Panther: Huey Newton and the Price of Black Power in America*, 1994.

NGO DINH DIEM. Son of a counselor to Emperor Thanh Thai, Ngo Dinh Diem was born in 1901 and claimed to descend from mandarins—a claim disputed by some. The third of six sons, Diem graduated first in his class from a Catholic school in Hue* and studied for the civil service at a French college in Hanoi.* Rising rapidly through administrative ranks, he became minister of the interior in 1933 but resigned two months later because of French unwillingness to grant Vietnam greater autonomy. An ardent nationalist and early opponent of communism, Diem retired from public life for twenty years, having nothing further to do with the French and refusing offers from the Japanese during World War II. His anticommunism strengthened when Vietminh forces killed one of his brothers and a nephew. Diem refused Ho Chi Minh's* offer to join his government, denouncing him as a "criminal." In 1950, Diem came to the United States, where he met Cardinal Spellman and Senators John Kennedy* and Mike Mansfield.* These contacts served Diem well when he accepted Emperor Bao Dai's 1954 offer to become prime minister of what would become the Republic of Vietnam. One of Diem's first acts was to request American assistance.

Diem might be described as a brilliant incompetent who beat the odds longer than anyone thought possible. Given his twenty-year retirement, he was not well known in Vietnam and had no following outside the Catholic community in an overwhelmingly Buddhist nation. Reclusive and paranoid, he depended almost exclusively on his family, refused to delegate authority, and did little to build a broadly based, popular government. Diem was surprisingly adept at meeting challenges to his government. In 1955 he rejected the reunification elections specified in the Geneva Accords, disposed of Emperor Bao Dai in a fraudulent election (winning 98.2 percent of the vote), neutralized the Cao Dai and Hoa Hao religious sects, and defeated the Binh Xuyen in open combat. He survived a 1960 coup attempt, which rendered him even more dependent on his immediate family, especially his brother Ngo Dinh Nhu.

Administratively, Diem could not set priorities, choosing to spend a long afternoon with a journalist while members of his government and the military waited for audiences. Governing through repression and intrigue, he quickly killed or imprisoned the remaining Vietminh infrastructure along with most other potential opponents. His oppressiveness and refusal to implement reforms tried the patience of the United States, which flirted with dumping him as early as 1955. By 1963, however, he was finished. The final blow was Ngo Dinh Nhu's* vicious attacks on Buddhist dissidents and the ensuing national paralysis. Although not involved in the coup, the United States signaled that it would accept a change in government. On November 1, the generals moved; Diem and his brother were murdered the next day.

After the coup, Diem was vilified, but Vietnamese attitudes toward Diem changed in the 1970s as the United States withdrew, and South Vietnam's fate became obvious. In South Vietnam's final weeks, Diem was rehabilitated as a courageous nationalist tragically victimized by the United States.

REFERENCES: Denis Warner, *The Last Confucian*, 1963; *Who's Who in the Far East and Australasia, 1961–1962*, 1962; Marvin Kalb and Elie Abel, *Roots of Involvement: The U.S. in Asia, 1784–1971*, 1971.

Samuel Freeman

NGO DINH NHU. Born in 1910, Ngo Dinh Nhu was educated at the Ecole des Chartes in Paris and then worked in the French colonial bureaucracy until penalized for nationalist activities. A master at organization, Nhu orchestrated Saigon demonstrations in September 1954, advocating a "third force" alternative to French colonialism or Ho Chi Minh.* The Can Lao Nhan Vi Cach Mang Dang was his primary effort at mass organization. Unfortunately, Nhu's "personalism" was based on a misinterpretation of French thinking and was so alien to Vietnamese thought and culture that no one understood it. The party was organized along the lines of communist cells, complete with fascist-styled storm troopers and an elaborate intelligence network. Nhu used the party to maintain the authority of the Ngo family rather than building democratic institutions or national unity.

Nhu recommended and administered the Strategic Hamlet Program. Like everything else in the Diem regime, it was poorly administered and riddled with corruption. Obsessed with numbers, Nhu pushed the construction of strategic hamlets more rapidly than they could be assimilated, often in unsecured areas. Government promises for equipment, material, and money were not kept. Villagers often had to pay bribes to receive promised supplies. The Vietcong* quickly subverted many hamlets; others simply disintegrated.

As head of the secret police, Nhu created thirteen internal intelligence units, which spied on one another as well as on potential dissidents. He also commanded Vietnamese Special Forces, effectively his personal army. With these resources Nhu frustrated numerous efforts to depose his brother, Ngo Dinh Diem,* who always viewed internal dissent as more threatening than the Vietcong. The corruption, brutality, and intrigue caught up with the Diem regime in 1963, when Nhu took on the Buddhists. After Nhu's Special Forces attacked Buddhist pagodas, the United States notified plotting generals that it would accept a coup. On November 1 the generals moved. Diem and Nhu were murdered that next day.

REFERENCES: Denis Warner, *The Last Confucian*, 1963; *Who's Who in the Far East and Australasia, 1961–1962*, 1962; Marvin Kalb and Elie Abel, *Roots of Involvement: The U.S. in Asia, 1784–1971*, 1971.

Samuel Freeman

NGO DINH NHU, MADAME. Born Tran Le Xuan (Beautiful Spring) in 1924 to a completely Gallicized Vietnamese family that had enriched itself in service to the French colonialists, Le Xuan dropped out of Hanoi's Lycee Albert Sarraut. She was fluent in French but never learned to write Vietnamese. In 1944 Tran Le Xuan married Ngo Dinh Nhu,* brother of Ngo Dinh Diem,* Prime Minister of Vietnam. Since Diem never married, Madame Nhu was essentially the First Lady of the Republic of Vietnam. Powerful in her own right, Madame Nhu issued decrees having the force of law banning divorce, adultery, prostitution, dancing, boxing, beauty contests, and fortune-telling, among other things. Considering herself a feminist, she lectured on women's issues and commanded her own parliamentary organization, the Women's Solidarity Movement.

Madame Nhu saw herself as the reincarnation of the Trung sisters, ancient leaders in the struggle for independence from China, but she was more a reincarnation of Marie Antoinette. She was incredibly insensitive to, and uncaring about, anyone outside the ruling clique or the sufferings that Diem's inept, corrupt, and increasingly brutal government imposed on the people. When Buddhist monks, including Thich Quang Duc, and a nun immolated themselves protesting Diem's government, she airily referred to them as Buddhist "barbecues." Nhu encouraged her outrageousness by adding that "if the Buddhists want to have another barbecue, I will be glad to supply the gasoline." Such statements helped consolidate American opposition to Diem, paving the way for the November 1963 coup. Madame Nhu was traveling in the United States, campaigning for support for the Diem regime, in November 1963, when Diem and her husband were assassinated. She then turned to a widowhood in Rome.

REFERENCES: Frances FitzGerald, *Fire in the Lake: The Vietnamese and the Americans in Vietnam*, 1972; Stanley Karnow, *Vietnam: A History*, 1983; Thomas D. Boettcher, *Vietnam, the Valor and the Sorrow*, 1985; *New York Times*, October 28–31, November 1–2, 1963.

Samuel Freeman

NGUYEN CAO KY. Nguyen Cao Ky was born September 8, 1930, in Son Tay, Tonkin, near Hanoi.* Ky was drafted into the Vietnamese National Army in 1950, served with distinction, and rose to the rank of lieutenant. He was trained as a pilot in France and Algeria in 1953 and 1954, and during the regime of Ngo Dinh Diem* he became an officer, eventually a lieutenant general in the South Vietnamese air force. Flamboyant and with an iron will, Ky first came to prominence in 1964, when he threatened to conduct an air strike against the headquarters of Nguyen Khanh* because of all of the squabbling during the military regime. Ky finally agreed to cooperate after a dressing-down by U.S. ambassador Maxwell Taylor,* and in 1965 he became prime minister, sharing power with General Nguyen Van Thieu.*

A dedicated elitist with decidedly Western tastes, Ky imposed brutal restrictions on the Buddhists—far more than even Ngo Dinh Diem had imposed—and invited their wrath. Throughout 1966 the Buddhists demanded Ky's ouster, but Ky continued in power. In 1967, he agreed, with considerable support from the United States, to let Thieu become the sole head of state, with Ky serving as vice president. Although Ky had promised Lyndon Johnson* he would strive to bring about a "social revolution" in Vietnam, he had no intention of upsetting the status quo of corruption and power that was enriching him and his family. Between 1967 and 1971, Ky's influence was gradually eclipsed as Thieu consolidated his own power, and in 1971 Thieu disqualified Ky from challenging him for the presidency of South Vietnam. Ngyuen Cao Ky fled South Vietnam before the Final Offensive and opened a liquor store in southern California.

REFERENCES: David Halberstam, *The Best and the Brightest*, 1972; Nguyen Cao Ky, *Twenty Years and Twenty Days*, 1976; George C. Herring, *America's Longest War: The United States in Vietnam, 1950–1975*, 1986.

Samuel Freeman

NGUYEN KHANH. Born in 1927, Nguyen Khanh grew up to be an incorrigible, untrustworthy schemer. He had to quit school in 1943 and joined the Vietminh in their campaign against the Japanese and the French, but the Vietminh soon expelled him. Khanh then went over to the French, who trained him for an officer's position in the Vietnamese National Army. In 1954 Khanh came to the support of Ngo Dinh Diem,* but in 1963 he also participated in the coup against him. Khanh then participated in a bloodless coup in January 1964 that put him in control of the government of South Vietnam. For the next year South Vietnam deteriorated under his convoluted leadership, with the Vietcong* gaining strength and his own government torn apart by corruption and internecine political warfare. In February 1965, Generals Nguyen Cao Ky* and Nguyen Van Thieu* ousted Khanh for good. He was exiled to the United States and took up residence in Palm Beach, Florida.

REFERENCES: *Who's Who in the Far East and Australasia, 1964–65,* 1965; Stanley Karnow, *Vietnam: A History,* 1983; Frances FitzGerald, *Fire in the Lake: The Vietnamese and the Americans in Vietnam,* 1972.

Samuel Freeman

NGUYEN NGOC LOAN. General Nguyen Ngoc Loan achieved infamy with the filmed summary execution of a Vietcong suspect in Saigon* during the Tet Offensive* in 1968. Widely reported in the United States, it contributed to the American people's increasing revulsion with the war. Loan attempted to justify the execution, explaining that the man had murdered a friend of his family. Nevertheless, the execution was in keeping with his reputation for ruthlessness, corruption, and brutality.

A northern-born Catholic, Loan first came into prominence in 1966, while serving as a colonel to Saigon's chief of police—a lucrative position that enabled him to control Saigon's extortion racket. Faced with the "Buddhist Crisis," Nguyen Cao Ky* placed him in charge of subduing rebellious I Corps. With loyal troops reinforced by tanks and airborne units, Loan attacked Danang pagodas that lodged resisting Buddhists and military units. In a series of firefights ending May 22, Loan regained control of the city, killing hundreds of rebel troops and civilians in the process. He then proceeded to lay siege to Hue,* prompting self-immolations by nine Buddhist priests and nuns in protest. After Loan pacified Hue, Ky instigated a public relations campaign to soften resentments. Prominent members of the uprising were treated leniently. Colonel Loan was ordered to clean up Hue, and he jailed hundreds, who remained behind bars for years without trial. Loan's efforts were rewarded with promotion to general and chief of the national police shortly thereafter. After the fall of South Vietnam in 1975, Loan fled to the United States.

REFERENCES: Frances FitzGerald, *Fire in the Lake: The Vietnamese and the Americans in Vietnam,* 1972; *Who's Who in the Far East and Australasia, 1961–1962,* 1962; Marvin Kalb and Elie Abel, *Roots of Involvement: The U.S. in Asia, 1784–1971,* 1971.

Samuel Freeman

NGUYEN THI BINH. Nguyen Thi Binh was born to a middle-class family in Saigon,* French Indochina, in 1927. Early on, especially as a student, she came to hate French rule and became a strident nationalist committed to Vietnamese independence. She fought against the French and then, during World War II, targeted the Japanese, who had occupied Vietnam. When the Americans showed up in the 1950s, she turned on them too. She was obsessed with the independence and reunification of Vietnam. Early in 1961, she joined the National Liberation Front (NLF), or Vietcong,* and by 1962 she was a member of its central committee and a committed communist. She traveled widely, explaining the NLF position to world leaders. When the Paris peace talks between the United States, North Vietnam, South Vietnam, and the NLF commenced in 1968, she moved to Paris to head the NLF delegation. Between 1968 and 1972, she served as the official spokesperson for the National Liberation Front, which had become known as the Provisional Revolutionary Government of Vietnam. In 1975, when North Vietnam conquered South Vietnam, she became minister of education in the Socialist Republic of Vietnam.
REFERENCES: John S. Bowman, ed., *The Vietnam War Almanac*, 1985; *Encyclopedia of the Third World*, vol. 3, 1929–1931, 1982.

NGUYEN VAN THIEU. Ngyuen Van Thieu was born in 1923 in Tri Thuy village in Ninh Thuan Province. Nguyen Van Thieu distinguished himself against the Vietminh after graduating from the Vietnamese Military Academy as an infantry lieutenant in 1949. Thieu also graduated from the U.S. Command and General Staff College in 1957. His major commands in the Army of the Republic of Vietnam, beginning in 1959, included the 21st Infantry Division and the 5th Infantry Division. He led a brigade of the 5th Division against Diem's presidential guard during the 1963 coup. Thieu continued to rise in power after the overthrow of Ngo Dinh Diem* and was instrumental, along with General Nguyen Cao Ky,* in bringing General Nguyen Khanh* to power in January 1964. By February 1965, Ky and Thieu had positioned themselves to take over the government. Surprisingly, the Ky–Thieu government was South Vietnam's longest. Although Ky originally was premier, and Thieu was chief of state and commander in chief of the armed forces, Thieu outmaneuvered Ky to become the presidential candidate (with Ky as vice president) in the 1967 elections.

While Thieu would have been more acceptable in 1965 to the United States than Ky, they were about equally acceptable by 1967. The primary American concern was that they not run against each other, splitting the military and raising prospects for civilian government or more coups. A Thieu–Ky ticket ensured military unity and their victory. However, Thieu managed only 35 percent of the vote when a surprise peace candidate ran unexpectedly strong second in elections marred by the double voting of military personnel and stuffed ballot boxes. When Ky attempted to run against him for president in 1971, Thieu outmaneuvered him again, disqualifying his candidacy on a technicality. Eliminating Ky prompted General Duong Van "Big" Minh to withdraw, leaving Thieu to run unopposed and to head the government until just before its collapse in April 1975.

Thieu bitterly opposed the proposed 1972 peace agreement. Calling it a sell-out, he delayed its signing until January 1973. To gain Thieu's assent, some minor modifications were effected. More important, Nixon* made secret promises regarding future American military support. In August 1974, Nixon resigned rather than face impeachment, and Gerald Ford became president. Congress passed the War Powers Resolution and other legislation restricting American involvement in Southeast Asia. When Thieu asked the United States to honor Nixon's promises, President Ford had neither the authority nor the sense of obligation to provide assistance. For the first time Thieu and South Vietnam stood alone.

The stability of Thieu's regime did not result from his establishing a popular government. Like its predecessors, it was noted for corruption, incompetence, and oppression. Stability resulted from Thieu's keeping the Vietnamese military command either unable or unwilling to mount a successful coup. This depended largely on maintaining the confidence of the United States. At bottom, American military and American money kept South Vietnam afloat, as demonstrated by its rapid disintegration once the support was terminated. Some criticize the United States for not coming to Thieu's assistance in 1975; however, a strong case can be made that since South Vietnam had failed to build a viable government after a massive, twenty-five-year effort, there were no meaningful prospects for ever building one. President Thieu now lives in Great Britain.

REFERENCES: *Who's Who in the Far East and Australasia, 1974–1975*, 1975; Stanley Karnow, *Vietnam: A History*, 1983; Edward Doyle and Terrence Maitland, *The Vietnam Experience: The Aftermath, 1975–1985*, 1985.

Samuel Freeman

NIEBUHR, REINHOLD. Reinhold Niebuhr was a theologian, ethicist, and political philosopher. Born in Wright City, Missouri, January 21, 1892, of first- and second-generation German immigrants, he became a significant spokesman for the social gospel. He was brought up in the Evangelical Synod of North America, which was related to the Lutheran and Calvinistic traditions. After attending denominational schools, he entered Yale Divinity School and received the B.D. and M.A. degrees. He spent most of his academic career at the Union Theological Seminary in New York. Rather than work on a doctorate, he became a pastor in 1915 because he "desired relevance rather than scholarship." That statement may be a key to understanding his thoughts. Late in life, he denied that he was a true theologian, preferring instead to describe himself as a "circuit-riding preacher with an interest in ethics."

During his pastorate in Detroit, Niebuhr was moved by the inhumanity manifested in the automobile industry toward the workers. Social evils were not being addressed. Questions about the evils of war further added to his disillusionment. In an attempt to relieve the dialectical tension, Niebuhr became a leader of the social gospel movement. He became a socialist and ran for political office, even though he had no hope of winning. By 1939, he became the leading opponent of the movement he had so vigorously supported. How could such a great change occur? One writer explained that it was the result of his dialectical thinking. "Usually the new idea was both a criticism and a transformation of the old."

Although he saw himself as moving to the right theologically and to the left politically, the conservative public called him liberal theologically, and the liberal politicians called him conservative. This difference in viewpoints was the result of his willingness to attack either extreme when he felt it was wrong. University professors criticized him for attacking liberalism, and the public sent a "flood of hate mail" for his criticism of Billy Graham.*

Niebuhr saw all issues as dialectical struggles between opposing forces. Faith and political activity, love and hate, right and wrong are examples of ethical controversies. However, according to one source, Niebuhr never imposed moral answers without giving consideration to the realities of the powers in conflict. Then he would attempt to bring religious faith into harmony with the political problems. Although it is not always possible because of dogmatism on either extreme, the Christian will be willing to persevere in the struggle.

Niebuhr's philosophical and ethical perspectives endeared him to such friends as Eleanor Roosevelt,* George Kennan,* Arthur Schelesinger, Jr.,* and Hubert Humphrey.* In 1964, he was awarded the President's Medal of Freedom by Lyndon B. Johnson.* Niebuhr wrote more than 1,000 published articles, reviews, sermons, and prayers. His major books included *Does Civilization Need Religion?* (1927), *Moral Man and Immoral Society* (1932), *Beyond Tragedy* (1937), *Christianity and Power Politics* (1941), *The Irony of American History* (1952), *The Self and the Dramas of History* (1957), and *Man's Nature and His Communities* (1965). Many have been collected and are available in numerous works. Reinhold Niebuhr died June 1, 1971.

REFERENCES: Kenneth Durkin, *Reinhold Niebuhr*, 1990; Richard Fox, *Reinhold Niebuhr: A Biography*, 1986.

Bobby J. James

NITZE, PAUL HENRY. Paul H. Nitze was born in Amherst, Massachusetts, January 16, 1907. He graduated cum laude from Harvard in 1928 and shortly thereafter became a vice president for the investment banking firm of Dillon, Reed, and Company. In 1940, Nitze became assistant to James V. Forrestal, undersecretary of the navy. In 1941, he was named financial director of the Office of the Coordinator of Inter-American Affairs, then under Nelson Rockefeller's* direction. During World War II, Nitze served on the Board of Economic Warfare and the Foreign Economic Administration, and after the war he was vice chairman of the U.S. Strategic Bombing Survey. Nitze moved to the State Department in 1946, helped develop the Marshall Plan, and in 1949 succeeded

George Kennan* as head of the State Department's policy planning staff. In 1956, Nitze wrote *U.S. Foreign Policy, 1945–1955.*

In 1960, President John F. Kennedy* appointed Nitze assistant secretary of defense for international security affairs, where he specialized in disarmament and military assistance plans. Nitze was secretary of the navy between 1963 and 1967 and deputy secretary of defense between 1967 and 1969. In that position he helped draft the San Antonio Formula and served on the Ad Hoc Task Force on Vietnam,* where he advised against further escalation of the war for fear of intervention from the People's Republic of China. Nitze resigned from the Defense Department when Richard Nixon* entered the White House in January 1969, although he served until 1974 as a member of the U.S. delegation to the Strategic Arms Limitations Talks. In 1981, Nitze was named head of the U.S. delegation to the Intermediate Range Nuclear Forces Negotiations with the Soviet Union, and in 1984, he was appointed arms control adviser to Secretary of State George Schultz. Later that year Nitze joined the faculty of Johns Hopkins University, where he began to explore environmental issues.

REFERENCES: *Current Biography*, 1962; *International Who's Who 1984–85*, 1986; "Brinkmanship on a Hot Border," *Time* 113, February 26, 1979, 39–40.

Joanna Cowden

NIXON, RICHARD MILHOUSE. Richard Milhouse Nixon was born in Yorba Linda, California, on January 9, 1913. Bright and extremely hardworking, he graduated from Whittier college in 1934 and from the Duke University Law School in 1937. He returned to Whittier to practice law and served in the U.S. naval reserve during World War II. After the war, the local Republican Party in Whittier, California, decided to nominate Nixon to run for a seat in the U.S. Congress. After a bitter campaign against Democrat Jerry Voorhis, which was characterized by smear tactics that Nixon enthusiastically endorsed, he won the election. He accused Voorhis of being so liberal that he must be a Communist sympathizer. The tactic worked, and Nixon acquired the *modus operandi* of much of his political career.

He was a conservative anti-Communist who made the Red Scare his own, parlaying it into higher, more prestigious political offices. In 1949, he rose to national prominence as the member of the House Un-American Activities Committee who pushed the Alger Hiss treason case. In 1950, Nixon was elected to the U.S. Senate after running a smear campaign against Democratic candidate Helen Douglas. In 1952, Dwight D. Eisenhower* selected Nixon as his vice-presidential running mate, and although critics accused Nixon of diverting campaign funds for personal use, he survived the crisis and the Eisenhower-Nixon ticket won the election.

Nixon was a faithful vice-president, often enduring intense criticism from journalists who resented his Red Scare politics, and in 1960 he won the Republican presidential nomination. He lost the election, however, to Democrat John F. Kennedy.* Two years later, Nixon staged a race for the California gover-

norship but lost to incumbent Pat Brown. It appeared that his political career
was over. But domestic unrest and the Vietnam War* in the 1960s destroyed
the Democratic Party's power base and resurrected Nixon's political career. He
won the Republican presidential nomination in 1968 and went on to defeat Vice-
President Hubert Humphrey* in the general election.

When he took office in 1969, Nixon appointed Henry Kissinger* as his national security advisor, and together they reconstructed U.S. foreign policy, at
least as it related to communism. Both men wanted to bring the Vietnam War
to an end without compromising U.S. credibility around the world. They wanted
''peace with honor'' in Vietnam and hoped to reach a functional accommodation
with the Communist world's two superpowers—the Soviet Union and the People's Republic of China. To end the Vietnam War, Nixon announced the ''Vietnamization'' program—a gradual withdrawal of U.S. troops from Vietnam and
the handing over of military equipment and military responsibility for the war
to the government of South Vietnam. But before signing any peace treaty with
North Vietnam, Nixon insisted on preservation of the government of South
Vietnam, with no Vietcong* participation in the South Vietnamese government
and withdrawal of all North Vietnamese troops from South Vietnam.

Between 1969 and 1972, however, North Vietnam refused to cooperate. Victory was in sight. U.S. troops levels steadily decreased as Vietnamization progressed, but South Vietnam appeared no more ready than before to assume full
responsibility for the conflict. To assist them, Nixon launched massive bombing
campaigns throughout Indochina, invaded Cambodia in 1970, and supported a
South Vietnamese invasion of Laos in 1971, but all to no avail. North Vietnam
refused to change its negotiating position—Vietcong participation in the government of South Vietnam, complete withdrawal of all U.S. forces from Indochina, and the right to leave all North Vietnamese troops in place in South
Vietnam.

As the presidential election approached in 1972, Nixon's sense of urgency
about the war in Vietnam increased. He desperately wanted to be reelected to
a second term. In 1968, he had promised American voters that he could find an
honorable, negotiated settlement to conflict, and he did not want to run for
reelection without having fulfilled that promise. Otherwise, Democratic critics
would crucify him in the campaign. Throughout 1972, as Henry Kissinger travelled around the world—Hanoi,* Paris, Moscow, and Beijing—the American
diplomatic position gradually changed to allow for North Vietnamese troops to
remain in place in South Vietnam after the complete withdrawal of all U.S.
forces. Summit meetings in the Soviet Union and the People's Republic of China
also launched what later became the detente foreign policy and gave Nixon the
assurance that Moscow and Beijing would not subvert the Vietnam peace accords. In October 1972, Nixon announced a tentative settlement, and he was
reelected in November by a landslide. The final agreements were signed in Paris
in January 1973.

The Watergate quagmire gradually destroyed the Nixon presidency. During the election campaign of 1972, zealous subordinates authorized a break-in at the Democratic Party headquarters in the Watergate complex in Washington, D.C. They botched the break-in and were arrested by Washington, D.C., police. A few days later, when Nixon learned of the arrest, he initiated a cover-up, trying to block formal investigations of the crime. During the next two years, the president consistently denied that he had engaged in such a cover-up, but when White House tapes revealed his complicity in August 1974, he resigned the presidency in disgrace. Only a pardon from President Gerald Ford kept him out of prison.

Nixon went almost into hiding for the next ten years, giving few interviews and saying little about public policy. Most Republican politicians wanted little to do with him because of the stigma attached to his administration. But late in the 1980s, Nixon slowly reentered public life, giving more interviews, delivering selected lectures, and writing articles and books about public affairs. He died on April 21, 1994.

REFERENCE: Stephen A. Ambrose, *Nixon*, 3 vols., 1987–1991.

NIXON DOCTRINE. Facing enormous political pressure because of economic problems, squeezes on the federal budget, antiwar opposition, and a new spirit of neoisolationism, President Richard M. Nixon* announced the Nixon Doctrine in a talk with journalists on Guam on July 25, 1969. While maintaining the protection of Southeast Asia and Japan by the "nuclear umbrella," the United States insisted that Asian soldiers, rather than American troops, would have to carry the burden of land warfare in the future. The Nixon Doctrine would not go into effect until after American disengagement from Vietnam and would not modify any existing U.S. commitments to the Southeast Asia Treaty Organization or any bilateral commitments to Japan, South Korea, Taiwan, or the Philippines. Critics charged that the Nixon Doctrine was based on a continuation of the containment* policy and actually made the United States more dependent on its Asian allies and more vulnerable to political instability in the area. President Nixon invoked the doctrine in 1971 to justify increased American economic and military assistance to Iran.

REFERENCE: Earl C. Ravenal, "The Nixon Doctrine and Our Asian Commitments," *Foreign Affairs* 49 (1971), 201–17.

NIXON AND THE SUPREME COURT. As he approached the presidential election of 1968, Richard M. Nixon* had developed what later became called the "southern strategy," a Republican plan to cut into the traditionally Democratic heartland of the South. In the election of 1964, despite his overwhelming loss nationwide, Barry Goldwater* had proven that a conservative Republican could do well in the South. In fact, except for his home state of Arizona, Goldwater had done well only in the Deep South. Nixon wanted to do just as well in the South.

At the same time, he did not want to alienate Republican moderates in the

Midwest, Northeast, and the border states. It would have been easy for Nixon to appeal to the South by denouncing the civil rights movement,* but he personally approved of the Civil Rights Act of 1964, and he feared that condemning the legislation would cost him more votes in the North than it would gain him in the South. Instead, Nixon decided to publicly proclaim the virtues of law and order, condemn antiwar protesters, and denounce the busing of children to achieve school integration, positions certain to endear him to conservative southerners. Privately, he also encouraged southern political leaders, Democrats as well as Republicans, that if he won the election, he would make sure that conservative southerners were appointed to the federal bench.

Governor George Wallace* of Alabama complicated the southern strategy when he announced his own third-party bid for the presidency, but Nixon kept the faith, still certain that if he could secure electoral votes in the upper South and border states, he would be able to win the election.

The first skirmish in the Supreme Court war was actually fought during the fall presidential campaign. Supreme Court chief justice Earl Warren* had presided over the most liberal period in the Court's history. Uncertain about the outcome of the election of 1968,* Warren decided to resign from the Court earlier than he had once planned in order to give President Lyndon B. Johnson* the chance to replace him with a young liberal who would preserve his judicial legacy. Johnson jumped at the opportunity and submitted the name of Supreme Court justice Abe Fortas,* his old friend and confidant, to replace Warren. Nixon and the Republicans shouted their opposition immediately, arguing that selection of Warren's replacement ought to be the prerogative of the next president, whoever he might be, not the current one. They vowed to fight confirmation in the Senate.

Fortas proved to be his own worst enemy. During the controversy over his appointment in October 1968, the press revealed that during his tenure on the Supreme Court, he had continued to advise the president politically and had accepted lecture fees, two practices that most jurists found unethical. The press had a field day with the news, and Republicans launched an ironclad filibuster in the Senate, which the Democrats could not stop. The Senate voted 45 to 43 to end the filibuster, but Senate rules required 59 votes to end it. Johnson withdrew the nomination. When Nixon won the election of 1968, he had the opportunity to fulfill his promise under the southern strategy.

Nixon's choice for chief justice was Warren Burger,* a conservative Republican to be sure, but not a southerner. When reporters revealed that Abe Fortas had accepted a lifetime retainer from a foundation guilty of stock manipulation, even while he served on the Supreme Court, his career was over. Fortas resigned on May 14, 1969. Nixon then submitted to the Senate the name of Clement Haynesworth to replace Fortas. Haynesworth, chief judge of the U.S. Court of Appeals for the fouth circuit, was a conservative southerner. This time, Democrats decided to get even for Republican opposition to Fortas. When it was revealed that Haynesworth had not excluded himself from cases in which he had stock interests, northern Democrats went after him with a vengeance, blocking his confirmation at all costs. The Senate rejected his confirmation by a vote of 55 to 45.

Their rejection of his nomination infuriated Nixon, who took the defeat personally. He came back with the nomination of G. Harold Carswell, a judge with the 5th Circuit of the U.S. Court of Appeals. Carswell was known in the judicial community as an intellectual lightweight, but Democrats knew they could not oppose him on those grounds; they had appointed enough of their own duds to the federal bench over the years. But when it was revealed that Carswell had written judicial opinions with racist sentiments early in his career, his chances for appointment to the Supreme Court were doomed. The Senate rejected him by a vote of 51 to 45. Nixon gave up the fight and nominated Harry Blackmun, who was confirmed unanimously in May 1970.

REFERENCE: Stephen Ambrose, *Nixon*, 3 vols., 1987–1991.

NOLTING, FREDERICK ERNEST. Frederick Nolting was born in Richmond, Virginia, on August 24, 1911. In 1933, he graduated from the University of Virginia, and after receiving a master's degree from Harvard in 1941, he returned to Virginia for his Ph.D. Nolting served in the U.S. Navy during World War II, and after the war he went to work for the State Department. He worked there in relative obscurity until 1955, when he was appointed a member of the U.S. delegation to the North Atlantic Treaty Organization (NATO). President Dwight D. Eisenhower* named him alternate permanent representative to NATO in 1957 and ambassador to South Vietnam in 1961.

In South Vietnam, Nolting became a personal friend and vociferous supporter of President Ngo Dinh Diem* and made it a personal mission to increase U.S. support—financial and military—for the South Vietnamese government. Between 1961 and 1963, however, Diem's erratic policies alienated most South Vietnamese and the John F. Kennedy* administration; in the process, Nolting lost political support. President Kennedy concluded that Nolting had identified himself too closely with the flawed regime in Saigon. In 1963, Kennedy replaced him with Henry Cabot Lodge, Jr.* Nolting then joined Morgan Guaranty Trust Company, an investment banking firm. In 1970, Nolting left Morgan Guaranty to join the faculty of the University of Virginia. Nolting died December 14, 1989.

REFERENCES: David Halberstam, *The Best and the Brightest*, 1972; Frederick Nolting, *From Trust to Tragedy: The Political Memoirs of Frederick Nolting, Kennedy's Ambassador to Diem's Vietnam*, 1988.

NORTH VIETNAMESE ARMY. In 1965, when President Lyndon B. Johnson* introduced regular U.S. combat troops into Vietnam,* most Americans assumed the war would end quickly, that the superiority of U.S. firepower and U.S. soldiers would quickly overwhelm the Vietcong* and the North Vietnamese Army (NVA). American air power would make it impossible for North Vietnam to keep its army supplied and reinforced in South Vietnam, and the U.S. strategy of attrition* would kill so many North Vietnamese soldiers that they would no longer be able to sustain the war effort. U.S. policymakers badly underestimated the NVA's commitment and resilience. The NVA was a formidable enemy.

In 1954, after the Vietminh victory over the French at Dien Bien Phu, Ho Chi Minh* formally organized the NVA. It consisted then of three infantry divisions and approximately 35,000 troops, many of them battle-hardened veterans of the French war. Their commander was Vo Nguyen Giap.* Ten years later, the NVA had fifteen infantry divisions and more than 125,000 troops, although they were equipped with dated, World War II equipment. By 1974, the NVA had jumped to 600,000 troops in eighteen infantry divisions; twenty independent infantry regiments; four armored regiments equipped with modern Soviet T-34, T-54, T-59, and PT-76 tanks; ten artillery regiments; twenty-four antiaircraft regiments; and fifteen surface-to-air (SAM) missile regiments—one of the finest armies in the history of the world.

REFERENCES: International Institute for Strategic Studies, *The Military Balance 1963–64*, 1963 and *The Military Balance, 1974–75*, 1975; Anthony Robinson, ed., *The Weapons of the Vietnam War*, 1983; Shelby M. Stanton, *The Rise and Fall of an American Army: U.S. Ground Forces in Vietnam, 1965–1973*, 1985.

NUCLEAR NONPROLIFERATION TREATY OF 1968. During the late 1950s and early 1960s, fear of thermonuclear warfare reached a fever pitch in the United States and Europe. Such films as *On the Beach,* *Fail Safe,* *The Bedford Incident*, and *Dr. Strangelove** elevated those fears even more, and political support for limits on nuclear weapons gained momentum. In the Nuclear Test Ban Treaty* of 1963, the United States and dozens of other nations agreed to end the atmospheric testing of nuclear weapons. Henceforth, signees to the treaty would test weapons only underground, where radioactive materials could not escape into the atmosphere.

There was also concern, however, about the proliferation of nuclear weapons. Most strategic observers were convinced that an increase in the number of countries possessing nuclear weapons would destabilize world politics and increase the likelihood of a nuclear exchange, if not between the superpowers, then between smaller rivals, such as India and Pakistan or Israel and Syria. The United States and the Soviet Union led the way in promoting the nonproliferation treaty. The two countries signed the treaty on May 31, 1968, and the United Nations General Assembly then approved the treaty by a vote of 95 to 4. More than fifty nations eventually signed, and it went into effect on March 5, 1970. The treaty prohibited the transfer of nuclear technology by a nuclear power to a nonnuclear power, and it also prohibited the manufacture or acquisition by other means of nuclear technology on the part of nonnuclear nations. By January 1976, ninety-six countries had signed the treaty.

REFERENCES: William Epstein, *The Last Chance*, 1976; Mason Willrich, *The Non-Proliferation Treaty*, 1969.

NUCLEAR REGULATORY COMMISSION. By the 1960s, criticism of the Atomic Energy Commission (AEC) began to appear on the grounds that a government agency responsible for regulating the atomic energy industry and protecting public health and safety should not also be involved in promoting the industry itself. The apparent discrepancy first came to light in 1956. The AEC had approved the construction of a 100-megawatt fast-breeder reactor in Lagoona Beach, Michigan, by the Power Reactor Development Company, even though the AEC's own safety experts had serious reservations about the project. There were other examples in subsequent years, and the rise of the environmental movement* in the 1960s intensified those concerns. In 1974, Congress passed the Energy Reorganization Act. It abolished the AEC and created the Nuclear Regulatory Commission (NRC) to protect public health and safety and the Energy Research and Development Administration to promote the uses of nuclear energy.
REFERENCE: Fred Clement, *The Nuclear Regulatory Commission*, 1989.

NUCLEAR TEST BAN TREATY (1963). The "Ban the Bomb" movement had been campaigning against the atmospheric testing of nuclear weapons ever since the mid-1950s. They argued that radioactive fallout from the tests was a public health hazard to the entire world. The Cuban missile crisis* of October 1962, which brought the world dangerously close to a thermonuclear conflict, elevated fears of nuclear weapons. On June 9, 1963, at American University in Washington, D.C., President John F. Kennedy* offered an olive branch to the Soviet Union. Rather than wallowing in Cold War* rhetoric, he called for a reduction in mutual suspicions because both superpowers had an interest in peace and an end to the arms race. He also proposed negotiations to end the atmospheric testing of nuclear weapons. "We all inhabit this small planet," Kennedy proclaimed. "We all breathe the same air. We all cherish our children's future. And we are all mortal."

The Soviet Union responded quickly to Kennedy's offer. Test ban talks between the United States and the Soviet Union had been taking place since the 1950s, but neither side had ever been inclined to seriously consider the permanent elimination of atmospheric testing. On June 10, the day after the president's American University speech, the two countries announced the beginning of a new round of negotiations. On July 15, the United States, Great Britain, and the Soviet Union began trilateral talks on the issue, and on August 5, 1963, negotiators signed a preliminary agreement in Moscow. All three nuclear powers agreed to conduct no more atmospheric tests of nuclear weapons. Nor could they test such weapons in outer space or under the water, only in underground installations from which no radioactive particles could escape. During the next month, ninety-six other nations signed the agreement. The U.S. Senate ratified the treaty on September 24, 1963, and it went into effect on October 10, 1963.
REFERENCE: Alonzo L. Hamby, *The Imperial Years: The U.S. since 1939*, 1976.

NUREYEV, RUDOLPH HAMETOVICH. Rudolph Nureyev was born March 17, 1938. At the time of his birth, his mother was traveling aboard a train in Siberian Russia, near Lake Baikal. His mother was an ethnic Tatar from Kazan, while his father was of Bashkir Muslim descent. Because his father was a soldier in the Russian army, the family moved frequently during Nureyev's youth, although he spent the World War II years in Moscow. They then moved to the city of Ufa in Bashkiria, a region of Russia east of the Ural mountains. There, Nureyev began taking ballet lessons. He toured briefly with the Ufa Ballet, coming to Moscow in 1955. Brilliant in his auditions, he was accepted into the school of the Kirov Ballet of Leningrad. Creative and physically gifted, Nureyev graduated in 1958 and was immediately given solo roles in the Kirov Ballet.

Within a year he was widely accepted as the greatest male dancer in the Soviet Union. But Nureyev was also an individualist who chafed under the political restrictions on artistic expression so common in his country. He was hardly a politician, but communist repressions irritated him. Nureyev came to national attention in the United States when, on June 17, 1961, he fled the Kirov Ballet at the Paris airport and requested political asylum. One week later, he was the highest-paid dancer in the world and performed with the Marquis de Cuevas Ballet in Paris. During the 1960s and 1970s, he performed brilliantly with virtually every major ballet company in the world. A talented athlete and peerless creative genius, Nureyev epitomized the creative spirit of the 1960s. He lived an extremely private personal life and died of AIDS-related complications on January 6, 1993.

REFERENCE: *New York Times*, January 7, 1993.

O

OAKES, RICHARD. Mohawk Richard Oakes, perhaps best known for his leadership during the American Indian occupation of Alcatraz Island,* 1969–1971, was born in 1941 on the St. Regis Indian Reservation in New York, the son of Art Oakes of St. Regis and Albany, New York. He attended Salmon River Central School until he was sixteen years old and quit during the eleventh grade because he felt the American school system failed to offer him anything relevant to his Indian culture and heritage. Oakes then began a brief career in the iron work industry, working both on and off reservation, including high steel work—assembling steel beams for skyscrapers—which was common among Mohawk Indian men. The early years of his life were spent in New York, Massachusetts, and Rhode Island before he moved to California. During that time, he attended Adirondack Community College in Glen Falls, New York, and Syracuse University. While traveling cross-country to San Francisco, Oakes visited several Indian reservations and became aware of their political and economic situations. Oakes worked at several jobs in San Francisco until he had an opportunity to enroll in San Francisco State College in February 1969 under the government's new economic opportunity program. During this time, he met and married Annie Marufo, a Kashia Pomo Indian from northern California, and adopted her five children.

Oakes was a leader in the November 1969 occupation of Alcatraz Island, an event that became the catalyst for the emerging Indian activism that continued into the 1970s. The occupation of Alcatraz Island was an attempt by Indian college students and urban Indian people to attract national attention to the failure of U.S. government policy toward American Indians. The press and many of the Indian occupiers recognized Oakes as the "Indian leader" on Alcatraz, even though Oakes never claimed that position. Oakes left Alcatraz Island in January 1970 following the death of his stepdaughter Yvonne Oakes, who died from a head injury after falling down a stairwell in a vacant building on Alcatraz

Island. After leaving Alcatraz Island, Oakes remained active in Indian social issues and was particularly instrumental in the Pomo and Pit River Indian movements to regain ancestral lands in northern California. He participated in the planning of additional occupations of federal property in northern California and at key places around the country.

On September 21, 1972, Oakes was shot and killed by Michael Morgan, a Young Men's Christian Association (YMCA) camp employee in Sonoma County, California. Oakes had gone to the camp to locate an Indian youth who was staying with the Oakes family. The camp employee was charged with involuntary manslaughter, but charges were later dropped on the grounds that Oakes had come "menacingly toward" him. Oakes was buried on his wife's reservation on September 27, 1970, with traditional religious rites. The murder of Oakes unified the various Indian protest groups and gave impetus to the Trail of Broken Treaties March, which was planned on the Rosebud Indian Reservation and scheduled to arrive in Washington, D.C., in time for the 1972 presidential campaign.

REFERENCES: Troy R. Johnson, *The Occupation of Alcatraz Island: Indian Self-Determination and the Rise of Indian Activism*, 1996; *New York Times*, September 22, 1972.

Troy Johnson

OCHS, PHIL. Phil Ochs was born in El Paso, Texas, December 19, 1940. He was raised in Queens, New York, and attended military school in Virginia. He went to Ohio State University to study journalism, but in Columbus, Ochs became interested in folk music. He moved to New York in 1961. There, in Greenwich Village, he became involved in the folk protest movement with Bob Dylan.* A critic of the Vietnam War,* Ochs had hits in 1965 with "I Ain't a' Marchin' " and "Draft Dodger Rag." Because of his antiwar posture, Ochs was banned from radio and television in the United States. After the release of his *Pleasures of the Harbor* album in 1967, Ochs moved to California, where he became interested in rock and roll. His 1968 album *Tape from California* contained antiwar folk tunes like "War Is Over." By that time Ochs had become a genuine folk hero to the antiwar counterculture,* even though he was suffering badly from depression. He committed suicide in 1976.

REFERENCE: Michael Schumacher, *There But for Fortune: The Life of Phil Ochs*, 1996.

OH! CALCUTTA! Oh! Calcutta! was conceived by Kenneth Tynan and released for public attendance in 1969. Tynan, whom *Newsweek* described in its June 16, 1969, issue as a "brilliant English critic" and the "literary manager of Britain's National Theatre," conceived this play as an evening of "gentle stimulation, where a fellow can take a girl he is trying to woo." The actual release of the play, however, caused much more controversy than Tynan's somewhat tame description implies. *Oh! Calcutta!* was surrounded by controversy and the hype associated with it and became a major hit in 1969.

Oh! Calcutta! was embroiled in controversy before it was ever released for general public viewing. This off-Broadway play was touted prior to its release as "elegant erotica" by Tynan. In reality, however, it was "an erotic review of sex, with frequent total nudity and simulated sexual activity by the actors." Due to this controversial material, the production participants were worried about the play's being shut down by authorities for being obscene. In fact, according to *Newsweek*, Hillard Elkins, who produced this play, extensively consulted "New York City officials to keep the play within the bounds of the law." The controversy surrounding its theatrical release aroused the public interest and turned the play into a megahit.

REFERENCES: *Newsweek*, June 16, 1969; *Time*, June 27, 1969.

John Hinson

O'HARE, MADALYN MURRAY. Madalyn Murray O'Hare was born in 1919 and grew up to become the leader of the American atheist movement. Throughout the 1950s she labored in obscurity, defending the separation of church and state against what she considered religious fanaticism. She particularly opposed the practice of mandatory prayers in public schools, and she launched a federal lawsuit against the practice. In its 1962 *Engle v. Vitale** decision, the Supreme Court essentially agreed with O'Hare's position, claiming that even a so-called nondenominational prayer was a violation of the establishment clause of the First Amendment. The decision raised, and continues to raise, bitter protests from fundamentalist groups in the United States and made Madalyn Murray O'Hare, in the words of one journalist, "[t]he most hated woman in America."

In 1963, O'Hare founded American Atheists, Inc., in Austin, Texas. From her base in Austin, she continued to campaign against what she considered to be religious intrusions in public life—such as Christmas pageants in public schools, prayers and public school events, and Christian musical presentations in public schools. In 1995, Madalyn Murray O'Hare mysteriously disappeared, and her whereabouts were still unknown in 1999.

REFERENCE: J. Gordon Melton, *The Encyclopedia of American Religions*, 1989.

OLE MISS. In 1962, Oxford, Mississippi, was the scene of the country's most raucous civil rights struggle. Early in September 1962, a federal court ordered the University of Mississippi ("Ole Miss") to admit James Meredith,* an African American, as a fully matriculated student. Mississippi governor Ross Barnett,* telling white Mississippians that they were facing the "moment of our greatest crisis since the War Between the States," resolved to disobey the court order. When Meredith arrived on campus on September 30, an unruly mob pelted him with bricks and stones, even though federal marshals were accompanying him.

President John F. Kennedy* went on national television,* calling for peace and understanding in Mississippi, but the white mobs were not swayed. Meredith exhibited extraordinary courage in staying with his commitment to attend the

University of Mississippi. The situation was more than a little dangerous. Two
people had already been killed in the rioting. Finally, Kennedy had to call out
federal troops to protect Meredith and guarantee that the federal integration
would be implemented. The federal troops did the job, and Meredith attended
class. He graduated from Ole Miss in 1963.
REFERENCE: Dan Elish, *James Meredith and School Desegregation*, 1994.

OLYMPIC BOYCOTT OF 1968. In the mid-1960s, the nonviolent civil disobedience tactics of Martin Luther King, Jr.,* in the civil rights movement*
gave way to the black power* rhetoric of people like Stokely Carmichael.* That
movement was reflected in American sports. A number of African-American
leaders began to see modern athletics as simply another example of exploitation
in the United States. Early in 1968, Professor Harry Edwards* of San Jose State
University organized a boycott of the New York Athletic Club's* annual track
meet in Madison Square Garden. Since the club would not admit blacks as
members, Edwards argued that black athletes should not compete in the meet.
The boycott proved to be a success. A number of major African-American track
and field stars refused to compete, and the meet's attendance and television
audiences declined dramatically.

Buoyed by his success in the New York Athletic Club meet, Edwards decided
to launch a similar boycott of the 1968 Olympic games in Mexico City. He
made a simple argument: why should black athletes bring glory to a country
that discriminated against them racially? Edwards organized the Olympic Project
for Human Rights to supervise the boycott. He insisted that black athletes all
over the world refuse to compete unlesss the International Olympic Committee
(IOC) ban South Africa and Rhodesia from the games until apartheid was destroyed, Avery Brundage was ousted as head of the IOC, Muhammad Ali* had
his license to box restored in the United States, and black coaches were added
to the U.S. Olympic team.

Avery Brundage and the IOC at first tried to dig in and hold out, but Edwards
had his first success when most black African nations agreed to join the boycott.
Mexico then decided to refuse admission to the country to any individual carrying South Africa and Rhodesian passports. In April 1968, the IOC caved in and
banned South Africa and Rhodesia from all international competition.

Flushed with success, Edwards tried to keep the boycott going in the United
States, since only one of his demands had been met. The assassination of Martin
Luther King, Jr., in April 1968 only made the urgency of the boycott more
immediate. Throughout the spring and summer of 1968, Edwards traveled
around the country speaking to black athletes, trying to muster support for the
boycott. To counter Edwards, the U.S. Olympic Committee sent the legendary
Jesse Owens on a nationwide speaking tour, in which he argued against politi-
cizing the Olympics. The boycott collapsed in the summer of 1968, when America's premier black athletes decided to compete.

The boycott may have stalled, but the influence of Harry Edwards at the

Mexico City games could not be denied. A number of black athletes wore black socks during the Olympic trials and during the games as a symbolic protest. Tommie Smith and Juan Carlos placed first and third in the 200-meter race, and at the medal awards ceremony, when the "Star Spangled Banner" was being played, they raised their arms in clenched, black-gloved fists in order "to give young African Americans something to be proud of, to identify themselves with." Their protest salute received major media coverage in the United States. So did boxer George Foreman's countersalute. An African American from Houston, Foreman won the gold medal in heavyweight Olympic boxing. After the bout, he paraded around the ring, proudly waving an American flag.
REFERENCE: Randy Roberts and James S. Olson, *Winning Is the Only Thing: Sports in America since 1945*, 1989.

ON THE BEACH. *On the Beach* was a popular 1960 film adaptation of Nevil Shute's 1959 novel of the same name. *On the Beach* had an illustrious cast, which included Gregory Peck, Ava Gardner, Fred Astaire, and Anthony Perkins. It is set in Australia after global thermonuclear war. The film deals with the horrifying possibility that nuclear war could kill all human beings on the planet. In this case, nuclear war and radiation have killed everyone north of the equator, and the radiation is spreading inexorably south of the equator, killing everything in its path. The people in southern Australia are simply counting the days until their own doom. Released at a time in the United States when fear of nuclear warfare was at a peak, the film precipitated an intense political debate. "Ban-the-Bomb"* activists hailed the movie as a realistic prophecy of what could happen to human beings, while conservatives labeled it a shrill, inaccurate exaggeration.
REFERENCE: *New York Times*, January 6, 1960.

ONE VERY HOT DAY. David Halberstam,* a reporter for the *New York Times*, won the Pulitzer Prize for his reporting on the Vietnam War.* He had a decidedly low opinion of the war, even in its early stages, and was convinced that the government of South Vietnam was too corrupt to survive. In 1967, Halberstam tried his hand at a fictional account of the war, and the result was *One Very Hot Day*, published in 1967. The book describes the activities of three officers—two Americans and one South Vietnamese—during one day of the war in the humid, sticky, hot environment of South Vietnam. Halberstam describes a war that has no purpose and writes of the meaningless deaths of soldiers and civilians. Vietnam was a futile, unwinnable conflict.
REFERENCES: Philip D. Biedler, *American Literature and the Experience of Vietnam*, 1982; David Halberstam, *One Very Hot Day*, 1967.

OPERATION CEDAR FALLS. Throughout the Vietnam War,* a region known as the Iron Triangle* posed repeated, serious challenges to U.S. forces. The Iron Triangle was located approximately twenty miles northwest of Saigon* and consisted of sixty square miles of swamps, rice paddies, heavy jungle, and rice plantations. The Vietcong* had been active in the Iron Triangle for years, and they had crisscrossed the region with elaborate underground tunnels and bunkers. The Vietcong were able to deploy thousands of troops to the Iron Triangle. General William Westmoreland,* commander of U.S. forces in Vietnam, considered the Iron Triangle a "dagger pointed at the heart of Saigon," since it was relatively easy for Vietcong forces to attack the city from their strongholds in the area. Westmoreland decided that it was strategically critical for the United States to destroy the Vietcong infrastructure in the Iron Triangle.

"Operation Cedar Falls" became the code name for the U.S. assault on the Iron Triangle. Since Westmoreland had decided on an all-out use of American firepower, artillery and aerial bombardment, it was necessary to remove all Vietnamese civilians from the region before the attack began. Once all noncombatants had been removed, Westmoreland would pulverize the area with artillery and air bombardment and deploy infantry and air cavalry troops to destroy enemy forces. On January 8, 1967, the forced evacuation of civilians commenced. Once the civilians had been placed in relocation camps, Westmoreland concluded that anybody left behind had to be Vietcong and would be subject to destruction. Westmoreland then ordered the complete destruction of Ben Suc,* a village known to be a hiding place for the Vietcong. Finally, he ordered the saturation bombardment of the Iron Triangle.

The ground battle lasted for eighteen days. U.S. troops from the 1st and 25th Infantry divisions, the 173rd Airborne Brigade, and the 11th Armored Cavalry participated in the operation. They were assisted by several units from the Army of the Republic of Vietnam (ARVN). The joint U.S.-ARVN attack force discovered an astonishing underground network of five-hundred tunnels stretching a total of twelve miles, complete with ammunition depots, field hospitals, and barracks. When the battle was finally over, the Vietcong had lost 775 troops compared to a U.S. total of 250. Westmoreland proudly announced Operation Cedar Falls a stunning American victory. Actually, the victory was less than stunning. Within six months, Vietcong troops had reoccupied the Iron Triangle and used it as a staging area for the Tet Offensive's* assault on Saigon at the end of January 1968.

REFERENCES: Bernard William Rogers, *Cedar-Falls-Junction City: A Turning Point,* 1974; Jonathan Schell, *The Village of Ben Suc,* 1967; Stafford Thomas, "Operation Cedar Falls," in James S. Olson, ed., *Dictionary of the Vietnam War,* 1988.

OPERATION DEWEY CANYON. During most of the Vietnam War,* U.S. marines found themselves conducting sesarch-and-destroy* missions in the mountainous jungles of I Corps, the northernmost region of South Vietnam. Between January 22, 1968, and March 19, 1969, which coincided with the Tet Offensive,* the 9th Marine Regiment conducted Operation Dewey Canyon there, in an attempt to cut the supply lines of the North Vietnamese Army* (NVA) from the A Shau Valley and the Da Krong Valley into Laos. During the course of Operation Dewey Canyon, the U.S. marines captured fifty-five tons of NVA supplies and killed 1,335 NVA soldiers.

REFERENCES: Shelby L. Stanton, *Vietnam Order of Battle*, 1981, and *The Rise and Fall of an American Army: U.S. Ground Troops in Vietnam, 1965–1973*, 1985; Keith William Nolan, *Into Laos. The Story of Dewy CanyonII/Lam Son 719*, 1986.

OPERATION JUNCTION CITY. During the course of the Vietnam War*— up to the Tet Offensive* of 1968, at least—a hotbed of Vietcong* activity was located in what was known as War Zone C of Tay Ninh Province in South Vietnam. General William Westmoreland,* commander of U.S. forces, decided to wipe out the Vietcong in War Zone C, and on February 22, 1967, he launched Operation Junction City to do so. It was a huge, combined United States Army– South Vietnamese search and destroy* campaign. The U.S. units involved included elements of the 1st, 4th, and 26th Infantry divisions, 196th Light Infantry Brigade, 11th Armored Cavalry, and the 173rd Airborne Brigade. Their primary target in War Zone C was the Vietcong 9th Division. The battle continued until May 14, 1967, by which time the Vietcong, having sustained more than 3,000 casualties, broke off the fighting and retreated across the Cambodian border to regroup. Westmoreland hailed Junction City as a great military victory, but the battle there in 1967 actually produced a new strategic reality, changing the nature of the conflict. When the Vietcong retreated into Cambodia, North Vietnam developed new routes along the Ho Chi Minh Trail* to supply them. The war had widened into Cambodia and put new pressures on the United States to attack enemy forces there.

REFERENCES: Shelby L. Stanton, *Vietnam Order of Battle*, 1981, and *The Rise and Fall of an American Army: U.S. Ground Troops in Vietnam, 1965–1973*, 1985; Bernard William Rogers, *Cedar Falls-Junction City: A Turning Point*, 1974.

OPERATION MENU. On March 18, 1969, the U.S. Air Force began Operation Menu, a series of secret, illegal B-52 bombings of National Liberation Front (NLF) and North Vietnamese army* (NVA) sanctuaries in eastern Cambodia. It continued for fifteen months until the Cambodian invasion of 1970, when it was renamed Operation Freedom Deal and expanded to include "targets" throughout Cambodia. Freedom Deal continued until Congress prohibited funds for bombing Cambodia effective August 15, 1973. By their end, 16,527 sorties had been flown, and 383,851 tons of bombs had been dropped.

General Creighton Abrams* had wanted to attack sanctuaries for some time; however, President Lyndon Johnson* repeatedly refused permission. When Richard Nixon* became president in January 1969, these requests were resubmitted with the justifications that striking sanctuaries would reduce NLF–NVA offensive capabilities, and the Central Office for South Vietnam* (COSVN) (the NLF–NVA command structure) had been located and could be destroyed by either ground or air attack. After initial hesitation, Nixon approved, for reasons of his own. The bombing was to "signal" Hanoi* that Nixon was "tougher" than Johnson and to lend credence to the "mad man" image he wanted to create among North Vietnamese leaders.

"Menu" was a series of attacks (meals) against NLF–NVA Base Areas: "Breakfast"—Base Area 353, twenty-five square kilometers near the Fishhook, inhabited by 1,640 Cambodians and the supposed headquarters of COSVN; "Lunch"—Base Area 609, located on the Laotian–Cambodian–Vietnamese borders and inhabited by 198 Cambodians: "Snack"—Base Area 351, 101 square kilometers in the Fishhook, including one town and 383 Cambodians; "Dinner"—Base Area 352, located in the Fishhook, including one town and 770 Cambodians; and "Dessert"—Base Area 350, located north of the Fishhook with 120 Cambodians. The military did not recommend bombing Base Areas 354, 704, and 707 because they had substantial Cambodian civilian populations. Nonetheless, Base Area 704 was authorized as "Supper" with 247 B-52 missions flown against it. In March 1970, Nixon authorized expanded bombing of Laos, including B-52 raids against the Plain of Jars.

Officially, Military Assistance Command, Vietnam claimed the base areas were not inhabited by Cambodian civilians, but private military reports indicated awareness of civilian presence and expectations of civilian casualties. These reports contended that although casualties should be light because the base areas were sparsely populated, and Cambodians lived apart from the NLF–NVAA, "some Cambodian casualties would be sustained . . . [and] the surprise effect of attacks would tend to increase casualties . . . [due to] probable lack of protective shelter around Cambodian homes." The number of Cambodians killed is unknown.

Nixon, very concerned that Operation Menu not become public knowledge, ordered elaborate security measures, which included falsification of military records, an offense punishable by court-martial under Article 107 of the *Uniform Code of Military Justice*, so there was absolutely no record of the bombings having occurred. Nixon and Henry Kissinger's* justification was that secrecy was necessary to protect Cambodia's Prince Norodom Sihanouk,* who gave his "tacit consent." They do not provide evidence to support this proposition, and Prince Sihanouk vehemently denies he consented, tacitly or otherwise.

REFERENCES: William Shawcross, *Sideshow: Kissinger, Nixon, and the Destruction of Cambodia*, 1979; John Morrocco, *The Vietnam Experience. Rain of Fire: Air War, 1969–1973*, 1984.

Samuel Freeman

OPERATION MONGOOSE. When Fidel Castro* and the communists came to power in Cuba in 1959, the Eisenhower* and later, the Kennedy* administrations vowed to overthrow them. Such a communist presence in the Western Hemisphere was intolerable. Operation Mongoose was a successor to Operation Pluto, both Central Intelligence Agency* (CIA) programs to eliminate Castro as a political force in Cuba. The CIA set up Zenith Technical Enterprises, placed it on the campus of the University of Miami, and gave it an annual budget of

$50 million. Its mission was to overthrow Castro. The company purchased hundreds of motorboats, hired hundreds of Cuban exiles, and began conducting paramilitary assaults on Cuba from the Florida Keys. At the same time, there was an increase in the filibustering and paramilitary campaigns of independent exile groups, such as the Second Naval Guerrilla group and Alpha 66. The CIA tried to assassinate Fidel Castro using its own agents and even hired Mafia contract killers to do the job. Organized crime had been as upset about the Castro revolution as the American corporations and upper-class Cubans had been. Once in power, Castro shut down the gambling casinos, eliminated much of the drug trafficking, and outlawed prostitution, all of which had been extremely lucrative to mob interests in the United States. At the same time, Operation Mongoose involved commando raids to sabotage Cuban railroads and public utility plants. By the early 1960s an astonishing 12,000 Cuban emigrés were on the payroll of the Central Intelligence Agency.

REFERENCE: James S. Olson and Judith E. Olson, *The Cuban-Americans: From Triumph to Tragedy*, 1995.

OPERATION PLUTO. See **CUBAN MISSILE CRISIS (1962)**.

OPERATION RANCH HAND. During the course of the Vietnam War,* the most difficult problem facing U.S. policymakers was dealing with the challenges posed by fighting a guerrilla war against an elusive enemy able to melt into civilian communities or disappear into forested jungles and swamps. In particular, Vietcong* troops managed to use geography to their advantage. Jungle cover was so heavy that U.S. air strikes had difficulty targeting enemy troop concentrations accurately or, for that matter, seriously disrupting the movement of supplies from North Vietnam through Laos and Cambodia and into South Vietnam. Also, U.S. military officials knew that the Vietcong often worked their own rice paddies, disguised as civilians, to produce the food they needed.

To address these challenges, American policymakers began toying with the idea of using herbicides—essentially environmental warfare—to destroy the jungle cover and rice paddies the Vietcong used to hide and support themselves. Herbicides, basically weed-destroying chemicals, had long been employed in American agriculture, but the government of Ngo Dinh Diem,* president of South Vietnam, opposed spraying large sections of the country in order to disable the Vietcong. President Diem suspected that such herbicidal spraying would also alienate large numbers of civilians who might suffer its deleterious effects.

As the Vietcong steadily gained strength in 1959 and 1960, posing an increasingly dangerous threat to his regime, Diem changed his mind, and in 1961 he ended his opposition to herbicidal warfare. His change of heart precipitated a debate among U.S. policymakers. Some believed that the use of defoliant chemicals would prove cheap and effective, while others claimed that such a program would have serious, long-term environmental consequences and subject the United States to accusations of brutality. However, in November 1961, President John F. Kennedy* approved the use of herbicides in Southeast Asia.

The U.S. Air Force Tactical Air Command dubbed the campaign Operation Ranch Hand and commenced the aerial spraying in January 1962. At first, the chemicals were used sparingly, but over time, the regions being sprayed increased dramatically in size. Beginning in late 1965 and continuing until September 1969, the Air Force also sprayed defoliant chemicals over Laos. Between the first spraying in January 1962 and February 1971, when General Creighton Abrams* officially terminated Operation Ranch Hand, 19.22 million gallons of herbicides were sprayed on nearly six million acres of land in South Vietnam. Nearly a half million gallons were dropped on Laos.

REFERENCES: William A. Buchingham, Jr., *Operation Ranch Hand: The United States Air Force and Herbicides in Southeast Asia, 1961–1971*, 1982; Roger D. Launius, ''Operation Ranch Hand,'' in James S. Olson, ed., *Dictionary of the Vietnam War*, 1988.

OPERATION ROLLING THUNDER. The strategic bombing attacks against North Vietnam during the Vietnam War* carried the code name Operation Rolling Thunder. The logic of the Lyndon B. Johnson* administration in implementing the attacks was to make North Vietnam think carefully about the costs of continuing the war in the south. Johnson decided to gradually escalate the range and intensity of the bombing until North Vietnam had been forced to the negotiating table. The president also hoped to disrupt the flow of strategic supplies from North Vietnam to South Vietnam. The raids began in March 1965, with all targets confined to North Vietnam south of the twentieth parallel.

Two months later, targets north of the twentieth parallel were hit, although American pilots were forbidden to drop any bombs within thirty miles of Hanoi and the Chinese border or within ten miles of Haiphong. But the North Vietnamese steadfastly refused to negotiate, and beginning in February 1967, President Johnson expanded the targets to include oil storage facilities, railroad yards, airfields, and electrical power plants. The Rolling Thunder raids were not stopped until April 1, 1968, when President Johnson announced an end to the bombing in hopes of bringing about a diplomatic settlement of the war. By that time, 640,000 tons of bombs had been dropped, and 922 American aircraft had been lost.

REFERENCES: Robert S. Browning III, ''Operation Rolling Thunder,'' in James S. Olson, ed., *Dictionary of the Vietnam War*, 1988; R. Frank Futrell et al., *Aces and Aerial Victories: The U.S. Air Force in Southeast Asia, 1981*; John Morrocco, *The Vietnam Experience. Thunder from Above: Air War, 1941–1968*, 1985.

ORBISON, ROY KELTON. Roy Orbison was born April 23, 1936, in Vernon, Texas. He started singing as a teenager, and after spending two years at North Texas State University, he started his own band, the Teen Kings. Country singer Johnny Cash convinced him to sign a contract with the blues/rockabilly label Sam Records in Memphis. Orbison's first record—''Ooby Dooby''—was a modest hit when released in 1956. He wrote songs for the next four years and developed his own singing style, fusing country and western with rhythm and blues. Blessed with a strong, clear, wide-ranging tenor voice with a uniquely haunting quality, Orbison's first huge hit—"Only the Lonely"—sold 2 million records in 1960. He followed that in the next several years with a string of similar hits, including "Crying," "I'm Hurting," "Dream Baby," "Leah," "In Dreams," "Falling," "Blue Bayou," "Oh, Pretty Woman," "It's Over," and "Goodnight." Orbison became a leading figure in the early development of rock and roll.

Other rock-and-roll stars eclipsed Orbison in the late 1960s and early 1970s, but when some of them began releasing new versions of his old songs in the late 1970s and early 1980s, his career revived. In 1987, he joined Bob Dylan,* George Harrison, Tom Petty, and Jeff Lynne to form the Travelling Wilburys, whose album by the same name made its way into the top ten of the pop charts. Roy Orbison died December 7, 1988. Bruce Springsteen* said of him, "Some rock-and-roll reinforces friendship and community, but for me, Roy's ballads were always best when you were alone and in the dark."

REFERENCE: *New York Times*, December 8, 1988.

ORGANIZATION OF AFRO-AMERICAN UNITY.

ORGANIZATION OF AFRO-AMERICAN UNITY. The Organization of Afro-American Unity (OAAU) was founded by Malcolm X* in New York City in 1964. A charismatic, dedicated leader of the Nation of Islam, Malcolm X was suspended from the group by Elijah Muhammad* in 1964 after making disparaging remarks about John F. Kennedy* and his assassination. He then founded the Muslim Mosque as his own group. Later in 1964, Malcolm X completed his pilgrimage to Mecca, and he returned a changed person. While in Mecca, he observed firsthand that Islam is a multiracial, multicultural faith, and he converted to the Sunni Muslim group. He then founded the OAAU to promote his new point of view. Malcolm X still preached black nationalism, but he abandoned the rhetoric of violence and separatism for interracial brotherhood and understanding. Pan-Africanism and socialism also became part of the OAAU agenda. After the assassination of Malcolm X, the Organization of Afro-American Unity disintegrated.

REFERENCES: J. H. Clark, ed., *Malcolm X*, 1969; Peter Goldman, *Malcolm X*, 1972.

OSWALD, LEE HARVEY. Lee Harvey Oswald was born October 18, 1939, in New Orleans. He was raised in Fort Worth, Texas. By the time he was fifteen, Oswald was a loner and already interested in Marxist ideas. In 1956, he enlisted in the Marine Corps, but his tour of duty was an unhappy one. Fellow marines remembered him as a man with a short temper who always seemed to be having an argument with somebody. He was court-martialed twice, once for possessing an unregistered firearm and then for speaking disrespectfully to officers. Oswald mustered out of the Marine Corps in September 1959, and one month later he was living in Moscow and trying to secure Soviet citizenship. He married a

Russian woman, and they returned to the United States in 1962. Oswald then became involved in pro-Fidel Castro* activities. In 1963, he settled in Dallas, Texas, and got a job at the Texas School Book Depository. On November 22, 1963, from the sixth floor in the building, Oswald fired the rifle shots that killed President John F. Kennedy.* Two days later, Oswald was murdered by Jack Ruby* in the Dallas jail.

REFERENCES: William Manchester, *The Death of a President*, 1965; *New York Times*, November 25, 1963; Gerald L. Posner, *Case Closed*, 1994.

THE OTHER AMERICA. *The Other America* was the title of Michael Harrington's* highly influential 1962 exposé of poverty in America.

OUTER SPACE TREATY (1967). In 1967, with both the United States and the Soviet Union engaged in a technological race to become the first country to place a human being on the moon, the issue of territoriality in outer space came to the forefront. Just as the European nations had to work out a way of dividing the world in the sixteenth and seventeenth centuries, the United States and the Soviet Union had to address the issue of political sovereignty on celestial bodies. On April 25, 1967, the two nations signed the Outer Space Treaty. The treaty underscored the need for the peaceful exploration of outer space; banned the existence of weapons of mass destruction in outer space; prohibited the establishment of military bases in outer space; and suspended all claims for sovereignty in outer space. The treaty was signed on January 1967 by sixty countries, including the United States, the Soviet Union, and Great Britain.

REFERENCE: Milton Katz, *Ban the Bomb*, 1987.

OZZIE AND HARRIET. See *THE ADVENTURES OF OZZIE AND HARRIET*.

P

PANTY HOSE. Du Pont began marketing the first nylons in 1940, and in 1959 Glen Raven Mills, a North Carolina textile firm, introduced Panti-Legs, the first panty hose. The company simply stitched existing nylon stockings to a large nylon crotch. The first version came in ten sizes, hardly enough to satisfy a mass market, but they were also clumsy and hard to keep form-fitting. During the early 1960s, new versions were greatly improved. Seams were eliminated, and the new panty hose fitted much better. They also came in dozens of sizes. Women purchased panty hose with enthusiasm because the product eliminated the need for garter belts. In 1970, Hanes Company introduced L'eggs, panty hose packaged in a plastic container and available in supermarkets and convenience stores.

REFERENCE: Jane Stern and Michael Stern, *Encyclopedia of Pop Culture*, 1992.

PARIS PEACE TALKS. On May 13, 1968, after three years of heavy combat, the United States, North Vietnam, South Vietnam, and the Vietcong began meeting in Paris to discuss a negotiated settlement of the war. The talks were less than productive. North Vietnam was not about to be deterred from its goal of unifying both Vietnams under communist control and steadfastly refused to agree to a withdrawal of their troops from South Vietnam. South Vietnam knew that ''unification'' was a euphemism for its own destruction. The parties spent months arguing over the size and shape of the table that they would eventually sit around once negotiations began. The United States, even after policymakers realized that Vietnam was not worth such an enormous American investment, refused to budge out of fear that the Soviet Union and the People's Republic of China would interpret compromise as weakness.

During the Richard Nixon* administration, national security adviser Henry Kissinger* began conducting secret negotiations with North Vietnam. By 1971, the United States was tired of the war and ready to compromise, and both Nixon and Kissinger believed that secret negotiations would make concessions easier. Eventually, the United States agreed to almost all of the enemy's demands: North Vietnamese troops were allowed to remain in South Vietnam, while all U.S. troops were withdrawn; the Vietcong* were permitted to participate in the government of South Vietnam; and all prisoners of war would be returned. On January 25, 1973, Henry Kissinger and Le Duc Tho* of North Vietnam signed the Paris Peace Accords. The documents, of course, were hardly worth the paper they were written on. Two years later, in April 1975, North Vietnam launched a huge offensive and seized control of South Vietnam. Vietnam had been re-united.

REFERENCES: Allen E. Goodman, *The Lost Peace: America's Search for a Negotiated Settlement of the Vietnam War*, 1978; Walter Dillard, *Sixty Days to Peace*, 1982.

PARTICIPATORY DEMOCRACY. The term ''participatory democracy'' was the rallying cry of the New Left* movement in the 1960s. It had its intellectual origins in the writings of C. Wright Mills,* whose books *White Collar* (1951) and *The Power Elite* (1956) described the American class structure and how the middle class had changed in the twentieth century from independent, self-employed people to hired professionals for corporate and government bureaucracies. A fundamental and self-perpetuating chasm separated the power elite in America from the masses, and the only way to change the system was through ''participatory democracy''—large-scale participation of the masses in voluntary organizations and local governments. Only then could the true potential of democracy be realized. In 1960, University of Michigan professor Arnold Kaufman wrote an essay, ''Participatory Democracy and Human Nature,'' in which he called on people to actively participate in the political process, as opposed to merely voting in elections. In the collective action of ''the people'' all problems could be solved. By the 1960s, New Left activists had picked up on the term ''participatory democracy.'' Tom Hayden,* a student of Kaufman at the University of Michigan, described the concept in the Port Huron Statement* of 1962, which became the effective constitution of the Students for a Democratic Society (SDS).*

But as radicalism evolved in the 1960s, participatory democracy came to mean different things to different people. To some it simply meant socialism, since they believed that true democracy and capitalism were fundamentally inconsistent with one another. They also came to see ''participatory democracy'' as a call for workers to rise up and seize control of industry. Others came to see democracy as inconsistent with traditional representative democracy and argued for what they called ''consensus politics''—direct, face-to-face negotiations until consensus was reached between competing groups. It was too easy, they claimed, for the power elite to manipulate and control the processes of representative democracy.

The antiwar movement* soon put the idea of personal, consensus politics to a test. In 1965, when opposition to the Vietnam War* blossomed into a political movement, Students for a Democratic Society found itself in its vanguard. They soon discovered, however, that without representative institutions, participatory democracy was just one round of endless meetings and ideological infighting. The movement needed organization and leadership, a sense of discipline, planning, and effective implementation, but SDS could not provide them. Participatory democracy collapsed quickly in the 1960s, although some argue that it has survived in the 1980s and 1990s in grassroots political organizations and the multiplication of advocacy groups.

REFERENCES: C. George Benello and Dimitrios Roussopoulos, eds., *The Case for Participatory Democracy*, 1972; Jane Mansbridge, *Beyond Adversary Democracy*, 1980.

PATTON. First released in 1968, the film *Patton* depicted the life of General George S. Patton, Jr., the military genius and political dunce of World War II who commanded a series of U.S. armies in North Africa, Sicily, and Italy and during the final assault on Germany. Directed by Franklin J. Schaffner with a screenplay by Francis Ford Coppola, the film starred George C. Scott as the near-legendary general. *Patton* captured the general in all of his outrageous genius, praising war as "man's most noble endeavor." George C. Scott was brilliant in his performance and won an Oscar as Best Actor.

But beyond the film's cinematic qualities, it had a political impact as well. At a time when the United States was in a debilitating, nasty, unpopular war in Vietnam and with the U.S. Army in a state of near collapse, *Patton* praised armies, generals, and combat. Also, President Richard M. Nixon* was mesmerized by the film, particularly by Patton's aggressiveness and willingness to disregard the political consequences of his decisions. Nixon had the film played many times in the White House during his five and a half years there and felt that it provided him with an emotional counter to the prevailing liberalism of the times.

REFERENCE: *New York Times*, August 14, 1968.

PAUL VI, POPE. Pope Paul VI was born as Giovanni Battista Montini on September 26, 1897, in Concesio, Brescia, Italy. He was ordained a Roman Catholic priest in 1920 and made his career in the papal diplomatic corps, serving in a variety of foreign posts and in 1952 becoming the Vatican's secretary of state. He was appointed archbishop of Milan in 1954 and created cardinal in 1958. On June 21, 1963, he was elected pope and assumed the title of Paul VI. In October 1965, Pope Paul VI made history when he became the first Roman Catholic pontiff in history to visit the United States. The visit was his personal acknowledgment that Roman Catholicism was alive and well in the United States—the largest single denomination in the country—and that the United States was the most powerful nation in the world. Pope Paul VI died on August 6, 1978.

REFERENCE: *New York Times*, August 7, 1978.

PAUL REVERE AND THE RAIDERS. Paul Revere and the Raiders was a popular rock-and-roll band of the 1960s. Formed in Portland, Oregon, in 1960, the group included Paul Revere, Mark Lindsay, Phil Volk, Michael Smith, and Drake Levin. Mark Lindsay was lead vocalist, and with his long hair, tied in a ponytail, he had a special appeal among the bubble-gum, teenybopper set. Known for their concert costumes—pseudo Revolutionary War outfits—they released a version of "Louie Louie" in 1963. It was completely eclipsed by the Kingsmen's version of the same song. The first hit single of Paul Revere and the Raiders—"Steppin' Out"—was released in 1965. They followed it with a string of hit singles, including "Just like Me" (1965), "Kicks" (1966), "Hungry" (1966), "The Clear Airplane Strike" (1966), "Good Thing" (1966), "Ups and Downs" (1967), and "Him or Me—What's It Gonna Be?" (1967). The group then broke up.
REFERENCE: Claudia M. Doege, *Paul Revere and the Raiders*, 1985.

PAULSEN, PATRICK. Patrick Paulsen was born 1927 in a small fishing village on the northern coast of the state of Washington. His family moved to southern California when he was a small child, and he was raised there. Paulsen served in the U.S. Marine Corps during World War II, and after leaving the service, he attended San Francisco City College. There he joined an acting group known as the Ric-y-tic Players. Paulsen made a living as a deadpan comedian in the West Coast club circuit in the 1950s, and in the 1960s he met up with Dick and Tom Smothers, who hired him to perform on their hit CBS television show *The Smothers Brothers Comedy Hour.** Paulsen won an Emmy award in 1968 for his comedy routine.

He is best remembered in American popular culture, however, because of the presidential campaigns he mounted in 1968 and in subsequent years. In a parody of American presidential politics, Paulsen organized the STAG party (Straight Talkin' American Government) and named himself its presidential nominee. Exploiting his persona as a deadpan loser, he managed to garner tens of thousands of votes from adoring fans, who preferred him to Hubert Humphrey,* George Wallace,* Richard Nixon,* George McGovern,* or any of the other presidential candidates of the 1960s and 1970s. Pat Paulsen died in Mexico on April 24, 1997.
REFERENCE: *New York Times*, April 26, 1997.

PEACE AND FREEDOM PARTY. The Peace and Freedom Party was founded in Ann Arbor, Michigan, in 1968 by Black Panthers* and white radicals. They nominated Eldridge Cleaver* for president and Douglas F. Dowd for vice president. The Peace and Freedom Party agenda opposed the Vietnam War,* called for black liberation and a general redistribution of wealth, and demanded that America prepare for social revolution. The Cleaver–Douglas ticket won 136,385 votes in the 1968 presidential election.
REFERENCE: Hanes Walton, Jr., *The Negro in Third-Party Politics*, 1969.

PEACE CORPS. In his inaugural address, President John F. Kennedy* told his countrymen, "Ask not what your country can do for you; ask what you can do for your country." The speech inspired an entire generation of young Americans. In 1961, the United States was engaged in a struggle for national survival with the Soviet Union. The most violent phase of the civil rights movement* had not begun yet, nor had the protest movement against the Vietnam War.* America was still naïve and optimistic, and the Peace Corps became a perfect symbol of that naïveté.

The idea for the Peace Corps actually originated in the Civilian Conservation Corps of the 1930s, when unemployed young men by the tens of thousands went to work in rural areas, building roads, fighting fires, and cleaning state and national parks. In the Cold War* climate of the early 1960s, with the United States and the Soviet Union competing for influence in the Third World, the idea of sending educated American volunteers to assist in the economic development of poor countries quickly captured the national imagination. John Kennedy proposed the Peace Corps during the presidential campaign of 1960. He also had in mind doing something to improve the image of Americans abroad. William J. Lederer and Eugene Bardick's best-selling novel *The Ugly American* in 1958 had described an American diplomatic corps composed of ignorant, arrogant political appointees who knew nothing about the language or culture of the country in which they were serving.

Soon after he took office in 1961, Kennedy launched the Peace Corps and put his brother-in-law, Sargent Shriver, in charge of it. Tens of thousands of Americans signed up to serve in a war against poverty, illiteracy, and disease in the Third World. The program became a permanent part of American foreign policy, but by the late 1960s it had been eclipsed in influence and popularity by the youth rebellion, civil rights movement, and antiwar protest. Tens of thousands of Americans participated in the program during the next decade, by which time the Peace Corps was emphasizing the recruitment of technical experts. In 1971, the Peace Corps, VISTA, and several other volunteer programs were combined into the federal government's ACTION agency.

REFERENCES: David Burner, *Making Peace with the Sixties*, 1996; Robert G. Carey, *The Peace Corps*, 1970.

PEALE, NORMAN VINCENT. Norman Vincent Peale was born May 31, 1898, in Bowersville, Ohio. His father was a Methodist minister. Peale graduated from Ohio Wesleyan College in 1920, worked as a journalist for a year in Ohio and Michigan, and then entered the school of theology at Boston University to study for the ministry. He became a full-time minister in 1924 with a small congregation in Brooklyn, New York. Peale was an instant success, and three years later the congregation of 3,000 was meeting in a new sanctuary. In 1927, Peale took the pastorship of the University Methodist Church in Syracuse, New York, and he added a radio ministry in 1932. He was unrivaled at raising money and attracting new church members.

Late in 1932, Peale accepted the pulpit of the Marble Collegiate Church in New York City. Marble Collegiate was a decrepit, poorly maintained former chapel of the Reformed Church. A new radio program—*The Art of Living*—made Peale a household name in the 1930s. Peale became a regular columnist for *Reader's Digest*, a popular speaker on the lecture circuit, and, in 1952, with his book *The Power of Positive Thinking*, a best-selling author. Critics charged Peale with confusing religion with success, but he remained a popular clergyman during the turbulent 1960s, a beacon of stability in a troubled time. In 1984, he wrote his twenty-second book, *The True Joy of Positive Living*, an autobiography. Norman Vincent Peale died December 24, 1993.

REFERENCES: Arthur Gordon, *Norman Vincent Peale: Minister to Millions*, 1958; *New York Times*, December 25, 1993; Norman Vincent Peale, *The True Joy of Positive Living*, 1984.

PENTHOUSE. During the 1950s and 1960s, Hugh Hefner's* *Playboy* magazine became the most popular soft-core men's magazine in the country. By the mid-1960s, Hefner was selling 6 million copies of *Playboy* a month, with millions of other men also having access to its articles, cartoons, interviews, and nude photographs. Hard-core pornography circulated as well, but it was still confined to the sleazy world of pulp-printed, black-and-white, trashy magazines. Compared to them, *Playboy* was a glossy, upscale, sophisticated, almost respectable monthly alternative.

But in 1967, Bob Guccione got the idea to publish a competitor to *Playboy*. He knew there was a market for a more hard-core magazine as long as it could have at least a facade of respectability, appeal to middle-class and upper-class men, and be sold in a variety of retail outlets, not just in adult bookstores. Men had to be able to purchase the magazine without undue embarrassment. Guccione knew that he had to craft a product that was as glitzy as *Playboy* but also more daring in its nudity and sexuality. In 1969, Guccione published the first issue of *Penthouse*. While *Playboy* featured big-busted, all-American, young white women, *Penthouse* was more likely to feature a racially diverse group of women. While Hefner made sure that *Playboy* models posed conservatively, with the focus on breasts and buttocks, Guccione made sure that his models posed provocatively, with genitalia clearly, even obviously, exposed to the viewer. The articles in *Penthouse* were sexually explicit, the cartoons more graphic, the advertisements more overt.

Guccione had hit a gold mine. Although *Penthouse* circulation never reached *Playboy*'s numbers, it was nevertheless a huge publishing success, attracting 3 million monthly readers by the early 1970s whose demographics put them at higher income and educational levels than *Playboy*'s readers. Guccione was still publishing *Penthouse* in the late 1990s.

REFERENCE: Gay Talese, *Thy Neighbor's Wife*, 1980.

PEOPLE'S PARK. In May 1967, to eliminate what they thought had become an eyesore near the campus, the University of California at Berkeley purchased several old houses, condemned the buildings, and had them razed. Two years later, community activists decided, without the university's approval, to convert the land into a park. They claimed a right, under John Locke's theory of capitalism, to convert unused property to the social good. In what they considered to be an act of liberation and spontaneity, the activists began planting grass and gardens on the land. The university disagreed, and on May 15, 1969, police came to the property and removed the "homesteaders," and bulldozers leveled the gardens. A riot then ensued, with demonstrators throwing rocks at police and police firing shotguns. One demonstrator was killed, and Governor Ronald Reagan* called out the National Guard to quell the rioting. Community activists accused the police, the university, and the National Guard of abuse of power, while university and city officials charged the demonstrators with trying to bring about a state of anarchy.

REFERENCE: David Burner, *Making Peace with the 60s*, 1996.

PERCY, CHARLES HARTING. Charles Percy was born in Pensacola, Florida, September 27, 1919. He graduated from the University of Chicago and joined the firm of Bell and Howell, but the outbreak of World War II took Percy into the U.S. Navy. He was honorably discharged in 1945 and returned to Bell and Howell. He rose quickly through the corporate ranks, becoming chief executive and chairman of the board in 1955. A liberal Republican, Percy accepted appointment from President Dwight D. Eisenhower* as special U.S. ambassador in 1956. He could not buck the Democratic landslide of 1964, losing his bid to become governor of Illinois, but he was elected to the U.S. Senate in 1966, a post he held until 1985. Over the years, as a Republican liberal, Percy found himself increasingly isolated in the party, which was growing more conservative. He retired to private business in 1985.

REFERENCES: Robert Hartley, *Charles H. Percy: A Political Perspective*, 1975; David Murray, *Charles Percy of Illinois*, 1968.

PERRY MASON. *Perry Mason* was one of the most successful dramatic programs in American television* history. Based on Earle Stanley Gardner's murder mysteries, the series starred Raymond Burr as defense attorney Perry Mason, Barbara Hale as his assistant, Della Street, William Hopper as private investigator Paul Drake, and William Talman as District Attorney Hamilton Burger. Perry Mason offered a murder-a-week to viewers, with Hamilton Burger always trying and failing to prosecute innocent people and send them to the electric chair. The first episode was broadcast on September 21, 1957, on CBS, and it continued as a weekly series until September 1966. CBS brought *Perry Mason* back to the screen briefly in 1973 and 1974. Perhaps in the irreverent 1960s, when so many Americans lost faith in their government, images of Perry Mason exposing government corruption and ineptitude on a weekly basis proved cathartic.

REFERENCES: Brian Kelleher, *The Perry Mason TV Show Book*, 1987; David Marc, *Demographic Vistas: Television in American Culture*, 1984.

PETER, PAUL, AND MARY. Peter, Paul, and Mary were a popular, influential folk group of the 1960s. Formed in New York City in 1961, the group included Peter Yarrow, Noel Paul Stookey, and Mary Travers. They signed a contract with Warner Brothers Records and had two hits in 1962—"Lemon Tree" and "If I Had a Hammer." They became popular on college campuses and were involved in the civil rights* and antiwar* movements during the 1960s. "Blowin' in the Wind," "Don't Think Twice, It's Alright," and "Puff the Magic Dragon" were other Peter, Paul, and Mary hits in 1963 and 1964. Peter, Paul, and Mary broke up in 1970.
REFERENCE: Patricia Romanowski and Holly George-Warren, eds., *The New Rolling Stone Encyclopedia of Rock and Roll*, 1996.

PETTICOAT JUNCTION. Petticoat Junction was one of the three rural-oriented situation comedies created for CBS by Paul Henning during the 1960s. It first aired September 24, 1963, and ran for seven years. The series originally starred Bea Benaderet as Kate Bradley, Edgar Buchanan as Uncle Joe Carson, Jeanine Riley as Billie Jo Bradley, Pat Woodell as Bobbie Jo Bradley, and Linda Kaye Henning as Betty Jo Bradley. Gunilla Hutton and, later, Meredith MacRae replaced Jeanine Riley, and Lori Saunders replaced Pat Woodell.

Petticoat Junction, in the rural sitcom tradition of the *Beverly Hillbillies*, provide entertainment in the outlandish predicaments of its characters. The series, however, offered reassurance about community and family during the turbulence of radicals, riots, and demonstrations in the 1960s. Kate Bradley provided a matriarchal version of stability similar to that of Sheriff Andy Taylor in *The Andy Griffith Show*. As fantasy television, *Petticoat Junction* provided a weekly escape to a world where problems could be solved in a single thirty-minute episode. The audience was given a glimmer of hope in this unrealistic consideration that all problems could be easily solved, and things would be fine in the end.

The series declined in popularity after Bea Benaderet, the actress playing the central character, died in 1968. Although the producers attempted to re-create a strong central character, they could not achieve their goal. *Petticoat Junction* was canceled on September 12, 1970, when CBS decided to discontinue its rural comedies. Today the series is still popular in rerun syndication in many rural areas throughout the United States.
REFERENCES: Tim Brooks and Earle Marsh, *The Complete Directory to Prime Time Network Shows: 1946–Present*, 1992; David Marc, *Demographic Vistas: Television in American Culture*, 1984.

Christopher Gore

PEYTON PLACE. Peyton Place was America's first prime-time soap opera. It stood in stark contrast to the squeaky-clean dramas and family situation comedies so common in the 1950s and early 1960s. The series, based on Grace Metalious' best-selling novel of the same name, was first broadcast by ABC on September 15, 1964. Its ensemble cast was headed by Dorothy Malone as Constance Mackenzie, Mia Farrow as Allison Mackenzie, Ed Nelson as Michael Rossi, Warner Anderson as Matthew Swain, and Ryan O'Neill as Rodney Harrington. *Peyton Place* was set in a small, prosperous New England town where extramarital affairs, crime, and pettiness were commonplace. When it was canceled on June 2, 1969, *Peyton Place* had appeared in 514 original episodes (the program was broadcast three times a week).

REFERENCE: Emily Toth, *Inside* Peyton Place: *The Life of Grace Metalious*, 1981.

PHAM VAN DONG. Pham Van Dong was born in Quang Nam Province of Annam, the French colony in Indochina, on March 1, 1906. He came from a highly educated, prosperous family and was educated at the French Lycée in Hue.* His closest friends during his student years were Vo Nguyen Giap* and Ngo Dinh Diem.* Pham soon developed a strong, anti-French, pro-Vietnamese nationalism, and he dedicated himself to the expulsion of France from Indochina and to the independence of Vietnam. French authorities charged him with sedition in 1930, and he spent the next eight years in prison. He then fled to China, where he met Ho Chi Minh* and became even more nationalistic. Pham Van Dong was one of the founding fathers of the Lao Dong Party, and, along with Vo Nguyen Giap and Ho Chi Minh, he spent the next thirty years as one of the triumvirate running Vietnamese affairs.

During World War II, Pham was active in fighting the Japanese, who had occupied French Indochina, and between 1945 and 1954 he worked just as hard at expelling the French, who finally were defeated at the Battle of Dien Bien Phu in 1954. He headed the Vietminh delegation at the Geneva Conference of 1954 and served as Ho Chi Minh's prime minister from 1950 to 1969. After Ho's death in 1969, Pham emerged as the most visible of North Vietnam's leaders and the one who negotiated with the United States. He proved to be a skilled, stubborn diplomat who was absolutely committed to the expulsion of the United States and the reunification of South Vietnam and North Vietnam into an independent nation. When North Vietnam conquered South Vietnam in 1975, Pham became prime minister of the new Socialist Republic of Vietnam. He remained there until 1986, when a series of disastrous economic setbacks forced his resignation.

REFERENCES: *Who's Who in Socialist Countries*, 1978; *Washington Post*, December 18, 1986.

PHOENIX PROGRAM. During the course of the Vietnam War,* U.S. officials faced a constant challenge in dealing with the guerrilla nature of the conflict. It was difficult to distinguish between civilian noncombatants and Vietcong* soldiers, who often enjoyed considerable support from South Vietnamese villagers. It was also obvious that the Vietcong and its political arm, the National Liberation Front,* enjoyed more political legitimacy among South Vietnamese civilians than their own government—the so-called Republic of Vietnam. Although the United States opted for a military approach to the war, hoping to destroy enemy resistance very quickly, they also engaged in counterinsurgency* efforts designed to erode the political loyalty of the South Vietnamese.

One effort staged by the Central Intelligence Agency* (CIA) to undermine the Vietcong was the Phoenix Program. Largely the design of William Colby,* the Phoenix Program had three primary objectives. First, the CIA hoped to identify South Vietnamese members of the National Liberation Front and then expose them, kill them, or turn their loyalties to South Vietnam. Second, the CIA hoped that the Phoenix Program would be able to secure the loyalties of South Vietnamese villagers in combatting the Vietcong. Third, it was hoped that Phoenix would erode the military capabilities of the Vietcong. Overall, the goal of the Phoenix Program was to stabilize and legitimize the government of South Vietnam.

Such hopes, however, were only pipe dreams. Phoenix was implemented by the government of South Vietnam, with substantial support from the CIA, and it soon spun out of control. Identifying Vietcong and "neutralizing,"* or killing them, became a political football. South Vietnamese government officials frequently targeted non-Vietcong who happened to be their political rivals or enemies, and large numbers of innocent people were killed. Some estimates put the number of Phoenix Program victims at 20,000, many of whom were not Vietcong at all. Corruption became endemic to the program as well. People identified as Vietcong, or even accused of being Vietcong, could buy their safety with payments to government officials. In the end, what debilitated the Vietcong was the Tet Offensive* of 1968, which resulted in the deaths of more than 80 percent of the Vietcong. The Phoenix Program continued, however, until 1972. REFERENCES: William Colby and Peter Forbath, *Honorable Men: My Life in the CIA*, 1978; John Prados, *Presidents Secret Wars: CIA and Pentagon Covert Operations Since World War II*, 1986; Stafford Thomas, "Phoenix Program," in James S. Olson, ed., *Dictionary of the Vietnam War*, 1988; Douglas Valentine, *The Phoenix Program*, 1990.

PIKE, JAMES ALBERT. James Albert Pike was born in Oklahoma City, Oklahoma, February 14, 1913. He was raised as a Roman Catholic in Hollywood, California. Although Pike intended to become a priest, he began a spiritual crisis at the University of Santa Clara, where he questioned the idea of papal infallibility and the church's conservative position on birth control. He dropped out of Santa Clara, claiming to be an agnostic, and transferred to the University of Southern California. There he was awarded a bachelor's degree and then a law degree. He earned a doctorate of laws at Yale and then took a job with the Securities and Exchange Commission in Washington, D.C., established his own law firm, and joined the Episcopal Church. During World War II, Pike served in the navy, and in 1945 he enrolled in the Union Theological Seminary in New York City.

Pike was ordained an Episcopal priest in 1946 and took a post as rector of Christ Church in Poughkeepsie, New York. He also served there as chaplain at Vassar College. Pike became chaplain of Columbia University in 1949 and chair of the Department of Religion. In 1952, he received the prestigious appointment as dean of the Cathedral of Saint John the Divine, the country's largest Episcopal congregation. His weekly television show—*The Dean Pike Show*—ran on ABC television from 1952 to 1958. In 1966, Pike became Episcopal bishop of California.

By that time, however, he had become extremely controversial because of his liberal views. Pike openly backed the civil rights movement,* called for an end to poverty, and ordained the first woman as an Episcopal minister. But what really alienated Pike from conservative Episcopalian officials was a December 1960 article in *Christian Century* in which he sincerely expressed doubts about the Trinity, the Virgin birth, and the Resurrection of Jesus Christ. Charges of heresy were leveled at Pike throughout the 1960s. The controversies spawned three of his books: *A Time for Christian Candor* (1964), *What Is This Treasure?* (1966), and *If This Be Heresy* (1967).

In the middle of the heresy controversy, Pike's personal life began to disintegrate. He had a severe drinking problem, and in 1967 it became public that his mistress had committed suicide. His son committed suicide, and his wife divorced him. Pike then turned to the paranormal, becoming involved in seances and attempts to reach the dead. His 1968 book *The Other Side* dealt with these concerns. He resigned his bishopric in 1968 and joined the faculty of the University of California at Santa Barbara. Pike formally left the church in 1969. He died September 8, 1969, in Israel when he became lost while driving his car in the Judaean desert.

REFERENCES: Hans W. Holzer, *The Psychic World of Bishop Pike*, 1970; Diane Kennedy Pike, *Search: The Personal Story of a Wilderness Journey*, 1970.

PLATH, SYLVIA. Sylvia Plath was born in Boston October 27, 1932. She graduated from Smith College in 1955 and then went to England on a Fulbright Fellowship. She married British poet Ted Hughes, and they had two children, but the marriage was a dysfunctional hell for Plath. She was a talented poet in her own right, but not until the end of her life did her full power find its way into print. Her poetic voice was brutal, frank, and extremely aggressive, but at the same time her work could make a legitimate claim to being witty. Plath's frustration with sexist society transformed her into a feminist who blamed most of her difficulties on her father and her husband. One of her most famous poems—"Daddy"—ended with "Daddy, daddy, you bastard, I'm through." Life became intolerable for Plath, and on February 11, 1963, when she was just thirty years old, she turned on the oven in her London flat, placed her head inside, and gassed herself to death. Among feminists, she became an icon and martyr after death, a woman whose life was cut short by what feminists considered the evil restrictions of a sexist society. In 1965, a collection of her poems was

published as *Ariel*. Plath is considered by many social historians to be the literary mother of modern feminism.
REFERENCES: *New York Times*, February 12–13, 1963.

PLAYBOY. See **HEFNER, HUGH MARSTON.**

POITIER, SIDNEY. Sidney Poitier was born February 20, 1927, in Miami, Florida. He was raised in the Bahamas and did not return to the United States until 1941. Poitier worked in New York City as a dishwasher until Pearl Harbor, when he joined the U.S. Army. After World War II, he returned to New York City and attended acting classes at the American Negro Theater, where he paid his tuition by doing janitorial work there. He broke into films with a small role in *No Way Out* in 1950, and he soon followed that with memorable performances in *Cry the Beloved Country* (1952), *Red Ball Express* (1952), *Go, Man, Go* (1954), *Blackboard Jungle* (1956), *Goodbye, My Lady* (1956), *Edge of the City* (1957), *Band of Angels* (1957), *The Defiant Ones* (1958), *Something of Value* (1959), and *Porgy and Bess* (1959). With each, Poitier improved his craft and developed into one of America's premier actors.

In 1959, he began a two-year run on Broadway with the hit play *Raisin in the Sun*, and in 1961 he made a movie of the same name. He became the first African American to win an Oscar as Best Actor, which the Academy of Motion Picture Arts and Sciences awarded him in 1965 because of his stunning performance in *Lilies of the Field*. Since then, Poitier has continued his career as an actor and a director, and among his best films have been *To Sir, with Love* (1967), *In the Heat of the Night* (1967), and *Guess Who's Coming to Dinner* (1968).
REFERENCES: Alvin H. Marill, *The Films of Sidney Poitier*, 1981; Sidney Poitier, *This Life*, 1980.

POLITICAL ASSOCIATION OF SPANISH-SPEAKING ORGANIZA-TIONS. In the 1960 presidential elections, Hector García of Texas formed Viva Kennedy* clubs in Texas to promote the candidacy of Senator John F. Kennedy* of Massachusetts. The clubs proved very successful, and after the election Garcia and several others formed a more permanent organization—the Political Association of Spanish-Speaking Organizations (PASSO). The group was to serve as an umbrella organization for all the Hispanic political and cultural associations in Texas. In 1963, PASSO joined the Teamsters' Union and elected five Hispanics to the city council of Crystal City, Texas. After that, its importance declined, and it was largely eclipsed by La Raza Unida.*
REFERENCE: Robert Cuellar, *A Social and Political History of the Mexican American Population of Texas, 1929–1963*, 1974.

POOR PEOPLE'S CAMPAIGN. In 1962, with the publication of Michael Harrington's* best-selling *Poverty in America*, large numbers of Americans became concerned about the plight of poor people. After the Civil Rights Act of 1964 and the Voting Rights Act* of 1965 had abolished most forms of de jure discrimination, many African-American leaders turned their attention to poverty as a key concern. Until black people enjoyed the same economic and educational opportunities as whites, they would always be second-class citizens in the United States. Martin Luther King, Jr.* was a leading figure in the campaign to end poverty in America. To bring attention to the problem, King began planning his famous Poor People's Campaign early in 1967. He wanted to invite representatives of poor people from around the country to camp out at the Mall in Washington, D.C., and express their concerns. When King was assassinated in April 1968, leadership of the Poor People's Campaign was assumed by his assistant, Ralph Abernathy.*

The Poor People's marchers arrived in Washington, D.C., on May 11, 1968. Reies Tijerina* and Corky Gonzales* were among the Mexican-American leaders. Thousands of marchers camped out on the grounds between the White House and the Capitol, constructing what came to be known as "Resurrection City," a series of makeshift, temporary, cardboard homes and tents. Abernathy demanded an end to the Vietnam War,* because it was diverting too much money away from social programs, and the expansion of Lyndon B. Johnson's* Great Society.* The marchers disbanded on June 23, 1968.

REFERENCE: Ralph Abernathy, *And the Walls Came Tumbling Down: An Autobiography*, 1989.

THE PORT HURON STATEMENT. The Port Huron Conference marked the founding of the Students for a Democratic Society* (SDS) at a United Automobile Workers (UAW) summer camp in 1962. Representatives included members from the National Student Association (NSA), the Student Nonviolent Coordinating Committee* (SNCC), the Young People's Socialist League, the Student Christian Movement, and the Young Democrats. Roughly five dozen students represented a handful of colleges. Tom Hayden* and Al Haber emerged as leaders. Political topics discussed included civil rights, Cold War* policy, and the quality of life in America. The conference ended at 5:00 A.M. on June 16 with the issuance of an agenda for action. This document was the Port Huron Statement.

The Port Huron Statement set the agenda and course of action until the 1968–1969 radicalization and breakup of the SDS. The statement called for social reform, not revolution. It opposed the U.S. role in the Cold War and opposed communism. Framers considered educational reform as essential in promoting political reform. They proposed a critique of American society, the use of nonviolence, and the support of traditional American ideals.

The *Introduction: Agenda for Action* developed a "generational" awareness in its approach to foreign and domestic politics. Most SDS members were born into modest comfort, attended universities, and expressed anxiety over the world they were to inherit. They affirmed American values but failed to see their application in the world. "As we grew, however, our comfort was penetrated by events too troubling to dismiss" (Hayden, Port Huron Statement). Racial hatred and bigotry forced students into action. Also, "the enclosing fact of the Cold War, symbolized by the presence of the Bomb, brought awareness that we ourselves, and our friends, and millions of abstract 'others'" we knew more directly because of our common peril, might die at any time" (Hayden). Those issues seemed covered by paradoxes. "All men are created equal" failed to apply in the South or in major cities of the North. Also, the peaceful intentions of U.S. foreign policy contradicted economic and military investments in the Cold War. The statement covered over sixty pages and addressed almost every reformist-liberal issue.

Direct application of democracy became a central theme of the Port Huron Statement. "Participatory democracy"* called for the dismantling of centralized bureaucracies. The statement proposed the establishment of "little democracies" in all aspects of American life. This included community control of schools. It advocated the establishment of citizen supervisory boards to control police. The document advocated greater worker input in industry. The SDS called for increased student participation in university decisions. Finally, it called for mobilization against war. The document essentially redefined the American Left and became the foundation for SDS activities in the 1960s.

REFERENCE: Cyril Levitt, *Children of Privilege: Student Revolt in the Sixties*, 1984.

Michael Hall

POWELL, ADAM CLAYTON, JR. Adam Clayton Powell, Jr., was born in New Haven, Connecticut, November 29, 1908. His father was a civil rights leader in his own right and pastor of the Abyssinian Baptist Church in Harlem. The younger Powell graduated from Colgate University in 1930 and then earned a master of fine arts degree from Columbia in 1932. In 1937, he replaced his father at the Abyssinian Baptist pulpit. Powell earned a reputation for fighting racial discrimination and providing jobs for his parishioners. He won election to the New York City council in 1941, and he was elected to Congress as a Democrat in 1945. During the next twenty years, because of congressional seniority rules, Powell became, as chair of the powerful House Education and Labor Committee, one of the most influential men in Washington, D.C.

Powell's political career began to unravel in 1966. He had traveled to Europe with his twenty-one-year-old black personal secretary, who also happened to be a former Miss Ohio, and a white woman attorney on the labor committee's payroll. New York City newspapers hyped the scandal, but it wasn't until news broke of Powell's misuing government funds for private vacations that he got into political trouble. On January 9, 1967, his House colleagues voted to take the committee chairmanship from him. One day later, the House of Representatives voted 364 to 64 to take away his seat in Congress.

The black community was outraged, arguing that had Powell been white, he would have survived in Congress. He resettled to the island of Bimini in the

Bahamas and from there won with a 74 percent vote total the special congressional election to replace him. He never assumed the seat, but he then won the election of 1968. In January 1969, the House voted to seat him, although fining him $25,000. Powell was somewhat redeemed in June 1969, when the U.S. Supreme Court ruled that his expulsion from Congress had been unconstitutional. Powell lost the election of 1970 and died April 4, 1972.

REFERENCE: Charles V. Hamilton, *Adam Clayton Powell, Jr.: The Political Biography of an American Dilemma*, 1991.

PRESLEY, ELVIS. Elvis Aron Presley was born in Tupelo, Mississippi, January 8, 1935. He did not originate the genre of rock and roll, yet he was singularly the most important entertainer to have ever performed it. Often referred to as the "King," he profoundly influenced the world's perceptions of popular music.

When he was thirteen, Presley's family moved to Memphis, Tennessee. There he was exposed to a thirty-year tradition of hillbilly and traditional blues music; there also, white youngsters were absorbing black styles of music, speech, and dress. He graduated from Humes High School in 1953 and worked as a driver for an electrical contracting company. Within one year he released his first single for the Sun Records label. The record, "That's All Right," was a traditional blues song by Arthur "Big Boy" Crudup. Presley's version, which bore little resemblance to the original, was rockabilly, and it marked a turning point in the history of American popular music.

In late 1955, Presley signed a contract with RCA. At the same time and more important, he signed a management contract with Colonel Tom Parker. Both agreements would last throughout his life. In early 1956, at RCA's Nashville studio, he recorded "Heartbreak Hotel," his first number one hit on national pop music charts. Over the next twenty-seven months, he recorded fourteen consecutive million-sellers, which became top-ten crossover hits on national pop, country, and rhythm-and-blues charts.

Presley was inducted into the U.S. Army in March 1958, not to resume his career for two years. When discharged, he made one important television appearance with Frank Sinatra before retreating from public performances to concentrate on a movie career. He made twenty-nine films, but none were particularly memorable.

During the next eight years, he continued to record, but with unremarkable results in either record sales or box office receipts. In 1968, he effected a successful comeback with a holiday television special. Soon after, he began the final phase of his career with a short stint in Las Vegas nightclubs, followed by a very successful extended tour.

Although he continued to record and perform, the last years of his life were troubled by rumors of drug use and mental instability. He died August 16, 1977, at the age of forty-two. Since his death, his mansion in Memphis, Graceland, has become a prominent tourist attraction, drawing millions of fans and curiosity-seekers. During his career, Elvis Presley recorded more than 100 ''top-40'' hits. In 1990, thirteen years after his death, both volumes of a retrospective video of the Presley career reached platinum sales, ranking in the top ten music videos sold.

REFERENCE: Robert Hall, *Elvis Presley*, 1986.

Sammie Miller

PRISONERS OF WAR. The most nagging problem faced by U.S. diplomats during the course of the Vietnam War* involved prisoners of war (POWs). Throughout the diplomatic discussions between 1965 and 1972, the only non-negotiable demand the United States made of North Vietnam and the Vietcong* was the return of all POWs. By 1972 the United States had compromised on all of its other demands, dropping its opposition to Vietcong participation in the government of South Vietnam and allowing North Vietnamese troops to remain in South Vietnam after the complete withdrawal of U.S. troops. The Paris Peace Accords, finally concluded in January 1973, included such provisions, and between February and April 1973, North Vietnam released 566 U.S. military POWs and 25 civilian POWs. Upon their release, it became abundantly clear that they had not been treated humanely according to the 1949 Geneva Convention on the treatment of prisoners of war. Torture, malnutrition, and poor medical treatment had been standard for the POWs.

REFERENCES: Reader's Digest, *POW: A Definitive History of the American Prisoner of War Experience in Vietnam, 1964–1973*, 1976; Guenter Lewy, *America in Vietnam*, 1978.

PSYCHO. *Psycho* was Alfred Hitchcock's masterpiece of film suspense. Released in 1960, *Psycho* starred Anthony Perkins, Janet Leigh, and Martin Balsam. Perkins played Norman Bates, a quiet, mousy motel keeper who was psychotic. He kept a skeleton of his dead mother in a rocking chair in the basement, dressed up in his mother's old clothes and wig, and murdered unsuspecting visitors to the motel. Although *Psycho* was considered one of the most tense, suspenseful, and frightening movies in Hollywood history, it was remarkably free of graphic violence. Hitchcock was a master director, and *Psycho* is an outstanding example of his creative genius.

REFERENCE: *New York Times*, September 20, 1960.

USS *PUEBLO*. The USS *Pueblo* was a U.S. Navy surveillance vessel sent to the Pacific Ocean to gather information. While sailing off the coast of North Korea on January 23, 1968, it was attacked and captured by North Korean patrol boats. Four of the eighty-three crewmen were injured from enemy fire, one of whom later died. In the next several months, the incident proved to be a landmark in U.S.–North Korean relations.

The crew was imprisoned in the port city of Wonson. The next day, Commander Lloyd Bucher announced over international radio that he had violated

North Korean waters and was involved in a U.S. spy mission. Meanwhile, negotiations between Korean and U.S. officials began. The Koreans adamantly refused to release the hostages, claiming that they had been captured in North Korean national waters. The incident put the United States in a difficult position. One week after the event, the North Vietnamese and Vietcong launched the Tet Offensive,* an all-out, carefully planned and coordinated attack on towns, cities, and military installations throughout South Vietnam. President Lyndon B. Johnson* did not want the *Pueblo* incident to escalate into a second war on the Asian continent. In a face-saving gesture, the president deployed 15,000 U.S. troops to the region. On March 4, 1968, Johnson received a letter signed by all eighty-two living crewmen demanding that the United States take full responsibility for the incident in exchange for their release.

The incident became a controversial political issue in the 1968 presidential election. Richard Nixon,* the Republican nominee, claimed that the *Pueblo* had been the wrong ship to carry out an intelligence mission, and he criticized the fact that no armed naval vessels had been in the region to lend assistance. Lyndon B. Johnson offered only the weakest of defenses, and when the president announced at the end of March that he would not seek reelection, the *Pueblo* disappeared from newspaper headlines.

The negotiations, however, continued. In December 1968, the United States signed an official apology, even though publicly denying any culpability. On December 22, 1968, the eighty-two surviving crewmen were released, along with the remains of the deceased sailor.

But the *Pueblo* incident was hardly over, at least as far as the navy was concerned. In 1969, an official inquiry began concerning the failure of *Pueblo* crew members to destroy valuable documents before capture, the poor defensive measures taken by the ship, and the reasons for Commander Bucher's confession. Bucher testified that he had only two guns with which to defend the ship and that once captured, he had been coerced into making the confession. He also expressed deep anger at the United States for its lack of intervention after the initial attack. Despite widespread sentiment that the crew and its commander be court-martialed, Secretary of the Navy John Chafee refused to pursue such charges, citing the crew's emotional suffering during eleven months of captivity.

North Korea is still in possession of the *Pueblo*. North Korea regards the ship as a ''shrine'' representing a victory over ''the most vicious enemy in the world.''

REFERENCES: Lloyd M. Bucher, *Bucher: My Story*, 1970; Robert A. Liston, *The Pueblo Surrender*, 1988.

Michael Smith

PUERTO RICAN AMERICANS. After the Spanish-American War, Puerto Rico became an American possession. There were about 1,500 Puerto Ricans in the continental United States by 1910 and more than 50,000 by 1930, but after World War II the migration became much larger. There were approximately

900,000 Puerto Ricans on the mainland in 1960, nearly 1.4 million in 1970, and about 2 million by 1990. With only 3,400 square miles of territory, a population of more than 2.5 million by 1960, and most capital controlled by U.S. corporations, Puerto Rico had severe economic problems. Because the economy revolved around sugar, tobacco, and coffee production, much employment was only seasonal. With jobs available on the mainland, airfare to New York City less than fifty dollars, and no immigration restrictions, the United States seemed the answer. Thousands went first as contract laborers working commercial farms from Florida to Massachusetts, but nearly all the Puerto Ricans ultimately settled in the cities, especially New York's urban ghettos in the Bronx, the South Bronx, the Lower East Side, Spanish Harlem, and the Williamsburg section of Brooklyn. By 1970 many school districts in New York City had a sizable Puerto Rican population, and there were other colonies throughout major northeastern cities.

Still, the immigrants had problems. Especially troubling was their lack of a firm ethnic identity. The United States granted Puerto Ricans citizenship in 1917 and the right to elect their own governor in 1947, but Puerto Rican politics always revolved around the question of independence versus commonwealth status (granted in 1952) or statehood. Color also challenged Puerto Rican ethnicity and divided the community. At home race had hardly been an issue; for centuries whites, blacks, mestizos, and mulattoes had mingled socially. But on the mainland a racial wedge split the community for the first time, with white Puerto Ricans aligning themselves with white Americans rather than with black Puerto Ricans and with black Puerto Ricans emphasizing their Spanish language to distinguish themselves from African Americans. In the 1960s, when the civil rights movement* gained momentum, white Puerto Ricans could not sympathize with calls for integration and cared little about de facto segregation. Finally, most Puerto Ricans entered the cities just as job opportunities were shifting to the suburbs, and employment required education and technical skills; they found only minimum-wage service jobs that would never lift them above the poverty line. Most Puerto Ricans joined the "working poor," people with jobs that do not generate enough income for a minimum standard of living.

Not until the 1960s did Puerto Ricans begin organizing in their own interests. Many joined the Democratic Party, and New York labor unions and Democratic politicians mounted campaigns to register Puerto Rican voters, but because of population dispersal and the Hispanic alienation from organizations, getting out the vote continued to be a major challenge. Some Puerto Rican groups concentrated on education as the way out of the ghetto. In 1961 the Puerto Rican Forum established Aspira to help young Puerto Ricans go to college. Aware that young people needed positive images, the Forum, Aspira, and the Conference on Puerto Rican Education became the most active groups in the Puerto Rican community. The Puerto Rican Legal Defense and Education Fund, a largely middle-class organization, promoted higher education and fought discrimination. Other Puerto Rican leaders promoted bilingualism and demanded bilingual teachers in schools, special programs to preserve the Spanish language, courses in Puerto Rican history and culture, and community participation in education. Arguing that the school system was top-heavy with Anglos and Jews, groups like the United Bronx Parents called for community control of schools, Puerto Rican administrators and teachers in predominantly Puerto Rican schools, and Puerto Rican paraprofessionals. Jewish and Anglo educators felt threatened, fearing the loss of their jobs or lack of promotions in favor of Puerto Ricans, and decentralization met bitter opposition from the New York United Federation of Teachers.

Other Puerto Ricans opted for economic action. The Puerto Rican Merchants Association encouraged small businesses, and the Puerto Rican Civil Service Employees Association promoted the interests of Puerto Rican government workers. Under the war on poverty program begun in 1965, the federal government funded a Puerto Rican Community Development Project, which sponsored drug treatment, summer jobs, job training, and school tutoring programs. Puerto Rican workers joined labor unions and eventually constituted a major segment of the International Ladies Garment Workers Union. A number of welfare rights groups demanded greater funding, fairer treatment of recipients, and more advertisements of benefits. The East Harlem Tenants Council organized for lower rents, safer apartments, and better maintenance from landlords. Puerto Rican social workers formed the Puerto Rican Family Institute to assist families coming to the mainland, and after securing funds from the Council against Poverty in 1965, the institute began marriage, employment, and family counseling.

Some Puerto Ricans turned to militancy. The Free Puerto Rico Now group and the National Committee for the Freedom of Puerto Rican Nationalist Prisoners advocated the use of violence to achieve Puerto Rican independence. During the 1960s the National Committee for Puerto Rican Civil Rights demonstrated for civil rights, affirmative action in the hiring of Puerto Rican teachers, policemen, and firemen, and Puerto Rican studies programs in schools. The Young Lords, a militant group of Puerto Rican students formed in the 1960s, demanded Puerto Rican studies programs in the city colleges, community control of community institutions, and an end to police brutality.

REFERENCES: Joseph P. Fitzpatrick, *Puerto Rican Americans: The Meaning of Migration to the Mainland*, 1987; Manuel Maldonado-Dennis, *The Emigration Dialectic: Puerto Rico and the USA*, 1980; Felix M. Padilla, *Puerto Rican Chicago*, 1987.

Q

QUASAR. Quasars were one of the most important scientific discoveries of the 1960s. Until then, most astrophysicists and cosmologists believed that the universe existed in a state of steady stability. Radiotelescopes, however, had long been providing puzzling evidence—abnormalities that existing theory could not explain. But in 1963, astronomer Maarten Schmidt of the California Institute of Technology postulated the existence of quasars—brightly burning clusters of matter containing more energy than 1 trillion stars like the earth's sun. Also, the quasars were receding from the earth at approximately 25,000 miles per second, proving that the universe was still expanding. Quasar theory gave rise to the so-called Big Bang* theory of the origin of the universe—that sometime between 10 billion and 20 billion years ago, the universe was born in a huge explosion of matter. The results of that explosion—brightly burning, rapidly receding quasars—meant that at some future date, the forces of gravity would slow the expansion and eventually bring about a huge collapse of the universe as all of its matter imploded.

REFERENCE: William J. Kaufman, *Galaxies and Quasars*, 1979.

R

RABBIT, RUN. *Rabbit, Run* is the title of John Updike's most famous best-selling novel. Published in 1960, *Rabbit, Run* featured Harry ''Rabbit'' Angstrom, an army veteran who finds himself trapped in a nameless working-class town of the 1950s. In an age when the American Dream supposedly embraced family, religion, and the pursuit of happiness, Rabbit cannot find happiness. All he can think of are earlier days when he had fewer responsibilities and more freedom. His wife is an alcoholic, and he is caught in a dead-end job. In a desperate and ultimately futile attempt to recapture that sense of personal liberation, Rabbit abandons his pregnant wife and runs off with another woman. Although Rabbit eventually returns to his wife, she unwittingly kills their baby daughter in a drunken stupor. The message of *Rabbit, Run* stood in sharp contrast to the dominant ethology of the 1950s.
REFERENCE: John Updike, *Rabbit, Run*, 1960.

RABBITS. During the Vietnam War,* the term ''rabbits'' was used by African-American soldiers* to refer to white soldiers.
REFERENCE: James S. Olson, ed., *Dictionary of the Vietnam War*, 1988.

RAMPARTS. During the 1960s and early 1970s, *Ramparts* was the premier New Left * magazine in the United States. It was founded in San Francisco in 1962. Under Warren Hinckle's brilliant leadership, *Ramparts* went from a circulation of 4,000 in 1964 to 250,000 in 1968. It peaked in 1968, however, and entered a long period of decline. By late in 1969, circulation was down to 125,000, and financial problems plagued the journal. Still, it was a major voice in support of the civil rights movement* and against the Vietnam War.* By the mid-1970s, many of *Ramparts* most important contributors—such as Eldridge Cleaver,* David Horowitz, and Pete Collier—began turning more conservative.

Internecine feuding and financial difficulties had also crippled *Ramparts*. Today, its circulation has stabilized at 200,000.
REFERENCE: Warren Hinckle, *If You Have a Lemon, Make Lemonade*, 1974.

RAND, AYN. Ayn Rand was born February 2, 1905, in St. Petersburg, Russia. She emigrated to the United States in 1926 after receiving her undergraduate degree in history from the University of Leningrad. The Bolshevik Revolution had an indelible impact on Rand's thinking. Totalitarian bureaucracies that destroyed individual initiative were certain, she believed, to ultimately destroy civilization as well. She became a naturalized U.S. citizen in 1931.

Rand published her first book in 1936—*We the Living*, a novel of the Russian Revolution. She followed it with a series of successful and influential books—*The Fountainhead* (1943), *Atlas Shrugged* (1957), *The Virtue of Selfishness* (1965), *Capitalism: The Unknown Ideal* (1966), and *The New Left: The Anti-Industrial Revolution* (1970). During the peak of the 1960s Great Society * faith in the ability of big government to ameliorate social problems, Rand became the godmother to conservatives and libertarians who believed only in the power of capitalism, the individual, and the market. Her heroes were brave men who defied the demands of bureaucracies, whether corporate or political. New Left * critics labeled her a fascist. Ayn Rand died in New York City March 6, 1982.
REFERENCES: Barbara Branden, *The Passion of Ayn Rand*, 1986; Sid Greenberg, *Ayn Rand and Alienation*, 1977; Douglas J. Uyl and Douglas B. Rasmussen, eds., *The Philosophic Thought of Ayn Rand*, 1984.

RAND CORPORATION. The Rand Corporation is a highly influential, nonprofit "think tank" corporation in the United States. In 1946, in Santa Monica, California, Douglas Aircraft Company formed Rand, naming the company after *R*esearch *and D*evelopment. Rand split from Douglas in 1948. During the early 1950s, Rand conducted research to evaluate the effectiveness of major American weapons systems under contracts with the Department of Defense. It broadened its research in the late 1950s to include national security resource allocation. During the Vietnam War,* the Rand Corporation also provided intelligence evaluations, frequently warning the Johnson* administration that American policy in Indochina was counterproductive and destined for failure.
REFERENCE: L. R. Smith, *The Rand Corporation*, 1966.

RANDOLPH, ASA PHILIP. A. Philip Randolph was born April 15, 1889, in Crescent City, Florida. An African-American activist even as a young man in the 1910s, he moved to New York City in 1911 and from 1917 to 1928 published *The Messenger*. In the paper, Randolph opposed U.S. entry into World War I and advised blacks not to enlist in the armed forces. A devoted socialist, Randolph organized the Brotherhood of Sleeping Car Porters in 1925, a union of African-American railroad porters. He served as president of the union from

1928 to 1968. He was the most prominent black labor leader in the United States.

Randolph's activism continued throughout his life. During World War II, he organized the famous March on Washington to protest employee segregation in defense industries. His threat led President Franklin D. Roosevelt to establish the Fair Employment Practices Commission. In 1963, Randolph chaired another March on Washington,* where Rev. Martin Luther King, Jr.,* gave his memorable "I Have a Dream" speech. Randolph actively backed President Lyndon B. Johnson's* antipoverty program in the 1960s. Randolph died May 16, 1979.
REFERENCES: Jarvis Anderson, *A. Philip Randolph: A Biographical Portrait*, 1973; *New York Times*, May 17, 1979.

RAPPING. In the 1960s, the term "rapping" emerged in the hippie* counterculture* as a slang expression describing the rapid-fire, obsessive conversations of an individual taking amphetamine drugs.
REFERENCE: Ruth Bronsteen, *The Hippy's Handbook—How to Live on Love*, 1967.

RAT PATROL. *Rat Patrol* was a popular television* war drama that defied the odds in the 1960s. At a time when military programs were increasingly unpopular with an American public frustrated over Vietnam,* *Rat Patrol* was a ratings success. It was first broadcast by ABC on September 12, 1968. *Rat Patrol* starred Christopher George as Sam Troy, Gary Raymond as Jack Moffitt, Lawrence Casey as Mark Hitchcock, Justin Tarr as Tully Pettigrew, and Hans Gudegast as Hauptman Han Dietrich. The "Rat Patrol" was a squad of American soldiers fighting in the North African deserts during World War II. An independent team of guerrilla fighters, they raced over the dunes in two machine gun-mounted jeeps, inflicting damage on the German army every week. The last episode was broadcast on September 16, 1968.
REFERENCE: Tim Brooks and Earle Marsh, *The Complete Directory to Prime Time Network and Cable TV Shows*, 1995.

RAWHIDE. *Rawhide* was a popular western television* series of the 1960s. CBS broadcast the first episode on January 9, 1959. Starring Clint Eastwood as Rowdy Yates, Eric Fleming as Gil Flavor, Sheb Wolley as Pete Nolan, and Paul Brinegar as Wishbone, *Rawhide* was set on the southern plains after the Civil War, where cowboys raised cattle and drove them to market, always trying to foil rustlers, Indians, and the elements. *Rawhide*'s last episode played on January 4, 1966.
REFERENCE: Richard Schickel, *Clint Eastwood: A Biography*, 1996.

RAY, JAMES EARL. On June 8, 1968, a forty-year-old habitual criminal, James Earl Ray, was arrested by Scotland Yard detectives at Heathrow Airport in London for the assassination of Dr. Martin Luther King, Jr.* Ray was born March 10, 1928, in Alton, Illinois, to Lucille Maher and George Ellis Ray. He was the eldest of seven children. His discipline problems started at an early age. He failed first grade and was described by school officials as "shiftless" and "seldom if ever polite." He dropped out of school in eighth grade and at sixteen got a job at a tannery. While there he was introduced to Nazism. He believed Hitler could make America all-white.

When he turned eighteen, he enlisted in the army and was sent to Bremerhaven, Germany. While there he began trading in cigarettes on the black market. Ray's medical history shows that he contracted gonorrhea, syphilis, pediculosis pubis (lice), and other sexually transmitted diseases while in Germany. He was finally discharged on December 23, 1948, for "ineptness and lack of adaptability to military service." This was after he had been arrested for being drunk and resisting arrest.

On January 1, 1949, he was arrested for a traffic violation. In September 1954, police arrested Ray for burglary, and in 1955 he was charged with "forging the endorsement on a U.S. Post Office money order." For this he served in the federal prison at Leavenworth, Kansas, until April 1958. He was arrested again October 10, 1959, for armed robbery twenty minutes after it occurred. He was sentenced to twenty years. In April 1967, Ray escaped from prison. He was a free man for about a year. On April 4, 1968, he killed Dr. Martin Luther King, Jr., who was standing on the balcony of the Lorraine Motel in Memphis, Tennessee. Ray denied that he had anything to do with the assassination and told his story like this: he bought a rifle in Birmingham and carried it to Memphis as he says he was instructed. He did not know anyone was going to be killed. When he heard the shot at 6:01 P.M. he was sitting in a white Mustang on Main Street. A man came running down the stairs, dropped the rifle on the sidewalk, jumped into the back of the Mustang, covered up with a sheet, and then told Ray to drive. About eight blocks from the rooming house, the man told Ray to stop, then jumped out of the car, after which Ray drove on to Atlanta. James Earl Ray was eventually convicted of murder and sentenced to life in prison.

He killed the most prominent civil rights leader the nation had ever known. Ironically, the death of Dr. King, who preached nonviolent protest, was followed by riots all over the country. People of all ethnic groups mourned the loss of one of America's greatest figures. Others would follow in the footsteps of Dr. King, but he will always be remembered as the man who started the civil rights movement* in America and the man who fought for equal rights for every American citizen.

In 1996, James Earl Ray fell seriously ill of liver disease. He was still proclaiming his innocence of the murder of Martin Luther King, Jr. Surprisingly, Ray's demands for a new trial gained momentum in 1997 when the family of Martin Luther King, Jr. began agreeing with Ray that such a judicial procedure was necessary. Some of King's family, including his wife, Coretta Scott King, worry that a conspiracy existed, and continues to exist, to cover up full disclosure of the information about the assassination, perhaps to protect prominent

politicians who might have participated in the assassination. Ray died April 23, 1998.
REFERENCES: *New York Times*, June 9–15, 1968.

Heather Toronjo

REAGAN, RONALD WILSON. Ronald Reagan was born February 6, 1911, in Tampico, Illinois. His father was an itinerant salesman, so Reagan grew up in a number of Illinois towns. He graduated from Eureka College in 1932 with a degree in economics and sociology and then took a job as a radio sportscaster in Davenport, Iowa. In 1937, while covering the Chicago Cubs spring training work on Catalina Island in California, Reagan was discovered by a movie scout. He signed a contract with Warner Brothers and acted in films and then television for the next thirty years. From 1947 to 1957 and again in 1959 and 1960, Reagan served as president of the Screen Actors Guild.

Reagan graduated from college as a New Deal Democrat, but during the red scare of the late 1940s and early 1950s, he steadily became more conservative. From 1954 to 1962, he hosted *General Electric Theater* and then *Death Valley Days* on prime-time television,* and in the process Reagan became one of the country's most recognizable personalities. He also became the darling of conservative Republicans at the GOP (Grand Old Party) national convention in San Francisco in 1964, when he delivered an electrifying speech endorsing Barry Goldwater* for the presidency. Handsome, charismatic, and blessed with a shrewd sense of timing and audience expectations, Reagan emerged from the Republican debacle of 1964 as a candidate in his own right. When he won the California gubernatorial election of 1966, Reagan became one of the most prominent conservatives in the United States.

He made unsuccessful bids for the Republican presidential nomination in 1968, was reelected governor in 1970, and again failed to receive the Republican nomination in 1972. His tenure as governor was noted for its budgetary austerity and cuts in social welfare programs. Reagan lost the Republican presidential nomination to Gerald Ford in 1976, but in 1980 he secured the nomination and defeated President Jimmy Carter for the presidency. Reagan survived an assassination attempt in 1981 and won a landslide reelection victory in 1984. He proved to be one of the most popular presidents in recent history, even though most scholars panned his tenure in the White House. He retired from politics in 1989.
REFERENCES: Bill Boyarsky, *Ronald Reagan: His Life and Rise to the Presidency*, 1981; Peter Hanaford, *The Reagans: A Political Portrait*, 1983.

RED POWER. The term ''red power'' has been used to describe the Indian civil rights movement* of the 1960s and 1970s, particularly the demands of Native American activists for equality, self-determination,* and the restoration of the landed estate and traditional hunting, fishing, and movement privileges. Some historians target the American Indian Chicago Conference* of 1961 as the real beginning of the modern red power movement, when a younger, more urban generation of Indian leaders challenged older, more traditional tribal leaders in the National Congress of American Indians for control of the Indian rights movement. Young men like Clyde Warrior (Ponca), Melvin Thom (Paiute), and Herbert Blatchford (Navajo) left the Chicago meeting discontented about the slow pace of change. They reconvened in Gallup, New Mexico, and formed the National Indian Youth Council,* which demanded an end to racism, ethnocentrism, and paternalism in American Indian policy and greater influence of Native Americans in the decision-making process of the Bureau of Indian Affairs.

By the mid-1960s, Indian activists were inspired and galvanized into action by the "black power"* movement among African Americans. Between 1964 and 1966, activists staged "fish-ins" to proclaim Indian independence from state fish and game laws. Such groups as the Indian Land Rights Association, the Alaska Federation of Natives, and the American Indian Civil Rights Council demanded the restoration of tribal lands, denouncing the idea of monetary compensation for the loss of the Indian estate. The Pan-Indian movement, led by people like Lehman Brightman and his United Native Americans, worked to overcome tribal differences and construct a united, powerful Indian political constituency in the United States.

In 1969, a Pan-Indian group known as Indians of All Tribes* occupied Alcatraz Island* in San Francisco, demanding its return to native peoples. Groups such as the American Indian Movement,* in addition to insisting on the restoration of tribal lands, demanded complete Indian control over the Bureau of Indian Affairs. In 1972, activists Hank Adams of the fish-ins and Dennis Banks* of the American Indian Movement organized the "Trail of Broken Treaties" caravan and traveled to Washington, D.C., to demand the complete revival of tribal sovereignty by repeal of the 1871 ban on future treaties, restoration of treaty-making status to individual tribes, the provision of full government services to unrecognized eastern tribes, a review of all past treaty violations, restitution for those violations, and elimination of all state court jurisdiction over American Indians. They also invaded and trashed the offices of the Bureau of Indian Affairs in Washington, D.C., to dramatize their demands.

By the early 1970s, however, the red power movement had increasingly developed into a campaign for self-determination. Although self-determination meant different things to different people, several controlling principles emerged during the debate over its merits. First, self-determination revolved around Indian control of the government agencies dealing most directly with them. The idea of having non-Indians administering Indian health, educational, and economic programs was unacceptable to self-determinationists. Second, self-determination called for an end to assimilationist pressures and a restoration of tribal values and culture. Allotment, citizenship, compensation, termination,* and relocation had all aimed at the annihilation of tribal cultures, and self-determinationists wanted to prevent the future emergence of such programs.

Third, self-determinationists insisted on maintaining the trust status of the tribes with the federal government.

Although many non-Indians saw self-determination and the continuance of the trust status as contradictory—a combination of paternalism and independence—self-determinationists were convinced that Indians needed the trust status to protect them from non-Indian majorities at the state and local level. Finally, self-determinationists hoped to bring about the economic development of reservation resources so that Indians could enjoy improving standards of living without compromising their cultural integrity or tribal unity. Many of the demands of self-determinationists were achieved when Congress passed the Indian Education Act of 1972, the Indian Finance Act of 1974, the Indian Self-Determination and Education Assistance Act of 1975, and the Indian Child Welfare Act of 1978.

REFERENCES: Steven Cornell, *The Return of the Native: American Indian Political Resurgence*, 1988; Laurence M. Hauptman, *The Iroquois Struggle for Survival: World War II to Red Power*, 1986; Alvin M. Josephy, Jr., *Red Power: The American Indians' Fight for Freedom*, 1971; James S. Olson and Raymond Wilson, *Native Americans in the Twentieth Century*, 1984.

REDDING, OTIS. Otis Redding was born in Dawson, Georgia, September 9, 1941. As an adolescent, he tried to copy the styles of Sam Cooke and Little Richard. He toured with several groups in the late 1950s and early 1960s, and he had his first hit—"These Arms of Mine"—in 1963. Redding became extraordinarily popular among black audiences in the urban club circuit. Along with James Brown,* he was one of the most popular black entertainers of the 1960s. In 1965 and 1966, a number of Redding's rhythm-and-blues hits also did well on the pop charts, including "Fa-Fa-Fa-Fa-Fa," "I've Been Loving You Too Long," "I Can't Turn You Loose," and "Respect" (made famous by Aretha Franklin*). Four days before his death in an airplane crash on December 10, 1967, Redding recorded "(Sittin' On) The Dock of the Bay," which became a number one hit on the pop charts in 1968.

REFERENCE: Jane Schiesel, *The Otis Redding Story*, 1973.

REDLINING. See CIVIL RIGHTS ACT OF 1968.

REPARATIONS. During the late 1960s, the idea of reparations emerged among black militants as a way for whites to compensate for the sins they had committed against black people throughout U.S. history. Patterned after the billions of dollars of reparations imposed on Germany by the Allied powers after World War I, the radical demand was a means through which the militants hoped to upstage more moderate leaders in the black community. The most spectacular moment in the campaign for reparations came in 1969, when James Forman, head of the Student Nonviolent Coordinating Committee,* calmly walked to the pulpit—uninvited—in the middle of Sunday services at the Riverside Church

in New York City and demanded that white churches offer up $500 million in reparations to compensate for their centuries of racism. The speech earned Forman headlines in newspapers throughout the country, and the National Council of Churches responded by establishing fund-raising organizations to funnel money to disadvantaged groups. More traditional black religious groups, such as the National Baptist Convention, roundly condemned Forman and the National Council of Churches for pandering to such a ridiculous demand, and little money ever found its way from white churches to the hands of poor black people. The demand for reparations was, however, one of the more spectacular episodes in the history of the civil rights movement* during the 1960s.
REFERENCE: David Burner, *Making Peace with the Sixties*, 1996.

RESURRECTION CITY. See **POOR PEOPLE'S CAMPAIGN** (1968).

REVENUE ACT OF 1964. The Revenue Act of 1964, also known as the Tax Reduction Act, was initiated by President John F. Kennedy* as an overhaul of the U.S. Internal Revenue Code of 1954. It resulted in nearly $13 billion in tax reductions. Kennedy wanted to reduce corporate and individual taxes as well as to restructure the income tax itself. The 1954 legislation, in his opinion, was essentially a "tax break" since it removed liquid capital from the economy by excessively high rates. Lower taxes, Kennedy believed, would put more discretionary money in consumer pockets and augment overall demand, which would in turn stimulate investment, production, and employment. It reduced the maximum personal tax rate from more than 90 percent to 70 percent and the maximum corporate rate from 52 percent to 48 percent. It became law early in 1964 under the Lyndon B. Johnson* administration.
REFERENCE: James S. Olson, ed., *Dictionary of United States Economic History*, 1992.

REVENUE-SHARING. "Revenue-sharing," or what President Richard Nixon* called his "New American Revolution," was the centerpiece of the president's domestic program. At the time, the administration wanted to cut federal spending. Revenue-sharing involved distributing federal money to cities and states in block grants rather than in the mandated programs of the past. The policy went into effect in 1973 with the distribution of $5.4 billion. The program soon became highly controversial, however, because governors and mayors discovered that they were actually receiving less money than before. By that time the program had become institutionalized, as so many federal programs do, but it did not set a permanent pattern for federal funding.
REFERENCE: Stephen E. Ambrose, *Nixon*, 1989.

RHEAULT CONTROVERSY. Colonel Robert Rheault was commander of the Fifth Special Forces Group in South Vietnam in 1969 when he was arrested for ordering the killing of a South Vietnamese Special Forces employee, whom Rheault learned was a secret agent of the Vietcong.* Eventually, the case had to be dismissed because the Central Intelligence Agency* (CIA) refused to release sensitive, classified documents to the prosecution. Rheault resigned from the Special Forces in 1969.

REFERENCE: Charles M. Simpson III, *Inside the Green Berets: The First Thirty Years*, 1983.

RIESMAN, DAVID. David Riesman has been described by one of his reviewers as an "unusually perceptive, sympathetic and ingenious interpreter of the social lives of college students, university intellectuals, suburbanites and factory workers." A lawyer turned sociologist, Riesman has enjoyed a large following since the publication of his first book, *The Lonely Crowd*, in 1950. His insight into American society has placed his works on the standard reading lists in colleges and universities around the country.

Riesman was born September 22, 1909, to Dr. David and Eleanor Riesman in Philadelphia. He attended William Penn Charter School before matriculating to Harvard. In 1931, he received his B.A. degree and then entered Harvard Law School. He received his law degree in 1934. He then worked as a clerk for Justice Louis D. Brandeis* of the Supreme Court for two years before beginning an academic career as professor of law at the University of Buffalo, where he remained from 1937 to 1941. From 1941 to 1946, he was the deputy assistant district attorney of New York County and also was legal adviser to the Sperry Gyroscope Company. In 1946, he moved to the University of Chicago. In 1947, he began his new career when he became a professor of social sciences at the University of Chicago.

The Lonely Crowd attracted widespread attention outside academic circles and established Riesman as one of the top sociologists of the nation. The book attempted to identify American character as shaped by American culture. The author's findings—that of the inner-, other-, and outer-directed characters—were soon established as the conventional typology in sociology. The two areas of Riesman's research over the years have been the examination of the American character in a changing society and the institution of higher education. These two themes can be seen in *Abundance for What? And Other Essays* and *The Academic Revolution*. In *Abundance for What?* Riesman again examined the character of Americans, only this time he looked at the effect of the Cold War* on American thought and character. Riesman stated that the Cold War had created a prosperity that was dependent on "military Keynesianism" and that this had created the need for more and more specialized career choices for the young. Riesman said that the Cold War had moved Americans toward conformity and blandness. He was pessimistic about their future.

In *The Academic Revolution*, Riesman, along with Christopher Jencks, examined the higher education system in America. They stated that the movement toward the creation of an academic professional class and the rising importance of a graduate degree had tended to block social equality, rather than broaden it. Without a graduate degree, students would face less chance of changing their

social position. They also studied the generational problems facing the universities at the time and cast a less than favorable eye on the student radicals. Riesman's career of constructive criticism of the American culture has earned him a following among academicians in several fields as well as the general public. His work has become the standard of its field.
REFERENCE: Seymour Martin Lipset, *Culture and Social Character: The Work of David Riesman*, 1961.

Steven D. Smith

THE RIFLEMAN. *The Rifleman* was a very popular television* western series of the late 1950s and early 1960s. First broadcast by ABC on September 30, 1958, it featured Chuck Connors as Lucas McCain, a homesteader in North Fork, New Mexico Territory, in the 1880s. The cast also included Johnny Crawford as Mark McCain and Paul Fix as Marshal Micah Torrance. Lucas McCain was handy with a gun, particularly with his specially designed Winchester rifle and its large ring, which allowed him to cock the weapon as he drew it. Lucas regularly came to the aid of Marshal Torrance, who could never seem to handle desperadoes on his own. The last episode was broadcast on July 1, 1963.
REFERENCE: Tim Brooks and Earle Marsh, *The Complete Directory to Prime Time Network and Cable TV Shows*, 1995.

THE RIGHTEOUS BROTHERS. The Righteous Brothers were an extremely popular vocal group of the early 1960s. Formed in Los Angeles in 1962, the duo included Bill Medley and Bobby Hatfield. Some critics said they represented the best (or the worst) of so-called blue-eyed soul. In 1964, their song "You've Lost That Lovin' Feeling" went to number one on the pop charts. During the next two years, they also put out several other major hits, including "Unchained Melody," "Ebb Tide," "Just Once in My Life," and "('You're My) Soul and Inspiration." The Righteous Brothers broke up in 1968.
REFERENCE: Patricia Romanowski and Holly George-Warren, eds., *The New Rolling Stone Encyclopedia of Rock and Roll*, 1996.

RIOTS IN THE 1960S. Although urban rioting is hardly a new phenomenon in world history, the riots of the 1960s in the United States reached unprecedented levels of damage, violence, injury, and death. Between 1964 and 1967, racial violence continued to escalate in major urban areas. The riots in New York, Los Angeles, Newark, and Detroit were all sparked by incidents involving white police officers and black citizens. Poor relations and communications between the police forces and the communities made peace talks futile. Although racial incidents served as the trigger, most analysts agree that the riots were fueled by the extremely poor socioeconomic conditions of the urban ghettos.

Between July 18 and 22, 1964, New York's predominantly black neighborhood of Harlem was engulfed in violence. At a rally protesting police brutality, speakers from the Congress of Racial Equality* urged the crowd to take action.

The crowd went to the police station to demand that a white police officer who shot a fifteen-year-old black youth be fired. As police tried to set up barricades, fighting led to rioting. Blacks looted stores, threw bricks, and hurled bottles; relative control was kept by officers' firing warning shots into the air.

However, the situation deteriorated rapidly after the funeral service for the slain youth, James Powell. Jesse Gray, a black nationalist, called on crowds to respond, which resulted in rioting by more than 1,000 African Americans in Harlem, Brooklyn, and Bedford-Stuyvesant. The estimated toll over the four days of rioting included twenty-five dead, 140 injured, 112 looted stores, 556 property damage reports, and 276 arrests. Only William Epton, leader of the Harlem Defense Council and the Progressive Labor Movement, was actually charged with inciting criminal anarchy, based on a Federal Bureau of Investigation (FBI) report. The police officer who shot James Powell was never indicted.

One year later in Watts, a district of Los Angeles, violence broke out over the arrest of a black man, Marquette Frye, by a white patrolman. When Frye's family tried to prevent the officer from taking Frye into custody, fighting ensued, and bystanders joined in. Rioting continued from August 11 through August 16. During the first two days, an estimated 7,000 youths were encouraged by their elders to loot stores, fight police, and stone cars. After the youths stole firearms and ammunition, they engaged the police in gunfights. The situation continued to deteriorate as many of the rioters began drinking alcohol. White motorists who accidentally entered Watts were beaten, and their cars were burned. Only business and property with signs saying "Negro Owned," "Blood," or "Brother" were spared from looting and fires started by Molotov cocktails.

Unlike the Harlem riot, the local police could not control the crowds. On the fourth day, 10,000 National Guardsmen were deployed to Watts. The troops used machine guns, rifles, tear gas, and roadblocks to regain control. By August 16, almost 15,000 peacekeepers were patrolling a forty-six-square-mile area. Although federal troops were not involved, President Lyndon B. Johnson* sent Undersecretary of Commerce LeRoy Collins to head a seven-member commission to discover the underlying and immediate causes of the riot and to recommend solutions.

After five months of study, the commission determined that this riot was spontaneous; 2 percent of the population simply exploded. The populace was angered by the following: (1) inflammatory speeches by civil rights leaders; (2) repeal of the California Fair Housing Act; and (3) disappointment with federal antipoverty programs. The commission also cited poor relations between the community and the police. Statistics showed thirty-four dead, 1,032 injured, 4,000 arrested, and close to $40 million in property damages. With these alarming numbers, the commission predicted further outbreaks.

Like the Harlem and Watts riots, the heat of the summer months increased tensions in Newark, New Jersey. After black taxi cab driver John Smith was arrested, false rumors spread through the black community that Smith had been beaten to death. This news, coupled with the defeat of a black city councilman candidate and the proposed development of a medical college on a site wanted by blacks for more housing, resulted in a riot July 12–17, 1967. Using typical rioting tactics, approximately 3,000 rioters gained control of downtown Newark and the West, East, and Central Wards. A spirit of cooperation developed among the rioters, who formed human chains to more easily remove stolen goods from the stores. Like the Watts riots, the National Guard was called for help. Almost 5,000 officers worked together to secure the perimeter, to enforce martial law, and to distribute emergency food rations to the community. After five days of chaotic fighting, the officers were tired, and there were several incidents of "friendly fire." After six days, the rioting ended. Every business in the riot zone was damaged in some manner; business losses exceeded $35 million. Casualties included twenty-six dead and 1,500 injured. Despite over 1,500 arrests, only 2 percent of Newark's population was involved in the rioting.

Less than one week later, Detroit experienced the worst rioting ever recorded in American history. Between July 23 and 30, forty-three people died, 2,000 were injured, and another 5,000 were left homeless. More than 7,000 persons were arrested in rioting that covered downtown Detroit and a seven-mile radius. In all, property damage ranged from $250 million to $500 million. The Detroit riot, however, was unique in several ways. First, it was biracial; both blacks and whites rioted together, not against one another. Next, citizens not involved in the rioting did not hide in their homes but helped firefighters by standing guard to protect them from the rioting. Also, the riot was not restricted to the ghettos; looting and firebombing spread to the suburbs. Officials realized that this was not an ordinary riot; in addition to 8,000 National Guardsmen, local officials requested federal military assistance.

By the end of the second day, President Lyndon B. Johnson* sent former secretary of defense Cyrus Vance to assess the situation; on July 24, the president announced on television* that he had issued orders for federal troops to quell the rioting in Detroit. Paratroopers and airborne divisions were deployed into Detroit and into Flint, Pontiac, and Grand Rapids, where other disturbances were beginning. Federal troops would fight for four days before rioting ceased. At the conclusion of the riot, the opinion of the media turned against the officers. The media cited alleged police brutality, and the courts actually indicted three officers for misconduct. Although the officers were later found innocent, the media and the public no longer viewed officers as heroes protecting society from evil elements.

Clearly, urban rioting had progressed over a three-year period from violent racial flare-ups to integrated destruction by the masses. Following the Detroit riot, President Johnson ordered a federal study to investigate urban violence. He also declared July 30, 1967, a National Day of Peace and Prayer for Reconciliation. Finally, he ordered new training in riot-control procedures for National Guardsmen. With this last measure, Johnson acknowledged that urban rioting would continue to be a problem in the United States. The riots following the assassination of Martin Luther King, Jr.,* in April 1968 proved him correct.

REFERENCES: Earl L. Brown, *Why Race Riots? Lessons from Detroit*, 1977; Spencer Crump, *Black Riots in Los Angeles*, 1966; Thomas F. Parker, ed., *Violence in the United States, 1956–1967*, 1974.

Lee Ann Lawrence

RIPON SOCIETY. The Ripon Society was organized in 1962 by seventeen graduate students at Harvard and the Massachusetts Institute of Technology. Liberal Republicans, they wanted to promote a more liberal political agenda in the Republican Party. John Saloma was the Ripon Society's first president. They wanted the Republican Party to embrace openly the civil rights movement* and the use of federal and state governments to ameliorate social and economic problems. Ripon Society members tended to back the candidacies of people like Governor Nelson Rockefeller* of New York, Senator Jacob Javits* of New York, Senator Charles Percy* of Illinois, Mayor John Lindsay* of New York City, and Governor George Romney* of Michigan.

REFERENCE: Edward H. Schapsmeier and Frederick H. Schapsmeier, *Political Parties and Civic Action Groups*, 1981.

ROBERTS, ORAL. Oral Roberts was born January 24, 1918, in Oklahoma, to a devout Pentecostal family. His father was an itinerant evangelist. In 1935, during a revival in Ada, Oklahoma, Roberts received what he believed to be his call from God to serve in the ministry. He soon joined his father on the evangelical circuit. A gifted, charismatic preacher who claimed the gift of healing, the younger Roberts soon developed a popular following. In 1938 he wrote his first book—*Salvation by the Blood*—and wrote his second book, *The Drama of the End Time*, in 1941. During the 1940s, he filled several different pastorates in Oklahoma and expanded his reputation as a healer. In 1947, he moved to Tulsa, Oklahoma, but he also took his healing revivals on the road and was soon playing to huge crowds.

In 1954, Roberts launched the modern era of televangelism with his television program *Your Faith Is Power*. Soon he was marketing his own magazine, comic books, and radio programs as well. By the 1960s, he was one of the most recognizable religious figures in the United States. He then began to build Oral Roberts University in Tulsa. As his ministry came to emphasize more evangelicalism than healing, he became increasingly acceptable to mainline Protestants. During the 1970s, Roberts was embroiled in controversy when he claimed that he had talked with a 900-foot-tall Jesus and was supposed to build a medical school. Despite the controversy, Roberts dedicated the "City of Faith" in 1981. He remains an active evangelist today.

REFERENCES: David E. Harrell, *Oral Roberts: An American Life*, 1985; Oral Roberts, *Oral Roberts' Life Story*, 1952.

ROBINSON V. CALIFORNIA. During the 1960s, the Supreme Court, under the leadership of Chief Justice Earl Warren,* staked out new constitutional ground on the Eighth Amendment issue of cruel and unusual punishment, narrowing the freedom of the state to punish individuals convicted of crimes. *Robinson v. California* was one such decision. Decided on June 25, 1962, with Justice Potter Stewart* writing the majority opinion, the Court declared unconstitutional a California law making narcotics addiction a criminal offense. To purchase, distribute, and sell illegal narcotics remained criminal offenses, but mere addiction to such a narcotic could not be considered a crime. Such legislation would be a violation of the Eighth Amendment's protection against cruel and unusual punishment.
REFERENCE: 370 U.S. 660 (1962).

ROCKEFELLER, NELSON ALDRICH. Nelson Rockefeller was born in Bar Harbor, Maine, July 8, 1908, to one of the world's richest families. He attended Dartmouth College from 1926 to 1930 and then entered the family business in New York City, managing real estate sales and development. From 1930 to 1935, he clerked at the family-owned Chase National Bank, and from 1935 to 1940, he served as chairman of the family-owned Creole Petroleum Company. But like so many children of the fabulously wealthy, Rockefeller could not find satisfaction in working to make more money for the world's already richest family.

He turned to public service, and in 1940 President Franklin D. Roosevelt appointed him coordinator of Inter-American Affairs. In 1944, he was appointed assistant secretary of state for Latin American affairs. Rockefeller returned to the family businesses in 1945 and held various volunteer posts in the Truman and Eisenhower* administrations. A liberal Republican, he accepted Eisenhower's appointment as chairman of the Advisory Committee on Government Organization as well as undersecretary of health, education, and welfare and special assistant on foreign policy. In 1958, Nelson Rockefeller defeated W. Averell Harriman* to become governor of New York.

He eventually served four terms as governor. His administrations were liberal ones, noted for their expansion of social welfare programs and increase in the size of the state budgets and annual deficits. During his stay at the governor's mansion in Albany, Rockefeller was a perennial also-ran for the Republican presidential nomination. In 1960, he lost out to Vice President Richard M. Nixon,* and in 1964 Senator Barry Goldwater* of Arizona edged him out for the nomination. When Rockefeller refused to endorse Goldwater in the general election, he earned the eternal ire of Republican conservatives. Rockefeller made another bid for the presidency in 1968, but GOP (Grand Old Party) conservatives vetoed him. Nixon got the nomination instead.

Nelson retired from public life in 1973, but in 1974 President Gerald Ford nominated him to serve as vice president of the United States. Spiro Agnew had resigned the vice presidency under criminal indictment in 1973, and Nixon had replaced him with Gerald Ford. When Nixon resigned amid the Watergate revelations of August 1974, and Ford succeeded to the presidency, the new president picked Rockefeller to replace him. Rockefeller served out Ford's term, but they lost the presidential election of 1976 to Jimmy Carter. Nelson Rockefeller then retired from private life and died of a heart attack January 26, 1979.

REFERENCES: Robert H. Connery and Gerald Benjamin, *Rockefeller of New York: Executive Power in the Statehouse*, 1979; Joseph E. Persico, *The Imperial Rockefeller: A Biography of Nelson A. Rockefeller*, 1982.

ROCKWELL, GEORGE LINCOLN. George Lincoln Rockwell was the leader of the American Nazi Party during the 1960s. A confirmed racist since his undergraduate years in college, Rockwell in 1958 founded the National Committee to Free America from Jewish Domination. Later that year he founded the American Nazi Party. Rockwell fancied himself a neo-Adolf Hitler, and he tried to run for president in 1964 and for governor of Virginia in 1965. The American Nazi Party was always badly divided by internecine personal and ideological warfare, which eventually became the source of Rockwell's demise. In 1966, he dismissed John Patler from the party for stirring up dissension between light- and dark-complexioned Nazis. Patler decided to get even. On August 26, 1967, he assassinated Rockwell.

REFERENCE: *New York Times*, August 27, 1967.

ROGERS, WILLIAM PIERCE. William P. Rogers was born at Norfolk, New York, June 23, 1913. He graduated from Colgate University in 1934, and in 1937 he earned a law degree at Cornell University, where he edited the law review. Rogers worked briefly with a Wall Street firm in 1937 before joining the staff of New York County district attorney Thomas E. Dewey, who was about to launch his campaign against racketeers. While serving on Dewey's staff, Rogers gained extensive experience as a trial lawyer. He was an officer with the U.S. Naval Reserve in the Pacific during World War II. After the war, Rogers returned to Dewey's staff briefly and then went to work as counsel to several congressional committees. During those years he came to know Congressman and, later, Senator Richard Nixon* and worked on the Alger Hiss case. In 1950, Rogers returned to private law practice and continued as a Nixon adviser. When Dwight D. Eisenhower* was elected president in 1952, Rogers became deputy attorney general. In October 1957, he became attorney general in the Eisenhower cabinet.

Between 1960 and 1968, Rogers practiced law, but when Richard Nixon entered the White House in 1969, Rogers became secretary of state. Nixon also named Henry Kissinger* to the post of special White House assistant on foreign affairs. From the beginning, Kissinger's influence was dominant. Nixon tended to be suspicious and secretive, and he distrusted the "Ivy League types" at the State Department. Rogers was always upstaged by Kissinger. The making of foreign policy had definitely shifted to the White House. Thus, William Rogers was often put in the position of explaining and defending policies before Congress and the nation that had been formulated by Nixon and Kissinger with little or no input from the State Department. This was especially true in the areas of Sino–Soviet and Vietnam policy. Rogers himself was often the subject of unkind chatter on the cocktail circuit. But he continued to serve until 1973, when he resigned to return to his private law practice. In 1986, he was chosen by the Reagan administration to head the investigation of the Challenger disaster.

REFERENCES: *Current Biography*, 1969; William P. Rogers, *Vietnam in Perspective*, 1969; Thomas G. Paterson, *American Foreign Policy*, 1983; *U.S. News & World Report*, February 24, 1986.

Joseph M. Rowe, Jr.

THE ROLLING STONES. The Rolling Stones are arguably considered today to be the greatest band in the history of rock and roll. They certainly have the most longevity. Formed in London, England, in 1962, the band included lead singer Mick Jagger, Keith Richards, Brian Jones, Bill Wyman, and Charlie Watts. Ian Stewart, their pianist, had stopped performing before they ever made their first hit record, but he had remained behind the scenes as part of the group. They based their music on Chicago blues and their performances on a defiant, in-your-face sexuality. During their first tour of the United States in 1964, they muted the most rebellious tones of their music and performance in part to satisfy what they considered to be morally "uptight"* American audiences. But they were only pale imitations of the Beatles.*

They did not become successful in the United States until 1965, when they returned with a vengeance, bringing all of their rebelliousness to an American concert tour. At a time when the Beatles offered the innocent rock and roll of "I Want to Hold Your Hand" and "Eight Days a Week," the Stones emphasized outright rebellion, nastiness, overt sexuality, drug worship, and rudeness. Many American critics severely attacked the Stones, but concert audiences and young record buyers responded positively. Their first American hit came in July 1965—"I Can't Get No Satisfaction." The song was powerful, feverish, irreverent, and menacing, and it carved out a special place for the Rolling Stones in American popular culture. Among their other major hits in the 1960s were "Paint It Black" (1966), "Ruby Tuesday" (1967), "Jumpin' Jack Flash" (1968), and "Honky Tonk Woman" (1969).

In their personal lives, the Stones exhibited voracious appetites for drugs and sex, fulfilling what fans came to expect of them. Brian Jones, in a drug stupor, drowned in a swimming pool in 1969, and later in the year, at their infamous Altamont,* California, rock concert, a concertgoer was beaten to death by security guards, who happened to be members of the Hell's Angels motorcycle gang. In the 1970s, the Stones quietly left behind their insolence and became fashionably decadent icons for a new decade, symbolized by their 1971 album *Sticky Fingers*. They continued to record and perform in the 1980s and 1990s, earning well-deserved, if notorious, reputations as the godfathers of rock and roll.

REFERENCE: Tony Sanchez, *Up and Down with the Rolling Stones*, 1996.

ROMNEY, GEORGE. George Romney was born in the Mormon colonies in Chihuahua, Mexico, on July 8, 1907. In the 1920s, he studied at the University of Utah and George Washington University, and in 1929 he joined the congressional staff of Senator David Walsh of Massachusetts, specializing in tariff issues. In 1930, Romney went to work as a lobbyist for the Aluminum Company of America (ALCOA). During the next twenty-three years, he worked for ALCOA and the Automobile Manufacturers Association, and in 1954 he became president of American Motors.

He became active in Michigan Republican Party politics, and in 1962 he was elected governor of the state. He soon earned a reputation as a pragmatic, liberal Republican and was reelected in 1964 and 1966. Romney was considering a run for the Republican presidential nomination in 1968, but his candidacy was ruined after he took a fact-finding trip to Vietnam. He had serious reservations about the war, and he told journalists that U.S. officials in Saigon* had ''brainwashed'' him. Americans associated the word ''brainwash'' with Communist activities during the Korean War, and Romney had trouble defending himself. He lost the New Hampshire primary to Richard Nixon,* and the loss derailed his candidacy. In 1969, President Nixon appointed Romney to his cabinet as secretary of housing and urban development. Romney retired in 1973 and died on July 26, 1995.

REFERENCES: Arthur Chamberlain, *George Romney*, 1971; Clark Mollenhoff, *George Romney: Mormon in Politics*, 1968; *New York Times*, July 27, 1995.

ROOSEVELT, ELEANOR ANNA. Eleanor Roosevelt was born October 11, 1884, in New York City. She married Franklin Delano Roosevelt. They had six children together, but his infidelity forced Eleanor Roosevelt to increasingly seek the meaning of her life outside their home. During his years as governor of New York (1929–1933) and president of the United States (1933–1945), she became a political figure in her own right, evolving, in the eyes of many, into the conscience of the nation. Her political philosophy was decidedly more liberal than that of her husband, and throughout his political career she continually pushed him to the left, advocating the use of the federal government to solve social and economic problems. After his death in 1945, she remained politically active, becoming in many ways the grand dame of the Democratic Party, the one individual whose endorsement all candidates sought. She also continued to pursue her humanitarian causes on a world scale. Eleanor Roosevelt died November 7, 1962.

REFERENCES: Jason Berger, *A New Deal for the World: Eleanor Roosevelt and American Foreign Policy*, 1981; Joseph P. Lasch, *Eleanor and Franklin*, 1971; J. William Youngs, *Eleanor Roosevelt: A Personal and Public Life*, 1985.

ROSTOW, WALT WHITMAN. Walt Whitman Rostow was born in New York City on October 7, 1916. Blessed with a brilliant analytical mind, he graduated from Yale in 1936 and went on to graduate studies at Oxford University as a Rhodes Scholar. In 1938, he returned to Yale to work on a Ph.D. in economics. He finished there in 1940. During World War II, Rostow worked in the Office of Strategic Services, a forerunner of the Central Intelligence Agency.* After the war, he spent several years with the state department, and in 1950 he joined the faculty of the Massachusetts Institute of Technology (MIT) as a professor of economic history.

During the 1950s, Rostow worked on the book that eventually made him the most prominent economic historian in the world. Published in 1960, *The Stages of Economic Growth* was an analysis of the process by which countries industrialize and modernize. From his research, Rostow concluded that the best way for the United States to fight Communist expansion in the Third World was to have a strong military posture as well as the social and economic resources to accelerate the process of urbanization and economic development. Once a country had modernized, communism would have little appeal for people, he argued, but it was imperative to protect these countries from Communist aggression until the process of modernization had run its course. Rostow also served as a foreign policy advisor to Senator John F. Kennedy* of Massachusetts during the late 1950s. When Kennedy became president in 1961, Rostow was named special assistant to the president for foreign security affairs. In that post, Rostow played a key role in the early formulation of U.S. policy toward Laos, Cambodia, and Vietnam.

During the Kennedy administration, as chairman of the policy planning council in the White House, Rostow developed what became known as the "Rostow thesis." The only way that externally supported, Third World radical insurgencies could be stopped, Rostow argued, was to accelerate the pace of economic development and escalate military measures to cut off the external support. Those ideas directly affected the Kennedy administration's approach to Vietnam and Laos. In 1963 and 1964, Rostow went to the state department, where he was put in charge of long-range analysis and planning in a broad range of foreign policy areas.

By June 1964, Rostow was back in the White House as President Lyndon B. Johnson's* closest adviser on Southeast Asian affairs. He quickly earned a reputation as a hardliner who advocated intense bombing of North Vietnam and an increased U.S. military presence in South Vietnam. Subjecting North Vietnam to heavy losses and maximum destruction from conventional weapons would end the war, Rostow claimed, because the North Vietnamese would soon realize that the conflict was destroying them. President Johnson bought into Rostow's logic, and in 1964 and 1965 the Vietnam War* dramatically escalated. On March 31, 1966, President Johnson appointed him special assistant to the president for national security affairs, succeeding McGeorge Bundy.* He remained there until Johnson left the White House in 1969.

Because of his reputation as an architect of a very unpopular war, Rostow had difficulty finding a university teaching position until he joined the faculty of the University of Texas, where he has continued to teach, lecture, and write. Since arriving on the Austin, Texas, campus, Rostow has written many books, including *The Division of Europe After World War II, 1946* (1981); *Eisenhower, Kennedy, and Foreign Affairs* (1985); *Essays on a Half-Century: Ideas, Policies, and Action* (1988); *Theorists of Economic Growth from David Hume to the Present* (1990); and *The Great Population Spike and After: Reflections on the 21st Century* (1998).

REFERENCES: Seymour Brown, *The Faces of Power: Constancy and Change in United States Foreign Policy from Truman to Johnson*, 1968; *Economics in the Long View: Essays in Honor of W. W. Rostow*, 1982; Roger D. Launius, "Walt Whitman Rostow," in James S. Olson, ed., *Dictionary of the Vietnam War*, 1988; W. W. Rostow, *Getting From There to Here*, 1978, and *The Diffusion of Power, 1957–1972*, 1972.

ROUTE 66. *Route 66* was a popular television* adventure series of the early 1960s. CBS broadcast the first episode on October 7, 1960. There is an innocence to *Route 66*, particularly when seen in the aftermath of the youth rebellion, counterculture,* and anti–Vietnam War* attitudes that sprouted in America in the mid- and late 1960s. Martin Milner played Todd Stiles, and George Maharis played Buz Murdock, two young men who crisscross the United States in a Corvette, looking for love, adventure, and fun. The last episode was broadcast on September 18, 1964.

REFERENCE: Tim Brooks and Earle Marsh, *The Complete Directory to Prime Time Network and Cable TV Shows*, 1995.

ROWAN AND MARTIN'S *LAUGH-IN.* *Laugh-In* emerged from the comic genius of Dan Rowan and Dick Martin, a stand-up comedy team that launched the comedy variety show on NBC. Its first episode premiered on January 22, 1968. The show's cast included Gary Owens, Ruth Buzzi, Goldie Hawn, Judy Carne, Lillie Tomlin, Henry Gibson, Arte Johnson, Jo Anne Worley, and a host of others. It was the perfect variety show for the 1960s. Irreverent and zany, the show poked fun at politicians and government policies and featured one-liners and cameo appearances by the rich and famous and unique, memorable performances by its ensemble cast. It rocketed to the top of the Nielsen ratings. The last episode was broadcast on May 14, 1973.

REFERENCE: Dan Rowan, *A Friendship*, 1986; *Rowan and Martin's* Laugh-In, 1969.

RUBIN, JERRY. Jerry Rubin was born in Cincinnati, Ohio, on July 14, 1938. In 1961, he graduated from the University of Cincinnati and went on to the University of California at Berkeley for graduate studies. At Berkeley, Rubin was soon deeply involved in Mario Savio's* Free Speech Movement.* As the Free Speech Movement merged into the antiwar movement,* Rubin became a radical student leader, heading up the militant Vietnam Day Committee (VDC).

He staged a series of antiwar* demonstrations, and VDC members blocked troop train movements in California. In 1968, Rubin and Abbie Hoffman* formed the Youth International Party,* also known as "Yippies." Yippies were committed to promoting the counterculture* and opposing the Vietnam War.* Rubin was a central figure in the antiwar demonstrations in Chicago during the 1968 Democratic Party presidential nominating convention, and he was arrested for conspiracy to riot. During the subsequent trial, he became known as one of the "Chicago 8."* Although he was convicted, the verdict was later overturned on appeal.

After 1973, with the end of the Vietnam War, Rubin fell out of the political and pop culture limelight and became a successful Wall Street stockbroker. Journalists often used him as a symbol of the transformation of the "Hippies" of the 1960s into the "Yuppies" of the 1980s. On November 15, 1994, he was hit by a car while crossing a street in Los Angeles. He died two weeks later, on November 28, 1994.

REFERENCES: *New York Times*, November 29, 1995; Jerry Rubin, *Growing (Up) at Thirty-Seven*, 1976; Nancy Zaroulis and Gerald Sullivan, *Who Spoke Up? American Protest Against the Vietnam War, 1963–1975*, 1984.

RUBY, JACK. Born Jacob Rubenstein in Chicago in 1911, Jack Ruby grew up in foster homes, dropped out of high school, and made a living in a variety of odd jobs. After a tour in the army air corps during World War II, he settled in Dallas and became a nightclub manager. At his nightclubs—the Vegas and the Carousel—Ruby gained a reputation as a friend of the police. He was occasionally arrested for liquor law violations but never convicted. Otherwise an obscure man, Ruby became famous—or infamous, depending on one's perspective—on November 24, 1963, when he murdered Lee Harvey Oswald,* the alleged assassin of President John F. Kennedy.* Ruby managed to make his way into the Dallas police station, and when Oswald was being transferred from a cell, Ruby shot him. A national television audience witnessed the murder. Ruby was convicted and sentenced to death for the crime. Ruby insisted, and the Warren Commission concurred, that there had been no organized conspiracy to murder the president and Oswald. Ruby's death sentence was commuted to life in prison, and he died of cancer January 3, 1967.

REFERENCE: *New York Times*, January 4, 1967.

RUDD, MARK. According to information in his Federal Bureau of Investigation (FBI) photo, Mark Rudd hailed from Irvington, New Jersey, and was born June 2, 1947. He entered Columbia University* in the fall of 1965 and became involved with the Students for a Democratic Society* (SDS). He became a leader in the Weathermen* faction of the SDS during the 1960s and led violent protests in Chicago in October 1969. Wanted by the law, he went underground to conduct a war of liberation against the United States. Rudd disappeared from FBI surveillance after 1971.

Rudd became an outspoken leader of the SDS and the New Left* during the Columbia University riots in the spring of 1968. The protests began on the morning of April 23, 1968. Police moved in and broke up the demonstration. Students responded by occupying Columbia University buildings. On April 27, the occupation of buildings ended when police stormed the campus and arrested scores of students. A general student strike resulted from the police action. During the strike, students learned that Columbia planned to demolish a hotel for transients in the Morningside Park neighborhood. This led to a takeover of the hotel by the SDS and neighborhood residents. President Grayson Kirk suspended Rudd and three other students in hopes of breaking the organization. Students responded by occupying several more buildings on campus, including the administration building. In the wake of the riots, SDS emerged as the dominant New Left organization, and William C. Sullivan of the Domestic Intelligence Department of the FBI launched counterintelligence operations against the SDS.

Rudd spun an ad hoc political philosophy together. At first, he refrained from labeling New Left thought or associating it with socialism or communism. Rudd refrained from attacking the establishment from the outside. Positive action in America depended on attacking the evil manifestations of capitalism. He believed that any blueprint for society produced utopian dreams and no real solutions. Ironically, Rudd believed the fruition of social change required a mass democratic, socialist movement. He envisioned the movement involved in the struggle against racism, supporting Third World liberation and against the capitalist and private enterprise system. For Rudd, there was no alternative in a system controlled by a few privileged power brokers. ''Liberal policies are as bad as the conservative policies.'' Furthermore, Rudd believed Americans and Third World nations were exploited by a few people with enormous wealth who controlled the political system. Revolution was the only answer.

By 1969, after the Chicago riots and the election of Richard Nixon,* Rudd became SDS party secretary. Rudd, Bernadine Dorhn, William Ayres, and their radical faction pushed for an agenda of revolution through violence as advocated in the ''Weatherman Papers.'' In October 1969, Rudd and his Weathermen arrived in riot gear in order to take on the Chicago police. Only 200–500 Weathermen of Rudd's promised 20,000 showed up. The strategy changed to vandalism against stores, expensive private property, and military recruiting stations. Susan Stern, a Weatherman from Seattle, claimed Rudd's major accomplishment involved the destruction of a Rolls Royce on Chicago's Gold Coast. He did, however, receive federal charges for interstate conspiracy to commit a riot. He fled and went underground. Although Rudd is still alive today, he has not been seen in public since 1970.

REFERENCES: Kirkpatrick Sale, *SDS: Ten Years toward a Revolution*, 1973; Nancy Zaroulis and Gerald Sullivan, *Who Spoke Up? American Protest against the Vietnam War, 1963–1975*, 1984.

Michael Hall

RUSK, DAVID DEAN. Born in Cherokee County, Georgia, February 9, 1909, Dean Rusk received an undergraduate degree from Davidson College in 1931 and then won a prestigious Rhodes Fellowship, which gave him the opportunity to attend Oxford. He joined the army during World War II and saw combat in Burma. After the war, Rusk went to work for the State Department, becoming assistant secretary of state for Far Eastern affairs in 1952. He earned a reputation for being a dedicated anticommunist. In 1952, Rusk left the State Department to become president of the Rockefeller Foundation. He was still with the Rockefeller Foundation in 1960, when John F. Kennedy* named him secretary of state. He also served as secretary of state under President Lyndon B. Johnson* from 1963 to 1969.

During the years of the Vietnam War,* Rusk was a hard-liner who supported the American military buildup and the use of force against North Vietnam and the Vietcong.* He repeatedly urged Johnson to launch bombing campaigns against North Vietnam, and he was most reluctant to negotiate with the communists. Even after the Tet Offensive* of 1968, Rusk advocated the deployment of more troops to South Vietnam. When he left the State Department in 1969, Rusk was widely considered the primary architect of the American debacle in Vietnam. After retiring from public life, Rusk returned to academe.

REFERENCES: Warren I. Cohen, *Dean Rusk*, 1980; Dean Rusk, *As I Saw It*, 1989.

RUSSELL, RICHARD BREVARD. A native Georgian, Richard Russell was born November 2, 1897, and received a law degree from the University of Georgia in 1918. He practiced law for three years and then was elected as a Democrat to the state legislature. Ten years later, at the age of thirty-three, he became the youngest governor in the history of Georgia. Russell won a seat in the U.S. Senate in the election of 1932, where he remained for the next thirty-eight years. He became a master of parliamentary maneuver and a formidable debater. Although he fought social welfare and civil rights legislation, Russell nevertheless won great respect among liberal senators because of his ability and integrity. By 1952, Russell was a major figure in the Democratic Party. He lost the presidential nomination to Adlai Stevenson* that year, but as chairman of the Senate Armed Services Committee and of the military expenditures subcommittee of the Appropriations Committee, Russell wielded vast influence over military policy.

As early as 1954, Russell warned Dwight D. Eisenhower* against sending arms and technicians to bolster French forces in Indochina. He once told John Foster Dulles that he was "weary of seeing American soldiers being used as gladiators to be thrown into every arena around the world." When Eisenhower decided to make the commitment, Russell said that he would "support the flag" but that "it is going to be a long drawn-out affair costly in both blood and Treasure." Russell remained faithful to his word. As long as American forces were fighting in Vietnam, he supported the policies of successive presidents. But he regretted the intervention, calling it "one of the great tragedies of our history.'' Throughout the summer and fall of 1970, Senator Richard Russell's health deteriorated. He had to enter Walter Reed Medical Center on December 8, 1970, and died there January 21, 1971, at the age of seventy-three.

REFERENCES: Gilbert C. Fite, *Richard B. Russell, Jr.: Senator from Georgia*, 1991; Robert Mann, *The Walls of Jericho: Lyndon Johnson, Hubert Humphrey, Richard Russell and the Struggle for Civil Rights*, 1988.

Joseph M. Rowe, Jr.

RUSTIN, BAYARD. Bayard Rustin was born to West Indian parents in Philadelphia in 1910. He attended school at several colleges in Pennsylvania before moving to New York City in 1936 and joining the Young Communist League. Rustin then became a Young Communist League oganizer on the campus of the City College of New York. An African American, Rustin protested racial segregation in the U.S. military and opposed war. But when the Soviet Union suddenly changed philosophy in 1939 and signed a nonaggression pact with Nazi Germany, Rustin resigned his Young Communist League membership in disgust.

Still interested in desegregation and world peace, Rustin joined forces with A. Philip Randolph* for the 1943 March on Washington to bring about integration in defense plants. He also became active in the Fellowship of Reconciliation,* in which he protested segregation in interstate transportation. In 1943, Rustin was convicted of draft evasion and sentenced to a federal penitentiary. When he was released from prison in 1947, Rustin organized the Journey of Reconciliation project, an early version of the 1961 freedom rides.* Rustin was arrested during his own ride into North Carolina in 1948 and spent several months on a prison chain gang.

In 1953, Rustin joined the War Resisters League,* and two years later he became an adviser to Rev. Martin Luther King, Jr.* He helped with the Montgomery bus boycott and then assisted in the founding of the Southern Christian Leadership Conference (SCLC).* Rustin resigned from the SCLC in 1960, when his homosexuality became widely known. Three years later, however, Rustin and King worked together in staging the 1963 March on Washington.

Rustin became director of the A. Philip Randolph Institute in 1963 and decided that the future of African Americans would best be served in an alliance with labor unions, churches, and liberal organizations. He bitterly denounced the black power* movement as political folly, arguing that radicalism would only isolate black people in American society. Bayard Rustin died in 1987.

REFERENCES: Bayard Rustin, *Strategies for Freedom*, 1976; Milton Viorst, *Fire in the Streets: America in the 1960s*, 1979.

S

SAIGON. Saigon, today known as Ho Chi Minh City, was the capital of the Republic of Vietnam (South Vietnam) from 1954 to 1975. It is located approximately forty-five miles up the Ben Nghe River from the South China Sea. REFERENCE: Virginia Thompson, *French Indochina*, 1968.

SALINGER, J. D. Jerome David Salinger was born in New York City January 1, 1919. He graduated from Valley Forge Military Academy in 1936 after being expelled from several preparatory schools and went on to attend New York University, Ursinus College, and Columbia University. At Columbia, he published his first short work of fiction in *Story*, an influential periodical founded by his writing instructor, Whit Burnett. Salinger's short works soon began appearing in *Esquire, Collier's, The Saturday Evening Post*, and most notably, *The New Yorker*. During the 1940s, he published ''I'm Crazy'' and ''Slight Rebellion of Madison,'' both of which introduced Holden Caulfield, the future narrator of *The Catcher in the Rye*.

Salinger is most famous for this controversial novel about the odyssey of teenage misfit and prep school dropout Holden Caulfield, a curious, self-critical, and compassionate moral idealist whose attitudes are controlled by a rigid hatred of hypocrisy. *Catcher in the Rye* is hilariously irreverent, a sarcastic critique of every established institution imaginable. During the late 1950s and throughout the 1960s, *Catcher in the Rye* became required reading in thousands of high school and college American-literature courses, influencing the thinking of millions of young American readers. Holden Caulfield became an antihero—a symbolic icon for a decade in which rejection of parents, church, military, and country became the rite of passage for an entire generation of educated young people. The organization, humor, and theme in *The Catcher in the Rye* all make it one of the most influential novels in American literary history. It created a pop culture icon that outlasted the age in which it was written, a fan club that forced Salinger into seclusion, and a generation with a new and unprecedented affinity for rebellion. It drew readers to his subsequent short fiction, *Nine Stories* (1953), and the novella collections *Franny and Zooey* (1955) and *Raise High the Roofbeam, Carpenters, and Seymour: An Introduction* (1963).

Salinger's personal life was very unstable. He married Sylvia (maiden name unknown) in September 1945 and divorced her in October 1947. He married Claire Douglas in 1955 and divorced her twelve years later; he had two children from the second marriage—Margaret Ann and Matthew. Salinger is currently living alone in rural New Hampshire and has not published under his own name since 1965. In seclusion, he hoped to avoid the millions of young people who viewed him as some kind of "Holy Grail" in the search for the meaning of life. Robert Coles once described Salinger as "an original and gifted writer, a marvelous entertainer, a man of the slogans and cliches the rest of us fall prey to." But truly, the only way to personify J. D. Salinger's character is simply with his favorite creation, Holden Caulfield.

REFERENCES: Frederick Gwynne, *The Fiction of J. D. Salinger*, 1979; Ian Hamilton, *In Search of J. D. Salinger*, 1988.

Bradley A. Olson

SALISBURY, HARRISON EVANS. Harrison Evans Salisbury was born in Minneapolis, Minnesota, on November 14, 1908. He went to work as a journalist for United Press in 1930 and travelled widely throughout the world on assignments. In 1948, he joined the staff of the *New York Times*. The *Times* named him their Moscow bureau chief, and Salisbury wrote from the Soviet Union until 1953. He then returned to New York, and in 1964 he was named assistant managing editor. In 1966, to get a first-hand look at the Vietnam War,* he travelled to Hanoi.* His articles stirred up controversy because he confirmed North Vietnamese allegations that U.S. bombing had caused widespread civilian casualties* and that the bombing was only stiffening North Vietnam's will to resist. His 1967 book *Behind the Lines: Hanoi, December 23, 1966-January 7, 1967* was equally controversial. Salisbury eventually became the dean of American journalism. He died July 5, 1993.

REFERENCES: *New York Times*, July 6, 1993; Harrison E. Salisbury, *Behind the Lines: Hanoi, December 23, 1966–January 7, 1967*, 1967.

SAN ANTONIO FORMULA. By the fall of 1967, President Lyndon B. Johnson* was deeply concerned about what the Vietnam War* was doing to his administration and was anxious to find an honorable exit from the conflict. On September 29, 1967, in San Antonio, Texas, he delivered a conciliatory speech in which he suggested an end to the bombing* of North Vietnam if Ho Chi Minh* would engage in serious diplomatic talks to achieve a settlement and if he would stop the infiltration of troops and supplies into South Vietnam during the negotiations. North Vietnam did not even respond to the overture. Journalists dubbed the speech the "San Antonio Formula." On March 31, 1968, Johnson reiterated the offer and unilaterally stopped the bombing of North Vietnam above the 19th parallel. But it was to no avail. North Vietnam was determined to see the war to a victorious conclusion.

REFERENCES: *New York Times*, September 30 and October 1, 1967.

SAVIO, MARIO. See **FREE SPEECH MOVEMENT**.

SCHLESINGER, ARTHUR MEIER, JR. Arthur M. Schlesinger, Jr., was born October 15, 1917, in Columbus, Ohio. His father was a distinguished Harvard historian, and the younger Scheslinger followed in his father's footsteps. He attended Harvard, and his senior thesis, a biography of Orestes A. Brownson, was published in 1939. Schlesinger then joined the Harvard faculty, even though he did not have a Ph.D. In 1945, his book *The Age of Jackson* (1945) earned him a Pulitzer Prize. A decade later, his trilogy *The Age of Roosevelt* firmly established him as one of America's leading historians. In 1961, Schlesinger was appointed special adviser to President John F. Kennedy,* who had been a student of Schlesinger's at Harvard, and he served until Kennedy's assassination on November 22, 1963. Partly as a way of dealing with his own grief, Schlesinger wrote *A Thousand Days*, a highly favorable assessment of the Kennedy administration.

Although Schlesinger supported President Lyndon B. Johnson's* Great Society* civil rights* and antipoverty programs, he parted company with the president over Vietnam. He published *The Bitter Heritage*, an assessment of U.S. policy in Vietnam, in 1966. In the book, he argued that U.S. policymakers had confused communism and nationalism, had backed Ngo Dinh Diem,* a corrupt fascist, and had employed conventional tactics in fighting a guerrilla war. Schlesinger questioned the logic of the domino theory* and claimed that the Chinese, long-time enemies of the Vietnamese, would not intervene in the war. After leaving Washington, D.C., Schlesinger returned to his teaching and writing career. Today he is professor emeritus at the City University of New York.

REFERENCES: Arthur M. Schlesinger, Jr., *A Thousand Days*, 1965, and *The Bitter Heritage*, 1966.

SEALE, BOBBY. Bobby Seale was born in Dallas, Texas, October 22, 1936. His family moved to Oakland, California, when he was a young man. In 1966, he joined Huey Newton* in founding the Black Panthers.* The Black Panthers' original mission was to stop police brutality against the African-American community in Oakland. Arming themselves with cameras and shotguns, Newton and Seale began patrolling ghetto streets, trying to document cases of police brutality and defending black victims. Rejecting the middle-class values of white society and the nonviolent, civil disobedience tactics of mainstream civil rights organizations, the Black Panthers appealed to unemployed young black men living in urban ghettos. They asserted the right to defend themselves against racist attacks by the white power structure, especially the police, imposed a militaristic discipline on members, advocated arming the black community, and espoused a militant machismo philosophy.

In 1968, Seale once again came to national attention as one of the so-called Chicago Eight*—a group of antiwar* protesters who had conducted massive anti–Vietnam War* demonstrations in the streets and parks around the site of the Democratic Party's 1968 national nominating convention in August 1968. They were indicted for violating the Anti-Riot Statute, or "H. Rap Brown Law,"* an article of the Civil Rights Act of 1968 designed to reduce rioting and civil disorder. More specifically, they were accused of conspiracy to cross state lines with intent to incite riots, interfere with the performance of duties of police officers and firemen, and teach the use of incendiary devices.

The trial began on September 24, 1969, before U.S. District Court judge Julius Jennings Hoffman. The trial was a raucous affair. Hoffman rejected most defense motions and mispronounced the names of defendants and their attorneys. Insults and epithets came from both sides of the bench. The defendants sought to make the Vietnam War, racism, and domestic repression the central issues of the trial. Seale asked for a postponement of the trial after his attorney was hospitalized, but Hoffman denied the request. Belligerent and unruly, Seale labeled Hoffman a racist, fascist pig. To keep Seale quiet, Hoffman had him gagged and chained to a metal chair. Seale continued to protest by banging his chains on the metal chair. Hoffman tried chaining him to a wooden chair, but Seale still managed to disrupt the proceedings. On November 5, Hoffman declared a mistrial for Seale, severed him from the case, and sentenced him to four years in prison on sixteen contempt charges.

By 1970, Seale's own political philosophy was changing from a racial to an economic focus. He decided that capitalism was the real problem facing African Americans and that only in a socialist system could they achieve justice and equality. He also eschewed armed violence for political organizations. In 1973, Seale ran unsuccessfully for mayor of Oakland. He resigned from the Black Panther Party in 1974. In recent years, Seale has worked as a faculty member at Temple University in Philadelphia and has made considerable money on the lecture circuit. At the 1996 Democratic National Convention in Chicago, Seale did a number of interviews recalling the events of the 1968 convention.

REFERENCE: Bobby Seale, *A Lonely Rage: The Autobiography of Bobby Seale*, 1978.

SEARCH AND DESTROY. During the Vietnam War,* General William Westmoreland*, commander of Military Assistance Command, Vietnam, employed the term "search and destroy" as a euphemism for the strategy of attrition* he had adopted in fighting the Vietcong* and the North Vietnamese Army (NVA).* Westmoreland was convinced that the massive superiority in firepower the United States enjoyed over the enemy would allow for a military victory. He intended to inflict so many casualties* on the Vietcong and NVA that North Vietnam would soon be unable to replace soldiers in the field and, therefore, would not be able to continue the war. To implement this strategy, Westmoreland devised the tactic of "search and destroy" missions, in which U.S. infantry in the army and marine corps actively sought out enemy troops by patrols in the field. Once contact was made with the enemy, the infantry would engage in a firefight and call in artillery and aerial bombardment. Westmoreland also believed that once the NVA troops had been decimated, the Army of the Republic of Vietnam* (ARVN) would be able to defeat the Vietcong.

The flaw in Westmoreland's strategic thinking was his confidence that the United States would be able to inflict enormous losses on the NVA and the Vietcong without sustaining serious losses of its own. But the NVA and Vietcong enjoyed the tactical initiative during the war and could choose when and where to fight giving them an advantage. Also, every year more than 200,000 young men in North Vietnam reached draft age. For the strategy of attrition to work, the United States would have had to kill more than that number of enemy troops every year. Westmoreland never managed to kill that many, and North Vietnam strengthened its army every year. North Vietnam was dedicated to inflicting so many losses on the United States that political support for the war in America would erode. Their assumption proved correct, especially after the Tet Offensive* of 1968. Although U.S. troops slaughtered the Vietcong by the tens of thousands, the Tet Offensive convinced most Americans that the war in Vietnam had become a futile quest, that victory was not in sight and very well might be impossible to achieve. When President Richard M. Nixon* took office, the "search and destroy" strategy began to crumble as U.S. troops were gradually withdrawn from South Vietnam.

REFERENCES: James S. Olson and Randy Roberts, *Where the Domino Fell: America and Vietnam 1945–1995*, 1995.

SEDAKA, NEIL. Neil Sedaka was born March 13, 1939, in Brooklyn, New York. He was a student at Juilliard in New York in 1958, when Connie Francis* bought his song "Stupid Cupid" and turned it into a hit. He also wrote her "Where the Boys Are," a hit in 1961. Sedaka himself began performing in 1959, and two of his songs were top twenty hits—"The Diary" and "I Go Ape." Blessed with a distinctive, high-pitched voice, Sedaka then put together a string of hits between 1959 and 1962, including "Oh! Carol," "Stairway to Heaven," "Calendar Girl," "Little Devil," "Happy Birthday, Sweet Sixteen," "Breaking Up Is Hard to Do," and "Next Door to an Angel." Sedaka's singing career faded beginning in 1963, but he continued to work as a successful song writer and producer.

REFERENCE: Neil Sedaka, *Laughter In the Rain: My Own Story*, 1982.

SEEGER, PETE. Pete Seeger was born in Patterson, New York, in 1919. His father was a music professor and an avowed pacifist. As a teenager, Seeger had already been politicized with leftist values. In 1936, he entered Harvard, but he was unhappy there and left in 1938. He got a job in New York with the Archives of American Folk Music, and he developed a deep, abiding interest in the genre.

In 1940, he joined Woodie Guthrie and formed the Almanac Singers. He joined the army and the Communist Party in 1942. A supporter of labor unions and the poor, Seeger wrote and sang folk ballads that inspired the American Left during the Cold War* and red scare.

In the late 1940s, Seeger formed the folk group the Weavers and recorded the hits "Goodnight Irene" and "If I Had a Hammer." By the early 1950s, however, Seeger had been blacklisted because of his Communist Party past, even though he had quit the party in 1948. Recording contracts and concert bookings were difficult to come by. Seeger survived on the college performance circuit and did some records with Folkway Records. Before a 1955 meeting of the House Un-American Activities Committee (HUAC), Seeger refused to testify and refused to take the Fifth Amendment, arguing that HUAC's very existence violated his First Amendment rights. The next year, he recorded the hit "Where Have All the Flowers Gone" and was indicted for contempt for Congress. Seeger fought the indictment in court for the next five years, but in 1961 he was convicted of contempt of Congress and sentenced to ten years in prison. An appellate court later overturned the conviction.

During the 1960s, the political climate in America became more favorable to Seeger's iconoclastic views. His version of "We Shall Overcome" became the theme song of the civil rights movement,* and Seeger spent a good deal of time in the early 1960s touring the South. In the late 1960s, he fought against the Vietnam War.* On the *Smothers Brothers Comedy Hour** in 1966, he sang "Waist Deep in the Big Muddy," an antiwar song that CBS censors cut from the program. At the insistence of the Smothers brothers, Seeger was invited back to sing it again, which he did, but CBS soon canceled the program. Since then, Seeger has turned his attention to environmental concerns.
REFERENCE: David King Dunaway, *How Can I Keep from Singing: Pete Seeger*, 1983.

SELF-DETERMINATION. The term "self-determination" is used to describe the general demands of the red power* movement during the 1960s and 1970s. A general disregard and disrespect for tribal independence and governance characterized the political leadership in Washington, D.C., during the nineteenth century. The history of federal agencies dealing with Native Americans indicates that early in this period all pertinent branches of the federal government were involved, including the president, the State and War Departments, Congress, and the courts. Most executive activities related to Native Americans were gradually concentrated in the Bureau of Indian Affairs.

Investigations into reservation living conditions in the 1960s uncovered serious problems and inconsistencies. Some directly involved the government administration of Indian affairs. Others, however, stemmed from disturbingly low levels of health, education, and income. Many Indian lands possess tremendous potential for development due to the abundance of commercially necessary natural resources. Congress was forced into action by Native American provocation during the late 1960s and early 1970s. The confrontation at Wounded Knee, the seizure of Alcatraz Island,* the Trail of Broken Treaties caravan to Washington, D.C., the formation of pro-native action groups exemplified by the founding of the American Indian Movement,* and other similar actions triggered self-determination reform.

White House encouragement hastened self-determination legislation. The administration of President John F. Kennedy* initiated early shifts away from the dichotomy of blanket paternalism and the total termination* of federal responsibility. The Lyndon B. Johnson* adminstration focused major attention on Indian affairs. Urban and rural Native Americans benefited from federal grant-in-aid programs. President Richard Nixon* sustained the pressure on Congress to allow Indian acts and decisions to determine the future of Native Americans. President Gerald Ford in January 1975 signed what has been termed "the Magna Carta for Indians." The Indian Self-Determination and Education Assistance Act formally renounced the threat of the termination policy and affected every segment of Indian life, on and off the reservations.

The act emphasized the strengthening of Native American sovereign leadership through tribal handling of federal funding for community operation. The purpose is to develop tribal government independence. Today, most of the programs formally administered by the Bureau of Indian Affairs are managed by the tribes themselves. Some tribal leaders have, however, criticized the manner in which the act has been implemented, claiming that the end result of the Self-Determination Act has been to duplicate the existing agencies of the federal government within tribal operations. They cite delays in contract approvals, red tape, and federal dictation of operational priorities as preventing full control of tribal affairs from resting within Native American society. Many tribes acknowledge fears that if they take advantage of the benefits offered by the Self-Determination Act, Congress will withdraw recognition of tribal sovereignty* and resume the disastrous termination policy.

REFERENCES: American Indian Policy Review Commission, *Final Report*, 1977; Roxanne Dunbar Ortiz, *Indians of the Americas: Human Rights and Self-Determination*, 1984; Jack D. Forbes, *Native Americans and Nixon: Presidential Politics and Minority Self-Determination, 1969–1972*, 1981; William T. Hagan, "Tribalism Rejuvenated: The Native American since the Era of Termination," *Western Historical Quarterly* 12 (January 1981), 5–16; Hurst Hannum, *Autonomy, Self-Determination and Sovereignty: The Accommodation of Conflicting Rights*, 1990; Sharon O'Brien, *American Indian Tribal Government*, 1989; Theodore W. Taylor, *American Indian Policy*, 1983.

David Ritchey

THE SELMA RIOTS. In 1965, civil rights activists switched the focus of their voter registration drives from Mississippi to Alabama. Alabama whites reacted with all of the frustration and fear of their Mississippi counterparts. The center of the voter registration campaign was the city of Selma, a former entrepôt in the slave trade. Early in 1965, hundreds of civil rights workers associated with the Student Nonviolent Coordinating Committee* descended on central Alabama. Sheriff Jim Clark of Selma and his deputies attacked the demonstrators in what rapidly escalated into a police riot. Black people attempting to register to vote were beaten by club-toting police and attacked by police dogs. Two civil rights activists were beaten to death.

The murders brought Martin Luther King, Jr.,* and the Southern Christian Leadership Conference* into the battle. A week after the killings, King staged a protest march from Selma to the state capitol in Montgomery. He did not personally attend. The marchers were barely out of town when Alabama state troopers attacked them with tear gas and clubs, all of which was broadcast over national television. As the demonstrators fled back toward town, they were attacked and gassed by Sheriff Clark's deputies. The protesters dispersed.

On March 21, 1965, however, the march commenced again, this time with Martin Luther King, Jr., among the demonstrators. President Lyndon B. Johnson* had federalized 3,000 members of the Alabama National Guard and stationed them all along the highway from Selma to Montgomery. Thousands of liberal whites and blacks from the North joined the marchers, and they made their way safely to the state capitol, where King delivered another of his moving speeches for equality and justice. That same night, however, civil rights worker Viola Liuzzo was murdered by Klansmen. Her death convinced President Johnson to move forward with the legislation that eventually became the Voting Rights Act* of 1965.

REFERENCES: David Burner, *Making Peace with the Sixties*, 1996; David J. Garrow, *Protest at Selma: Martin Luther King, Jr., and the Voting Rights Act of 1965*, 1978; Frank Parker, *Black Votes Count: Political Empowerment in Mississippi after 1965*, 1990; Amelia Robinson, *Bridge across Jordan: The Story of the Civil Rights Struggle in Selma*, 1991.

SESAME STREET. In 1969, television producer Joan Ganz Cooney, an executive with the Public Broadcasting Corporation, acted on a long-held wish and developed a new children's program. Despairing of the wasteland that had become commercial children's television, with its cookie-cutter cartoons, situation comedies, and white, middle-class suburban images, Cooney wanted to provide a creative, alluring children's program that would appeal to urban ethnic as well as suburban white audiences and deliver knowledge to children. She hoped the program would help prepare all children, but especially urban minority children, for success in school. She named the program *Sesame Street*.

Puppeteer Jim Henson created a motley crew of Muppet characters, including Big Bird, Bert, Ernie, and Cookie Monster. The Public Broadcasting Corporation distributed the program, and it became enormously popular among white and black, poor and middle-class, and urban and rural children. *Sesame Street* programs still exist today, although critics argue that its commercial success has diluted its original mission and that it has not really had a measurable impact on the reading and math scores of its viewers.

REFERENCE: Wilbur Schramm, *The Second Harvest of Two Research-Producing Events: The Surgeon-General's Inquiry and Sesame Street*, 1976.

SEVEN DAYS IN MAY. *Seven Days in May* was a popular 1964 film about an attempted military overthrow of the U.S. government. Directed by John Frankenheimer with a screenplay by Rod Serling that was based on Fletcher Knebel and Charles Bailey's novel *Seven Days in May*, the film starred Kirk Douglas as Colonel Martin Casey, Burt Lancaster as General James Scott, Frederic March as President Jordan Lyman, and Edmond O'Brien as Senator Raymond Clark. Colonel Casey uncovers a secret plot, planned by General Scott, to overthrow President Lyman, who he believes is too liberal, too accommodationist, and too soft on communism. As such, the film is a precursor of the antimilitary attitudes that became so endemic to American culture in the late 1960s.
REFERENCE: *New York Times*, February 20, 1964.

SEX AND THE SINGLE GIRL. *Sex and the Single Girl* was the title of Helen Gurley Brown's best-selling 1962 book. Many social historians trace the beginning of the modern woman's movement to publication of *Sex and the Single Girl*, although others insist Betty Friedan's* *The Feminine Mystique* inaugurated the new era. The sexual revolution* was just beginning in 1962, and Brown rejected the prevailing cultural ethos of the early 1960s that the measure of a woman's success in Amerian society was marriage and motherhood. She encouraged single women to develop their minds and their lives, to seek out career success, to become economically independent, to compete in a man's world, and to enjoy an active, fulfilling sex life. *Sex and the Single Girl* was eventually published in twenty-eight countries and was one of the great publishing successes of the 1960s.
REFERENCE: Lucille Falkoff, *Helen Gurley Brown: The Queen of Cosmopolitan*, 1992.

THE SEXUAL REVOLUTION. Historians today look to the decade of the 1960s as an era of great social change in the United States, particularly regarding issues of gender and sexuality. It was the decade of the so-called sexual revolution, in which traditional standards of behavior and morality seemed to be changing very rapidly. The idea of the "new morality" flew in the face of convention, especially the traditional moral standard of confining sexual relations to monogamous married couples. The counterculture* promoted different notions, and praise for the so-called virtues of premarital sex, homosexuality, group sex, free love, wife swapping, and pornography surfaced into the popular culture. Many Americans, of course, had little tolerance for such ideas. Nathan Eldon Tanner, a leader of the Mormon Church, spoke, for example, of the "new morality as nothing more than the same old immorality."

Regardless of the debate in the United States over the merits of the "new morality," social change was accelerating. A series of important demographic, technological, and cultural developments was at the foundation of changing values about sexuality. In 1959, the first group of "baby boomers"—people born after the end of World War II—reached their teenage years. The demographic profile of the American population grew steadily younger throughout the decade, and by the mid-1960s, tens of millions of Americans were entering the years of their greatest sexual activity. Sex is not, of course, the domain of only the young, but hormonal realities being what they are, younger people are more sexually active than older people. It is hardly surprising, therefore, that sex became an obsessive preoccupation of the decade.

Science and technology also made their contribution to the sexual revolution. In 1960, the Searle pharmaceutical company and several other drug manufacturers began marketing the birth control pill. Development of the birth control pill had not been intended to create some sort of moral confrontation; rather, it was intended for use by married couples to ensure that procreation would be brought about at an appropriate, predesignated time, enabling the family to control its numbers and plan its economic future. Birth control was intended to promote sexual happiness and domestic tranquillity. The "pill," as it was widely called, was touted as a boost to romance, in part because its use did not interrupt the act of copulation, and it was not a burden to the woman because it was taken orally on a daily basis, like vitamins. Pregnancy was not a concern to either partner, which made for a stress-free environment and encouraged sexual activity.

Changing gender attitudes also contributed to the sexual revolution. Women like Helen Gurley Brown, and Betty Friedan,* who wrote *The Feminine Mystique* (1963), rejected the traditional notions that sex for women was nothing more than an act of procreation and that the true measure of a woman's happiness could be found only inside the home. Instead, they encouraged women to seek happiness and fulfillment outside the realm of marriage and motherhood, to build successful careers, and to enjoy sex as a physical and emotional pleasure, not just a wifely duty. Because of the availability of the birth control pill, women's advocates could also speak openly and even encouragingly about premarital and extramarital sex, both of which had long been taboos in traditional value systems. No longer were single women to be criticized or pitied.

Finally, the appearance of hippies* and the counterculture in the later 1960s promoted sexual activity. In their rejection of most American institutions, the counterculture also discarded traditional moral assumptions. Celibacy, chastity, and monogamy, which most American religious traditions had long upheld as positive virtues, became objects of ridicule to hippies, who accused their elders of being "uptight."* Sexual pleasure became an end in itself, a value in its own right, not simply a means of binding a husband to a wife and a wife to a husband.

The sexual revolution had a direct impact on American popular culture. New sexual attitudes were readily apparent in such books as Jacqueline Susann's* *Valley of the Dolls* and Helen Gurley Brown's *Sex and the Single Girl*; films like *Midnight Cowboy,* *I Am Curious (Yellow),* *The Fox,* *The Pawnbroker*, and *Bob and Carol and Ted and Alice*; plays like *Oh! Calcutta!** and *Hair**; soft-core pornographic magazines like *Penthouse*; and television programs like *Peyton Place.** Advertisers shamelessly employed sexuality to market products;

college campuses began to permit coeducational dormitories; and federal courts narrowly defined obscenity and dramatically restricted governmental powers of censorship. First Amendment advocates claimed that American society had never been so free.

But there was also a dark side to the sexual revolution. During the 1960s, the divorce rate in the United States spiraled up to the point that nearly one out of every two marriages failed. The number of single mothers, especially teenage mothers, skyrocketed. Most of them dropped out of school, ended up on welfare, and became trapped in a long-term cycle of poverty. Venereal diseases—particularly syphilis and gonorrhea—reached epidemic proportions. The number of illegal abortions and the number of women dying from them increased to such an extent that demands for legalization of abortion gained momentum. Also, the stage was set for the arrival in the United States of the AIDS virus in the 1970s. REFERENCES: Anthony Giddens, *The Transformation of Intimacy: Sexuality, Love, and Eroticism in Modern Societies*, 1992; Lawrence Lipton, *The Erotic Revolution*, 1965; Gay Talese, *Thy Neighbor's Wife*, 1980.

SHAPIRO V. THOMPSON, WASHINGTON V. LEGRANT, REYNOLDS V. SMITH.

During the 1950s and 1960s, the Supreme Court under Chief Justice Earl Warren* pursued a consistent legal goal of undermining de jure segregation, restricting the powers of the state, and expanding the rights of individuals. They were especially concerned with issues of personal privacy, which found expression in *Shapiro v. Thompson, Washington v. Legrant*, and *Reynolds v. Smith*, all of which involved the individual right to travel across state lines. To discourage welfare recipients from relocating to states with higher cash benefits, a number of states passed one-year residency requirements. Any individual applying for state welfare benefits had to be a resident of the state, and residency could not be awarded until the individual had lived in the state for twelve months. The Court overturned such laws as violations of due process and equal protection.
REFERENCE: 394 U.S. 618 (1969).

SHEEN, FULTON JOHN.

Fulton J. Sheen was born May 8, 1895, in El Paso, Texas. He attended St. Paul's Seminary in Minneapolis and was ordained a Roman Catholic priest in 1919. He then did graduate work at the Catholic University of America in Washington, D.C., and the Catholic University of Louvain, Belgium. He also studied at the Sorbonne in Paris as well as the Angelicum and Gregorian in Rome. After a stint as a parish priest in Peoria, Illinois, Sheen joined the faculty of the Catholic University of America. His first book—*God and Intelligence in Modern Philosophy*—was published in 1925, and he followed it with sixty-five more. His last book—*Treasure in Clay*—was published posthumously in 1980.

Although Sheen continued to write and publish widely, his fame was not to come as an academic. In 1930, he launched the *Catholic Hour* on NBC Radio, and the program made him the best-known Roman Catholic in the United States. In 1950, he became national director of the Society for the Propagation of the Faith. Sheen's radio program gave way to television* in 1952, and from then until 1968 he appeared on weekly television, primarily ABC's prime-time *Life Is Worth Living* and then *The Bishop Fulton Sheen Program*. On screen, Sheen served up commonsense homilies and a conservative, anticommunist commentary on world affairs. In addition to becoming a television personality, Sheen served as the auxiliary bishop of New York from 1951 to 1966, when he was appointed bishop of Rochester, New York. He retired from the diocese in 1969 and died December 9, 1979.

REFERENCES: D. P. Noonan, *Missionary with a Mike: The Bishop Sheen Story*, 1968, and *The Passion of Fulton Sheen*, 1972.

SHEPARD, ALAN BARTLETT, JR. Alan Bartlett Shepard, Jr. was born in East Derry, New Hampshire, November 18, 1923. He graduated from the U.S. Naval Academy at Annapolis, Maryland, in 1944 and was commissioned. He went into naval aviation, and during the 1950s he served as a test pilot. In 1959, Shepard was selected as one of the original U.S. astronauts for the National Aeronautics and Space Administration* (NASA). He remained on active duty for the navy, although he was posted to NASA. As part of Project Mercury, he became the first American to fly in space on May 5, 1961, when he successfully completed a suborbital flight. In 1965, Shepard was named chief of the astronaut office for NASA. He commanded the Apollo 14 mission in 1971 and became the fifth man to walk on the moon. On lunar soil, Shepard took out a golf club and ball and hit, in the moon's weak gravitational field, what he now claims is the longest drive in history. Upon his return, he was promoted to the rank of rear admiral. He retired from NASA and the navy in 1974 and went into real estate in Houston.

REFERENCES: John M. Logsdan, *The Decision to Go to the Moon: Project Apollo and the National Interest*, 1976; National Aeronautics and Space Administration, *NASA Historical Data Book*, 1988; Alan Shepard and Deke Slayton, *Moon Shot: The Inside Story of America's Race to the Moon*, 1994.

SHORT-TIMER. The term ''short-timer'' became a euphemism for a soldier whose tour of duty in Southeast Asia was about to come to an end. Vietnam was not like earlier U.S. wars, when soldiers served ''for the duration'' and had no idea when they would be able to go home. Instead, U.S. Army troops served for twelve months and U.S. marines for thirteen months. Soldiers knew, to the day, when they would be rotated out of Vietnam for other assignments or for mustering out of the military. For obvious reasons, ''short-timers'' were the envy of soldiers who still had most of their tours of duty ahead of them. ''Short-timers'' often advertised their status by placing calendars on their helmet covers or by carrying a ''short-timer's stick,'' with knife notches indicating the number of days left to serve. At the same time, "short-timers" also worried constantly about the possibility of being killed in action with only a few days left to serve. REFERENCE: Dudley Acker, "Short-Timer," in James S. Olson, ed., *Historical Dictionary of the Vietnam War*, 1988.

SIHANOUK, NORODOM. Norodom Sihanouk was born in Cambodia in 1922; in 1941, French imperial authorities crowned him king of Cambodia. He was only a puppet monarch, however, until 1954, when Cambodia received its independence. Sihanouk soon found himself walking a political tightrope between the People's Republic of China and North Vietnam and between North Vietnam and the United States. He tried to maintain Cambodia's neutrality, but it became increasingly difficult as North Vietnamese troops deployed into Cambodia and the Vietcong* used Cambodian sanctuaries to escape U.S. military retaliation. In 1969, Sihanouk finally acquiesced to American demands for permission to bomb North Vietnam Army* installations in Cambodia, but the Richard Nixon* administration still viewed him as a political obstacle to successful pursuance of the war. In March 1970, with the assistance of the United States, Cambodian military Leader Lon Nol deposed Sihanouk, who then went to China, where he unsuccessfully tried to stage a recovery of his power. After the Khmer Rouge reign of terror in the 1970s, Sihanouk returned to Cambodia as king, but his power was limited. His son, Norodom Ranariddh, became premier in the 1990s. As late as May 1996, Khmer Rouge communists were still trying to assassinate Sihanouk.
REFERENCES: William Shawcross, *Sideshow: Kissinger, Nixon, and the Destruction of Cambodia*, 1979; Norodom Sihanouk, *Sihanouk Reminiscences*, 1992.

"SILENT MAJORITY" SPEECH. President Richard Nixon's* November 3, 1969, "silent majority" speech was made in response to the massive antiwar protest of the Moratorium Day demonstration* of October 15 and in anticipation of the moratorium days set for mid-November. In this televised speech, Nixon both attacked the antiwar movement* as subversive of his administration's policies and outlined a plan of action for the future. He made a patriotic appeal to "the great silent majority" of Americans to support his search for a "just and lasting peace" as an alternative to immediate withdrawal, which, he stated, would lead to "a collapse of confidence in American leadership, not only in Asia but throughout the world."

Nixon outlined the history of American involvement in Vietnam since his inauguration and stated that the previous administrations had "Americanized the war," but his administration would henceforth "Vietnamize the search for peace." To this end, he described a plan of withdrawal of American forces from Vietnam to correspond with the buildup and strengthening of South Vietnam's forces. He then attacked the antiwar movement as a "vocal minority" and stated that "North Vietnam cannot defeat or humiliate the United States. Only Americans can do that." Despite the White House claim of 80,000 letters and telegrams of support following the speech, the Moratorium Day demonstrations of mid-November exceeded their October counterparts. Nevertheless, Nixon's appeal to patriotism and his promise of Vietnamization* and the consequent return of American troops marked the beginning of the end of the massive antiwar demonstrations of the Vietnam era.

REFERENCES: *New York Times*, November 4–5, 1969.

Linda Alkana

SILENT SPRING. See **CARSON, RACHEL**.

SILVER ACT OF 1963. The Silver Act of 1963 repealed the Silver Purchase Act of 1934. By the 1960s, silver was in short supply, so the new law permitted the Treasury Department to withdraw all silver certificates—currency redeemable in pure silver—from circulation. The government no longer had to purchase new silver from mines at fixed prices, a change that allowed silver prices to seek a market-determined level.

REFERENCE: James S. Olson, ed., *Dictionary of United States Economic History*, 1991.

SIMON AND GARFUNKEL. Simon and Garfunkel were an extraordinarily popular vocal group of the 1960s. Formed in New York City in 1962, the duo included Paul Simon and Arthur Garfunkel. The two began harmonizing together in the sixth grade, singing doo-wop* hits. They recorded the minor hit "Hey, Schoolgirl" as Tom and Jerry in 1957, broke up, and then came together again in 1962. They recorded an album entitled *Wednesday Morning*, and one of its songs—"Sounds of Silence"—went to the top of the pop charts in 1965 and became an early example of a genre that became known as "folk rock." Four of their singles and three albums reached the top thirty in 1966, including "I Am a Rock" and "Homeward Bound." In 1967, they had another number one hit—"Mrs. Robinson," part of the sound track to the film *The Graduate*.* Their last collaboration of the 1960s, the album *Bridge over Troubled Waters*, reached number one in the spring of 1970. Simon and Garfunkel then broke up.

REFERENCE: Patricia Romanowski and Holly George-Warren, eds., *The New Rolling Stone Encyclopedia of Rock and Roll*, 1996.

SING ALONG WITH MITCH. Mitch Miller was a highly successful music recorder in the 1950s, heading up Columbia Records' recording division. He abhorred rock and roll, not only for what he considered its musical shortcomings but because it had sent his music—old-fashioned melodies—into a severe decline. Miller instinctively knew that millions of other Americans shared his frustration, and he sold an idea to NBC. The first episode of *Sing Along with Mitch* appeared on January 27, 1961, featuring musical performances with lyrics printed as subtitles on the screen, allowing the audience to sing along. Miller became an overnight celebrity, and *Sing Along with Mitch* appeared weekly until

its last episode on September 2, 1966. By that time, rock and roll had buried the old melodies.
REFERENCE: Tim Brooks and Earle Marsh, *The Complete Directory to Prime Time Network and Cable TV Shows*, 1995.

SIRHAN, SIRHAN BISHARA. Sirhan Bishara Sirhan, born March 19, 1944, was a Jerusalem-born Palestinian with Jordanian citizenship. In January 1957, the Sirhan family immigrated to the United States, where they took up permanent residence. Shortly after their arrival, however, the family broke up in discord, the mother moving to California with the five children and the father remaining in New York until he eventually returned to Jordan. While growing up, Sirhan Sirhan learned that several of his Jordanian relatives had died at the hands of Israeli soldiers. He dreamed of returning to Jordan, which he considered his homeland, and avenging their deaths. Sirhan was an exemplary student whose fantasies included political fame. At the age of twenty-four, Sirhan, then a stock clerk, committed an act that assured that his name would never be forgotten.

At 12:15 A.M. on June 5, 1968, in the kitchen of the Ambassador Hotel in Los Angeles, Sirhan emptied eight rounds of his cheap .22 caliber pistol, killing Senator Robert F. Kennedy* of New York. Senator Kennedy was celebrating his victory in the California Democratic presidential primary. Papers later found in Sirhan's home indicated that Kennedy needed to be killed before June 5, the first anniversary of Israel's smashing victory over Syria, Jordan, and the United Arab Republic in the Six-Day War. Kennedy seemed to be the likely Democratic nominee for president, and he was a firm supporter of Israel.

The Kennedy name was a legend in the United States and around the world. Robert Kennedy was the nostalgic likeness of his older brother John, who had been assassinated in 1963. News of the senator's death shocked the nation and affected people around the world. In the United States, businesses closed, sports and social events were postponed, political candidates put their campaigns on hold, and the Democratic Party was thrown into turmoil. Kennedy's death, along with that of Martin Luther King, Jr.,* two months earlier, contributed to the growing mood of cynicism in the United States. Sirhan Sirhan was convicted of premeditated first-degree murder and sentenced to life in prison. Today, he is still serving that sentence in a California penitentiary.
REFERENCES: Arthur M. Schlesinger, Jr., *Robert F. Kennedy and His Times*, 1979; *New York Times*, June 6–12, 1968.

Jennifer Sherman

SIT-INS. The so-called sit-in became one of the most successful tactics of the nonviolent phase of the civil rights movement.* In February 1960, four young students at North Carolina A&T, an all-black state college, decided to protest segregation in Greenville, North Carolina's, restaurants and lunch counters. One of the students was Jesse Jackson,* who would go on to become one of the most prominent civil rights leaders in U.S. history. The four students entered Woolworth's department store in downtown Greenville, took seats at the store lunch counter, which catered only to whites, and demanded to be served. The store would not comply, and the students refused to leave. They had to be carried out of Woolworth's by police. The next day, eighty-five North Carolina A&T students crowded into Woolworth's, disrupting normal business and making a complete nuisance of themselves, driving away white customers and making Woolworth's the object of nationwide contempt.

The sit-in was successful and led to the desegregation of the lunch counter. Civil rights activists then exported the tactic from North Carolina to the rest of the South, adding stores, theaters, and doctors' offices to the list of sites suitable for sit-ins. Throughout the South, business proprietors had to cave in to integration in order to prevent complete disruption of business operations.

REFERENCES: William Chafe, *Civilities and Civil Rights: Greensboro, North Carolina, and the Black Struggle for Freedom*, 1980; James H. Laue, *Direct Action and Desegregation, 1960–1962*, 1989; Martin Oppenheimer, *The Sit-In Movement of 1960*, 1989.

SIX-DAY WAR. In June 1967 war once again erupted in the Middle East. The belligerents included Egypt, Syria, and Israel, with the Egyptians and Syrians receiving considerable assistance from the Soviet Union and from other Arab nations. The war lasted only six days, with the Israelis administering a crushing defeat on the Arab armies. Claiming the need to do so because of national security, Israel seized control of the Golan Heights on the Syrian frontier and large segments of the Sinai Peninsula, formerly Egyptian territory. Israeli forces also took complete control of the city of Jerusalem and several regions on the west bank of the Jordan River. The United States sided with Israel, and the war led to the severing of U.S. diplomatic relations with Egypt and Syria.

REFERENCE: Robert W. Stookey, *America and the Arab States*, 1975.

SKATEBOARDING. Skateboarding became a fad during the 1960s, just when surfing* was becoming extraordinarily popular. At first the skateboard—roller skates attached to a thirty-inch-by-eight-inch board—was used by surfers to remain in shape even when they could not be at the beach riding the waves. Jan and Dean's 1964 pop hit "Sidewalk Surfin' " launched the craze, and by the end of the year nearly 100 companies manufactured skateboards. The First Annual Skateboard Championship brought 10,000 competitors to Anaheim Stadium in 1965.

REFERENCE: Patricia Romanowski and Holly George-Warren, eds., *The New Rolling Stone Encyclopedia of Rock and Roll*, 1996.

SMITH, MARGARET CHASE. Born Margaret Madeline Chase December 14, 1897, in Skowhegan, Maine, she taught in the public schools until becoming secretary to her husband, Clyde Harold Smith, when he entered Congress in 1937. With the death of her husband in 1940, she won a special election to fill the vacancy and entered Congress as a Republican. She was reelected four times. In 1948, she was elected to the U.S. Senate, the only woman serving there at the time. A moderate Republican, Smith was reelected in 1954, 1960, and 1966. She retired from the Senate in 1969. Margaret Chase Smith died October 29, 1995.

REFERENCES: Frank Graham, *Margaret Chase Smith: Woman of Courage*, 1964; *New York Times*, October 30, 1995.

SMOKING. See **SURGEON GENERAL'S REPORT**.

THE SMOTHERS BROTHERS COMEDY HOUR. The Smothers Brothers Comedy Hour was first broadcast by CBS on February 5, 1967. The Smothers Brothers were a singing-comedy act that had gained national fame during the folk music popularity explosion of the early 1960s. In a midseason attempt to steal viewers from NBC's *Bonanza*,* CBS gave the brothers their own show on Sunday night. It quickly became very popular and extremely controversial. Among the more controversial shows was one in September 1967 in which the special guest was the folksinger Pete Seeger,* making his first appearance on television* after a sixteen-year blacklisting. He was scheduled to perform his virulently antiwar* song "Waist Deep in the Big Muddy," but the network cut the segment when Seeger, backed by the Smothers Brothers, refused to cut the most controversial verse.

In February 1968, after a long battle with CBS, Tommy Smothers once again introduced Seeger on the show, and this time he was allowed to perform the song in its entirety. The Smothers Brothers continued to battle the network and its censors, but they were finally canceled in 1969, even though the program was still extremely popular. The final straws were an interview with Joan Baez,* who made a reference to her husband's prison term for draft* evasion, and a segment featuring Dr. Benjamin Spock.* Using a technical clause in the Smothers Brothers contract relating to their furnishing the network affiliates with a broadcast tape prior to the showing, the network claimed breach of contract when the final tape of the April 14 show featuring Spock was several days late getting to the affiliates. It was later shown that the network censors kept sending back parts of the tape for editing until it was too late for the show to furnish the final tape to the affiliates. The Smothers Brothers would sue CBS and win their case. The last episode of the show was broadcast in May 1970.

REFERENCE: Thomas Finton, *A Historical Analysis of the CBS–Smothers Brothers Controversy*, 1977.

SNYDER, GARY. Gary Snyder was one of the leading figures of the beat* generation of the 1950s and early 1960s. He was born May 8, 1930, in San Francisco. He graduated from Reed College in Oregon in 1951 and then did graduate work at Indiana University and the University of California at Berkeley. Interested in nature and ecology, Snyder worked as a forest ranger for a time in the early 1950s and then went to Japan, where he studied Buddhism. There he acquired a Buddhist sense of discipline in terms of the relationship of the individual to the larger world. He began writing prolifically in the late 1950s, arguing that throughout human history, beneath the surface issues of petty politics and mundane greed, existed a "great subculture" transcending time and space, manifesting itself differently in different times, such as shamanism in the premodern world, Quakerism in the seventeenth century, and the hippie* movement in the twentieth century. All of these movements rejected authority, elevated individual human nature, and preached connections between the natural and spiritual worlds. Snyder's philosophy rejected modern technology, promoted the use of simple crafts, and advocated a low-energy consumption existence, loyalty to bodily impulses, and respect for nature. In 1972, his writings were collected and published as *The Old Ways*.

REFERENCES: Bruce Cook, *The Beat Generation*, 1971; John Arthur Maynard, *Venice West: The Beat Generation in Southern California*, 1991; Steven Watson, *The Birth of the Beat Generation, 1944–1960*, 1995.

SONNY AND CHER. Salvatore Bono was born February 16, 1935, in Detroit, and Cherilyn Sarkasian LaPier was born May 20, 1946, in El Centro, California. They married in 1964 and became very popular hippie*-style pop singers. After several unsuccessful releases, they made a number one hit in 1965—"I Got You Babe." Bono wrote and produced the record, as well as the string of hits that followed: "Baby Don't Go," "The Beat Goes On," "Laugh at Me," "All I Really Wanna Do," and "You Better Sit Down Kids." Their career as a duo peaked then, although they made two top ten hits in 1971–1972—"All I Ever Need Is You" and "A Cowboy's Work Is Never Done." They had a successful, if short, Las Vegas career, and their *Sonny and Cher* television* variety show gave them a national profile. Sonny and Cher divorced in 1975. Sonny Bono died in a skiing accident on January 6, 1998.

REFERENCE: Thomas Braun, *Sonny and Cher*, 1978.

SONTAG, SUSAN. Susan Sontag was born in New York City in 1933, raised in Tucson and Los Angeles, and educated at Berkeley and Harvard. Brilliant, trendy, and intellectually fashionable, she wrote *Benefactor* (1963), *Against Interpretation* (1966), *Death Kit* (1967), *Trip to Hanoi* (1968), *Styles of Radical Will* (1969), and *Art of Revolution* (1970). A contemporary critic of American culture, she wrote that "most people in this society who aren't utterly mad are, at best, reformed or potential lunatics." After visiting North Vietnam, she decided that country epitomized patriotism, neighborliness, joy, and faith in the human condition. She reserved the sharpest barbs in her verbal arsenal, not surprisingly, for her own culture. There is no hope for the West, no redemption for "what this particular civilization has wrought upon the world. The white race is the cancer of human history." She was especially eloquent in her descriptions of American degradation, a decline inherent in a lack of genuine guilt over rampant consumerism, social alienation, bourgeois expectations, moral bankruptcy, psychological impotence, and the inability to communicate or sustain relationships.

Nor did intellectuals escape her wrath. In what many critics considered an anti-intellectual diatribe, she raged against the flight from feeling in modern literary criticism, the futile attempt by scholars to interpret literature, to reduce its contents to convenient intellectual categories. All it created, she argued, was the "perennial, never consummated project of interpretation," which is inherently "reactionary, impertinent, cowardly, and stifling." She went on to argue that "the world, our world, is depleted, impoverished enough. Away with all duplicates of it, until we again experience more immediately what we have." Interpretation buries the aesthetic experience, preventing people from coming to terms emotionally with art. "The effusion of interpretation of art today poisons our sensibilities." The plague of the modern mind, Sontag reasoned, is too much thinking, not enough feeling.

In the 1970s, after a bout with breast cancer, Sontag put her fertile mind to work examining the relationship between disease and culture. Her 1977 book *Illness as Metaphor* rested on the premise that cultures mythologize what they do not understand, producing an endless series of very potent and potentially misleading metaphors. For cancer, as for tuberculosis in an earlier generation, society tried to find psychosocial etiologies for the disease. Since cancer has defied understanding for so long, it has produced a particularly large and intoxicating lexicon of metaphors. So does AIDS, which Sontag wrote about in her 1989 book, *AIDS and Its Metaphors*.
REFERENCE: Liam Kennedy, *Susan Sontag*, 1995.

SOUL. "Soul" was a musical form that emerged late in the 1950s from African-American rhythm and blues. It took a secular approach to gospel rhythms and added the funk rhythms. Otis Redding,* Wilson Pickett, the Impressions, Marvin Gaye,* the Temptations, Smokey Robinson, the Supremes,* and Aretha Franklin* were all part of early soul music. The term "soul" was also an African-American slang term in the mid-1960s that meant real, sincere, and authentic.
REFERENCE: Patricia Romanowski and Holly George-Warren, eds., *The New Rolling Stone Encyclopedia of Rock and Roll*, 1996.

SOUL ON ICE. See **CLEAVER, ELDRIDGE**.

THE SOUND OF MUSIC. *The Sound of Music* was the most commercially successful film of the 1960s and perhaps the most watched movie in film history. Released in 1965, it was based on the 1959 Rogers and Hammerstein Broadway hit of the same name. It starred Christopher Plummer as Admiral Georg von Trapp and Julie Andrews* as Maria, the novice-nanny who eventually marries von Trapp. The film is set in the pre–World War II Austrian countryside, shortly after the 1938 German *Anschluss* that made Austria part of Germany. The admiral has no intention of serving in the Third Reich's navy, and eventually he must flee Austria for Switzerland, bringing his family with him across the Alps. *The Sound of Music* was the perfect film for America in the early 1960s: naive, optimistic, and generous of spirit.

REFERENCE: *New York Times*, March 3, 1965.

SOUTHERN CHRISTIAN LEADERSHIP CONFERENCE. The Southern Christian Leadership Conference (SCLC) emerged out of the Montgomery, Alabama, bus boycott of 1956. Rev. Martin Luther King, Jr.,* had established the Montgomery Improvement Association to implement the boycott, and his success in desegregating the public transportation system of Montgomery brought him national attention. In January 1957, just after city officials in Montgomery agreed to desegregate the buses, black ministers from ten southern states met at the Ebenezer Baptist Church in Atlanta and formed the Southern Christian Leadership Conference. They elected King as the SCLC's first president.

With the goals of achieving the desegregation of public facilities, public schools, and public transportation, as well as protecting the right to vote, SCLC leaders urged black people to refuse to cooperate with the institutions of a segregated society. They urged nonviolent civil disobedience and mass protest to achieve their objectives. Because of its close ties to the black church, which was by far the most influential institution in African-American society, the SCLC soon became the most powerful voice among southern blacks in the civil rights movement.* When Congress finally passed the Civil Rights Act of 1964 and the Voting Rights Act* of 1965, it was reacting to initiatives first established by the Southern Christian Leadership Conference.

The Southern Christian Leadership Conference retained its preeminent position in the civil rights movement until the assassination of Martin Luther King, Jr., in April 1968. The SCLC elected Ralph Abernathy* to succeed King, but he had none of King's charisma and few of his administrative abilities. Under Abernathy, the SCLC continued with the Poor People's Campaign,* which King had planned. By that time, however, the SCLC had been eclipsed in visibility by more militant black power* groups. The SCLC still exists today as an interracial, civil rights advocacy group.

REFERENCE: David J. Garrow, *Bearing the Cross: Martin Luther King, Jr., and the Southern Christian Leadership Conference*, 1986.

SPACE RACE. When the Soviet Union launched the satellite *Sputnik*, on October 4, 1957, the United States experienced a technological identity crisis. At the time, the Cold War* rivalry was at its peak, and each side was committed to proving the superiority of its own ideology and the society it had spawned. Beating the United States into space was a public relations coup for the Soviet Union, and in the wake of that crisis, Congress established in 1958 the National Aeronautics and Space Administration* (NASA). During the next two years, a number of existing military space programs were transferred to the new agency, but the fortunes of the U.S. space program did not develop very well. While the Soviet Union was putting increasingly heavy payloads into earth orbit, demonstrating the overwhelming superiority of the country's rocket thrusters, NASA was presiding over a series of dismal failures, most of them broadcast over national television. While Russian rockets apparently functioned flawlessly, American rockets underwent a series of spectacular failures, blowing up on the launch pads or veering out of control like a child's Roman candle on the Fourth of July.

In 1959, America's space fortunes finally appeared to improve. Vanguard rocket launches became somewhat more successful, and on April 10, 1959, the National Aeronautics and Space Administration introduced the first American astronauts to the public. Project Mercury, in which an American astronaut would be squeezed into a tiny capsule and launched into space, was designed to vault the United States ahead of the Soviet space program. The first seven men selected were military test pilots: John Glenn,* Alan Shepard,* Virgil Grissom,* Wally Schirra, Donald Slayton, Gordon Cooper, and Scott Carpenter. The astronauts became instant celebrities.

But the Russians soon had another humiliation to serve. Just when the American program seemed to be off and running, the Soviet Union upstaged the United States once again. On April 12, 1961, the Russians placed cosmonaut Yuri Gagarin in orbit around the earth in the space capsule *Vostok*. The *Vostok* circled the earth for more than four days before returning Gagarin safely. The Soviet Union exploded with excitement and pride, and Americans ate humble pie, wondering whether the Russian juggernaut could be stopped.

The Soviet space victory posed a serious political problem to the John F. Kennedy* administration, which was already in hot water. The bungled Bay of Pigs* invasion in Cuba was also in the headlines, and it appeared that at the moment of the Soviet Union's greatest triumph, the United States was in the midst of an ignominious defeat. The young president needed some good news, and he needed a crusade to reestablish American technological superiority over the Russians. He had been in the White House barely two months before predictions of the great American decline began, apparently, to be fulfilled.

Kennedy did not have to wait long. Three weeks after Gagarin's momentous flight, NASA's Project Mercury finally yielded results. On May 5, 1961, astronaut Alan Shepard, aboard the Project Mercury space capsule *Freedom 7*, successfully completed a suborbital flight into space. Less than twenty minutes in duration, Shepard's flight was hardly a match for Gagarin's marathon, but it was enough to inject confidence into the American space program and make Alan Shepard a certifiable American hero. Kennedy sensed the political capital to be earned from successes in space. On May 25, 1961, he addressed Congress and said, ''I believe that this nation should commit itself to achieving the goal, before this decade is out, of landing a man on the moon and returning him safely to earth.'' The race to the moon was on.

Virgil ''Gus'' Grissom became the second American in space in July. Aboard the Mercury spacecraft *Liberty Bell*, Grissom made the same suborbital flight that Shepard had done. But upon his reentry and splashdown, Grissom nearly drowned when a detonator malfunction blew off the *Liberty Bell*'s hatch cover prematurely, before the navy's rescue team arrived on the scene. Seawater filled the capsule. Due to the additional weight of the seawater, the rescue helicopter was unable to retrieve the capsule. Fortunately, the astronaut was unharmed. Grissom's suborbital flight and near-fatal accident proved crucial in developing a new life vest for astronauts and a new survival kit that included such things as shark repellent. It also set the stage for John Glenn's* orbital flight.

But the suborbital flights, popular though they were, were pale comparisons to the Russian space program, which was regularly launching cosmonauts into multiple orbits of the earth. The third Mercury flight was designed to prove that the United States could do the same. Astronaut John H. Glenn, Jr., had been selected to become the first American to fly in orbit around the earth. The flight took place in February 1962. Glenn was launched into earth orbit in his Mercury space capsule. He almost died during the return to earth, when the heat shield of his capsule malfunctioned, but the American public did not really hear of the extent of his problem until much later. Finally, the American space program seemed to match its Soviet counterpart.

The Mercury program then gave way to the Gemini program, in which American astronauts orbited the earth in two-man spacecrafts. Gemini's string of successful launches prepared the way for the Apollo program—a three-man spacecraft engineered to take American astronauts to the moon. But on June 27, 1967, astronauts Virgil Grissom, Edward H. White, and Roger B. Chaffee of the *Apollo 1* crew became the first casualties of the American space program. During a practice session in the *Apollo 1* capsule, the crew experienced a number of problems. When the capsule was pressurized with pure oxygen at thirty-six pounds per square inch to simulate flight conditions, the crew noticed a strange, faint odor. Scientists stopped the simulation and took samples of the air in the capsule, but they detected nothing unusual. The capsule was repressurized, and the simulation continued. But at 6:30 P.M., an electrical spark ignited the oxygen. Due to the pressurization of the cabin, the heat reached nearly 2,000 degrees; heat-resistant materials melted, and the crew died in a matter of seconds. After the *Apollo 1* tragedy, the National Aeronautics and Space Administration developed elaborate new safety procedures, and the Apollo capsule had to be redesigned.

After the *Apollo 1* disaster, NASA reengineered its program and again set its sight on the moon. In 1968 and early 1969, a series of successful Apollo flights had placed American astronauts in orbit around the moon and returned them to earth. The crusade came to fruition on July 21, 1969, when astronaut Neil Armstrong walked on the moon. The Apollo 11 spacecraft *Columbia* had taken Armstrong, Edwin ''Buzz'' Aldrin, and Michael Collins into a lunar orbit, and then Armstrong and Aldrin took a lunar landing vehicle named *Eagle* to the surface of the moon. Armstrong was the first to step out of the *Eagle* and onto the moon, remarking as he did so, ''That's one small step for man, one giant leap for mankind.'' A few minutes later, Aldrin joined Armstrong, and they planted a U.S. flag on the moon. The two astronauts collected rock samples for more than two hours, took hundreds of photographs, and then got back aboard the *Eagle*.

Back at home, hundreds of millions of people watched live video of the visit to the moon, and most of the world viewed the event as a triumph of American technology, victory over the Soviet Union in the space race. The *Eagle* left the moon after twenty-one hours and rendezvoused with *Columbia*, where Collins was awaiting the return of Armstrong and Aldrin. The astronauts returned to earth on July 24, splashing down safely in the Pacific Ocean. The space race was over, and the United States had won. Capitalism, most Americans concluded, was indeed superior in every way to communism.

REFERENCES: John M. Logsdan, *The Decision to Go to the Moon: Project Apollo and the National Interest*, 1976; National Aeronautics and Space Administration, *NASA Historical Data Book*, 1988; Alan Shepard and Deke Slayton, *Moon Shot: The Inside Story of America's Race to the Moon*, 1994.

SPARTACUS. Directed by Stanley Kubrick, *Spartacus* starred Kirk Douglas,* Tony Curtis, Jean Simmons, John Ireland, Laurence Olivier, and Peter Ustinov. By 1960 Hollywood's political war between liberals and conservatives had moved to a celluloid battlefield. Epic films like *The Robe* and *Ben Hur* in the mid-1950s popularized the Jewish struggle for freedom in the Roman Empire, and *Spartacus*, the story of the uprising of slaves against their Roman masters, was released in 1960. *Spartacus* was based on Howard Fast's novel of the same name. During the late 1940s and 1950s, Fast was blacklisted in Hollywood because of his links to the Communist Party. Kirk Douglas, whose politics were quite liberal, loved *Spartacus* and bought the movie rights. A liberal Democrat, Douglas detested the excesses of the red scare* and decided to hire Dalton Trumbo, one of the Hollywood Ten, who was still blacklisted and ghostwriting scripts, to write the screenplay for *Spartacus*. Douglas was making a political statement in *Spartacus*—celebrating the liberation of oppressed people and using previously oppressed actors and writers to do the job.

REFERENCE: Kirk Douglas, *The Ragman's Son: An Autobiography*, 1988.

SPECIAL FORCES. In 1952, the U.S. Army established the Special Forces, a military unit whose purpose was to fight guerrilla wars behind enemy lines. By the time of the Vietnam War,* the Special Forces had developed into the army's main unit for sustaining counterinsurgency* activities in a military conflict. The 1st U.S. Army Special Forces Group was formed in Japan in June 1957, and several months later elements of the 1st Special Forces were deployed to Na Trang, South Vietnam, to train Army of the Republic of Vietnam (ARVN) commandos. President John F. Kennedy* had a fascination for counterinsurgency tactics, and his interest gave the Special Forces an elan they had not possessed before. Over the opposition of many army senior officers, he author-ized the wearing of the distinctive ''green beret,'' which gave the Special Forces its nickname. Kennedy expanded the Special Forces from 2,500 to 10,000 troops, and in 1963 he had the Special Forces assume control of the Central Intelligence Agency's* (CIA) counterinsurgency program in South Vietnam.

On October 1, 1964, the Fifth Special Forces Group arrived in Vietnam and established its headquarters at Nha Trang. The first border camp, where Mon-tagnard tribesmen received military training to assist ARVN, had been placed at Ban Me Thuot in 1961, but the Fifth Special Forces expanded the program, building it up to 42,000 troops and dozens of border camps. The camps were located along supply and infiltration* routes. In 1966, the Special Forces mission changed somewhat when they were ordered to organize Mobile Strike Forces to attack Vietcong* and North Vietnamese Army* bases. They also administered thousands of educational, welfare, and medical projects for South Vietnamese civilians. The last Special Forces units departed South Vietnam in March 1971. REFERENCE: Shelby M. Stanton, *Green Berets At War*, 1985.

SPECK, RICHARD. Richard Speck was born in Monmouth, Illinois, Decem-ber 6, 1941. He was one of eight children born to Benjamin and Mary Margaret Speck. When Richard was six, his father died. His mother remarried a Texan named Carl Lindberg. The family moved to Dallas in 1950. Speck's adolescence foreshadowed his dark future. He dropped out of school in the ninth grade, and he was arrested for the first time at age thirteen for starting a fire in a used car lot. The police arrested him forty times over the next eleven years, and he served two jail sentences.

In 1960, Speck married fifteen-year-old Shirley Malone and had a daughter by her before receiving a two-year sentence at the Texas Department of Cor-rections prison in Huntsville, Texas. He had been convicted of burglary and forgery. A divorce followed his release from prison, and in March 1966 Speck returned to Monmouth. In April, he moved to Chicago, where he worked off and on as a seaman and earned a reputation for heavy drinking and barroom brawling.

On July 12, 1966, Speck learned that a job had fallen through, and he spent most of the next day drinking. He left a bar about 10:30 P.M. and walked to a suburban neighborhood. There he knocked on the door of an apartment con-taining six young women students from the South Chicago Community Hospital School of Nurses. One of the young women opened the door, and Speck forced his way in. He told the students that he would not hurt them but would only tie them up. He claimed to need money to get to New Orleans. He bound each of the young women with strips of bedsheets. Three other students then entered the apartment, and Speck tied them up too. Then he led each woman, one at a time, into a back room where he systematically strangled and stabbed them. He also raped one of the victims. One of the nurses, Corazon Atienza, managed to hide under a bed and remained safe. Speck forgot how many nurses he had actually killed. Atienza heard an alarm clock ring at 5:30 A.M. and waited an hour before emerging from her hiding place. She found the bodies of her eight friends and climbed onto a ledge, screaming, "They are all dead! My friends are all dead! Oh, God, I'm the only one alive."

Atienza described the murderer to police, and by the next day detectives had matched fingerprints with Speck's. Upon learning that he was a suspect, Speck attempted to commit suicide by slashing his wrists. He was taken to Cook County Hospital, and a doctor recognized his tattoo—"Born to Raise Hell"—from previous care and called the police. Nine months later, a jury deliberated less than an hour before convicting him of murder. He was sentenced to death, but in 1972 the Supreme Court struck down the death penalty. Speck was resentenced to eight consecutive terms of 50 to 150 years. He died of a heart attack December 5, 1991.

Speck's heinous crime horrified America. No longer could people assume that they were safe, even in their own homes. Five years after his death, he returned to the headlines when Illinois prison authorities discovered several videotapes. Speck had smuggled a video camera into the penitentiary and produced several pornographic films of homosexual acts between himself and other inmates. He also commented on what a wonderful life he enjoyed in prison—all the sex, drugs, and alcohol he needed to be happy. The tapes precipitated a political scandal in Illinois and calls for an investigation into the criminal justice system.
REFERENCES: Dennis L. Brio, *The Crime of the Century: Richard Speck and the Murder of Eight Student Nurses*, 1993; *New York Times*, July 14–16, 1966, and December 6, 1991.

Cory Toole

SPEED. See **METHAMPHETAMINE**.

SPELLMAN, FRANCIS JOSEPH. Francis Joseph Spellman was born May 4, 1889, in Whitman, Massachusetts. He graduated from Fordham University in 1911 and was ordained a Roman Catholic priest. Spellman then attended the North American College in Rome, and in 1916 he became a parish priest in Roxbury. Two years later, Spellman headed the Cathedral of the Holy Cross in Boston, and in 1922 he was appointed vice chancellor of the diocese of Boston, a position he held until 1925. That year, Spellman became an attaché to the papal secretary of state in Rome. In 1932, he was appointed auxiliary bishop of Boston. He was known for his patience, tolerance, and emotional equilibrium. In 1939, he became archbishop of New York, and he received the red cap of a cardinal in 1946. Francis Cardinal Spellman remained at the head of the New York archdiocese for the rest of his life. He was an outspoken opponent of fascism and communism, a gifted administrator, and one of the most prominent Catholics of his time. He died December 2, 1967.
REFERENCES: Robert I. Gannon, *The Cardinal Spellman Story*, 1962; *New York Times*, December 3, 1967.

SPOCK, BENJAMIN McLANE. Benjamin McLane Spock was born May 2, 1903, in New Haven, Connecticut. He graduated from Yale in 1929 and took a medical degree from Columbia in 1933. He specialized in pediatrics and psychiatry and served a tour of duty in the navy during World War II. While on duty, he wrote *The Common Sense Book of Baby and Child Care*. It was published in 1946 and eventually became one of the most successful books in American publishing history. The timing of the book could not have been more propitious. The first infants of the post–World War II "baby boom" were just being born, and Dr. Spock offered their mothers revolutionary advice on child raising. Until his book, parents were usually advised to raise their infants on firm, strict schedules, feeding them well-defined diets and making them sleep, play, and eat on a timeline. Spock's book advised mothers to relax, to understand that each child and each parent were unique and that no firm rules could be applied to everybody. By the late 1950s, Benjamin Spock had become the authoritative voice on child care in the United States.

He was also politically active by that time. He opposed the testing of nuclear weapons because of radioactive contamination, and from 1963 to 1967 Spock served as president of the National Committee for a Sane Nuclear Policy.* He was also a bitter, outspoken critic of U.S. involvement in Vietnam. He actively participated in acts of civil disobedience to protest the draft,* advising young men not to register for the selective service, to burn their draft cards, and not to report for physicals. In 1968, he was convicted of conspiracy to violate draft laws, but the conviction was overturned on appeal. Spock ran for president in 1972 on the People's Party ticket but managed to receive only 78,000 votes. After Vietnam, he continued his activism, protesting nuclear weapons, nuclear power plants, and U.S. defense spending. In 1996, at the age of ninety-three, Spock was still lecturing about politics and medicine. Spock died March 16, 1998.

REFERENCE: Lynn Z. Bloom, *Doctor Spock: Biography of a Conservative Radical*, 1972.

SPRING MOBILIZATION TO END THE WAR IN VIETNAM. The Spring Mobilization to End the War in Vietnam was organized on November 26, 1966, to sponsor antiwar* demonstrations in the spring of 1967. Veteran peace activist A. J. Muste* was chairman of the group, and its four vice chairmen were David Dellinger,* editor of *Liberation*; Edward Keating, publisher of *Ramparts*; Sidney Peck, a professor at Case Western Reserve University; and Robert Greenblatt, a professor at Cornell University. In January 1967, they named the Reverend James Luther Bevel, a close associate of Martin Luther King, Jr.,* as director of the Spring Mobilization to End the War in Vietnam. During the next four months, they prepared for mass demonstrations, one scheduled for New York City and the other for San Francisco, and on April 15, 1967, the demonstrations occurred. More than 125,000 marched in New York City against the war—including Martin Luther King, Jr.,* James Luther Bevel, and Benjamin

Spock*—and another 60,000 marched in San Francisco, making the Spring Mobilization larger than any previous antiwar demonstration in U.S. history.
REFERENCES: Thomas Powers, *The War At Home*, 1985; *New York Times*, April 16–18, 1967.

STEPPENWOLF. Steppenwolf was a rock-and-roll band formed in Los Angeles in 1967. Included in the group were John Kay, Michael Monarch, Goldy McJohn, Rushton Moreve, and Jerry Edmonton. They were a psychedelic rock band that made the transition to heavy metal (a term coined in their first hit single, "Born to Be Wild"). Their first album, *Steppenwolf*, went to number six on the pop charts, and their second—*Steppenwolf the Second*—was even more successful, thanks to its megahit single "Magic Carpet Ride." "Born to Be Wild" then became part of the sound track of the film *Easy Rider*,* which strengthened Steppenwolf's image as a heavy metal, biker band. Their 1969 album *At Your Birthday Party* also penetrated the top ten on the album charts, with its hit single "Rock Me." Among their last hit singles were "Move Over" and "Heh Lawdy Mama." Although Steppenwolf remained popular on the concert circuit, their streak at the top of the pop music charts was over.
REFERENCE: John Kay, *Magic Carpet Ride: The Autobiography of John Kay and Steppenwolf*, 1994.

STEVENSON, ADLAI EWING. Adlai Stevenson was born February 5, 1900, in Los Angeles. He graduated from Princeton in 1922, spent two years at Harvard Law School without getting a degree, and finally received a law degree from Northwestern University in 1926. Stevenson then joined a prominent Chicago law firm and went into private practice. He spent some time with the Agricultural Adjustment Administration in Washington, D.C., in 1933 before returning to the law firm of Cutting, Moore, and Sidley. In 1941, Stevenson became special assistant to Secretary of the Navy Frank Knox. He became assistant to the secretary of state in 1945 and worked on formation of the United Nations. By that time Stevenson was a faithful Democrat. He served as governor of Illinois from 1949 to 1953.

In 1952, Stevenson won the Democratic presidential nomination and ran against Dwight D. Eisenhower.* Eisenhower defeated him again in 1956. Stevenson was known for his intellect, his internationalism in foreign affairs, and his moderate-to-liberal position on domestic concerns. In spite of his two electoral defeats, Stevenson continued to be a major force in the Democratic Party. President John F. Kennedy* appointed Stevenson to the post of ambassador to the United Nations in 1961. Stevenson remained there until his death February 14, 1965.
REFERENCE: Bert Cochran, *Adlai Stevenson: Patrician among the Politicians*, 1969.

STEWART, POTTER. Potter Stewart was born January 23, 1915, in Jackson, Michigan. He graduated from Yale in 1937 and earned his law degree there in 1941. His family was well connected in Ohio politics—Stewart's father was a justice on the state supreme court. The younger Stewart took a Wall Street job in 1941, but soon after the Japanese attack on Pearl Harbor, he joined the navy. After the war, he worked briefly for the same firm but then relocated to Cincinnati, Ohio, to practice there. A devoted Republican, Stewart supported Senator Robert Taft's bid for the GOP (Grand Old Party) presidential nomination in 1952, but he then actively supported Dwight D. Eisenhower* in 1952 and 1956. In 1954, Eisenhower appointed him to the U.S. Court of Appeals for the Sixth District, and in 1958 the president placed him on the Supreme Court.

Stewart began his tenure on the Warren Court as a consistent, conservative dissenter, but by the early 1960s he had moved more closely to the legal center. On civil rights, he upheld school desegregation opinions but disagreed with busing to achieve integration. He voted for vigorous enforcement of fair employment statutes, but he drew the line at affirmative action* regulations that resembled racial quotas. On issues of civil liberties for criminal defendants and prison inmates, Potter usually sided with police. He was the only dissenter in the Court's decision to outlaw compulsory prayer recitations. Stewart retired from the Court in 1984 and died December 7, 1985.
REFERENCE: *New York Times*, December 8, 1985.

STONEWALL INN RIOTS. The Stonewall Inn was a gay bar on Christopher Street in New York City's Greenwich Village. Located in Sheridan Square, the Stonewall Inn seemed scandalous to nearby straight residents, who preferred a quiet, conservative neighborhood. Stonewall patrons tended to be young non-whites, often teenage runaways living in the East Village. Drag queens paraded in and out of Stonewall, and the inn advertised its all-but-naked "go-go boy" entertainers. Even though patrons minded their own business, neighborhood residents often complained to the police, and vice squads frequently surprised Stonewallers, conducting harassment raids, roughing up the patrons, and arresting a few on charges of lewd conduct. Until June 1969, the patrons of the Stonewall Inn and other local gay bars acquiesced passively to the treatment they received at the hands of public officials.

During New York City elections, the gay community had to be especially on guard. Zealous politicians, anxious to drum up votes among conservative straights, often unleashed the vice squads, who raided Times Square pornographic theaters and bookstores, rounded up prostitutes and their johns, invaded shooting galleries to arrest heroin addicts, and went gay-bashing, engaging in virtual hit-and-run attacks on gay bars. Usually, as soon as the elections were over, life returned to normal, with the police ignoring the drug addicts, prostitutes, and gays. But 1969 was a municipal election year. Incumbent mayor John Lindsay* appeared to be on the political ropes, with his reelection campaign mired in charges of incompetence and bloated budgets. Desperate to turn the campaign around, his staff sent the word out to police precinct captains to get some headlines by arresting "perverts." John Lindsay wanted the *Daily News*, the *Post*, and the *Times* to report his aggressive campaign to "clean up" the city. A new police captain had taken over a few weeks earlier at Manhattan's Sixth Precinct, and he had already, for his own pleasure, conducted a series of raids on gay bars in Greenwich Village. The police always had an excuse, because the Stonewall Inn operated without a liquor license. When the police captain found out that City Hall wanted some more raids, he jumped at the opportunity.

Just before midnight on June 27, 1969, two detectives, accompanied by several uniformed officers, met at the Sixth Precinct headquarters, discussed the raid, and headed out to Christopher Street. They anticipated having a little fun—screaming epithets, nightsticking some "fags," and arresting a few drag queens. They backed a paddy wagon up to the entrance of the Stonewall Inn and then strutted their way in, loudly asking to see the liquor license and pushing the customers around. The police frisked each patron, ostensibly looking for drugs, and then released them one by one out the front door. Three drag queens, the bartender, and a bouncer, who loudly protested what he called "police brutality," were arrested on a variety of charges, including public lewdness, selling alcohol without a state license, and resisting arrest.

A crowd had gathered outside, across Christopher Street, as soon as the paddy wagon parked, and they waited to see what would transpire. They seemed passive enough at first, like any other group of onlookers waiting for a show. Suddenly, however, the temper of the crowd changed. They started jeering the police, shouting epithets and making catcalls and obscene gestures of their own. Two policemen then came out of the Stonewall Inn, trying to wrestle a lesbian into the paddy wagon. She was not cooperating at all—kicking, twisting, biting, and screaming, putting up a struggle every inch of the way. The police grappled and kicked back, calling her "butch" and "bitch" and "dyke." What had been a police raid quickly escalated into a gay rebellion. Cobblestones, bottles, full beer cans, and coins rained down on police. Like a medieval army of old trying to storm a fortified castle, several men uprooted a parking meter and used it as a battering ram, pounding it repeatedly against the doors of the Stonewall Inn. The police retreated into the bar and called for backup after several Molotov cocktails exploded through the windows and set the Stonewall Inn ablaze. Reinforcements soon poured into Sheridan Square, but marauding groups of gay protesters attacked police cars, turning them over or setting them on fire, spooked police horses, and continued the hailstorm of rocks and bottles. The free-for-all continued into the early morning hours of June 28.

It started up again the next evening. Overnight, "gay power" graffiti slogans had been spray-painted on walls throughout Greenwich Village and at scattered sites in Lower Manhattan. Clusters of angry gay men and lesbians dotted Christopher Street, and the police showed up 400 strong, in full riot gear, complete with helmets, plastic face masks, bullet-proof vests, shields, and nightsticks. On the corner of Greenwich Avenue and Christopher Street, several dozen drag queens, shouting "Save our sister," attacked a group of police who were clubbing a young man. Over the course of the next several hours, the rioting intensified, with police battling a crowd of more than 2,000 people. Allen Ginsberg,* a leading beat* writer and one of the founding fathers of the 1960s countercul- ture,* showed up at Christopher Street several days later and remarked to a reporter for the *Village Voice*: "You know, the guys there were so beautiful. They've lost that wounded look that fags all had ten years ago." The days of routine gay-bashing, as accepted police policy in New York City, were num- bered.

In the weeks following the Stonewall Riots, gays and lesbians settled into intense discussions about their political future. The Stonewall Inn riots on June 27–28, 1969, had galvanized them, raising their consciousness into a "we're not going to take it anymore" mentality. Gay leaders in New York City formed the Gay Liberation Front late in July, proclaiming their rejection of society's "attempt to impose sexual roles and definitions of our nature. We are stepping outside these roles and simplistic myths. We are going to be who we are." Similar groups sprouted on college campuses and in major cities around the country. When New York City police raided several gay bars in August 1970, thousands of gay men and women staged a protest march from Times Square to Greenwich Village. When antigay articles appeared in the media, gay activists stormed the publishers' New York offices, demanding retractions and organizing boycotts against the newspapers and magazines. The Stonewall Inn riots had given birth to a new civil rights constituency.
REFERENCES: *New York Times*, June 28–30, and July 1–2, 1969.

STRAIGHT. The term "straight" had a dual meaning during the 1960s. Within the counterculture,* "straight" was used to refer to white, middle-class culture, which youthful rebels found synonymous with materialism, stress, and anomie. In the subculture of homosexuals, the term "straight" was already being used to describe heterosexuals, with the term "gay" being used for homosexuals.
REFERENCES: Ruth Bronsteen, *The Hippy's Handbook—How to Live on Love*, 1967; Lewis Yablonsky, *The Hippie Trip*, 1968.

STRATEGIC ARMS LIMITATION TALKS. The Strategic Arms Limitation Talks (SALT) were organized late in the 1960s when Soviet and United States officials were both interested in opening formal talks concerning reductions in nuclear arsenals. The nuclear arms race was expensive and dangerous, with each side able to destroy its enemy several times over. The first round of negotiations opened early in 1969 and were known as SALT I. After three years of discus- sions, the two countries signed a series of treaties limiting strategic weapons production, outlawing the development of antiballistic missile systems, and im- proving the hot-line communication network.
REFERENCE: Thomas W. Wolfe, *The SALT Experience*, 1975.

STUDENT NONVIOLENT COORDINATING COMMITTEE. The Student Nonviolent Coordinating Committee (SNCC) was founded in Raleigh, North

Carolina, in 1960 by a group of sixteen African-American and white students to promote racial desegregation in the United States. The leading figures in its founding were James Forman and Robert Moses. The successful sit-ins* at North Carolina A&T College in 1960 inspired the founders of SNCC. SNCC grew rapidly in its early years, recruiting college students from around the country. SNCC set up field offices in cities throughout the South.

SNCC volunteers then set out to dismantle Jim Crow* segregation. Using the tactics of nonviolent civil disobedience, they intentionally violated segregation laws, using drinking fountains and rest rooms labeled for whites only, entering areas where African Americans were prohibited, and participating in the freedom rides* to desegregate interstate transportation facilities. They also worked to register black voters in the South and founded the Freedom Democratic Party* in Mississippi.

In 1966, Stokely Carmichael* became president of the Student Nonviolent Coordinating Committee, and under his leadership SNCC became increasingly militant. Carmichael described Martin Luther King, Jr.,* and Roy Wilkins* of the National Association for the Advancement of Colored People (NAACP) as hapless "Uncle Toms." He openly protested Vietnam as a racist war. But SNCC rhetoric escalated even as the civil rights movement* succeeded with the Civil Rights Act of 1964, the Voting Rights Act* of 1965, and affirmative action* programs. When Richard Nixon* de-escalated the Vietnam War* beginning in 1969, SNCC lost its reason for being. In 1970, SNCC renamed itself the Student Coordinating Committee, but the movement gradually disintegrated in the early 1970s.

REFERENCES: David Burner, *Making Peace with the Sixties*, 1996; Emily Stoper, *The Student Nonviolent Coordinating Committee: The Growth of Radicalism in a Civil Rights Organization*, 1989; Howard Zinn, *SNCC: The New Abolitionists*, 1964.

STUDENTS FOR A DEMOCRATIC SOCIETY. In 1960, the Students for a Democratic Society (SDS) first emerged from a traditional socialist organization—the League for Industrial Democracy. Two years later, University of Michigan student Tom Hayden* galvanized SDS when the organization adopted the Port Huron Statement,* which called for personal responsibility and participatory democracy* in order to truly democratize America. Hayden provided SDS with extraordinary leadership during the next several years, and with the emergence of the civil rights movement* and the antiwar movement,* SDS was blessed with two excellent reasons for being. SDS organizers helped the Student Nonviolent Coordinating Committee* register black voters in the South, organized "teach-ins"* at colleges and universities protesting escalation of the Vietnam War* and increased draft* calls, and protested against university administrations, which SDS considered antistudent and authoritarian. They were also at the forefront of the antipoverty* campaign and were leaders in the tactics of mass protest. By 1968, Hayden had established 350 chapters of SDS at colleges and universities around the country, and SDS membership exceeded

100,000 people. SDS participated actively in the massive protests in Chicago at the Democratic National Convention* in 1968.

But at the peak of its influence, SDS began to self-destruct, as had so many left-wing groups in U.S. history. Ideological and tactical arguments soon fractured SDS as its leadership argued about the best way to bring about revolutionary change. By 1969, SDS had produced such splinter groups as the Revolutionary Youth Movement, the Worker–Student Alliance, the Progressive Labor Party, and the Weathermen.* Late in 1969, when Weathermen terrorists adopted bombings as a tactical initiative, SDS went into permanent decline.
REFERENCES: Todd Gitlin, *The Sixties: Years of Hope, Days of Rage*, 1987; Kirkpatrick Sale, *SDS*, 1973.

SUPER BOWL. The first of what became the greatest sports event in American history was played in 1967. It later became known as the ''Super Bowl,'' a final play-off between the championship team of the National Football League and the championship team in the rival American Football League. It was known that year as the World Championship Game, with the Green Bay Packers of the National Football League defeating the Kansas City Chiefs of the American Football League by a score of 35 to 10. In 1969, the name Super Bowl was given to the annual championship game, which is played each January.
REFERENCE: Lorrine Glennon, ed., *Our Times: An Illustrated History of the 20th Century*, 1995.

SUPER BOWL III (1969). In 1966, when the American Football League and the National Football League agreed to merge into a biconference National Football League (National Football Conference [NFC] and American Football Conference [AFC]), a great rivalry was born. Throughout the country, American sports fans considered the AFC inferior in talent and strategy to the older NFC. In the first two championship games, which later became known as Super Bowls, the NFC confirmed public attitudes. Vince Lombardi's* Green Bay Packers won both games convincingly. Few people expected a different outcome in Super Bowl III.

The Baltimore Colts approached Super Bowl III as overwhelming favorites. Few people expected the lowly New York Jets to prevail over the Colts and their legendary quarterback, Johnny Unitas. But three days before the game Joe Namath,* the loudmouthed quarterback for the Jets, lifted a double Scotch in his hand and told reporters, ''We'll win. I guarantee it.'' The bold prediction set the stage for the most memorable game in professional football history. Baltimore fans and NFC supporters around the country gleefully waited for the opportunity to watch the Colts destroy Namath.

But it was not to be. On January 12, 1969, in Miami, Florida, Joe Namath lived up to his prediction. When the game was over, the Jets and the American Football Conference had won their first Super Bowl. The 16 to 7 upset let football fans throughout the United States know that the AFC was a true competitor to the NFC. As the 1960s came to an end, so did the stereotype of the invincible National Football Conference.

REFERENCE: Bruce Chadwick, *Joe Namath*, 1995.

Travis Tatum

THE SUPREMES. The Supremes were an extraordinarily popular singing group of the 1960s. The three members of the group—Diana Ross, Florence Ballard, and Mary Wilson—were childhood friends living in Detroit in 1961, when they signed a contract with Motown* Records. Their first hit came in 1964 with ''Where Did Our Love Go?'' which quickly became number one on *Billboard* magazine's both black and white music charts. During the rest of the decade, the Supremes added twelve more number one records to the country's hit parade, including ''Stop! In the Name of Love'' (1965), ''Back in My Arms Again'' (1965), ''I Hear a Symphony'' (1965), ''You Can't Hurry Love'' (1966), ''You Keep Me Hangin On' '' (1966), ''Love Is Here and Now You're Gone'' (1967), ''The Happening'' (1967), ''Reflections'' (1967), and ''Love Child'' (1968). Diana Ross left the group in 1970 for a solo career, and without her the Supremes never again matched their 1960s popularity, although they did release several hit records in the 1970s. The Supremes were one of the most commercially successful rock groups of the 1960s.

REFERENCES: Loren D. Estleman, *Motown*, 1991; Diana Ross, *Secrets of a Sparrow: Memoirs*, 1993.

SURFING. During the 1960s, the sport of surfing became extremely popular in California and the Atlantic coastal beaches, and in between the two coasts, ''surfing culture'' mesmerized teenagers. It came to symbolize the carefree, ''dropping-out'' lifestyle that the 1960s claimed to idealize. Surfing became a state of mind in Iowa as much as it was in Laguna Beach, California. In the mid-1950s, the development of lightweight, fiberglass surfboards made ''hot-dogging'' (trick riding) practically an art form. Bright-colored, baggy swimming trunks and blond, peroxide-dyed hair became pop culture icons, as did station wagons, which allowed surfers to carry their boards to the beach. Rock groups like the Beach Boys* and Jan and Dean picked up on the craze and transformed it into part of American popular culture. So did the ''beach party'' films of people like Frankie Avalon and Annette Funicello. In 1966, Bruce Brown's film *The Endless Summer* captured the surfing lifestyle in documentary form, following two young surfers on their worldwide quest for the perfect wave. During the early 1960s, surfing seemed so American—sunny, healthy, outdoorsy, and innocent. Social protest and rebellion later in the 1960s tarnished the image of American innocence, and the surfer culture declined somewhat on the national level.

REFERENCE: John M. Kelly, Jr., *Surf and Sea*, 1965.

SURGEON GENERAL'S REPORT. In 1960, more than 55 percent of adults in the United States smoked cigarettes. Scientists had long believed that tobacco use increased the risk of cancer and cardiovascular disease, but the tobacco industry consistently denied any correlation. Lung cancer had increased dramatically since World War II, probably because of the number of young men who began smoking during World War I, when tobacco companies distributed cigarettes free to servicemen. In the mid-1950s, the U.S. surgeon general's office commissioned ten independent biomedical investigations into the relationship between smoking and lung cancer. All ten studies confirmed the relationship, and in 1964 the surgeon general issued the famous report proclaiming that cigarette smoking posed a serious threat to public health. In 1966, the surgeon general required warning labels to be placed on all packages of cigarettes. Bans on television advertising of cigarettes soon followed. The actions of the surgeon general had a dramatic, long-term impact on smoking in the United States. By the mid-1990s, fewer than 27 percent of American adults smoked.

REFERENCE: Wilbur Schramm, *The Second Harvest of Two Research-Producing Events: The Surgeon-General's Inquiry and Sesame Street*, 1976.

SURVIVAL OF AMERICAN INDIANS ASSOCIATION. The Survival of American Indians Association was established in 1964. Its founders consisted largely of Nisqually and Puyallup Indians concerned about preserving Native American fishing rights in western Washington. Its original leader was Hank Adams.* Today, the association has a membership of 500 people and continues to be an advocate for Indian rights.

REFERENCE: Armand S. La Potin, ed., *Native American Voluntary Organizations*, 1987.

SUSANN, JACQUELINE. Born in Philadelphia in 1918, Jacqueline Susann was perhaps the most popular novelist of the 1960s, even though critics would credit her only with inventing a new literary genre—glittering, trashy fiction about the lives of famous people. The only praise highbrow critics would give Susann was that she was a good "storyteller." She also pioneered the coast-to-coast series of appearances and book signings that have become so common in the publishing industry. Jacqueline Susann was a self-promoter without peer. Primarily an entertainer who got her start in show business on local television, she turned celebrity watching into an industry by writing thinly veiled, keep-them-guessing-who-it-is melodramas about rich and famous people. Susann's talent for self-promotion and exciting, if superficial, fiction helped her sell millions of books in the 1960s and early 1970s. She took the business of book promotion out of the hands of the literary elite and put it on radio and television.

In 1964 her first best-seller—*Every Night, Josephine!*—was published. The book was about her pet dog, or at least about whom the dog met during her walks along 57th Street in New York City—Richard Burton, Elizabeth Taylor, Greta Garbo, Michael Rennie, Laurence Harvey, and a host of others. *Josephine* sold 1.7 million copies. In 1966, *Valley of the Dolls* topped even that record. "Dolls" was a euphemism for pills, and the novel was about the sex-crazed, pornographic, drug-filled lives of fictional Hollywood celebrities. The book was the first mainstream, best-selling novel in American history to explicitly describe female sexuality and eroticism. Literary critics panned the shallow characterizations and silly plot, but readers bought the book by the millions, and it spent twenty-eight weeks at the top of the best-seller lists. Susann became a celebrity herself, appearing on every radio program and television news and talk show possible. Her 1969 book, *The Love Machine*, remained number one for twenty-six weeks. Her third novel—*Once Is Not Enough*—was published in 1973. Jacqueline Susann died September 22, 1974, of breast cancer.

REFERENCES: *New York Times*, September 23, 1974; Barbara Seaman, *Lovely Me: The Life of Jacqueline Susann*, 1987.

T

TANANA-YUKON DENA' NENA' HENASH. Established in June 1962, Tanana-Yukon Dena' Nena' Henash (Our Land Speaks) was a group of Athabascan chiefs from central Alaska. An early leader was Charles Ryan, one of the Metlakatla people. They first met to protest Alaskan state restrictions on their traditional hunting rights. The Statehood Act of 1958 had supposedly guaranteed those rights, but the law also permitted state authorities to open up 102 million acres of Athabascan land to public domain access. The Athabascan chiefs campaigned to make sure that land near their villages was not designated as part of that public domain and that they retained all hunting, fishing, and mineral rights there. The organization also demanded improved federal health care programs, escrow accounts for Indian oil and gas revenues, and economic training for young people. Most of their demands were achieved in the Alaska Native Claims Settlement Act of 1971.

REFERENCES: Robert D. Arnold, *Alaska Native Land Claims*, 1978; David S. Case, *Alaska Natives and American Laws*, 1984; Armand S. La Potin, *Native American Voluntary Organizations*, 1986.

THE TATE-LABIANCA MURDERS. Early Saturday morning, August 9, 1969, actress Sharon Tate, who was eight months pregnant, Jay Sebring, Abigail Folger, Voytek Frykowski, and Steven Earl Parent were brutally murdered in the Los Angeles home of Tate and her husband, film director Roman Polanski. The next morning, Leon and Rosemary LaBianca were killed at their home. In both murders, the victims were tortured, repeatedly stabbed, shot, beaten, and hanged. The words ''Pig,'' ''Rise,'' and ''Helter Skelter'' were smeared on the walls in the victims' blood.

Charles Manson and four members of his cultlike hippie* ''family'' were charged with their murders. Manson (aka Jesus Christ, God, the Devil, Soul, Charles Willis Manson) was tried along with Susan Atkins (aka Sadie) and

Patricia Krenwinkel (aka Katie) for conspiracy and seven counts of first-degree murder. In the same trial, Leslie van Houten (aka Lulu) was tried for conspiracy and two counts of murder, as she was not present at the Tate murders. Charles "Tex" Watson was later tried separately for conspiracy and seven counts of first-degree murder.

Each defendant had several attorneys over the duration of the trial; all were expected to follow Manson's orders, or they were removed by their respective clients. In one extreme case, Ronald Hughes was murdered by "family" members on the outside after he refused to listen to Manson's ridiculous demands. During most of the trial, Irving Kanarek, Paul Fitzgerald, Daye Shinn, and Maxwell Keith represented Manson, Krenwinkel, Atkins, and van Houten, respectively. The prosecution was led by Vincent T. Bugliosi, deputy district attorney, who was assisted by Aaron Stovitz, Steven Kays, and Donald Musichi. The original judge was William Keene, but Manson filed an affidavit of prejudice and requested his removal from the case. Judge Keene had no argument and removed himself. Judge Charles H. Older was then assigned to the case and seemed to please the defense.

The trial was a three-ring circus. The prosecution was forced to subpoena all known members of the family in order to prevent them from intimidating potential witnesses. Lynette (aka Squeaky) Fromme led a vigil outside the courthouse, recruiting new family members and proclaiming the trial the "second crucifixion of Christ." Inside, the prosecution was plagued by numerous objections from defense attorney Kanarek, many of which were totally inappropriate. The defendants' outlandish behavior in the courtroom ranged from frequent outbursts to attempting to attack Judge Older and trying several times to prejudice the jury. In the latter instances, the defense always followed with a motion for mistrial, but the judge consistently denied it, claiming that he was not going to allow the defendants to benefit from their own misbehavior.

The star prosecution witness was Linda Kasabian, a family member who had been present at both murders. In exchange for her testimony, she was granted immunity. Kasabian spent a total of seventeen days on the stand, remaining a strong, credible witness the whole time. She testified that Manson was in complete control of family members, even to the extent of knowing their most personal and intimate thoughts. In fact, several family members believed him to be Jesus Christ. Manson preached from the Bible about Revelation 9. He employed the Bible, along with lyrics from Beatles'* songs, to convince the family of what he called "Helter Skelter."

Helter Skelter was a type of Armageddon between the races, where black people would rise up and destroy the entire white race, except for the family, which would live in a bottomless pit in the desert to escape the civil war in the United States. Manson also believed that the Beatles were sending him messages in their lyrics to incite Helter Skelter. He planned to frame some African Americans for the murders in an attempt to start the racial conflict. He purposely left a wallet from one of the murders in the street, hoping that a black man would find it and use the credit cards, thereby incriminating himself.

The defense case was hopeless. The lawyers attempted to represent their clients the best way that they could, but they found it difficult to discredit Linda Kasabian while their clients were carving Xs into their foreheads and chanting in Latin. The girls also insisted on testifying despite their lawyers' objections. Their testimony was so damning that the prosecution did not even bother to cross-examine. On March 29, 1971, the jury returned and sentenced all four defendants to death. However, on February 18, 1972, the death penalty was abolished in California, and their sentences were reduced to life in prison. Later, the state reinstated the death penalty, but Manson and the young women were unaffected because the act was not retroactive. All four are still currently serving their sentences.

The murders and the sensational trial captured the attention of America. It showed the dark side of the counterculture* of the 1960s and left a vivid reminder that the decade was not all peace, free love, and happiness.

REFERENCES: Vincent Bugliosi, *Helter Skelter: The True Story of the Manson Murders*, 1974; Ed Sanders, *The Family: The Manson Group and Its Aftermath*, 1989.

Margaret Peck

TAYLOR, MAXWELL DAVENPORT. Maxwell Taylor was born August 26, 1901, in Keytesville, Missouri. He graduated fourth in his class at West Point in 1922. He became a second lieutenant in the corps of engineers but did not receive the rank of captain until 1935. Promotions were few and far between in the peacetime army. Fluent in French and Spanish, Taylor taught languages at West Point from 1927 to 1932. After graduating from the Field Artillery School and the General Staff School, Taylor was posted to Tokyo as an embassy attaché. His real assignment was to learn Japanese. In 1939, Taylor became military attaché in Beijing, China.

After finishing course work at the Army War College in 1940, Taylor became chief of staff to General Matthew Ridgway, who then commanded the 82d Infantry Division. The 82d was the nucleus of the army's two new airborne divisions. When World War II broke out, Taylor was perfectly positioned for promotion. As a paratroop commander, he was on the cutting edge of one of the great innovations in infantry warfare. By December 1942, Taylor was promoted to brigadier general. He became artillery commander of the 82d Airborne and deployed to Europe in March 1943. Six months later, Taylor agreed to sneak incognito into Rome, which was occupied by Italian troops and surrounded by German troops, to determine the feasibility of an airborne assault there. At great risk to his own life, he decided that the invasion was ill advised. He made his way back through German lines and was awarded a Silver Star for bravery. Two months later, he was promoted to major general and given command of the 101st Airborne. As part of D-Day in June 1944, Taylor parachuted into Normandy with his troops. In September 1944, he led the 101st in its invasion of the Netherlands.

In 1945, Taylor became superintendent of West Point. After serving as commander of U.S. forces in Europe from 1949 to 1953, he took command of the Eighth Army in Korea and was there when the armistice ended the Korean War. He became army chief of staff in 1955. At the age of fifty-four, Taylor had reached the summit of his profession.

But he was a troubled chief of staff. The development of nuclear weapons and long-range bombers had given the air force priority, as well as naval aircraft carriers. Taylor bitterly opposed the ''massive retaliation'' defense policy of the Eisenhower* administration, arguing that too heavy dependence on nuclear weapons would limit U.S. ability to respond to the great variety of possible military threats. He called instead for ''flexible response''—a balanced military policy that would allow for guerrilla warfare, counterinsurgency,* conventional warfare, and nuclear warfare. In frustration, Taylor resigned from the army in 1959. He then wrote a book entitled *The Uncertain Trumpet*, explaining his point of view.

The book impressed John F. Kennedy,* who brought Taylor out of retirement as military adviser to the president in 1961. In September 1962, Kennedy named Taylor chairman of the Joint Chiefs of Staff. He remained there, advocating escalation of the U.S. military effort in Vietnam, until 1965, when President Lyndon B. Johnson* named him ambassador to South Vietnam. Taylor retired from the army in 1969. Among other works, he is also the author of *Responsibility and Response* (1967) and *Precarious Security* (1976). Maxwell Taylor died April 20, 1987.

REFERENCES: Douglas Kinnard, *The Certain Trumpet: Maxwell Taylor and the American Experience*, 1991; *New York Times*, April 21, 1987.

TAYLOR-ROSTOW MISSION OF 1961. Almost as soon as he took office in 1961, President John F. Kennedy* grew concerned over reports he was receiving about the progress of the war in Vietnam. In October 1961, he sent General Maxwell D. Taylor* and his deputy Walt W. Rostow* to investigate the situation in South Vietnam. They concluded that the government of President Ngo Dinh Diem* was weak and that his support among peasants was eroding. They told Kennedy he should increase military aid, deploy larger numbers of military advisers, and place an 8,000-man logistical U.S. task force in South Vietnam to serve as soldiers and/or economic and political workers. They assured Kennedy that the increases would not lead to similar increases in Communist strength because they assumed that North Vietnam was too vulnerable to U.S. air power. Kennedy accepted some of the recommendations, which led to an escalation of the war.

REFERENCE: Douglas Kinnard, *The Certain Trumpet: Maxwell Taylor and the American Experience*, 1991.

THE TEACHINGS OF DON JUAN. *The Teachings of Don Juan: A Yaqui Way of Knowledge* was the title of Carlos Castaneda's enormously popular 1968 book. At the time, Castaneda was a graduate student in anthropology at the University of California at Los Angeles. He claimed to have gone on a spiritual journey throughout the American Southwest, and in a small Arizona town he met Don Juan, a Yaqui Indian shaman who taught him the meaning of life. Castaneda's spiritual enlightenment—his introduction to an entirely new reality—came about because Don Juan introduced him to peyote and psilocybin mushrooms, both hallucinogenic drugs. Published just when the psychedelic values of the 1960s were reaching their peak, *The Teachings of Don Juan* was part travelogue, part ethnography, part anthropology, and part parapsychology. Scholars today still do not know if *The Teachings of Don Juan* is simple fiction or autobiography, but the book earned an enormous international audience in the 1960s.

REFERENCE: Carlos Castaneda, *The Teachings of Don Juan: A Yaqui Way of Knowledge*, 1968.

TEACH-INS. Soon after the United States began bombing North Vietnam in the wake of the Gulf of Tonkin* Resolution in August 1964, antiwar sentiment escalated dramatically. On March 10, 1965, when 3,000 U.S. marines landed at Danang, South Vietnam, to begin the Americanization of the war, several antiwar faculty members at the University of Michigan organized "teach-ins," patterned after the civil rights "sit-ins"* that took place in 1960. More than 3,000 students attended the "teach-in," where faculty members explained their opposition to the war. Soon, similar teach-ins were taking place at dozens of campuses across the country. On May 15, 1965, a total of 122 campuses participated in a national teach-in. Such antiwar activists as Tom Hayden* and Jane Fonda* also organized mini teach-ins at coffeehouses and bars near U.S. military installations, so that the GIs could be exposed to the antiwar argument. The teach-ins proved to be the beginning of a broad-based antiwar movement* that eventually swept the country and undermined political support for the U.S. military effort in Southeast Asia.

REFERENCES: Dick Cluster, ed., *They Should Have Served That Coffee*, 1979; David Cortright, *Soldiers in Revolt*, 1975; Samuel Freeman, "Teach-Ins," in James S. Olson, ed., *Dictionary of the Vietnam War*, 1988; Todd Gitlin, *The Sixties: Years of Hope, Days of Rage*, 1987; Kirkpatrick Sale, *SDS*, 1973.

TELEVISION. During the 1960s, television became the most important communications media in the United States, eclipsing radio, film, and print as the primary method by which Americans acquired information and entertained themselves. Advertisers paid more and more money to the networks to sell their products, and America's already thriving consumer culture expanded even more. Critics charged that television entertainment played to the lowest common denominator of the viewing public, and that as a result, programming was juvenile and unsophisticated. Television executives knew which programs would be watched and which would be ignored, so television in the 1960s was replete with situation comedies, westerns, soap operas, and sporting events.

The power of television to influence public policy first became evident during the violent confrontations in the early 1960s between civil rights protestors and law enforcement officials in the South. As tens of millions of Americans watched acts of police brutality against nonviolent demonstrators, the civil rights movement* acquired the moral upper hand in the debate over integration and the right to vote. When tens of millions of American television viewers witnessed Jack Ruby* murder Lee Harvey Oswald* in November 1963, conspiracy theories about the assassination of President John F. Kennedy* multiplied. Beginning with the presidential debates between John Kennedy and Richard Nixon* in 1960, television became the most powerful force in American politics.

The era of the 1960s will also be remembered as the ''decade of hard news,'' when Walter Cronkite* at CBS and Chet Huntley and David Brinkley at NBC made the prime time evening news a staple of American television. Tens of millions tuned in each evening to watch a summary of daily international events and stories about Washington, D.C. politics. In the process, news anchors like Cronkite became arbiters of American political opinion.

Nothing more clearly reveals the influence of television on American life in the 1960s than the Vietnam War.* Between 1964 and 1975, the war in Vietnam was broadcast nightly in two and three-minute segments on American television. It was the first war to be significantly ''covered'' by television, the first war in which television, as opposed to the print media, was the primary means of informing the public about the course and the nature of the conflict. Critics charged that television telescoped events, selected film for its dramatic quality, and had a built-in liberal bias. They also believed that commercial television's message was aimed at the viewers' emotions rather than their intellect. The result, they insisted, was inaccurate coverage, distortion, and ultimately propaganda. Military and political leaders in particular used the arguments of television critics to suggest that television ''lost'' the war in Vietnam.

Television's defenders argued that coverage of the war had been accurate and fair, especially compared to the one-sided, biased slant coming out of the Pentagon and U.S. military headquarters in Saigon.* The major networks argued that their coverage compared favorably, in terms of accuracy, with that of the print media, and that when there were mistakes, they often originated with Pentagon and State Department reports, which were frequently loaded with errors, omissions, and exaggerations.

The Tet Offensive* of 1968 became a symbol of the power of television to shape public opinion. The Vietcong* offensive had caught the U.S. military completely off guard, and even though U.S. forces recovered quickly and delivered a death blow to the Vietcong, the entire event was a political disaster at home in the United States. In November 1967, General William Westmoreland* had predicted the imminent demise of enemy resistance, and suddenly that resistance seemed more powerful than ever. The Tet Offensive, complete with Vietcong* troops inside the U.S. embassy compound in Saigon, made its way into the evening news, and whatever support remained for the Vietnam War crumbled.

REFERENCES: Michael Arlen, *Living Room War*, 1969; Eric Barnouw, *Tube of Plenty: The Evolution of American Television*, 1975; Peter Braestrup, *Big Story: How the American Press and Television Reported and Interpreted the Crisis of Tet 1968 in Vietnam and Washington*, 1983; Jorge Lewinski, *The Camera at War*, 1978; J. Fred McDonald, Television and the Cold War: The Video Road to Vietnam, 1985.

TERMINATE WITH EXTREME PREJUDICE. During the 1960s, it was learned that within the covert operations section of the Central Intelligence Agency,* the term ''terminate with extreme prejudice'' was a euphemism for assassination.

REFERENCE: James S. Olson, ed., *Dictionary of the Vietnam War*, 1988.

TERMINATION. After World War II, a conservative mood blanketed America, and people yearned for more tranquil times when change had been slower and values more constant. Voices from the past sounded again. The National Council of Churches had commissioned a study of its mission system in 1944, and talk of assimilating the Indians reemerged. Anglo conformity had returned to Indian affairs. At the same time, the postwar boom in recreational camping turned the attention of white land developers back to the reservations. They wanted to turn Indian land into large commercial farms or resort developments, to employ Indian land ''productively.'' Ever since 1934, western congressmen had unsuccessfully tried to repeal the Indian Reorganization Act, dissolve the tribes, nullify their corporate authority, and remove Indian land from its trust status.

Conservative whites wanted to resolve all Native American land claims against the federal government and assimilate the Indians. Some tribes had been trying for years to recover damages from the federal government for fraudulent treaty arrangements, and to settle those disputes Congress created the Indian Claims Commission in 1946. Indians immediately filed 852 claims for more than $1.2 billion, each claim arguing that the government had undervalued the land when the first treaties were negotiated. When the commission ceased to operate in 1978, over $800 million had been awarded on 285 claims out of the 852 originally filed.

It became obvious that satisfactory settlement of all the claims would be impossible, but the attempt did pave the way for the ''termination'' program. In 1950, President Harry Truman appointed Dillon S. Myer commissioner of Indian affairs. Previously employed by the War Relocation Authority, Myer was an assimilationist who had tried to scatter Japanese Americans among the general population in 1945. He brought that same commitment to the Bureau of Indian Affairs (BIA), hoping to dissolve the reservations and disperse Native Americans throughout the country. On August 1, 1953, Congress inaugurated the termination program, passing resolutions removing federal authority over all Indian tribes, ending their status as wards of the United States, and granting them all the privileges of citizenship. State and local governments were to take legal jurisdiction over the reservations, and federal authority would be terminated.

During the Eisenhower* administration, Congress "terminated" several tribes in western Oregon, the Alabama-Coushattas in Texas, the Utes and Paiutes in Utah, the Klamaths in Oregon, and the Menominis in Wisconsin. More than 1.6 million acres of reservation land fell into white hands between 1953 and 1956. Without federal funds and with tribal corporate power negated, "terminated" Indians had no means of livelihood and sold their land to support themselves. The Klamaths and Menominis suffered especially heavy losses. Ralph Nader* denounced termination while he was editor of the *Harvard Law School Record* in 1957, and a number of liberal journals, including *Christian Century, Harper's,* and the *Nation,* openly criticized government policy. The National Congress of American Indians, a Native American lobbying group formed in 1944, condemned termination, as did the Indian Rights Association and the Association of American Indian Affairs. By 1956 the antitermination movement had become so strong that Eisenhower called a halt to the termination program except in cases where individual tribes requested it. Once again the federal government was supporting tribal control of Indian land.

Many Indian tribes were terminated throughout the United States, but by the early 1960s, termination had become increasingly unpopular. The civil rights movement* had raised the national consciousness about the problems of America's ethnic minorities, and Indian activists began demanding the restoration of tribal sovereignty. Termination was not formally reversed until 1970, when the Richard Nixon* administration successfully promoted its repeal. Not until 1988, however, did Congress pass an omnibus measure repealing termination—the Repeal of Termination Act—which prohibited Congress from ever terminating or transferring BIA services without the express permission of the involved tribes.

REFERENCES: Russel Lawrence Bars and James Youngblood Henderson, *The Road: Indian Tribes and Political Liberty,* 1980; John R. Wander, *"Retained by the People": A History of American Indians and the Bill of Rights,* 1994; Wilcomb E. Washburn, *Red Man's Land, White Man's Law,* 1971.

TET OFFENSIVE. In November 1967, General William Westmoreland* appeared before a joint session of Congress and promised that the end of the Vietnam War* was in sight. He argued that enemy resources—human and matériel—were so depleted that the ability to fight in the field was rapidly disappearing. President Lyndon B. Johnson* took heart at the news, hoping that the Vietnam nightmare would soon end. As Westmoreland was speaking, it appeared that enemy forces were preparing for a massive offensive against isolated American military installations at such places as Khe Sanh,* Con Thien,* and

Pleiku.* Hoping that the enemy was planning a frontal assault and that his forces would be able to decimate them, Westmoreland relocated large numbers of troops from South Vietnamese cities and placed them in the countryside where the alleged offensives would begin.

But North Vietnam and the Vietcong* had a surprise for Westmoreland and the United States. The supposed offensives against Con Thien and Khe Sanh were only diversionary measures. While American troops prepared for rural offensives, the Vietcong staged a massive offensive against most South Vietnamese cities. They launched the offensive on January 31, 1968, on the annual Vietnamese new year's celebration known as Tet. The attack caught the United States and the South Vietnamese off-guard. Enemy troops overran several provinces and seized control of several cities. Bloody hand-to-hand combat took place in Hue.*

The communist objectives at Tet were to inspire a spontaneous uprising of South Vietnamese peasants against their own government, inflict a military defeat on the United States, and bring about the downfall of South Vietnam. They achieved none of those objectives. The government of South Vietnam survived, the peasants did not rebel, and the United States killed up to 70,000 Vietcong in the fighting. After the Tet Offensive, the Vietcong were finished as a military force.

But the tactical failure of the communists at Tet actually proved to be a strategic victory. They may have lost the battle in Vietnam and failed to achieve their objectives, but during Tet the commmunists won the war. Back in the United States, the Tet Offensive was a political disaster. Coming so soon after Westmoreland's predictions of victory, the offensive convinced most Americans that the Vietnam War was unwinnable. It led to President Lyndon B. Johnson's withdrawal from the 1968 presidential race and then to President Richard M. Nixon's* formulation of the Vietnamization program.

REFERENCES: Peter Braestrup, *Big Story: How the American Press and Television Reported and Interpreted the Crisis of Tet 1968 in Vietnam and Washington*, 1983; James S. Olson and Randy Roberts, *Where the Domino Fell: America and Vietnam 1945–1995*, 1995.

THALIDOMIDE. Thalidomide was a drug developed in the 1950s by Chemie Grunenthal, a West German firm. The drug reduced nausea in pregnant women and had a sedative effect for nervousness and insomnia. In 1957, the company released it for sale in Europe. Thalidomide was not distributed in the United States because it did not meet the testing guidelines of the Food and Drug Administration (FDA), particularly the requirement to assess its effects on unborn fetuses. By 1961, it was obvious that a disaster had occurred, and Chemie Grunenthal pulled the drug off the market. Thalidomide caused stillbirths and severe birth defects in fetuses. The most common defect was phocomelia, which left newborn babies with short, stublike arms and legs and useless hands and feet. Some of them also had hearing, vision, and gastrointestinal defects.

In 1962, Dr. Helen B. Taussig and Dr. Frances Kelsey of the FDA went public with the news, warning women not to take the drug. The only way American women could get access to thalidomide was to travel abroad. Sherri Finkbine, an Arizona woman whose husband had been acquiring the drug for her during business trips to Germany, decided to have an abortion. The decision precipitated a huge outburst of protest from people who opposed abortion. Finkbine remained on the front pages in the United States until she went to Sweden and had the abortion. Neonatologists there confirmed that her baby suffered from phocomelia. More than 10,000 babies around the world were born with the defect between 1958 and 1962, only twelve of whom were in the United States. But the controversy provided one of the early right-to-life, right-to-choose battles in recent U.S. history.

REFERENCE: William McBride, *Killing the Messenger*, 1994.

THAT GIRL. *That Girl* was a zany, 1960s television* situation comedy on ABC. First broadcast on September 8, 1966, the series starred Marlo Thomas as Ann Marie and Ted Bessell as Don Hollinger, an engaged New York City couple. She is an aspiring actress, and he is an executive with *Newsview* magazine. The last episode was telecast on September 10, 1971. *That Girl* is considered one of the first television series to feature a single woman.

REFERENCE: Tim Brooks and Earle Marsh, *The Complete Directory to Prime Time Network and Cable TV Shows*, 1995.

THICH QUANG DUC. On June 11, 1963, a Buddhist monk sat down at a busy intersection in Saigon, South Vietnam, and doused himself with gasoline. He then set himself on fire and sat there, absolutely immobile, until the fire consumed him. While he burned to death, a dozen photojournalists recorded his immolation, and the wire services picked up the suicide and broadcast it around the world that evening. At the time of his death, Thich Quang Duc was a sixty-six-year-old Buddhist monk who opposed the corrupt regime of President Ngo Dinh Diem* of South Vietnam. Quang Duc had tired of Diem's oppression of Buddhists, and he wanted to make a political statement for the world to see. It worked. His death received maximum exposure in the United States and helped undermine support for Diem in the John F. Kennedy* administration. Self-immolation is a traditional form of protest in many regions of Asia, but Quang Duc's death violated the sensibilities of policymakers in Washington and was a critical factor in convincing them that Diem was incapable of governing South Vietnam. Diem's imperious reaction to the suicide did not help his cause in Washington, D.C. He joked about the death and then escalated his oppression of Buddhists, which only provoked more Buddhist self-immolations and more anti-Diem demonstrations in Saigon. Thich Quang Duc's self-sacrifice marked the beginning of the end of the Diem regime.

REFERENCES: *New York Times*, June 12–15, 1963; Stafford Thomas, "Thich Quang Duc," in James S. Olson, ed., *Dictionary of the Vietnam War*, 1988.

THOMAS, NORMAN MATTOON. Norman Thomas was born November 20, 1884, in Canton, Ohio. He considered a career in the ministry after graduating from Union Theological Seminary in New York City, but he soon left the ministry and helped found the Fellowship of Reconciliation* and edited its magazine, *World Tomorrow.* Thomas was an avowed pacifist. In 1917, he helped found the National Civil Liberties Union, which became the American Civil Liberties Union. Because of his antiwar and civil libertarian views, Thomas became a socialist in 1920. From 1922 to 1937, he worked for the League for Industrial Democracy.

During the 1920s, Thomas ran for several statewide posts on the socialist ticket in New York, and in 1928 he was the Socialist Party's nominee for president of the United States. Thomas ran for the presidency again in 1932 (when he received 884,781 votes), 1936, 1940, 1944, and 1948. During World War II, he fought U.S. participation in the conflict and called repeatedly for peace. During the 1950s, Thomas helped organize the Committee for a Sane Nuclear Policy, and he was a bitter opponent of the Vietnam War.* Norman Thomas died December 19, 1968.

REFERENCES: James Durham, *Norman Thomas: A Biography, 1884–1968,* 1969; W. A. Swanberg, *Norman Thomas: The Last Idealist,* 1976.

THREE DOG NIGHT. Three Dog Night was formed in Los Angeles in 1967. The group consisted of Danny Hutton, Chuck Hegron, Cory Wells, Mike Allsup, Jimmy Greenspoon, Joe Schermie, and Floyd Sneed. In the late 1960s and early 1970s, Three Dog Night had a run of eighteen consecutive releases that made it into the top twenty on the pop charts. They became known for their three-part harmony vocal leads. Included in their hit records were "One," "Easy to Be Hard," "Eli's Coming," "Mama Told Me," and "Liar." Their popularity peaked in 1971, however, and the band then went into a long period of decline.

REFERENCE: Jimmy Greenspan, *One Is the Loneliest Number: On the Road and Behind the Scenes with the Legendary Rock Band, Three Dog Night,* 1991.

THURMOND, STROM. Strom Thurmond was born in Edgefield, South Carolina, on May 12, 1902. He graduated from Clemson College in 1923 and then taught school for several years, reading law privately and becoming involved in local county Democratic Party politics. He won a seat in the state senate in 1933 and served until 1938, when he began work as a circuit judge. Thurmond remained there until 1946, when he was elected governor of South Carolina. He came to national attention in 1948 when he battled the Democratic Party over its civil rights position at the national convention. Thurmond was diametrically opposed to any extension of civil rights to black people. He then declared his own candidacy for president, running as a "Dixiecrat" for the insurgent States Rights Party. His candidacy sent a wave of fear through Democrats, but Harry Truman still managed to win reelection as president.

Thurmond served as governor until 1951, when he began practicing law privately in Aiken, South Carolina. He had been admitted to the South Carolina bar in 1930. In 1954, Thurmond ran for a seat in the U.S. Senate and won, beginning a career that continues today. Increasingly uncomfortable as a Democrat because of the party's more liberal bent, Thurmond switched allegiances in 1964, declaring himself a Republican and working diligently for the election of Barry Goldwater as president.

During the 1960s and 1970s, Strom Thurmond staked out his political ground as an inveterate opponent of civil rights legislation, the welfare state, environmentalism, and federal regulation. He no longer openly espoused his states rights philosophy, but every vote he cast in the Senate reflected that point of view. In terms of U.S. foreign policy, he was an outspoken anti-Communist and supporter of a hardline approach to the Soviet Union, the People's Republic of China, and North Vietnam. He supported of President Lyndon B. Johnson,* at least far as the Vietnam War* was concerned, but he often expressed frustration that the United States did not employ *more* firepower against the Vietcong* and North Vietnamese Army.* In 1966, he criticized the president for pursuing a "no-win" policy in Vietnam. Thurmond urged President Johnson to unleash all of America's firepower to deliver a punishing blow to North Vietnam.

Thurmond backed Richard M. Nixon* for the presidency in 1968, and Nixon later credited Thurmond with delivering the southern delegate votes needed for the nomination. In return, Nixon gave Thurmond extraordinary influence in the selection of federal judges and other appointments. Thurmond was reelected to the U.S. Senate in 1960, 1966, 1972, 1978, 1984, 1990, and 1996. Most recently, during the impeachment trial of President Bill Clinton, Thurmond presided as the senior Republican.

REFERENCES: Nadine Cohodas, *Strom Thurmond and the Politics of Southern Change*, 1993; Roger D. Launius, "Strom Thurmond," in James S. Olson, ed., *Dictionary of the Vietnam War*, 1988.

TIJERINA, REIES LÓPEZ. Reies López Tijerina was born outside San Antonio, Texas, in 1926, to a family of migrant laborers. He spent the early years of his adulthood as an itinerant evangelist for the Assembly of God Church, but in 1950 he left the church. Within a few years, Tijerina became interested in the process by which Mexican Americans* in the Southwest lost their land to Anglo settlers. Working as a janitor in Albuquerque, he spent a great deal of his leisure hours in archival collections, researching the issue. In February 1963, he founded the Alianza Federal de Mercedes, or Federal Alliance of Grants, to promote the return of the land to its original owners or their descendants. With all of his evangelistic preaching skills, Tijerina traveled throughout northwestern New Mexico, winning converts to his cause. By 1966, alliance membership exceeded 20,000 people.

Tijerina then turned to insurgent tactics to promote the land issue. In mid-1966, he led a sixty-mile protest march from Santa Fe to Albuquerque and presented his demands to Governor Jack Campbell. A few months later, Tijerina led an alliance group in an invasion and "takeover" of Kit Carson National Forest, which he then proclaimed was the Republic of Rio Chama. Federal authorities arrested Tijerina. He then disbanded the Alianza Federal de Mercedes and quickly established the Alianza Federal de Pueblos Libres, or Federal Alliance of Free Towns.* In June 1967, Tijerina led a raid on the Tierra Amarilla courthouse to release ten jailed alliance members. He was eventually arrested and spent nearly three years in a federal penitentiary. He was paroled in July 1971, and by that time his politics had become much less radical. He was still preoccupied with the land title issue, but his means had turned more peaceful.

In the 1980s, Tijerina took off on an anti-Semitism crusade, claiming that Jews were responsible for the loss of Hispanic land titles and for the historical and continuing discrimination against Mexican Americans in the United States. Since then, mainstream Chicano* activists have maintained some distance from Tijerina.

REFERENCES: Patricia B. Blawis, *Tijerina and the Land Grants*, 1971; Richard Gardner, *Grito! Reies Tijerina and the New Mexico Land Grant War of 1967*, 1970; Peter Nabakov, *Tijerina and the Courthouse Raid*, 1969.

TILLICH, PAUL JOHAANNES. Paul Tillich was born in Starzeddel, Germany, August 20, 1886. He did undergraduate work at the University of Berlin in 1904, the University of Tübingen in 1905, and the University of Halle from 1905 to 1907. He earned the Ph.D. from the University of Breslau in 1911. During World War I Tillich served as a chaplain in the German army. During the next fifteen years, he taught in Marburg, Dresden, Leipzig, and Frankfurt, establishing a reputation as Germany's leading theologian and philosopher. When the Nazis came to power in Germany in 1933, Tillich lost his professorship at the University of Frankfurt. He emigrated to the United States and took up a professorship at the Union Theological Seminary in New York. After twenty-two years at Union, he moved to Cambridge, Massachusetts, as a university professor at Harvard. He completed his academic career at the University of Chicago, joining the faculty there in 1962.

In the United States, Tillich's intellectual reputation grew even more, until he was recognized as the leading theologian in the Western world. In such books as *The Shaking of the Foundations* (1948), *The Protestant Era* (1948), *Systematic Theology* (1951–1963), *The Courage to Be* (1952), *Dynamics of Faith* (1957), and *On the Boundary* (1966), Tillich expounded his existentialist conviction that the central dynamic in Western culture was the isolation, despair, and estrangement of human beings trapped in an ambiguous existence. Yet, there was still a message of hope in Tillich's philosophy. God was the "essence of being" whose reality was expressed in the natural world. For Tillich, the life of Christ transcended the despair of human beings. Jesus had been human and had undergone and overcome the isolation and estrangement of life. Through Jesus, God extended reconciliation and hope to alienated human beings. Tillich denied that there could be any final authority on Christian religion because cultural circumstances constantly changed. He died October 22, 1965.

REFERENCES: Carl J. Armbruster, *The Vision of Paul Tillich*, 1967; David H. Kelsey, *The Fabric of Paul Tillich's Theology*, 1967; *New York Times*, October 23, 1965.

TINKER V. DES MOINES INDEPENDENT COMMUNITY SCHOOL DISTRICT. The so-called Warren Court of the 1950s and 1960s justifiably earned its reputation as the most liberal Supreme Court in U.S. history. Its point of view was particularly evident in civil liberties decisions, especially in First Amendment freedom of speech and freedom of the press controversies. One example is *Tinker v. Des Moines Independent Community School District*, decided by a 7 to 2 vote on February 24, 1969, with Justice Abraham Fortas* writing the majority opinion. A number of students in the Des Moines public schools had taken to wearing black armbands to protest the Vietnam War.* School officials prohibited the practice on disciplinary grounds. The Court declared such prohibitions unconstitutional violations of the First Amendment freedom of speech. The Constitution, the Court concluded, protects symbolic speech as well as oral speech, as long as such speech is not disruptive and harmful to others.

REFERENCE: 393 U.S. 503 (1969).

***THE TONIGHT SHOW,* STARRING JOHNNY CARSON.** NBC launched *The Tonight Show* in 1954, with Steve Allen serving as the host of the daily, late-night talk show. Jack Paar took over the hosting job in 1957, and Johnny Carson replaced him in 1962. For the next thirty years, *The Tonight Show* was an American entertainment staple, with millions tuned in to Carson's comic monologue and noncontroversial repartee with guests from the political, sports, and entertainment worlds. The last episode was broadcast on May 22, 1992.

REFERENCE: Laurence Leamer, *King of the Night: The Life of Johnny Carson*, 1989.

TRADE EXPANSION ACT OF 1962. The Trade Expansion Act of 1962 replaced the Reciprocal Trade Agreements Act of 1934 and authorized President John F. Kennedy* to negotiate mutual tariff reductions of up to 50 percent with other countries. The negotiations began in 1967 as the "Kennedy Round."

REFERENCE: James S. Olson, ed., *Dictionary of United States Economic History*, 1991.

TRANSPORTATION, DEPARTMENT OF. The Department of Transportation (DOT) was established in 1966 as a Cabinet-level federal agency. It became an umbrella agency designed to coordinate federal transportation policy. Included in the DOT were the following federal agencies: the United States Coast Guard, the Federal Aviation Administration, the Federal Highway Administration, the Federal Railroad Administration, the National Highway Traffic Safety Administration, the Urban Mass Transit Administration, the Saint Lawrence Sea-

way Development Corporation, and the Research and Special Programs Administration.
REFERENCE: Grant M. Davis, "The Department of Transportation: A Study on Organizational Futility," *Public Utility Fortnightly* 87 (May 27, 1971): 29–33.

TRANSCENDENTAL MEDITATION. See MAHARISHI MAHESH YOGI.

TRIP. In the 1960s, the term "trip" emerged in the hippie* counterculture* as a slang expression for being high on a hallucinogenic drug. One could have either a "good trip" or a "bad trip." Later in the 1960s, the term "trip" had become a more generic reference to any adventure. A tour in Vietnam, for example, was a "bad trip," as was contaminated heroin.
REFERENCE: Ruth Bronsteen, *The Hippy's Handbook—How to Live on Love*, 1967.

TRUE GRIT. True Grit was the 1969 film that finally won John Wayne* an Oscar as Best Actor. In the movie, Wayne plays Rooster Cogburn, a federal marshall who tracks down fugitives in the Old West. Rooster Cogburn is a classic frontier hero, an independent man free of women and families. He lives by himself, except for a Chinese cook and a house cat, and spends his time on the trail of criminals. In that sense, he is a familiar figure in western popular literature—free, without fear, and willing to confront enormous odds on his own. Wayne's favorite scene in the film was the climatic confrontation between Rooster Cogburn and the murderous gang of Ned Pepper. Everyone is on horseback, facing one another across a grassy meadow. When Cogburn announces his insistence on bringing the men to justice, Pepper calls out, "Bold talk for a one-eyed fat-man." An outraged Cogburn does a one-eyed double-take and retorts, "Fill your hands, you son of a bitch!" He then spurs his horse forward in a frontier joust, holding the reins in his teeth, firing a rifle with his right hand and a pistol with his left, sending the evil ones to their just rewards.
Rooster Cogburn also possesses an undeniable warmth and vulnerability. On-screen over the years, Wayne had symbolized men who were apparently free of the usual laws of physiology. They could eat, drink, and smoke as they pleased without suffering physical consequences. But Rooster Cogburn is a corpulent, old, bloated, flatulent, profane, one-eyed lawman who can barely get out of bed in the morning. In one scene, he falls off his horse, dead drunk after a long day's ride, and, failing several times to get on his feet, says to his companions, "We'll camp here for the night." Unlike other John Wayne characters over the years who are free of women and families, Cogburn falls under the virtuous spell of fourteen-year-old Mattie Ross, whose determination more than matches his own. He worries about her, taking her to the doctor to make sure that a snake-bitten hand heals, and trying to talk her out of her cynicism. As Rooster Cogburn, Wayne conveyed strength, subtle emotions, and a beguiling humor, even creating a campy caricature of himself while preserving the film's credi-

bility. In the closing scene, he bids Ross farewell, inviting her to "come see a fat old man sometime." Then he jumps his horse over a fence and rides off into the sunset. For film critic Vincent Canby, "The last scene in the movie is so fine it will probably become Wayne's cinematic epitaph."
REFERENCE: Randy Roberts and James S. Olson, *John Wayne American*, 1995.

TUNNEL RATS. During the Vietnam War,* the term "tunnel rat" was used by American soldiers to refer to those among them who were specially trained to enter North Vietnamese and Vietcong* underground tunnels and search and destroy* enemy troops. In South Vietnam, there were hundreds of miles of tunnels the Vietcong used for living areas, storage depots, hospitals, and ordnance factories.
REFERENCE: Tom Mangold and John Penycate, *The Tunnels of Cu Chi*, 1985.

TWENTY-THIRD AMENDMENT. For many years, the residents of the District of Columbia had complained that they were not represented in Congress and could not vote in presidential elections. District advocates claimed that such restrictions amounted to disfranchisement in a democratic society. As the population of the District of Columbia became increasingly African-American after World War II, those complaints began to assume racial overtones. Finally, on June 16, 1960, Congress passed the proposed Twenty-Third Amendment to the Constitution, which allowed members of the District of Columbia to vote in presidential elections and awarded the same number of electoral votes they would have, based on their population, if they had representatives in Congress. The requisite number of states had ratified the amendment by March 29, 1961, when it went into effect.
REFERENCE: *New York Times*, March 30, 1961.

TWENTY-FOURTH AMENDMENT. As the civil rights movement* gained momentum in the early 1960s, the continuing vitality of the poll tax in most southern states seemed increasingly racist and unjustifiable to large numbers of Americans. Southern whites maintained the poll tax because it kept large numbers of African Americans, who also tended to be poor, from voting. On August 27, 1964, Congress passed the proposed Twenty-Fourth Amendment to the Constitution, which banned the poll tax. The requisite number of states ratified the amendment by January 23, 1964, when it went into effect.
REFERENCE: *New York Times*, January 24, 1964.

TWENTY-FIFTH AMENDMENT. The assassination of President John F. Kennedy* on November 22, 1963, with Vice President Lyndon B. Johnson* so near in the motorcade, raised questions among many Americans about presidential succession, particularly if the president and the vice president were killed accidentally or in a conspiracy. The Twenty-Fifth Amendment addressed the question by declaring that in the event of the death of the president and vice president, the speaker of the House of Representatives would succeed to the presidency. The amendment then designated the order of succession to the presidency in the event of the death of the speaker of the house. The amendment also provided for the transfer of presidential powers to the vice president in the case of the disabling of the president. Congress passed the amendment on July 6, 1966, and it was ratified by the final state on February 10, 1967.

REFERENCE: *New York Times*, February 11, 1967.

TWIGGY. Twiggy, whose real name is Leslie Hornby, was born in the cockney section of London September 19, 1949. In elementary school, she acquired the nickname "Sticks" by her classmates because of her extremely thin figure. At the age of fifteen, she dropped out of school and told her twenty-five-year-old boyfriend, Nigel Davies, that she wanted to become a model. Davies offered to help Twiggy make her way in the fashion world. He took Twiggy to a top London hairdresser, who cropped and lightened her hair. Mr. Leonard, the hairdresser, then placed a photograph of Twiggy in his front window as an advertisement. Shortly after, Twiggy's picture appeared in the *London Daily Express* with the caption "This is the face of 1966."

Twiggy began to accept bookings as a model in London, with Davies as her manager. A few months later her popularity took her to Paris, where she was featured on covers and in layouts of *Elle, Vogue*, and *Paris Match*. During this period, Davies also established a clothing company called Twiggy Enterprises, Ltd., to be directed by Twiggy's parents and himself. All clothing was subject to Twiggy's final approval. Twiggy Enterprises successfully marketed the Twiggy line of clothes throughout Great Britain.

Her popularity grew rapidly after she spent seven weeks in 1967 touring America and being photographed in New York. Upon arrival in New York, she charged $120 an hour to be photographed, but the rate soon doubled to $240. She took the fashion world by storm. When she arrived in the United States, her reception outdid that of the Beatles* in hysteria and popularity. Twiggy was a five-foot, six-inch, ninety-one-pound high school dropout whose bobbed hair, triple-lashed eyes, and skinny figure became the fashion craze of the late 1960s. Young, liberated, and mod, she popularized miniskirts,* knit tops, striped stockings, and the thinnest of bodies. Fashion historians consider her the first modern supermodel who single-handedly destroyed the so-called full, well-rounded, ideal body that had dominated popular culture for the previous century.

REFERENCES: Annalee Gold, *75 Years of Fashion*, 1975; *New York Times*, April 28, 1967; Elizabeth Wilson, *Adorned in Dress*, 1987.

Karen Russell

THE TWILIGHT ZONE. *The Twilight Zone* first appeared on CBS television* on October 2, 1959. The creation of playwright Rod Serling, the series ran through September 1965, earning a cult following. *The Twilight Zone* was essentially a science fiction anthology, without a permanent cast, whose stock-in-

trade was whimsy, the occult, and ironic twists of fate in the lives of the characters. The show was especially popular among younger audiences.
REFERENCE: Joel Engel, *Rod Serling*, 1989.

TWIST. The twist was a dance craze that swept through the United States and then the rest of the world in 1960. Chubby Checker,* a twenty-year-old rock and roller from Philadelphia, first popularized the dance. A free-form dance that featured twisting body gyrations, the twist could be performed without a partner. The twist was a perfect symbol of the 1960s, when the age of individualism reached its apogee. The twist actually originated in Harlem in the 1950s, but when Checker performed the song and dance on *American Bandstand* in 1960, white teenagers accepted it with extraordinary enthusiasm. Permutations on the twist—such as the frug and the mashed potato—appeared later in the decade.
REFERENCE: Lorraine Glennon, ed., *Our Times: The Illustrated History of the 20th Century*, 1995.

2001: A SPACE ODYSSEY. Directed by Stanley Kubrick, *2001: A Space Odyssey* was released in 1968. It was based on a science fiction story by Arthur C. Clarke and starred Keir Dullea as an astronaut/hero. A fantasy dealing with the evolution of human intelligence from the age of cavemen to the age of supercomputers, *2001* was science fiction with intellectual sophistication and moral complexity. Its special effects were spectacular, its imagery enigmatic, its music spellbinding. Critics at first panned the film, calling it cold, incoherent, and arrogant, but it was a huge commercial success, mesmerizing audiences with its technical wizardry and allowing endless speculation about the meaning of its plot.
REFERENCE: *New York Times*, April 4, 1968.

U

U-2 CRISIS. For several years during the late 1950s, the United States, from military bases in Turkey, had flown high-altitude reconnaissance missions over the Soviet Union. It was essentially a covert operation of the Central Intelligence Agency* (CIA). CIA pilots flew U-2 aircraft, which were capable of hovering above Soviet radar and were equipped with high-altitude photographic equipment. But in May 1960, Soviet surface-to-air missiles shot down an American U-2 and captured the pilot, Francis Gary Powers, who had parachuted out of the falling aircraft. At first, the United States denied Soviet accusations of espionage, claiming it was only a weather flight over Turkey that had gone astray.

But when the Soviet Union displayed Powers at a press conference, exposing the U.S. explanation as a lie, the Eisenhower* administration came clean, explaining that the U-2 reconnaissance flights had been going on for years. President Dwight D. Eisenhower and Soviet premier Nikita Khrushchev* were scheduled for a summit meeting at the end of May, but an angry Khrushchev scuttled the meetings. Eisenhower canceled future U-2 flights, but technology was already rendering the aircraft obsolete. The United States now had satellites in orbit that were capable of photographing the same regions of the Soviet Union. Powers was sentenced to a long prison term at hard labor, but in 1963 he was traded for an East German spy and released.

REFERENCES: John L. Gaddis, *Russia, the Soviet Union, and the United States*, 1978; Paul Y. Hammond, *Cold War and Detente*, 1975.

THE UGLY AMERICAN **(Book).** *The Ugly American* is the title of a powerful, influential novel of the late 1950s and early 1960s. William J. Lederer and Eugene Burdick's *The Ugly American* was published in 1958 and spent seventy-eight weeks on the best-seller list. The book sold 4 million copies and was made into a movie starring Marlon Brando. *The Ugly American* is set in the fictionalized Southeast Asian country of Sarkhan. The book focuses on the failures of

American foreign policy and the diplomats who were hopelessly ill equipped to carry out that policy. The leading character is Colonel Hillandale, who happens to be bright and able, moving through Sarkhan winning the trust of the indigenous people and weaning them away from communism. Unfortunately, few of the other Americans in the novel are as capable.

The real enemy in *The Ugly American* is the U.S. foreign service. Although communication is its main function, the foreign service is unable to communicate in the language of the host country. Chosen too often for their "personal wealth, political loyalty, and the ability to stay out of trouble," America's ambassadors rarely have any applicable foreign language training. They hear only what their interpreters want them to hear, obtain from newspapers only what their readers want them to obtain, and are subject to costly leaks and security problems. Isolated in the cities, they spend their days entertaining visiting American VIPs, socializing with other Western diplomats, and occasionally meeting with members of the local elite. They ignore the vast percentage of the population who live in rural poverty and speak only their own language. They have no knowledge of their enemy. They have not read the works of Mao Zedong,* Karl Marx, or Vladimir Lenin. Instead they believe that American dollars will lead to victory. The communists in *The Ugly American*, on the other hand, speak the native language and work closely with rural peasants, building loyalties and political support. The United States was losing the fight for the Third World, but it could still win against communism. In that sense, the novel is a jeremiad. The solution is to fill the Third World with more Colonel Hillandales—competent, confident, and linguistically gifted Americans who can show the virtues of democracy and capitalism.

REFERENCE: William J. Lederer and Eugene Burdick, *The Ugly American*, 1958.

Randy Roberts

THE UGLY AMERICAN (Film). *The Ugly American* was a 1963 film based on William J. Lederer and Eugene Burdick's best-selling 1958 novel of the same name. The film starred Marlon Brando as Harrison Carter MacWhite, the do-gooder American diplomat whose intentions in Southeast Asia are decent but whose modest abilities and naïveté prevent him from fulfilling his own expectations. MacWhite is the newly appointed ambassador to Sarkhan, a South Vietnam–like Southeast Asian country caught in its own struggle with communist insurgents. Elegant, self-assured, and charming, MacWhite encompasses all the good that America appears to be in the world, but he is also obtuse about real world problems and their solutions, just as the United States turned out to be in Vietnam.

REFERENCE: *New York Times*, April 12, 1963.

UNION OF CONCERNED SCIENTISTS. The Union of Concerned Scientists was founded in 1969 by several scientists and academics at the Massachusetts Institute of Technology. They also opened an office in Washington, D.C. The

Union of Concerned Scientists was primarily concerned with nuclear arms reduction and the economic, safety, and medical issues associated with the use of domestic nuclear power. They became the recognized experts on these issues and regularly testified before Congress and served on various study commissions dealing with nuclear power issues.

REFERENCE: Loree Bykerk and Ardith Maney, *U.S. Consumer Interest Groups: Institutional Profiles*, 1995.

UNITED FARM WORKERS UNION. Although the New Deal achieved remarkable gains in the status of American workers, migrant farm laborers were still largely unprotected by the law. In 1962, César Chávez* established the Farm Workers Association to represent them, and in 1965 he changed its name to the National Farm Workers Association (NFWA). The NFWA successfully struck commercial rose grafters in McFarland, California, in May 1965, and three months later they joined the Filipino workers of the Agricultural Workers Organizing Committee in striking the commercial grape farmers in Delano, California.

Chávez headed the union, and from the beginning it was as much a social and cultural phenomenon as it was a labor movement. He also launched a nationwide boycott of California grapes until growers had recognized the union. During the NFWA's famous "March to Sacramento"* in the spring of 1966, Schenley Industries recognized the union. Chávez then targeted the Di Giorgio farms. By that time, the union ran into opposition from the International Brotherhood of Teamsters, which resented the NFWA's territorial gains and claimed that the union was more interested in assisting Chicano* and Filipino workers than poor white workers. The teamsters even cooperated with Di Giorgio. To increase its strength, the NFWA merged with the Agricultural Workers Organizing Committee in 1967 to form the United Farm Workers Organizing Committee of the American Federation of Labor–Congress of Industrial Organizations (AFL–CIO). The boycott of nonunion grapes proved very successful, and in 1970 the major growers signed contracts with the union. In 1972, the United Farm Workers Organizing Committee became the United Farm Workers.

REFERENCES: Dick Meister and Anne Loftis, *A Long Time Coming: The Struggle to Unionize America's Farm Workers*, 1977; Paul Fusco and George D. Horowitz, *La Causa, the California Grape Strike*, 1970; Jacques E. Levy, *César Chávez: Autobiography of La Causa*, 1975.

UNITED MEXICAN AMERICAN STUDENTS. The United Mexican Americans Students (UMAS) organization was a Chicano* group formed in Los Angeles in 1967. They campaigned for civil rights and for the election of Chicano candidates to political office among heavily Mexican-American constituencies. In 1969, UMAS's name was changed to the Movimiento Estudiantil Chicano de Aztlán.

REFERENCE: Matt S. Meier and Feliciano Rivera, *Dictionary of Mexican American History*, 1981.

UNITED NATIVE AMERICANS. United Native Americans was founded in 1968 by Lehman L. Brightman, whose own militancy was an outgrowth of the termination* movement of the 1950s and 1960s. Based in San Francisco, United Native Americans was one of the leading organizations in the "red power"* movement. Brightman was a severe critic of the Bureau of Indian Affairs (BIA) in particular and federal Indian policy in general, and he also attacked such groups as the National Congress of Americans, which he felt was so moderate that its policies amounted to an alliance with the BIA. Brightman demanded Indian control of the BIA, restoration of tribal lands, and complete civil rights for Native Americans. From 1968 to 1977, United Native Americans published a journal entitled *Warpath*.

REFERENCE: Armand S. La Potin, *Native American Voluntary Organizations*, 1986.

UNITED STATES V. OREGON **(1969).** For thousands of years, various Native American peoples fished for salmon along the Columbia River. When white settlers began arriving in the Columbia River basin of what is today Washington and Oregon in the 1840s and 1850s, the tribes ceded land title to the federal government but negotiated treaties retaining their hunting, fishing, and meeting rights at "usual and accustomed places." But in the twentieth century, logging activities and river pollution began to compromise the salmon harvests. Even worse, construction of hydroelectric dams along the Columbia and Snake Rivers inundated traditional fishing sites.

In the 1960s, to protect their fishing rights, a number of tribes sued in the federal courts. One of those cases—*United States v. Oregon*—was decided by the Supreme Court in 1969. It ruled that Native American fishing rights did not come from white people but had originated with Indian peoples. Treaties had guaranteed indigenous peoples the right to fish at their accustomed places and to enjoy jurisdictional control over their own fishing activities. The Court also ordered that the federal government, state governments, and Indian tribes establish cooperative machinery to manage salmon resources. The decision led to the establishment of the Columbia River Inter-Tribal Fish Commission in 1977 to implement Native American jurisdictional authority and to coordinate fishing activities.

REFERENCES: Russel Lawrence Barsh and James Youngblood Henderson, *The Road: Indian Tribes and Political Liberty*, 1980; Vine DeLoria and Clifford M. Lytle, *American Indians, American Justice*, 1983; H. Barry Holt and Gary Forrester, *Digest of American Indian Law: Cases and Chronology*, 1990; Stephen L. Pevar, *The Rights of Indians and Tribes: The Basic ACLU Guide to Indian and Tribal Rights*, 1992; John R. Wunder, *"Retained by the People": A History of American Indians and the Bill of Rights*, 1994; Wilcomb E. Washburn, *Red Man's Land, White Man's Law: The Past and Present Status of the American Indian*, 1971; Charles F. Wilkinson, *American Indians, Time and the Law*, 1987.

UNITED STATES V. ROBEL. The Supreme Court under Chief Justice Earl Warren* earned a reputation for limiting the powers of the state and enhancing the rights and freedoms of individuals. That was especially true in how the Court interpreted First Amendment issues during the 1960s, including the freedom of association clause, in cases involving questions of political loyalty. The Court decided *United States v. Robel* on December 11, 1967, with Chief Justice Earl Warren writing the majority opinion. The vote had been 6 to 2. The case involved the constitutionality of a section of the Subversive Activities Control Act of 1950, which forbade employment in defense industries to members of subversive organizations. The Court overturned the legislation as an unconstitutional violation of the First Amendment right to freedom of association.
REFERENCE: 389 U.S. 258 (1967).

UNITED STATES V. WADE. During the tenure of Chief Justice Earl Warren* (1953–1960), the Supreme Court assumed the most liberal constitutional profile in U.S. history, narrowing the powers of government officials and broadening the rights of individuals. A series of decisions revolving around the right-to-counsel clause of the Sixth Amendment substantially increased the rights of criminal defendants. One such case was *United States v. Wade*, decided by a unanimous vote on June 12, 1967. The issue to be resolved dealt with whether a suspect forced to stand in a police lineup for identification purposes had the right to have his or her legal counsel present. The Court decided in favor of defendants. Police could not force them to stand in identification lineups without the presence of their counsel.
REFERENCE: 388 U.S. 218 (1967).

THE UNTOUCHABLES. *The Untouchables* was a popular television* detective and police dramatic series of the late 1950s and early 1960s. Its setting was the organized crime chaos of Chicago during the Prohibition era of the late 1920s and early 1930s. ABC first broadcast *The Untouchables* on October 15, 1959. Narrated by Walter Winchell, *The Untouchables* revolved around the crime-fighting exploits of government agent Elliot Ness, played by Robert Stack. Ness was a squeaky-clean, humorless crime fighter. The last episode was broadcast on September 10, 1963.
REFERENCE: Tim Brooks and Earle Marsh, *The Complete Directory to Prime Time Network and Cable TV Shows*, 1995.

UPTIGHT. The term ''uptight'' became part of the lexicon of the 1960s. Generally, it described an older generation of Americans who came of age during the Great Depression and World War II. The counterculture* considered them hopelessly conventional and conservative about matters of sexuality, music, and politics. ''Uptight'' was an adjective used to refer to an individual whose values were conservative and middle-class.
REFERENCE: Ruth Bronsteen, *The Hippy's Handbook—How to Live on Love*, 1967.

V

VAN DUSEN, HENRY PITNEY. Henry Van Dusen was born December 11, 1967, in Philadelphia. He graduated from Princeton in 1919, earned a divinity degree at the Union Theological Seminary in New York in 1924, and finally took a Ph.D. at the University of Edinburgh in 1932. He spent the rest of his career at the Union Theological Seminary as professor of systematic theology until 1945 and president until 1963. Van Dusen was the author of *The Plain Man Seeks for God* (1933), *God in These Times* (1935), *World Christianity: Yesterday, Today and Tomorrow* (1947), *Life's Meaning* (1951), *One Great Hope* (1961), and *The Vindication of Liberal Theology* (1963).

During his lifetime, Van Dusen became the world's leading ecumenist; he was the central figure in establishing the World Council of Churches in 1948, and he played a direct role in its activities until 1961. His theology was eminently liberal, a perfect match for the cultural and political mood of the 1960s in the United States. For Van Dusen, there was no final arbiter of truth in the universe, only honest people striving to define truth for themselves. The church, he believed, should also be committed to social reform. A longtime member of the Euthanasia Society, Van Dusen took his own life on February 13, 1975, after a long struggle with the debilitating effects of a stroke.
REFERENCE: *New York Times*, February 14, 1975.

VATICAN II. Perhaps the most momentous event in the religious history of the 1960s in the United States was the Vatican II conference of the Roman Catholic Church. The last Vatican Council had been convened in 1873, and in October 1962 Pope John XXIII assembled Vatican Council II, or Vatican II. The purpose of the meetings, which lasted until December 1965, was to discuss the place of the church in a changing world. More than 2,500 people participated in the sessions.

The charge Pope John XXIII gave the participants was to restore the church to a central role in world affairs by bridging the gap between communism and capitalism, the West and the East, and the developed world and the Third World, as well as to update ancient rituals, ceremonies, and liturgies. Vatican II eventually issued sixteen documents outlining important ecclesiastical reforms. After Vatican II, the mass could be performed in Latin or in a vernacular language, lay parishioners could participate more directly in church liturgies, Catholics were called on to work with non-Catholics in solving social problems, and church members were urged to read the Bible on their own rather than letting their spiritual studies revolve only around existing church dogma. Pope John did, however, stand firm in his opposition to contraception, abortion, and clerical celibacy.

REFERENCE: James S. Olson, *Catholic Immigrants in America*, 1987.

VIETCONG. The term ''Vietcong'' was coined by South Vietnamese president Ngo Dinh Diem* in the 1950s as a reference to ''Vietnamese communists.'' Coming from him, it was more epithet than definition. The Vietcong were primarily South Vietnamese communists committed to the overthrow of the American-backed government of the Republic of Vietnam. During the late 1950s and early 1960s, the Vietcong became a formidable army in South Vietnam, supported by Russian and Chinese supplies brought to them down the Ho Chi Minh Trail.* The inability of South Vietnamese troops to prevail militarily against the Vietcong ultimately led to the U.S. escalation of the conflict. The Vietcong remained a powerful fighting force until the Tet Offensive* of 1968, in which they suffered huge losses at the hands of American troops. After Tet, Vietnam was largely a war against North Vietnamese forces.

REFERENCE: James S. Olson and Randy Roberts, *Where the Domino Fell: America and Vietnam 1945–1995*, 1995.

VIETNAM VETERANS AGAINST THE WAR. Vietnam Veterans against the War (VVAW) was founded in 1967 after six veterans who marched together in an antiwar* demonstration decided veterans needed their own antiwar organization. Its membership ultimately included several thousand veterans and a few government infiltrators. The VVAW participated in most major antiwar activities, including the 1968 Democratic National Convention* in Chicago. Government officials saw VVAW from its inception as a special threat because Vietnam veterans had a unique credibility. Furthermore, officials feared their capacity for violence, although VVAW demonstrations were always among the most peaceful and orderly.

With Jane Fonda's* financial assistance, VVAW conducted the Detroit ''Winter Soldier Investigation'' (February 1971), where numerous veterans testified about ''war crimes'' they either witnessed or perpetrated. Selected testimonies were published in *The Winter Soldier Investigation* (1972). Speaking at the hearings, prompted in part by VVAW outrage over the assertion that the My Lai massacre was an aberration resulting from soldiers' having ''gone berserk,'' executive secretary Al Hubbard stated, "The crimes against humanity, the war itself, might not have occurred if we, all of us, had not been brought up in a country permeated with racism, obsessed with communism, and convinced beyond a shadow of a doubt that we are good and most other countries are inherently evil." The government and its supporters denounced the proceedings and made several attempts to discredit testimony given.

On April 19, 1971, the VVAW began "Dewey Canyon III." (Dewey Canyon* I and II were military operations in Laos.) It included over 1,000 veterans, led by men in wheelchairs and mothers of men killed in combat who held a memorial service at the Tomb of the Unknown Soldier and then were refused permission to lay wreaths on graves of fallen comrades at Arlington Cemetery (although after much haggling 200 were permitted to lay wreaths the next day). They camped on the mall in defiance of a court order, which was rescinded after it was realized that it would be poor public relations to arrest peaceful combat veterans. On April 23, 1971, more than 1,000 veterans threw medals they had won in Vietnam over police barricades on the Capitol steps.

Subsequent activities included several protests in December 1971 of the heaviest bombing of North Vietnam since 1968 and at the 1972 Republican convention in Miami, for which eight members (and two sympathizers) were tried on contrived criminal conspiracy charges. In July 1974, about 2,000 members demonstrated in Washington demanding universal amnesty for draft* resisters and deserters, implementation of the Paris peace treaty, ending aid to Nguyen Van Thieu* and Lon Nol, Richard Nixon's* impeachment, and a universal discharge with benefits for all Vietnam veterans. In all its activities, the VVAW had an overriding goal: to make the nation realize, in the words of cofounder Jan Barry, "the moral agony of America's Viet Nam war generation—whether to kill on military orders and be a criminal, or to refuse to kill and be a criminal."

REFERENCES: David W. Levy, *The Debate over Vietnam*, 1991; Thomas Powers, *Vietnam: The War at Home, Vietnam and the American People, 1964–1968*, 1984; Melvin Small, *Johnson, Nixon, and the Doves*, 1988; Kathleen J. Turner, *Lyndon Johnson's Dual War: Vietnam and the Press*, 1985; Sandy Vogelgesang, *The Long Dark Night of the Soul: The American Intellectual Left and the Vietnam War*, 1974; Nancy Zaroulis and Gerald Sullivan, *Who Spoke Up? American Protest against the War in Vietnam, 1963–1975*, 1984.

Samuel Freeman

VIETNAM WAR. The roots of American involvement in Vietnam go back to World War II. At the time, Vietnam was a French colony, but Vietnamese nationalists had long chafed under foreign domination. For centuries, they fought against Chinese occupation of Vietnam, and no sooner had they expelled the Chinese imperialists in the early nineteenth century than French imperialists arrived and imposed a new form of colonialism. French politicians and their Vietnamese surrogates dominated the political bureaucracy, seized land and businesses from the Vietnamese, and imposed Roman Catholicism on the country. Vietnamese nationalists launched a guerrilla campaign against the French, but French military power was too great.

Japan then did what the Vietnamese could not do. When Germany overran France in 1940, Japan occupied a Vietnam that France could no longer defend. Vietnamese nationalists, led by Ho Chi Minh,* then turned on the Japanese, fighting a guerrilla war to push them out of Vietnam. Vietnam did not want an Asian imperialist master any more than it wanted a Western master. In fact, Ho Chi Minh worked with the Office of Strategic Services, the forerunner of the Central Intelligence Agency* (CIA), during World War II. In return for intelligence information and the return of American pilots shot down over the South China Sea, the United States armed Ho Chi Minh's 5,000-man army.

As World War II came to a close, President Franklin D. Roosevelt actually contemplated liberating Vietnam from French control. The Vietnamese, he thought, were ready for independence. But France, a key U.S. ally during the war, would have none of it, and Great Britain also opposed Vietnamese independence. If France lost Vietnam, what would prevent Great Britain from losing India or Hong Kong or Malaya? When Franklin Roosevelt died in April 1945, so did Vietnam's hopes for independence. The new president, Harry Truman, had too many things on his mind, and Vietnam was not one of them. When World War II ended, France moved back to Indochina and reimposed its colonial control of Cambodia, Laos, and Vietnam.

Ho Chi Minh and his army, now known as the Vietminh, resumed their guerrilla war against the French. Within a matter of two years, whatever sympathy the United States had once had for Ho Chi Minh evaporated. He was a communist, a devoted follower of Karl Marx and Nicolai Lenin, and he believed that only in communism could the Vietnamese ever really enjoy true freedom, equality, and justice. He was also, as he had always been, a genuine nationalist who wanted to see Vietnam independent and free of all foreign occupation or domination. But as the United States entered the years of the red scare and the Cold War,* in which a global struggle for the survival of democracy and communism was beginning, Ho Chi Minh's communism became far more important in American eyes than his nationalism. By 1950, the United States was providing hundreds of millions of dollars in military assistance to France, hoping that the French would be able to defeat the communists and maintain control of their colony.

It was not to be. France steadily lost ground in Vietnam, and Ho Chi Minh recruited an army of more than 100,000 highly skilled, committed troops. In the spring of 1954, when French forces were about to undergo a humiliating defeat at the hands of the Vietminh at Dien Bien Phu, France appealed for U.S. military intervention. It wanted American air support and, if necessary, American ground troops to rescue the embattled French Expeditionary Corps. President Dwight D. Eisenhower* ultimately decided not to intervene, and Dien Bien Phu fell to the Vietnamese communists.

With the French Empire in Vietnam crumbling, the United States worked to preserve a noncommunist base of some kind there. The domino theory* was gaining ground among American policymakers, who believed that if Vietnam fell to communism, a chain reaction of falling dominos would begin that might eventually bring all of Southeast Asia and perhaps East Asia under communist control. In the Geneva Accords of 1954, the United States managed to see to the division of Vietnam at the seventeenth parallel. North Vietnam would be communist, and South Vietnam would be noncommunist. In 1956, free elections would be held to reunite the country.

Ho Chi Minh became the leader of the Democratic Republic of Vietnam (North Vietnam), and Ngo Dinh Diem,* an anticommunist Vietnamese nationalist, became president of the Republic of Vietnam (South Vietnam). The free elections were never held. When the CIA determined that Ho Chi Minh would win handily in the north and the south, the elections were canceled. Ho Chi Minh then began recruiting sympathetic Vietnamese into a southern army, which became known as the Vietcong. The Vietcong then launched a guerrilla war against the American-backed regime of Ngo Dinh Diem.

Diem was a corrupt, anti-Buddhist Roman Catholic whose self-serving policies soon alienated most South Vietnamese and made Ho Chi Minh's recruiting much easier. The Vietcong kept gaining ground, and President Dwight Eisenhower had to send in hundreds of U.S. military advisers to train the South Vietnamese army. By the time Eisenhower left the White House, more than 700 U.S. troops had been deployed to South Vietnam. The Vietcong continued, however, to gain ground, and by September 1963 more than 16,000 U.S. military advisers were in-country. Ngo Dinh Diem was assassinated by his own generals on November 1, 1963, and three weeks later, President John F. Kennedy* was assassinated in Dallas, Texas. Vice President Lyndon B. Johnson* then became president of the United States.

Throughout 1964 and early 1965, the U.S. position in South Vietnam continued to deteriorate. Instability became endemic in the government of South Vietnam, with rebellions and coup d'états becoming commonplace. The Army of the Republic of Vietnam (ARVN) was hopelessly weak, and the Vietcong continued to gain ground. Johnson had to send several thousand additional U.S. military advisers to South Vietnam in an attempt to stem the tide. After the Gulf of Tonkin incident* during the first week of August 1964, the president began a bombing campaign over North Vietnam (Bombing of Southeast Asia*). The war was widening.

By early 1965, it was clear that if the United States did not introduce regular ground troops into South Vietnam, communists would overrun the country in a matter of months. By this time, the president knew that the war was getting out of hand, but he refused to disengage, not wanting to be ''the first president to lose a war.'' In March 1965, Johnson deployed the first contingent of U.S. Marines to Vietnam, and by the end of the year more than 184,000 American ground troops were in the country. Casualties* began to mount.

Despite the growing American commitment, the government of South Vietnam grew weaker, and the Vietcong, now sustained by troops and supplies from North Vietnam, grew stronger. American military officials kept raising the "minimum number of troops" necessary to win the war, and by the end of 1966 more than 325,000 American soldiers were fighting in Vietnam.

The war was clearly out of control. It was creating serious economic problems. Until 1965, when President Lyndon B. Johnson introduced U.S. ground troops into the conflict, the Vietnam War had only a minor impact on the American economy. But as the war escalated, government expenditures increased dramatically. President Lyndon B. Johnson wanted to fight the Vietnam War as well as maintain his Great Society* domestic programs. In 1964, federal spending totaled $118 billion. It had been $118 billion in 1964 as well, and $111 billion in 1963. But in 1966 federal spending jumped to $134 billion and then to $158 billion in 1967, $179 billion in 1968, $185 billion in 1969, $197 billion in 1970, $212 billion in 1971, $232 billion in 1972, and $247 billion in 1973. The total federal debt increased from $286 billion in 1960 to $458 billion in 1973. The large-scale federal spending fueled an inflationary spiral during the late 1960s. Since cutting federal spending was impossible for Johnson because of his domestic agenda, the only alternative was a tax increase, but the Vietnam War was politically unpopular, and Johnson did not feel he could secure much of a tax increase as a way of dampening consumer purchasing power. When inflation reached 6 percent in 1968, Congress passed a 10 percent income tax surcharge in hopes of slowing spending and lessening inflation, but it was too little too late. Although the Vietnam War's most dramatic impact on American society was social and political, it did set in motion the inflationary spiral that plagued the economy throughout the 1970s and 1980s.

At home, Johnson faced an antiwar movement* that was gaining in strength, criticism from U.S. allies around the world, and an enemy in Vietnam that seemed intractably committed. By the end of 1967, General William Westmoreland* promised Johnson that the end of the war was in sight, that the presence of nearly 500,000 U.S. troops had finally overwhelmed the enemy. The news gratified Johnson, who wanted to have Vietnam behind him before the 1968 presidential election.

But it was not to be. On January 31, 1968, just three weeks before the New Hampshire primary, the Vietcong launched the Tet Offensive.* They attacked U.S. and South Vietnamese forces all over the country, and although American forces managed to repel the attack and inflict huge casualties on the Vietcong, the Tet Offensive proved to be a strategic and political disaster at home. The Vietnam War appeared to be a never-ending quagmire with victory as far away as it had been in 1965. Senator Eugene McCarthy* almost upset the president in New Hampshire, Senator Robert Kennedy* of New York then declared his intention to take the nomination away from the president, and at the end of March, Lyndon Johnson bowed out of the race, announcing that he would stop the bombing of North Vietnam and not run for reelection.

The Republicans smelled blood in the presidential election of 1968,* calling for law and order at home and a diplomatic solution to the Vietnam War. Robert Kennedy was assassinated in June 1968, and Hubert Humphrey* won the Democratic presidential nomination. Richard Nixon* became the GOP (Grand Old Party) nominee, and George Wallace* mounted a third-party campaign. In November, Nixon eked out a narrow victory and entered the White House in January 1969.

During the election campaign, Nixon had implied, if not outright promised, that his administration would be able to find "peace with honor" in Vietnam. Once he took the oath of office in January 1969, he had to make good on the promise. He soon announced what he called "Vietnamization"*—the gradual withdrawal of American troops and the handing of the war over to the Army of the Republic of Vietnam. During the next four years, Nixon steadily reduced the troop level from 543,000 Americans to only 50 in 1973. In order to secure an agreement from North Vietnam, he launched an enormous bombing campaign in December 1972, after which North Vietnam finally agreed to the peace settlement.

Ironically, North Vietnam had dictated the terms. Ever since the beginning of the Paris peace talks in 1968, North Vietnam had insisted on the withdrawal of all U.S. troops from Indochina, the right of the Vietcong to participate in the government of South Vietnam, and the continuing presence of North Vietnamese soldiers in South Vietnam. For years the United States refused to negotiate on those terms, but by 1972, with most American troops gone, all the United States wanted was to get back the prisoners of war.* The Vietnam War, arguably the most misguided political and military crusade in American history, ended in January 1973. Two years later, in March 1975, North Vietnamese troops easily conquered South Vietnam.

REFERENCE: James S. Olson and Randy Roberts, *Where the Domino Fell: America and Vietnam, 1945–1995*, 1995.

VIETNAMIZATION. President Richard Nixon* used the term "Vietnamization" to describe the process by which he gradually withdrew U.S. forces from Vietnam and turned the war over to the Army of the Republic of Vietnam. Actually, for decades the U.S. presence in Vietnam had ostensibly been to buy time until South Vietnamese forces were trained and ready for successful engagement. With the antiwar movement* gaining momentum in the United States, Nixon decided it was politically necessary for the United States to disengage. Between 1969 and 1973, he reduced the number of U.S. troops from 543,000 to only 50. As American troops withdrew, South Vietnamese troops took over the fighting. The policy did not work, at least in terms of saving South Vietnam from a communist takeover. In the spring of 1975, North Vietnamese forces seized control of the country.

REFERENCE: James S. Olson and Randy Roberts, *Where the Domino Fell: America and Vietnam, 1945–1995*, 1995.

THE VIRGINIAN. The Virginian was a popular television* western of the 1960s. Like *Bonanza** and *Gunsmoke,** it survived the general decline of television westerns during the decade. The first episode was broadcast by NBC on September 19, 1962. Loosely based on Owen Wister's classic 1902 novel *The Virginian*, the series was set in the Wyoming Territory of the 1890s. Among other leading stars, the cast included Lee J. Cobb as Judge Henry Garth, James Drury as the Virginian, Doug McClure as Trampas, Gary Clarke as Steve, and Pippa Scott as Molly Wood. *The Virginian* was unique because it was television's first attempt at a ninety-minute weekly program. The last episode was broadcast on September 8, 1971.
REFERENCE: Tim Brooks and Earle Marsh, *The Complete Directory to Prime Time Network and Cable TV Shows*, 1995.

VISTA. See VOLUNTEERS IN SERVICE TO AMERICA.

VIVA KENNEDY CLUBS. Because of his Roman Catholicism and Democratic credentials, John F. Kennedy* appealed to many Mexican Americans* during the election of 1960.* Hector García and Carlos McCormick of the American G.I. Forum established a group called Viva Kennedy to rally Mexican-American support for Kennedy's candidacy. Viva Kennedy clubs were established in towns and cities throughout the Southwest, and they enjoyed an enthusiastic reception among Mexican Americans. The Viva Kennedy clubs played an important part in Kennedy's victory, and after the election, the organizers of the Viva Kennedy movement in Texas established Mexican Americans for Political Action, a group that evolved into the Political Association of Spanish-Speaking Organizations.
REFERENCE: Matt S. Meier and Feliciano Rivera, *Dictionary of Mexican American History*, 1981.

VO NGUYEN GIAP. Vo Nguyen Giap was born in Quang Binh Province, Vietnam, in 1912. He became interested in revolutionary politics as an adolescent, and while attending law school at the University of Hanoi,* he joined the Lao Dong Party, Vietnam's primary communist organization. A bitter opponent of the French Empire, Giap engaged in anti-French political activities and was exiled in 1939. His wife was arrested and died in a French prison in 1941. Giap joined forces with Ho Chi Minh* and helped organize the Vietminh, Ho's military force. During World War II, the Vietminh fought against Japanese occupation forces in Vietnam. In 1946, Ho Chi Minh named Giap commander in chief of Vietminh forces.

Giap then turned his attention to harassing French forces engaged in the reoccupation of Vietnam. Vietminh troops increased in numbers and strength during the late 1940s and early 1950s, and by 1953 Giap was in charge of an army of 300,000 troops. He inflicted a massive military defeat on the French at Dien Bien Phu in May 1954. France then surrendered its imperial foothold in Indochina. At the Geneva Conference of 1954, Vietnam was divided at the seventeenth parallel into South Vietnam and North Vietnam, with reunification elections scheduled for 1956.

When the United States refused to allow the elections, primarily because intelligence reports indicated that Ho Chi Minh would win in both the north and south, the Vietminh launched a military crusade against the government of South Vietnam. For the next sixteen years, Giap engineered the North Vietnamese and Vietcong military campaigns against American and South Vietnamese forces. Although he frequently committed tactical errors, especially in allowing frontal assaults on American positions, Giap managed to sustain the conflict indefinitely, inflicting unacceptably large casualties* on American forces. Giap and Ho Chi Minh knew that Americans would soon tire of a seemingly endless war. After the disastrous Eastertide Offensive of 1972, in which the North Vietnamese army took more than 100,000 casualties, Giap was relieved of his command and replaced by Van Tien Dung, who masterminded the final defeat of South Vietnam in 1975. Nevertheless, Vo Nguyen Giap remains a genuine Vietnamese hero today and lives in Hanoi.
REFERENCE: Vo Nguyen Giap, *Unforgettable Months and Years*, 1975.

LOS VOLUNTARIOS. In 1963, Rodolfo ''Corky'' Gonzales* established Los Voluntarios and headquartered the organization in Denver. Its initial purpose was to end police brutality against Mexican Americans* by monitoring police activities. Los Voluntarios was an incipient civil rights organization that was later absorbed by the Crusade for Justice* group.
REFERENCE: Matt S. Meier and Feliciano Rivera, *Dictionary of Mexican American History*, 1981.

VOLUNTEERS IN SERVICE TO AMERICA. Also known as VISTA, Volunteers in Service to America was a federal program created with passage of the Equal Opportunity Act* on August 30, 1964. John F. Kennedy's* Peace Corps* had been enormously popular among young people, but a few critics charged that the United States should not be dissipating its resources abroad when there were enough problems here at home. President Lyndon B. Johnson* took that criticism to heart and used it to justify VISTA, a similar program that served poverty-stricken regions of the United States. VISTA volunteers served in inner-city schools, urban hospitals, rural health clinics, Indian reservations, and a variety of other settings. The program still exists today.
REFERENCES: T. Zane Reeves, *The Politics of the Peace Corps and VISTA*, 1988; Marvin Schwartz, *In Service to America: A History of VISTA in Arkansas, 1965–1985*, 1988.

VOTING RIGHTS ACT OF 1965. The Voting Rights Act of 1965, also known as the Civil Rights Act of 1965, was one of the most significant pieces of civil rights legislation in U.S. history. The civil rights movement* had focused most of its energies in the 1950s and early 1960s on ending de jure segregation in American public life. A series of Supreme Court decisions, combined with the Civil Rights Act of 1964, had largely achieved that objective, at least on paper. But civil rights activists also realized that until African Americans exercised the franchise in large numbers, they would have no real permanent political power in the United States. During the early 1960s, when groups such as the Southern Christian Leadership Conference* and the Student Nonviolent Coordinating Committee* had tried to register black voters in the South, they had encountered violent resistance from whites. Hispanic voters in Texas and other parts of the Southwest often experienced similar intimidation.

President Lyndon B. Johnson* decided to address the problem, and he pushed through Congress the Voting Rights Act, which became law on August 6, 1965. The legislation banned all literacy tests for voting and authorized the use of federal marshals to observe and supervise elections where literacy tests had been used in the past and where less than half of all eligible voters were actually registered. As a result of the law, the number of black and Hispanic voters participating in local, state, and national elections increased markedly.
REFERENCE: David J. Garrow, *Protest at Selma: Martin Luther King, Jr., and the Voting Rights Act of 1965*, 1978.

VOYAGE TO THE BOTTOM OF THE SEA. Loosely based on Irwin Allen's 1961 film *Voyage to the Bottom of the Sea*, the television* series *Voyage to the Bottom of the Sea* was first broadcast by ABC on September 14, 1964. It featured Richard Basehart as Admiral Harriman Nelson, commander of the *Seaview*, a gigantic submarine that explored the depths of the world's oceans, fought alien creatures and human malcontents, and tried to protect the world from destruction. The science fiction drama was popular Sunday night fare until its last broadcast on September 15, 1968.
REFERENCE: Tim Brooks and Earle Marsh, *The Complete Directory to Prime Time Network and Cable TV Shows*, 1995.

W

WAGON TRAIN. *Wagon Train* was one of the most popular western dramas in television* history. Included in its cast were Ward Bond as Major Seth Adams, Robert Horton as Flint McCullough, Terry Wilson as Bill Hawks, and Frank McGrath as Charlie Wooster. Its setting was the trail from St. Joseph, Missouri, to California in the 1860s, before the completion of the transcontinental railroad, and the weekly programming revolved around the dangers—Indians, cutthroats, deserts, snakes, and mountains—that members of the wagon train faced during their cross-country journey. NBC first broadcast the series on September 18, 1957, and produced *Wagon Train* until 1962, when ABC took over. The last episode was broadcast on September 5, 1965.
REFERENCE: Tim Brooks and Earle Marsh, *The Complete Directory to Prime Time Network and Cable TV Shows*, 1995.

WALLACE, GEORGE CORLEY. George C. Wallace was born August 25, 1919, in Clio, Alabama. His father was a farmer. Wallace grew up in Clio and then worked his way through the University of Alabama. He received a law degree there in 1942 and then joined the U.S. Army for the duration of World War II. In 1946 and 1947, he served as an assistant attorney general of Alabama, and he won a seat in the state legislature in 1947. There he earned a reputation as somewhat of a liberal for denouncing the Ku Klux Klan and as a definite populist. Reelected three times, Wallace served there until 1953, when he accepted appointment as a state circuit judge. He lost a bid for the governorship of Alabama in 1958, largely because he offered moderate enough views on racial issues to earn the endorsement of the National Association for the Advancement of Colored People (NAACP). He vowed never to let race defeat him again. Wallace practiced law for the next four years in Clanton, Alabama. In 1963, he was elected to the state's highest office. His campaign theme was "Segregation now! Segregation tomorrow! Segregation forever!"

Wallace entered the governor's mansion just in time to confront the federal court-ordered integration of the University of Alabama. On June 11, 1963, he tried personally to block the door to the University of Alabama so that black students could not enter. It was political posturing at its worst, since federal troops were present to make sure that integration occurred, but Wallace became a hero to white segregationists throughout Alabama. He also began to secure a national following by preaching states' rights and an end to the "dictatorship of federal courts."

In 1964, Wallace declared himself a candidate for the Democratic presidential nomination. He stunned political insiders by securing 30 percent of the vote in Wisconsin and 45 percent in Maryland. When the Republican Party nominated conservative senator Barry Goldwater* of Arizona, however, Wallace withdrew from the Democratic race. But in his opposition to the social changes sweeping the country, Wallace had managed to develop a following in the working-class neighborhoods of northern cities. One year later, he refused to provide state troopers to protect Martin Luther King, Jr.'s,* civil rights march from Selma to Montgomery.

Under the Alabama Constitution, Wallace could not run for reelection in 1966, but his wife, Lurleen Wallace, did run and won by a landslide. He became the power behind the throne. When 1968 rolled around, the antiwar,* civil rights,* and black power* movements had alienated millions of white people, and Wallace was prepared to exploit their discontent. He declared himself a third-party presidential candidate in 1968, promising victory in Vietnam and law and order at home. Tough, charismatic, and blunt to a fault, Wallace picked retired air force general Curtis LeMay* as his running mate. The Wallace–Lemay ticket, represented by the American Party,* won more than 9 million popular votes (13.5 percent of the total) and forty-seven electoral votes in the election of 1968.

In 1970, Wallace won the governorship of Alabama again, and in 1972 he declared himself a candidate for the Democratic presidential nomination. He did well in several early primaries, but during a campaign stop in Laurel, Maryland, on May 15, 1972, he was shot. Wallace survived the assassination attempt, but it left him paralyzed from the waist down and ended his run for the White House. He won a third term as governor in 1975, and a year later he flirted with running for the Democratic presidential nomination, but his health was simply not good enough for the stresses of the campaign. Wallace remained a loyal Democrat for the rest of his political career. After leaving the governor's mansion in 1979, Wallace publicly apologized to the state's African Americans for some of the things he had said and positions he had defended during his career. He died September 13, 1998.

REFERENCES: Jody Carlson, *George C. Wallace and the Politics of Powerlessness: The Wallace Campaigns for the Presidency, 1964–1976*, 1981; Marshall Frady, *Wallace*, 1970.

WAR RESISTERS LEAGUE. Founded in 1923, the War Resisters League (WRL) is a secular pacifist organization. It opposed American participation in

World War II, the Korean War, and Vietnam, as well as protesting draft* laws
and the use of taxes for military purposes. In the early 1960s, David Dellinger*
was the leader of the WRL, and in the spring of 1964 he sponsored several draft
card-burning demonstrations. The WRL organized the first nationwide protest
demonstration against the Vietnam War* in December 1964. For the next nine
years, the WRL sponsored teach-ins* against the war and counseled young men
on how to avoid the draft. In more recent years, the WRL opposed the Persian
Gulf War.
REFERENCE: Pauline Maier, *The Old Revolutionaries*, 1980.

WARHOL, ANDY. Andy Warhol was born Andrew Warhola, Jr., to Czech
immigrant parents October 28, 1928, in Forest City, Pennsylvania. Not until
later in his life did he alter his name, date, and place of birth to create a mysterious identity. Warhol's celebrated birthday is on August 6, 1930. He claimed
many cities for his place of birth, most commonly, Pittsburgh. Warhol spent
much of his childhood in bed with chorea, otherwise known as "Saint Vitus'
dance," a disorder of the nervous system. When he was not bedridden, Warhol
enjoyed movies and idolized the glamour of Hollywood. He worked in a department store in Pittsburgh decorating the show windows. In 1945, he went to
the Carnegie Institute of Technology, now known as Carnegie–Mellon University. Throughout college his classmates labeled him shy, timid, and naive, but
he was admired for his outrageous and even scandalously controversial art. In
college Warhol developed the techniques that stayed with him throughout the
rest of his artwork.

In the early 1950s, he moved to New York City, where he became a commercial artist with *Glamour* magazine. He did not gain notoriety in the art world,
however, until 1962, when he launched his exhibition of the Campbell's soup
cans. For art historians, Warhol stands as a significant departure from the abstract impressionism so common to the 1950s. He pioneered the use of photographic silk screening on canvas and bold employment of colors. Among his
best-known works are "200 Soup Cans" (1962), "Green Coca-Cola Bottles"
(1962), "Two Dollar Bills" (1962), "Marilyn Monroe" (1962), and "Self-
Portraits" (1964–1966). He became known as the "King of Pop Art." His
purpose was to create art that expressed the dehumanization and institutionali-
zation of modern life. His art was not meant to be interesting or pleasing to the
eye; on the contrary, he wanted it to appear dull and boring. Warhol is most
famous for his repetitive art in which he used his own technique of photographic
silk screening. He used everyday packaging like the Coke bottle and the Campbell's soup can or such superstar celebrities as Marilyn Monroe* and Elvis
Presley.* He also did many paintings with comic strip characters like Superman
and Dick Tracy.

He made films with the same purpose in mind. The film *Empire* does nothing
but focus on the Empire State Building for eight hours. Through his film *The
Lonesome Cowboys* (1968), one can see the revolution of lifestyle and political

thought of the 1960s—unrepressed sexuality, social negativism, and political nihilism. Warhol's films epitomized the prevailing culture and morality of the decade. Among his other films were *The Chelsea Girls* and *Blue Movie*. Andy Warhol died February 26, 1987; while hospitalized for gall bladder surgery, he suffered a massive cardiac arrhythmia.

REFERENCES: Richard Morphet, *Warhol*, 1971; Victor Brockis, *The Life and Death of Andy Warhol*, 1989.

Jessica Carlson

WARNKE, PAUL CULLITON. A native of Webster, Massachusetts, Paul Warnke was born January 31, 1920, and graduated from Yale in 1941 and the Columbia University Law School in 1948. He practiced law in Washington, D.C., until 1966, when he was named general counsel for the Department of Defense. Between 1967 and 1969, Warnke served as assistant secretary of defense for international security affairs. During those years, he came to be a vigorous opponent, within the Defense Department, of the Vietnam War.* Warnke was convinced that it was the wrong war in the wrong place and that the United States would be unable to prevail. He had great influence over Secretary of Defense Clark Clifford,* and General William Westmoreland* would later blame Warnke for converting Clifford from a hawk* to a dove* about Vietnam. Later, Warnke became one of Clifford's law partners. When Richard Nixon* won the election of 1968, Warnke found himself exiled from political power with the rest of the Democrats; so he returned to private practice and continued to work on antiwar programs for the Democratic National Committee. Warnke returned to government service in 1977 during the Jimmy Carter administration as director of the Arms Control and Disarmament Agency and chief negotiator of the second Strategic Arms Limitation Treaty (SALT II). His appointment was quite controversial because of his open opposition to the Vietnam War and because he opposed deployment of the B-1 bomber and the Trident nuclear submarine. Although Warnke had no illusions about Soviet benevolence, he did believe that both countries had the capacity to destroy one another many times over and that weapons reduction was essential to world peace. Warnke continued to work on the SALT II treaty until his resignation in October 1978. Since then he has been a member of the Council on Foreign Relations.

REFERENCES: *Current Biography*, 1986; Paul Warnke, "Apes on a Treadmill," *Foreign Policy* 18 (1975).

WARREN, EARL. Earl Warren was born March 19, 1891, in Los Angeles. He took his undergraduate and law degrees at the University of California at Berkeley in 1914 and then joined the staff of the Oakland, California, district attorney's office. Anxious for a political career, Warren earned his credentials as a prosecutor, serving as deputy assistant district attorney of Alameda County from 1920 to 1923, chief deputy district attorney of Alameda County from 1923 to 1925, and district attorney of Alameda County from 1925 to 1938. As district attorney, he earned a reputation for being an enemy of organized crime and political corruption. A Republican, Warren won the election of 1938 and became attorney general of California, a post he held until his election as governor of California in 1942.

During the war, Warren was an outspoken conservative, enthusiastically supporting the internment of Japanese Americans and speaking out about the dangers of communism. He was reelected in 1946 and 1950. At the Republican National Convention of 1952, Warren surprised conservatives by throwing his support behind General Dwight D. Eisenhower.* Warren's endorsement proved crucial to Eisenhower's nomination and election. When Chief Justice Fred Vinson died in 1953, Eisenhower repaid his debt to Warren by nominating him as chief justice of the Supreme Court. Eisenhower, who later said picking Warren was the "biggest damn-fool mistake I ever made," thought the California governor would become a conservative bastion on the federal bench.

He surprised everyone. The political philosophy of the Warren Court became abundantly clear in 1954 with the *Brown v. Board of Education of Topeka, Kansas* decision. Segregated public schools were declared unconstitutional, and during the rest of his tenure, the Warren Court became known for its support of individual civil rights, civil liberties, voting rights, and personal privacy. Warren became the judicial symbol of the 1960s. The Warren Court was the most liberal in U.S. history, evidenced by the *Brown* decision as well as by *Baker v. Carr,* * Engel v. Vitale,* * Gideon v. Wainwright,* * Escobedo v. Illinois,* * Miranda v. Arizona,* * Loving v. Virginia,* * and *Gaston County v. United States.* * Earl Warren died December 29, 1971.

REFERENCES: D. J. Herda, *Earl Warren: Chief Justice for Social Change*, 1995; Arnold Rice, *The Warren Court, 1953–1969*, 1987; G. Edward White, *Earl Warren: A Public Life*, 1983.

WARREN COMMISSION. See THE KENNEDY ASSASSINATION.

WARS OF NATIONAL LIBERATION. Karl Marx's historical determinism predicted class revolutions around the world, and in a Moscow speech on January 6, 1961, Soviet Premier Nikita Khrushchev* claimed that "wars of national liberation" were leading the world down the path to socialism. He also offered the leaders of indigenous rebellions against "fascism and capitalism" the military and financial support of the Soviet Union. President John F. Kennedy* decided that Khrushchev intended to promote Communist interests that way instead of by direct confrontations with the United States. Not surprising, Kennedy came to see Communist political movements in Asia, Latin America, and Africa as part of a grand Soviet strategy. He therefore put a premium on development of effective counterinsurgency* programs to thwart wars of national liberation, a policy that took the United States into the jungles of Vietnam.

REFERENCE: *New York Times*, January 7–8, 1961.

WASTED. During the Vietnam War,* the term "waste" took on additional meaning. U.S. soldiers used the term "wasted" as a euphemism for killing people, particularly Vietcong and North Vietnamese troops and South Vietnamese civilians. "I really wasted that guy," a GI might say. The term was also used to describe the mercy killing of a fellow GI, whose wounds were so serious that he could not survive. The term ended up being employed in two contexts. First, it referred to "worthless" people who did not deserve to live, and second, it was used as a reference to unnecessary deaths, such as accidental killings.
REFERENCE: Samuel Freeman, "Wasted," in James S. Olson, ed., *Dictionary of the Vietnam War*, 1988.

WATTS, ALAN WILSON. Alan Watts was born January 6, 1915, in Chislehurst, Kent, England. He attended King's School in Canterbury, where he became enamored with Buddhist ideas. Watts did not go to college but worked in the family business and continued to study Buddhism. In 1935, he published his first book, *The Spirit of Zen*. Watts married a wealthy Buddhist in 1938 and moved to New York City. In the United States, he decided to reevaluate his religious thinking by attending the Seabury-Western Theological Seminary in Evanston, Illinois. There he began fusing Buddhist and Christian ideas. He wrote *The Meaning of Happiness* in 1940 and was ordained an Episcopalian minister in 1945. He was appointed chaplain at Northwestern University, where he wrote two more books: *Behold the Spirit* and *Supreme Identity*.

Watts then moved to California and became a faculty member at the Academy of Asian Studies and in 1956 published *The Way of Zen*. The book made him a popular lecturer and a guru of the fledgling Zen Buddhism movement, which became popular in the countercultural atmosphere of the 1960s. By that time, Watts was again in the midst of personal religious turmoil. He divorced his wife and began experimenting with psychedelic drugs, which he came to believe liberated him from the conventions of modern society. In 1962, Watts wrote *The Joyous Cosmology*. The book made him a guru of the hippie* movement and the counterculture's* leading advocate of Eastern religions. He also became more openly critical of Christianity's need to condemn self-interest, sex, and pleasure, a point of view he expressed in his book *The Two Hands of God* (1963). By 1967 Watts was deep into meditation and had became a "flower child."

By the early 1970s, Watts reached the peak of his influence, widely perceived as a gifted, charismatic mystic. Personally, however, he was drowning in a sea of drugs and alcohol. Alan Watts died November 16, 1973. Among his other books are *This Is It* (1960), *Psychotherapy East and West* (1961), *Beyond Theology* (1964), *The Book: On the Taboos against Knowing Who You Are* (1973), and his autobiography, *In My Own Way* (1973).
REFERENCES: David Clark, *The Pantheism of Alan Watts*, 1976; David Stuart, *Alan Watts*, 1976; Alan Watts, *In My Own Way*, 1973.

WATTS REBELLION. See RIOTS IN THE 1960s.

WAYNE, JOHN. John Wayne was born Marion Mitchell Morrison May 25, 1907, in Winterset, Iowa. When he was still a child, the family moved to California, and he was raised in Glendale, a suburb of Los Angeles. He graduated second in his class at Glendale High School and won a football scholarship to the University of Southern California. During the summer after his freshman year, he got a job working at the Fox Studio in Hollywood, where he met John Ford, the legendary director. Within a few months, he quit school and went to work full-time in the movie business.

He appeared in several bit roles in 1926 and 1927, but in 1928 director Raoul Walsh saw Wayne on the Fox Studio lot and hired him for the lead in his epic film *The Big Trail*. At that point in his career, Morrison took the stage name John Wayne. A box office flop, *The Big Trail* put Wayne's career on hold. For the next ten years he made dozens of B westerns and serials, becoming a familiar face to audiences in the small towns of the West, Midwest, and South. Wayne's big break came in 1939, when John Ford gave him a starring role as the Ringo Kid in *Stagecoach*.

During World War II and just after, Wayne made a number of films that projected him to superstardom in American popular culture. His war movies—*Flying Tigers, Reunion in France, Pittsburgh, The Fighting Seabees, Back to Bataan*, and *They Were Expendable*—made him Hollywood's most important male lead. By the end of the war, for millions of Americans, John Wayne truly *was* America. In the postwar years, he made films like *Red River, Fort Apache, The Sands of Iwo Jima, Hondo*, and *The Searchers*. As cowboy or soldier, Wayne displayed a hardened implacability, a determined inflexibility that marked his best film roles and actual life. Although his distinctive diction has been often imitated, he is better remembered for what he did on-screen rather than for what he said. He restored order. Sometimes his methods were harsh, occasionally his manner was gruff, but always the result was the same. He affirmed that there was a rough sense of justice at work and that if good was not always rewarded, evil was always punished.

During the 1950s and 1960s, Wayne also earned his reputation as a committed anticommunist and political conservative. He was an outspoken patriot who minced few words in his love for his country and in his disdain for those who criticized it. He made a series of films in the 1960s, including *North to Alaska, The Comancheros, The Man Who Shot Liberty Valance, Hatari!, How the West Was Won, The Longest Day, Donovan's Reef, McLintock!, Circus World, The Greatest Story Ever Told, In Harm's Way, The Sons of Katie Elder*, and *Cast a Giant Shadow*. Wayne received a Best Actor Oscar for his performance as Rooster Cogburn in *True Grit*.*

During the 1970s, Wayne continued to act and to speak out on political issues. By that time, of course, he had become a certifiable popular culture icon and perhaps the most recognizable face on the planet. His last film—*The Shootist*—was released in 1976. John Wayne died June 11, 1979.

REFERENCE: Randy Roberts and James S. Olson, *John Wayne, American*, 1995.

WEATHERMEN. The Weathermen originated from within leadership circles in the Students for a Democratic Society* (SDS). The SDS leadership became dominated by militants who advocated a more aggressive agenda than outlined in the Port Huron Statement* of 1962. This statement, partially authored by Tom Hayden* of Michigan State University, outlined SDS objectives: participatory democracy,* community control of schools, community control of police, students sharing power in universities, workers sharing power in running plants, change from within, reform rather than revolution, and opposition to the Cold War* but denunciation of communism. Riffs developed in the SDS as the Vietnam War* intensified, and riots broke out at Columbia University* and elsewhere by the late 1960s. These external events stimulated a reaction within the SDS that led to the rise of the Weathermen.

Premonitions of the split appeared at the 1968 national convention at Michigan State. Eight hundred people attended the convention, 300 of whom were undercover police. Two factions appeared to fight for control of the national leadership. One group of Maoists, the Progressive Labor Party (PL), proposed an alliance between students and workers. The PL held sway over Michigan State SDSers and delegates from other state universities. Leaders asked members to turn from drugs and middle-class countercultural conventions that alienated blue-collar workers. Another faction developed around Bernadette Dorhn, Columbia SDS student Mark Rudd, and such Ann Arbor-based radicals as Jim Mellen, Bill Ayers, Diana Oughton, and Terry Robbins. They hoped to unite with the Black Panthers,* the Vietcong,* and other Third World nationalist movements. With each scathing exchange between the two groups, a spirit of militancy intensified, and factionalism increased. In the end, the second group won majority control of party leadership.

By the time of the 1969 convention, the revolutionary faction had positioned themselves to enact drastic changes in the SDS mission. Mark Rudd and John Jacobs, his mentor, drafted a paper that became known as the ''Weatherman Paper.'' Rudd made it public to the Columbia SDS chapter and printed it in *New Left Notes*. Out of the convention chaos Rudd became party secretary. Dorhn and Mellen announced their manifesto: ''You don't need a weatherman to know which way the wind blows,'' whose title was taken from Bob Dylan's cryptic song ''Subterranean Homesick Blues.'' The manifesto condemned white-collar workers as counterrevolutionary racists, supported the Black Panthers, and declared a guerrilla war against the United States. They openly supported communism and advocated violence as a means to achieve that political objective. As the convention gave birth to the Weathermen, the SDS died. In the process, the organization membership fell from more than 100,000 people to only several thousand.

The leadership of the Weathermen believed it needed to demonstrate its power for members to believe in the revolution, to gain respect from Black Panthers, and to demonstrate solidarity with the North Vietnamese and other Third World revolutionaries. Weathermen and Black Panthers came to consider the police as the focus of their attacks. The Weathermen launched its ''Days of Rage''* rampage in Chicago on October 8, 1969, and attacked neighborhoods, business firms, and an army induction center. Rudd had promised to bring 20,000 people to Chicago, but only 250 showed up. Actually, the Weathermen refrain that the working-class was counterrevolutionary and college students hopelessly bourgeois doomed it. They could barely generate enough members to stay active.

The bottom fell out of the organization in the spring of 1970, when a bomb exploded in a New York City townhouse, killing three Weatherpeople—Terry Robbins, Diana Oughton, and Ted Gold. One cop who went into the ruins discovered enough undetonated bombs to ''level a whole block.'' The Weathermen went underground, but the misjudgments, violence, and twisted reasoning continued. In June 1970, the Weathermen held a ''War Council'' in Flint, Michigan, and endorsed Charles Manson* as a heroic figure. The War Council called for a violent campaign against government buildings—not people. Weathermen bombed the U.S. Capitol Building, government installations in Pittsburgh (the ''perfect pig city'' due to the high number of blue-collar workers), and several draft boards. But their campaign was futile. An arrogant elitism alienated them from any constituencies they might have been able to attract. The Weathermen were largely neutralized by 1971.

REFERENCE: Irwin Unger, *The Movement: A History of the American New Left, 1959–172*, 1988.

Michael Hall

WEAVER, ROBERT CLIFTON. Robert Weaver was born in Washington, D.C., in 1907. He specialized in economics at Harvard University, earning his bachelor's degree in 1929, master's degree in 1931, and Ph.D. in 1934. During the New Deal years of the Franklin D. Roosevelt administration, Weaver served as an adviser to Secretary of the Interior Harold Ickes and became unofficial leader of the so-called black cabinet, a group of African-American, pro-New Deal civil servants. After World War II, Weaver lectured at Northwestern University and served as the chairman of several foundations. In 1955, he was appointed rent commissioner for New York state, and in 1960 he became vice chairman of the New York City housing and redevelopment board. In 1961, President Lyndon B. Johnson* named him secretary of housing and urban development, making Weaver the first African American ever to hold a cabinet position. Weaver became president of Baruch College in New York City in 1969. Among his many books are *Negro Labor: A National Problem* (1946), *The Negro Ghetto* (1948), *The Urban Complex* (1964), and *Dilemmas of Urban America* (1965). Robert Weaver died in 1994.

REFERENCE: *Who's Who in America, 1984–1985*, 1986.

WEIGHT WATCHERS. In 1961 Jean Nieditch, a thirty-seven-year-old suburban homemaker, founded Weight Watchers. She had fought a battle with her own weight throughout her life, and when she hit 214 pounds in 1960, Nieditch decided to do something about it. During the 1960s, the American fascination with thin female bodies was intensifying, and Nieditch decided that it was impossible to lose weight alone. She started a support group with six of her friends. They would exchange ideas, share concerns, and weigh each other on a weekly basis. She lost 70 pounds in a year and began establishing similar support groups through the New York metropolitan region. In 1963, she founded Weight Watchers International. To the weekly support group regimen, she added a diet that featured low-fat protein and plenty of fruits and vegetables. Women would pay a modest weekly fee to participate in a local support group. Weight Watchers functioned as a franchise outfit, eventually adding its own food line. It was a phenomenal success, and in 1970 Weight Watchers sported more than 125 local franchises. Nieditch was a multimillionaire.

REFERENCE: Denise Ditz, *Throw Darts at a Cheesecake*, 1992.

WEISNER, JEROME BERT. Jerome Bert Weisner was born May 30, 1915, in Dearborn, Michigan. He worked his way through the University of Michigan, graduating in 1937 with a degree in mathematics and electrical engineering. He later earned a master's degree and the Ph.D. in electrical engineering. During World War II, Weisner worked at the Massachusetts Institute of Technology's (MIT) Radiation Laboratory, and after the war he joined the faculty there. A gifted scientist and leader, he directed MIT's research laboratory of electronics from 1952 to 1961. Weisner backed John F. Kennedy's* bid for the White House in 1960, and early in 1961 the new president named Weisner special assistant to the president for science and technology. In the post, he played a key role in developing the Nuclear Test Ban Treaty* of 1963. Early in 1964, after Kennedy's assassination, Weisner returned to MIT as dean of science, and in 1966 he was named MIT's thirteenth president. He served as president for nine years. Jerome Weisner died October 22, 1994.

REFERENCE: *New York Times*, October 23, 1994.

WESBERRY V. SANDERS. Throughout the 1960s, the Supreme Court continued the trends launched when Earl Warren* became chief justice in 1953. Very consistently, the Court struck down all forms of de jure segregation, expanded the rights of individuals, narrowed the powers of government, and labored to make sure that the Fifteenth Amendment's protection of voting rights was expanded. One of the most important of the voting rights decisions of the Warren Court was the *Wesberry v. Sanders* decision of February 17, 1964. By a 6 to 3 vote, with Justice Hugo Black* writing the majority opinion, the Court ordered that significant disparities in the population of congressional districts within the same state were unconstitutional. What *Baker v. Carr** did to state legislative districts, *Wesberry v. Sanders* did to congressional districts.

REFERENCE: 376 U.S. 1 (1964).

WESTMORELAND, WILLIAM CHILDS. Born in Spartanburg County, South Carolina, March 26, 1914, William Westmoreland graduated from West

Point in 1936. He saw combat in North Africa, Sicily, France, and Germany during World War II, and by the Korean War he had command of his own regimental combat team. After Korea, Westmoreland did a turn as superintendent of West Point and head of the 101st Airborne division. In 1964, he was given command of all American forces in South Vietnam. During his command, Westmoreland emphasized military conquest over pacification, and as a result the United States had to continually escalate its commitment there. Westmoreland kept promising victory if only he could have more troops. He was fighting a war of attrition* and intended to kill so many communist troops that the enemy could not continue to fight. At the end of 1967, with more than 540,000 troops, Westmoreland told Congress that victory was in sight.

Two months later, the Tet Offensive* shattered all of the general's promises. The Vietcong* and North Vietnamese launched an offensive that caught American troops off-guard. Although Westmoreland responded brilliantly and inflicted a massive military defeat on communist forces, he had lost all of his credibility at home. Americans were sick of the war and wanted out. Less than two months after Tet, President Lyndon B. Johnson* announced that he would not seek reelection and that he would work for a negotiated peace in Paris. In July 1968, Westmoreland completed his tour of duty in Vietnam and became chief of staff of the U.S. Army. He retired from active duty in 1972. Ten years later, he surfaced again into the public consciousness when CBS News accused him of intentionally misleading Congress and the public about the real number of enemy troops in Vietnam. Westmoreland filed a libel suit that was eventually settled out of court.

REFERENCES: David Halberstam, *The Best and the Brightest*, 1972; William Westmoreland, *A Soldier Reports*, 1976; Samuel Zaffiri, *Westmoreland*, 1994.

WHEELER, EARLE GILMORE. Born January 13, 1908, Earle Gilmore Wheeler graduated from West Point in 1932 and went into the infantry. After serving in China from 1937 to 1939, he returned to the United States, where he specialized in logistics and troop training. Wheeler rose quickly through the ranks, did extremely well at the National War College, and became a full general in 1962. He was appointed chairman of the Joint Chiefs of Staff in 1964 and found himself playing a leading role in the formation of Vietnam policy. With the Gulf of Tonkin* incident, Wheeler continually urged President Lyndon B. Johnson* to adopt more aggressive military policies toward Vietnam. By 1965, he was a strong advocate of Americanization of the war, since he was certain that American troops could quickly defeat the communist enemy. Even as late as 1967, with the war going badly and the American public turning against the conflict, Wheeler continued to urge escalation. When Richard Nixon* became president in 1969, Wheeler remained unrepentant, counseling the president to increase the bombing of North Vietnam, expand the war into Cambodia and

Laos, and carry out an all-out war on North Vietnam. Earl Wheeler retired in 1970 and died December 18, 1975.

REFERENCE: *New York Times*, December 19, 1975.

WHITE, BYRON RAYMOND. Byron White was born in Fort Collins, Colorado, in 1917. He graduated Phi Beta Kappa from the University of Colorado in 1938 and was a Rhodes Scholar at Oxford University in 1939. There he met John F. Kennedy.* During the early years of World War II, White served in the navy and then returned to earn his law degree from Yale. He clerked for Supreme Court justice Fred Vinson from 1946 to 1947, when he returned to Denver to practice law. During the presidential election of 1960,* he served as chairman of the National Citizens for Kennedy group. Kennedy named him deputy attorney general in 1961 and then justice of the Supreme Court in 1962.

During his term on the Court, White was generally a conservative. Although he was considered a centrist on the Warren Court, White could be depended on to oppose the expansion of the rights of criminal defendants. He dissented in the 1966 *Miranda v. Arizona* * decision. White favored expansion in the civil rights of minorities, but he dissented in the *Roe v. Wade* (1973) decision expanding abortion rights. White resigned from the Court in 1993.

REFERENCES: Bob Italia, *Byron White*, 1992; *New York Times*, March 20, 1993.

WHITMAN, CHARLES. Charles Whitman was born June 24, 1941, in Lake Worth, Florida. He was an Eagle Scout and altar boy while growing up. He served six years in the marine reserves. He won the sharpshooting prize for his division. Friends described him as a model citizen and student. His father had been strict but fair and a fanatic about guns. The younger Whitman enrolled at the University of Texas (UT) at Austin, planning to earn a degree in mathematical engineering. He ended up in architectural engineering because it provided an outlet for his artistic feelings. During his last semester, Whitman took fourteen hours of courses and worked part-time to help support his wife. Over the course of a decade, Whitman had been treated several times by psychiatrists. One doctor remembered his confessing that he often "thought of going up on the tower with a deer rifle and start shooting people." Still, the psychiatrist claimed that at the time, Whitman displayed none of the outward signs of insanity.

On August 1, 1966, Whitman acted out his fantasy. Before driving to the UT campus, he murdered his wife and his mother. He then climbed to the twenty-ninth floor observation deck of the UT administration building, some 280 feet above the rest of the campus. He killed a clerk on the way. He took with him a 6mm rifle with a 4x telescope, a Remington .35 caliber pump rifle, a .30 caliber reconditioned army carbine, a sawed-off 12-gauge shotgun, a .357 magnum pistol, a 9mm luger, and a Bowie knife. He also carried with him plenty of ammunition, canned peaches, canned sausages, and a roll of toilet paper.

During a ninety-minute shooting spree from the observation deck, Whitman shot forty-seven people, killing sixteen of them. The carnage did not end until Romero Martinez, an Austin police officer, climbed quietly to the observation deck and, accompanied by three other policemen, fired six rounds into Whitman. Martinez then finished Whitman off with the blast of a shotgun. The four police officers then carried Whitman's body down to the first floor of the administration building. The Charles Whitman rampage was one of the worst instances of mass murder in U.S. history.

REFERENCES: *Austin-American Statesman*, August 2–8, 1966.

Eugene M. Addison III

THE WHO. The rock group the Who was formed in 1964 by three former classmates of the Acton County Grammar School in the Shephard's Bush district of West London. The group consisted of lead singer Roger Daltry, a welder; lead guitarist and songwriter Peter Townsend, an art student; and bass guitarist John Entwhistle, a tax office employee. They were subsequently joined by former plaster salesman Keith Moon, who, as drummer, became one of rock music's unchallenged legends.

The Who were the modernist representative of the British invasion* of American pop music in the 1960s, of which the Rolling Stones* and the Beatles* constituted the other major components. They debuted in the United States in 1967 and began a two-decade tradition of top-forty American hits. They appeared the same year at the Monterey Pop Festival and in 1969 at Woodstock.* They became known for anarchic lyrics, gymnastic performances, and the ritual on-stage destruction of band instruments. Their defining early work was "My Generation," which captured youthful imaginations.

The group is credited with pioneering the hybrid art form of rock opera. After he became interested in Eastern mysticism, Townsend wrote *Tommy*, the story of a young boy who was deaf, dumb, and blind. The full-length rock opera was first conceived as an album as well as a live performance. After its world premiere in 1969, the Who became the biggest concert attraction in rock, whose performances were attended by the likes of Jacquelyn Kennedy Onassis. *Tommy* catapulted Who record sales into the tens of millions but weakened their traditional rock-oriented audience base.

From 1965 to 1983, the Who enjoyed continued stardom in the uncertain world of American popular music, despite internal disputes and the death in 1978 of drummer Keith Moon. The group regularly toured Europe and the United States until 1982, when it performed its "final" tour. In late 1983, Townsend announced the group's breakup. *Tommy* enjoyed a revival in a Broadway adaptation in 1993. Its opening set a record for one-day ticket sales. Three weeks later it received eleven nominations for Tony Awards and won five.

REFERENCE: Gene Busnar, *Super Stars of Rock*, 1984.

Sammie Miller

WHO'S AFRAID OF VIRGINIA WOOLF? *Who's Afraid of Virginia Woolf?* is the title of Edward Albee's Tony Award–winning 1962 Broadway play. The play revolves around two couples living in a small, liberal arts college town. The men are faculty members, one a senior professor whose point of view has degenerated into raw cynicism, the other a junior professor anxious to do whatever it takes to secure tenure. Both couples have left a faculty party for a nightcap at the home of the senior professor. During the rest of the evening, in alcohol-driven rages, the senior professor and his wife engage in a bitter, raucous argument that exposes the petty, vacuous pathos of their lives. The young couple is forced to watch the display and wonder if they are looking into their own futures. *Who's Afraid of Virginia Woolf?* won Albee a New York Drama Critics' Award. In 1966, the play was made into a film starring Elizabeth Taylor, Richard Burton, George Segal, and Sandy Dennis.
REFERENCE: *New York Times*, October 28, 1962.

WHY ARE WE IN VIETNAM? *Why Are We in Vietnam?* is the title of Norman Mailer's* 1967 novel. Although the novel's settings are Texas, New York City, and the Brooks Range of Alaska, it is an antiwar* story without ever being directly in Vietnam. A cast of characters—D. J. Jellicoe, Rusty Jellicoe, Alice Lee Jellicoe, Medium Asshole Pete, Medium Asshole Bill, and Tex Hud—end up in the Brooks Range of Alaska on a hunting trip. There, in a pristine and naturally savage environment, they use all the hunting technology they can muster and literally slaughter wolves, caribou, bighorn sheep, and bears. The carnage is extraordinary and, in Norman Mailer's mind, symbolic of what American military technology was doing to the life and habitat of Southeast Asia.
REFERENCE: Norman Mailer, *Why Are We in Vietnam?*, 1967.

THE WILD WILD WEST. *The Wild Wild West* was an improbable, if popular, television* series during the 1960s. First broadcast by CBS on September 17, 1965, it featured Robert Conrad as James T. West and Ross Martin as Artemus Gordon, two secret service agents working for the Ulysses S. Grant administration in the 1860s and 1870s. They engaged in elaborate schemes to foil the designs of evil men and invented so many fantastic devices to achieve their ends that the series was actually part western, part science fiction, part James Bond.*
The last episode was telecast on September 7, 1970.
REFERENCE: R. M. Cangey, *Inside The Wild Wild West*, 1996.

WILKINS, ROY. Roy Wilkins was born in St. Louis, Missouri, in 1901, and raised in Minneapolis. He graduated from the University of Minnesota in 1923, working his way through school by doing odd jobs and editing the *St. Paul Appeal*, an African-American newspaper. He then moved to Kansas City, Missouri, to work on the staff of the *City Call*, another African-American newspaper, and there he had his first experiences with segregation. Missouri's Jim Crow* system raised his political conscience, and he joined the local chapter of the National Association for the Advancement of Colored People (NAACP). Wilkins was a patient, even-tempered man who despised discrimination, and he soon became a powerful influence in the national NAACP.

In 1931, Wilkins moved to New York City to work as assistant executive secretary to Walter White, head of the NAACP. Three years later, he was named editor of the NAACP's official publication—*Crisis*. That year, he was arrested for the first time for leading a demonstration in Washington, D.C., against Attorney General Homer Cummings, who had refused to include lynching as a major crime in the United States. Throughout the 1930s, Wilkins kept up his crusade against the lynching of African Americans. In the 1940s, Wilkins fought for the desegregation of the armed forcs. He was the primary planner of the NAACP legal strategy that led to the famous *Brown v. Board of Education* decision in 1954. When Walter White died in 1955, Wilkins assumed the position of executive secretary of the NAACP. From that position, he was at the forefront of the NAACP's fight against segregation during the late 1950s and throughout the 1960s. Roy Wilkins resigned from his post as executive director of the NAACP in 1977. He died September 8, 1981.
REFERENCE: *New York Times*, September 9, 1981.

WISE OLD MEN. During the last few years of Lyndon B. Johnson's* administration, the term "Wise Old Men" was used to refer to a group of elder statesmen advising the president about foreign affairs in general and Vietnam in particular. Included in the group were W. Averell Harriman,* Dean Acheson,* Paul Nitze,* George Kennan,* John McCloy, Robert Lovett, and Charles Bohlen, each of whom possessed extensive knowledge and experience in European affairs but little familiarity with Indochina. At first, they had urged the president to be "tough" and escalate the U.S. commitment, but by early 1968 they had turned against the war. On March 25, 1968, at a painful meeting, they advised the president to end the war, one way or another. Several days later, Johnson announced that he would not seek reelection.
REFERENCE: Walter Isaacson and Evan Thomas, *The Wise Men. Six Friends and the World They Made*, 1986.

WITH IT. The term "with it," as in "He's really with it," became a slang expression in the 1960s to refer to an individual who was young, rebellious, and into the sex, drug, fashion, long-hair, and rock-and-roll culture of the 1960s. The expression actually had its origins in England and came to the United States with the so-called British invasion* of rock groups in the mid-1960s.
REFERENCE: Ruth Bronsteen, *The Hippy's Handbook—How to Live on Love*, 1967.

WOLFMAN JACK. "Wolfman Jack" was the stage name of Robert Weston Smith, a Brooklyn native who went into the radio broadcasting business. Throughout the 1950s, he bounced from station to station, changing his name with each move, trying to establish for himself a foothold in the industry. He

did so in 1960, when he went to work for XERF Radio in Via Cuncio, Mexico, a town nine miles south of Del Rio, Texas. XERF had a huge 250,000-watt broadcasting unit that could be heard all around the Southwest and into the Midwest. During daytime hours, XERF broadcast a relatively standard fare of news, sports, and religious programming, but at midnight, Smith became Wolfman Jack and switched to rock and roll. Free of Federal Communications Commission regulations, Wolfman Jack sold advice, sex pills, diet pills, drugs, and outrageous iconoclasm over the air. In 1973, George Lucas featured Wolfman Jack in his film *American Graffiti*. Throughout the 1970s and 1980s, Wolfman Jack continued to be an icon of the pop music scene. He died in 1996.
REFERENCE: Wolfman Jack, *Have Mercy!*, 1995.

WOMEN STRIKE FOR PEACE. On November 1, 1962, nearly 50,000 women participated in a one-day strike around the country to protest the atmospheric testing of nuclear weapons. Strikers were particularly concerned about the impact of nuclear fallout on children's health. Dagmar Wilson was the leader of the strike. They campaigned widely for a ban on nuclear testing, and in 1963, when President John F. Kennedy* negotiated with the Soviet Union the Nuclear Test Ban Treaty,* Women Strike for Peace (WSP) took considerable credit for the success. Since then, the WSP has continued to campaign for reductions in the number of nuclear weapons.
REFERENCE: Sarah Slavin, *U.S. Women's Interest Groups*, 1995.

WONDER, STEVIE. Stevie Wonder was born in 1951 as Steveland Judkins Morris. Blind from birth, Morris was a gifted musical talent, and in 1962 Barry Gordy of Motown* Records signed him to a contract. The subsequent album— *Little Stevie Wonder, the 12-Year-Old Genius*—was released in 1963 and became a huge hit. Wonder also enjoyed an extraordinary longevity in American popular music. He started as a harmonica player and vocalist, but over the years, Wonder developed an expertise with the piano, drums, organ, and synthesizer. He also added reggae and rap to his rock-and-roll and soul repertoire. By 1996, Stevie Wonder had released fifty-six top ten hits and twenty-three hit albums in his career.
REFERENCES: John Swenson, *Stevie Wonder*, 1986.

THE WONDERFUL WORLD OF WALT DISNEY. The *Wonderful World of Walt Disney* is the longest-running prime-time program in American television* history. It was first broadcast on October 27, 1954, by ABC. NBC picked up the series in 1961, CBS in 1981, ABC again in 1986, and NBC in 1988. *Walt Disney* was the perfect television vehicle for marketing the creative talent of Walt Disney Studios. It was a weekly anthology of cartoons, films, live-action adventures, documentaries, nature stories, and made-for-television dramas. The last episode was broadcast on September 9, 1990.

REFERENCE: Steven Watts, *The Magic Kingdom: Walt Disney and the American Way of Life*, 1997.

WOODSTOCK. The Woodstock Music and Art Fair is considered by social historians today to be the ultimate event of the youth rebellion of the 1960s. Held on the Max Yasgur farm near the town of Bethel in upstate New York, from August 12 to August 17, 1969, Woodstock attracted more than 400,000 concertgoers and some of the most famous rock-and-roll, blues, folk, and soul performers of the 1960s, including Joan Baez*; Crosby, Stills, Nash, and Young; Janis Joplin*; Jimmie Hendrix*; the Who*; Sly and the Family Stone; Jefferson Airplane*; and Santana. The physical facilities were atrocious. Torrential rains turned the farm into a giant quagmire, and concert organizers, grossly underestimating the size of the crowd, did not provide nearly enough portable toilets, food stands, and water facilities. In spite of the difficulties, however, concertgoers had the experience of their young lives. Woodstock was a lovefest of rebellion, drugs, sex, and music, the perfect symbol of everything good and bad that the counterculture* of the 1960s represented. In subsequent years, Woodstock assumed legendary proportions, becoming one of the most powerful and enduring icons of the 1960s.

REFERENCES: *New York Times*, August 16–18, 1969.

X

XIMENES, VICENTE TREVIÑO. Vicente Treviño Ximenes was born in Floresville, Texas, in 1919. As a bombardier, he flew fifty missions in the army air corps during World War II. In 1945, he mustered out of the army with the rank of major. After the war, Ximenes returned home and entered college. He received an undergraduate degree from the University of New Mexico in 1950 and a master's degree there in 1951. Ximenes joined the faculty there in 1951 and also established a local branch of the American G.I. Forum. In 1957–1958, he served as national president of the forum. During the early and mid-1960s, he worked for the Agency for International Development,* and in 1967 President Lyndon B. Johnson* named Ximenes head of the Inter-Agency Committee on Mexican-American Affairs. He also served a term as a member of the U.S. Equal Opportunity Commission.

REFERENCE: ''Vicente T. Ximenes—Educator, Economist,'' *La Luz* 6 (August 1977).

Y

YIPPIES. See **YOUTH INTERNATIONAL PARTY**.

YOUNG, WHITNEY M., JR. Whitney M. Young, Jr., was born in Lincoln Ridge, Kentucky, in 1922. He received his undergraduate degree from Kentucky State College in 1941. In 1947, Young earned his M.S.W. from the University of Minnesota and began his career as a social worker. In 1954, he was appointed dean of the school of social work at Atlanta University. Young was still holding that position when he was appointed president of the National Urban League in 1961.

Young's tenure as head of the National Urban League was a difficult one. The National Urban League's primary focus was the creation of jobs for black people, and Young worked closely with white business and political leaders to achieve that objective. Naturally, his rhetoric was based on interracial cooperation. But in the black power* atmosphere of the late 1960s, Young seemed too accommodationist to black militants, who often called him an "Uncle Tom." Young spoke eloquently about the need for civil rights, but he also believed passionately that black success could be achieved only within the existing social and economic system. Whitney Young died in 1971 during a trip to Africa.
REFERENCE: Nancy J. Weiss, *Whitney M. Young, Jr., and the Struggle for Civil Rights*, 1989.

YOUNG AMERICANS FOR FREEDOM. The Young Americans for Freedom was founded in Sharon, Connecticut, in 1960 to promote a conservative political agenda in the United States. Its leader was William F. Buckley, Jr.,* and in their so-called Sharon Statement, they called for downsizing of the federal government, laissez-faire economics, libertarian social policies, and a tough foreign policy stance toward the Soviet Union. During the 1960s, the Young Americans for Freedom grew substantially among white, middle-class, and upper-class students, and they endorsed Barry Goldwater's* presidential campaign in 1964 and tried to make Governor Ronald Reagan* of California the Republican standard-bearer in 1968. When the conservative revival swept America in the 1980s, most prominent Republican conservatives had once been members of the Young Americans for Freedom.

REFERENCE: Lee Edwards and Anne Edwards, *You Can Make the Difference*, 1968.

YOUTH INTERNATIONAL PARTY. The Youth International Party, also known as "yippies," was created by Abbie Hoffman,* Jerry Rubin,* and several other antiwar protesters after the October 1967 March on the Pentagon. It was a loose, amorphous, poorly organized political movement that glorified opposition to the Vietnam War * and support of the youth rebellion and the counterculture.* For a time early in 1968, a yippie was any hippie* headed for the Democratic National Convention* in Chicago. In essence, the yippie movement politicized cultural rebellion.

But yippies posed a problem to more traditional elements of the New Left.* They generated a carnival atmosphere at their gatherings, promoting the bizarre and absurd as often as they demanded rationality. They attracted media attention, but they also embarrassed more traditional antiwar Democrats. Antiauthoritarian and antitraditional, the yippie movement actually rejected the traditional politics that socialists and liberals venerated. Its carnival strategy—they nominated a pig for president in 1968—was designed to mock traditional social and political institutions. "Don't trust anyone over thirty" was their byword. For the most part, the yippie phenomenon ended after the Democratic National Convention in Chicago in 1968 and the Chicago Eight* trial in September 1969.

REFERENCE: Joseph R. Urgo, "Comedic Impulses and Societal Propriety: The Yippie Carnival," *Studies in Popular Culture* 10 (1987).

YZAGUIRRE, RAÚL. Raúl Yzaguirre was born July 22, 1939, in San Juan, Texas. As a teenager he came to know Dr. Hector García of the American G.I. Forum, and in high school Yzaguirre enthusiastically organized a local forum chapter. He graduated from high school in 1958 and joined the air force. While stationed at Andrews Air Force Base, he took classes part-time at the University of Maryland and established the National Organization for Mexican American Services, a Washington, D.C.,-based activist group. When he left the air force, Yzaguirre finished his bachelor's degree at George Washington University. In 1969, he founded Interstate Research Associates, a Chicano* research and consulting firm. Yzaguirre assumed the directorship of the National Council of La Raza in 1974. He has continued to lead the group since then and has also founded the Forum of National Hispanic Organizations and the National Committee on the Concerns of Hispanics and Blacks.

REFERENCE: "Interview with Raúl Yzaguirre," *La Luz* 1 (March 1973).

Z

ZAP. In the 1960s, the term "zap" emerged in the hippie* counterculture* as a slang expression for victory or the elimination of an enemy or an obnoxious entity or idea.

REFERENCE: Ruth Bronsteen, *The Hippy's Handbook—How to Live on Love*, 1967.

ZAPRUDER FILM. On the morning of November 22, 1963, Abraham Zapruder went to Dealey Plaza in Dallas, Texas, to get a glimpse of President and Mrs. John F. Kennedy* during their visit to the city. He brought along a cheap, handheld home movie camera to record the event. A black Lincoln convertible carried the President and First Lady. As the car turned left at the Texas School Book Depository Building, Zapruder pushed the button on the camera and began filming the motorcade. But at precisely 12:30 P.M., shots rang out, and Zapruder eyewitnessed and recorded what happened. President Kennedy was shot in the head and neck by a hidden assassin. He was pronounced dead at 1:00 P.M.

As the shooting took place, Zapruder screamed again and again, "They killed him! They killed him!" The Zapruder film proved to be the only camera footage taken of the Kennedy assassination* and served as an important piece of primary evidence in the Warren Commission's investigation of the tragedy.

REFERENCE: Gerald L. Posner, *Case Closed*, 1994.

ZHOU ENLAI. Zhou Enlai was born in China in 1896. When he was a student in France in 1921, he joined the Communist Party. Three years later, he returned to China and joined Sun Yat-sen's Kuomintang reform movement. Zhou barely escaped several years later when Jiang Jieshi (Chiang Kai-shek*) purged all Communists from the Kuomintang. He became a close friend and associate of Mao Zedong,* whom Zhou believed was a brilliant theorist and just the man to lead China's peasant masses in insurrection. Always a faithful follower of Mao, Zhou played a leading role in the Chinese Revolution of 1949, which expelled

Jiang Jieshi and the Kuomintang from the mainland. In the new People's Republic of China, Zhou served as foreign minister from 1949 and 1958, and from 1949 until his death in 1976 he also served as premier of the country.

Because of the two-thousand year old rivalry between China and Vietnam, Zhou was also suspicious of Ho Chi Minh's* intentions, and even while he kept North Vietnam rich in war supplies, he used his influence to urge a negotiated settlement. The expansion of the war, so close to China's southern frontier, always worried Zhou. He was also anxious to improve U.S.-China relations, and the Vietnam War* was an obstacle to normalization. Such a normalization, he believed, would strengthen China vis-a-vis the Soviet Union. Although U.S. policymakers, worried about the Chinese entering the Vietnam War,* on the side of North Vietnam, as they had done during Korea, Zhou had no such intentions. On the contrary, he wanted the Vietnam War ended as soon as possible, since he feard its potential to destabilize Asian politics. He played a leading role in securing President Richard Nixon's* epic visit to Beijing in 1972. Zhou Enlai died on January 8, 1976.

REFERENCES: Chae-Jin Lee, *Zhou Enlai: The Early Years*, 1994; Dorothy Hoobler, *Zhou Enlai*, 1986; *New York Times*, January 9, 1976.

ZIPPO WAR. The "Zippo" has long been the lighter of preference for American outdoorsmen. "Zippo" lighter is considered very reliable because it produces a dependable flame even under poor weather conditions, such as light rain, high humidity, and heavy winds. Not surprising, U.S. soldiers in Vietnam preferred Zippo lighters. The term "Zippo War" evolved from the frequency with which U.S. troops on search-and-destroy* missions employed Zippo lighters to burn down the homes of suspected Vietcong.* Sometimes, GIs used Zippo lighters to burn down whole villages. In retaliation, the Vietcong used discarded Zippo lighters to make booby traps* which, if picked up by a soldier who thought the lighter had been discarded, would detonate in his hands when ignited. Sometimes, "zippo" was also used to refer to an M2A17 flamethrower, another weapon used to root Vietcong out of tunnels and to burn homes.

REFERENCES: Samuel Freeman, "Zippo War," in James S. Olson, ed., *Dictionary of the Vietnam War*, 1988; Morley Safer, *Flashbacks*, 1990.

Chronology of the 1960s

1960

January

The U.S. population totals 179,245,000 people.

The Sabin oral polio vaccine begins to be administered in the United States.

The United States and Japan sign a mutual security treaty.

February

The sit-in movement begins in Greensboro, North Carolina.

April

Congress passes the Civil Rights Act.

May

An American U-2 high-altitude reconnaissance aircraft is shot down by surface-to-air missiles over the Soviet Union.

Caryl Chessman, the so-called Red Light Bandit and rapist, is executed in California.

June

The Supreme Court decides the *Elkins v. United States* case.

July

Civil war erupts in what used to be the Belgian Congo in Africa.

John F. Kennedy wins the Democratic presidential nomination.

Richard Nixon wins the Republican presidential nomination.

October

The first of the televised Kennedy–Nixon presidential debates takes place.

November

John F. Kennedy narrowly defeats Richard Nixon in the presidential election.

Antischool desegregation riots break out in New Orleans.

The Supreme Court decides the *Gomillion v. Lightfoot* case.

December

U.S. troop levels in Vietnam at the end of 1960 reach 900 people.

1961

January

The United States severs diplomatic relations with Cuba.

John F. Kennedy succeeds Dwight D. Eisenhower as president. Dean Rusk succeeds Christian A. Herter as secretary of state. Robert S. McNamara succeeds Gordon Gray as secretary of defense.

February

The Senecas demand on February 12, 1961, that construction of Kinzua Dam be stopped.

March

President John F. Kennedy creates the Peace Corps.

The twenty-third Amendment to the Constitution, which gives residents of the District of Columbia the right to vote in presidential elections, goes into effect.

April

A Central Intelligence Agency-backed army of Cuban exiles conducts the unsuccessful invasion of Cuba at the Bay of Pigs.

May

The minimum wage is raised to $1.25 an hour.

President John Kennedy tells Congress of his intention to place a man on the moon before the decade is up.

President John Kennedy signs legislation establishing the Alliance for Progress between the United States and Latin America.

Alan Shepard completes a successful suborbital flight in a Mercury spacecraft, becoming the first American in space.

Freedom riders begin their civil rights protests in the South.

The Geneva Conference on Laos begins.

June

President John F. Kennedy and Soviet Premier Nikita Khrushchev hold a summit conference in Vienna.

August

Nikita Khrushchev orders construction of the Berlin Wall, separating East Berlin and West Berlin.

October

Roger Maris of the New York Yankees hits his sixty-first home run to break Babe Ruth's single-season record.

December

U.S. troop levels in Vietnam reach 3,200 people.

1962

February

John Glenn, in a Mercury spacecraft, becomes the first American to orbit the earth.

President Kennedy authorizes American military personnel in South Vietnam to return fire if they are fired upon.

March

The U.S. Supreme Court makes its decision in the *Baker v. Carr* case.

April

The Defense Department orders the integration of all military reserve units.

The steel companies announce a price increase and precipitate a power struggle with the Kennedy administration.

June

The Supreme Court decides the *Engle v. Vitale* case.

July

The Geneva Accords on Laos are signed.

September

The political crisis over the admission of James Meredith, an African American, to the University of Mississippi in Oxford, Mississippi, begins.

October

Who's Afraid of Virginia Woolf? opens on Broadway.

Congress passes the Trade Expansion Act.

The Cuban missile crisis between the United States and the Soviet Union brings the world to the brink of nuclear annihilation.

November

President John F. Kennedy signs an executive order outlawing racial discrimination in housing units built or purchased with federal funds.

December

U.S. troop levels in Vietnam reach 11,300 people.

1963

January

The Battle of Ap Bac is fought in South Vietnam.

March

The Supreme Court decides the *Gideon v. Wainwright* case.

June

The United States and the Soviet Union agree to the establishment of a "hot line" communication between Washington, D.C., and Moscow to help avoid tragic miscalculations during international emergencies. The hot line is a direct result of the Cuban missile crisis.

The University of Alabama is desegregated.

Medgar Evers is assassinated in Jackson, Mississippi.

July

The United States bans all financial transactions with Cuba.

August

The United States, the Soviet Union, and Great Britain sign the Nuclear Test Ban Treaty, outlawing the atmospheric testing of nuclear weapons.

The Freedom March, in which Martin Luther King, Jr., gave his "I Have a Dream" speech, brings hundreds of thousands of civil rights demonstrators to Washington, D.C.

September

An African-American church is bombed in Birmingham, Alabama, killing four black children.

November

Ngo Dinh Diem is assassinated in South Vietnam.

John F. Kennedy is assassinated in the United States.

Lee Harvey Oswald, the alleged murderer of President John F. Kennedy, is murdered in Dallas.

President Lyndon B. Johnson establishes the Warren Commission to investigate the assassination of John F. Kennedy.

December

U.S. troop levels in Vietnam reach 16,300 people.

1964

January

President Johnson announces his "War on Poverty."

The twenty-fourth Amendment to the Constitution, which outlawed the poll tax, goes into effect.

The surgeon general issues his report on the health hazards of cigarette smoking.

Hello, Dolly! opens on Broadway.

February

The Beatles begin their first American concert tour.

Cassius Clay (Muhammad Ali) wins the heavyweight boxing title for the first time.

President Lyndon B. Johnson removes all American dependents from South Vietnam.

Congress passes the Tax Reduction Act.

April

President Lyndon B. Johnson signs the Agricultural Act.

May

The Supreme Court decides the *Griffin v. County School Board of Prince Edward County* case.

June

The Supreme Court decides the *Escobedo v. Illinois* case.

July

Congress passes the Civil Rights Act.

Senator Barry Goldwater of Arizona receives the 1964 Republican presidential nomination.

August

The Gulf of Tonkin incident occurs in the South China Sea, and Congress passes the Gulf of Tonkin Resolution.

Congress passes the Economic Opportunity Act.

Three young civil rights workers—James Chaney, Andrew Goodman, and Michael Schwerner—are murdered in Mississippi.

President Lyndon B. Johnson receives the 1964 Democratic presidential nomination.

A racial rebellion erupts in Philadelphia.

September

Fiddler on the Roof opens on Broadway.

November

President Lyndon Johnson wins a landslide victory over Barry Goldwater in the presidential election.

Vietcong troops attack the U.S. air base at Bien Hoa in South Vietnam.

December

U.S. troop levels in Vietnam reach 23,300 people.

Vietcong troops kill two U.S. soldiers at the Brinks Hotel in Saigon, South Vietnam.

1965

February

Vietcong troops attack a U.S. Special Forces compound in Pleiku, South Vietnam. The United States responds with a bombing campaign over North Vietnam.

Malcolm X is assassinated in New York City.

March

The first contingent of U.S. ground troops arrives in Danang, South Vietnam.

Martin Luther King, Jr., leads the five-day civil rights March from Selma to Montgomery, Alabama.

Civil rights worker Viola Liuzzo is murdered in Alabama.

April

Congress passes the Elementary and Secondary Education Act.

President Lyndon Johnson sends U.S. troops into the Dominican Republic to prevent a communist takeover there.

President Lyndon B. Johnson authorizes U.S. troops in South Vietnam to conduct offensive operations against the enemy.

The Supreme Court decides the *Griffin v. California* case.

May

The National Teach-In Day opposing the Vietnam War is held on college campuses throughout the country.

The Battle of Ba Gia is fought in South Vietnam.

Reporters first use the term ''credibility gap'' to describe the Johnson administration.

June

The Supreme Court decides the *Griswold v. Connecticut* case.

July

Congress approves the medicare program.

The Watts racial rebellion breaks out in Los Angeles.

Carol Doda, with her silicone breasts, begins performing topless at the Condor Club in San Francisco.

August

Congress passes the Voting Rights Act.

September

Congress creates the Department of Housing and Urban Welfare.

Congress creates the National Endowment for the Arts and the National Endowment for the Humanities.

César Chávez and the National Farm Workers Union begin a strike against grape growers in California.

October

Congress passes the Immigration and Nationality Act.

Pope Paul VI becomes the first Roman Catholic pontiff to visit the United States.

Coordinated antiwar protests take place in forty U.S. cities.

November

A massive power outage cuts off electricity throughout the Northeast and upper Midwest.

More than 25,000 antiwar protesters demonstrate in Washington, D.C.

Battle of Ia Drang Valley occurs in South Vietnam.

December

U.S. troop levels in Vietnam reach 184,300 people.

To date, 636 U.S. military personnel have been killed in action in the Vietnam War.

President Lyndon B. Johnson temporarily suspends the bombing of North Vietnam and invites the enemy to the negotiation table.

1966

January

Senator J. William Fulbright begins the Senate Foreign Relations Committee hearings on the Vietnam War.

February

The Nisqually Indians stage a fish-in in Washington State on February 15, 1966, to protest state laws requiring only hook and line fishing.

May

Stokely Carmichael popularizes the "black power" slogan.

Mame opens on Broadway.

June

James Meredith is shot while making a solo civil rights march from Memphis, Tennessee, to Jackson, Mississippi.

The U.S. Supreme Court decides the *Miranda v. Arizona* case.

July

Martin Luther King, Jr., takes his civil rights movement to Cicero, Illinois.

Racial rebellion erupts in Chicago.

Richard Speck murders eight student nurses in Chicago.

August

Charles Whitman murders sixteen people after barricading himself in a tower at the University of Texas at Austin.

September

Congress increases the minimum wage to $1.40 per hour.

October

Congress creates the Department of Transportation.

Jack Ruby is convicted of the murder of Lee Harvey Oswald.

The Black Panther Party is formed in Oakland, California.

November

Cabaret opens on Broadway.

December

U.S. troop levels in Vietnam reach 385,300 people.

To date, 6,644 U.S. military personnel have been killed in action in the Vietnam War.

1967

January

A fire on the launch pad at Cape Kennedy, Florida, kills Apollo astronauts Virgil Grissom, Edward H. White, and Roger Chaffee.

The village of Ben Suc is destroyed in South Vietnam.

February

The twenty-fifth Amendment, providing for presidential disability and succession, goes into effect.

Representative Adam Clayton Powell is denied his seat in the ninetieth Congress.

March

The Brown Beret organization is founded.

April

The Spring Mobilization Committee organizes huge, nationwide protests against the Vietnam War.

The U.S. Senate ratifies the Outer Space Treaty with the Soviet Union.

Muhammad Ali refuses induction into the U.S. Army.

May

The Battle of Dak To begins in South Vietnam.

June

The Six-Day War breaks out between Israel and the Arab states.

Israeli planes and torpedo boats attack the USS *Liberty* in the Mediterranean.

A summit between President Lyndon Johnson and Soviet premier Alexei Kosygin takes place at Glassboro State College in New Jersey.

The General Agreement on Trade and Tariffs is signed by the United States and forty-five other countries.

July

Racial rebellions erupt in Newark, New Jersey, and Detroit.

September

Nguyen Van Thieu is elected president of South Vietnam.

The Battle of Con Thien begins in South Vietnam.

November

Senator Eugene McCarthy of Minnesota announces his candidacy for the 1968 Democatic presidential nomination.

The U.S. population reaches 200,000,000 people.

Hair premieres off-Broadway in New York City.

December

U.S. troop levels in Vietnam reach 485,600 people.

To date, 16,021 U.S. military personnel have been killed in action in the Vietnam War.

1968

January

Vietcong and North Vietnamese forces launch the Tet Offensive.

North Korea seizes the USS *Pueblo* and imprisons its crew.

February

The Kerner Report is issued.

Richard M. Nixon announces his intention to seek the 1968 Republican presidential nomination.

Senator Eugene McCarthy almost upsets President Lyndon B. Johnson in the New Hampshire presidential primary.

March

President Johnson unilaterally announces a halt to most U.S. bombing of North Vietnam.

Senator Robert F. Kennedy of New York announces his candidacy for the 1968 Democratic presidential nomination.

The My Lai massacre takes place in South Vietnam.

President Lyndon Johnson announces that he will not run for reelection.

The National Council on Indian Opportunity is founded.

April

Congress passes the Civil Rights Act providing for open housing.

Congress passes the American Indian Civil Rights Act.

Martin Luther King, Jr., is assassinated in Memphis, Tennessee, and racial rebellions erupt in urban centers all over the United States.

Columbia University is paralyzed by student demonstrations.

The Poor People's March arrives in Washington, D.C.

Vice President Hubert Humphrey announces his candidacy for the 1968 Democratic presidential nomination.

The Club of Rome is established.

May

Preliminary peace talks between the United States and North Vietnam begin in Paris.

June

Senator Robert F. Kennedy is assassinated in Los Angeles.

Earl Warren announces his intention to resign as chief justice of the U.S. Supreme Court.

President Lyndon Johnson announces his selection of Abraham Fortas to replace Earl Warren as chief justice of the Supreme Court.

Congress passes an income tax surcharge bill to help finance the Vietnam War.

July

The United States, the Soviet Union, and fifty-nine other countries sign the Nuclear Nonproliferation Treaty.

A racial rebellion erupts in Cleveland, Ohio.

The American Indian Movement is founded in Minneapolis.

August

Richard Nixon wins the 1968 Republican presidential nomination.

Hubert Humphrey wins the 1968 Democratic presidential nomination.

A racial rebellion erupts in Miami, Florida.

October

The Great White Hope opens on Broadway.

President Lyndon B. Johnson halts the bombing of North Vietnam.

President Lyndon Johnson withdraws the name of Abraham Fortas to become the next chief justice of the Supreme Court.

December

U.S. troop levels in Vietnam reach 536,100 people.

To date, 30,610 U.S. military personnel have been killed in action in the Vietnam War.

The Mohawk Blockade of the Cornwall Bridge in upstate New York takes place on December 18, 1968.

1969

January

Richard M. Nixon is inaugurated president of the United States, with William Rogers as secretary of state and Melvin Laird as secretary of defense. Henry Kissinger is named national security adviser.

The New York Jets win Super Bowl III.

March

The U.S. Senate ratifies the Nuclear Nonproliferation Treaty.

April

CBS cancels *The Smothers Brothers Comedy Hour*.

A black student rebellion shuts down Cornell University.

The number of U.S. military personnel in Vietnam peaks at 543,300.

June

President Richard M. Nixon announces the withdrawal of 25,000 U.S. troops from Vietnam.

The Cuyahoga River in Cleveland, Ohio, catches on fire.

Warren Burger is confirmed as the next chief justice of the U.S. Supreme Court.

July

Dr. Benjamin Spock is convicted of conspiracy to counsel young men to resist the draft.

President Richard M. Nixon proclaims the Nixon Doctrine.

Senator Edward Kennedy is involved in the infamous automobile accident on Chappaquiddick Island in Massachusetts.

August

The Manson "family" murders actress Sharon Tate and four others at her Los Angeles home.

The Woodstock Music and Art Fair is held in upstate New York.

September

The trial of the Chicago Eight begins in Chicago.

Ho Chi Minh dies.

The New York Mets win the World Series.

October

The first Vietnam Moratorium Day demonstrations.

The Department of Health, Education, and Welfare bans the use of cyclamates, an artificial sweetener.

November

President Richard Nixon announces the Vietnamization program.

The My Lai massacre is first reported in the American press.

The second Vietnam Moratorium Day demonstrations take place.

The first of the Strategic Arms Limitation Talks begin between the United States and the Soviet Union.

President Richard Nixon signs legislation introducing the lottery system for selective service.

Indians of All Tribes occupy Alcatraz Island in San Francisco Bay.

The Senate rejects the nomination of Clement Haynsworth as a justice of the U.S. Supreme Court.

December

Congress passes an income tax reform bill.

U.S. troop levels in Vietnam drop to 475,200 people.

To date, 40,024 U.S. military personnel have been killed in action in the Vietnam War.

Selected Bibliography

AFRICAN AMERICANS

Anderson, Alan B., and George W. Pickering. *Confronting the Color Line: The Broken Promise of the Civil Rights Movement in Chicago.* 1986.

Barnes, Catherine A. *Journey from Jim Crow: The Desegregation of Southern Transit.* 1983.

Bartley, Numan V. *The Rise of Massive Resistance: Race and Politics in the South during the 1950s.* 1969.

Beifuss, Joan Turner. *At the River I Stand: Memphis, the 1968 Strike, and Martin Luther King.* 1989.

Belfrage, Sally. *Freedom Summer.* 1965.

Blumberg, Rhoda Lois. *Civil Rights: The 1960s Freedom Struggle.* 1991.

Branch, Taylor. *Parting the Waters: America in the King Years, 1954–63.* 1988.

Brooks, Thomas R. *Walls Come Tumbling Down: A History of the Civil Rights Movement, 1940–1970.* 1974.

Cagin, Seth, and Philip Dray. *We Are Not Afraid: The Story of Godman, Schwerner, and Chaney and the Civil Rights Campaign in Mississippi.* 1988.

Carson, Clayborne. *In Struggle: SNCC and the Black Awakening of the 1960s.* 1981.

Chafe, William. *Civilities and Civil Rights: Greensboro, North Carolina, and the Black Struggle for Freedom.* 1980.

Clark, E. Culpepper. *The Schoolhouse Door: Segregation's Last Stand at the University of Alabama.* 1993.

Cleaver, Eldridge. *Soul on Ice.* 1968.

David, Jay, and Elaine Crane, eds. *The Black Soldier: From the American Revolution to Vietnam.* 1971.

Dittmer, John. *Local People: The Struggle for Civil Rights in Mississippi.* 1994.

Eissen-Udom, E. U. *Black Nationalism: A Search for an Identity in America.* 1962.

Fairclough, Adam. *"To Redeem the Soul of America": The Southern Christian Leadership Conference from King to the 1980s.* 1987.

Fisher, Randall M. *Rhetoric and American Democracy: Black Protest through Vietnam Dissent.* 1985.

Garrow, David J. *Protest at Selma: Martin Luther King, Jr. and the Voting Rights Act of 1965.* 1978.

———. *Bearing the Cross: Martin Luther King, Jr., and the Southern Christian Leadership Conference.* 1986.

———. *Chicago, 1966: Open-Housing Marches, Summit Negotiations and Operation Breadbasket.* 1989.

Graham, Hugh Davis. *The Civil Rights Era: Origins and Development of a National Policy, 1960–1965.* 1990.

Haines, Herbert. *Black Radicals and the Civil Rights Mainstream, 1954–1970.* 1988.

Halpern, Stephen C. *On the Limits of the Law: The Ironic Legacy of Title VI of the 1964 Civil Rights Act.* 1995.

Hamilton, Charles V. *Adam Clayton Powell, Jr.: The Political Biography of an American Dilemma.* 1991.

Hill, Herbert, and James E. Jones, eds. *Race in America: The Struggle for Equality.* 1993.

Honey, Michael K. *Southern Labor and Black Civil Rights: Organizing Memphis Workers.* 1993.

Lawson, Steven D. *In Pursuit of Power: Southern Blacks and Electoral Politics, 1965–1982.* 1985.

Lincoln, C. Eric. *The Black Muslims in America.* 1973.

Marable, Manning. *Black American Politics: From the Washington Marches to Jesse Jackson.* 1985.

———. *Race, Reform, and Rebellion: The Second Reconstruction in Black America, 1945–1982.* 1991.

McAdam, Doug. *Political Process and the Development of Black Insurgency, 1930–1970.* 1982.

———. *Freedom Summer.* 1988.

McCord, William. *Mississippi: The Long Hot Summer.* 1965.

McMillen, Neil R. *Dark Journey: Black Mississippians in the Age of Jim Crow.* 1989.

Mills, Nicholas. *Like a Holy Crusade: Mississippi 1964—The Turning of the Civil Rights Movement.* 1992.

Morris, Aldon D. *The Origins of the Civil Rights Movement: Black Communities Organizing for Change.* 1984.

Newby, I. B. *Challenge to the Court: Social Scientists and the Defense of Segregation, 1954–1966.* 1969.

Oates, Stephen B. *Let the Trumpet Sound: The Life of Martin Luther King, Jr.* 1982.

Payne, Charles. *I've Got the Light of Freedom: The Organizing Tradition and the Mississippi Freedom Struggle.* 1995.

Peake, Thomas R. *Keeping the Dream Alive: A History of the Southern Christian Leadership Conference.* 1986.

Powledge, Fred. *Free at Last? The Civil Rights Movement and the People Who Made It.* 1991.

Ralph, James R. *Northern Protest: Martin Luther King, Jr., Chicago, and the Civil Rights Movement.* 1993.

Rothschild, Mary Aiken. *A Case of Black and White: Northern Volunteers and the Southern Freedom Summer, 1964–1965.* 1982.

Sitkoff, Harvard. *The Struggle for Black Equality, 1954–1992.* 1993.

Smith, Robert C. *They Closed Their Schools: Prince Edward County, Virginia, 1951–1964*. 1965.

Stoper, Emily. *The Student Nonviolent Coordinating Committee: The Growth of Radicalism in a Civil Rights Organization*. 1989.

Terry, Wallace. *Bloods: An Oral History of the Vietnam War by Black Veterans*. 1984.

Weisbrot, Robert. *Freedom Bound: A History of America's Civil Rights Movement*. 1990.

Whalen, Charles, and Barbara Whalen. *The Long Debate: A Legislative History of the 1964 Civil Rights Act*. 1985.

Wilkinson, J. Harvie. *From Brown to Bakke: The Supreme Court and School Integration, 1954–1978*. 1979.

Williams, Juan. *Eyes on the Prize: America's Civil Rights Years*. 1987.

Witherspoon, William R. *Martin Luther King, Jr.: To the Mountain Top*. 1985.

Wright, Nathan, Jr. *Black Power and Urban Unrest*. 1967.

X, Malcolm, and Alex Haley. *The Autobiography of Malcolm X*. 1964.

ANTIWAR MOVEMENT

Bacciocco, Edward J. *The New Left in America: Reform to Revolution, 1956–1970*. 1974.

Bannan, John, and Rosemary Bannan. *Law, Morality and the Courts: Peace Militants and the Courts*. 1975.

Baskir, Lawrence M., and William A. Strauss. *Change and Circumstance: The Draft, The War and the Vietnam Generation*. 1978.

Belfrage, Cedric, and James Aronson. *Something to Guard: The Stormy Life of the National Guardian, 1947–1967*. 1978.

Berman, William C. *William Fulbright and the Vietnam War: The Dissent of a Political Realist*. 1988.

Bloom, Lynn Z. *Doctor Spock: Biography of a Conservative Radical*. 1972.

Braestrup, Peter. *Big Story: How the American Press and Television Reported and Interpreted the Crisis of Tet 1968 in Vietnam and Washington*. 1978.

Breins, Wini. *The Great Refusal: Community and Organization in the New Left: 1962–1969*. 1982.

Brodie, Bernard. *Vietnam: Why We Failed in War and Politics*. 1973.

Cantor, Milton. *The Divided Left: American Radicalism, 1900–1975*. 1978.

Capps, Walter H. *The Unfinished War: Vietnam and the American Conscience*. 1982.

Carroll, Peter N. *It Seemed Like Nothing Happened: The Tragedy and Promise of America in the 1970s*. 1982.

Chomsky, Noam. *American Power and the New Mandarins*. 1967.

Clecak, Peter. *Radical Paradoxes: Dilemmas of the American Left, 1945–1970*. 1974.

Coffin, William Sloane. *Once to Every Man: A Memoir*. 1977.

Cooney, Robert, and Helen Michalowski, eds. *The Power of the People: Active Nonviolence in the United States*. 1977.

Cortright, David. *Soldiers in Revolt: The American Military Today*. 1975.

DeBenedetti, Charles, and Charles Chatfield. *An American Ordeal: The Antiwar Movement of the Vietnam Era*. 1990.

Finn, James. *Protest: Pacifism and Politics*. 1968.

Fisher, Randall M. *Rhetoric and American Democracy: Black Protest through Vietnam Dissent*. 1985.

Fowler, Robert Booth. *Believing Skeptics: American Political Intellectuals, 1945–1964.* 1976.

Gausman, William F. *Red Stains on Vietnam Doves.* 1989.

Halberstam, David. *The Making of a Quagmire: America and Vietnam during the Kennedy Era.* 1964.

————. *Ho.* 1971.

Hall, Mitchell K. *Because of Their Faith: CALCAV and Religious Opposition to the Vietnam War.* 1990.

Hallen, Daniel C. *The Uncensored War: The Media and Vietnam.* 1989.

Halstead, Fred. *Out Now! A Participant's Account of the American Movement against the Vietnam War.* 1978.

Harris, David. *Dreams Die Hard.* 1982.

Hayden, Tom. *Reunion: A Memoir.* 1988.

Heath, G. Lewis, ed. *Mutiny Does Not Happen Lightly: The Literature of the American Resistance to the Vietnam War.* 1976.

Larner, Jeremy. *Nobody Knows: Reflections on the McCarthy Campaign of 1968.* 1978.

Levy, David W. *The Debate over Vietnam.* 1991.

Lewy, Guenter. *Peace and Revolution: The Moral Crisis of American Pacifism.* 1988.

Lyttle, Bradford. *The Chicago Anti-Vietnam War Movement.* 1988.

McGill, William J. *The Year of the Monkey: Revolt on Campus, 1968–69.* 1982.

Meconis, Charles. *With Clumsy Grace: The American Catholic Left, 1961–1977.* 1979.

Mehnert, Klaus. *Twilight of the Young: The Radical Movements of the 1960s and Their Legacy.* 1976.

Miller, James. *"Democracy Is in the Streets": From Port Huron to the Siege of Chicago.* 1987.

Powers, Thomas. *Vietnam: The War at Home, Vietnam and the American People, 1964–1968.* 1984.

Rothman, Stanley, and S. Robert Lichter. *Roots of Radicalism: Jews, Christians, and the New Left.* 1982.

Sale, Kirkpatrick. *SDS.* 1974.

Small, Melvin. *Johnson, Nixon, and the Doves.* 1988.

Smith, Curt. *Long Time Gone: The Years of Turmoil Remembered.* 1982.

Stavis, Ben. *We Were the Campaign: New Hampshire to Chicago for McCarthy.* 1970.

Surrey, David S. *Choice of Conscience: Vietnam Era Military and Draft Resisters in Canada.* 1982.

Turner, Kathleen J. *Lyndon Johnson's Dual War: Vietnam and the Press.* 1985.

Unger, Irwin. *The Movement: A History of the American New Left, 1959–1972.* 1974.

Useem, Michael. *Conscription, Protest, and Social Conflict: The Life and Death of a Draft Resistance Movement.* 1973.

Vogelgesang, Sandy. *The Long Dark Night of the Soul: The American Intellectual Left and the Vietnam War.* 1974.

Wittner, Lawrence S. *Rebels against War: The American Peace Movement, 1933–1983.* 1984.

Zaroulis, Nancy, and Gerald Sullivan. *Who Spoke Up? American Protest against the War in Vietnam, 1963–1975.* 1984.

Zinn, Howard. *SNCC: The New Abolitionists.* 1965.

ASIAN AMERICANS

Chan, Sucheng. *Asian Americans: An Intrepretive History*. 1991.

Downey, Bruce T., and Douglas P. Olney, eds. *The Hmong in the West: Observations and Reports*. 1982.

Freeman, James M. *Hearts of Sorrow: Vietnamese American Lives*. 1989.

Grant, Bruce. *The Boat People*. 1979.

Jensen, Joan. *Passage from India: Asian Indian Immigrants in North America*. 1988.

Kelly, Gail P. *From Vietnam to America: A Chronicle of the Vietnamese Immigration to the United States*. 1977.

Kim, Hyung-chan Kim. *The Korean Diaspora*. 1977.

Kim, Hyung-chan Kim, and Wayne Patterson, eds. *The Koreans in America, 1882–1974*. 1974.

Kimura, Yukiko. *The Japanese-Americans: Evolution of a Subculture*. 1976.

Lasker, Bruno. *Filipino Immigration to the United States*. 1969.

Ogawa, Dennis. *From Japs to Japanese: An Evolution of Japanese-American Stereotypes*. 1971.

Pido, Antonio J. A. *The Filipinos in America*. 1986.

Rutledge, Paul. *The Vietnamese Experience in America*. 1992.

Saran, Parmatma. *The Asian Indian Experience in the United States*. 1985.

Strand, Paul, and Woodrow Jones, Jr. *Indochinese Refugees in America: Problems of Adaptation and Assimilation*. 1985.

Sung, Betty Lee. *Chinese American Intermarriage*. 1990.

Sutter, Valerie. *The Indochinese Refugee Dilemma*. 1990.

Takaki, Ronald. *Strangers from a Different Shore: A History of Asian Americans*. 1989.

Tsai Shi-shan, Henry. *The Chinese Experience in America*. 1986.

Wain, Barry. *The Refused: The Agony of the Indochinese Refugees*. 1981.

Yanagisako, Sylvia Junko. *Transforming the Past: Tradition and Kinship among Japanese Americans*. 1985.

BEATNIKS

Beard, Rick, and Leslie Berlowitz, eds. *Greenwich Village: Culture and Counterculture*. 1993.

Cook, Bruce. *The Beat Generation*. 1971.

Doherty, Brian, ed. *The Beat Generation Writers*. 1995.

Halsey, Edmund Foster. *Understanding the Beats*. 1992.

Maynard, John Arthur. *Venice West: The Beat Generation in Southern California*. 1991.

Smith, Richard Cándida. *Utopia and Dissent: Art, Poetry, and Politics in California*. 1995.

Stephenson, Gregory. *The Daybreak Boys: Essays on the Literature of the Beat Generation*. 1990.

Sukenick, Ronald. *Down and In: Life in the Underground*. 1987.

Tonkinson, Carole, ed. *Big Sky Mind: Buddhism and the Beat Generation*. 1995.

Tytell, John. *Naked Angels: The Lives and Literature of the Beat Generation*. 1976.

Watson, Steve. *The Birth of the Beat Generation, 1944–1960*. 1995.

CAMPUS PROTEST

Avorn, Jerr L., et al. *Up against the Ivy Wall: A History of the Columbia Crisis*. 1968.

Eichel, Lawrence F., et al. *The Harvard Strike*. 1970.

Flacks, Richard. *Youth and Social Change*. 1971.

Foster, Julian, and Durward Long, eds. *Protest! Student Activism in America*. 1970.

Fueur, Lewis. *The Conflict of Generations: The Character and Significance of Student Movements*. 1969.

Glazer, Nathan. *Remembering the Answers: Essays on the American Student Revolt*. 1970.

Goines, David Lance. *The Free Speech Movement: Coming of Age in the 1960s*. 1993.

Grant, Joanne, ed. *Confrontation on Campus: The Columbia Pattern for the New Protest*. 1969.

Grossvogel, David, and Cushing Strout. *Divided We Stand: Reflections on the Crisis at Cornell*. 1971.

Heirich, Max. *The Beginning: Berkeley, 1964*. 1968.

———. *The Spiral of Conflict: Berkeley, 1964*. 1971.

Horowitz, Helen Lefkowitz. *Campus Life: Undergraduate Cultures from the End of the Eighteenth Century to the Present*. 1987.

Kahn, Roger. *The Battle for Morningside Heights: Why Students Rebel*. 1970.

Lee, Calvin B. T. *The Campus Scene, 1900–1970*. 1970.

Levitt, Cyril. *Children of Privilege: Student Revolt in the Sixties*. 1984.

Lipset, Seymour Martin. *Rebellion in the University*. 1971.

McGill, William J. *The Year of the Monkey: Revolt on Campus, 1968–69*. 1982.

Orrick, William H., Jr. *Shut It Down! A College in Crisis: San Francisco State College, October 1968–April 1969*. 1969.

Rorabaugh, W. J. *Berkeley at War: The 1960s*. 1989.

Westby, David L. *The Clouded Vision: The Student Movement in the United States in the 1960s*. 1976.

COUNTERCULTURE

Braden, William. *The Age of Aquarius: Technology and the Cultural Revolution*. 1970.

Cox, Craig. *Storefront Revolution: Food Co-ops and the Counterculture*. 1994.

Dickstein, Morris. *Gates of Eden: American Culture in the Sixties*. 1977.

Eisen, Jonathan. *Altamont: Death of Innocence in the Woodstock Nation*. 1970.

King, Richard. *The Party of Eros: Radical Social Thought and the Realm of Freedom*. 1972.

Lee, Martin A., and Bruce Shlain. *Acid Dreams: The CIA, LSD, and the Sixties Rebellion*. 1985.

Lobenthal, Joel. *Radical Rags: Fashions of the Sixties*. 1990.

Miller, Thomas. *The Hippies and American Values*. 1991.

Perry, Charles. *Haight-Ashbury: A History*. 1984.

Roszak, Theodore. *The Making of a Counter Culture: Reflections on the Technocratic Society and Its Youthful Opposition*. 1969.

Stein, David Lewis. *Living the Revolution: The Yippies in Chicago*. 1969.

Stevens, Jay. *Storming Heaven: LSD and the American Dream*. 1987.

Urgo, Joseph R. *Novel Frames: Literature as Guide to Race, Sex, and History in America.* 1991.

von Hoffman, Nicholas. *We Are the People Our Parents Warned Us Against.* 1968.

Whitmer, Peter O. *Aquarius Revisited: Seven Who Created the Sixties Counterculture That Changed America.* 1987.

Wolfe, Burton H. *The Hippies.* 1968.

Yinger, Milton. *Countercultures: The Promise and the Peril of a World Turned Upside Down.* 1982.

FILM

Adair, Gilbert. *Vietnam on Film.* 1981.

Alloway, Lawrence. *Violent America: The Movies 1946–1964.* 1971.

Auster, Albert, and Leonard Quart. *How the War Was Remembered: Hollywood and Vietnam.* 1988.

Brownlow, Kevin. *The War, the West and the Wilderness.* 1979.

Dittmar, Linda, and Gene Michaud, eds. *From Hanoi to Hollywood: The Vietnam War in American Film.* 1990.

Henricksen, Margot. *Dr. Strangelove's America: Society and Culture in the Atomic Age.* 1997.

Jowett, Garth. *Film: The Democratic Art.* 1976.

Ray, Robert B. *A Certain Tendency of the Hollywood Cinema, 1930–1980.* 1985.

Shaheen, Jack G. *Nuclear War Films.* 1978.

Sklar, Robert. *Movie-Made America: A Cultural History of American Movies.* 1975.

Smith, Julian. *Looking Away, Hollywood and Vietnam.* 1975.

Wilson, James C. *Vietnam in Prose and Film.* 1982.

Wood, Robin. *Hollywood from Vietnam to Reagan.* 1986.

FOREIGN POLICY

Abel, E. S. *The Missiles of October: Twelve Days to World War III.* 1966.

Allison, G. T. *Essence of Decision: Explaining the Cuban Missile Crisis.* 1971.

Baral, Jaya. *The Pentagon and the Making of U.S. Foreign Policy.* 1978.

Blaufarb, D. S. *The Counterinsurgency Era: U.S. Doctrine and Performance, 1950 to the Present.* 1977.

Bohlen, Charles E. *Witness to History, 1929–1969.* 1973.

Buszynski, Leszet. *Soviet Foreign Policy and Southeast Asia.* 1986.

Cady, John. *The United States and Burma.* 1976.

Cairnes, James Ford. *The Eagle and the Lotus: Western Intervention in Vietnam, 1847–1968.* 1969.

Calleo, David. *The Atlantic Fantasy: The United States, NATO and Europe.* 1970.

Chakrabartty, H. R. *China, Vietnam and the United States.* 1966.

Chayes, Abram. *The Cuban Missile Crisis: International Crises and the Role of Law.* 1974.

Chen, King C. *Vietnam and China, 1938–1954.* 1969.

Edmonds, Robin. *Soviet Foreign Policy, 1962–1973: The Paradox of a Superpower.* 1975.

Havens, Thomas R. *Fire across the Sea: The Vietnam War and Japan.* 1987.

Holsti, Ole R., and James N. Rosenau. *American Leadership in World Affairs: Vietnam and the Breakdown of Consensus.* 1984.

Hoopes, Townsend. *The Limits of Intervention.* 1970.

Hsiao, Gene T., ed. *The Role of External Powers in Indochina.* 1973.

Johnson, Haynes B. *The Bay of Pigs.* 1964.

Kattenburg, Paul M. *The Vietnam Trauma in American Foreign Policy, 1945–1975.* 1980.

King, Peter, ed. *Australia's Vietnam.* 1983.

Kissinger, Henry A. *White House Years: The Memoirs of Henry A. Kissinger.* 1979.

———. *Years of Upheaval: The Memoirs of Henry A. Kissinger.* 1982.

Pachter, H. M. *Collision Course: The Cuban Missile Crisis and Coexistence.* 1963.

Palmer, David R. *Summons of the Trumpet: U.S.–Vietnam in Perspective.* 1978.

Papp, Daniel S. *Vietnam: The View from Moscow, Peking, Washington.* 1981.

Patti, Archimedes. *Why Vietnam? Prelude to America's Albatross.* 1981.

Pike, Douglas. *Vietnam and the Soviet Union: Anatomy of an Alliance.* 1987.

Porter, D. Gareth. *A Peace Denied: The United States, Vietnam, and the Paris Agreement.* 1976.

Rosenberger, Leif. *The Soviet Union and Vietnam: An Uneasy Alliance.* 1986.

Rosie, George. *The British in Vietnam: How the Twenty-Five Years War Began.* 1970.

Ross, Douglas A. *In the Interests of Peace: Canada and Vietnam, 1954–1973.* 1984.

Shafer, D. Michael, ed. *The Legacy: The Vietnam War in the American Imagination.* 1990.

Sullivan, Marianna P. *France's Vietnam Policy: A Study in French–American Relations.* 1978.

Sutter, Robert G. *Chinese Foreign Policy after the Cultural Revolution: 1966–1977.* 1978.

Taylor, Charles. *Snow Job: Canada, the United States and Vietnam (1954–1973).* 1974.

Thies, Wallace. *When Governments Collide: Coercion and Diplomacy in the Vietnam Conflict, 1964–1968.* 1980.

Wyden, Peter. *Bay of Pigs: The Untold Story.* 1979.

Zagoria, Donald S., ed. *Soviet Policy in East Asia.* 1983.

GENERAL BACKGROUND

Anderson, Terry. *The Movement and the Sixties: Protest in America from Greensboro to Wounded Knee.* 1995.

Berman, Ronald. *America in the Sixties: An Intellectual History.* 1970.

Blum, John Morton. *Years of Discord, 1961–1974.* 1991.

Burner, David, Robert Marcus, and Thomas West. *A Giant's Strength: America in the Sixties.* 1971.

Burns, Stewart. *Social Movements of the 1960s: Searching for Democracy.* 1990.

Chalmers, David. *And the Crooked Places Made Straight: The Struggle for Social Change in the 1960s.* 1991.

Farber, David. *The Age of Great Dreams: America in the 1960s.* 1994.

———, ed. *The Sixties: From Memory to History.* 1994.

Freeman, Jo, ed. *Social Movements of the Sixties and Seventies.* 1983.

Gitlin, Todd. *The Sixties: Years of Hope, Days of Rage.* 1987.

Halberstam, David. *The Best and the Brightest.* 1972.

Hodgson, Geoffrey. *America in Our Time: From World War II to Nixon—What Happened and Why.* 1978.

Knight, Douglas. *Streets of Dreams: The Nature and Legacy of the 1960s.* 1989.

Matusow, Allen J. *The Unraveling of America: A History of Liberalism in the 1960s.* 1984.

Mendel-Reyes, Meta. *Reclaiming Democracy: The Sixties in Politics and Memory.* 1995.

Morgan, Edward P. *The Sixties Experience: Hard Lessons about Modern America.* 1991.

Morrison, Joan, and Robert K. Morrison, eds. *From Camelot to Kent State: The Sixties in the Words of Those Who Lived It.* 1987.

O'Neill, William L. *Coming Apart: An Informal History of America in the 1960s.* 1971.

Sayres, Sohnya, Anders Stephenson, Stanley Aronowitz, and Frederic Jameson, eds. *The 60s Without Apology.* 1984.

Steigerwald, David. *The Sixties and the End of Modern America.* 1995.

Stern, Jane, and Michael Stern. *Sixties People.* 1990.

Tischler, Barbara L., ed. *Sights on the Sixties.* 1992.

Viorst, Milton. *Fire in the Streets: America in the 1960s.* 1979.

HISPANIC AMERICANS

Abalos, David T. *Latinos in the United States: The Sacred and the Political.* 1987.

Balseiro, J. A., ed. *The Hispanic Presence in Florida: Yesterday and Today: 1513–1976.* 1977.

Bonachea, Ramón L., and Marta San Martín. *The Cuban Insurrection, 1952–1959.* 1973.

Bonsal, Philip W. *Cuba, Castro, and the United States.* 1971.

Boswell, Thomas D., and James R. Curtis. *The Cuban–American Experience: Culture, Images and Perspectives.* 1983.

Bourne, Peter G. *Fidel: A Biography of Fidel Castro.* 1986.

Cortés, Carlos E., ed. *The Cuban Exiles in the United States.* 1980.

———. *The Cuban Experience in the United States.* 1980.

———. *Cuban Refugee Programs.* 1980.

Cripps, Louise L. *The Spanish Caribbean: From Columbus to Castro.* 1979.

Domínguez, Jorge I. *Cuba: Order and Revolution.* 1978.

Dominguez, Virginia R. *From Neighbor to Stranger: The Dilemma of Caribbean Peoples in the United States.* 1970.

Fagan, Richard R., Richard M. Brody, and Thomas J. O'Leary. *Cubans in Exile: Disaffection and Revolution.* 1968.

Farber, Samuel. *Revolution and Reaction in Cuba, 1933–1960.* 1976.

Fitzpatrick, Joseph P. *Puerto Rican Americans: The Meaning of Migration to the United States.* 1987.

Gallagher, Patrick Lee. *The Cuban Exile. A Socio-Political Analysis.* 1980.

Gann, L. H., and Peter J. Duignan. *The Hispanics in the United States: A History.* 1987.

Garcia, Maria. *Mexican-Americans: Leadership, Ideology, and Identity, 1930–1960.* 1989.

Gernard, Renee. *The Cuban Americans.* 1988.

Gomez-Quinones, Juan. *Chicano Politics: Reality and Promise, 1940–1990.* 1990.

Gonzales, Edward. *Cuba under Castro: The Limits of Charisma.* 1974.

Griswold del Castillo, Richard. *La Familia: Chicano Families in the Urban Southwest, 1848 to the Present.* 1984.

Hendricks, Glenn. *The Dominican Diaspora: From the Dominican Republic to New York City, Villages in Transition.* 1974.

Horowitz, Ruth. *Honor and the American Dream: Culture and Identity in a Chicano Community.* 1983.

Llanas, José. *Cuban Americans: Masters of Survival.* 1982.

Llerena, Mario. *The Unsuspected Revolution: The Birth and Rise of Castroism.* 1978.

Maril, Robert Lee. *Poorest of Americans: The Mexican Americans of the Lower Rio Grande Valley of Texas.* 1989.

Masud-Piloto, Felix Roberto. *With Open Arms: Cuban Migration to the United States.* 1988.

McNally, Michael J. *Catholicism in South Florida, 1868–1968.* 1984.

Mormino, Gary R., and George E. Pozzetta. *The Immigrant World of Ybor City: Italians and Their Latin Neighbors in Tampa, 1885–1985.* 1987.

Padilla, Felix M. *Puerto Rican Chicago.* 1987.

Palmer, Ransford W. *In Search of a Better Life: Perspectives on Migration from the Caribbean.* 1990.

Paterson, Thomas G. *Contesting Castro: The United States and the Triumph of the Cuban Revolution.* 1994.

Pedraza-Bailey, Silvia. *Political and Economic Migrants in America: Cubans and Mexicans.* 1985.

Pérez, Louis A., Jr. *Cuba and the United States: Ties of Singular Intimacy.* 1990.

Portes, Alejandro, and Robert L. Bach. *Latin Journey: Cuban and Mexican Immigrants in the United States.* 1985.

Ridge, Martin. *The New Bilingualism: An American Dilemma.* 1981.

Rodriguez, Clara P. *Puerto Ricans: Born in the U.S.A.* 1989.

Romo, Ricardo. *East Los Angeles: History of a Barrio.* 1983.

Sanchez Jankowski, Martin. *City Bound: Urban Life and Political Attitudes among Chicano Youth.* 1986.

Smith, Robert Freeman. *The United States and Cuba: Business and Diplomacy, 1917–1960.* 1960.

Suchlicki, Jaime. *University Students and Revolution in Cuba, 1920–1968.* 1969.

———. *Cuba, from Columbus to Castro.* 1974.

Vélez-Ibañez, Carlos. *Bonds of Mutual Trust: The Cultural Systems of Rotating Credit Associations among Urban Mexicans and Chicanos.* 1983.

Welch, Richard E., Jr. *Response to Revolution. The United States and the Cuban Revolution, 1959–1961.* 1985.

Weyr, Thomas. *Hispanic U.S.A.: Breaking the Melting Pot.* 1988.

JOHNSON ADMINISTRATION

Berman, Larry. *Planning a Tragedy: The Americanization of the War in Vietnam.* 1982.

———. *Lyndon Johnson's War: The Road to Stalemate in Vietnam.* 1989.

Bornet, Vaughn. *The Presidency of Lyndon Johnson.* 1983.

Califano, Joseph. *The Triumph and Tragedy of Lyndon Johnson: The White House Years.* 1991.

Conkin, Paul. *Big Daddy from the Pedernales.* 1986.

Gans, Herbert. *The War against the Poor: The Underclass and Antipoverty Policy.* 1995.

Goldman, Eric. *The Tragedy of Lyndon Johnson.* 1969.

Johnson, Lyndon Baines. *The Vantage Point: Perspectives of the Presidency, 1963–1969.* 1971.

Kaplan, Marshall, and Peggy Cucity, eds. *The Great Society and Its Legacy: Twenty Years of U.S. Social Policy.* 1986.

Kearns, Doris. *Lyndon Johnson and the American Dream.* 1976.

Miller, Merle. *Lyndon: An Oral Biography.* 1980.

Roberts, Charles. *LBJ's Inner Circle.* 1965.

Smith, R. B. *An International History of the Vietnam War: The Johnson Strategy.* 1990.

Turner, Kathleen J. *Lyndon Johnson's Dual War: Vietnam and the Press.* 1985.

KENNEDY ADMINISTRATION

Aliano, Richard A. *American Defense Policy from Eisenhower to Kennedy: The Politics of Changing Military Requirements, 1957–1961.* 1976.

Beschloss, Michael R. *The Crisis Years: Kennedy and Khrushchev 1960–1963.* 1992.

Fairlie, Henry. *The Kennedy Promise: The Politics of Expectation.* 1973.

Galloway, John. *The Kennedys and Vietnam.* 1990.

Giglio, James. *The Presidency of John F. Kennedy.* 1971.

Hersh, Seymour. *The Dark Side of Camelot.* 1997.

Hilsman, Roger. *To Move a Nation: The Politics of Foreign Policy in the Administration of John F. Kennedy.* 1967.

Miroff, Bruce. *Pragmatic Illusions: The Presidential Politics of John F. Kennedy.* 1976.

Newman, John M. *JFK and Vietnam: Deception, Intrigue, and the Struggle for Power.* 1992.

Nolting, Frederick. *From Trust to Tragedy: The Political Memoirs of Frederick Nolting, Kennedy's Ambassador to Diem's Vietnam.* 1988.

O'Donnell, Kenneth, and David Powers. *"Johnny, We Hardly Knew Ye."* 1978.

Parmet, Herbert. *JFK: The Presidency of John F. Kennedy.* 1983.

Reeves, Thomas. *A Question of Character. A Life of John F. Kennedy.* 1991.

Rust, William J. *Kennedy in Vietnam: American Foreign Policy, 1960–1963.* 1987.

Salinger, Pierre. *With Kennedy.* 1966.

Schlesinger, Arthur M., Jr. *A Thousand Days: John F. Kennedy in the White House.* 1965.

———. *Robert Kennedy and His Times.* 1978.

Smith, R. B. *An International History of the Vietnam War: The Kennedy Strategy.* 1987.

Sorensen, Theodore. *Kennedy.* 1965.

Walton, Richard J. *Cold War and Counterrevolution: The Foreign Policy of John F. Kennedy.* 1972.

Wills, Gary. *The Kennedy Imprisonment: A Meditation on Power.* 1982.

NATIVE AMERICANS

Barsh, Russel Lawrence, and James Youngblood Henderson. *The Road: Indian Tribes and Political Liberty.* 1980.

Berkhofer, Robert E., Jr. *The White Man's Indian: Images of the Indian from Columbus to the Present*. 1978.

Boldt, Menno. *Surviving as Indians: The Challenge of Self-Government*. 1994.

Burnette, Robert, and John Koster. *The Road to Wounded Knee*. 1974.

Burt, Larry W. *Tribalism in Crisis: Federal Indian Policy, 1953–1961*. 1982.

Burton, Lloyd. *American Indian Water Rights and the Limits of Law*. 1993.

Cadwalader, Sandra A., and Vine Deloria, Jr., eds. *The Aggressions of Civilization: Federal Indian Policy since the 1880s*. 1984.

Churchill, Ward, and Jim Vander Wall. *Agents of Repression: The FBI's Secret Wars against the Black Panther Party and the American Indian Movement*. 1988.

Cornell, Steven. *The Return of the Native: American Indian Political Resurgence*. 1988.

Deloria, Vine, Jr. *We Talk, You Listen: New Tribes, New Turf*. 1970.

———. *God Is Red*. 1973.

———. *Behind the Trail of Broken Treaties*. 1974.

———. *Custer Died for Your Sins: An Indian Manifesto*. 1988.

Dunbar Ortiz, Roxanne. *Indians of the Americas: Human Rights and Self-Determination*. 1984.

Forbes, Jack D. *Native Americans and Nixon: Presidential Politics and Minority Self-Determination, 1969–1972*. 1981.

Fortunate Eagle, Adam. *Alcatraz! Alcatraz! The Indian Occupation of 1969–1971*. 1992.

Friesen, Carol. *Disputed Jurisdiction and Recognition of Judgments between Tribal and State Courts*. 1990.

Green, Donald E., and Thomas V. Tonnesen, eds. *American Indians: Social Justice and Public Policy*. 1991.

Green, L. C., and Olive P. Dickson. *The Law of Nations and the New World*. 1989.

Greenberg, Pam, and Jody Zelio. *States and the Indian Gaming Regulatory Act*. 1992.

Grinde, Donald A., Jr., and Bruce E. Johansen. *Exemplar of Liberty: Native America and the Evolution of Democracy*. 1991.

Gross, Emma R. *Contemporary Federal Policy toward American Indians*. 1989.

Guillemin, Jeanne. *Urban Renegades: The Cultural Strategy of the American Indians*. 1975.

Hannum, Hurst. *Autonomy, Self-Determination and Sovereignty: The Accommodation of Conflicting Rights*. 1990.

Hertzberg, Hazel W. *The Search for an American Indian Identity: Modern Pan-Indian Movements*. 1971.

Johnson, Troy R. *The Occupation of Alcatraz Island: Indian Self-Determination and the Rise of Indian Activism*. 1996.

Johnston, Basil H. *Indian School Days*. 1989.

Josephy, Alvin J., Jr. *Red Power: The American Indians' Fight for Freedom*. 1971.

———. *Now That the Buffalo's Gone: A Study of Today's American Indians*. 1984.

Levitan, Sar A., and Barbara Hetrick. *Big Brother's Indian Programs, with Reservations*. 1971.

Levitan, Sar A., and William B. Johnson. *Indian Giving: Federal Programs for Native Americans*. 1979.

Lincoln, Kenneth. *Native American Renaissance*. 1983.

Lyden, Fremont J., and Lyman H. Legters, eds. *Native Americans and Public Policy*. 1992.

McNickle, D'Arcy. *Native American Tribalism: Indian Survivals and Renewals*. 1973.

Meyer, William. *Native Americans: The New Indian Resistance.* 1971.

Nagel, Joane. *American Indian Ethnic Renewal: Red Power and the Resurgence of Identity and Culture.* 1995.

Neils, Elaine M. *Reservation to City: Indian Migration and Federal Relocation.* 1971.

Orfield, Gary. *A Study of the Termination Policy.* 1965.

Parman, Donald L. *The Indians in the American West during the Twentieth Century.* 1994.

Pommershein, Frank. *Braid of Feathers: American Indian Law and Contemporary Tribal Life.* 1995.

Senese, Guy B. *Self-Determination and the Social Education of Native Americans.* 1991.

Sorkin, Alan L. *American Indians and Federal Aid.* 1971.

————. *The Urban American Indian.* 1978.

Steiner, Stan. *The New Indians.* 1968.

Stern, Kenneth S. *Loud Hawk: The United States and the American Indian Movement.* 1994.

Vizenor, Gerald. *Manifest Manners: Postindian Warriors of Survivance.* 1994.

Waddell, Jack O., and O. Michael Watson, eds. *The American Indian in Urban Society.* 1971.

Wells, Robert N., Jr., ed. *Native American Resurgence and Renewal.* 1994.

NEW LEFT

Bacciocco, Edward J. *The New Left in America: Reform to Revolution, 1956 to 1970.* 1974.

Bone, Christopher. *The Disinherited Children: A Study of the New Left and the Generation Gap.* 1977.

Breines, Wini. *Community and Organization in the New Left, 1962–1968: The Great Refusal.* 1982.

Buhle, Paul, ed. *History and the New Left: Madison, Wisconsin, 1950–1970.* 1989.

Calvert, Gregory Nevala. *Democracy from the Heart: Spiritual Values, Decentralism, and Democratic Idealism in the Movement of the 1960s.* 1991.

Collier, Peter, and David Horowitz. *Destructive Generation: Second Thoughts about the Sixties.* 1989.

Conlin, John. *The Troubles: A Jaundiced Glance Back at the Movement of the 1960s.* 1982.

Davis, James Kirkpatrick. *Assault on the Left: The FBI and the Sixties Antiwar Movement.* 1997.

Friedman, Michael. *The New Left of the Sixties.* 1972.

Gann, Lewis H., and Peter Duignan. *The New Left and the Cultural Revolution of the 1960s: A Reevaluation.* 1995.

Gitlin, Todd. *The Whole World Is Watching: Mass Media in the Making and Unmaking of the New Left.* 1980.

Goldwin, Robert, ed. *How Democratic Is America? Responses to the New Left Challenge.* 1971.

Goode, Stephen. *Affluent Revolutionaries: A Portrait of the New Left.* 1974.

Grosse, Van. *Where the Boys Are: Cuba, Cold War America, and the Making of the New Left.* 1993.

Isserman, Maurice. *If I Had a Hammer . . . The Death of the Old Left and the Birth of the New Left.* 1987.

Levy, Peter B. *The New Left and Labor in the 1960s.* 1994.

Lewy, Guenter. *Peace and Revolution: The Moral Crisis of American Pacifism.* 1988.

Miller, James. *"Democracy Is in the Streets": From Port Huron to the Siege of Chicago.* 1987.

Myers, R. David, ed. *Toward a History of the New Left: Essays from within the Movement.* 1989.

Newfield, Jack. *A Prophetic Minority: The American New Left.* 1966.

Rand, Ayn. *The New Left: The Anti-Industrial Revolution.* 1975.

Rothman, Stanley, and S. Robert Lichter. *Roots of Radicalism: Jews, Christians and the New Left.* 1982.

Sargent, Lyman Tower. *New Left Thought: An Introduction.* 1972.

Stolz, Matthew F., ed. *Politics of the New Left.* 1971.

Unger, Irwin, and Debi Unger. *The Movement: A History of the American New Left.* 1974.

Vickers, George. *The Formation of the New Left: The Early Years.* 1975.

Wald, Alan W. *Writing from the New Left: Essays on Radical Culture and Politics.* 1994.

Woods, James L. *New Left Ideology: Its Dimensions and Development.* 1975.

NIXON ADMINISTRATION

Forbes, Jack D. *Native Americans and Nixon: Presidential Politics and Minority Self-Determination, 1969–1972.* 1981.

Kissinger, Henry A. *White House Years.* 1979.

––––––. *Years of Upheaval.* 1982.

Nixon, Richard M. *RN: The Memoirs of Richard Nixon.* 1978.

Shawcross, William. *Sideshow: Kissinger, Nixon, and the Destruction of Cambodia.* 1979.

Szulc, Tad. *The Illusion of Peace: Foreign Policy in the Nixon Years.* 1978.

THE SOUTH

Bartley, Numan V. *The Rise of Massive Resistance: Race and Politics in the South during the 1950s.* 1969.

Bartley, Numan V., and Hugh D. Graham. *Southern Politics and the Second Reconstruction.* 1975.

Belknap, Michal R. *Federal Law and Southern Order: Racial Violence and Constitutional Conflict in the Post-Brown South.* 1987.

Black, Earl, and Merle Black. *Politics and Society in the South.* 1987.

Bloom, Jack. *Class, Race, and the Civil Rights Movement: The Political Economy of Southern Racism.* 1987.

Davidson, Chandler, and Bernard Grofman, eds. *Quiet Revolution in the South: The Impact of the Voting Rights Act, 1965–1990.* 1994.

Goldfield, David. *Black, White, and Southern: Race Relations and Southern Culture 1940 to the Present.* 1990.

Jacoway, Elizabeth, and David R. Colburn. *Southern Businessmen and Desegregation.* 1982.

Lawson, Steven F. *Black Ballots: Voting Rights in the South, 1944–1969.* 1976.

———. *In Pursuit of Power: Southern Blacks and Electoral Politics, 1965–1982.* 1985.

———. *Running for Freedom: Civil Rights and Black Politics in America since 1941.* 1991.

Lesher, Stephan. *George Wallace: American Populist.* 1994.

McMillen, Neil R. *The Citizens' Council: Organized Resistance to the Second Reconstruction, 1954–1964.* 1971.

Parker, Frank. *Black Votes Count: Political Empowerment in Mississippi after 1965.* 1990.

Watters, Pat, and Reese Cleghorn. *Climbing Jacob's Ladder: The Arrival of Negroes in Southern Politics.* 1967.

Wilhoit, Francis M. *The Politics of Massive Resistance.* 1973.

TELEVISION

Barnouw, Eric. *Tube of Plenty: The Evolution of American Television.* 1975.

Castleman, Harry. *Watching TV: Four Decades of American TV.* 1982.

Lowe, Carl, ed. *TV and American Culture.* 1981.

McDonald, J. Fred. *Television and the Cold War: The Video Road to Vietnam.* 1985.

Rollins, Peter C., and David H. Cuthbert. *Television's Vietnam: The Impact of Visual Images.* 1983.

Sklar, Robert. *Prime Time America: Life on and behind the Television Screen.* 1988.

Taylor, Ella. *Prime-Time Families: Television Culture in Postwar America.* 1989.

Winship, Michael. *Television.* 1988.

URBAN RIOTS

Bullock, Paul, ed. *Watts: The Aftermath by the People of Watts.* 1969.

Button, James W. *Black Violence: Political Impact of the 1960s Riots.* 1978.

Fine, Sidney. *Violence in the Model City: The Cavanaugh Administration and the Detroit Riot of 1967.* 1989.

Harris, Fred R., and Tom Wicker, eds. *The Kerner Report: The 1968 Report of the National Advisory Commission on Civil Disorders.* 1988.

Horne, Gerald. *Fire This Time: The Watts Uprising and the Meaning of the 1960s.* 1997.

VIETNAM WAR

Andrew, Bruce. *Public Constraint and American Policy in Vietnam.* 1976.

Arnett, Peter, and Michael Maclear. *The Ten Thousand Day War.* 1981.

Austin, Anthony. *The President's War.* 1971.

Ball, George W. *The Past Has Another Pattern.* 1982.

Baral, Jaya. *The Pentagon and the Making of U.S. Foreign Policy.* 1978.

Baritz, Loren. *Backfire: A History of How American Culture Led Us into Vietnam and Made Us Fight the Way We Did.* 1984.

Barnet, Richard J. *Roots of War.* 1972.

Berman, Larry. *Planning a Tragedy: The Americanization of the War in Vietnam.* 1982.
———. *Lyndon Johnson's War: The Road to Stalemate in Vietnam.* 1989.
Blum, Robert M. *Drawing the Line: The Origin of the American Containment Policy in East Asia.* 1982.
Braestrup, Peter, ed. *Vietnam as History: Ten Years after the Paris Peace Accords.* 1984.
Brodie, Bernard. *War and Politics.* 1973.
Brown, MacAlister, and Joseph J. Zasloff. *Apprentice Revolutionaries: The Communist Movement in Laos, 1930–1985.* 1986.
Burke, John P., and Fred I. Greenstein. *How Presidents Test Reality: Decisions on Vietnam, 1954 and 1965.* 1991.
Campagna, Anthony S. *The Economic Consequences of the Vietnam War.* 1991.
Capps, Walter H. *The Unfinished War: Vietnam and the American Conscience.* 1990.
———, ed. *The Vietnam Reader.* 1990.
Charlton, Michael, and Anthony Moncrief. *Many Reasons Why: The American Involvement in Vietnam.* 1978.
Clifford, Clark. *Counsel to the President: A Memoir.* 1991.
Cohen, Warren. *Dean Rusk.* 1980.
Cooper, Chester. *The Lost Crusade: America in Vietnam.* 1972.
Davidson, Phillip B. *Vietnam at War: The History, 1945–1975.* 1988.
Dommen, Arthur J. *Conflict in Laos.* 1971.
———. *Laos: The Keystone of Indochina.* 1985.
Donovan, John C. *The Cold Warriors: A Policy-Making Elite.* 1974.
Drachman, Edward R. *United States Policy toward Vietnam, 1940–1945.* 1970.
Eisenhower, Dwight D. *The White House Years: Mandate for Change 1953–1956.* 1963.
———. *The White House Years: Waging Peace 1956–1961.* 1965.
Ellsberg, Daniel. *Papers on the War.* 1972.
Evans, Rowland, and Robert Novak. *Lyndon B. Johnson: The Exercise of Power.* 1966.
Fall, Bernard. *Street without Joy.* 1961.
———. *Viet-Nam Witness 1953–1966.* 1966.
———. *Hell in a Very Small Place.* 1967.
———. *Last Reflections on a War.* 1967.
———. *Anatomy of a Crisis: The Laotian Crisis of 1960–1961.* 1969.
Fincher, E. B. *The Vietnam War.* 1980.
FitzGerald, Francis. *Fire in the Lake: The Vietnamese and the Americans in Vietnam.* 1972.
Galloway, John. *The Gulf of Tonkin Resolution.* 1970.
———. *The Kennedys and Vietnam.* 1971.
Gardner, Lloyd C. *Approaching Vietnam: From World War II through Dienbienphu.* 1989.
Gelb, Lawrence, and Richard K. Betts. *The Irony of Vietnam: The System Worked.* 1979.
Geyelin, Philip. *Lyndon B. Johnson and the World.* 1969.
Gibbons, William C. *The U.S. Government and the Vietnam War, 1961–1964.* 1975.
Goldman, Eric. *The Tragedy of Lyndon Johnson.* 1969.
Goulden, Joseph C. *Truth Is the First Casualty.* 1968.
Graebner, Norman A. *Nationalism and Communism in Asia: The American Response.* 1977.
Grinter, Lawrence E., and Peter M. Dunne. *The American War in Vietnam: Lessons, Legacies, and Implications for Future Conflicts.* 1987.

Halberstam, David. *The Making of a Quagmire: America and Vietnam during the Kennedy Era.* 1964.

———. *The Best and the Brightest.* 1972.

Harriman, W. Averell. *America and Russia in a Changing World: A Half Century of Personal Observation.* 1971.

Hartmann, Robert T. *Palace Politics: An Inside Account of the Ford Years.* 1980.

Hayes, S. P., ed. *The Beginning of American Aid to Southeast Asia: The Griffin Mission of 1950.* 1971.

Heardon, Patrick H. *The Tragedy of Vietnam.* 1991.

Herring, George C. *America's Longest War: The United States and Vietnam, 1950–1975.* 1986.

Humphrey, Hubert H. *The Education of a Public Man: My Life and Politics.* 1976.

Isaacs, Arnold R. *Without Honor: Defeat in Vietnam and Cambodia.* 1983.

Isaacson, Walter, and Evan Thomas. *The Wise Men: Six Friends and the World They Made.* 1986.

Joes, Anthony J. *The War for South Vietnam: Nineteen Fifty-Four to Nineteen Seventy-Five.* 1989.

Johnson, Lyndon Baines. *The Vantage Point: Perspectives of the Presidency, 1963–1969.* 1971.

Kahin, George McT., and John W. Lewis. *The United States in Vietnam: An Analysis in Depth of the History of American Involvement in Vietnam.* 1967.

Kalb, Marvin, and Elie Abel. *Roots of Involvement: The U.S. in Asia 1784–1971.* 1971.

Karnow, Stanley. *Vietnam: A History.* 1984.

Kattenburg, Paul. *The Vietnam Trauma in American Foreign Policy, 1945–1975.* 1980.

Kearns, Doris. *Lyndon Johnson and the American Dream.* 1976.

Kendrick, Alexander. *The Wound Within: America in the Vietnam Years, 1945–1974.* 1974.

Kirk, Donald. *Wider War: The Struggle for Cambodia, Thailand, and Laos.* 1971.

Kissinger, Henry A. *White House Years.* 1979.

———. *Years of Upheaval.* 1982.

Kolko, Gabriel. *Anatomy of a War: Vietnam, the United States, and the Modern Historical Experience.* 1985.

Krepinevich, Andrew F., Jr. *The Army and Vietnam.* 1986.

Lee, Sam. *The Perfect War.* 1990.

Lewy, Guenter. *America in Vietnam.* 1978.

Lodge, Henry Cabot. *The Storm Has Many Eyes: A Personal Narrative.* 1973.

Lomperis, Timothy J. *The War Everyone Lost—And Won: America's Intervention in Vietnam's Twin Struggles.* 1984.

Louis, William Roger. *Imperialism at Bay: The United States and the Decolonization of the British Empire.* 1978.

Manhattan, Avro. *Vietnam: Why Did We Go?* 1984.

McCloud, Bill. *What Should We Tell Our Children about Vietnam?* 1990.

McLaughlin, Martin. *Vietnam and World Revolution: A Trotskyite Analysis.* 1985.

McQuaid, Kim. *The Anxious Years: America in the Vietnam-Watergate Era.* 1989.

Miller, Merle. *Lyndon: An Oral Biography.* 1980.

Millett, Allan R., ed. *A Short History of the Vietnam War.* 1978.

Miroff, Bruce. *Pragmatic Illusions: The Presidential Politics of John F. Kennedy.* 1976.

Morrison, Wilbur. *Vietnam: The Winnable War.* 1990.

Moss, George. *Vietnam: An American Ordeal.* 1989.

Newman, John M. *JFK and Vietnam: Deception, Intrigue, and the Struggle for Power.* 1992.

Nickelsen, Harry. *Vietnam.* 1989.

Nixon, Richard M. *RN: The Memoirs of Richard Nixon.* 1978.

———. *No More Vietnams.* 1980.

———. *The Real War.* 1980.

———. *Nineteen Ninety-Nine Victory without War.* 1988.

Nolting, Frederick. *From Trust to Tragedy: The Political Memoirs of Frederick Nolting, Kennedy's Ambassador to Diem's Vietnam.* 1988.

O'Donnell, Kenneth, and David Powers. *"Johnny, We Hardly Knew Ye."* 1978.

Olson, James S. *Dictionary of the Vietnam War.* 1988.

Olson, James S., and Randy Roberts. *Where the Domino Fell: America and Vietnam, 1945–1990.* 1991.

Osborne, Milton. *Before Kampuchea: Preludes to Tragedy.* 1979.

Palmer, Bruce, Jr. *The Twenty-Five-Year War: America's Military Role in Vietnam.* 1984.

Palmer, Dave. *Summons of the Trumpet: America and Vietnam in Perspective.* 1978.

Palmer, Gregory. *The McNamara Strategy and the Vietnam War: Program Budgeting in the Pentagon, 1960–1968.* 1978.

Patti, Archimedes L. *Why Vietnam? Prelude to America's Albatross.* 1981.

Podhoretz, Norman. *Why We Were in Vietnam.* 1982.

Poole, Peter. *Eight Presidents and Indochina.* 1978.

Ravenal, Earl C. *Never Again: Learning from America's Foreign Policy Failures.* 1978.

Reeves, Richard. *A Ford Not a Lincoln.* 1975.

Reeves, Thomas C. *A Question of Character: A Life of John F. Kennedy.* 1991.

Rose, Lisle Abbott. *Roots of Tragedy: The United States and the Struggle for Asia, 1945–1953.* 1976.

Rostow, W. W. *The Diffusion of Power, 1957–1972.* 1972.

Rotter, Andrew J. *The Path to Vietnam: Origins of the American Commitment to Southeast Asia.* 1989.

Rusk, Dean. *As I Saw It: The Memoirs of Dean Rusk.* 1990.

Rust, William J. *Kennedy in Vietnam: American Foreign Policy, 1960–1963.* 1987.

Salinger, Pierre. *With Kennedy.* 1966.

Salisbury, Harrison, ed. *Vietnam Reconsidered: Lessons from a War.* 1984.

Schell, Jonathan. *The Village of Ben Suc.* 1967.

Schlesinger, Arthur M., Jr. *A Thousand Days: John F. Kennedy in the White House.* 1965.

———. *The Bitter Heritage: Vietnam and American Democracy, 1941–1966.* 1967.

———. *Robert Kennedy and His Times.* 1978.

Sharp, Melvin. *The Vietnam War and Public Policy.* 1991.

Sharp, U. S. G. *Strategy for Defeat: Vietnam in Retrospect.* 1978.

Shawcross, William. *Sideshow: Kissinger, Nixon, and the Destruction of Cambodia.* 1979.

———. *The Quality of Mercy: Cambodia, Holocaust, and Modern Conscience.* 1984.

Sheehan, Neil. *The Bright and Shining Lie: John Paul Vann and America in Vietnam.* 1988.

Short, Anthony. *The Origins of the Vietnam War.* 1989.

Smith, R. B. *An International History of the Vietnam War. Volume 1: Revolution versus Containment, 1955–1961.* 1984.

———. *An International History of the Vietnam War: The Kennedy Strategy.* 1987.

———. *An International History of the Vietnam War: The Johnson Strategy.* 1990.

Sorensen, Theodore. *Kennedy.* 1965.

Stevenson, Charles A. *The End of Nowhere: American Policy toward Laos since 1954.* 1972.

Sullivan, Michael P. *The Vietnam War: A Study in the Making of American Foreign Policy.* 1985.

Summers, Harry G., Jr. *On Strategy: A Critical Analysis of the Vietnam War.* 1982.

Szulc, Tad. *The Illusion of Peace: Foreign Policy in the Nixon Years.* 1978.

Taylor, Maxwell D. *Swords and Plowshares.* 1972.

Thayer, Thomas. *Vietnam: War without Fronts.* 1985.

Thies, Wallace J. *When Governments Collide: Coercion and Diplomacy in the Vietnam Conflict, 1964–1968.* 1980.

Trewhitt, Henry. *McNamara.* 1971.

Turley, William S. *The Second Indochina War: A Short Political and Military History, 1945–1975.* 1986.

Turner, Kathleen J. *Lyndon Johnson's Dual War: Vietnam and the Press.* 1985.

Vance, Cyrus. *Hard Choices.* 1983.

Walt, Lewis W. *Strange War, Strange Strategy.* 1976.

Westmoreland, William. *A Soldier Reports.* 1976.

Windchy, Eugene G. *Tonkin Gulf.* 1971.

Young, Marilyn. *The Vietnam Wars, 1945–1990.* 1991.

VIETNAM WAR IN LITERATURE

Anisfield, Nancy, ed. *Vietnam Anthology: American War Literature.* 1985.

Baritz, Loren. *Backfire: A History of How American Culture Led Us into Vietnam and Made Us Fight the Way We Did.* 1985.

Ehrhart, W. D., ed. *Carrying the Darkness: The Poetry of the Vietnam War.* 1989.

Heath, G. Lewis, ed. *Mutiny Does Not Happen Lightly: The Literature of the American Resistance to the Vietnam War.* 1976.

Lewis, Lloyd B. *The Tainted War: Culture and Identity in Vietnam War Narratives.* 1985.

Lomperis, Timothy J., and John Clark Pratt, eds. *Reading the Wind: The Literature of the Vietnam War.* 1987.

Louvre, Alf, and Jeffrey Walsh, eds. *Tell Me Lies about Vietnam: Cultural Battles for the Meaning of the War.* 1988.

Melling, Philip H. *Vietnam in American Literature.* 1990.

Myers, Thomas. *Walking Point: American Narratives of Vietnam.* 1988.

Newman, John. *Vietnam War Literature.* 1982.

Walsh, Jeffrey, and James Aulich, eds. *Vietnam Images: War and Representation.* 1989.

Wilson, James C. *Vietnam in Prose and Film.* 1982.

WOMEN

Baker, Mark. *Nam: The Vietnam War in the Words of the Men and Women Who Fought There.* 1981.

Emerson, Gloria. *Winners and Losers: Battles, Retreats, Gains, Losses, and Ruins from a Long War.* 1977.

Evans, Sara. *Personal Politics: The Roots of Women's Liberation in the Civil Rights Movement and the New Left.* 1979.

Freedman, Dan, and Jacqueline Rhoads. *Nurses in Vietnam: The Forgotten Veterans.* 1987.

Friedan, Betty. *The Feminine Mystique.* 1963.

Giddings, Paula. *When and Where I Enter: The Impact of Black Women on Race and Sex in America.* 1984.

Holm, Jeanne. *Women in the Military: An Unfinished Revolution.* 1982.

Jeffords, Susan. *The Remasculinization of America: Gender and the Vietnam War.* 1989.

Kennedy, Leon. *Susan Sontag.* 1995.

Marshall, Kathryn. *In the Combat Zone: An Oral History of American Women in Vietnam.* 1987.

Norman, Elizabeth. *Women at War: The Story of Fifty Military Nurses Who Served in Vietnam.* 1990.

Salvin, Sarah. *U.S. Women's Interest Groups.* 1995.

Saywell, Shelley. *Women in War.* 1985.

Walker, Kieth. *A Piece of My Heart: The Stories of 26 American Women Who Served in Vietnam.* 1985.

Walsh, Patricia L. *Forever Sad the Hearts.* 1982.

Index

Boldface pages locate main entries.

About the Contributors

EUGENE M. ADDISON III is an undergraduate student at Sam Houston State University in Huntsville, Texas.

LINDA ALKANA teaches history at California State University, Long Beach.

JESSICA CARLSON is an undergraduate student at the Maryland Institute, College of Art, in Baltimore.

EMILY CASON is an undergraduate student at Abilene Christian University in Texas.

JOANNA COWDEN is an historian at California State University, Chico.

AMBER DURDEN is an undergraduate student at Texas A&M University in College Station.

SAMUEL FREEMAN is a political scientist at the University of Texas, Pan American, in Edinburgh.

CHRISTOPHER GORE is an assistant director of admissions at Midwestern State University in Wichita Falls, Texas.

MICHAEL HALL teaches history for Houston Community College in Texas.

ADAM HARWELL is an undergraduate student at Texas A&M University in College Station.

JOHN HINSON is living and working in Cleveland, Texas.

JERRY JAY INMON is a graduate student in the parks and recreation program at Texas A&M University in College Station.

BOBBY J. JAMES is a graduate student at Sam Houston State University in Huntsville, Texas.

TROY JOHNSON is an historian at California State University, Long Beach.

SEAN A. KELLEHER is a political scientist at the University of Texas at the Permian Basin in Odessa.

ANDREW KOEHL is an undergraduate at the California Institute of Technology in Pasadena.

LEE ANN LAWRENCE lives in Cypress, Texas.

MARCUS D. LEFLORE is an undergraduate at Texas A&M University in College Station.

MELISSA M. MILLER is an undergraduate student at Sam Houston State University in Huntsville, Texas.

SAMMIE MILLER lives in Huntsville, Texas.

CAROL NGUYEN is an undergraduate student at the University of Texas at Austin.

BRADLEY A. OLSON is an undergraduate student at the University of Pennsylvania in Philadelphia.

JAMES S. OLSON is Distinguished Professor of History at Sam Houston State University in Huntsville, Texas.

MARGARET PECK is an undergraduate student at the University of Texas at Austin.

LAURIE PIERCE is an undergraduate student at the University of Texas at Austin.

CARLOS RAINER is a third-year law student at the University of Texas at Austin.

DAVID RITCHEY teaches at the Spring Creek campus of Collin County Community College in Plano, Texas.

RANDY ROBERTS is Professor of History at Purdue University in West Lafayette, Indiana.

JOSEPH M. ROWE, JR., is Professor of History at Sam Houston State University in Huntsville, Texas.

KAREN RUSSELL is an undergraduate student at Southern Methodist University in Dallas, Texas.

MEAGHAN J. SAMUELS is an undergraduate student at the University of Texas at Austin.

JENNIFER SHERMAN is an undergraduate student at Texas A&M University in College Station.

MICHAEL SMITH is an undergraduate student at Louisiana State University in Baton Rouge.

STEVEN D. SMITH teaches history in the Houston Independent School District in Texas.

TRAVIS TATUM is an undergraduate student at Texas A&M University in College Station.

TRACY THOMPSON is an undergraduate student at Houston Community College in Texas.

CORY TOOLE is an undergraduate student at Texas A&M University at Austin.

HEATHER TORONJO is an undergraduate student at Texas A&M University in College Station.

ALEXANDER PINH VILAYTHONG is an undergraduate student at Texas A&M University in College Station.

ANNE G. WOODWARD is an undergraduate student at Southwestern University in Georgetown, Texas.

WILLIAM WOOTEN is a graduate student in history at Texas A&M University in College Station.

BRAD WUERGLER is an undergraduate student at Austin College in Sherman, Texas.

ISBN 0-313-29271-X

90000>

HARDCOVER BAR CODE